Advances in Information Security and Privacy

Advances in Information Security and Privacy

Editors

Gianluca Lax
Antonia Russo

MDPI • Basel • Beijing • Wuhan • Barcelona • Belgrade • Manchester • Tokyo • Cluj • Tianjin

Editors
Gianluca Lax
DIIES Dept.
University Mediterranea of
Reggio Calabria
Reggio Calabria
Italy

Antonia Russo
DIIES Dept.
University Mediterranea of
Reggio Calabria
Reggio Calabria
Italy

Editorial Office
MDPI
St. Alban-Anlage 66
4052 Basel, Switzerland

This is a reprint of articles from the Special Issue published online in the open access journal *Applied Sciences* (ISSN 2076-3417) (available at: www.mdpi.com/journal/applsci/special_issues/information_security_privacy).

For citation purposes, cite each article independently as indicated on the article page online and as indicated below:

LastName, A.A.; LastName, B.B.; LastName, C.C. Article Title. *Journal Name* **Year**, *Volume Number*, Page Range.

ISBN 978-3-0365-5296-5 (Hbk)
ISBN 978-3-0365-5295-8 (PDF)

© 2022 by the authors. Articles in this book are Open Access and distributed under the Creative Commons Attribution (CC BY) license, which allows users to download, copy and build upon published articles, as long as the author and publisher are properly credited, which ensures maximum dissemination and a wider impact of our publications.

The book as a whole is distributed by MDPI under the terms and conditions of the Creative Commons license CC BY-NC-ND.

Contents

About the Editors vii

Gianluca Lax and Antonia Russo
Advances in Information Security and Privacy
Reprinted from: *Appl. Sci.* **2022**, *12*, 7995, doi:10.3390/app12167995 1

Yara Alghofaili, Albatul Albattah, Noura Alrajeh, Murad A. Rassam and Bander Ali Saleh Al-rimy
Secure Cloud Infrastructure: A Survey on Issues, Current Solutions, and Open Challenges
Reprinted from: *Appl. Sci.* **2021**, *11*, 9005, doi:10.3390/app11199005 5

Aisha Zahid Junejo, Manzoor Ahmed Hashmani and Mehak Maqbool Memon
Empirical Evaluation of Privacy Efficiency in Blockchain Networks: Review and Open Challenges
Reprinted from: *Appl. Sci.* **2021**, *11*, 7013, doi:10.3390/app11157013 41

Yi-Fan Tseng and Shih-Jie Gao
Decentralized Inner-Product Encryption with Constant-Size Ciphertext
Reprinted from: *Appl. Sci.* **2022**, *12*, 636, doi:10.3390/app12020636 69

Ming-Te Chen and Hsuan-Chao Huang
A Practical and Efficient Node Blind SignCryption Scheme for the IoT Device Network
Reprinted from: *Appl. Sci.* **2021**, *12*, 278, doi:10.3390/app12010278 85

Volodymyr Maksymovych, Mariia Shabatura, Oleh Harasymchuk, Mikolaj Karpinski, Daniel Jancarczyk and Pawel Sawicki
Development of Additive Fibonacci Generators with Improved Characteristics for Cybersecurity Needs
Reprinted from: *Appl. Sci.* **2022**, *12*, 1519, doi:10.3390/app12031519 99

Moin Uddin, Muhammad Muzammal, Muhammad Khurram Hameed, Ibrahim Tariq Javed, Bandar Alamri and Noel Crespi
CBCIoT: A Consensus Algorithm for Blockchain-Based IoT Applications
Reprinted from: *Appl. Sci.* **2021**, *11*, 11011, doi:10.3390/app112211011 111

Xianyun Xu, Huifang Chen and Lei Xie
A Location Privacy Preservation Method Based on Dummy Locations in Internet of Vehicles
Reprinted from: *Appl. Sci.* **2021**, *11*, 4594, doi:10.3390/app11104594 131

Daan Storm van Leeuwen, Ali Ahmed, Craig Watterson and Nilufar Baghaei
Contact Tracing: Ensuring Privacy and Security
Reprinted from: *Appl. Sci.* **2021**, *11*, 9977, doi:10.3390/app11219977 147

Minjung Park and Sangmi Chai
AI Model for Predicting Legal Judgments to Improve Accuracy and Explainability of Online Privacy Invasion Cases
Reprinted from: *Appl. Sci.* **2021**, *11*, 11080, doi:10.3390/app112311080 165

Francesco Buccafurri, Vincenzo De Angelis, Maria Francesca Idone, Cecilia Labrini and Sara Lazzaro
Achieving Sender Anonymity in Tor against the Global Passive Adversary
Reprinted from: *Appl. Sci.* **2021**, *12*, 137, doi:10.3390/app12010137 181

Kashif Naseer Qureshi, Luqman Shahzad, Abdelzahir Abdelmaboud, Taiseer Abdalla Elfadil Eisa, Bandar Alamri and Ibrahim Tariq Javed et al.
A Blockchain-Based Efficient, Secure and Anonymous Conditional Privacy-Preserving and Authentication Scheme for the Internet of Vehicles
Reprinted from: *Appl. Sci.* **2022**, *12*, 476, doi:10.3390/app12010476 . . . . **205**

Viktor Taneski, Marko Kompara, Marjan Heričko and Boštjan Brumen
Strength Analysis of Real-Life Passwords Using Markov Models
Reprinted from: *Appl. Sci.* **2021**, *11*, 9406, doi:10.3390/app11209406 . . . . **225**

Vitalii Yesin, Mikolaj Karpinski, Maryna Yesina, Vladyslav Vilihura and Stanislaw A. Rajba
Technique for Evaluating the Security of Relational Databases Based on the Enhanced Clements–Hoffman Model
Reprinted from: *Appl. Sci.* **2021**, *11*, 11175, doi:10.3390/app112311175 . . . . **257**

Vitalii Yesin, Mikolaj Karpinski, Maryna Yesina, Vladyslav Vilihura and Kornel Warwas
Ensuring Data Integrity in Databases with the Universal Basis of Relations
Reprinted from: *Appl. Sci.* **2021**, *11*, 8781, doi:10.3390/app11188781 . . . . **281**

Sung-Soo Jung, Sang-Joon Lee and Ieck-Chae Euom
Delegation-Based Personal Data Processing Request Notarization Framework for GDPR Based on Private Blockchain
Reprinted from: *Appl. Sci.* **2021**, *11*, 10574, doi:10.3390/app112210574 . . . . **295**

Marko Hölbl, Boštjan Kežmah and Marko Kompara
Data Protection Heterogeneity in the European Union
Reprinted from: *Appl. Sci.* **2021**, *11*, 10912, doi:10.3390/app112210912 . . . . **325**

About the Editors

Gianluca Lax

Gianluca Lax is an Associate Professor of Computer Science at the University Mediterranea of Reggio Calabria, Italy. In 2005, he received his Ph.D. in computer science from the University of Calabria. In 2018, he got the habilitation as a Full Professor of Computer Science. Since 2018, he is the Coordinator of a master's degree in Information Technologies for Telecommunications Engineering. His research interests include privacy, information security, and social network analysis. He is an author of more than 150 papers published in leading international journals and conference proceedings.

Antonia Russo

Antonia Russo is a Postdoctoral Researcher at the University Mediterranea of Reggio Calabria. In 2022, she received her Ph.D. in Information Engineering from the University Mediterranea of Reggio Calabria. Her research interests include security, privacy, access control, and social network analysis.

Editorial

Advances in Information Security and Privacy

Gianluca Lax * and Antonia Russo

Department of Information Engineering, Infrastructure and Sustainable Energy (DIIES), University Mediterranea di Reggio Calabria, 89122 Reggio Calabria, Italy
* Correspondence: lax@unirc.it; Tel.: +39-965-167-3304

1. Introduction

Due to the recent pandemic crisis, many people are spending their days smart working and have increased their use of digital resources for both work and entertainment. This means that the amount of digital information handled online has dramatically increased, and a significant increase in the number of attacks, breaches, and hacks has been observed. This Special Issue aims to establish the state of the art in protecting information by mitigating information risks. This objective is reached by presenting both surveys on specific topics and original approaches and solutions to specific problems. In total, 16 papers have been published in this Special Issue; the following sections provide summaries of these papers grouped by the topics they address.

2. Surveys

Two papers were selected to present an overview of the state of the art in two important topics. Alghofaili Yara et al. [1] present a comprehensive survey regarding security issues at four cloud infrastructure levels: application, network, host, and data. They investigate the most prominent issues that may affect the cloud computing business model with regard to infrastructure and the current solutions used to mitigate different security issues at each of these levels. The second survey published in this Special Issue regards the use of blockchain technology in the development of privacy protocols [2]. This survey classifies the existing solutions based on blockchain fundamental building blocks (smart contracts, cryptography, and hashing) and investigates the evaluation criteria used to validate these techniques. The key factors that strengthen or weaken blockchain privacy are identified, and an evaluation framework to analyze the efficiency of blockchain-based privacy solutions is also formulated.

3. Cryptographic Primitives

Low-level cryptographic algorithms are very important because they are used to build cryptographic protocols for security. In this Special Issue, four papers discuss this topic. Tseng Yi-Fan and Shih-Jie Gao [3] define a new form of inner product encryption to provide fine-grained access control to secure distributed system architectures. The main advantages of this scheme are that it is the first decentralized scheme with constant-size ciphertext and it reduces encryption/decryption costs compared to the state of the art. A new scheme supporting digital signature, encryption, and delegation is proposed in [4]. This scheme requires limited memory space and power; therefore, it has been designed to be used in IoT devices with resource limitations. An important cryptographic primitive is the generation of pseudorandom sequences, because they are especially used in information security. Maksymovych Volodymyr et al. [5] define a new Additive Fibonacci generator scheme in which the introduction of additional structural elements ensures the operation of generators with arbitrary values of the recurrent equation modulus. This innovation improves the statistical characteristics of generators and expands the scope of their use in cryptography, particularly in streaming ciphers. In this section, the proposal presented in [6] is included,

Citation: Lax, G.; Russo, A. Advances in Information Security and Privacy. *Appl. Sci.* 2022, 12, 7995. https://doi.org/10.3390/app12167995

Received: 8 August 2022
Accepted: 8 August 2022
Published: 10 August 2022

Publisher's Note: MDPI stays neutral with regard to jurisdictional claims in published maps and institutional affiliations.

Copyright: © 2022 by the authors. Licensee MDPI, Basel, Switzerland. This article is an open access article distributed under the terms and conditions of the Creative Commons Attribution (CC BY) license (https:// creativecommons.org/licenses/by/ 4.0/).

in which a new consensus algorithm is proposed because consensus algorithms are the basis for blockchains. The primary purpose of this algorithm is to improve scalability in terms of validation and verification rates; for this reason, the new algorithm was designed to be used in scenarios in which a limited delay is tolerated. The results of the validation show that the proposed algorithm improves the state of the art in terms of the efficiency of block generation time and transactions per second.

4. Privacy

The topic of privacy has received significant attention in this Special Issue, and four articles discuss this topic. In the field of location-based service, the provision of dummy locations is used to preserve users' privacy. Xu Xianyun, Huifang Chen, and Lei Xie [7] present a dummy location selection algorithm to maximize the anonymous entropy and the effective distance of the candidate location set consisting of the vehicle user's location and dummy locations. This solution ensures the uncertainty and dispersion of selected dummy locations. This proposal is innovative because a trustable third-party server is not needed. Privacy concerns in contact tracing applications are studied in [8], and the conclusion that decentralized solutions are preferable to centralized solutions leads the authors to propose a framework that provides a roadmap on building contact tracing applications within the EU. The framework is validated against common threats and compared with three leading European contact-tracing implementations. The possibility that a firm is involved in privacy infringement cases resulting in legal causations is studied in [9]. This study exploits machine learning and text analysis to build a model that can predict legal judgment using information related to societal factors and technological development. Tor is the most popular anonymous communication protocol used to protect the personal privacy of its users. The study presented in [10] highlights that anonymity is broken if an adversary can monitor the traffic at the bounds of the Tor circuit. Thus, the authors propose an improvement of the protocol based on probabilistic encryption to effectively protect users' privacy.

5. Authentication

In the field of the Internet of Vehicles, achieving both the privacy and traceability of nodes is a challenging task. To address this need, Qureshi Kashif Naseer et al. [11] present an authentication scheme based on blockchain to provide vehicle nodes with mechanisms to become anonymous and take control of their data during the data communication process. The proposed scheme has been implemented by utilizing Hyperledger Fabric as a blockchain and provides conditional privacy to users and vehicles to ensure the anonymity, traceability, and unlinkability of data sharing among vehicles. Passwords are the most commonly used mechanism for authentication, and the use of password checkers to prevent users from creating easy-to-guess passwords is considered the best practice. The study presented in [12] analyzes how Markov models can help create a more effective password checker that would be able to check the probability of a given password to be chosen by an attacker. The authors determine that one Markov model is insufficient for the creation of a more effective password checker, and multiple Markov models are required to carry out strength calculations for a wide range of passwords.

6. Database Security

The obtainment of convincing evidence of database security and the quantification of a measure of database security is an important topic. Yesin Vitalii et al. [13] present a technique for the evaluation of the security of relational databases based on the enhanced theoretical Clements–Hoffman model. The degree of security is calculated on the basis of an integral quantitative metric that is the reciprocal of the total residual risk associated with the possibility of implementing threats in relation to a database object when using security measures. The main techniques implemented in accordance with the recommendations of the Clark–Wilson model to ensure the integrity of data and persistent stored database modules are studied in [14]. The authors propose a mechanism to ensure the integrity of the data and programs of databases based on the provisions of the relational database theory, the Row Level Security technology, the potential of the modern blockchain model, and the capabilities of the database management system on the platform of which databases with the universal basis of relations are implemented. By applying this mechanism, it is guaranteed that the stored data and programs remain correct, unaltered, undistorted, and preserved.

7. Regulation

The General Data Protection Regulation (GDPR) is the most important regulation regarding data protection and privacy in the European Union. Ensuring the reliability and integrity of the personal data processing request records of a data subject to enable its utilization according to the GDPR requirements is the challenge investigated in [15]. In this paper, the authors propose a notarization framework using a private blockchain to allow the data subject to delegate requests to process personal data. In this framework, the requests are handled by a data controller, and the generated data request and processing result data are stored in the blockchain ledger and notarized via a trusted institution of the blockchain network. This framework has been implemented with Hyperledger Fabric to demonstrate the fulfillment of system requirements and the feasibility of implementing a GDPR compliance audit for the processing of personal data. A comparison of the legislation on data protection topics in the various EU member states is studied in [16]. The study is limited to 19 states whose national supervisory authorities agreed to participate in the research by answering a prepared survey about data protection issues. Among many other findings, an interesting result is that in most of the cases, member states do not have any additional/specific legislation on data protection.

Acknowledgments: This issue would not have been possible without the contributions of the authors, reviewers, and the editorial team of *Applied Sciences*. Congratulations to all authors; we are sure that their research will receive many downloads and citations in the coming years. We would like to thank the editorial team of *Applied Sciences* for always being present during the whole process of the creation of this Special Issue.

Conflicts of Interest: The authors declare no conflict of interest.

References

1. Alghofaili, Y.; Albattah, A.; Alrajeh, N.; Rassam, M.; Al-rimy, B. Secure Cloud Infrastructure: A Survey on Issues, Current Solutions, and Open Challenges. *Appl. Sci.* **2021**, *11*, 9005. [CrossRef]
2. Junejo, A.; Hashmani, M.; Memon, M. Empirical Evaluation of Privacy Efficiency in Blockchain Networks: Review and Open Challenges. *Appl. Sci.* **2021**, *11*, 7013. [CrossRef]
3. Tseng, Y.; Gao, S. Decentralized Inner-Product Encryption with Constant-Size Ciphertext. *Appl. Sci.* **2022**, *12*, 636. [CrossRef]
4. Chen, M.; Huang, H. A Practical and Efficient Node Blind SignCryption Scheme for the IoT Device Network. *Appl. Sci.* **2022**, *12*, 278. [CrossRef]
5. Maksymovych, V.; Shabatura, M.; Harasymchuk, O.; Karpinski, M.; Jancarczyk, D.; Sawicki, P. Development of Additive Fibonacci Generators with Improved Characteristics for Cybersecurity Needs. *Appl. Sci.* **2022**, *12*, 1519. [CrossRef]
6. Uddin, M.; Muzammal, M.; Hameed, M.; Javed, I.; Alamri, B.; Crespi, N. CBCIoT: A Consensus Algorithm for Blockchain-Based IoT Applications. *Appl. Sci.* **2021**, *11*, 11011. [CrossRef]
7. Xu, X.; Chen, H.; Xie, L. A Location Privacy Preservation Method Based on Dummy Locations in Internet of Vehicles. *Appl. Sci.* **2021**, *11*, 4594. [CrossRef]
8. Storm van Leeuwen, D.; Ahmed, A.; Watterson, C.; Baghaei, N. Contact Tracing: Ensuring Privacy and Security. *Appl. Sci.* **2021**, *11*, 9977. [CrossRef]
9. Park, M.; Chai, S. AI Model for Predicting Legal Judgments to Improve Accuracy and Explainability of Online Privacy Invasion Cases. *Appl. Sci.* **2021**, *11*, 11080. [CrossRef]
10. Buccafurri, F.; De Angelis, V.; Idone, M.; Labrini, C.; Lazzaro, S. Achieving Sender Anonymity in Tor against the Global Passive Adversary. *Appl. Sci.* **2022**, *12*, 137. [CrossRef]
11. Qureshi, K.; Shahzad, L.; Abdelmaboud, A.; Elfadil Eisa, T.; Alamri, B.; Javed, I.; Al-Dhaqm, A.; Crespi, N. A Blockchain-Based Efficient, Secure and Anonymous Conditional Privacy-Preserving and Authentication Scheme for the Internet of Vehicles. *Appl. Sci.* **2022**, *12*, 476. [CrossRef]

12. Taneski, V.; Kompara, M.; Heričko, M.; Brumen, B. Strength Analysis of Real-Life Passwords Using Markov Models. *Appl. Sci.* **2021**, *11*, 9406. [CrossRef]
13. Yesin, V.; Karpinski, M.; Yesina, M.; Vilihura, V.; Rajba, S. Technique for Evaluating the Security of Relational Databases Based on the Enhanced Clements-Hoffman Model. *Appl. Sci.* **2021**, *11*, 11175. [CrossRef]
14. Yesin, V.; Karpinski, M.; Yesina, M.; Vilihura, V.; Warwas, K. Ensuring Data Integrity in Databases with the Universal Basis of Relations. *Appl. Sci.* **2021**, *11*, 8781. [CrossRef]
15. Jung, S.; Lee, S.; Euom, I. Delegation-Based Personal Data Processing Request Notarization Framework for GDPR Based on Private Blockchain. *Appl. Sci.* **2021**, *11*, 10574. [CrossRef]
16. Hölbl, M.; Kežmah, B.; Kompara, M. Data Protection Heterogeneity in the European Union. *Appl. Sci.* **2021**, *11*, 10912. [CrossRef]

Review

Secure Cloud Infrastructure: A Survey on Issues, Current Solutions, and Open Challenges

Yara Alghofaili [1], Albatul Albattah [1], Noura Alrajeh [1], Murad A. Rassam [1,2,*] and Bander Ali Saleh Al-rimy [3]

[1] Department of Information Technology, College of Computer, Qassim University, Buraydah 51452, Saudi Arabia; 411207305@qu.edu.sa (Y.A.); 411207333@qu.edu.sa (A.A.); 411200195@qu.edu.sa (N.A.)
[2] Faculty of Engineering and Information Technology, Taiz University, Taiz 6803, Yemen
[3] Faculty of Engineering, Universiti Teknologi Malaysia, Johor Bahru 81310, Malaysia; bander@utm.my
* Correspondence: m.qasem@qu.edu.sa

Abstract: Cloud computing is currently becoming a well-known buzzword in which business titans, such as Microsoft, Amazon, and Google, among others, are at the forefront in developing and providing sophisticated cloud computing systems to their users in a cost-effective manner. Security is the biggest concern for cloud computing and is a major obstacle to users adopting cloud computing systems. Maintaining the security of cloud computing is important, especially for the infrastructure. Several research works have been conducted in the cloud infrastructure security area; however, some gaps have not been completely addressed, while new challenges continue to arise. This paper presents a comprehensive survey of the security issues at different cloud infrastructure levels (e.g., application, network, host, and data). It investigates the most prominent issues that may affect the cloud computing business model with regard to infrastructure. It further discusses the current solutions proposed in the literature to mitigate the different security issues at each level. To assist in solving the issues, the challenges that are still unsolved are summarized. Based on the exploration of the current challenges, some cloud features such as flexibility, elasticity and the multi-tenancy are found to pose new challenges at each infrastructure level. More specifically, the multi-tenancy is found to have the most impact at all infrastructure levels, as it can lead to several security problems such as unavailability, abuse, data loss and privacy breach. This survey concludes by giving some recommendations for future research.

Keywords: cloud computing; secure cloud infrastructure; application security; network security; host security; data security

1. Introduction

The idea behind cloud computing is to provide all possible facilities such as software, IT infrastructure, and services to its customers for use over the internet. Cloud computing systems are large-scale, heterogeneous collections of autonomous systems and flexible computational architecture. This technology is emerging, as it is considered the first choice for businesses that do not want to deal with the in-house maintenance of systems and a development team [1]. Many businesses, such as Amazon AWS, Google, IBM, Sun, Microsoft, and many others, are developing efficient cloud products and technology [2]. In cloud technology, data are shared via virtual data centers from the customers and the organization [2].

Cloud computing has evolved as a popular and universal paradigm for service-oriented computing where computing infrastructure and solutions are delivered as a service. The cloud has revolutionized the abstraction and use of computing infrastructure through its features (e.g., self-service on-demand, broad network access, resource pooling, etc.), making cloud computing desirable [3]. However, security is the biggest challenge, and concerns regarding cloud computing continue to arise as we witness an increasing number of new developments in cloud computing platforms [4]. In the post-COVID-19 world, it is clear that more people and businesses are adopting cloud services, software, and infrastructure, as they can be accessed anytime, and from anywhere. To handle security risks, several research works and developments, such as in [5–8], have been proposed. Nonetheless, there are still more opportunities for new techniques to make the cloud more secure. Most of the existing techniques for securing the cloud do not focus on the new types of security risks that might face the cloud computing infrastructure. Hence, they cannot detect attacks or vulnerabilities that might come from the cloud service provider's side or the consumer's side. Furthermore, very few existing works have examined the different levels of cloud infrastructure altogether. Due to the high importance of investigating such issues, this paper conducted an extensive survey on the issues that the cloud computing infrastructure faces at different levels (application, host, network, and data level). It also presents the existing solutions used to mitigate these issues. Additionally, this paper highlights some open challenges that still need to be solved and suggest directions for future work. To the best of our knowledge, this study is the first effort to provide a systematic review of associated security issues and solutions based on cloud levels (application, host, network, and data level). The following are the main contributions of this study:

1. Conducting a systematic evaluation of 103 articles on cloud infrastructure in connection with attacks and defenses.
2. Providing a new taxonomy for a systematic review of cloud infrastructure levels.
3. Investigating four levels that aim to cover all vulnerabilities that might come from the cloud service provider's side or the consumer's side.
4. Identifying the limitations of the examined studies and highlighting the open research challenges and proposed directions for future work.

The rest of this paper is divided into eight sections: the methodology of this study is presented in Section 2. The background on cloud computing is given in Section 3. The current security issues that cloud infrastructure faces at different levels are investigated in Section 4. Section 5 presents the solutions proposed to solve the related security issues in the literature. The open challenges that still need to be solved are presented in Section 6. Section 7 suggests some future directions. The paper is concluded in Section 8.

2. Methodology

This study was based on the systematic literature review (SLR). The phases in this study are divided into three, which are depicted in Figure 1.

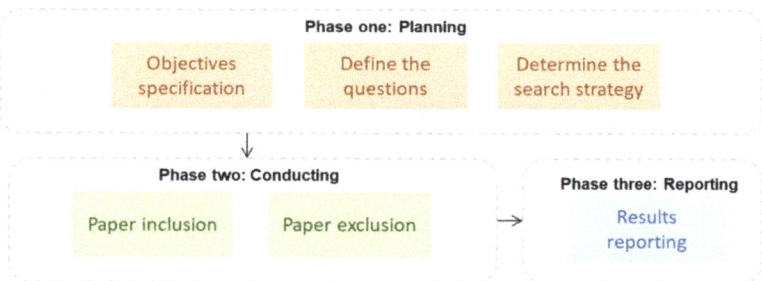

Figure 1. The methodology of the study.

2.1. Planning the Review Phase

This phase contains three sub-phases: obtaining the research objectives, defining the research questions, and determining the search strategy used in the study.

2.1.1. Research Objectives

The following are the study's primary objectives:

1. To quantify and expand upon the current state-of-the-art literature on secure cloud infrastructure to provide a new taxonomy.
2. To present an in-depth review of various issues and solutions that are used in cloud infrastructure at various levels (application, host, network, and data).
3. To highlight the limitations and pitfalls of the current solutions in terms of research challenges and future opportunities.

2.1.2. Research Questions

The study considers answering two important questions, which are described below, to achieve the objectives.

Q1: What are the well-known issues and the proposed solutions in cloud infrastructure at its various levels?

Q2: What are some of the security issues that could stymie widespread cloud computing adoption?

2.1.3. Search Strategy

During this study, various academic digital databases are used to extract related studies, including Springer, IEEE Xplore, ScienceDirect, ACM Digital Library, Arxiv, and some other related international conferences, as shown in Figure 2. These databases are considered to be sufficient for covering the most up-to-date and reliable literature on cloud infrastructure issues and existing security solutions. The literature search was extensively conducted from 2011 to 2020, as shown in Figure 3. This study queried major libraries, utilizing a combination of various search keywords that evolved utilizing a reduplicate operation to maximize the number of pertinent studies in order to obtain accurate search results (optimal results). Therefore, the most used combinations of words included: "Cloud Computing", "Secure Cloud Infrastructure", "Application Security", "Network Security", "Host Security", and "Data Security". Based on these keywords, the studies were grouped into different categories to map the pertinent studies based on cloud infrastructure levels, such as application, network, host, and data. This procedure includes extracting from the abstracts of the studies some keywords and concepts that reflect the contributions of the studies.

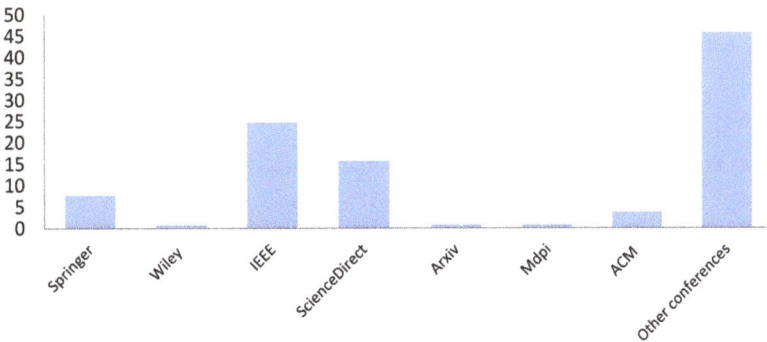

Figure 2. Number of papers selected from each academic database.

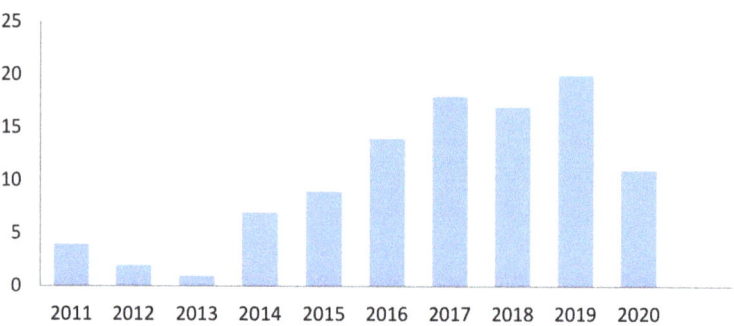

Figure 3. Number of papers selected over years.

2.2. Conducting the Review Phase

This phase defines the criteria of inclusion and exclusion followed in this study. For inclusion,

1. The publication was written in English.
2. The publication addressed the issue or solutions for cloud infrastructure security covering one or more levels.
3. The publication was more than 4 pages.

For exclusion,

1. The publication was written in a language other than English.
2. The publication discussed cloud infrastructure from a non-secure side.
3. The publication did not cover any level of cloud infrastructure.
4. The publication was less than 4 pages.

2.3. Reporting the Results Phase

The search yielded a total of 531 publications. After eliminating duplicated publications, the total number decreased to 326. A total of 74 publications did not fulfill the inclusion criteria and were thus eliminated. Among the remaining 252 publications, 149 did not cover the security of cloud infrastructure at any level and thus were removed. A total of 103 publications are recognized as being relevant among the remaining publications.

3. Cloud Computing Background and Terminologies

The idea behind cloud computing is not new. In the 1960s, John McCarthy envisioned that computing services will be offered to the general public as a utility [3]. The term "cloud" has also been used in various aspects, such as the concept of widespread ATM networks in the 1990s and the e-commerce outlets currently used by hundreds of millions of people around the world. However, the term only started to gain momentum after Google's CEO Eric Schmidt defined a "cloud" as the business model of offering services across the Internet in 2006 [9]. In 2011, the National Institute of Standards and Technology (NIST) defined cloud computing as a paradigm for allowing convenient, ubiquitous, and on-demand network access to a shared pool of configurable computing resources such as servers, storage, services, applications, and networks that can be quickly provisioned and released with minimal interaction or management effort from service providers. This cloud paradigm consists of five essential attributes, three service delivery models, and four deployment models [3], as shown in Figure 4 (which is adapted from the study in [10]).

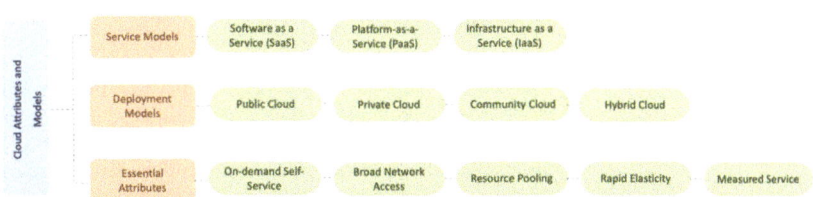

Figure 4. Cloud attributes and models.

3.1. Cloud Essential Attributes

NIST summarized the cloud computing attributes as the following [3]:

On-demand self-service (Pay-as-you use): A consumer will be able to unilaterally save on computing capabilities such as network storage and server time as the consumer's needs will be satisfied automatically without the need for human interaction with all service providers.

Broad network access: Some capabilities are available through the network and can be accessed through standard techniques that promote utilization via thick client platforms or heterogeneous devices such as laptops, tablets, mobile phones, and workstations.

Resource pooling (multi-tenancy): Service providers are involved in pooling computing resources to several multiple consumers through a multi-tenant model. It is also defined by various virtual and physical resources assigned and reassigned approbate to consumer demand.

Rapid elasticity: The capabilities are released and provided rapidly to scale both internally and externally commensurate to a request. Additionally, the consumer has some capabilities for provisioning, although they often appear to be unlimited. They can be assigned in any quantity and at any time.

Measured service: Cloud systems can automatically control and optimize resource utilization by leveraging metering to services such as active user accounts processing, storage, and bandwidth. Resource use can also be controlled, reported, and monitored to provide transparency for both consumers and providers.

3.2. Cloud Stockholders

Many actors play a major role in cloud computing, as shown in Table 1.

Table 1. Cloud Stakeholders.

Stakeholders in Cloud	Definition
Service Providers	The cloud computing systems are owned and operated by service providers and deliver service to third parties. The providers will be responsible for maintaining and upgrading systems, such as Google, Microsoft, IBM, Oracle, Amazon, and Sun [11]
Consumers	The effective subscribers purchase the services and use the system based on their operational expenses from service providers [11].
Enablers	Organizations that facilitate adoption, utilization and delivery to selling services in cloud computing [11].
Regulators	International entities that penetrate the other stakeholders [11].

3.3. Cloud Computing Services Delivery Models

A cloud services delivery model consists of three primary models that become more established and formalized. These models are software-as-a-service (SaaS), platform-as-a-service (PaaS), and infrastructure-as-a-service (IaaS). These three primary models are commonly referred to as an SPI model.

3.3.1. Software as a Service (SaaS)

Software as a service (SaaS) is a software distribution model that allows the consumer to access applications hosted by service provider infrastructure over a network. Concretely, the SaaS model provides software to customers, which are mostly end users who subscribe to ready-to-use applications (Bokhari et al., 2018). Moreover, the SaaS model has been associated with a pay-as-you-go attribute that offers cloud consumers a service that enables them to access the software from a web browser without any complexity regarding installation, maintenance, and high initial cost [12,13]. MS Office 365, Google Apps, Salesforce, CISCO Webex and DropBox are examples of SaaS's real-world applications. From a security standpoint, user awareness is the major contributor to SaaS security. Nevertheless, the SaaS provider needs to impose a set of security policies like multi-factor authentication, password complexity, and retention to make sure that users follow the due security requirements. Security measures are another aspect that SaaS providers should have in place to protect users' data and make them accessible for legitimate use all the time.

3.3.2. Platform-as-a-Service (PaaS)

Platform-as-a-service (PaaS) refers to a group of software and development tools hosted by the provider's servers. It offers developers a platform to build their applications without any concern about what lies underneath the service. The PaaS model also facilitates the effective management of the software development life cycle from the planning until maintenance phases. Furthermore, the platform uses programming languages such as Java, Python, and Net, among other tools that enable consumers to create custom applications [12,13]. WordPress, GoDaddy, and AWS are examples of PaaS products that many developers and programmers rely upon nowadays. In the PaaS paradigm, security is a shared responsibility between the developers and service providers. On the one hand, developers need to adopt security standards and best practices when building their applications. For instance, the developer needs to make sure that the application is free from bugs and flaws. It is also necessary to test and mitigate any vulnerability that attackers could exploit to break into and compromise users' data. On the other hand, the reliability of PaaS technology is crucial for a safe and secure application development environment. For instance, some application development environments such as C++ are infamous in memory management, leaving the window open for attackers to carry out several attacks, such as stack overflow. Another vulnerability that attackers could exploit is the lack of proper authentication inherited from some RDBMSs such as Oracle, which allows users authenticated at the OS level to login the database with admin privileges with no username/password.

3.3.3. Infrastructure as a Service (IaaS)

Infrastructure as a service (IaaS) is a single-tenant model where the cloud computing service provider dedicates resources that are only shared with contracted consumers based on pay-per-use fees. The IaaS model helps to minimize the need for a large initial investment in computing hardware such as networking devices, processing power, and servers. The model can also add or release computing resources quickly and cost-effectively [12]. With the spreading of multiple cloud delivery models, it is often difficult to identify the limits of security accountability. Both cloud service providers (CSPs) and customers are responsible for security. Figure 5 (which is adapted from [14]) shows cloud computing services delivery models' responsibilities. Examples of the IaaS include Amazon Web Services, CISCO Meta-cloud, MS Azure, and Google Compute Engine (GCE). Again, the security of the infrastructure used by customers is imperative, as it is the first line of defense that protects the system's perimeter. In this regard, attackers could target the infrastructure in many ways, such as denial of service (DoS) and malware, and most of the time, the PaaS security is the responsibility of the service provider.

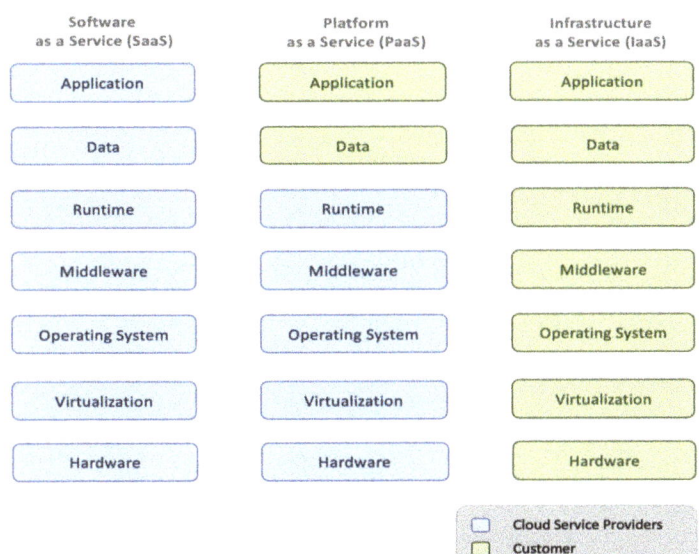

Figure 5. Cloud computing services delivery models' responsibilities.

3.4. Cloud Computing Deployment Models

The first critical step to take is to choose the appropriate type of cloud to be implemented by an institution, as it guarantees an effective implementation process [14]. According to [15], institutions that have been unsuccessful in implementing a deployment model have done so by choosing the wrong type of cloud. Before determining the best form of cloud to use, institutions must first analyze their data to avoid chances of failure. However, the security aspect is overlooked by many of the customers when opting-in for cloud services due to the misconception about the efficacy of the security embedded into cloud services. Many organizations that adopt cloud computing rely totally on the security applied by the cloud service providers. Consequently, malicious actors could exploit client-side vulnerability to compromise the systems of one or more tenants. Four models have been completely incorporated in every type of cloud-based system in accordance with management requirements and the senility of data. These models include public cloud, private cloud, community cloud, and hybrid cloud.

3.4.1. Public Cloud

The public cloud is often referred to as an external cloud. This type of cloud is open to all users or large groups of users via the Internet, with ownership being retained by cloud service providers. It is run by the provider and enables users to access any data through the internet. The public cloud offers cost-effective and elastic ways of deploying IT solutions [10,16]. However, Internet connectivity imposes many security threats to the services and systems hosted by the cloud, including, but not limited to, DoS, malware, ransomware, and advanced persistent threat (APT) attacks.

3.4.2. Private Cloud

The private cloud is often referred to as the internal cloud. This type is dedicated to a single user, group, or institution. It may be operated by the service provider or a third party and may work on-site or off-site. Although more secure, private clouds are more costly. A private cloud is also hosted within the institution's firewall; thus, users within an institution can access it over the intranet [14]. In contrast to public clouds, private clouds are less secure due to the limitation in resources and expertise dedicated to the services and systems, let alone the security. As a result, some components might not be well-protected, which allows malicious actors to carry out attacks by exploiting these weakly secured components.

3.4.3. Community Cloud

The community cloud serves specific communities with shared interests, such as missions, policies, security requirements, and compliance considerations. It can be managed by institutions themselves or by a third party on-site or off-site. The community cloud provides greater privacy, protection, and policy compliance standards [16]. The security of community clouds relies on the degree of security-awareness of the community and how critical the security is for community business. For instance, a cloud for federal agencies contains sensitive data that, if exposed, could compromise national security. As such, the security measures should be intrinsic to such clouds.

3.4.4. Hybrid Cloud

This type of cloud deployment occurs due to the diversity of an institution's requirements. It is a mix of two or more models (public, private, or community) to implement cloud services. It allows institutions to host sensitive data or applications on the private cloud and non-sensitive data or applications on the public cloud [16]. However, the hybridization between clouds poses several security risks due to the federation between clouds with different and incompatible security measures. Attackers, consequently, expose vulnerabilities in one or more clouds to break into the entire system.

3.5. Existing Surveys

Various survey papers have analyzed the security concerns relating to cloud computing over the last decade. Most of the reviewed literature has contributed significantly to the management of cloud security issues [17]. One such survey in [18] explored the common security concerns of cloud use. In addition, the authors presented some solutions to security risks according to user data sensitivity in cloud architecture.

A study by [19] highlighted the security issues for data transfer in a cloud. This survey provided sensible solutions for tackling possible threats. A survey in [20] presented a taxonomy and survey of cloud services in terms of cloud infrastructure vendors and revenue. It proposed a taxonomy of the services containing some categories such as computing, networking services, databases, storage, analytics, and machine learning. The computing, networking, and storage of all cloud vendors provide a strong product in terms of functionality and are considered the core of cloud computing. On the other hand, the databases, machine learning, and data analytics products of all cloud vendors offer a variety of different choices concerning streaming capabilities, data processing and orchestration, building blocks, and machine learning.

A survey in [21] focused on the security issues facing cloud entities. The entities involved the cloud customer, the cloud service provider, and the data owner. Additionally, the study focused on the crypto cloud with various communication-, storage-, and service-level agreements. Additionally, it included the necessary updates to research the causes and effects of different cyber-attacks.

A study by [22] discussed the various data protection issues in a multi-tenant system in cloud computing and suggested approaches to address security issues. This survey, however, focused more on data privacy rather than security.

A study in [23] provided a proper definition of cloud computing and different cloud architecture layers. Additionally, the study compared three service models (SaaS, PaaS, and IaaS) with deployment models (private, public, and community). The authors discussed the information security requirements of the private and public cloud. In addition, they discussed the main issues and challenges of cloud computing related to security.

A survey in [24] focused more on how we can recognize many forms of threats that often occur in cloud computing environments. In this paper, the author's contribution was in classifying the types of threats based on service resources in the context of the cloud. Based on the description and scope of the types of threats, this classification was defined.

A study in [25] discussed the design of software-defined networks (SDNs) and cloud computing environments with regard to DDoS attack situations and recognition instruments in cloud computing conditions. Additionally, this survey study discussed how to fabricate exploratory conditions and utilize simulation instruments for DDoS attacks and identification.

In the study of [26], a survey reviewed and evaluated major attacks targeting the security of Cloud Computing and presented solutions and potential countermeasures to serve as a benchmark for comparative research. This study lacked techniques to solve some major security challenges.

The authors in [27] reviewed technologies that allow for privacy-aware outsourcing of storage and processing of sensitive data to public clouds. The authors reviewed masking methods for outsourced data based on data splitting and anonymization, in addition to cryptographic methods covered by other surveys. These methods were then compared in terms of operations supported by masked outsourced data, overheads, and the impact on data management.

A narrative review by [28] showed integral end-to-end mapping of cloud security requirements, identifying threats, known vulnerabilities, and recommended remedies. It also contributed to the identification of a unified taxonomy for security requirements, threats, vulnerabilities, and countermeasures for end-to-end mapping. It also highlighted security challenges in other related fields, such as trust-based security models, cloud-enabled big data applications, the Internet of Things (IoT), the software defined network (SDN), and network function virtualization (NFV).

The study in [29] conducted a systematic literature review of the integration as a service between trusted computing and cloud computing for infrastructure as a service (IaaS). Cloud computing integration and trusted computing can create a new infrastructure architecture as a service that encourages more cloud service tenants to trust cloud service providers.

A survey in [17] provided security issues and requirements for the cloud and identified threats and known vulnerabilities. The work presented a new classification of recent security solutions that exist in this area. It presented a series of documented policies, procedures and processes that define a secure way to manage the cloud environment to identify the vulnerability and increase confidence in an ever-connected world.

In [30], the authors investigated the key contemporary security problem in cloud computing and provided the best practices for service providers and organizations hoping to manage cloud services. Table 2 presents a summary of the existing related surveys in terms of their contributions and the levels of infrastructure they covered. It summarizes existing survey papers in cloud infrastructure over the period from 2016 to 2020. As noticed, most of these surveys were conducted at only one level of cloud infrastructure. For instance, the surveys in [19,20,23,28], focused on only the data level, while the survey in [24] focused on only the application level. Moreover, a survey [26] was conducted on the network level and another paper [30] on the host level.

There have been some works performed at two or more levels in cloud infrastructure, such as the studies conducted in [18,22,25]. In addition, the studies in [21,27,29,31], considered all infrastructure levels. Nevertheless, [20] considered a public cloud only, and also for cloud services in terms of cloud infrastructure vendors and revenue. Meanwhile the survey in [27] focused more on how to manage the data in the public cloud. The study in [29] was a narrative review without any analyses of the reviewed materials. Lastly, the survey in [31] was limited to the analyses of security from the provider's perspective.

To conclude, the existing survey papers in cloud infrastructure security are not comprehensive enough. They do not cover the security of all levels of cloud infrastructure, i.e., host, network, application and data. Some of the reported surveys are limited to one or more levels. In addition, some surveys do not consider all perspectives of customers and service providers. Our proposed survey is different, such that it conducts an extensive review of issues that faced all levels of cloud computing infrastructure with a proper analysis of such issues. Then, it discusses the existing solutions used to mitigate these issues. Finally, the survey highlights the open issues and challenges, and gives directions for future research.

Table 2. Summary of existing surveys.

Reference	Contribution	Data	Application	Host	Network
[18]	The study reviewed the security issues regarding user data sensitivity on cloud architecture.	√			
[19]	The study focused on identified cloud computing security issues during data migration to the cloud and presented solutions for resolving potential threats.	√			
[20]	The survey performed a taxonomy to compare key services that are regularly used by cloud applications.	√	√	√	√
[21]	This study focused on the crypto cloud with various Communication, Storage, and Service Level Agreements.		√		√
[22]	The survey focused on data privacy.	√			
[23]	The study highlighted the security requirements for cloud computing.		√		
[24]	The study was classifying types of threats based on service resources in the context of the cloud.	√	√		
[25]	The study reviewed DDoS techniques used in cloud computing.				√
[26]	The study evaluated major attacks targeting the security of Cloud Computing.	√	√	√	√
[27]	The study reviewed technologies that allow for privacy-aware outsourcing of storage and processing of sensitive data to public clouds.	√			
[17]	The study provided security issues and requirements for the cloud, identified threats, and known vulnerabilities.	√	√		√
[30]	The study is more about the security from providers perspectives.	√	√	√	√
This survey	Provides an extensive survey on issues that cloud computing infrastructure faced at its levels (Application, Host, and Network and data level). Presents some existing solutions used to mitigate these issues. Highlights some open challenges that still need to be solved.	√	√	√	√

4. Security Issues in Cloud Computing Infrastructure

Four main levels should be considered when planning for and applying security in cloud infrastructure, which are data level, application level, network level, and the host level [31]. These levels are shown in Figure 6.

According to [31], these levels are described as in the following paragraphs.

Security at the data level refers to providing protection for data at rest and in transit to protect the data from loss or leakage, which significantly impact data security and privacy. Malicious actors could compromise the data exchanged between the systems within the cloud, referred to as data in transit. Sniffing and man-in-the-middle (MITM) are the common attacks against data in transit within cloud ecosystem. In addition, several threats including, but not limited to, data leakage, hijacking, manipulation and eradication can affect the confidentiality, integrity, and availability of the data at rest.

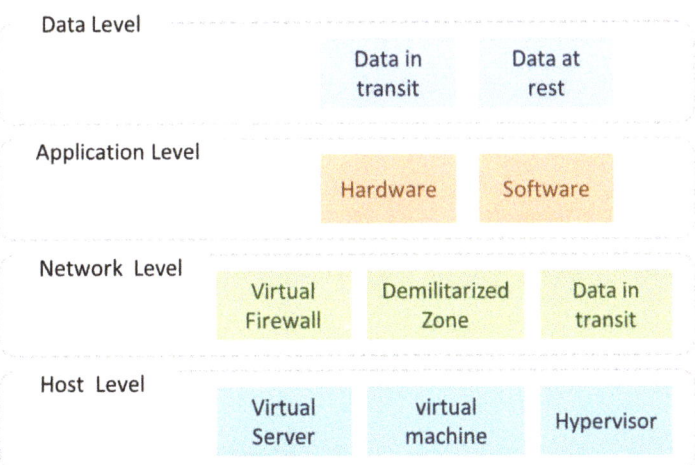

Figure 6. Cloud infrastructure levels.

Application level: Security at this level refers to providing protection for applications when utilizing the hardware and software resources to prevent the attackers to get control over these applications. The most major threats at this level are denial of service (DoS) attacks that affect software applications.

Network level: Security at this level refers to providing protection for the network when using a virtual firewall, demilitarized zone (DMZ), and data in transit. For this purpose, information about different types of firewalls should be monitored, collected, and maintained.

Host level: Security at this level refers to providing security for the host when using a virtual server, hypervisor, and virtual machine. It is important to collect the information about the system log files to know when and where the applications have been logged.

At each level, the main CIA components should be evaluated when protecting cloud infrastructure. Along with the growing popularity of cloud-based systems, the security problems introduced by adapting this technology are increasing. Although cloud computing has many advantages, it is vulnerable to various types of attacks. Attackers are consistently seeking to find weaknesses to attack the infrastructure of cloud computing [32]. The following subsections explore the security issues in the different levels of cloud infrastructure.

4.1. Data-Level Issues

Data breaches, loss, segregation, virtualization, confidentiality, integrity, and availability are the issues faced at this level. Figure 7 depicts these issues and the following subsections discuss them in detail.

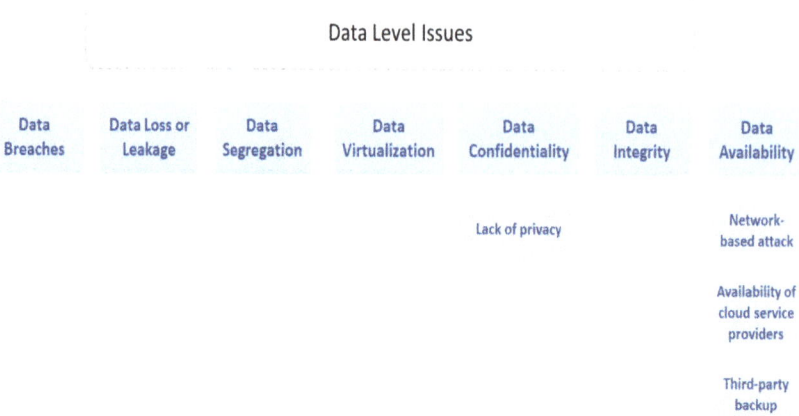

Figure 7. Data Level Issues.

4.1.1. Data Breach Issues

Data breaches are a critical security issue that needs to be focused on in the cloud infrastructure. Because large amounts of data from different users are stored in the cloud, a malicious user can access the cloud in such a way that the entire cloud environment is vulnerable to a high-value attack. Breaches can occur due to various accidental transmission problems [33]. The shared resources in the cloud make it easy for adversaries to target the data in the cloud infrastructure using many types of attacks. These attacks can be classified into several categories, including data loss and data leakage.

4.1.2. Data Loss or Leakage Issues

Data are transferred from data centers to the client's systems and are transmitted from one execution mode to multiple execution mode, which may cause data loss or leakage. Even though data are stored away from the client system, there could be a possibility of data loss or leakage. As a result, data leakage is becoming a critical security issue among the various security issues in the cloud environment [34]. The loss and/or leakage of data may be carried out by internal threat actors such as disgruntled employees, contractors, and other partners. Likewise, external actors could gain access to the cloud infrastructure and disclose, delete, or lock the data they may locate. This could be done with the aid of a wide range of tools and tricks such as malware, identity theft, and password brute force. To protect data in the cloud environment from being leaked, two main types of countermeasures are employed, namely encryption and watermarking. However, encryption cannot protect data at rest if intruders manage to gain access into the cloud using valid credentials. As such, it is imperative to scrutinize cloud access requests and ensure that they come from legitimate users.

4.1.3. Data Segregation Issues

Multi-tenancy is one of the key features of cloud computing. Since multi-tenancy allows multiple users to store data on cloud servers, there is a possibility of data intrusion. Utilizing the shared environment, intruders could gain access using the credentials of an unaware user. Data can also be intruded by injecting a client code or using any application with known vulnerabilities. There is therefore a need for security measures to control the access to shared environments or isolate the data of each user in multi-tenant environments [33].

4.1.4. Data Virtualization Issues

Due to the high mobility and elasticity features of the cloud, VMs along with data can easily be moved from their original location to another. This might lead to loss of the metadata fully or partially, which can cause many service interruptions and an unpleasant experience. For instance, the user might face difficulties in copying or cloning the data, as the movement of sensitive data in the form of metadata causes the loss of these data and the hazard of errors [21].

4.1.5. Data Confidentiality Issues

Often, the confidentiality in a cloud system policy focuses on protecting data during transfers between entities. In addition, it is concerned with data privacy, where customer data must not be disclosed to unauthorized parties at any time. Data are stored on remote servers and can be hosted by single or multi-cloud providers based on the content such as data, videos, etc. This raises several security concerns with regard to the security, compatibility and interoperability between the different cloud service providers. Data confidentiality is one of the essential criteria when data are stored on a remote server. Such confidentiality could be compromised due to the miscoordination between the cloud service providers that co-host the data, which opens one or more vulnerabilities that threat actors can exploit. To maintain confidentiality, understanding and classification of data, users should be aware of the data stored in the cloud and their accessibility [33].

4.1.6. Data Integrity Issues

Integrity issues arise in such an environment due to data being stored remotely and at multiple locations [35]. Such a distributed environment evokes special attention to the integrity when storing and retrieving the data in multiple places, where many errors could occur, such as manipulating, losing, or corrupting these data fragments. Although these issues could occur due to system internal errors, hackers can inflict such damages as well. The system should be so secure that only the legitimate user can access and/or modify the data. In a cloud-based environment, data integrity must be maintained correctly to prevent data loss. In general, data integrity could be avoided by applying several security measures like hashing, salting, timestamping, and digital signatures. The repeatedly used data integrity protection methods provide information about changes in data and checksums to verify the integrity of the data [36].

4.1.7. Data Availability Issues

Data should be available for authorized users at all times. The user must also have control over their data. There are currently three major threats to data availability, which are the network-based attack, the availability of cloud service providers and third-party backup of data collected by cloud service providers. The threat actors could launch massive DoS attacks against the targeted cloud, preventing users from accessing resources on the cloud. Attackers could also erase data on cloud storage or take one or more data storage offline. Therefore, cloud service providers should avoid a single point of failures situation by applying the concept of redundancy on network, service, and data storage levels. Data recovery after an accident, such as a hard disk crash, destruction and natural disasters, should be assured by the cloud provider [36].

4.2. Application-Level Issues

Many issues arise at the application level, as shown in Figure 8. These issues are related to availability, authentication, insecure APIs, malicious insiders, and end user attacks. The following subsections elaborate on these issues.

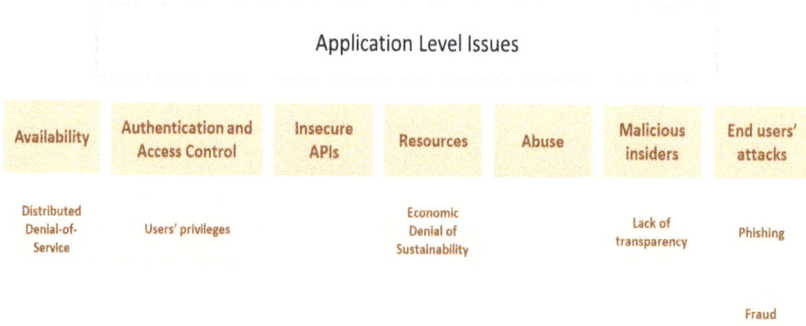

Figure 8. Application-level issues.

4.2.1. Availability Issues

The cloud should be available at all times, and robust to any security threat or user misbehavior. This is a basic, yet difficult, problem in the cloud. Compared to multi-clouds, the issue of availability in a single cloud is very critical. The application availability refers to making it accessible to the user [35]. Distributed denial-of-service attacks (DDoS) are one of the major threats to an application's availability on the cloud. These attacks have become complex and continue to develop rapidly, making it more difficult to identify and tackle them [37]. The major aim for the attacker is to block legal users and take control over resources and services so that the customer will not be able to use the application hosted on the cloud.

4.2.2. Authentication and Access Control Issues

Many issues also came in the context of access control and authentication. These issues come in the form of unauthorized access/use/of the resources on the cloud. In the access control context, the elasticity feature in IaaS introduces several security issues due to the rapid change in the infrastructure configurations, which makes one or more applied access controls outdated. Therefore, an agile and adaptive authentication approach needs to be incorporated into cloud-based applications. There is also a need for mechanisms that enforce a proper configuration and change management [38].

Although the multi-tenancy feature in IaaS facilitates the usage of infrastructure through sharing resources among multiple customers, this causes some issues related to accessing these resources from authenticated, yet unauthorized users. Therefore, proper access controls that solve such conflict need to be in place [38].

In addition, the flexibility of IaaS allows the consumer to configure virtual machines. This could be a security issue, as the misconfiguration of VMs may lead to security violations due to overlooking some security parameters during the creation of the VM. Additionally, there is a need for an approach constructed on role-based access control [38]. In the authentication context, cloud authentication techniques are typically only one party or open access, such that the cloud service provider does not have a platform for multiple user interface authentication, resulting in unauthorized or vulnerable access to the cloud space [39].

4.2.3. Insecure APIs

Cloud APIs are usually used to connect with other systems at all levels of the infrastructure, network, host and application services. These APIs are used for different tasks, such as access and control network and VM infrastructure resources in IaaS, access cloud services (e.g., storage) in PaaS, and link cloud infrastructure to applications in SaaS [40]. However, those APIs, if not secured properly, could be utilized by malicious actors as a platform to carry out many types of attacks against the applications on the cloud. The security of different cloud providers depends upon the security of the APIs. Numerous cloud security problems will result in a poor set of APIs and interfaces. Generally, cloud providers sell their APIs to third parties to provide consumers with services. Nevertheless, weakly secured APIs can be used by hackers to access security keys and sensitive information. Consequently, the encrypted customer data in the cloud can be read using the encryption keys, which violates access control and authentication standards, and compromises data integrity, availability and confidentiality [40].

4.2.4. Resources Issues

A cloud offers computing platforms rich resources where payment is based on the usage of the cloud resources, known as "pay-as-you-use" or utility computing. However, resource-exhaustion attacks like DDoS could consume many resources on the server and cloud infrastructure, which leads to overcharging the customer and/or depleting the quota the user subscribed to. In such instances, the primary aim of the attack is to render cloud computing unsustainable by targeting the cloud adopter's economic resources. Thus, the economic denial of sustainability (EDoS) attack represents a new form of DDoS attack [41].

4.2.5. Abuse of Cloud Computing

IaaS providers provide their customers with unrestricted computing, networking, and storage capacities. These providers sometimes offer a "frictionless" registration process that allows those with a valid credit card to register and start using cloud services. Clients sometimes get limited trial periods free of charge. By exploiting anonymity through these registrations and various templates, spammers have misused malicious software. These kinds of attacks have typically targeted PaaS and IaaS providers. Cloud providers must be concerned about issues such as malicious data hosting, password cracking, key cracking, the building of rainbow tables, the launching of dynamic attack points, CAPTCHA, control, and botnet command solving farms [34].

4.2.6. Malicious Insiders Issues

Malicious insiders pose a threat to customers due to the lack of transparency between cloud providers and customers' procedures to the services. In insider attacks, malicious actors have legitimate access privileges to the resources, which makes it difficult to identify whether what he/she is doing is malicious. This kind of issue normally starts at the very beginning with the hiring process. Sometimes, the visibility of hiring standards and practices for the employees is low. Such a situation often seems to attract attackers who attempt to perform espionage and facilitate organized crime. Malicious insiders cause data breaches, loss, and/or falsification [34].

4.2.7. End Users' Attacks

There are many attacks on cloud users, such as phishing and fraud, that can affect the infrastructure of cloud services. Phishing and fraud are ways to steal a legitimate user's identity, such as credentials and credit card information. Usually, phishing is performed by sending the user an email containing a connection to a fraudulent website that looks like a legitimate one. When the user visits the fraudulent website, the username and password are sent to the attacker, who can use them to attack the cloud. Another type of phishing and fraud is to send the user an email claiming to be from the provider of cloud services and to ask the user to provide his/her credentials for maintenance purposes [42]. Although attacks targeting the end user on the cloud look similar to those on conventional systems, they are not identical, as cloud users can gain access from different platforms, which gives the attacker more options to break into the system.

4.3. Network Level Issues

The issues at this level involve attacks on availability, integrity and confidentiality, as shown in Figure 9.

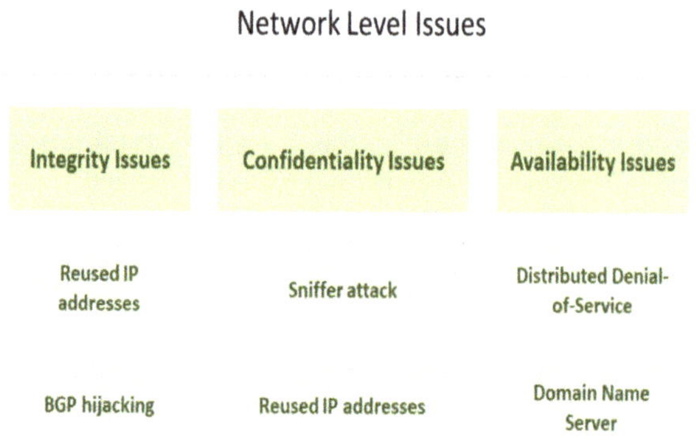

```
                        Network Level Issues

        ┌─────────────────┐  ┌──────────────────────┐  ┌──────────────────┐
        │ Integrity Issues│  │Confidentiality Issues│  │Availability Issues│
        └─────────────────┘  └──────────────────────┘  └──────────────────┘

             Reused IP                                   Distributed Denial-
             addresses              Sniffer attack           of-Service


                                                          Domain Name
             BGP hijacking       Reused IP addresses         Server
```

Figure 9. Network level Issues.

4.3.1. Integrity Issues

Integrity refers to the confidence in the protection against changes by unauthorized persons. The issues of integrity came in many contexts in cloud infrastructure [36]. In the context of the network, IP addresses are seized by corrupting the Internet routing tables by BGP hijacking or prefix hijacking. Normally, the border gateway protocol (BGP) is utilized to stabilize the network and transfer the packets from one path route to another route if the original path is down. However, attackers could hijack the BGP and redirect the data to other destinations. BGP hijacking leads to data leakages, and compromises the integrity and sometimes availability [43]. In addition, in the cloud environment, IP addresses are usually reassigned and reused. This occurs when customers change their location. The old "aged" IP can be assigned to other customers. This might lead to increased risk when reusing an existing IP address for a new device/customer happens faster than removing its old assignment from DNS caches [44].

4.3.2. Confidentiality Issues

Issues regarding confidentiality are rising due to the growing number of cloud users working in a multi-tenant environment, where compromising one system could lead to a chain of subsequent compromises in other systems. Sniffing attack is the most prominent issue. This occurs in a cloud environment when unencrypted packets of data are transferred between two entities in the cloud. These packets can, therefore, be captured, leading to the exploitation of confidential information. In a cloud environment, the existence of an entity with a promiscuous mode in the network node highly suggests that data in the node are being monitored by an attacker [44]. In addition, the reused IP addresses lead to the compromising of confidentiality, if not handled properly when reassigned to another user [44].

4.3.3. Availability Issues

Many of the issues come in the context of network availability, such as DDoS and DNS attacks. DDoS floods the customer with useless traffic for an infinite period, rendering resources or services inaccessible. The primary aim is to take control over resources (bandwidth of network or time of CPU) such that they cannot provide services to the legal consumers. The other aim is to hide the attacker's identity by imitating legal web application traffic and creating many agents to launch a DDOS attack [34]. The attacker typically hides their identity by spoofing the victim's IP address portion of a packet header. This makes it very hard to identify the source of an attack. Most providers cannot cover this attack, since they are unable to differentiate between good traffic and bad traffic. A conventional solution has been increasing the number of resources [34]. With regard to the domain name server (DNS), servers play a critical role in cloud infrastructure, given that the failure of DNS will most likely lead to the cloud's lockdown, rendering the data inaccessible. DNS in the cloud infrastructure is exploited to execute large-scale attacks to damage cloud data services. Some common attacks on the DNS infrastructure include DDoS attacks, modified data attacks, corrupted data attacks, man-in-the-middle attacks, and DNS ID spoofing attacks. These attacks compromise server availability [44].

4.4. Host-Level Issues

At the host level, visualization and data storage issues are the main concern, as shown in Figure 10.

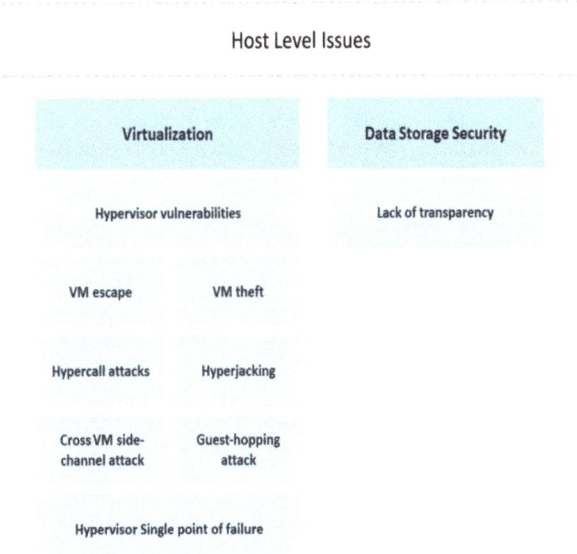

Figure 10. Host Level Issues.

4.4.1. Virtualization Issues

The concept of the cloud is based on virtualization, in which many guest VMs share common physical hardware. Malicious actors can target the virtualization elements, such as the hypervisor and virtual machines [45]. Therefore, securing the hypervisor in cloud environments is necessary, as hackers can use it to compromise all VMs built based on it [46]. Many of the issues raised in the context of virtualization and hypervisor issues [21] can be summarized as follows:

Hypervisor Vulnerabilities

To run multiple guest VMs and applications simultaneously on a single host machine and to provide isolation between the guest VMs, a hypervisor or virtual machine manager (VMM) is generated. While hypervisors are supposed to be vigorous and stable, they are vulnerable to attacks. When attackers take control of the hypervisor, it will be under their full control, and all the VMs and data will be accessible to them. The greater control offered by the bottom layers in the virtual machine is another reason hackers consider the VMM a potential target. Compromising a VMM also allows attackers to access the underlying physical device and applications they host. Many of the well-known attacks (e.g., Hyperjacking, Bluepill, etc.) inject rootkits based on VMs that can mount or change the current rogue hypervisor to take full control of the environment. Since the hypervisor runs underneath the host OS, standard security measures make it difficult to detect these types of attacks [45].

VM Theft

Virtual machine (VM) theft is another virtualization-related attack that can hit cloud environments. For this attack to mount and run, an attacker copies a VM over the network or to a portable storage medium. This could be done by utilizing the migration utility on the hypervisor. Nevertheless, to trigger unauthorized migration of the guest VM to its cloud infrastructure, an intruder may also tamper with the VMM control panel that handles live migration [47]. As such, securing the hypervisor could help in mitigating the VM theft attack.

VM Escape

Virtual machines are intended to support a strong separation between hosts and VMs. However, the operating system's vulnerabilities running within the VM can help attackers to inject malware, which not only can affect the current VM but also bypass the VMM layer into the other VMs on the same hypervisor. This allows the malware to gain access to the host machine and initiate sustainable attacks, utilizing the set of backdoors they open [45].

Hyper Jacking

Hyper jacking is an attack in which, inside a virtual machine (VM) host, a hacker takes control over the hypervisor that generates the virtual environment. This attack aims to target the operating system of the virtual machines. Therefore, the software of the attacker can run, and its existence will be completely hidden from the applications on the VMs [45].

Hyper-Call Attacks

Hyper-call attacks involve an intrusion into the VM using well-defined hyper-call interfaces by an unauthorized guest VM by exploiting vulnerabilities in the hyper-call handler of a VMM. Such attacks could lead to a shift in the functionality of the VMM or a "host crash" when a malicious code with VMM privileges is executed [47].

Guest-Hopping Attacks

Guest-hopping attacks include any failure of separation between shared infrastructures. An attacker tries to access one virtual machine by accessing another virtual machine hosted on the same hardware. The Forensics and VM debugging instruments are one of the potential mitigations of the guest hopping attack to observe any attempts to manipulate VM [42].

Hypervisor Single Point of Failure

The hypervisor technology that regulates the access of VMs to physical resources is the basis of current virtualized environments and is critical for the overall functionality of the system. Therefore, hypervisor failure due to the overuse of hardware or device faults leads to overall system collapse [45]. This is known as single-point-of-failure, which originates from lacking redundant hypervisor and/or underlying hardware. Therefore, a robust cloud environment should implement the high availability approach, in which critical components are redundant. In such a setup, if one component failed, the redundant component takes over the workload. This kind of operation is normally transparent to end users and they do not experience any interruption in the cloud services.

Cross VM Side-Channel Attack

In a side-channel attack, the attacker establishes a hidden channel over shared hardware resources from which he/she collects important information. During this attack, hackers monitor victim's activities and collect information such as cryptographic keys, username, and passwords. Although side-channel attacks have been around for a long time in conventional systems, with the advent of cloud technologies, where the basic concept is to share resources, their effect is growing by several folds [48].

4.4.2. Data Storage Security Issue

Since user data are stored in the server set of the cloud service provider (CSP) that operates concurrently and in a distributed way, the integrity and the confidentiality of the data stored at the CSP must be maintained. This can be achieved by ensuring that CSP employees have restricted access to user data and strict security procedures to ensure that only authorized employees gain control and access to CSP servers. In addition, well-defined data backups and redundant data storage can be used by the CSP to make data recovery possible [42]. However, the transparency between the user and the service provider may play a decisive role in this matter [34], as the customer is aware of the storage sites, the policies followed, as well as the protection methods followed.

Table 3 summarizes the security issues discussed above at every level of the cloud infrastructure. It highlights the threats exhibited at each level and the cloud features affected, in addition to the impact on security measures.

Table 3. Summary of security issues.

Security Issue	Threats	Level Effected	Feature Affected by	Impact on Security	Reference
Availability	DDoS	Application level/Network level	Multi-tenancy and Elasticity	Compromised the availability	[36,38]
	DNS attacks	Network level	Multi-tenancy and Elasticity	Compromised the availability	[34,44]
	Unavailability data	Application level/Host level/Network level/Data level	Multi-tenancy	Compromised the data availability	[37]
Integrity	Data modification	Application level/Host level/Network level/Data level	Multi-tenancy and Elasticity	Change on data that lead to loss of integrity	[36,37]
	Prefix Hijacking	Network level	Multi-tenancy and Elasticity	Affected integrity and availability	[44]
	Reused IP Addressing	Network level	Multi-tenancy and Elasticity	Compromised integrity and confidentiality	[45]
Confidentiality	Lack of data confidentiality	Application level/Host level/Network level/Data level	Flexibility and Multi-tenancy	Impact the data privacy	[44]
	Sniffer Attacks	Network level	Elasticity	Affected confidentiality	[45]
	Reused IP Addressing	Network level	Elasticity	Compromised integrity and confidentiality	[45]
Authentication and Access Control	Sharing resources	Application level	Multi-tenancy	Violate access control standards	[39,40]
	Misconfiguration	Application level	Flexibility	Compromised access control standards	[39,40]
	Unauthorized/ vulnerable access	Application level	Flexibility, Multi-tenancy and Elasticity	Violate authentication and access control standards	[39,40]

Table 3. Cont.

Security Issue	Threats	Level Effected	Feature Affected by	Impact on Security	Reference
Virtualization	Hypervisor vulnerabilities	Host level	Multi-tenancy and Elasticity	Can cause damage to the entire system	[46]
	VM theft	Host level/Network level	Flexibility	Effect the network and storage	[48]
	VM escape	Host level	Flexibility	Cause a vulnerability to OS	[46]
	Hyperjacking	Host level	-	Take control over OS	[46]
	Hyper-call	Host level	Elasticity	Shift the functionality of VMM and host crash	[48]
	Guest-hopping attack	Host level	Multi-tenancy	Lead to access VM	[43]
	Hypervisor Single point of failure	Host level	Multi-tenancy	Can cause damage to the entire system	[46]
	Cross VM side-channel attack	Host level	Multi-tenancy	in the valuable information	[48]
	Data virtualization	Application level/Host level/Network level/Data level	Elasticity	Data loss and cause damage to the data	[22]
Insecure API's	Insecure API's	Application level	Flexibility, Multi-tenancy and Elasticity	Violate access control and authentication but also loss of data integrity, availability and confidentiality	[41]
Resources	EDoS	Application level	On-demand services (Pay-as-you use)	Effected the costs of the resources	[42]
Abuse of Cloud Computing	User's abuse	Application level	Multi-tenancy	It can cause malicious data hosting, password cracking, key cracking, the building of rainbow tables, launching of dynamic attack points	[35]
Malicious Insiders	Insider users	Application level	Multi-tenancy	Data Breaches	[35]
End users' attacks	Phishing Fraud	Application level	Multi-tenancy	Steal user's identity	[42]
Data Storage Security	Data Storage Issues (e.g., lack of transparency)	Host level	Multi-tenancy	Data Breaches	[43]
Data Loss or Leakage	Data Loss or Leakage	Application level/Host level/Network level/Data level	Multi-tenancy	loss of data integrity, availability and confidentiality	[35]
Data Segregation	injecting a client code or using any application	Application level/Host level	Multi-tenancy	loss of data integrity, availability and confidentiality	[34]

As shown in Table 4, the most affected cloud feature is multi-tenancy. The reason for this might be related to the interaction between the customers who share the same environment and/or resources. In addition, attackers could carry out utilizing the interface used by customers to interact with the service provider.

In addition, it can be noticed that most security issues affect the application level and data level rather than the network level, but the most serious issues threaten the host level. This fact should be taken seriously, as damage to the host can damage the entire system, including the shared spaces. The following subsections present the proposed solutions in the literature for the issues discussed in this section. The solutions will be discussed based on the levels as well as the issues discussed in the same manner.

5. Related Existing Solutions in Cloud Levels

This section presents solutions proposed in the literature based on the different cloud infrastructure levels. This includes the data, application, network, and host levels. More details about those solutions are discussed in the following subsections.

5.1. Solutions at Data Level

Through the transition from conventional computing models to the Internet-based cloud model, there is a great need for emphasizing data security and privacy. Data loss or data leakage can significantly affect the organization's business and ruin the trust in its brand. A study in [49] investigated the audit in the cloud computing environment. Data auditing involves examining various features that include data confidentiality, integrity, remanence, provenance and lineage. According to the study, there are a range of basic techniques in each of these features that could satisfy the needs of cloud service users for data auditing, except data remanence, which is still an open issue within public cloud services. As concluded, the study found that despite many available techniques to address user auditing issues in the data auditing area, cloud providers have so far focused more on infrastructure security auditing than data auditing.

The authors in [50] focused on the issue of data integrity verification by a third-party auditor for client data that resides on a cloud storage server (CSS). The study suggested a protocol for dynamic data updates using the modified Chameleon Authentication Tree (MCAT). They also demonstrated the security of their optimized auditing protocol by proving that it is resistant to replay, replace, and forge attacks.

A study in [51] proposed a classification technique based on various parameters. The parameters were defined based on different dimensions. It is intended to have security levels based on content type and accessibility. According to the authors, data security can be provided based on the level of protection needed. Depending on the data set classified as dimensions, the corresponding security provisions for storage can be applied.

In [52], the authors proposed a secure data classification-based cloud computing model. The proposed model minimizes the total time necessary to secure data by applying TLS, AES and SHA cryptographic algorithms based on the classified data type. The proposed model has been tested and the results show the reliability and efficient existence of the proposed model.

In [53], the authors proposed a framework for privacy-preserving out-sourced classification in cloud computing (POCC). Using POCC, the evaluator can train a classification model securely over data encrypted with different public keys, that are outsourced to multiple data providers. Based on Gentry's scheme, the authors used a proxy fully homomorphic encryption technique to protect the privacy of sensitive data.

The work in [36] defined the data security modeling design in cloud computing. Data security in all cloud storage layers was discussed. Based on this study, the standard cloud storage uses a three-level cloud data security model that can be expanded to a fourth level responsible for data integrity checks. The paper introduced the design of a four-level data security model in cloud computing that describes each part of cloud data security using Petri nets.

The authors in [54] proposed a framework to protect big data in the cloud computing environment. The Map Reduce framework was used to find the number of users logging into the cloud data center. The proposed framework protects the mapping of different data elements to each provider using the meta cloud data storage interface. While this proposed approach requires a high degree of implementation effort, it offers valuable information for a cloud computing environment that can have a high impact on future systems.

A study in [55] proposed a framework consisting of various techniques and specialized procedures that can protect the data efficiently from the owner to the cloud and then to the user. Data protection strategies include a secure socket layer (SSL) and MAC, which are used to check the integrity of data, to encode the data, and divide it into three sections of the cloud. The division of data into three sections offers additional protection and more accessibility. The proposed method achieves the availability, reliability, and integrity of data travelling through the server owner to the cloud and from the cloud to the customer. In addition, it also offers more flexibility and allows the user to retrieve files from the cloud by searching for encrypted data.

The study in [56] identified problems related to cloud data storage, such as data breaches, data theft, and cloud data unavailability. The study proposed potential solutions to those issues. The proposed solutions addressed issues related to identity management and access control. However, there are many issues related to access control and identity management that are still unsolved, such as weak credentials that can easily be reset, denial of service attack to lock the account for a period of time, weak logging and monitoring capabilities, and XML wrapping attacks on web pages.

The authors in [57] proposed a new technique called match-then-decryption, in which a matching phase is added before the decryption phase. This technique works by computing special components in ciphertexts used to verify whether the private key attribute matches the hidden access policy in ciphertexts without decryption. Formal security analyses and comparisons showed that the suggested solutions simultaneously ensure privacy attributes and increase the efficiency of decryption for outsourced cloud data storage.

In [58], the authors proposed a system to enhance the RSA algorithm by increasing the key size to strengthen the encryption process. The proposed algorithm reduces the time required for encryption and decryption by dividing the file into blocks and enhances the strength of the algorithm by increasing the key size. This power paves the way for users to store data in the cloud efficiently.

The study in [59] used elliptic curve cryptography (ECC) to encrypt data in the cloud environment because the key size used by ECC is very small. Owing to the small key size of the ECC, the computing power is reduced, and the energy consumption is minimized. This study showed that ECC is fast and more effective for data protection in a cloud computing environment and reduces computing power and also improves performance.

The authors in [60] suggested a hybrid algorithm to improve cloud data security using an encryption algorithm. To improve cloud security, this study combined homographic and blowfish encryption algorithms. The blowfish algorithm was used to generate a security key. A symmetric key block was used for both decryption and encryption. Homographic encryption, on the other hand, provides confidentiality of data and prevents storing the information in plain text at any stage.

In [61], the authors proposed a novel lightweight encryption algorithm consisting of combining a symmetric algorithm for encrypting data and an asymmetric one for distributing keys. This combination allows users to benefit from successful asymmetric encryption protection and rapid symmetric encryption performance while maintaining uses' rights to protected and permitted access to data. The findings reveal that the lightweight algorithm's processing time is faster than state-of-the-art cryptographic algorithms.

In the study [8], the authors suggested a hybrid layered approach to protect the data of the user, along with a combination of a lattice-based security technique. A new approach was introduced for responsibilities and roles examination using the lattice model. The AES and RSA algorithms were used to provide sensitive data with more and better protection.

The study in [60] proposed a hybrid algorithm to enhance the security of cloud data using an encryption algorithm. It combined homographic encryption and blowfish encryption to enhance cloud security. However, this hybrid algorithm does not appear to be effective in practice, as the homographic encryption is extremely slow and computationally expensive, to the point that it is not currently practical. In addition to that, the blowfish algorithm does not provide authentication and non-repudiation because more than one person might share the same key. Additionally, there are some drawbacks in this method of decryption, as it takes up more time and bandwidth.

To conclude, the proposed solutions for cloud data protection vary between data auditing, encryption, classification, and secure data modeling. However, these techniques are still not fully mature and face many problems. In Section 6, some open challenges are highlighted, followed by future research recommendations in Section 7.

5.2. Solutions at Application Level

To mitigate risks at the application level, several solutions have been proposed by researchers. For instance, a study in [62] provided a novel "Scale Inside Out" technique that decreases the Resource Utilization Factor to a minimum value during attacks to rapidly absorb the DDoS attack. In addition to other co-located facilities, the recommended solution sacrifices victim service resources and provides certain resources to the prevention service to assess the availability during the attack. According to the study, the experimental evaluation indicates a decrease of up to 95% in total attack downtime of the victim's service in addition to significant improvements in attack detection and reporting time and downtime of co-located facilities.

A contribution in [63] suggested a method to limit the effects of economic denial of service (EDoS) attacks on cloud applications. This method was dependent on the adoption of the service level agreement (SLA) supplemented by an intrusion prevention scheme (IPS).

Another effort in [64] suggested a new method that used an artificial neural network (ANN) along with the genetic algorithm (GA) for EDoS attack detection in the cloud. The classification was carried out using an ANN that classifies the customer of the cloud server and minimizes the EDoS attacks in the cloud environment, while the GA was used to optimize the attributes of each server using appropriate fitness functions.

Researchers in [5] proposed an approach to mitigate EDoS attacks in the SDN-based cloud computing environment. An unsupervised deep learning technique called long short-term memory (LSTM) was used as a multivariate time series anomaly detection model. The main concept was to try to predict the values of a cloud customer's resource use (memory use, CPU load, etc.). The experiments were conducted with different EDoS attack levels and proved that the proposed approach was an effective and innovative solution for SDN-based cloud defense of EDoS attacks according to the authors.

Another study in [37] designed a technique for identifying cloud computing DDoS attacks. This technique employs machine learning algorithms such as support vector machine (SVM), naive Bayes (NB), and random forest (RF) for classification. The study was carried out using Tor Hammer as an attacking tool on a cloud environment, and a new dataset for the intrusion detection technique was developed.

A study in [65] discussed various authentication schemes used in cloud computing and proposed a framework for using passphrase-based multifactor authentication to make cloud resources more secure. The primary comparison of authentication models reinforced the level of security and the disadvantages of corresponding schemes in the cloud computing environment. The passphrase in the proposed scheme ensures secure passwords and provides extra security for the SSH key pair. In [66], the authors proposed an authentication-based AES and MD5 technique for data encryption to protect the data and the login of the users over the cloud at the time of login.

The authors in [67] proposed a novel security model for authentication-supported cloud computing. The model introduced a new idea for a biometric security system based on fingerprint recognition. The proposed method automated the verification process to match human fingerprints, where fingerprints are used to identify the individuals and verify their identity. Users are authenticated based on the fingerprint templates, which must be given based on random numbers generated each time. The experimental results showed that the proposed system outperforms the single-fingerprint authentication system.

The researchers in [68] recently proposed a novel hash-based, multi-factor, secure mutual authentication scheme that includes mathematical hashing properties, certificates, nonce values, traditional user IDs and password mechanisms. The strength of the proposed authentication procedure was evaluated using the GNY belief logic and the Scyther method. The results show that the proposed scheme can prevent the man-in-the-middle, replay and forgery attacks.

In another recent study [69], the Seamless Secure Anonymous Authentication Scheme (S-SAAS) was proposed to establish a secure session for cloud-based mobile edge computing. This proposed protocol used elliptic-curve cryptography, one-way hash function and less expensive operation to provide seamless connectivity. In addition, this proposed protocol applied a new random integer to withstand potential attacks and satisfies important security features.

The authors in [70] recently proposed a novel pairing-free multi-server authentication protocol based on ECC for the MCC environment. The proposed scheme not only offers computational cost-efficiency but also preserves the features of costly pairing schemes, such as the achievement of secure mutual authentication, anonymity and scalability. The strength of the scheme is theoretically illustrated by the formal security model.

The authors in [71] developed various models for information and resource sharing among tenants in an IaaS cloud using the Open Stack platform as a reference. The models encourage a tenant to engage its IT resources with other tenants in a controlled method. Nevertheless, the VMs need to be restricted in network access so that malicious software is incapable of transmitting the information in an uncontrolled manner.

The work in [72] proposed a novel access control framework for security and privacy issues in the cloud environment. The proposed framework was based on dynamic trustworthiness. Access control that is based on dynamic trustworthiness is applied to decrease the possibility to perform unauthorized activities and to make sure that only authorized users can access cloud resources. The result show that the system identifies malicious behavior to avoid any unauthorized access, will enhance the security of cloud computing, and will therefore lead to an increased trust degree of users.

The authors in [73] proposed a hybrid access control framework called iHAC that enables combining the features of type enforcement and role-based access control. The proposed framework enables flexible access control and is unified for IaaS clouds environments. In addition, a VMM-based access control technique was designed to restrict the VM's behaviors to the underlying resources in a fine-grained method. The experimental results show that the iHAC framework helps to make true access control decisions with an acceptable performance overhead.

Another study in [74] proposed a dynamic access control approach to solve the multifarious security breaches that occur in the cloud. This approach tends to secure data in the cloud that should address the interrelationship between the requestor, data that are requested, and the action that will be performed on the data. Furthermore, the study considered the user for granting access control dynamically. The result only presented an initial implementation of the proposed approach.

A recent study in [75] proposed a blockchain-based access control framework called AuthPrivacyChain and privacy protection in clouds. All authorization that is linked to transactions is posted through the user to the blockchain. Moreover, the framework was designed based on an enterprise operation system (EOS) blockchain to access the permission and the information as a further description of blockchain transactions. Additionally, AuthPrivacyChain provides access control, authorization revocation and authorization. The experimental results show that only legal users can access resources, but AuthPrivacyChain cannot prevent attacks from external users.

A study in [76] proposed an approach for cloud identity management with privacy and security improvements based on blockchain. This approach provides a mechanism for authentication and decentralized trust. In the trust model, the cloud service providers (CSPs) do not require pre-configured parameters or rules to establish interactive trust relationships. Therefore, this approach manages trust relationships between the clients and CSPs effectively and ensures secure IaaS for cloud federations. The results show the effectiveness of the proposed identity management blockchain-based approach while improving privacy and security capabilities.

The authors in [77] proposed a novel dynamic trust model for federated identity management (FIM) based on fuzzy cognitive maps. This model aimed at evaluating trustworthiness relationships between unknown entities dynamically and securely which makes FIM more flexible and scalable to be maintained and deployed in the cloud. Furthermore, the proposed model provides a set of trust features that serve as a basis for quantifying and modeling the trust level of unknown entities.

The study in [78] introduced a framework that enables the CSPs to supply the identity and access management (IAM) as a public cloud service, which is also called IAMaaS. This framework aims at ensuring that the collection of identities complies with the cloud. According to the authors, the IAMaaS can work perfectly with an existing on-premise platform in a hybrid manner to promote the capacity of security. In addition, the IAMaaS enables users to define the virtual private area in cloud space to enhance the security and protection of their resources.

The researchers in [79] proposed an identity management system (IDMS) to preserve the security of communication among servers and clients in cloud computing. The proposed system relied on the dual certificate manager (DCM) technique for authorizing and authenticating users to avoid privacy violations. The DCM technique uses token-based terminology for tracking and easy data access, which lead to downsizing the domain of the attacks. Additionally, this technique was commonly applied for the SSL/TLS protocol to protect data transmission.

To conclude, the review of solutions in the literature at the application level revealed that solutions at this level focused on the use of IDS/IPS techniques to mitigate the risks associated with DDoS and EDoS. These techniques have certain limitations, such as ineffectiveness when dealing with complex and unknown patterns of attacks, while the cloud needs techniques that can detect and/or prevent sophisticated attacks. In addition, the existing access control and identity management solutions (e.g., traditional firewall, encryption, and virtualized access control) at this level are not appropriate to promote security, because these solutions have a deficiency in managing the privileges the trust relationships needed to prevent the internal/external attackers. Consequently, the researchers should incorporate advanced techniques such as blockchain.

Moreover, numerous models used various techniques for authentication, but there are many barriers against implementing these techniques, such as the different testing environments and the use of a small amount of data during the verification process. This does not give confidence in the suitability of the models in the cloud computing environment even. Additionally, biometric systems are emerging as one of the best solutions to improve authentication security and privacy. Biometric systems play a key role in government and commercial applications outsourced to the cloud. Therefore, security and privacy are the biggest concerns for users. Unfortunately, most of these techniques are complex, impractical, and time-consuming.

5.3. Solutions at Network Level

In [80], the authors proposed SNORT as an intrusion detection system to defend against DoS and DDoS attacks in cloud computing. The DDoS attack floods the server with a huge number of needless packets and makes it unavailable to legal consumers. The proposed system depends on some written rules to detect and prevent DDoS attacks. Similarly, the authors in [81] proposed an approach to identify and filter a variety of DDoS attacks in cloud environments. This approach is based on the GARCH model and an artificial neural network (ANN). GARCH is used to estimate the value of variances and to figure out any possible anomalies in the real traffic relative to the actual value of variances. The ANN is used to identify the traffic after discarding values that are less than a certain threshold into regular traffic and anomalous traffic.

A recent study in [6] presented a technique for the consumers to encrypt and push the data blocks randomly in the P2P network based on blockchain. There are several data centers and multiple users in a distributed cloud, and this may sometimes pose a problem in file block replica placement. Therefore, the blockchain approach seems to be the perfect technique in terms of file security and network transmission delay.

Another study in [82] proposed a dynamic proof to communication-efficient recovery and supporting public audibility from data corruptions through irretrievability schemes. In this study, the data were divided into two parts: coding operation and data block which are performed for all blocks individually. The proposed approach can be applied to storage to minimize the update impact on the remote data. Any attempt to update will therefore impact only on small codeword symbols. In addition, an efficient data reform strategy is proposed in case of a server breakdown.

The authors in [83] summarized all types of attacks on DNS that exploit the DNS infrastructure. According to the authors, the most used DNS technique is the use of firewalls, which are considered one of the best practices in setting up DNS servers. Furthermore, the dynamic DNS firewall and appropriate signatures protect against whole potential attack surfaces.

The study [84] designed a software-as-a-service (SaaS) model that was called Open-Pipe. The OpenPipe model adopted a hybrid control mode that was applied with two hierarchical control levels, in which a software-defined networks (SDN) controller forms the higher level, and the local controllers comprise the lower level. The SDN worked to separate the control plane from the data plane to provide network virtualization and programmability. A lab demo was performed to verify the effectiveness of openPipe.

The study [85] presented several security approaches that were used to prevent unauthorized access to cloud computing environments, such as certificates (e.g., Public Key Infrastructure), a high level of authentication and authorization, and different encryption methods (e.g., symmetric and asymmetric key algorithms).

The authors in [86] proposed a Bayesian network-based weighted attack path modeling technique to model attack paths. They also proposed an optimized algorithm to find the shortest attack path from multiple sources based on key nodes and key edges. Not only does the algorithm find the shortest path, but it also resolves any existing ties between equal weight paths.

A study in [87] proposed a Hypervisor Level Distributed Network Security (HLDNS) framework to be deployed on each cloud server. Each server monitors the network traffic between the VMs and the other components such as the virtual network, the internal network, and the external network for intrusion detection. The study tested the proposed HLDNS framework on a cloud-tested NIT Goa by performing various attacks in real-time using recent intrusion detection datasets such as UNSW-NB15 and CICIDS-2017. The results of the experiments were encouraging.

The authors in [88] focused on detecting the DDoS attack by developing a deep learning classifier. The users' service requests are collected and grouped as log information. Some important features of the log file are selected for classification using the Bhattacharya distance measure to reduce the training time of the classifier. From the simulation results, it was concluded that the proposed TEHO-based DBN classifier yielded improved detection performance.

At this level, more emphasis was given to solve the DoS/DDoS attacks by using IDS/IPS techniques. However, these techniques are not accurate (e.g., generate a false alarm for legal requests), and deal with unique or single attacks only. In addition, these solutions did not deal with IP spoofing, while attackers use this kind of attack with

DoS/DDoS to overload networks. Consequently, they were unable to differentiate between good traffic and bad traffic. In addition, very few efforts have been made to address prefix hijacking attacks, while it is a major problem.

Another important point is that more attention is given to the availability of the network by solving DNS issues using firewalls; however, there are several forms of DNS attacks such as a man-in-the-middle attack, modified data attack, DNS ID spoofing attack, corrupted data attack, and DDOS attack that cannot be solved by using the traditional firewalls and can be overcome by other techniques.

5.4. Solutions at Host Level

The authors in [89] investigated the virtual machines and hypervisor intrusion detection method, VMHIDS, as a technique in the virtualized cloud environment to detect and prevent hypervisor attacks. This method protected both the hypervisor and virtual machines from cloud environment attacks, either internal or external. The continuous hypervisor or VM monitoring with VMHIDS made it possible to analyze real-time events for automated detection and blocking malicious events. VMHIDS monitors and keeps track of each file and process that interacts with the hypervisor. As VMHIDS is placed on both VMs and hypervisors, it is easy to detect new attacks or suspected attacks on hypervisors for faster prevention.

A study in [90] proposed a host-based intrusion detection model that provides security as a service at the host level in the cloud. This model alerts the host to malicious activities inside the system. Furthermore, a KNN classifier has been used to classify the system call traces that allow integration of new training documents. The result showed that the proposed method achieved high detection accuracy.

The authors in [91] developed a prevention model for DDOS attacks over hypervisor environments. This model was based on host-based intrusion detection defense system. In other words, the model was based solely on IDS modeling and then incorporated into the hypervisor environment with IPS. To identify and configure the cloud server, the prevention model uses principal component analysis and linear discriminant analysis with a hybrid, nature-inspired metaheuristic algorithm named Ant Lion optimization for feature selection. An artificial neural network is then used as a classifier. The results indicate that the model was able to detect malicious activities and block the malicious IP by sending it to the blacklist.

Another study in [92] suggested a framework to decrease the co-located VM attack on the same hypervisor. This was done by implementing virtual machine security policies when an illegal transfer or copy of live VMs into a suspicious hypervisor occurs. The preset data traffic rate monitoring between two VMs and the VSwitch node helped to detect VM confusion at a particular time point. The results show that the framework decreases the risk associated with the VM running upon this suspected hypervisor. This framework, however, focused only on the live migration from one hypervisor to another hypervisor of single VMs.

A study in [34] proposed various ways to secure the servers by using IDS, by storing hashed values, as the data in the cloud are naturally plaintext. The study suggested that multiple applications that run on single servers must be separated. Furthermore, the threshold that monitors server load and prevents DOS attacks should be determined. Finally, data replication is necessary to ensure the availability of data and that the server works all of the time.

In [93], the authors proposed an in-and-out-of-the-box virtual machine and hypervisor by using a prevention system and intrusion detection. The goal of this work was to detect vulnerabilities including persistent attacks such as DoS attacks and stealthy self-hiding rootkits. The experiments were conducted on the open-source host that is based on IDS, also known as Open-Source Security Event Correlator (OSSEC). The experimental results show that OSSEC IDS effectively detects rootkits and DoS attacks in both Linux and Windows operating systems.

A study in [94] discussed the virtualization issues in cloud computing infrastructure. According to the study, the major threats for cloud infrastructure are distributed side-channel attacks that can be used to exploit sensitive information from various parts of a distributed system. Furthermore, they sketched an approach for the reduction in side-channel attacks utilizing an autonomic system.

The researchers in [95] suggested a framework that used the VM monitoring script to obtain the status of the VMs to defend the VMs from an attack. As part of the kernel-based virtual machine manager (KVM), a smart virtualization monitoring system was integrated by sending the status of each VM running on a hypervisor. The intelligent device classifies and actively rectifies attack patterns. Via the cloud API, the appropriate action that should be taken will be communicated.

In [7], the authors proposed a Security-aware Virtual Machine Placement Algorithm (SMOOP) based on multi-objective optimization to search for a pare-to-optimal method to reduce cloud's overall security risks. SMOOP assessed cloud security from four perspectives: hypervisor vulnerabilities, networking, co-residence, and VM vulnerabilities. The proposed vulnerability assessment was location-specific and spans multi dimensions. Compared to existing solutions, the experimental findings indicate the efficacy of the proposed method and the enhancement.

A study in [96] evaluated the private cloud infrastructure tools called Ceilometer and Monasca to test the ability of information collected in a short time to detect the resource constraints and determine the effect of resource consumption of host systems. Both tools were analyzed, and the evaluation revealed that the Monasca achieved better performance than Ceilometer.

The authors in [97] implemented signature-based network intrusion detection (NIDS) such as OSSEC as host-based IDS and SNORT for the detection of intrusions at the cloud VM instances and network level. In addition, the study discussed the flow of traffic and monitoring on various occasions. The results show that the proposed systems were able to detect attacks on host VMs and can send alerts to the organization.

A recent study in [98] introduced a new hypervisor-based cloud IDS that utilizes online multivariate statistical change analysis to detect anomalous network behaviors. In the proposed system, the hypervisor benefits from a collection of instances to introduce an instance-oriented new feature mode that exploits the correlated and individual behaviors of instances to enhance the detection capability. The proposed approach was evaluated using a newly collected cloud intrusion dataset that includes a wide diversity of attack vectors.

According to [99], a parameterized scheduling policy focused on minimizing the makespan, combined with an energy-efficiency policy based on the hibernation of every virtual machine whenever possible, could reduce the energy consumption of large-scale data centers without affecting the overall performance of cloud computing systems. In the same work, the authors described a model for reducing energy consumption in cloud computing environments that can reduce the energy consumption of a cloud computing system by up to 45%. The proposed model is divided into two parts: an energy-aware independent batch scheduler and a set of energy-efficiency policies for idle VM hibernation. The experimental results show the good performance of the proposed model.

Furthermore, in [100], the online non-clairvoyant scheduling algorithm Highest Scaled Importance First (HSIF) method was proposed, in which HSIF chooses an active job with the highest scaled importance to minimize the sum of scaled importance-based flow time and energy consumed. The use of HSIF in data centers and battery-based devices reduces power consumption and improves computing capability.

To determine which cloud scheduling solution is more important to select, this paper [101] proposed an energy-efficient task-scheduling algorithm based on best-worst (BWM) and the technique for order preference by similarity to ideal solution (TOPSIS). The experimental results demonstrate that, when compared to its counterparts, the proposed approach can effectively reduce energy consumption. Furthermore, the proposed approach can significantly improve VM utilization, making it suitable for exploring large-scale problems.

In addition, the SCORE tool was defined in this paper [102] as an extension to the Google Omega lightweight simulator, which is devoted to the simulation of energy-efficient monolithic and parallel-scheduling models as well as the execution of heterogeneous, realistic, and synthetic workloads. Empirical tests were used to evaluate the simulator. The experiment results confirm that SCORE is a performant and reliable tool for testing energy efficiency, security, and scheduling strategies in cloud computing environments.

At this level, the majority of solutions employed IDS/IPS models to detecting and preventing hypervisor attacks and identifying malicious activities inside the system. However, the cloud is a large-scale and heterogeneous environment that needs to mitigate the risks of hypervisors in multiple VMs, while some studies, such as [93], focused on mitigating risks on hypervisors in single VMs only. Furthermore, some solutions were customized to specific scenarios, known patterns of attacks, or even specific software [92,94]. To conclude, the proposed solutions should consider some serious attacks such as the distributed side-channel attacks while designing their detection or prevention techniques. These attacks are major threats to cloud infrastructures that can be used to exploit sensitive data from various parts of a distributed system [95]. The host-level techniques are still not fully mature, in which these techniques need to immediately respond, automatically block malicious events, and take appropriate action to prevent attacks from happening.

Table 4 presents a summary of the existing solutions in the literature according to the four levels discussed in the previous subsections.

Table 4. Summary of existing solutions in the literature.

Level Name	Techniques	Limitations	References
Data Level	Data loss or leakage used a technique to secure data are by applying encryption mechanisms like TLS, AES and SHA Classification technique to have security levels for data	The encryption techniques are still not fully mature and face many problems The available technique to classification is consumes resources	[9,37,50–62]
Application Level	IDS/IPS techniques were used to solve DDoS attacks in cloud applications and services IDS/IPS techniques were used to solve EDoS attacks The techniques to solve poor authentication are identity management system (IDMS), and also some authentication based on AES and MD5	The existing techniques deal with simple DDoS attacks only, while the nature of the cloud needs techniques can prevent and detect the complex attacks and unknown patterns The techniques used to solve simple attacks Testing environments and use a small amount of data are considered barriers against implementation. The traditional access control and identity management are not suitable to promote security	[6,38,63–80]
Network Level	The existing techniques using a IDS/IPS to solve DoS and DDoS attacks The techniques of DNS issues vary between dynamic firewalls and IDS	Some of DDoS/DoS techniques did not deal with IP spoofing where these attacks often use IP spoofing to overload networks; therefore, it is unable to differentiate between good traffic and bad traffic These techniques did not take into consideration some of the serious attacks such as Man in the middle attack, modified data attack, DNS ID spoofing attack, corrupted data attack, . . . etc.	[7,81–89]

Table 4. *Cont.*

Level Name	Techniques	Limitations	References
Host Level	The techniques to solve the virtual machines and hypervisor issues are intrusion detection and VM monitoring	These techniques were limited their techniques to specific scenarios, known patterns of attacks or even specific software Techniques need more focus on other types of attacks such as distributed side-channel attacks while designing their detecting or preventing techniques	[8,35,90–102]

6. Open Challenges

While cloud computing has been widely embraced by businesses and industries, cloud computing research is still immature. Many of the current gaps regarding the cloud infrastructure have not been completely addressed, while new challenges continue to arise. The following subsections summarize the most important open challenges that need to be studied further.

Securing Hypervisor

An insecure hypervisor is a serious challenge that threatens cloud computing. It can damage the entire system [21]. Traditional detection/prevention solutions are not efficient enough with the dynamic nature of the cloud. The cloud needs context-aware solutions to differentiate between normal and abnormal behaviors. Additionally, any proposed solution should take immediate action to avoid damaging the cloud infrastructure or disrupting the normal operations.

Third-party Auditing

The popularity and rapid growth of cloud-based information storage services have generated controversy about the integrity of cloud-based data, which can be lost or destroyed because of unavoidable hardware-software failures and/or human-related errors. The third-party auditor should provide expert integrity verification services. During public auditing of cloud information, the content of the private information of the individual client should not be revealed to any public verifier. As a result, a new major issue regarding privacy, and more specifically the leakage of data privacy to third-party auditors, has been being introduced. It remains a difficult research challenge to establish solutions that ensure the integrity of cloud storage security and privacy.

Data Availability

Under security breaches, the system must be able to continue its normal operations. Availability also refers to the data, software and hardware available to approved users based on demand. System availability incorporates the capacity of the framework to carry out operations at all times. Data availability, protection, and data security stand out amongst the most perplexing challenges of the cloud environment up to now.

Data Remanence

Data remanence is the presence of residual data even after deletion, reformatting, or reallocation of it to another person. This is a major threat to the confidentiality of deleted files (passwords, encryption keys, government data, financial or health data, etc.). Data remanence may be discovered by computer forensics and other various techniques. In addition, it is possible to find and recover files that might have been removed from a computer [103]. Cloud providers have not fully addressed data remanence, and this issue is even ignored by some cloud providers, even though it is one of the most critical issues.

Network security

At the network level, the proposed security mechanisms were presented to be defensive in IaaS, such as a dynamic DNS firewall that protects against attack, as mentioned in [83]. However, there are still a lot of attacks that cannot be resolved with a traditional firewall. The DNS attack is an increased risk in cloud computing due to the several attacks that are identified as a consequence of it. In addition, there are few research efforts about reusing IP addresses, which leads to serious data and system breaches from a customer security perspective.

Access control and Identity Management

Due to the obvious cloud-specific characteristics, conventional access control and identity management techniques are not suitable for promoting IaaS security. New technologies such as blockchain and computational intelligence should be used in this regard to provide sufficient security in this new computing environment.

Authentication

Most authentication solutions are time-consuming and complex. Existing studies tested their techniques via simulation with a small amount of data, less complex resources and a smaller number of users. However, the cloud in reality has a huge number of users and other complex features. Therefore, more effort should be given to developing techniques that take into consideration all of these constraints. Moreover, authentication techniques are usually for one party, and the cloud service provider does not have a platform for multiple user interface authentication.

7. Future Recommendations

Based on the open challenges discussed so far, this section recommends some future research directions.

Securing Hypervisor

To distinguish between normal and abnormal behaviors, the cloud requires context-aware solutions to detect new and emerging attack patterns and respond immediately to prevent any possible harm to the cloud infrastructure. This should also take into account the dynamic nature of the cloud environment and the mobility of its customers. Additionally, customer preferences and his/her level of security awareness should be considered when building these solutions.

Third-party Auditing

Some recommendations for developing third-party auditing solutions should consider the following characteristics:

Third-party auditing should be performed without retrieving a copy of the data; therefore, privacy is maintained.

The data should be divided into parts and stored in an encrypted format in the cloud storage, thereby maintaining the confidentiality of the data.

Verifying data integrity at the client's request to check whether the stored data are tampered with and inform the user as such.

Data Availability

How to store data is also key to ensuring data availability. Some techniques can be used to ensure data availability and could be a focus for future research in securing cloud infrastructure as in the following points:

- Data backups must be stored separately or in a distributed network. This means that the user will not lose information permanently if the storage part degrades or fails.
- Update backups periodically, so that the user can restore the most current data versions.
- Data loss prevention (DLP) tools help to minimize data violations and data center physical damage. These tools use cloud-based secure storage from third parties to avoid loss of data. Some DLP tools provide monitoring, blocking of threats, and forensic analysis.
- Object storage uses advanced erasure coding to ensure data availability. Erasure coding blends data with parity data, and then breaks and distributes them throughout the storage environment. This could prevent component failure since users only need a subset of the shared data for data restoration.

Data Remanence

These solutions can be used to remove or minimize the presence of residual data as mentioned below.

- Sterilization, also known as purging, refers to removing confidential information from a storage system to avoid ant recovery by a known method or technique.
- Data encryption is an effective data protection method.

Network security

Some security recommendations for network security can be summarized as follows:

- The internal communication of the cloud must adopt secure communication techniques such as HTTPS, and also the transmission channel must be encrypted by TLS.
- Using anomaly detection solutions for HTTP requests that can effectively prevent any malicious network intrusion behaviors.
- The cloud can use public security services such as web application firewalls (WAF), virtual firewalls, virtual bastion machines, virtual host protection and virtual database audit systems.

Access control and Identity management

The following are some security considerations for access control and identity management that should be considered by future research.

- The cloud must be accessed only by the access key authentication.
- The cloud must apply some security operation management such as (A) situation awareness that sort all assets and business systems in the cloud, (B) safe operation and maintenance that provide unified account management, unified authority management, unified interface management and unified ID authentication.
- Single sign-on (SSO), currently applied in many cloud environments, could be incorporated with blockchain-based self-sovereign identity management approaches. This will give customers more autonomy in keeping and managing their credentials in a unified and more private manner.

Authentication

There is a need for authentication mechanisms that can deal with complex resources, a large number of users, and the heterogeneous nature of the cloud without consuming time. Furthermore, there is a need for authentication techniques for multiple user interface authentication. Blockchain technology could be utilized to design stronger authentication mechanisms.

8. Conclusions

Despite bringing many benefits, the cloud computing paradigm imposes serious concerns in terms of security and privacy, which are considered hurdles in the adoption of the cloud at a very large scale. Customers and organizations in the cloud should be aware of threats, attacks and vulnerabilities, as security awareness is considered the first step to ease the adoption of the cloud. This paper discussed the concerns and challenges in the cloud computing infrastructure at various levels (Application, Network, Host, Data). To deal with these challenges, several existing solutions were introduced to alleviate them. Many existing gaps, however, have not been fully resolved, and new problems continue to appear due to the shared, virtualized, distributed, and public nature of the cloud. Subsequently, this paper focused on various solutions to address security issues at different levels in the cloud infrastructure.

Funding: The APC was funded by Deanship of Scientific Research, Qassim University.

Acknowledgments: The researcher(s) would like to thank the Deanship of Scientific Research, Qassim University for funding the publication of this project.

Conflicts of Interest: The authors declare no conflict of interest.

References

1. Elsherbiny, S.; Eldaydamony, E.; Alrahmawy, M.; Reyad, A.E. An extended Intelligent Water Drops algorithm for workflow scheduling in cloud computing environment. *Egypt. Inf. J.* **2018**, *19*, 33–55. [CrossRef]
2. Hanen, J.; Kechaou, Z.; Ben Ayed, M. An enhanced healthcare system in mobile cloud computing environment. *Vietnam J. Comput. Sci.* **2016**, *3*, 267–277. [CrossRef]
3. Mell, P.; Grance, T. *The NIST Definition of Cloud Computing*; Nation-al Institute of Standards and Technology: Gaithersburg, MD, USA, 2011.
4. Hatwar, S.V.; Chavan, R. Cloud Computing Security Aspects, Vulnerabilities and Countermeasures. *Int. J. Comput. Appl.* **2015**, *119*, 46–53. [CrossRef]
5. Dinh, P.T.; Park, M. Dynamic Economic-Denial-of-Sustainability (EDoS) Detection in SDN-based Cloud. In Proceedings of the 2020 Fifth International Conference on Fog and Mobile Edge Computing (FMEC), Paris, France, 20–23 April 2020.
6. Karajeh, H.; Maqableh, M.; Masa'deh, R. Privacy and security issues of cloud computing environment. In Proceedings of the 23rd IBIMA Conference Vision, Valencia, Spain, 13–14 May 2020.
7. Han, J.; Zang, W.; Chen, S.; Yu, M. Reducing Security Risks of Clouds Through Virtual Machine Placement. In Proceedings of the IFIP Annual Conference on Data and Applications Security and Privacy, Philadelphia, PA, USA, 19–21 July 2017.
8. Saravanan, N.; Umamakeswari, A. Lattice based access control for protecting user data in cloud environments with hybrid security. *Comput. Secur.* **2021**, *100*, 102074. [CrossRef]
9. Vaquero, L.M.; Rodero-Merino, L.; Caceres, J.; Lindner, M. *A Break in the Clouds: Towards a Cloud Definition*; ACM: New York, NY, USA, 2008.
10. Siddiqui, S.; Darbari, M.; Yagyasen, D. A Comprehensive Study of Challenges and Issues in Cloud Computing. In *Soft Computing and Signal Processing*; Springer: Singapore, 2019; pp. 325–344.
11. Marston, S.; Li, Z.; Bandyopadhyay, S.; Ghalsasi, A. Cloud Computing—The Business Perspective. *Decis. Support Syst.* **2011**, *51*, 176–189. [CrossRef]
12. Kuyoro, S.; Ibikunle, F.; Awodele, O. Cloud computing security issues and challenges. *Int. J. Comput. Netw.* **2011**, *3*, 247–255.
13. Alajmi, Q.; Sadiq, A.S.; Kamaludin, A.; A Al-Sharafi, M. Cloud Computing Delivery and Delivery Models: Opportunity and Challenges. *Adv. Sci. Lett.* **2018**, *24*, 4040–4044. [CrossRef]
14. Diaby, T.; Rad, B.B. Cloud Computing: A review of the Concepts and Deployment Models. *Int. J. Inf. Technol. Comput. Sci.* **2017**, *9*, 50–58. [CrossRef]
15. Chauhan, V.K.; Bansal, K.; Alappanavar, P. Exposing cloud computing as a failure. *Int. J. Eng. Sci. Technol.* **2012**, *4*, 1320–1326.
16. Bamiah, M.A.; Brohi, S.N. Exploring the cloud deployment and service delivery models. *Int. J. Res. Rev. Inf. Sci.* **2011**, *1*, 77–80.
17. Tabrizchi, H.; Rafsanjani, M.K. A survey on security challenges in cloud computing: Issues, threats, and solutions. *J. Supercomput.* **2020**, *76*, 9493–9532. [CrossRef]
18. An, Y.Z.; Zaaba, Z.F.; Samsudin, N.F. Reviews on Security Issues and Challenges in Cloud Computing. *IOP Conf. Ser. Mater. Sci. Eng.* **2016**, *160*, 012106. [CrossRef]
19. Faheem, M.; Akram, U.; Khan, I.; Naqeeb, S.; Shahzad, A.; Ullah, A.; Mushtaq, M.F. Cloud Computing Environment and Security Challenges: A Review. *Int. J. Adv. Comput. Sci. Appl.* **2017**, *8*, 183–195. [CrossRef]
20. Sikeridis, D.; Papapanagiotou, I.; Rimal, B.P.; Devetsikiotis, M. A Comparative taxonomy and survey of public cloud infrastructure vendors. *arXiv* **2017**, arXiv:1710.01476.
21. Subramanian, N.; Jeyaraj, A. Recent security challenges in cloud computing. *Comput. Electr. Eng.* **2018**, *71*, 28–42. [CrossRef]
22. Kumar, P.R.; Raj, P.H.; Jelciana, P. Exploring Data Security Issues and Solutions in Cloud Computing. *Procedia Comput. Sci.* **2018**, *125*, 691–697. [CrossRef]
23. Bokhari, M.U.; Makki, Q.; Tamandani, Y.K. A Survey on Cloud Computing. In *Big Data Analytics*; Advances in Intelligent Systems and Computing; Springer: Singapore, 2018; Volume 654, pp. 149–164.
24. Abdurachman, E.; Gaol, F.L.; Soewito, B. Survey on Threats and Risks in the Cloud Computing Environment. *Procedia Comput. Sci.* **2019**, *161*, 1325–1332. [CrossRef]
25. Dong, S.; Abbas, K.; Jain, R. A Survey on Distributed Denial of Service (DDoS) Attacks in SDN and Cloud Computing Environments. *IEEE Access* **2019**, *7*, 80813–80828. [CrossRef]
26. Alhenaki, L.; Alwatban, A.; Alamri, B.; Alarifi, N. A Survey on the Security of Cloud Computing. In Proceedings of the 2019 2nd International Conference on Computer Applications & Information Security (ICCAIS), Riyadh, Saudi Arabia, 1–3 May 2019.
27. Domingo-Ferrer, J.; Farràs, O.; Ribes-González, J.; Sánchez, D. Privacy-preserving cloud computing on sensitive data: A survey of methods, products and challenges. *Comput. Commun.* **2019**, *140*, 38–60. [CrossRef]
28. Kumar, R.; Goyal, R. On cloud security requirements, threats, vulnerabilities and countermeasures: A survey. *Comput. Sci. Rev.* **2019**, *33*, 1–48. [CrossRef]
29. Ibrahim, F.A.M.; Hemayed, E.E. Trusted Cloud Computing Architectures for infrastructure as a service: Survey and systematic literature review. *Comput. Secur.* **2019**, *82*, 196–226. [CrossRef]
30. Qureshi, A.; Dashti, W.; Jahangeer, A.; Zafar, A. Security Challenges over Cloud Environment from Service Provider Prospective. *Cloud Comput. Data Sci.* **2020**, *1*, 1–48. [CrossRef]
31. Saini, H.; Saini, A. Security Mechanisms at different Levels in Cloud Infrastructure. *Int. J. Comput. Appl.* **2014**, *108*, 1–6. [CrossRef]

32. Inukollu, V.N.; Arsi, S.; Ravuri, S.R. Security Issues Associated with Big Data in Cloud Computing. *Int. J. Netw. Secur. Appl.* **2014**, *6*, 45–56. [CrossRef]
33. Rao, R.V.; Selvamani, K. Data Security Challenges and Its Solutions in Cloud Computing. *Procedia Comput. Sci.* **2015**, *48*, 204–209. [CrossRef]
34. Aich, A.; Sen, A. Study on Cloud Security Risk and Remedy. *Int. J. Grid Distrib. Comput.* **2015**, *8*, 155–166. [CrossRef]
35. Farsi, M.; Ali, M.; Shah, R.A.; Wagan, A.A.; Kharabsheh, R. Cloud computing and data security threats taxonomy: A review. *J. Intell. Fuzzy Syst.* **2020**, *38*, 2517–2527. [CrossRef]
36. Balogh, Z.; Turčáni, M. Modeling of data security in cloud computing. In Proceedings of the 2016 Annual IEEE Systems Conference (SysCon), Orlando, FL, USA, 18–21 April 2016.
37. Wani, A.R.; Rana, Q.P.; Saxena, U.; Pandey, N. Analysis and Detection of DDoS Attacks on Cloud Computing Environment using Machine Learning Techniques. In Proceedings of the 2019 Amity International Conference on Artificial Intelligence (AICAI), Dubai, United Arab Emirates, 4–6 February 2019.
38. Al Amri, S.M.; Guan, L. Infrastructure as a service: Exploring network access control challenges. In Proceedings of the 2016 SAI Computing Conference (SAI), London, UK, 13–15 July 2016.
39. Sharma, A.; Keshwani, B.; Dadheech, P. Authentication issues and techniques in cloud computing security: A review. In Proceedings of the International Conference on Sustainable Computing in Science, Technology and Management (SUSCOM), Jaipur, India, 26–28 February 2019.
40. Kazim, M.; Zhu, S.Y. A survey on top security threats in cloud computing. *Int. J. Adv. Comput. Sci. Appl.* **2015**, *6*. [CrossRef]
41. Al-Haidari, F.; Sqalli, M.; Salah, K. Evaluation of the impact of EDoS attacks against cloud computing services. *Arab. J. Sci. Eng.* **2015**, *40*, 773–785. [CrossRef]
42. Turab, N.M.; Abu Taleb, A.; Masadeh, S.R. Cloud Computing Challenges and Solutions. *Int. J. Comput. Netw. Commun.* **2013**, *5*, 209–216. [CrossRef]
43. Sermpezis, P.; Kotronis, V.; Dainotti, A.; Dimitropoulos, X. A Survey among Network Operators on BGP Prefix Hijacking. *ACM SIGCOMM Comput. Commun. Rev.* **2018**, *48*, 64–69. [CrossRef]
44. Mohiuddin, I.; Almogren, A.; Alrubaian, M.; Al-Qurishi, M. Analysis of network issues and their impact on Cloud Storage. In Proceedings of the 2019 2nd International Conference on Computer Applications & Information Security (ICCAIS), Riyadh, Saudi Arabia, 1–3 May 2019.
45. Tank, D.; Aggarwal, A.; Chaubey, N. Virtualization vulnerabilities, security issues, and solutions: A critical study and comparison. *Int. J. Inf. Technol.* **2019**, 1–16. [CrossRef]
46. Krishna, S.R.; Rani, B.P. Virtualization Security Issues and Mitigations in Cloud Computing. In *Proceedings of the First International Conference on Computational Intelligence and Informatics*; Springer: Singapore, 2017; pp. 117–128.
47. Rakotondravony, N.; Taubmann, B.; Mandarawi, W.; Weishäupl, E.; Xu, P.; Kolosnjaji, B.; Protsenko, M.; De Meer, H.; Reiser, H.P. Classifying malware attacks in IaaS cloud environments. *J. Cloud Comput.* **2017**, *6*, 26. [CrossRef]
48. Saxena, S.; Sanyal, G.; Srivastava, S.; Amin, R. Preventing from Cross-VM Side-Channel Attack Using New Replacement Method. *Wirel. Pers. Commun.* **2017**, *97*, 4827–4854. [CrossRef]
49. Rasheed, H. Data and infrastructure security auditing in cloud computing environments. *Int. J. Inf. Manag.* **2014**, *34*, 364–368. [CrossRef]
50. Singh, A.P.; Pasupuleti, S.K. Optimized Public Auditing and Data Dynamics for Data Storage Security in Cloud Computing. *Procedia Comput. Sci.* **2016**, *93*, 751–759. [CrossRef]
51. Shaikh, R.; Sasikumar, M. Data Classification for Achieving Security in Cloud Computing. *Procedia Comput. Sci.* **2015**, *45*, 493–498. [CrossRef]
52. Tawalbeh, L.; Darwazeh, N.S.; Al-Qassas, R.S.; AlDosari, F. A Secure Cloud Computing Model based on Data Classification. *Procedia Comput. Sci.* **2015**, *52*, 1153–1158. [CrossRef]
53. Li, P.; Li, J.; Huang, Z.; Gao, C.-Z.; Chen, W.-B.; Chen, K. Privacy-preserving outsourced classification in cloud computing. *Clust. Comput.* **2017**, *21*, 277–286. [CrossRef]
54. Manogaran, G.; Thota, C.; Kumar, M.V. MetaCloudDataStorage Architecture for Big Data Security in Cloud Computing. *Procedia Comput. Sci.* **2016**, *87*, 128–133. [CrossRef]
55. Sood, S.K. A combined approach to ensure data security in cloud computing. *J. Netw. Comput. Appl.* **2012**, *35*, 1831–1838. [CrossRef]
56. Vurukonda, N.; Rao, B.T. A Study on Data Storage Security Issues in Cloud Computing. *Procedia Comput. Sci.* **2016**, *92*, 128–135. [CrossRef]
57. Zhang, Y.; Chen, X.; Li, J.; Wong, D.S.; Li, H.; You, I. Ensuring attribute privacy protection and fast decryption for outsourced data security in mobile cloud computing. *Inf. Sci.* **2017**, *379*, 42–61. [CrossRef]
58. Amalarethinam, I.G.; Leena, H. Enhanced RSA Algorithm with Varying Key Sizes for Data Security in Cloud. In Proceedings of the 2017 World Congress on Computing and Communication Technologies (WCCCT), Tiruchirappalli, India, 2–4 February 2017; IEEE: Tiruchirappalli, India, 2017; pp. 172–175.
59. Khan, I.A.; Qazi, R. Data Security in Cloud Computing Using Elliptic Curve Cryptography. *Int. J. Comput. Commun. Netw.* **2019**, *1*, 46–52.

60. Sajay, K.R.; Babu, S.S.; Vijayalakshmi, Y. Enhancing the security of cloud data using hybrid encryption algorithm. *J. Ambient. Intell. Hum. Comput.* **2019**, 1–10. [CrossRef]
61. Belguith, S.; Jemai, A.; Attia, R. Enhancing data security in cloud computing using a lightweight cryptographic algorithm. In Proceedings of the Eleventh International Conference on Autonomic and Autonomous Systems, Rome, Italy, 24–29 May 2015.
62. Somani, G.; Gaur, M.S.; Sanghi, D.; Conti, M.; Rajarajan, M. Scale Inside-Out: Rapid Mitigation of Cloud DDoS Attacks. *IEEE Trans. Dependable Secur. Comput.* **2018**, *15*, 959–973. [CrossRef]
63. Ficco, M.; Rak, M. Economic denial of sustainability mitigation in cloud computing. In *Organizational Innovation and Change*; Springer International Publishing: Cham, Switzerland, 2016; pp. 229–238.
64. Nautiyal, S.; Wadhwa, S. A Comparative Approach to Mitigate Economic Denial of Sustainability (EDoS) in a Cloud Environment. In Proceedings of the 2019 4th International Conference on Information Systems and Computer Networks (ISCON), Mathura, India, 21–22 November 2019.
65. Rehman, F.; Akram, S.; Shah, M.A. The framework for efficient passphrase-based multifactor authentication in cloud computing. In Proceedings of the 2016 22nd International Conference on Automation and Computing (ICAC), Colchester, UK, 7–8 September 2016.
66. Ojha, S.; Rajput, V. AES and MD5 based secure authentication in cloud computing. In Proceedings of the 2017 International Conference on I-SMAC (IoT in Social, Mobile, Analytics and Cloud) (I-SMAC), Palladam, India, 10–11 February 2017.
67. Rajeswari, P.; Raju, S.V.; Ashour, A.S.; Dey, N. Multi-fingerprint unimodel-based biometric authentication supporting cloud computing. In *Intelligent Techniques in Signal Processing for Multimedia Security*; Springer: Cham, Switzerland, 2017; pp. 469–485.
68. Devipriya, K.; Lingamgunta, S. Multi Factor Two-way Hash-Based Authentication in Cloud Computing. *Int. J. Cloud Appl. Comput.* **2020**, *10*, 56–76. [CrossRef]
69. Deebak, B.; Al-Turjman, F.; Mostarda, L. Seamless secure anonymous authentication for cloud-based mobile edge computing. *Comput. Electr. Eng.* **2020**, *87*, 106782. [CrossRef]
70. Irshad, A.; Chaudhry, S.A.; Alomari, O.A.; Yahya, K.; Kumar, N. A Novel Pairing-Free Lightweight Authentication Protocol for Mobile Cloud Computing Framework. *IEEE Syst. J.* **2021**, *15*, 3664–3672. [CrossRef]
71. Zhang, Y.; Krishnan, R.; Sandhu, R. Secure Information and Resource Sharing in Cloud Infrastructure as a Service. In Proceedings of the 2014 ACM Workshop on Information Sharing & Collaborative Security, Scottsdale, AZ, USA, 3 November 2014; pp. 81–90.
72. Banyal, R.K.; Jain, V.K.; Jain, P. Dynamic Trust Based Access Control Framework for Securing Multi-Cloud Environment. In Proceedings of the 2014 International Conference on Information and Communication Technology for Competitive Strategies—ICTCS '14, Udaipur, India, 14–16 November 2014.
73. Zhou, C.; Li, B. iHAC: A Hybrid Access Control Framework for IaaS Clouds. In Proceedings of the 2014 IEEE/ACM 7th International Conference on Utility and Cloud Computing, London, UK, 8–11 December 2014.
74. Auxilia, M.; Raja, K. Dynamic Access Control Model for Cloud Computing. In Proceedings of the 2014 Sixth International Conference on Advanced Computing (ICoAC), Chennai, India, 17–19 December 2014.
75. Yang, C.; Tan, L.; Shi, N.; Xu, B.; Cao, Y.; Yu, K. AuthPrivacyChain: A Blockchain-Based Access Control Framework with Privacy Protection in Cloud. *IEEE Access* **2020**, *8*, 70604–70615. [CrossRef]
76. Bendiab, K.; Kolokotronis, N.; Shiaeles, S.; Boucherkha, S. WiP: A novel blockchain-based trust model for cloud identity management. In Proceedings of the 2018 IEEE 16th Intl Conf on Dependable, Autonomic and Secure Computing, 16th Intl Conf on Pervasive Intelligence and Computing, 4th Intl Conf on Big Data Intelligence and Computing and Cyber Science and Technology Congress (DASC/PiCom/DataCom/CyberSciTech), Athens, Greece, 12–15 August 2018.
77. Bendiab, G.; Shiaeles, S.; Boucherkha, S.; Ghita, B. FCMDT: A novel fuzzy cognitive maps dynamic trust model for cloud federated identity management. *Comput. Secur.* **2019**, *86*, 270–290. [CrossRef]
78. Sharma, D.H.; Dhote, C.; Potey, M. Identity and Access Management as Security-as-a-Service from Clouds. *Procedia Comput. Sci.* **2016**, *79*, 170–174. [CrossRef]
79. Khajehei, K. Preserving Privacy in Cloud Identity Management Systems Using DCM (Dual Certificate Management). *Int. J. Wirel. Microw. Technol.* **2018**, *8*, 54–65. [CrossRef]
80. Hassan, Z.; Odarchenko, R.; Gnatyuk, S.; Zaman, A.; Shah, M. Detection of Distributed Denial of Service Attacks Using Snort Rules in Cloud Computing & Remote Control Systems. In Proceedings of the 2018 IEEE 5th International Conference on Methods and Systems of Navigation and Motion Control (MSNMC), Kyiv, Ukraine, 16–18 October 2018.
81. Badve, O.P.; Gupta, B.; Yamaguchi, S.; Gou, Z. DDoS detection and filtering technique in cloud environment using GARCH model. In Proceedings of the 2015 IEEE 4th Global Conference on Consumer Electronics (GCCE), Osaka, Japan, 27–30 October 2015.
82. Jouini, M.; Rabai, L.B.A. A. A security framework for secure cloud computing environments. In *Cloud Security: Concepts, Methodologies, Tools, and Applications*; IGI Global: Hershey, PA, USA, 2019; pp. 249–263. [CrossRef]
83. Rajendran, B.; Shetty, P. Domain Name System (DNS) Security: Attacks Identification and Protection Methods. In Proceedings of the International Conference on Security and Management (SAM), Las Vegas, NV, USA, 30 July–2 August 2018.
84. Liang, K.; Zhao, L.; Chu, X.; Chen, H.-H. An Integrated Architecture for Software Defined and Virtualized Radio Access Networks with Fog Computing. *IEEE Netw.* **2017**, *31*, 80–87. [CrossRef]
85. Maithili, K.; Vinothkumar, V.; Latha, P. Analyzing the Security Mechanisms to Prevent Unauthorized Access in Cloud and Network Security. *J. Comput. Nanosci.* **2018**, *15*, 2059–2063. [CrossRef]

86. Zimba, A.; Chen, H.; Wang, Z. Bayesian network based weighted APT attack paths modeling in cloud computing. *Future Gener. Comput. Syst.* **2019**, *96*, 525–537. [CrossRef]
87. Patil, R.; Dudeja, H.; Modi, C. Designing an efficient security framework for detecting intrusions in virtual network of cloud computing. *Comput. Secur.* **2019**, *85*, 402–422. [CrossRef]
88. Velliangiri, S.; Karthikeyan, P.; Kumar, V.V. Detection of distributed denial of service attack in cloud computing using the optimization-based deep networks. *J. Exp. Artif. Intell.* **2021**, 1–20. [CrossRef]
89. Dildar, M.S.; Khan, N.; Bin Abdullah, J.; Khan, A.S. Effective way to defend the hypervisor attacks in cloud computing. In Proceedings of the 2017 2nd International Conference on Anti-Cyber Crimes (ICACC), Abha, Saudi Arabia, 26–27 March 2017.
90. Deshpande, P.; Sharma, S.C.; Peddoju, S.K.; Junaid, S. HIDS: A host based intrusion detection system for cloud computing environment. *Int. J. Syst. Assur. Eng. Manag.* **2018**, *9*, 567–576. [CrossRef]
91. Jaber, A.N.; Zolkipli, M.F.; Shakir, H.A.; Jassim, M.R. Host based intrusion detection and prevention model against DDoS attack in cloud computing. In Proceedings of the International Conference on P2P, Parallel, Grid, Cloud and Internet Computing, Barcelona, Spain, 8–10 November 2017.
92. Ramamoorthy, S.; Rajalakshmi, S. A Preventive Method for Host Level Security in Cloud Infrastructure. In *Proceedings of the 3rd International Symposium on Big Data and Cloud Computing Challenges (ISBCC–16')*; Springer: Cham, Switzerland, 2016; pp. 3–12.
93. Kumara, A.; Jaidhar, C. Hypervisor and virtual machine dependent Intrusion Detection and Prevention System for virtualized cloud environment. In Proceedings of the 2015 1st International Conference on Telematics and Future Generation Networks (TAFGEN), Kuala Lumpur, Malaysia, 26–28 May 2015.
94. Bazm, M.-M.; Lacoste, M.; Südholt, M.; Menaud, J.-M. Isolation in cloud computing infrastructures: New security challenges. *Ann. Telecommun.* **2019**, *74*, 197–209. [CrossRef]
95. Deshpande, S.M.; Ainapure, B. An Intelligent Virtual Machine Monitoring System Using KVM for Reliable And Secure Environment in Cloud. In Proceedings of the 2016 IEEE International Conference on Advances in Electronics, Communication and Computer Technology (ICAECCT), Pune, India, 2–3 December 2016.
96. Gomez-Rodriguez, M.A.; Sosa-Sosa, V.J.; Gonzalez-Compean, J.L. Assessment of Private Cloud Infrastructure Monitoring Tools. In Proceedings of the 6th International Conference on Data Science, Technology and Applications, Madrid, Spain, 26–28 July 2017.
97. Mahajan, V.; Peddoju, S.K. Deployment of Intrusion Detection System in Cloud: A Performance-Based Study. In Proceedings of the 2017 IEEE Trustcom/BigDataSE/ICESS, Sydney, NSW, Australia, 1–4 August 2017. [CrossRef]
98. Aldribi, A.; Traoré, I.; Moa, B.; Nwamuo, O. Hypervisor-based cloud intrusion detection through online multivariate statistical change tracking. *Comput. Secur.* **2020**, *88*, 101646. [CrossRef]
99. Fernández-Cerero, D.; Jakóbik, A.K.; Grzonka, D.; Kołodziej, J.; Fernández-Montes, A. Security supportive energy-aware scheduling and energy policies for cloud environments. *J. Parallel Distrib. Comput.* **2018**, *119*, 191–202. [CrossRef]
100. Singh, P.; Khan, B.; Vidyarthi, A.; Alhelou, H.H.; Siano, P. Energy-Aware Online Non-Clairvoyant Scheduling Using Speed Scaling with Arbitrary Power Function. *Appl. Sci.* **2019**, *9*, 1467. [CrossRef]
101. Khorsand, R.; Ramezanpour, M. An energy-efficient task-scheduling algorithm based on a multi-criteria decision-making method in cloud computing. *Int. J. Commun. Syst.* **2020**, *33*, e4379. [CrossRef]
102. Fernández-Cerero, D.; Fernández-Montes, A.; Jakóbik, A.; Kołodziej, J.; Toro, M. SCORE: Simulator for cloud optimization of resources and energy consumption. *Simul. Model. Pract. Theory* **2018**, *82*, 160–173. [CrossRef]
103. Aissaoui, K.; Idar, H.A.; Belhadaoui, H.; Rifi, M. Survey on data remanence in Cloud Computing environment. In Proceedings of the 2017 International Conference on Wireless Technologies, Embedded and Intelligent Systems (WITS), Fez, Morocco, 19–20 April 2017.

Review

Empirical Evaluation of Privacy Efficiency in Blockchain Networks: Review and Open Challenges

Aisha Zahid Junejo [1,*], Manzoor Ahmed Hashmani [1,2] and Mehak Maqbool Memon [1]

1. Department of Computer and Information Science, Universiti Teknologi PETRONAS (UTP), Seri Iskandar 32610, Malaysia; manzoor.hashmani@utp.edu.my (M.A.H.); mehak_19001057@utp.edu.my (M.M.M.)
2. High Performance Cloud Computing Centre (HPC3), Universiti Teknologi PETRONAS (UTP), Seri Iskandar 32610, Malaysia
* Correspondence: aisha_19001022@utp.edu.my

Citation: Junejo, A.Z.; Hashmani, M.A.; Memon, M.M. Empirical Evaluation of Privacy Efficiency in Blockchain Networks: Review and Open Challenges. *Appl. Sci.* **2021**, *11*, 7013. https://doi.org/10.3390/app11157013

Academic Editor: Gianluca Lax

Received: 8 July 2021
Accepted: 26 July 2021
Published: 29 July 2021

Publisher's Note: MDPI stays neutral with regard to jurisdictional claims in published maps and institutional affiliations.

Copyright: © 2021 by the authors. Licensee MDPI, Basel, Switzerland. This article is an open access article distributed under the terms and conditions of the Creative Commons Attribution (CC BY) license (https://creativecommons.org/licenses/by/4.0/).

Abstract: With the widespread of blockchain technology, preserving the anonymity and confidentiality of transactions have become crucial. An enormous portion of blockchain research is dedicated to the design and development of privacy protocols but not much has been achieved for proper assessment of these solutions. To mitigate the gap, we have first comprehensively classified the existing solutions based on blockchain fundamental building blocks (i.e., smart contracts, cryptography, and hashing). Next, we investigated the evaluation criteria used for validating these techniques. The findings depict that the majority of privacy solutions are validated based on computing resources i.e., memory, time, storage, throughput, etc., only, which is not sufficient. Hence, we have additionally identified and presented various other factors that strengthen or weaken blockchain privacy. Based on those factors, we have formulated an evaluation framework to analyze the efficiency of blockchain privacy solutions. Further, we have introduced a concept of privacy precision that is a quantifiable measure to empirically assess privacy efficiency in blockchains. The calculation of privacy precision will be based on the effectiveness and strength of various privacy protecting attributes of a solution and the associated risks. Finally, we conclude the paper with some open research challenges and future directions. Our study can serve as a benchmark for empirical assessment of blockchain privacy.

Keywords: anonymity; confidentiality; blockchain privacy; privacy precision; smart contracts; cryptography; privacy attributes; privacy risks

1. Introduction

The elimination of an intermediary trusted party provided by the technology of blockchain is changing the verifiability, universal accessibility, and degree of autonomy over tokenized digital assets of any kind, resulting in a revolution on plethora of diverse scenarios. Introduced with the advent of Bitcoin [1], blockchains have been profusely researched and experimented over the years for a copious set of applications. These applications include banking and finance [2], supply chain management systems [3], electronic health records [4], Internet of Things (IoT) [5] and education [6]. Apart from disintermediation, the extended flexibility of blockchain has been exploited for all these application areas to address the issues of centralization, security, data integrity, and scalability [7]. Blockchain systems are decentralized [8] having no centralized, trusted authority for record verification and system maintenance. These systems rather hold each peer in the network accountable for protecting the integrity of the data and assets. Using mathematics and computation, the authenticity of records is verified by each participant [9] in the network before any of those are stored on the chain. The data, thereby, becomes, (i) more secure as there is no single point of failure, (ii) more transparent as each node in the network maintains the copy of the ledger and, (iii) more consistent as modification at any single point will be easily detectable. Since the data integrity in blockchain networks is achieved through public verification and storage of the records, hence the data on a public blockchain is readily available for anyone to download and access. As a result, a risk of privacy breach of the user involved in a transaction exists.

Privacy can be defined as the ability of a user to seclude themselves from sharing their confidential information and/or choose the extent of information disclosure in a shared setting. In blockchain networks, the term "privacy" is used for two aspects, i.e., user privacy and data privacy of the transactions. These two types of transaction privacy in blockchains are elaborated below:

1. User Privacy (Anonymity)

User privacy is the ability to convert the real identity of a blockchain user into something that cannot be identified, and further ensuring that the original identity also remains unobtainable [10]. This type of privacy is more commonly known as anonymity. It conceals the real-world identity of the user by masking the users' real network address with a computer-generated address.

2. Data Privacy (Confidentiality)

Hiding the contents of a transaction keeps blockchain data privacy intact. Data privacy is also referred to as confidentiality. At the most basic level, the data contents in a transaction are usually encrypted to maintain confidentiality in the network. Maintaining data confidentiality ensures that the transaction contents are free from unauthorized accessing, meddling and altering.

Despite all the glorious features of the blockchains, the tendency of these systems towards privacy disclosure is a worrisome issue nowadays [11]. Some may argue that the data on blockchain is encrypted and thus user assets are protected. However, privacy does not only refer to the data in blockchains, it also refers to protecting identity of participants in the network [12] as mentioned earlier. Deanonymization [13] of users in the network is a huge privacy issue. Analyzing transaction relationships, patterns, time, and links is possible. This creation of links between various transactions makes it convenient to trackback to the head node and determine the identities of transaction initiator and receiver. The details in this regard are given in [14] and are beyond the scope of this paper. According to [15], leakage of an individual's identity in blockchain results in disclosure of its corresponding transaction information. Therefore, using a blockchain jeopardizes the assets of a user by opening these to unauthorized exposure. Besides that, it is also envisioned that in the era of quantum computing, it will be easier to decrypt the codes and break the hashes [16] of blockchain networks.

Blockchain privacy can be achieved by strengthening the vulnerabilities of the blockchain architectural design. The fundamental building blocks of a blockchain system include hashing [17], cryptography [18], consensus [19] and smart contracts [20]. Each of these building blocks tend to either strengthen or weaken the privacy of the system. In this paper, we present a detailed description of these building blocks and their role in achieving privacy. This will help the blockchain enthusiasts to comprehend the issue in hand at deeper levels. Realizing the potential hazard of blockchain's privacy issue, numerous blockchain researchers and enthusiasts are working towards the issue. Some are digging deeper into the causes and factors resulting in privacy breach [14,16,21,22] while others are trying to provide a viable and universally accepted solution to the problem [23–25]. Despite the extensive research the issue persists. We argue that the reason behind the problem persistence is a result of the following:

1. Lack of literary resources for understandability of various blockchain components and features with respect to their effect on privacy.
2. Unavailability of a proper evaluation criteria that judges the efficiency privacy of a solution.
3. Absence of a concrete quantifiable value to empirically assess the degree of privacy offered by a solution.

Hence a comprehensive awareness of the role of each blockchain component towards privacy protection is much needed for ability to create better privacy preserving solutions. Moreover, proper analysis mechanism of these solutions is required to accurately evaluate the potential of each solution. Therefore, in this study, we bridge the said gap in literature by presenting a comprehensive review and solutions to the aforementioned existing issues. To accomplish the task, we first discuss the issue of privacy in detail. Further, we present a survey and classification of the privacy preserving solutions based on blockchain component/feature exploited for privacy provision. To the best of our knowledge, no manuscript has presented such classification so far. Next, we discuss the criteria and parameters adopted by several research works to evaluate these classified privacy solutions in blockchains. Most of the evaluations are performance based which is not sufficient with respect to privacy. This is because a solution might be utilizing lesser computational resources and consequently resulting in weaker privacy protection. Therefore, it is hard to judge the strength of a solution merely based on computing resources used. Hence, we introduce more parameters that affect the degree of privacy protection. These parameters include various features that make privacy protection stronger, and several features that can breach the privacy. Subsequently, we formulate a validation framework that considers these introduced parameters to empirically analyze the potential of the privacy technique under study. Calculation carried out based on the values of these parameters results in a singular value ranging between 0 and 1 (with 0 being no privacy preserved and 1 being maximum privacy preservation). We term this value as privacy precision in the formulated framework. To essentially evaluate any solution, considering both, pros and cons is significant. Our aspirations with this research are that it will be used as a benchmark when assessing blockchain based privacy solutions.

1.1. Gap Analysis and Contribution

We surveyed numerous articles relating to blockchain privacy, classified privacy protecting solutions based on the fundamental blockchain component targeted. During the survey, we found that most of these solutions are evaluated based on the computational performance and proof-of-concept, which is not acceptable. Therefore, research on privacy solutions for blockchain is not progressing significantly. To bridge this gap, this research study was carried out. The originality and contribution of this article is multifold:

1. Novel Classification of Privacy Solutions with respect to Blockchain Components

   We present a novel classification of existing privacy preserving solutions in blockchain networks based on the component involved in privacy protection. We classify the existing solutions into the categories of hashing, cryptographic primitives and smart contracts, all of which are significant components of blockchain functionality. To the best of our knowledge, such a classification has yet not been presented anywhere in the literature at the time of writing this manuscript. The purpose of this classification is to highlight the state-of-the-art methods preserving privacy in correspondence to the fundamentals to be tuned. This will be beneficial for the concerned individuals to make an informed decision about building a better privacy protecting blockchain for their applications.

2. Emphasizing on Insufficiency of State-of-the-Art Privacy Evaluation Criteria for Estimating the Potential of a Solution

   We extensively studied evaluation criteria adopted in various blockchain based privacy solutions for analysis. Using the literary evidence, we show that the evaluation is done mainly based on performance and proof of concept. However, we argue that such analysis is not sufficient to evaluate the privacy provided by a technology merely based on system performance, computational cost, and time and hence a proper framework with different criteria and parameters must be introduced for the evaluation. Therefore, we come to our third major contribution which is mentioned next.

3. Proposing Novel Framework to Empirically Evaluate Privacy Solutions (Beyond Performance)

To support the argument, we further present a framework with around 10 different criteria and sub-criteria, divided as privacy attributes and risks, that can effectively evaluate and quantify any blockchain based privacy solution irrespective of its category. With this, we also introduce the concept of privacy precision that is the empirical value calculated based on the efficiency of chosen parameters. This empirical value, ranging from 0 to 1, quantifies the degree of privacy provided by a solution.

To the best of our knowledge, none of the contributions have been published in any study so far.

1.2. Organization of the Paper

The organization of the rest of the paper is depicted in Figure 1 for a quick glance and elaborated as follows.

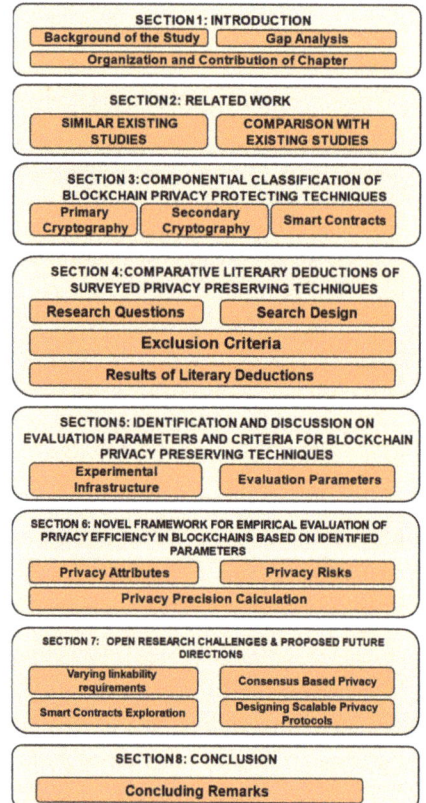

Figure 1. Organization of the paper.

In Section 2, we present related studies briefly and compare our work with existing work in the literature. Next, in Section 3, we present various fundamental components responsible for smooth functionality and integrity of the blockchain and highlight how each of these components can be used to strengthen the privacy. We also present critical analysis and comparison of the state-of-the-art blockchain privacy preserving solutions, classified based on their structural design. Then, in Section 4, some current trends with respect to blockchain privacy are presented. The section also highlights applications where blockchain privacy protocols are being used. We then show how the privacy degree is evaluated by each of these solutions and how these parameters (taken into consideration) are insufficient to be used as benchmark for privacy evaluation, in Section 5. Consequently, in Section 6 we proposed a privacy evaluation framework for blockchain networks that was designed considering all important features and risks affecting blockchain privacy. The evaluation framework will empirically analyze any privacy protecting solution of the blockchain networks. However, there are still a few key challenges that need to be considered. We present those open research challenges in Section 7. Finally, we conclude the paper in Section 8 along with some inferences derived throughout the paper.

2. Related Work

One of the most widely researched areas in the field of blockchain networks is the domain of preserving blockchain privacy. The reason being the growing concern of several industries and business enterprises to protect their data and trade secrets from unauthorized access. In this section, we first briefly discuss the importance of privacy in blockchain networks. Next, we present the related surveys that have been conducted in past focusing on blockchain privacy. Finally, we compare this survey with existing surveys in the domain to highlight the significance and novelty of the research presented in this paper.

Several business enterprises and various organizations are keen on deploying the technology for their day-to-day record keeping and business management. However, the only hurdle they are currently facing is privacy disclosure in the blockchains. This restricts the large scale applications of the technology [14]. Thus, a huge number of privacy solutions are proposed in literature. Besides that, multiple authors are contributing towards the evaluations of these solutions by presenting their surveys and reviews in the domain. One such survey is presented in [21]. In this survey, the authors have classified the fundamental techniques to preserve privacy i.e., mixing services and cryptographic primitives, and compared them based on the type of privacy preserved in each solution. Similarly, another article [26] broadly classified and compared cryptographic protocols in blockchain networks. Similar other studies were presented in [11,14,22] and more. The study presented in this paper is novel in a way that none of these surveys classified the privacy preserving solutions based on fundamental components of blockchain utilized. Moreover, this survey extensively discusses the evaluation criteria for the privacy preserving solutions, which to the best of our knowledge had not been published anywhere at the time of writing this manuscript. Moreover, this survey also introduces a multi-factor validation framework for appropriate evaluation of privacy preserving techniques considering all the features and risks.

Distinguishing Factors of Related Work

We carried out a comprehensive comparison of our research work with existing surveys. For the comparison, we identified the following criteria:

1. What is the publication year of the article? (YEAR)
2. How many citations does the article have? (CITE)
3. Whether the article is mainly centered around privacy concerns in blockchain? (PRIV-CEN)
4. If the article reviews existing cryptographic privacy techniques to retain transaction privacy? (CRYPT)
5. If the article reviews existing smart contract-based privacy techniques to retain transaction privacy? (SC)
6. Does the article shed a light on how these privacy techniques are evaluated and validated? (VAL)
7. Does the article provide sufficient information on open research challenges? (ORC)

The results of the comparison are depicted in Table 1.

From the table, it is evident that none of the existing work have focused on analyzing the validation requirements and state-of-the-art parameters, hence it becomes extremely important to address this limitation. Therefore, in this study we comprehensively report the validation strategies and criteria for blockchain privacy preserving techniques.

Table 1. A seven criteria comparison of various review articles on blockchain based privacy techniques.

Article	YEAR	CITE	PRIV-CEN	CRYPT	SC	VAL	ORC
[21]	2019	281	Yes	Yes	No	No	Yes
[11]	2019	64	Yes	Yes	No	No	Yes
[27]	2020	12	Yes	Yes	No	No	Yes
[28]	2019	83	No	No	No	No	Yes
[14]	2020	1	Yes	Yes	No	No	Yes
[29]	2020	2	Yes	Yes	No	No	No
[30]	2020	57	Yes	No	No	No	Yes
This survey	2021	-	Yes	Yes	Yes	Yes	Yes

3. Componential Classification of Blockchain Privacy Protecting Techniques

In today's era, data is constantly being generated at a significant pace [31]. This significant generation of data from several sources demands secure and reliable storage and exchange systems. Usually, the data is stored on cloud servers, however, this brings new concerns regarding data privacy, duplication and fine-grained access control [32], to the forefront. Thus, the technology of blockchain is being explored and utilized in various applications to investigate its effect and impact on record storage management and communication systems.

In its simplest terms, a blockchain can be referred to as database. This is because it is ledger that is responsible for storing data using data structure of a block [33]. The blockchain database exists on multiple computers at the same time to reduce the risk of data theft or loss [34]. These multiple computers or servers are called the participants, or "nodes" of the blockchain network. The data stored in blockchain database takes the form of a transaction. For example, if Alice wants to send a simple text message of "Hello" to Bob, it will be communicated and stored as a transaction. This transaction will consist of sender's key, receiver's key, and time stamp (i.e., the time when the transaction took place). The authenticity of these transactions in a blockchain network is validated via cryptography, making it an important component of the blockchain design [35]. Blockchains use two kinds of cryptographic algorithms. The first ones lie in the category of primary cryptography and includes asymmetric cryptography and hashing [36], whereas the second category is secondary cryptography which deals with providing additional security and privacy to the systems [26]. We discuss both the categories in detail later in this section.

When a transaction is initialized, it is propagated to all the participants in the network for verification [37]. The protocols and rules of this verification must be agreed upon by all the participants in the network. Hence, just like an ordinary agreement signed between trading parties, a digital agreement is enforced in the blockchain. Such digital agreements are called smart contracts [38]. Every node joining the chain, thus, provides its consent to abide by the rules of regulation, pre-coded into these contracts. Smart contracts [39] are responsible for provision of trust-less environment among participating nodes, integrity of data on chain, clear communication among peers, transparency and much more. These contracts are decentralized and immutable, so the blockchain nodes are assured of the integrity of these contracts. Since the seamless communication of blockchain is highly reliant on Smart Contracts, hence these can be intelligently programmed to transfer user assets in such a way that user and data privacy are retained. Moreover, these contracts are lightweight and require lesser computing resources as compared to the tradition cryptographic protocols. Furthermore, when smart contracts are used in conjunction with cryptographic schemes, they produce more promising results in terms of preserving blockchain privacy. More details on this are given further in this section. Another integral part of blockchain for maintaining justness of the blockchain system is known as consensus. This essential algorithms are responsible for conserving blockchain's efficiency and safety [40]. These algorithms do so by reaching a mutual agreement about the latest state of the blockchain. Several consensus algorithms are present in literature and can be used according to the application's requirement. However, consensus is not directly linked to strengthening blockchain privacy and hence is out of the scope of this paper. Interested readers may refer to [19] for details. A depiction of blockchain components that aid in privacy protection is illustrated in Figure 2. Blockchain fundamental building blocks (to preserve privacy) namely, public key cryptography [41], hashing [17] and smart contracts [42] are further elaborated in subsequent sections.

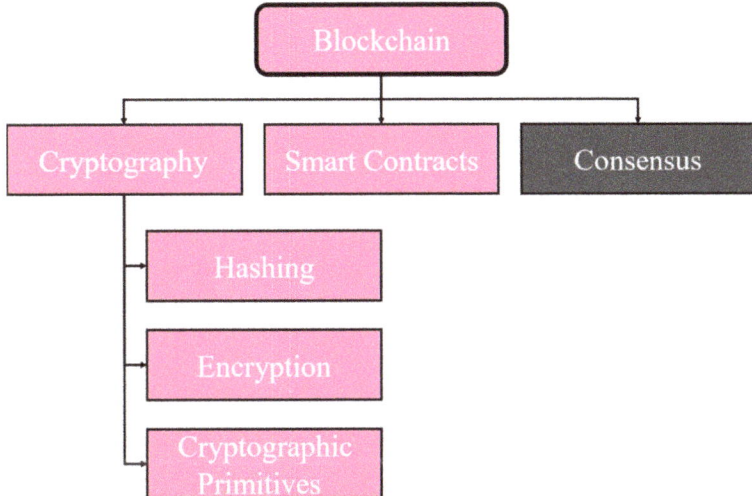

Figure 2. Blockchain components for privacy protection.

3.1. Effect of Blockchain's Primary Cryptography on Privacy

Cryptography is a technique of data storing and transmission in a certain form such that it is only interpretable by the intended user [43]. Besides safeguarding data from theft and alteration, cryptography may also be used for user authentication purposes [44]. Blockchain networks highly rely on cryptography for network integrity and data sharing. Cryptography is enforced in blockchains to accomplish the three basic information security tasks i.e., confidentiality (or data privacy), integrity or authentication (user privacy) and non-repudiation [45]. While it is deemed as an impeccable solution for online information security, cryptography does not guarantee complete protection of assets. However, it is an efficient method of shielding the data which minimizes the impact of unauthorized penetration if it does occur.

Fundamentally, two kinds of cryptographic algorithms are used in blockchains. The first one is known as asymmetric or public-key cryptography [46], and the second one is called hashing [47] both of which are elaborated further in this section.

3.1.1. Public Key Cryptography/Encryption

Blockchain uses asymmetric or public key cryptography to maintain reliability of the network. Public key cryptography uses a pair of keys, known as public and private keys, for data encryption and decryption. Public keys are distributed among the network participants for communication while private keys are kept private and protected from unauthorized access [48].

A study [49] exploited asymmetric cryptography for provision of privacy in eHealthcare system. The idea that the authors worked on was providing the medical data to the researchers for statistical analysis while ensuring that the privacy of the patients is not breached. Incorporating asymmetric cryptography in blockchain networks ensures accomplishment of two out of three information security properties, i.e., authentication and confidentiality [50].

Blockchain Solution for User Authentication

In most platforms, a user is authenticating by entering a password before he could utilize any of the services. This implies that if the main server of the platform is hacked, the hacker will get access to each user's password. Blockchain solves this problem by using asymmetric cryptography instead. For any user to participate in blockchain network, he must create his own pair of public and private keys. Public key is meant to be shared among the blockchain users to enable incoming transactions whereas private key must be kept secret.

Any transaction that is initiated by the user must be digitally signed by the user. This signature is generated using the private key of the user [51]. This signature can be verified by other participants using the public key of the signer. A signature generated using the private key of a user cannot be forged by any other user as he does not have access to the private key that generated the signature. However, the ownership of the transaction can easily be verified by anyone knowing the public key of the user. This serves as a means of authenticating that a certain transaction originated from a particular user, which cannot be denied by the sender. This property of inability of denying the validity of something is known as non-repudiation [52] in information security.

Blockchain Solution for Data Confidentiality

Using asymmetric cryptography also ensures data confidentiality or information privacy in blockchain networks. Blockchain networks are public in nature since it is the participants that verify communication between two parties instead of intermediary party [53]. Hence, all the transactions from one end to the other end will be propagated to the entire network for anyone to see. However, public–private key cryptography in blockchain networks ensures that the data is concealed and can only be viewed by the intended receiver. If a transaction is meant to be received and seen by user A, it must be encrypted using public key of user A. This transaction can now only be decrypted by the private key of user A [54], which implies that even if an adversarial user is listening to the network, he will not be able to see the contents of the transaction. Hence the confidentiality of the transaction contents will be intact, and data will travel across the network very securely. Although, this emphasizes the fact that private keys should be kept safe and guarded.

Besides maintaining information security properties, encryption has greater benefits to offer in the domain of blockchain privacy for various applications. A number of research articles, nowadays, are working on searching encrypted data stored in blockchain, while preserving the privacy of the data. This technique is known as searchable encryption. This kind of encryption is used to protect privacy and authenticity of data when enterprises store their sensitive records in external data centers [55]. Some studies [56] use single word searches while other advanced studies [57] present effective mechanisms to enable multi-keyword searches on the encrypted data in blockchains. Protecting data privacy using searchable encryption is a great concept but it is out of the scope of this manuscript since it covers blockchain fundamental privacy issues. Interested readers may refer to [57] for further study on the subject.

3.1.2. Hashing

Hashing is an integral component in the blockchain networks for maintaining the network consistency and reliability. Data is run through a hashing function to generate a kind of digital fingerprint that is essentially unique to the data file. The purpose of hashing the data is not for concealing it, rather allowing the verification that data is pure and not tampered with. This verification is convenient as modification of even a single character in the data will change the hash completely. The point of hashing is not to hide data, but to allow verification that the data has not been tampered with in any fashion. Moreover, the hash of a data cannot be "unhashed" or restored back into the original data. Hashing is a method used to verify the integrity of a message or file [58].

Blockchain Solution for Data Integrity

One of the most significant and prized features of blockchains is immutability [59]. Immutability simply refers to ensuring that the records in the chain have not been tampered with. This property of blockchain validates the integrity and truthfulness of the data in the chain.

Blockchain transactions are grouped together and stored into blocks. The blocks consisting of various transactions are chained together. Each block in the blockchain has a unique identifier (i.e., hash) [60]. The hash of each block is generated using a hashing function based on the hash of the previous block, list of transactions and time of publication (as illustrated in Figure 3). Even a slightest change in any of these can cause the entire block hash to be refreshed, highlighting tampering of the data. This makes it very complicated for any adversary to modify the data as it must make changes on every node of the entire decentralized network, which is practically impossible [61]. Thus, the integrity of the data is kept intact.

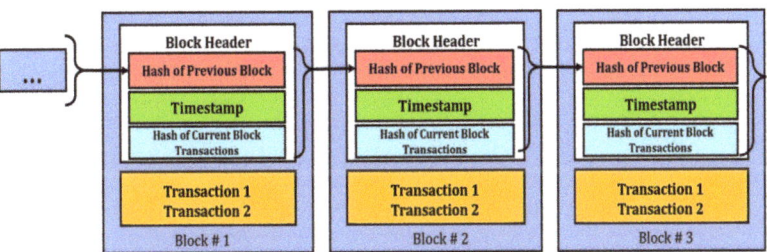

Figure 3. Structure of block.

3.2. Effect of Blockchain's Secondary Cryptography on Privacy

Due to public nature of blockchains, anyone can join the network at any point of time. Permission from any centralized or intermediary authorization is not required. As a result, bad actors can also join the network and gain access to the flow of transactions in the network. These bad actors can use various tricks and techniques to breach the privacy of users involved in various transactions. However, using secondary cryptography, it is possible to strengthen data confidentiality, user privacy, and minimize flow of metadata across the network [26]. Currently, the most widely used cryptographic techniques to achieve blockchain privacy are multi-party computation, ring signatures, homomorphic encryption, zero-knowledge proofs, and variants of all of these. In this section, we expounded the privacy protection by cryptography.

3.2.1. Multi-Party Computation for Achieving Blockchain Privacy

Multi-Party Computation (MPC), also referred to as Secure Multi-Party Computation (SMPC) is a privacy preserving cryptographic protocol. SMPC enables mutually distrusting distributed parties to jointly compute an arbitrary functionality without revelation of their own private inputs and outputs [62]. Consider a distributed environment with multiple parties P_i where $\{i = 1, 2, \ldots n\}$ having private inputs x_i wishing to compute an arbitrary functionality $f(x)$ jointly, such that $f(x_1, \ldots, x_n) = y_1, \ldots, y_n$. As soon as the computation completes, each party P_i is required to acquire its own corresponding output y_1 without obtaining any other kind of information [63].

The basic goal of SMPC is the construction of secure protocols that allow several mutually distrusted participants to collaborate for computation of an objective function in a joint fashion, using their own set of inputs. A study presented in [64] proposed an SMPC based solution for strengthening blockchain based privacy. In this solution, the user would store his data on the public ledger after encrypting it with his own secret key. Further, the solution exploited the features of smart contracts to enhance the security. When a user needs his private data in a smart contract, he decrypts the value using his key and uses the decrypted value as its local input to the SMPC protocol. The demonstration of the idea was presented using three parties only. Another study [65] also implemented SMPC for better privacy protection in blockchain based application. The study claims to have 66% more efficiency than existing solutions. However, since the claim was not backed up by any experiments, the authenticity of the claim is questionable.

3.2.2. Homomorphic Encryption for Achieving Blockchain Privacy

Homomorphic encryption is a cryptographic technique that allows computation to be performed on the encrypted data without accessing the secret key. The computation results obtained are same as that of the original data. Moreover, it utilizes proxy re-encryption technology to protect the selected ciphertext from being attacked [66]. It can also be seen as an extended version of either symmetric-key or public-key cryptography. In [67], homomorphic encryption was deployed to enhance blockchain security. Various privacy and security breaching attacks, such as collision attack, primage attack and wallet theft attacks were the motivation behind the study. The two homomorphic encryption techniques used for the study were Goldwasser-Micali and Paillier encryption schemes [68] for data privacy. The preliminary results presented in the study portrayed that these two schemes had a lower processing time and greater resilience against aforementioned attacks.

3.2.3. Ring Signatures for Achieving Blockchain Privacy

Numerous kinds of signatures are present in cryptography. However, to achieve anonymity in blockchain networks, ring signatures and its variants are used. Ring signatures, introduced in 2001 [69], work on the idea of involving various network participants to form a ring and create a signature based on the private key of ring creator and public keys of other participants in the ring. Doing this will reveal to the verifiers that one of the participants have signed the transaction without giving out the information of who exactly has signed the transaction. Thereby achieving anonymity and unforgeability [70]. Ring signatures were extended [71] to traceable ring signatures and adopted for the formation of Ring-Coin. In this case, anyone impersonating another person in the ring to sign the same message will risk revealing his identity immediately. This idea was further deployed for prevention of double-spending attack in blockchain and thereby became the basis of CryptoNote [72] with a slight modification.

A ring signature-based scheme was proposed [73] to strengthen the privacy in blockchain networks. This work combined ring signatures with elliptic curve cryptography for privacy enhancement. The study does not describe any experimentations performed for evaluation; however, it gives mathematical proofs testifying that the proposed mechanism was efficient.

3.2.4. Zero-Knowledge Proofs for Achieving Blockchain Privacy

Zero-Knowledge Proofs (ZKPs) are the most widely used cryptographic methods enabling transfer of assets across a decentralized, distributed, peer-to-peer blockchain network with improved privacy. The objective of zero-knowledge proofs is to attest the legitimacy of a transaction with zero knowledge offered to the verifier related to the transaction. The notion of ZKPs involve the prover to articulate a formal proof as an evidence of a particular assertion being true without provision of any extended and useful information to verifying party [74]. In blockchain networks, a variant of ZKP, known as Non-Interactive Zero-knowledge Proof (NIZK proof), is extensively utilized as it drastically reduces communication complexity. It is not desirable to deploy the extensive communication requirements of simple ZKPs. NIZK proofs must meet the following three properties:

1. Completeness: Everything that is true has a proof.
2. Soundness: Everything that can be proved is true.
3. Zero knowledge: Only the proven statement is revealed.

A commonly known application of NIZK is Zerocoin [75]. It utilizes NIZK for provision of user anonymity by involving mechanism of preventing transaction graph analysis, i.e., breaks the traces of coins. However, it is unsuccessful in achieving so because of several reasons including fixed coin denominations, conversion of anonymous coins into non-anonymous before payments, and unconcealed transaction amounts. To overcome these limitations, another application of NIZK named Zerocash [76] was introduced. Zerocash provided data confidentiality as well as user anonymity. Additionally, transaction size and verification time were also considerably reduced. Zerocash uses ZK-SNARKS. However, the NIZK protocol experiences high computation outlays specially in the proof generation phase of ZK-SNARKs protocol used in Zcash.

3.3. Effect of Smart Contracts on Privacy

Smart contracts are digital contracts consisting of rules and regulations, mutually agreed upon by all the parties in a decentralized network [77]. They are self-executing programs which run automatically and are tamper-proof. They are written in high-level programming languages and allow the developers along with the users to express complex behavioral requirements and patterns. The recent developments in the technology of blockchain networks revived the perception and enabled the formation of smart contracts that were originally envisioned by Szabo in 1994. Smart contracts are a significant part of the blockchains as they ensure simple business trading among two mutually distrusting parties without the intervention of any third intermediary. It allows disintermediation in the blockchains which is one of the technology's key features. Moreover, the correct use of smart contracts can ensure added security to the blockchain transactions. However, ensuring the correctness of the contracts is a challenging task because of the vulnerabilities of computer programs to the faults and failures [78].

Fundamentally, much work on privacy protecting using smart contracts has yet not been achieved in literature. However, smart contracts coupled with one or more cryptographic techniques and to address the issue of blockchain privacy, have been witnessed. One such example is presented in [23]. Particularly, Hawk [23] will automatically compile a smart contract into a cryptographic protocol. This compiled program has two parts, the first one deals with execution of major function, whereas the later one protects the users. For transaction encryption and verification, Hawk uses zero-knowledge proofs. Another smart contract based privacy solution is presented in [79]. It offers a solution to the secrecy of smart contract execution and uses advanced cryptographic primitives to support zero-knowledge proofs. Additionally, the data in Enigma is distributed among various nodes unlike the conventional blockchain data storage schemes (i.e., maintaining the copy of ledger of every node). The study in [80] utilizes Enigma protocol for privacy preservation on hybrid blockchain platforms. It highlights the inefficacy of centralized (off-chain) and decentralized (on-chain) platforms when implementing smart contracts individually and proposes a hybrid approach. The authors in the study split the smart contracts a part of which was executed on an off-chain contract and the other part was executed on Rinkeby [81], an Ethereum test network. This concept was adopted in [82]. All the smart contract functions requiring higher computation or consisting of sensitive information are included in the off-chain part of the contract to be signed and executed by concerned participants only. All the unanimous agreements are done off-chain.

4. Comparative Literary Deductions of Surveyed Privacy Preserving Techniques

4.1. Comparison of Surveyed Techniques

The studies surveyed in the above subsections are compared in this section for further analysis. We identified five criteria to contrast the privacy preserving techniques based on exploitation of different blockchain components. These identified criteria include

(1) component utilized, (2) underlying technique, (3) whether experiments have been performed to validate the solution or not, (4) type of results presented (i.e., performance based, feature based or mathematical proofs, (5) main contribution of the study and finally (6) grade of the solution. Performance based results include parameters such as execution time, computational complexity, memory utilized, throughput and so on, whereas feature-based experiments include parameters such as encryption strength, type of privacy (i.e., anonymity or confidentiality) and other such attributes. We assign these solutions a grade of 1–4 with 1 being the lowest grade and 4 being the highest. The grades are assigned on the basis of four factors, i.e., construction of the protocol to preserve privacy, implementation details provided, extensive validation of the results, and efficiency of privacy preserved. The results of the comparison are summarized in Table 2 as follows.

Table 2. Comparative analysis of privacy preserving techniques.

Study	Component	Technique	Experimental Validation (Y/N)	Type of Results	Main Contribution	Grade
[43]	Primary Cryptography	Public-Key Cryptography	Yes	Performance-Based	Direct transfer of patient centric data between the patient and researchers, ensuring patient anonymity	2
[83]	Primary Cryptography	Hashing	Yes	Performance-Based	Leveraging of blockchain in cloud data provenance using hashing	4
[55]	Secondary Cryptography	Multi-Party Computation	Yes	Performance-Based	Execution of SMPC protocol as a part of smart contract to protect user data privacy in smart contracts	3
[56]	Secondary Cryptography	Multi-Party Computation	No	N/A	Optimization of existing SMPC protocols	1
[58]	Secondary Cryptography	Homomorphic Encryption	Yes	Performance and Feature Based	Discussion of homomorphic and non-homomorphic encryption techniques w.r.t privacy and highlighting the significance of homomorphic encryption in blockchain privacy preservation, using preliminary experiments	2
[64]	Secondary Cryptography	Ring Signatures	No	Mathematical Proofs	This work combined ring signatures with elliptic curve cryptography for privacy enhancement	3
[67]	Secondary Cryptography	Zero-Knowledge Proofs	Yes	Mathematical Proofs and Performance-Based	Construction of decentralized anonymous payment (DAP) schemes enabling concealment of transaction origin, destination and contents	4
[22]	Smart Contracts	–	Yes	Performance-Based	Restriction of blockchain transaction storage for public view. Instead, usage of private smart contracts to encrypt data	4
[70]	Smart Contracts	–	Yes	Performance-Based	Utilizes verifiable secret-sharing for optimization of SMPC using private contracts	3
[73]	Smart Contracts	–	Yes	Performance-Based	Splitting of smart contracts into on and off chain contracts to enhance privacy and scalability of the blockchain network	2

4.2. Survey Research Methodology for Literary Deductions

The methodology adopted to conduct the survey is depicted in Figure 4. The goal of our research is to understand intrinsic concepts of blockchain with respect to privacy to understand the mechanisms of better privacy preserving techniques' formulation and appropriate evaluation. This will consequently result in wider adoption of the technology in privacy centric applications that are currently hesitant to deploy their systems to blockchains. Hence, the formulated research questions to achieve the study goal are:

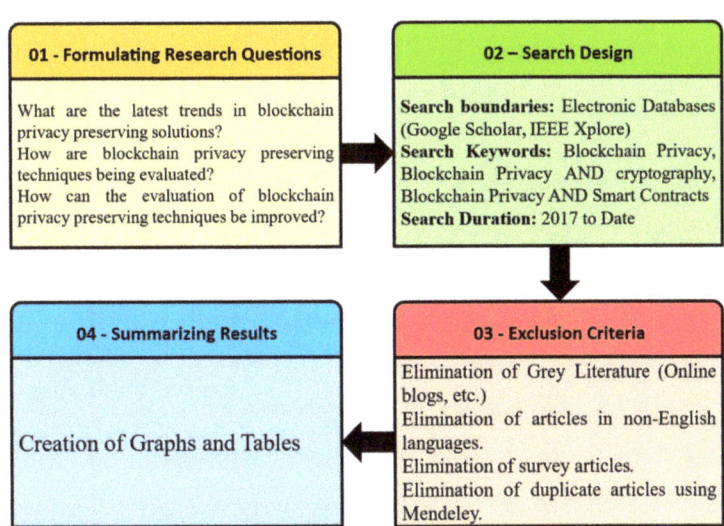

Figure 4. Survey methodology.

RQ1: *What are the latest trends in blockchain privacy preserving solutions?*

RQ2: *How are blockchain privacy preserving techniques being evaluated?*

RQ3: *How can the evaluation of blockchain privacy preserving techniques be improved?*

For this survey, we used Google Scholar and IEEE Xplore digital repositories. The keywords used for our results were "Blockchain Privacy", "Blockchain Privacy AND cryptography" and "Blockchain Privacy AND Smart Contracts". We considered the data of past 5 years (i.e., 2017–2021) and picked up the first 300 results for our analysis. We excluded survey articles as they were not needed for the analysis. Moreover, we excluded manuscripts that either belonged to techniques of privacy breaching attacks or did not have any significant contribution to the body of the knowledge. We also excluded any articles that were not written in English language. Grey literature and duplicate articles were also removed for the analysis. The inclusion and exclusion criteria are comprehensively depicted in Table 3. We classified these articles based on the core mechanism of preserving privacy i.e., cryptography, smart contracts, hybrid of both or others. The last category included solutions that used deep learning, differential privacy, federated learning, clustering, and other computing approaches to retain privacy in blockchain based networks. The basic goal was to find out the blockchain based privacy preserving techniques that are currently being researched and experimented. The results of the analysis are summarized in subsequent sections.

Table 3. Comparative analysis of privacy preserving techniques.

Inclusion Criteria	Exclusion Criteria
Articles are no more than 5 years old (i.e., published in range of 2017–2021)	Survey articles on blockchain privacy
Articles must be related to blockchain privacy preserving techniques	Privacy breaching attacks on blockchain networks
Articles must be written in English language	Grey literature (i.e., online blogs, etc.)

4.3. Results of Literary Deductions

The results of the analysis are presented in the graph depicted in Figure 5. The graph shows yearly distribution of articles based on blockchain privacy that were taken into consideration, with respect to aforementioned classes.

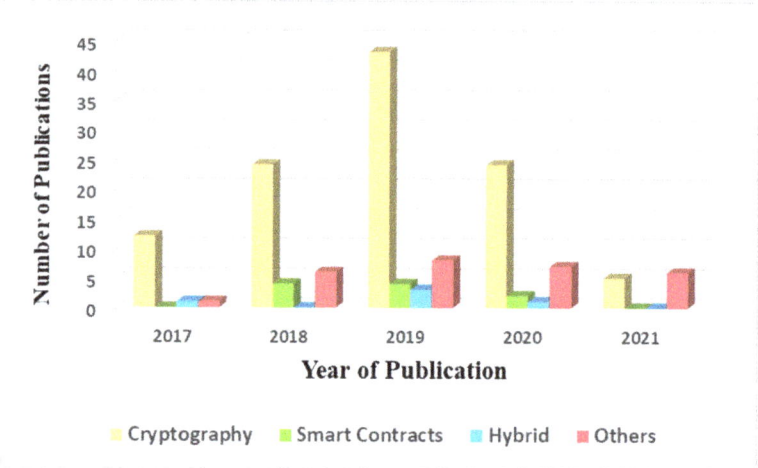

Figure 5. Latest trends in blockchain based privacy preserving solutions.

From the graph obtained (Figure 5), we can see most of the studies surveyed used cryptography for privacy protection. The majority of these studies used simple data encryption techniques including Attribute Based Encryption [84], Content Extraction Signature [85,86], RSA algorithm and others. The rest of them utilized ring signatures [73,87], zero-knowledge proofs [88,89] and other commonly known cryptographic techniques. Besides cryptographic techniques, a number of studies used machine learning approaches [90,91] for preserving blockchain privacy, followed by a very low number of studies exploring smart contracts [92–94] for the task. Furthermore, most of the papers surveyed leveraged blockchain privacy mechanisms into various application areas that require protecting data privacy. These applications include ad-hoc vehicular networks [95–97], healthcare [98–101], crowdsourcing [102,103], e-voting [104,105] and more. Several IoT applications such as protecting sensor data, body area networks, vehicular parking systems were also identified as potential application areas that requiring greater privacy guarantees. A pie chart depicting these privacy centric applications found in literature is given as Figure 6.

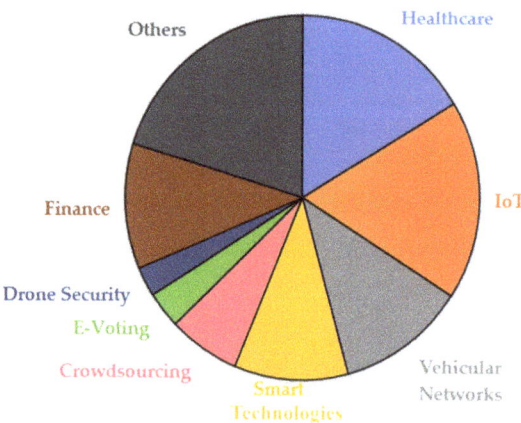

Figure 6. Privacy centric applications in blockchain networks.

We derived a few deductions from the literary findings in this section. These findings are elaborated below:

Deduction 1: *From Table 1, we can infer that most of the experiments were based on the performance. However, stronger privacy guarantees are not directly proportional to utilization of lesser computational resources. Hence, performance-based experimentations and results cannot be completely relied on when considering privacy strength of a technique. This deduction is comprehensively studied and analyzed further in Section 5.*

Deduction 2: *Another deduction that was inferred from the articles studied was that the smart contracts (despite their abundant usage in blockchains) are not largely studied for privacy protection in comparison to cryptography. Smart contracts play a major role in development of the blockchain networks, hence exploiting their full potential will result in promising privacy protection in blockchains.*

Deduction 3: *As inferred from the literary surveyed articles, healthcare record management systems and supply chains, Internet of Things (IoT) based sensor data management systems, financial applications, and vehicular communication networks are the topmost privacy centric applications, followed by smart technologies, crowdsourcing, federated and deep learning data management and so on.*

5. Identification and Discussion on Evaluation Parameters and Criteria for Blockchain Privacy Preserving Techniques

Due to the technology of blockchain having huge privacy concerns, extensive research is being conducted into this domain. Following which, numerous privacy-preserving solutions have been proposed in literature. In previous sections, we discussed those solutions in detail and in this section, we investigated and presented the state-of-the-art methods, parameters, and metrics to evaluate the degree of privacy provided by these solutions. Numerous privacy-preserving solutions were comprehensively examined to analyze underlying experimental infrastructure utilized for the evaluation, the evaluation parameters used for performance analysis followed by the nature of the solution i.e., if it is a fundamental privacy solution or applied. The fundamental solution refers to the privacy preserving solutions that strengthen the blockchain privacy whereas the applied solution corresponds to solutions that leverage blockchain for strengthening privacy in other application scenarios. The findings are summarized in Table 4.

Table 4. Summary of state-of-the-art blockchain privacy evaluation parameters.

Study	Experimental Infrastructure	Evaluation Criteria/Parameters	Fundamental/Applied
[106]	Mining Nodes: 20 Wallet Nodes: 20 Transaction Frequency: 5 s Consensus: Proof of Work Arduino MKR1000 32-bit ARM Cortex-M0 + MCU 32 KB of SRAM and 256 KB of flash Raspberry Pi Zero W with a 1 GHz single-core CPU and 512 MB RAM	Request Processing Time Transaction Size Block Creation Time	Applied (Pervasive Computing)
[107]	Programming Language: R-Programming Language System Software: Ubuntu 18.04 LTS with GPU Quadro P6000 RAM: 32-GB	Privacy-Level Index (Pindex) Dissimilarity level (DISS) Information Loss Accuracy FAR	Applied (Smart Power Networks)
[108]	Three test chains, (Kylin, Jungle, Local), Blockchain, Cloud were used. Over 100 tests performed Alibaba Cloud 2 core RAM: 8 GB Storage: 100 G System Software: Ubuntu 16.04	Authorization Time, Throughput vs. Delay Time Overhead Hash Cost Overhead	Applied (Cloud Access Control)

Table 4. Cont.

Study	Experimental Infrastructure	Evaluation Criteria/Parameters	Fundamental/Applied
[25]	Programming Language: Solidity Test net: Rinkeby (Ethereum), Geth Processor: Intel Core i7 Clock: 2.7 GHz RAM: 16 GB	Gas Cost Time Overhead	Fundamental
[76]	Multiple machines used for experiments. Machine 1: Processor: Intel Core i7-2620M Clock: 2.70 GHz RAM: 12 GB Machine 2: Processor: Intel Core i7-4770 Clock: 3.40 GHz RAM: 16 GB	Key Generation Time Key Size Proof Size Block Verification Time Transaction Latency Block Propagation Time Setup Time	Fundamental
[109]	System Software: Ubuntu 16.04 Processor: Intel Core i5-6200U Clock: 2.3 GHz RAM: 8 GB We used the Programming: BouncyCastle's Java library for Curve 25519	Protocol Run Time Ring Size	Fundamental
[23]	Amazon EC2 r3.8xlarge Virtual Machine RAM: 27 GB	Key Generation Time Proving Time Verification Time Evaluation Key Size Proof Size Verifier Key Size	Fundamental
[110]	Operating System: Ubuntu 18.04 Processor: Intel Core i7 Clock: 2.9 GHz RAM: 8 GB Testnet: Hyperledger Caliper Multiple Phase Experiments Experimental Rounds/Phase: 30	Throughput Latency Time Send Rate	Applied (IoT Data Sharing in Smart Cities)
[82]	Contracts Programming: Solidity Off-chain Signature Programming: JavaScript Testnet: Kovan, Ethereum	Gas Cost	Fundamental

From the table, it is evident that most of the evaluations are based on time, throughput, and memory required. All these parameters are dependent on computational resources. This means that the better the hardware machine used, the better will be the performance of the evaluated technique. None of these parameters take into account the level of privacy provided by a solution. When Bitcoin [15], Ring CT [109], Zerocash [76] were introduced, each of these claimed to provide privacy protection to user identity and user assets. The performance results given also depicted the same. However, the attacks [13,111–114] in later studies showed the vulnerabilities in proposed solutions, which when exploited, deanonymized the users for up to 90%. This is a highly significant number. Therefore, that makes it remarkably clear that computational performance-based experiments and proof-of-concept are not sufficient to judge the efficiency of a privacy preserving solution. This implies that more factors or parameters should be considered for evaluation. Another finding that we inferred from the survey is elaborated in deduction 4 given below:

Deduction 4: *Another discovery to be highlighted here, is that most of the privacy preserving frameworks are deployed using Ethereum [115] platform with Solidity [116] as programming language and tested using official Ethereum test networks. This means that Ethereum is a better platform when it comes to programming privacy related applications.*

6. Novel Framework for Empirical Evaluation of Privacy Efficiency in Blockchains Based on Identified Parameters

Since current evaluation parameters for blockchain based privacy solutions are insufficient, hence we further surveyed the literature to find more parameters for validation. From the survey, we found a number of essential characteristics that a blockchain based solution shall possess. Moreover, we also found out the parameters and criteria to evaluate those characteristics or features. Further, we also formulate a validation framework that will efficiently verify the ability of a proposed blockchain privacy solution. This work is loosely based on [7]. However, the problem with the study is that the study is focused on a limited type of privacy preserving solutions i.e., related to Internet of Things (IoT) networks. Moreover, the solution presented in the study [7] considers various parameters based on their presence or absence, it does not account for the degree of usefulness and efficiency of each parameter which is highly essential. Therefore, we enhanced the solution by first removing any parameters specific to IoT applications, to facilitate diverse applications. Next, we introduce some new parameters that have greater or at least equivalent significance in terms of privacy protection (details are mentioned later in this section). Moreover, we also introduce some performance evaluators to evaluate the efficiency of given parameters to assist in determining how effective a parameter is in preserving the privacy of the given technique. Since this work is loosely based on [7], hence, the weights taken for each of the characteristic are same as in the study. We discuss those parameters, performance evaluators, and the corresponding framework in detail in this section.

To evaluate the solution, we will calculate privacy precision of each solution. To do so, we divided the surveyed factors in two categories, i.e., privacy attributes and privacy risks. Privacy attributes consist of the factors that strengthen the privacy if present in a solution whereas privacy risks correspond to weaknesses of a solution, i.e., the risks that the solution is vulnerable to. Next, we use these attributes and risks to analyze privacy preserving solutions with different perspectives and collectively calculate its worth as a numeric value. The evaluation framework is elaborated in subsequent sections.

6.1. Privacy Attributes—Parameters Strengthening the Privacy

The identified privacy attributes for our framework are shown in Table 5. Along with the performance evaluators to validate the performance and efficiency of each attribute. The weighting vector $\vec{W_A}$ represents the weights of these five attributes of the privacy features, where:

$$\vec{W_A} = (w_1, w_2, \ldots w_5) = (3, 2, 2, 3, 2) \tag{1}$$

Table 5. Privacy attributes.

Privacy Attributes (A_i)	Total Evaluators (E_T)	Evaluators (E_i)	Weight (W_i)	Proportionality (R)
Encryption	3	Encryption Time	3	−1
		Memory Utilization		−1
		Throughput		1
Transactional Anonymity	2	Time	2	−1
		Space (Memory)		−1
Pseudonymous ID	2	Key Length	2	1
		Cipher Algorithm		1
Anonymity Group	1	Group Size	3	1
IP Protection	1	Percentage of nodes accessing transaction traffic	2	−1
Max Weight			12	

The maximum privacy achievable by a solution will be,

$$Maximum\ Privacy = \sum_{i=1}^{5} w_i = 12 \qquad (2)$$

The privacy attributes of a solution are expressed as a privacy attribute vector $\vec{A}$ where

$$\vec{A} = (A_1, A_2, \ldots, A_5) \qquad (3)$$

Each attribute (A) has some performance evaluators (E) to quantify how good the attribute is for preserving privacy. To calculate attribute value of each attribute, the values of evaluators are summed up. Note that each evaluator E has a different proportionality R. The attribute value is calculated as,

$$A_i = \sum_{i=1}^{E_{Ti}} E_i^{Ri} \qquad (4)$$

where A_i: score of ith attribute, E_i: value obtained of the ith performance evaluator, R_i: proportionality of the evaluator to strengthen the privacy. The value of R_i is 1 for directly proportional and -1 for inversely proportional, E_{Ti}: total evaluators for ith attribute.

Once we have A_i for each attribute, we will normalize the obtained value between 0 and max weight of the characteristic (W_i) using the following equation,

$$A_n = \frac{(A_i - min(d))^*(max(n) - min(n))}{max(d) - min(d)} \qquad (5)$$

where, $min(d)$: minimum Data Value Obtained, $max(d)$: maximum Data Value Obtained, $min(n)$: minimum Range Value, $max(n)$: maximum Range Value, A_n: normalized A_i.

The $min(d)$ and $max(d)$ values are taken as 0 and 100, respectively. Here, 0 indicates no privacy and 100 indicates complete privacy. Moreover, the values of $min(n)$ and $max(n)$ will be 0 and weight of the attribute. Substituting the values, the equation becomes,

$$A_n = \frac{A_i * w_i}{100} \qquad (6)$$

After normalized attribute values have been achieved, the normalized privacy attribute vector will be:

$$\vec{A_n} = (A_{n1}, A_{n2}, \ldots, A_{n5}) \qquad (7)$$

We will calculate the privacy weightage of each attribute by multiplying it with its corresponding weight. Hence, we propose that the overall attribute privacy P_A may be calculated as,

$$P_A = \vec{A_n} \cdot \vec{W_A} = \sum_{i=1}^{5} A_{ni} \times w_i \qquad (8)$$

6.2. Privacy Risks—Parameters Breaching the Privacy

Attributes or features aiding privacy of the blockchains are not enough to validate the efficiency of the solution. Evaluating its resilience against various well-known attacks and risks is also essential. Hence, we surveyed the literature for potential threats towards blockchain privacy. The identified risks for our framework are listed in Table 6.

Table 6. Privacy risks.

Privacy Risks (R_i)	Total Evaluators (E_T)	Evaluators (E_i)	Weight (v_i)
Linkability	2	Traffic Correlation / Address Correlation	1
Insider Adversary	2	Data Leakage / Data Propagation to Adversary	1
Performance	2	Computational Burden (Time, Storage, Clock Speed) / Memory Issue	1
Scalability	1	Transactions Per Second	1
Max Weight			4

We consider each criterion to be of equal effect and give a weight of one to all of them. For each of the risks present in the privacy solution, a negative value will be generated.

The weighting vector $\vec{V_R}$ represents the weights of these four risks of privacy, where:

$$\vec{V_R} = (v_1, v_2, \ldots v_4) = (1, 1, 1, 1) \quad (9)$$

The maximum privacy risk achievable by a solution will be,

$$Maximum\ Privacy = \sum_{i=1}^{4} v_i = 4 \quad (10)$$

The privacy risks of a solution are expressed as a privacy risk vector $\vec{R}$ where,

$$\vec{R} = (R_1, R_2, \ldots, R_4) \quad (11)$$

Each risk (R) has some performance evaluators (E) to quantify how good the attribute is for preserving privacy. To calculate risk value of each risk, the values of evaluators are summed up. Hence the risk value is calculated as,

$$R_i = \sum_{i=1}^{E_{T_i}} E_i \quad (12)$$

where, R_i: score of ith attribute, E_i: value obtained of the ith performance evaluator, E_{T_i}: total evaluators for ith attribute.

Once we have R_i for each risk, we will normalize the obtained value between 0 and max weight of the characteristic (v_i) using the following equation,

$$A_n = \frac{(A_i - min(d))^*(max(n) - min(n))}{max(d) - min(d)} \quad (13)$$

where, $min(d)$: minimum Data Value, $max(d)$: maximum Data Value, $min(n)$: minimum Range Value, $max(n)$: maximum Range Value, R_n: normalized R_i

The $min(d)$ and $max(d)$ values are taken as 0 and 100, respectively. Here, 0 indicates no privacy and 100 indicates complete privacy. Moreover, the values of $min(n)$ and $max(n)$ will be 0 and weight of the risk which is 1. Substituting the values, the equation becomes,

$$R_n = \frac{R_i}{100} \quad (14)$$

After normalized attribute values have been achieved, the normalized privacy attribute vector will be:

$$\vec{R_n} = (R_{n1}, R_{n2}, \ldots, R_{n4}) \quad (15)$$

We will calculate the privacy weightage of each attribute by multiplying it with its corresponding weight. Therefore, the overall attribute privacy P_A will be calculated as,

$$P_R = \vec{R_n} \cdot \vec{V_R} = \sum_{i=1}^{5} R_{ni} \times v_i \tag{16}$$

6.3. Privacy Precision

To calculate privacy precision, we first calculate the privacy resultant as,

$$\mathbb{R} = P_A - P_R \tag{17}$$

Practically a solution cannot provide all privacy features and the maximum privacy protection is not feasible. Similarly, the maximum risk cannot be assigned to a privacy-preserving solution. We have the minimum privacy resultant (-4) when a solution leaves all privacy risks and has no privacy feature. In a similar fashion, the maximum privacy resultant (12) is achieved when a solution offers all privacy features with no privacy risk. It is worth noting that these values are based on the criteria introduced in Tables 4 and 5 and will be changed if other criterion weighing scales are used.

We introduce privacy precision that is a quantifiable value to present the degree of privacy provided by a solution. To calculate privacy precision, we normalize the values of privacy resultant. Hence, using the privacy resultant, maximum and minimum privacy values achieved, and min–max normalization [117], we can calculate the privacy precision as,

$$Privacy\ Precision = \frac{Privacy\ Resultant - min(privacy)}{max(privacy) - min(privacy)} = \frac{\mathbb{R} - (-4)}{12 - (-4)} = \frac{\mathbb{R} + 4}{16} \tag{18}$$

Thus, the final value of Privacy Precision will range from 0 to 1. The grading model defined for the framework is shown in Table 7. Here, we define three (03) grades, namely, poor, good and excellent. Any solution that achieves less than 0.3 precision score is termed as poor, this is because such a low value represents that a solution either has insufficient number of privacy features to make it strong or it is prone to privacy breaching risks. In both the cases, solution is inefficient. For any solution that has a privacy precision of more than 0.3 but less than 0.6, the solution is considered as a good or fair solution as it contains moderately efficient features and has more resilience against the privacy breaching attacks. Finally, any solution that has a privacy precision of more than 0.6, is termed as an excellent solution. Such solutions are scalable, computationally intensive, and preserve privacy to a greater extent. A privacy preserving solution having precision score of 1 has all the features of privacy and no associated risks, hence it provides complete anonymity and confidentiality in blockchain transactions.

Table 7. Privacy precision grading model.

Grading	Precision Value
Poor	$0 \leq Precision \leq 0.3$
Good	$0.31 \leq Precision \leq 0.6$
Excellent	$0.61 \leq Precision \leq 1$

7. Open Research Challenges and Proposed Future Directions

In our study, we found out some open research challenges that must be considered for wider adoption of the blockchain technology in privacy-centric applications. These research challenges include:

1. Challenge 1: Varying linkability requirements.

   Although we proposed the existing solutions to be evaluated based on linkability analysis, however, the linking techniques and heuristics vary from solution to solution based on their design. Different techniques have different heuristics and methods of linkability and deanonymization of users. This means different techniques can be assessed differently and may yield different results. They do not have a uniform form of evaluation.

   Proposed Future Direction: A comprehensive literature survey and extensive research on uniform characteristics of blockchain based privacy solutions should be carried out for design of a uniform linkability attack. Common heuristics and similar data will enable justified comparison on the basis of transaction linking.

2. Challenge: Consensus Based Privacy

   We classified the existing solutions based on the fundamental blockchain component associated with enhancing the privacy. Consensus protocols are an integral part of blockchain networks as they are responsible for maintaining integrity, validity, and authenticity of the blockchain network. However, protecting privacy using consensus is yet an underexplored area.

   Proposed Future Direction: Research and analysis in consensus-based privacy protection is much needed to protect data eavesdropping. The effect of strengthening consensus to preserve transaction anonymity and confidentiality should be explored. Design of some consensus protocols that will secure privacy in blockchain combined with cryptography and/or smart contracts is expected to yield promising results in future.

3. Challenge: Smart Contracts Exploration

   Major portion of blockchain deployment and functionality is achieved through self-executing smart contracts, hence utilizing them in an efficient way will add a layer of privacy protection in blockchain systems. The findings of our survey as presented in Section 3, depict that although smart contracts are widely being used for various application scenarios, still they are comparatively underexplored in comparison to cryptographic primitives for privacy preservation.

   Proposed Future Direction: Investigating the constructs of smart contracts and using appropriate encryption schemes will add an additional layer of privacy in blockchain transactions. Hence, it is suggested to conduct further research and experiments using solidity smart contracts as Ethereum and Solidity are privacy-friendly blockchain platforms.

4. Challenge 4: Designing Scalable Privacy Protocols

   Various privacy preserving solutions, such as ZKSNARKS and other variants of zero-knowledge proofs provide good privacy protection, however, it comes with a cost of higher consumption of computational resources. Since verifying proof to approve a transaction requires advanced mathematics, it takes longer to verify the transaction. For applications that require a high number of transactions per minute, such as finance and banking systems, the ZKPs tend to produce the problem of transaction scalability. A proper balance between greater privacy preservation and provision of appropriate scalability requirements remains an unsolved challenge to the date.

   Proposed Future Direction: It is suggested to design a scalable privacy protocol that not only preserves privacy but also does not create scalability issues in the network. For this, the concept of zero-knowledge proofs can be taken as a starting point and some fundamental changes in its architecture may be produced to reduce the size of proofs thereby also retaining their efficiency. This will reduce the verification time in ZKPs.

8. Conclusions

In this study, we carried out an extensive survey relating to privacy preserving solutions in blockchains. We presented classification of the solutions based on the blockchain component for greater understandability of blockchain's privacy strengths and vulnerabilities. This will enable blockchain engineers and researchers to design and develop better privacy preserving solutions. Several concluding remarks derived from the study include:

- Utilization of optimum (less) computational resources is not directly proportional to stronger privacy guarantees. Therefore, we cannot rely on performance-based experimentations and results to analyze the potential strengths and shortcomings of the proposed privacy preserving solution.
- A comprehensive validation framework to analyze a privacy preserving solution from different perspectives is required and hence we proposed a novel validation framework to accomplish the task.
- Blockchain networks intensively rely on smart contracts for smooth execution, however, they are not studied and experimented to their full potential for achieving privacy. Therefore, we provide initial basis that will open further avenues of research in this area.
- Ethereum test networks, and Solidity smart contracts programming are extensively being used for development and testing of blockchain privacy preserving techniques.

We infer that this study will enable successful development, deployment, testing, and empirical evaluation of privacy preserving techniques in blockchain networks, being a key driving force for future development of blockchain technology and its applications in various privacy-centric domains.

Author Contributions: Manuscript preparation and conceptualization, A.Z.J., M.A.H.; research methodology design and data analysis and visualization, A.Z.J., M.M.M.; critical comparison, A.Z.J., M.A.H.; survey deductions, A.Z.J.; validation framework design, A.Z.J., M.A.H.; proof-reading, editing and formatting, M.A.H., M.M.M. All authors have read and agreed to the published version of the manuscript.

Funding: The research work is funded by Yayasan Universiti Teknologi PETRONAS—Fundamental Research Grant (YUTP-FRG): 015LC0-158(YUTP) and Centre of Graduate Studies (CGS), Universiti Teknologi PETRONAS (UTP), Malaysia

Institutional Review Board Statement: Not Applicable.

Informed Consent Statement: Not Applicable.

Acknowledgments: The authors extend their deep regards and acknowledgement to Universiti Teknologi PETRONAS for provision of resources and materials for the completion of this research work.

Conflicts of Interest: The authors declare no conflict of interest.

References

1. Junejo, A.Z.; Memon, M.M.; Junejo, M.A.; Talpur, S.; Memon, R.M. Blockchains Technology Analysis: Applications, Current Trends and Future Directions—An Overview. *Lect. Notes Netw. Syst.* **2020**, *118*, 411–419. [CrossRef]
2. Chen, Y.; Bellavitis, C. Blockchain disruption and decentralized finance: The rise of decentralized business models. *J. Bus. Ventur. Insights* **2020**, *13*, e00151. [CrossRef]
3. Dutta, P.; Choi, T.M.; Somani, S.; Butala, R. Blockchain technology in supply chain operations: Applications, challenges and research opportunities. *Transp. Res. Part. E Logist. Transp. Rev.* **2020**, *142*, 102067. [CrossRef]
4. Siyal, A.A.; Junejo, A.Z.; Zawish, M.; Ahmed, K.; Khalil, A.; Soursou, G. Applications of Blockchain Technology in Medicine and Healthcare: Challenges and Future Perspectives. *Cryptography* **2019**, *3*, 3. [CrossRef]
5. Hassan, M.U.; Rehmani, M.H.; Chen, J. Privacy preservation in blockchain based IoT systems: Integration issues, prospects, challenges, and future research directions. *Futur. Gener. Comput. Syst.* **2019**, *97*, 512–529. [CrossRef]
6. Hashmani, M.A.; Junejo, A.Z.; Alabdulatif, A.A.; Adil, S.H. Blockchain in Education–Track ability and Traceability. In Proceedings of the 2020 International Conference on Computational Intelligence (ICCI), Bandar Seri Iskandar, Malaysia, 8–9 October 2020; pp. 40–44. [CrossRef]
7. Firoozjaei, M.D.; Lu, R.; Ghorbani, A.A. An evaluation framework for privacy-preserving solutions applicable for blockchain-based internet-of-things platforms. *Secur. Priv.* **2020**, *3*, 1–28. [CrossRef]
8. Zhang, C.; Ni, Z.; Xu, Y.; Luo, E.; Chen, L.; Zhang, Y. A trustworthy industrial data management scheme based on redactable blockchain. *J. Parallel Distrib. Comput.* **2021**, *152*, 167–176. [CrossRef]
9. Kumar, R.; Tripathi, R.; Marchang, N.; Srivastava, G.; Gadekallu, T.R.; Xiong, N.N. A secured distributed detection system based on IPFS and blockchain for industrial image and video data security. *J. Parallel. Distrib. Comput.* **2021**, *152*, 128–143. [CrossRef]

10. De Haro-Olmo, F.J.; Varela-Vaca, Á.J.; Álvarez-Bermejo, J.A. Blockchain from the perspective of privacy and anonymisation: A systematic literature review. *Sensors* **2020**, *20*, 7171. [CrossRef]
11. Bernabe, J.B.; Canovas, J.L.; Hernandez-Ramos, J.L.; Moreno, R.T.; Skarmeta, A. Privacy-Preserving Solutions for Blockchain: Review and Challenges. *IEEE Access* **2019**, *7*, 164908–164940. [CrossRef]
12. Nguyen, B.M.; Dao, T.C.; Do, B.L. Towards a blockchain-based certificate authentication system in Vietnam. *PeerJ Comput. Sci.* **2020**, *2020*, e266. [CrossRef]
13. Biryukov, A.; Tikhomirov, S. Deanonymization and Linkability of Cryptocurrency Transactions Based on Network Analysis. In Proceedings of the 2019 IEEE European Symposium on Security and Privacy (EuroS P), Stockholm, Sweden, 17–19 June 2019; pp. 172–184. [CrossRef]
14. Junejo, A.Z.; Hashmani, M.A.; Alabdulatif, A.A. A survey on privacy vulnerabilities in permissionless blockchains. *Int. J. Adv. Comput. Sci. Appl.* **2020**, *11*, 130–139. [CrossRef]
15. Nakamoto, S. Bitcoin: A Peer-to-Peer Electronic Cash System. *Decentralized Bus. Rev.* **2008**, *1*, 21260.
16. Karame, G.; Capkun, S. Blockchain security and privacy. *IEEE Secur. Priv.* **2018**, *16*, 11–12. [CrossRef]
17. Dasgupta, D.; Shrein, J.M.; Gupta, K.D. A survey of blockchain from security perspective. *J. Bank. Financ. Technol.* **2019**, *3*, 1–17. [CrossRef]
18. Raikwar, M.; Gligoroski, D.; Kralevska, K. SoK of Used Cryptography in Blockchain. *IEEE Access* **2019**, *7*, 148550–148575. [CrossRef]
19. Khan, D.; Jung, L.T.; Hashmani, M.A.; Waqas, A. A Critical Review of Blockchain Consensus Model. In Proceedings of the 2020 3rd International Conference on Computing, Mathematics and Engineering Technologies (iCoMET), Sukkur, Pakistan, 29–30 January 2020; pp. 1–6. [CrossRef]
20. Singh, A.; Parizi, R.M.; Zhang, Q.; Choo, K.K.R.; Dehghantanha, A. Blockchain smart contracts formalization: Approaches and challenges to address vulnerabilities. *Comput. Secur.* **2020**, *88*, 101654. [CrossRef]
21. Feng, Q.; He, D.; Zeadally, S.; Khan, M.K.; Kumar, N. A survey on privacy protection in blockchain system. *J. Netw. Comput. Appl.* **2019**, *126*, 45–58. [CrossRef]
22. Cui, Y.; Pan, B.; Sun, Y. A Survey of Privacy-Preserving Techniques for Blockchain. In *Artificial Intelligence and Security*; Springer: Berlin/Heidelberg, Germany, 2019; pp. 225–234.
23. Kosba, A.; Miller, A.; Shi, E.; Wen, Z.; Papamanthou, C. Hawk: The Blockchain Model of Cryptography and Privacy-Preserving Smart Contracts. In Proceedings of the 2016 IEEE Symposium on Security and Privacy (SP), San Jose, CA, USA, 22–26 May 2016; pp. 839–858. [CrossRef]
24. Wu, H.; Zheng, W.; Chiesa, A.; Popa, R.A.; Stoica, I. DIZK: A distributed zero knowledge proof system. In Proceedings of the 27th USENIX Security Symposium, Baltimore, MD, USA, 15–17 August 2018; pp. 675–692.
25. Li, C.; Palanisamy, B. Decentralized Privacy-Preserving Timed Execution in Blockchain-Based Smart Contract Platforms. In Proceedings of the 25th IEEE International Conference High Performance Computing HiPC 2018, Bengaluru, India, 17–20 December 2019; pp. 265–274. [CrossRef]
26. Wang, L.; Shen, X.; Li, J.; Shao, J.; Yang, Y. Cryptographic primitives in blockchains. *J. Netw. Comput. Appl.* **2019**, *127*, 43–58. [CrossRef]
27. Peng, L.; Feng, W.; Yan, Z.; Li, Y.; Zhou, X.; Shimizu, S. Privacy preservation in permissionless blockchain: A survey. *Digit. Commun. Netw.* **2020**, *124*, 577–580. [CrossRef]
28. Mohanta, B.K.; Jena, D.; Panda, S.S.; Sobhanayak, S. Blockchain technology: A survey on applications and security privacy Challenges. *Internet Things* **2019**, *8*, 100107. [CrossRef]
29. Satybaldy, A.; Nowostawski, M. Review of techniques for privacy-preserving blockchain systems. In Proceedings of the BSCI 2020 Proceedings 2nd ACM International Symposium Blockchain Secure Critical Infrastructure, Co-located with AsiaCCS, Taipei, Taiwan, 6 October 2020; pp. 1–9. [CrossRef]
30. Ferrag, M.A.; Shu, L.; Yang, X.; Derhab, A.; Maglaras, L. Security and Privacy for Green IoT-Based Agriculture: Review, Blockchain Solutions, and Challenges. *IEEE Access* **2020**, *8*, 32031–32053. [CrossRef]
31. Bellini, E.; Bellini, P.; Cenni, D.; Nesi, P.; Pantaleo, G.; Paoli, I.; Paolucci, M. An IOE and big multimedia data approach for urban transport system resilience management in smart cities. *Sensors* **2021**, *21*, 435. [CrossRef]
32. Premkamal, P.K.; Pasupuleti, S.K.; Singh, A.K.; Alphonse, P.J.A. Enhanced attribute based access control with secure deduplication for big data storage in cloud. *Peer Peer Netw. Appl.* **2021**, *14*, 102–120. [CrossRef]
33. Chang, S.E.; Chen, Y. When blockchain meets supply chain: A systematic literature review on current development and potential applications. *IEEE Access* **2020**, *8*, 62478–62494. [CrossRef]
34. Ellervee, A.; Matulevicius, R.; Mayer, N. A comprehensive reference model for blockchain-based distributed ledger technology. *CEUR Workshop Proc.* **2017**, *1979*, 320–333.
35. Zheng, Z.; Xie, S.; Dai, H.; Chen, X.; Wang, H. An Overview of Blockchain Technology: Architecture, Consensus, and Future Trends. In Proceedings of the 2017 IEEE International Congress on Big Data (BigData Congress), Honolulu, HI, USA, 25–30 June 2017; Volume 2017, pp. 557–564. [CrossRef]
36. Khalid, Z.M.; Askar, S. Resistant Blockchain Cryptography to Quantum Computing Attacks. *Int. J. Sci. Bus.* **2021**, *5*, 116–125.
37. Jiang, S.; Cao, J.; Wu, H.; Yang, Y. Fairness-based Packing of Industrial IoT Data in Permissioned Blockchains. *IEEE Trans. Ind. Inform.* **2020**, *3203*, 1–11. [CrossRef]

38. Ante, L. Smart contracts on the blockchain—A bibliometric analysis and review. *Telemat. Inform.* **2021**, *57*, 101519. [CrossRef]
39. Rouhani, S.; Deters, R. Security, performance, and applications of smart contracts: A systematic survey. *IEEE Access* **2019**, *7*, 50759–50779. [CrossRef]
40. Du, M.; Ma, X.; Zhang, Z.; Wang, X.; Chen, Q. A review on consensus algorithm of blockchain. In Proceedings of the 2017 IEEE International Conference on Systems, Man, and Cybernetics (SMC), Banff, AB, Canada, 5–8 October 2017; pp. 2567–2572. [CrossRef]
41. Gamage, H.T.M.; Weerasinghe, H.D.; Dias, N.G.J. A Survey on Blockchain Technology Concepts, Applications, and Issues. *SN Comput. Sci.* **2020**, *1*, 114. [CrossRef]
42. Wang, S.; Ouyang, L.; Yuan, Y.; Ni, X.; Han, X.; Wang, F.Y. Blockchain-Enabled Smart Contracts: Architecture, Applications, and Future Trends. *IEEE Trans. Syst. Man Cybern. Syst.* **2019**, *49*, 2266–2277. [CrossRef]
43. Costa, D.G.; Figuerêdo, S.; Oliveira, G. Cryptography in wireless multimedia sensor networks: A survey and research directions. *Cryptography* **2017**, *1*, 4. [CrossRef]
44. Zhai, S.; Yang, Y.; Li, J.; Qiu, C.; Zhao, J. Research on the Application of Cryptography on the Blockchain. *J. Phys. Conf. Ser.* **2019**, *1168*, 032077. [CrossRef]
45. Chen, C.L.; Deng, Y.Y.; Weng, W.; Chen, C.H.; Chiu, Y.J.; Wu, C.M. A traceable and privacy-preserving authentication for UAV communication control system. *Electron* **2020**, *9*, 62. [CrossRef]
46. Chandra, S.; Paira, S.; Alam, S.S.; Sanyal, G. A comparative survey of symmetric and asymmetric key cryptography. In Proceedings of the 2014 International Conference on Electronics, Communication and Computational Engineering (ICECCE), Hosur, India, 17–18 November 2014; pp. 83–93. [CrossRef]
47. Martínez, V.G.; Hernández-Álvarez, L.; Encinas, L.H. Analysis of the cryptographic tools for blockchain and bitcoin. *Mathematics* **2020**, *8*, 131. [CrossRef]
48. Aydar, M.; Çetin, S.C.; Ayvaz, S.; Aygün, B. Private key encryption and recovery in blockchain. *arXiv* **2019**, arXiv:1907.04156.
49. Mahore, V.; Aggarwal, P.; Andola, N.; Raghav; Venkatesan, S. Secure and privacy focused electronic health record management system using permissioned blockchain. In Proceedings of the 2019 IEEE Conference on Information and Communication Technology, Allahabad, India, 6–8 December 2019; pp. 1–6. [CrossRef]
50. Tutorials Point. Blockchain-Public Key Cryptography. Available online: https://www.tutorialspoint.com/blockchain/blockchain_public_key_cryptography.htm (accessed on 1 July 2021).
51. Shen, B.; Guo, J.; Yang, Y. MedChain: Efficient healthcare data sharing via blockchain. *Appl. Sci.* **2019**, *9*, 1207. [CrossRef]
52. Ali, Q.E.; Ahmad, N.; Malik, A.H.; Ali, G.; Rehman, W.U. Issues, challenges, and research opportunities in intelligent transport system for security and privacy. *Appl. Sci.* **2018**, *8*, 1964. [CrossRef]
53. Firdaus, M.; Rhee, K.H. On blockchain-enhanced secure data storage and sharing in vehicular edge computing networks. *Appl. Sci.* **2021**, *11*, 414. [CrossRef]
54. Goel, A.; Agarwal, A.; Vatsa, M.; Singh, R.; Ratha, N. DeepRing: Protecting deep neural network with blockchain. In Proceedings of the 2019 IEEE/CVF Conference on Computer Vision and Pattern Recognition Workshops (CVPRW), Long Beach, CA, USA, 16–17 June 2019; pp. 2821–2828. [CrossRef]
55. Li, H.; Tian, H.; Zhang, F.; He, J. Blockchain-based searchable symmetric encryption scheme. *Comput. Electr. Eng.* **2019**, *73*, 32–45. [CrossRef]
56. Tahir, S.; Rajarajan, M. Privacy-Preserving Searchable Encryption Framework for Permissioned Blockchain Networks. In Proceedings of the 2018 IEEE International Conference on Internet of Things (iThings) and IEEE Green Computing and Communications (GreenCom) and IEEE Cyber, Physical and Social Computing (CPSCom) and IEEE Smart Data (SmartData), Halifax, NS, Canada, 30 July–3 August 2018; pp. 1628–1633. [CrossRef]
57. Jiang, S.; Xie, S.; Dai, H.N.; Chen, W.; Chen, X.; Weng, J.; Imran, M. Privacy-preserving and efficient multi-keyword search over encrypted data on blockchain. In Proceedings of the 2019 IEEE International Conference on Blockchain (Blockchain), Atlanta, GA, USA, 14–17 July 2019; pp. 405–410. [CrossRef]
58. Conley, J.P. *Encryption, Hashing, PPK, and Blockchain: A Simple Introduction*. Vanderbilt University Department of Economics Working Papers 19-00013, Vanderbilt University Department of Economics. 2019. Available online: https://econpapers.repec.org/paper/vanwpaper/vuecon-sub-19-00014.htm (accessed on 5 May 2021).
59. Moreno, J.; Serrano, M.A.; Fernandez, E.B.; Fernández-Medina, E. Improving Incident Response in Big Data Ecosystems by Using Blockchain Technologies. *Appl. Sci.* **2020**, *10*, 724. [CrossRef]
60. Dabbagh, M.; Choo, K.K.R.; Beheshti, A.; Tahir, M.; Safa, N.S. A survey of empirical performance evaluation of permissioned blockchain platforms: Challenges and opportunities. *Comput. Secur.* **2021**, *100*, 102078. [CrossRef]
61. Iqbal, M.; Matulevičius, R. Comparison of Blockchain-Based Solutions to Mitigate Data Tampering Security Risk. *Lect. Notes Bus. Inf. Process.* **2020**, *361*, 13–28. [CrossRef]
62. Zhao, C.; Zhao, S.; Zhao, M.; Chen, Z.; Gao, C.Z.; Li, H.; Tan, Y.A. Secure Multi-Party Computation: Theory, practice and applications. *Inf. Sci.* **2019**, *476*, 357–372. [CrossRef]
63. Zhou, J.; Feng, Y.; Wang, Z.; Guo, D. Using secure multi-party computation to protect privacy on a permissioned blockchain. *Sensors* **2021**, *21*, 1540. [CrossRef]
64. Benhamouda, F.; Halevi, S.; Halevi, T. Supporting private data on Hyperledger Fabric with secure multiparty computation. *IBM J. Res. Dev.* **2019**, *63*, 1–8. [CrossRef]

65. Innocent, A.A.T.; Prakash, G. Blockchain applications with privacy using efficient multiparty computation protocols. In Proceedings of the 2019 PhD Colloquium on Ethically Driven Innovation and Technology for Society (PhD EDITS), Bangalore, India, 18 August 2019. [CrossRef]
66. Yan, X.; Wu, Q.; Sun, Y. A Homomorphic Encryption and Privacy Protection Method Based on Blockchain and Edge Computing. *Wirel. Commun. Mob. Comput.* **2020**, *2020*, 8832341. [CrossRef]
67. Yaji, S.; Bangera, K.; Neelima, B. Privacy preserving in blockchain based on partial homomorphic encryption system for ai applications. In Proceedings of the 2018 IEEE 25th International Conference on High Performance Computing Workshops (HiPCW), Bengaluru, India, 17–20 December 2019; Volume 2018, pp. 81–85. [CrossRef]
68. Ji, H.; Xu, H. A Review of Applying Blockchain Technology for Privacy Protection. *Adv. Intell. Syst. Comput.* **2020**, *994*, 664–674. [CrossRef]
69. Rivest, R.L.; Shamir, A.; Tauman, Y. How to leak a secret. *Lect. Notes Comput. Sci.* **2001**, *2248*, 552–565. [CrossRef]
70. Wu, Y. An E-voting System based on Blockchain and Ring Signature. Master's Thesis, University of Birmingham, Birmingham, UK, 2017.
71. Fujisaki, E.; Suzuki, K. Traceable Ring Signature. In *Public Key Cryptography—PKC 2007*; Lecture Notes in Computer Science; Okamoto, T., Wang, X., Eds.; Springer: Berlin/Heidelberg, Germany, 2007; Volume 4450, pp. 181–200.
72. Van Saberhagen, N. CryptoNote v 2.0. White Paper, October 17, Semantics Scholar 2013. Available online: https://www.semanticscholar.org/paper/CryptoNote-v-2.0-Saberhagen/5bafdd891c1459ddfd22d71412d5365de723fb23 (accessed on 5 May 2021).
73. Li, X.; Mei, Y.; Gong, J.; Xiang, F.; Sun, Z. A blockchain privacy protection scheme based on ring signature. *IEEE Access* **2020**, *8*, 76765–76772. [CrossRef]
74. Zhang, R.; Xue, R.; Liu, L. Security and privacy on blockchain. *ACM Comput. Surveys* **2019**, *52*, 39. [CrossRef]
75. Miers, I.; Garman, C.; Green, M.; Rubin, A.D. Zerocoin: Anonymous Distributed E-Cash from Bitcoin. In Proceedings of the 2013 IEEE Symposium on Security and Privacy, Berkeley, CA, USA, 19–22 May 2013; pp. 397–411. [CrossRef]
76. Ben-Sasson, E.; Chiesa, A.; Garman, C.; Green, M.; Miers, I.; Tromer, E.; Virza, M. Zerocash: Decentralized Anonymous Payments from Bitcoin. In Proceedings of the 2014 IEEE Symposium on Security and Privacy, Berkeley, CA, USA, 18–21 May 2014; pp. 459–474. [CrossRef]
77. Cong, L.W.; He, Z. Blockchain Disruption and Smart Contracts. *Rev. Financ. Stud.* **2019**, *32*, 1754–1797. [CrossRef]
78. Zheng, Z.; Xie, S.; Dai, H.N.; Chen, W.; Chen, X.; Weng, J.; Imran, M. An overview on smart contracts: Challenges, advances and platforms. *Futur. Gener. Comput. Syst.* **2020**, *105*, 475–491. [CrossRef]
79. Shrobe, H.; Shrier, D.L.; Pentland, A. CHAPTER 15 Enigma: Decentralized Computation Platform with Guaranteed Privacy. In New Solutions for Cybersecurity. Available online: https://ebin.pub/new-solutions-for-cybersecurity-mit-connection-science-amp-engineering-mit-connection-science-amp-engineering-0262535378-9780262535373.html (accessed on 6 June 2021).
80. Molina-Jimenez, C.; Sfyrakis, I.; Solaiman, E.; Ng, I.; Wong, M.W.; Chun, A.; Crowcroft, J. Implementation of Smart Contracts Using Hybrid Architectures with On and Off–Blockchain Components. In Proceedings of the 2018 IEEE 8th International Symposium on Cloud and Service Computing (SC2), Paris, France, 18–21 November 2018; pp. 83–90. [CrossRef]
81. Kohli, M. Ethereum—Fund And Deploy Smart Contract To RinkeBy Test Network. 2019. Available online: https://medium.com/the-capital/ethereum-fund-and-deploy-smart-contract-to-rinkeby-test-network-790562f5a9bc (accessed on 3 June 2021).
82. Li, C.; Palanisamy, B.; Xu, R. Scalable and privacy-preserving design of on/off-chain smart contracts. In Proceedings of the 2019 IEEE 35th International Conference on Data Engineering Workshops (ICDEW), Macao, China, 8–12 April 2019; pp. 7–12. [CrossRef]
83. Liang, X.; Shetty, S.; Tosh, D.; Kamhoua, C.; Kwiat, K.; Njilla, L. ProvChain: A Blockchain-Based Data Provenance Architecture in Cloud Environment with Enhanced Privacy and Availability. In Proceedings of the 2017 17th IEEE/ACM International Symposium on Cluster, Cloud and Grid Computing (CCGRID), Madrid, Spain, 14–17 May 2017; pp. 468–477. [CrossRef]
84. Wu, A.; Zhang, Y.; Zheng, X.; Guo, R.; Zhao, Q.; Zheng, D. Efficient and privacy-preserving traceable attribute-based encryption in blockchain. *Ann. Telecommun.* **2019**, *74*, 401–411. [CrossRef]
85. Sutton, A.; Samavi, R. Blockchain enabled privacy audit logs. In *Lecture Notes in Computer Sciencce*; Spriger: Berlin/Heidelberg, Germany, 2017; Volume 10587, pp. 645–660. [CrossRef]
86. Liu, J.; Li, X.; Ye, L.; Zhang, H.; Du, X.; Guizani, M. BPDS: A blockchain based privacy-preserving data sharing for electronic medical records. In Proceedings of the 2018 IEEE Global Communications Conference (GLOBECOM), Abu Dhabi, United Arab Emirates, 9–13 December 2018.
87. Jivanyan, A.; Mamikonyan, T. Hierarchical One-out-of-Many Proofs With Applications to Blockchain Privacy and Ring Signatures. In Proceedings of the 2020 15th Asia Joint Conference on Information Security (AsiaJCIS), Taipei, Taiwan, 20–21 August 2020; pp. 74–81. [CrossRef]
88. Gabay, D.; Akkaya, K.; Cebe, M. Privacy-Preserving Authentication Scheme for Connected Electric Vehicles Using Blockchain and Zero Knowledge Proofs. *IEEE Trans. Veh. Technol.* **2020**, *69*, 5760–5772. [CrossRef]
89. Li, W.; Guo, H.; Nejad, M.; Shen, C.-C. Privacy-Preserving Traffic Management: A Blockchain and Zero-Knowledge Proof Inspired Approach. *IEEE Access* **2020**, *8*, 181733–181743. [CrossRef]
90. Firoozjaei, M.D.; Ghorbani, A.; Kim, H.; Song, J. Hy-Bridge: A Hybrid Blockchain for Privacy-Preserving and Trustful Energy Transactions in Internet-of-Things Platforms. *Sensors* **2020**, *20*, 928. [CrossRef]

91. Kumar, P.; Gupta, G.P.; Tripathi, R. TP2SF: A Trustworthy Privacy-Preserving Secured Framework for sustainable smart cities by leveraging blockchain and machine learning. *J. Syst. Archit.* **2021**, *115*, 101954. [CrossRef]
92. Hu, J.; He, D.; Zhao, Q.; Choo, K.-K.R. Parking Management: A Blockchain-Based Privacy-Preserving System. *IEEE Consum. Electron. Mag.* **2019**, *8*, 45–49. [CrossRef]
93. Pouraghily, A.; Islam, M.N.; Kundu, S.; Wolf, T. Poster Abstract: Privacy in Blockchain-Enabled IoT Devices. In Proceedings of the 2018 IEEE/ACM Third International Conference on Internet-of-Things Design and Implementation (IoTDI), Orlando, FL, USA, 17–20 April 2018; pp. 292–293. [CrossRef]
94. Pranto, T.H.; Noman, A.A.; Mahmud, A.; Haque, A.K.M.B. Blockchain and smart contract for IoT enabled smart agriculture. *PeerJ Comput. Sci.* **2021**, *7*, e407. [CrossRef]
95. Li, M.; Zhu, L.; Lin, X. Efficient and Privacy-Preserving Carpooling Using Blockchain-Assisted Vehicular Fog Computing. *IEEE Internet Things J.* **2019**, *6*, 4573–4584. [CrossRef]
96. Pu, Y.; Xiang, T.; Hu, C.; Alrawais, A.; Yan, H. An efficient blockchain-based privacy preserving scheme for vehicular social networks. *Inf. Sci.* **2020**, *540*, 308–324. [CrossRef]
97. Lu, Z.; Liu, W.; Wang, Q.; Qu, G.; Liu, Z. A Privacy-Preserving Trust Model Based on Blockchain for VANETs. *IEEE Access* **2018**, *6*, 45655–45664. [CrossRef]
98. Zhang, A.; Lin, X. Towards Secure and Privacy-Preserving Data Sharing in e-Health Systems via Consortium Blockchain. *J. Med. Syst.* **2018**, *42*, 140. [CrossRef] [PubMed]
99. Omar, A.; Rahman, S.; Basu, A.; Kiyomoto, S. *In MediBchain: A Blockchain Based Privacy Preserving Platform for Healthcare Data*; Springer: Berlin/Heidelberg, Germany, 2017; pp. 534–543. [CrossRef]
100. Al Omar, A.; Bhuiyan, M.Z.A.; Basu, A.; Kiyomoto, S.; Rahman, M.S. Privacy-friendly platform for healthcare data in cloud based on blockchain environment. *Futur. Gener. Comput. Syst.* **2019**, *95*, 511–521. [CrossRef]
101. Jiang, S.; Cao, J.; Wu, H.; Yang, Y.; Ma, M.; He, J. Blochie: A blockchain-based platform for healthcare information exchange. In Proceedings of the 2018 IEEE International Conference on Smart Computing (SMARTCOMP), Taormina, Italy, 18–20 June 2018; pp. 49–56. [CrossRef]
102. Xu, X.; Liu, Q.; Zhang, X.; Zhang, J.; Qi, L.; Dou, W. A Blockchain-Powered Crowdsourcing Method With Privacy Preservation in Mobile Environment. *IEEE Trans. Comput. Soc. Syst.* **2019**, *6*, 1407–1419. [CrossRef]
103. Wang, J.; Sun, G.; Gu, Y.; Liu, K. ConGradetect: Blockchain-based detection of code and identity privacy vulnerabilities in crowdsourcing. *J. Syst. Archit.* **2021**, *114*, 101910. [CrossRef]
104. Hardwick, F.S.; Gioulis, A.; Akram, R.N.; Markantonakis, K. E-Voting With Blockchain: An E-Voting Protocol with Decentralisation and Voter Privacy. In Proceedings of the 2018 IEEE International Conference on Internet of Things (iThings) and IEEE Green Computing and Communications (GreenCom) and IEEE Cyber, Physical and Social Computing (CPSCom) and IEEE Smart Data (SmartData), Halifax, NS, Canada, 30 July–3 August 2018; pp. 1561–1567. [CrossRef]
105. Zhang, W.; Yuan, Y.; Hu, Y.; Huang, S.; Cao, S.; Chopra, A.; Huang, S.A. Privacy-Preserving Voting Protocol on Blockchain. In Proceedings of the 2018 IEEE 11th International Conference on Cloud Computing (CLOUD), San Francisco, CA, USA, 2–7 July 2018; pp. 401–408. [CrossRef]
106. Le, T.; Mutka, M.W. Capchain: A privacy preserving access control framework based on blockchain for pervasive environments. In Proceedings of the 2018 IEEE International Conference on Smart Computing (SMARTCOMP), Taormina, Italy, 18–20 June 2018; pp. 57–64. [CrossRef]
107. Keshk, M.; Turnbull, B.; Moustafa, N.; Vatsalan, D.; Choo, K.K.R. A Privacy-Preserving-Framework-Based Blockchain and Deep Learning for Protecting Smart Power Networks. *IEEE Trans. Ind. Inform.* **2020**, *16*, 5110–5118. [CrossRef]
108. Yang, C.; Tan, L.; Shi, N.; Xu, B.; Cao, Y.; Yu, K. AuthPrivacyChain: A Blockchain-Based Access Control Framework with Privacy Protection in Cloud. *IEEE Access* **2020**, *8*, 70604–70615. [CrossRef]
109. Yuen, T.H.; Sun, S.F.; Liu, J.K.; Au, M.H.; Esgin, M.F.; Zhang, Q.; Gu, D. RingCT 3.0 for Blockchain Confidential Transaction: Shorter Size and Stronger Security. *Lect. Notes Comput. Sci.* **2020**, *12059 LNCS*, 464–483. [CrossRef]
110. Makhdoom, I.; Zhou, I.; Abolhasan, M.; Lipman, J.; Ni, W. PrivySharing: A blockchain-based framework for privacy-preserving and secure data sharing in smart cities. *Comput. Secur.* **2020**, *88*, 101653. [CrossRef]
111. Möser, M.; Soska, K.; Heilman, E.; Lee, K.; Heffan, H.; Srivastava, S.; Hogan, K.; Hennessey, J.; Miller, A.; Narayanan, A. An Empirical Analysis of Traceability in the Monero Blockchain. *Proc. Priv. Enhancing Technol.* **2018**, *2018*, 143–163. [CrossRef]
112. Kumar, A.; Fischer, C.; Tople, S.; Saxena, P. A Traceability Analysis of Monero's Blockchain. In *Computer Security—ESORICS 2017*; Lecture Notes in Computer Science; Foley, S., Gollmann, D., Snekkenes, E., Eds.; Springer: Cham, Switherland, 2017; Volume 10493, pp. 153–173.
113. Biryukov, A.; Khovratovich, D.; Pustogarov, I. Deanonymisation of Clients in Bitcoin P2P Network. In Proceedings of the 2014 ACM SIGSAC Conference on Computer and Communications Security, Scottsdale, AZ, USA, 3–7 November 2014; pp. 15–29. [CrossRef]
114. Koshy, P.; Koshy, D.; McDaniel, P. An Analysis of Anonymity in Bitcoin Using P2P Network Traffic. In Proceedings of the International Conference on Financial Cryptography and Data Security, Christ Church, Barbados, 3–7 March 2014; pp. 469–485. [CrossRef]
115. Chen, H.; Pendleton, M.; Njilla, L.; Xu, S. A Survey on Ethereum Systems Security: Vulnerabilities, Attacks, and Defenses. *ACM Comput. Surv.* **2020**, *53*, 1–43. [CrossRef]

116. Dannen, C. Introducing ethereum and solidity: Foundations of cryptocurrency and blockchain programming for beginners. *Introd. Ethereum Solidity Found. Cryptocurrency Blockchain Program. Begin.* **2017**, 1–185. [CrossRef]
117. Tulyakov, S.; Jaeger, S.; Govindaraju, V.; Doermann, D. Review of Classifier Combination Methods_TulyakovEtAl-2008. In *Machine Learning in Document Analysis and Recognition*; Studies in Computational Intelligence; Marinai, S., Fujisawa, H., Eds.; Springer: Berlin/Heidelberg, Germany, 2007; Volume 386, pp. 1–26.

Article

Decentralized Inner-Product Encryption with Constant-Size Ciphertext

Yi-Fan Tseng *[ID] and Shih-Jie Gao

Department of Computer Science, National Chengchi University, Taipei 11605, Taiwan; j23793276@gmail.com
* Correspondence: yftseng@cs.nccu.edu.tw

Abstract: With the rise of technology in recent years, more people are studying distributed system architecture, such as the e-government system. The advantage of this architecture is that when a single point of failure occurs, it does not cause the system to be invaded by other attackers, making the entire system more secure. On the other hand, inner product encryption (IPE) provides fine-grained access control, and can be used as a fundamental tool to construct other cryptographic primitives. Lots of studies for IPE have been proposed recently. The first and only existing decentralized IPE was proposed by Michalevsky and Joye in 2018. However, some restrictions in their scheme may make it impractical. First, the ciphertext size is linear to the length of the corresponding attribute vector; second, the number of authorities should be the same as the length of predicate vector. To cope with the aforementioned issues, we design the first decentralized IPE with constant-size ciphertext. The security of our scheme is proven under the ℓ-DBDHE assumption in the random oracle model. Compared with Michalevsky and Joye's work, ours achieves better efficiency in ciphertext length and encryption/decryption cost.

Keywords: inner product encryption; decentralized inner product encryption; constant-size ciphertext

Citation: Tseng, Y.-F.; Gao, S.-J. Decentralized Inner-Product Encryption with Constant-Size Ciphertext. *Appl. Sci.* **2022**, *12*, 636. https://doi.org/10.3390/app12020636

Academic Editor: Gianluca Lax

Received: 5 October 2021
Accepted: 6 January 2022
Published: 10 January 2022

Publisher's Note: MDPI stays neutral with regard to jurisdictional claims in published maps and institutional affiliations.

Copyright: © 2022 by the authors. Licensee MDPI, Basel, Switzerland. This article is an open access article distributed under the terms and conditions of the Creative Commons Attribution (CC BY) license (https://creativecommons.org/licenses/by/4.0/).

1. Introduction

Identity-based encryption (IBE) was first introduced by Shamir [1] in 1985, which allows a sender to use the recipient's identity to encrypt a message. An identity is a unique string directly linking to a user, e.g., an email address, a student ID number, an employee ID, etc. The first IBE scheme was proposed by Boneh and Franklin [2] in 2001. Though IBE reduces the management cost for traditional public key infrastructures, a drawback of IBE is that an encrypted datum can be only shared at a coarse-grained control level. This may not be suitable in the real world because the sender should know the particular recipient in advance. In a system, there may be a lot of users, and the identities of recipients may be uncertain when a message is encrypted. To solve the issue, Katz, Sahai and Waters [3] conceptualized inner product encryption (IPE) in 2008. In an IPE scheme, each ciphertext is associated with an attribute vector $\vec{Y}$ that can be decrypted by a private key associated with a predicate vector $\vec{X}$ if and only if the inner product of $\vec{X}$ and $\vec{Y}$ is zero, denoted by $<\vec{X},\vec{Y}>=0$. IPE can be viewed as the generalization for several cryptographic primitives. For example, given two identities, ID, ID', we can encode it into two vectors, $\vec{X}=(ID,1), \vec{Y}=(-1,ID')$, and we have

$$ID = ID' \Leftrightarrow <\vec{X},\vec{Y}>=0.$$

Thus, we are able to represent the functionality of IBE using IPE. Since then, lots of IPE scheme have been proposed [4–11]. In additional to its theoretical value, IPE provides lots applications in fine-grained access control as well. Using the encoding technique, IPE can be converted into many types of one-to-many encryption, such as broadcast encryption [12–14], attribute-based encryption [15–17] and subset predicate encryption [18–20]. Therefore, by adopting IPE, one can realize multiple kinds of flexible access control using only a single cryptographic primitive. Recently, more applications for

IPE have been developed, e.g., privacy-preserving video streaming [21], access control for WBAN [22], secure keyword searching [23] and outsourced data integration [24]. It shows the possibility for the application of IPE in various environments.

Traditionally, IPE is a centralized architecture, which needs a trusted server to issue private keys for all users. However, a centralized paradigm may not be practical in a real-world environment. In practice, the privileges of a user are usually given by different authorities. In addition, a centralized architecture would suffer from the problem of a single point of failure. To cope with these problems, Michalevsky and Joye gave the first Decentralized IPE (DIPE) scheme [25] in 2018. In a DIPE scheme, there are multiple authorities. For a user, each authority will output a partial private key for this user, without interaction with each other.

After studying the DIPE scheme of Michalevsky and Joye, we found two problems. One problem is the large ciphertext size. In their scheme, the ciphertext size is $\mathcal{O}(nk)$ group elements, where n is the length of attribute/predicate vector and k is the parameter of k-linear assumption. Since k can be viewed as a part of the security parameter, which is a constant, the ciphertext size is linear to the length of attribute/predicate vector. Another problem is that, in their scheme, each authority is responsible for issuing a private key for only an element in the user's predicate vector. This setting brings two disadvantages. First, unlike to decentralized attribute-based encryption [26–28], where the attributes of a user is independent to each other, the elements in a predicate vector for a user are usually closely bonded. Second, since each authority issues a partial private key for one element in a predicate vector, the number of authorities must equal to the length of predicate vector, which may not be practical, i.e., in the scheme of [25], an authority cannot responsible for multiple attributes, which is common in practice.

1.1. Contribution

In this manuscript, we propose a novel DIPE scheme with constant-size ciphertexts, and we give a formal security proof for the selective IND-CPA security under q-DBDHE assumption. We also modify the way an authority produces private keys from predicate vectors due to the aforementioned issue. In addition, we implement our construction in Python with Charm-Crypto library and C with PBC library to evaluate the performance.

1.2. Organization

In Section 2, we introduce the notations and complexity assumption used in our manuscript, and the definition of decentralized inner product encryption. The security of DIPE is defined in Section 2, as well. In Section 3, we describe our proposed scheme in detail and show the correctness. In Section 4, we give the formal security proof for our scheme. In Section 5, we show the comparison results between our scheme and the DIPE scheme in [25]. Finally, we conclude our work in Section 6.

2. Preliminaries

In this section, we introduce the definition and security requirements of decentralized inner product encryption. In addition, we demonstrate the notation and complexity assumption used in our work.

2.1. Notation

Given a set S, "randomly choose an element x from the set S" is denoted as $x \xleftarrow{\$} S$. For algorithm A, we write $x \leftarrow A$ to denote "x is the output by running A". The symbol "$\perp$" means a failed decryption that recovers the certain message unsuccessfully. "PPT" algorithm means "probabilistic polynomial time" algorithm that can run in polynomial-bounded time.

2.2. Bilinear Maps and Complexity Assumption

Let $\mathbb{G}$ and $\mathbb{G}_T$ be two multiplicative cyclic groups with prime order p. A map e is called a bilinear map if the following properties hold:

1. **Bilinearity**: For $u, v \in \mathbb{G}$, and $a, b \in \mathbb{Z}_p$, the equation $e(u^a, v^b) = e(u, v)^{ab}$ holds.
2. **Non-Degeneracy**: Assume g is the generator of $\mathbb{G}$, then, $e(g, g) \neq 1$.
3. **Computability**: For $u, v \in \mathbb{G}$, there exists an efficient algorithm to compute $e(u, v)$.

Next, we show the complexity assumption, the ℓ-decisional bilinear Diffie–Hellman exponent (ℓ-DBDHE) assumption [29,30], which the security of our scheme based on.

Definition 1 (The ℓ-Decisional Bilinear Diffie–Hellman Exponent Problem). *Let $\mathbb{G}$ be a group. g is a generator of $\mathbb{G}$, and $\gamma, s \xleftarrow{\$} \mathbb{Z}_p$ are two integers. Given a tuple:*

$$(g, g^\gamma, g^{\gamma^2}, \ldots, g^{\gamma^\ell}, g^{\gamma^{\ell+2}}, \ldots, g^{\gamma^{2\ell}}, g^s, T),$$

decide if $T = e(g, g)^{\gamma^{\ell+1} s}$ or $T \xleftarrow{\$} \mathbb{G}_T$ is a random element of $\mathbb{G}_T$.

Let $T_0 = (g, g^\gamma, g^{\gamma^2}, \ldots, g^{\gamma^\ell}, g^{\gamma^{\ell+2}}, \ldots, g^{\gamma^{2\ell}}, g^s)$. For an algorithm $\mathcal{A}$, the advantage of $\mathcal{A}$ in solving the ℓ-DBDHE problem is defined as:

$$\text{Adv}_{\mathcal{A}}^{\ell\text{-DBDHE}} = \left| \Pr[\mathcal{A}(T_0, T = e(g, g)^{\gamma^{\ell+1} s}) = 1] - \Pr[\mathcal{A}(T_0, T \xleftarrow{\$} \mathbb{G}_T) = 1] \right|.$$

Definition 2 (The ℓ-Decisional Bilinear Diffie–Hellman Exponent Assumption). *We say that the ℓ-decisional bilinear Diffie–Hellman exponent assumption holds if for all PPT algorithms, $\text{Adv}_{\mathcal{A}}^{\ell\text{-DBDHE}}$ is negligible.*

2.3. Definition of Decentralized Inner Product Encryption

The difference between DIPE and IPE is that a private key of DIPE is generated by multiple authorities, while a private key of IPE is generated by a centralized authority.

2.3.1. System Model

A DIPE scheme contains three roles, i.e., sender, receiver and authorities. A sender is a participant of the system who transfers the encrypted data to the receiver. The data are encrypted by an attribute vector before delivered to receiver. Authorities are responsible for issuing partial keys for receivers who make a request to obtain partial keys. The authorities will issue partial keys according to the predicate vector of the receiver. A receiver is a participant who wants to receive encrypted data. After a receiver receives all the partial keys from the authorities, the receiver will perform a decryption procedure to recover the data.

2.3.2. Definition of DIPE

A decentralized inner product encryption scheme consists of five PPT algorithms: **Setup, AuthSetup, KeyGen$_{A_i}$, Encrypt** and **Decrypt**. Unlike the single authority construction, in DIPE, the private key of a user is generated by multiple authorities. Each authority A_i computes a "partial key sk_i" of a user using its master secret key and the user's predicate vector. The full private key of a user is $\{sk_i\}_{i=1,\ldots,n}$, where n is the number of authorities:

- $Setup(1^\lambda)$. An authority in the system or a third party will run the algorithm. Taking as input a security parameter 1^λ, the algorithm outputs a public parameter pp.
- $AuthSetup(pp, i)$. All authorities will run the algorithm. Taking as inputs a public parameter pp, and a number i, the algorithm outputs a master secret key MSK_i and a public key PK_i of each authority, where i is the index of authority.
- $KeyGen_{A_i}(pp, MSK_i, GID, \vec{X})$. All authorities will run the algorithm. Taking as inputs a public parameter pp, a master secret key MSK_i, a global identity GID and a predicate vector $\vec{X}$, the algorithm outputs a partial key of the private key associated with $\vec{X}$ generated by i_{th} authority. Note that the description of $\vec{X}$ will be included in the partial keys.
- $Encrypt(pp, \{PK_i\}_{i=1,\ldots,n}, M, \vec{Y})$. A sender will run the algorithm. Taking as inputs a public parameter pp, all the public keys of each authority $\{PK_i\}_{i=1,\ldots,n}$, a message

M and an attribute vector $\vec{Y}$, the algorithm outputs a ciphertext C associated with $\vec{Y}$. Note that the description of $\vec{Y}$ will be included in the ciphertext.

- $Decrypt(\{sk_i\}_{i=1,\ldots,n}, C)$. A receiver will run the algorithm. Taking as inputs all the partial key of private keys of each authority $\{sk_i\}_{i=1,\ldots,n}$, a ciphertext C and an attribute vector $\vec{Y}$, the algorithm outputs a message M or $\perp$.

Correctness. For $pp \leftarrow Setup(1^\lambda)$, $(PK_i, MSK_i) \leftarrow AuthSetup(pp, i)$, $sk_i \leftarrow KeyGen_{A_i}(pp, MSK_i, GID, \vec{X})$, $C \leftarrow Encrypt(pp, \{PK_i\}_{i=1,\ldots,n}, M, \vec{Y})$, where $i = 1, \ldots, n$, we have that:
- If $\langle \vec{X}, \vec{Y} \rangle = 0$, then $Decrypt(\{sk_i\}_{i=1,\ldots,n}, C) = M$.
- If $\langle \vec{X}, \vec{Y} \rangle \neq 0$, then $Decrypt(\{sk_i\}_{i=1,\ldots,n}, C) = \perp$.

2.3.3. Security Model

The security definition used in our manuscript is the security against indistinguishability under selective chosen-plaintext attacks (sIND-CPA). "Indistinguishability" means that given a ciphertext, which is the encryption of one of two messages chosen by an adversary, the adversary tries to tell which of the two messages is encrypted. In addition, "chosen-plaintext attacks" means that an adversary is allowed to obtain the ciphertext for the plaintext of its choice. Finally, "selective" means that an adversary chooses a target vector and submits to the challenger before Setup phase.

Definition 3 (The sIND-CPA Security). *Let $\mathcal{A}$ be a probabilistic polynomial-time adversary. We define our security via the following interactive game between $\mathcal{A}$ and a challenger $\mathcal{C}$:*

- *Initialization.*
  $\mathcal{A}$ chooses an attribute vector $\vec{Y}^* = (y_1^*, y_2^*, \ldots, y_\ell^*)$ and sends $\vec{Y}^*$ to $\mathcal{C}$.
- *Setup.*
  $\mathcal{C}$ runs the Setup algorithm to generate PK_i and MSK_i, where $1 \leq i \leq n$, is the index of authority. $\mathcal{C}$ sends $PK_1, \ldots, PK_n$ and $MSK_1, \ldots, MSK_{n-1}$ to $\mathcal{A}$.
- *Phase1.*
  $\mathcal{A}$ can make polynomially times queries of the following oracle.
  - KeyExtract oracle: $\mathcal{A}$ sends a predicate vector $\vec{X}$ and a global identity GID to $\mathcal{C}$, and $\mathcal{C}$ returns the private key of $\vec{X}$. There is a restriction, that is, $\langle \vec{X}, \vec{Y}^* \rangle \neq 0$.
- *Challenge.*
  $\mathcal{A}$ submits two distinct messages M_0, M_1 of the same length to $\mathcal{C}$. $\mathcal{C}$ then randomly chooses $\beta \in \{0, 1\}$ and generates ciphertexts $C^* = Encrypt(pp, \{PK_i\}_{i=1,\ldots,n}, M_\beta, \vec{Y}^*)$. Then, $\mathcal{C}$ sends C^* to $\mathcal{A}$.
- *Phase2.*
  Same as Phase1.
- *Guess.*
  $\mathcal{A}$ will output a bit $\beta' \in \{0, 1\}$ and win the game if $\beta' = \beta$.
  The advantage of $\mathcal{A}$ winning the game is defined as:

$$\mathbf{Adv}_{\mathcal{A}}^{\mathsf{sIND\text{-}CPA}} = \left| Pr[\beta' = \beta] - \frac{1}{2} \right|.$$

A DIPE scheme is sIND-CPA secure if for all PPT adversaries $\mathcal{A}$, $\mathbf{Adv}_{\mathcal{A}}^{\mathsf{sIND\text{-}CPA}}$ is negligible.

3. The Proposed Scheme

In this section, we present our decentralized inner product encryption scheme with constant-size ciphertexts. The notations used in the proposed scheme are defined in Table 1.

Table 1. Notations.

Notation	Description
$\mathbb{G}$	a bilinear group with prime order p
$\mathbb{G}_T$	a bilinear group by pairing of the element of $\mathbb{G}$
e	a bilinear mapping; $e : \mathbb{G} \times \mathbb{G} \to \mathbb{G}_T$
g	a generator of $\mathbb{G}$
n	total number of authorities
ℓ	the length of predicate/attribute vector
A_i	ith authority
pp	public parameter
PK_i	public key of authority i
MSK_i	master secret key of authority i
$\vec{X}$	a predicate vector
$\vec{Y}$	an attribute vector
GID	an identity of a receiver
M	a message

Setup(1^λ)

The algorithm performs the following steps:

1. Randomly choose bilinear groups $\mathbb{G}, \mathbb{G}_T$ of prime order p with a generator $g \xleftarrow{\$} \mathbb{G}$;
2. Choose an one-way hash function, $H : \{0,1\}^* \times \mathbb{Z}_p^\ell \to \mathbb{G}$;
3. Output the public parameter $pp = \{g, H\}$.

AuthSetup(pp, i)

Each authority A_i in the system performs the following steps to generate its public key and its master secret key:

1. Choose $\bar{\alpha}_i \xleftarrow{\$} \mathbb{Z}_p$;
2. Choose $\alpha_{0,i} \xleftarrow{\$} \mathbb{Z}_p$;
3. Choose $\alpha_{1,i}, \alpha_{2,i}, \ldots, \alpha_{\ell,i} \xleftarrow{\$} \mathbb{Z}_p$;
4. Output a public key of authority i, $PK_i = \{g^{\alpha_{0,i}}, g^{\alpha_{1,i}}, \ldots, g^{\alpha_{\ell,i}}, Z_i = e(g,g)^{\bar{\alpha}_i}\}$;
5. Output a master secret key of authority A_i, $MSK_i = \{g^{\bar{\alpha}_i}, \alpha_{0,i}, \alpha_{1,i}, \ldots, \alpha_{\ell,i}\}$.

KeyGen$_{A_i}$($pp, MSK_i, GID, \vec{X} = (x_1, \cdots, x_\ell)$)

Each authority A_i in the system performs the following steps to generate a part of private key for receivers in the system"

1. Return failure symbol $\perp$ if $x_1 = 0$;
2. Output the private key $sk_i = \{D_0, D_{1,i}, \{K_{j,i}\}_{j=2,\ldots,\ell}\}$, where

$D_0 = H(GID, \vec{X})$
$D_{1,i} = g^{\bar{\alpha}_i} \cdot H(GID, \vec{X})^{\alpha_{0,i}}$
$\{K_{j,i} = H(GID, \vec{X})^{-\alpha_{1,i} \frac{x_j}{x_1}} \cdot H(GID, \vec{X})^{\alpha_{j,i}}\}_{j=2,\ldots,\ell}$.

Unlike the **KeyGen** algorithm in [25], we use the entire predicate vector $\vec{X}$ in **KeyGen**$_{A_i}$ performed by a single authority A_i.

Encrypt($pp, \{PK_i\}_{i=1,\ldots,n}, M, \vec{Y} = (y_1, \ldots, y_\ell)$)

A sender computes the ciphertext for a message $M \in \mathbb{G}_T$ and an attribute vector $\vec{Y} = (y_1, \ldots, y_\ell)$ by the following steps:

1. Choose $s \xleftarrow{\$} \mathbb{Z}_p$;
2. Output the ciphertexts as $C = \{E_0, E_1, E_2\}$, where

$E_0 = M \cdot (\prod_{i=1}^n Z_i)^s$
$E_1 = ((\prod_{i=1}^n g^{\alpha_{0,i}}) \cdot (\prod_{i=1}^n g^{\alpha_{1,i}})^{y_1} \cdot \ldots \cdot (\prod_{i=1}^n g^{\alpha_{\ell,i}})^{y_\ell})^s$
$E_2 = g^s$.

Decrypt($\{sk_i\}_{i=1,\ldots,n}, C$)

To decrypt, a receiver uses the private key $\{sk_i\}_{i=1,\ldots,n}$ to recover the message M from a ciphertext C as follows:

1. If $\langle \vec{X}, \vec{Y} \rangle = 0$, perform the following computation; otherwise, return $\bot$;
2. Compute

$$(\prod_{i=1}^n Z_i)^s = (\prod_{i=1}^n e(g,g)^{\bar{\alpha}_i})^s = \frac{e((\prod_{i=1}^n D_{1,i}) \cdot (\prod_{i=1}^n K_{2,i})^{y_2} \ldots (\prod_{i=1}^n K_{\ell,i})^{y_\ell}, E_2)}{e(E_1, D_0)}.$$

3. Compute $M = E_0 / (\prod_{i=1}^n Z_i)^s$.

Correctness

The correctness of the decryption algorithm is described as follows. For convenience, let $\bar{\alpha} = \sum_{i=1}^n \bar{\alpha}_i$, $\alpha_j = \sum_{i=1}^n \alpha_{j,i}$, for $j = 0, \ldots, \ell$. It is enough to show that

$$e(g,g)^{\bar{\alpha}_0 s} = \left(\prod_{i=1}^n e(g,g)^{\bar{\alpha}_i}\right)^s = \frac{e((\prod_{i=1}^n D_{1,i}) \cdot (\prod_{i=1}^n K_{2,i})^{y_2} \ldots (\prod_{i=1}^n K_{\ell,i})^{y_\ell}, E_2)}{e(E_1, D_0)}.$$

We first take a look at the numerator:

$$\prod_{i=1}^n D_{1,i} = \prod_{i=1}^n g^{\bar{\alpha}_i} \cdot H(GID, \vec{X})^{\alpha_{0,i}} = g^{\sum_{i=1}^n \bar{\alpha}_i} \cdot H(GID, \vec{X})^{\sum_{i=1}^n \alpha_{0,i}} = g^{\bar{\alpha}} \cdot H(GID, \vec{X})^{\alpha_0}$$

$$\prod_{i=1}^n K_{j,i} = \prod_{i=1}^n H(GID, \vec{X})^{-\alpha_{1,i}\frac{x_j}{x_1}} \cdot H(GID, \vec{X})^{\alpha_{j,i}} = H(GID, \vec{X})^{\frac{-x_j}{x_1}\sum_{i=1}^n \alpha_{1,i} + \sum_{i=1}^n \alpha_{j,i}}$$

$$= H(GID, \vec{X})^{\alpha_1(\frac{-x_j}{x_1}) + \alpha_j},$$

where $j = 2, \ldots, \ell$. Using the fact that

$$\langle \vec{X}, \vec{Y} \rangle = 0 \Leftrightarrow \sum_{i=1}^\ell x_i y_i = 0 \Leftrightarrow y_1 = \frac{\sum_{i=2}^\ell (-x_i y_i)}{x_1},$$

we have:

$$(\prod_{i=1}^n D_{1,i}) \cdot (\prod_{i=1}^n K_{2,i})^{y_2} \ldots (\prod_{i=1}^n K_{\ell,i})^{y_\ell}$$
$$= g^{\bar{\alpha}} \cdot H(GID, \vec{X})^{\alpha_0} \cdot (H(GID, \vec{X})^{\alpha_1(\frac{-x_2}{x_1}) + \alpha_2})^{y_2} \cdot \ldots \cdot (H(GID, \vec{X})^{\alpha_1(\frac{-x_\ell}{x_1}) + \alpha_\ell})^{y_\ell}$$
$$= g^{\bar{\alpha}} \cdot H(GID, \vec{X})^{\alpha_0} \cdot (H(GID, \vec{X}))^{\alpha_1 \frac{\sum_{i=2}^\ell (-x_i y_i)}{x_1} + \sum_{i=2}^\ell \alpha_i y_i}$$
$$= g^{\bar{\alpha}} \cdot H(GID, \vec{X})^{\alpha_0} \cdot H(GID, \vec{X})^{\alpha_1 y_1 + \sum_{i=2}^\ell \alpha_i y_i}$$
$$= g^{\bar{\alpha}} \cdot H(GID, \vec{X})^{\alpha_0} \cdot H(GID, \vec{X})^{\sum_{i=1}^\ell \alpha_i y_i}.$$

Thus, the numerator is:

$$e(g^{\bar{\alpha}} \cdot H(GID, \vec{X})^{\alpha_0} \cdot H(GID, \vec{X})^{\sum_{i=1}^\ell \alpha_i y_i}, E_2)$$
$$= e(g^{\bar{\alpha}} \cdot H(GID, \vec{X})^{\alpha_0} \cdot H(GID, \vec{X})^{\sum_{i=1}^\ell \alpha_i y_i}, g^s)$$
$$= e(g,g)^{\bar{\alpha}s} \cdot e(H(GID, \vec{X}), g)^{(\alpha_0 + \sum_{i=1}^\ell \alpha_i y_i)s}.$$

In addition, the denominator is:

$$
\begin{aligned}
e(E_1, D_0) &= e(((\prod_{i=1}^{n} g^{\alpha_{0,i}}) \cdot (\prod_{i=1}^{n} g^{\alpha_{1,i}})^{y_1} \cdot \ldots \cdot (\prod_{i=1}^{n} g^{\alpha_{\ell,i}})^{y_\ell})^s, H(GID, \vec{X})) \\
&= e(g^{\sum_{i=1}^{n} \alpha_{0,j}} \cdot g^{y_1 \sum_{i=1}^{n} \alpha_{1,j}} \cdot \ldots \cdot g^{y_\ell \sum_{i=1}^{n} \alpha_{\ell,j}}, H(GID, \vec{X}))^s \\
&= e(g^{\alpha_0} \cdot g^{\alpha_1 y_1} \cdot \ldots \cdot g^{\alpha_\ell y_\ell}, H(GID, \vec{X}))^s \\
&= e(g^{\alpha_0 + \sum_{i=1}^{\ell} \alpha_i y_i}, H(GID, \vec{X}))^s \\
&= e(H(GID, \vec{X}), g)^{(\alpha_0 + \sum_{i=1}^{\ell} \alpha_i y_i)s}.
\end{aligned}
$$

Finally, we have:

$$\frac{\text{numerator}}{\text{denominator}} = \frac{e(g,g)^{\bar{\alpha}s} \cdot e(H(GID, \vec{X}), g)^{(\alpha_0 + \sum_{i=1}^{\ell} \alpha_i y_i)s}}{e(H(GID, \vec{X}), g)^{(\alpha_0 + \sum_{i=1}^{\ell} \alpha_i y_i)s}} = e(g,g)^{\bar{\alpha}s}.$$

4. Security Proof

In this section, we will prove the sIND-CPA security for the proposed under the ℓ-DBDHE assumption in the random oracle model.

Theorem 1. *The proposed DIPE scheme is sIND-CPA secure if the q-DBDHE assumption holds.*

Proof. Assume there is a polynomial-time adversary that can win the sIND-CPA game with a non-negligible advantage. Then, we construct a PPT challenger $\mathcal{C}$ able to solve the ℓ-DBDHE problem as follows:

First of all, $\mathcal{C}$ is given an instance of the q-DBDHE problem, that is,

$$\left(g, g^\gamma, g^{\gamma^2}, \ldots, g^{\gamma^\ell}, g^{\gamma^{\ell+2}}, \ldots, g^{\gamma^{2\ell}}, g^s, T\right),$$

where T is $e(g,g)^{\gamma^{\ell+1}s}$ or a random element of $\mathbb{G}_T$. Then, $\mathcal{C}$ interacts with $\mathcal{A}$ in the game as follows.

Initialization.
$\mathcal{A}$ first sends the target vector $\vec{Y}^* = (y_1^*, y_2^*, \ldots, y_\ell^*)$ to $\mathcal{C}$.

Setup.
Without loss of generality, we may assume that $\mathcal{A}$ can obtain the first $n-1$ master secret keys MSK_i of authorities, where $i = 1, \ldots, n-1$:

1. Set $(g^{\alpha_{1,n}}, g^{\alpha_{2,n}}, \ldots, g^{\alpha_{\ell,n}}) = (g^\gamma, g^{\gamma^2}, \ldots, g^{\gamma^\ell})$. Define $\vec{\alpha}_n = \langle \alpha_{1,n}, \alpha_{2,n}, \ldots, \alpha_{\ell,n} \rangle$;
2. Choose $\delta \xleftarrow{\$} \mathbb{Z}_p$;
3. Compute $Z_n = e(g,g)^{\bar{\alpha}_n} = e(g^\gamma, g^{\gamma^\ell})$ and $g^{\alpha_{0,n}} = \left((g^\gamma)^{y_1^*}(g^{\gamma^2})^{y_2^*} \ldots (g^{\gamma^\ell})^{y_\ell^*}\right)^{-1} \cdot g^\delta$;
4. For $i = 1, \ldots, n-1$, $\mathcal{C}$, compute PK_i and MSK_i following the **AuthSetup**(pp, i) shown in Section 3;
5. Send to $\mathcal{A}$ the public keys $\{PK_i\}_{i=1,\ldots,n} = \{g^{\alpha_{0,i}}, g^{\alpha_{1,i}}, \ldots, g^{\alpha_{\ell,i}}, Z_i = e(g,g)^{\bar{\alpha}_i}\}_{i=1,\ldots,n}$, and the master secret key s $\{MSK_i\}_{i=1,\ldots,n-1} = \{g^{\bar{\alpha}_i}, \alpha_{0,i}, \alpha_{1,i}, \ldots, \alpha_{\ell,i}\}_{i=1,\ldots,n-1}$.

Here, we implicitly set

$$\bar{\alpha}_n = \gamma^{\ell+1}, \qquad \alpha_{0,n} = -\langle \vec{\alpha}_n, \vec{Y}^* \rangle + \delta, \qquad \{\alpha_{j,n} = \gamma^j\}_{j=1\ldots,\ell}.$$

Phase 1.
$\mathcal{C}$ maintains a hash list, H-list, to store the mapping result of $H(GID, \vec{X})$. Then, $\mathcal{A}$ is allowed to query the following oracles:

- Hash oracle:

This oracle takes $\vec{X} \in \mathbb{Z}_p^\ell$ and $GID \in \{0,1\}^*$ (global identity) as input and outputs an element of $\mathbb{G}$. If there exists a record $(GID, \vec{X}, v_k, V_k)$ in the H-list, return V_k. Otherwise, the oracle performs the following steps:

1. If $\langle \vec{X}, \vec{Y}^* \rangle = 0$, then randomly choose $V_k \xleftarrow{\$} \mathbb{G}$ and return V_k to $\mathcal{A}$;
2. Choose $v_k \xleftarrow{\$} \mathbb{Z}_p^*$;
3. Implicitly set

$$t = \frac{x_1 \gamma^\ell + x_2 \gamma^{\ell-1} + \ldots + x_\ell \gamma}{\langle \vec{X}, \vec{Y}^* \rangle} + v_k$$

by computing

$$V_k = g^t = (g^\gamma)^{\frac{x_\ell}{\langle \vec{X}, \vec{Y}^* \rangle}} \cdot \ldots \cdot (g^{\gamma^{\ell-1}})^{\frac{x_2}{\langle \vec{X}, \vec{Y}^* \rangle}} \cdot (g^{\gamma^\ell})^{\frac{x_1}{\langle \vec{X}, \vec{Y}^* \rangle}} \cdot g^{v_k}.$$

This can be efficiently computed with the instance of q-DBDHE problem;

4. Return $H(GID, \vec{X}) = V_k$ to $\mathcal{A}$ and store $(GID, \vec{X}, v_k, V_k)$ into the H-list.

- KeyExtract oracle:

Upon receiving a vector $\vec{X} = (x_1, x_2, \ldots, x_\ell)$ and a global identity GID from $\mathcal{A}$, where $\langle \vec{X}, \vec{Y}^* \rangle \neq 0$ (As shown in Definition 3, $\mathcal{A}$ is not allowed to make a KeyExtract query with $\langle \vec{X}, \vec{Y}^* \rangle = 0$, otherwise $\mathcal{A}$ can break the security trivially.) $\mathcal{C}$ performs as follows. For $i = 1, \ldots, n-1$, sk_i can be easily computed using the algorithm **KeyGen**$_{A_i}(pp, MSK_i, GID, \vec{X})$ shown in Section 3 since $\mathcal{C}$ knows MSK_i. As for sk_n, it can be computed from the instance of the ℓ-DBDHE problem by the following steps:

1. Query $V_k = H(GID, \vec{X})$ and set $D_0 = V_k$. Let $D_0 = g^t$, where

$$t = \frac{x_1 \gamma^\ell + x_2 \gamma^{\ell-1} + \ldots + x_\ell \gamma}{\langle \vec{X}, \vec{Y}^* \rangle} + v_k.$$

Note that v_k can be found in the H-list;

2. For $j = 2, \ldots, \ell$, compute

$$K_{j,n} = H(GID, \vec{X})^{-\alpha_{1,n} \frac{x_j}{x_1}} \cdot H(GID, \vec{X})^{\alpha_{j,n}} = (g^{-\alpha_{1,n} \frac{x_j}{x_1}} g^{\alpha_{j,n}})^t.$$

One can note that, in the exponent of $K_{j,n}$,

$$(-\alpha_{1,n} \frac{x_j}{x_1} + \alpha_{j,n}) t = (-\gamma \frac{x_j}{x_1} + \gamma^j) \cdot (\frac{x_1 \gamma^\ell + x_2 \gamma^{\ell-1} + \ldots + x_\ell \gamma}{\langle \vec{X}, \vec{Y}^* \rangle} + v_k),$$

the only unknown term is $\gamma^{\ell+1}$. However, the coefficient of $\gamma^{\ell+1}$ is

$$-\frac{x_j}{x_1} \cdot \frac{x_1}{\langle \vec{X}, \vec{Y}^* \rangle} + \frac{x_j}{\langle \vec{X}, \vec{Y}^* \rangle} = 0, j = 2, \ldots, \ell.$$

Thus, $K_{j,n}$ can be easily computed using the knowledge of $\vec{X}, \vec{Y}^*$ and the instance $(g, g^\gamma, g^{\gamma^2}, \ldots, g^{\gamma^\ell}, g^{\gamma^{\ell+2}}, \ldots, g^{\gamma^{2\ell}})$ of the ℓ-DBDHE problem;

3. Compute

$$D_{1,n} = g^{\bar{\alpha}_n} \cdot H(GID, \vec{X})^{\alpha_{0,n}} = g^{\bar{\alpha}_n + \alpha_{0,n} t}.$$

One can note that the exponent of $D_{1,n}$ is

$$\bar{\alpha}_n + \alpha_{0,n} t$$
$$= \gamma^{\ell+1} + (-\langle \vec{\alpha}_n, \vec{Y}^* \rangle + \delta) \cdot t$$
$$= \gamma^{\ell+1} + (-\langle \vec{\alpha}_n, \vec{Y}^* \rangle) \cdot \left(\frac{x_1 \gamma^\ell + x_2 \gamma^{\ell-1} + \ldots + x_\ell \gamma}{\langle \vec{X}, \vec{Y}^* \rangle} + v_k \right) + \delta t$$
$$= \gamma^{\ell+1} - \frac{(\alpha_1 y_1^* + \alpha_2 y_2^* + \ldots + \alpha_\ell y_\ell^*)(x_1 \gamma^\ell + x_2 \gamma^{\ell-1} + \ldots + x_\ell \gamma)}{\langle \vec{X}, \vec{Y}^* \rangle} - \langle \vec{\alpha}_n, \vec{Y}^* \rangle \cdot v_k + \delta t$$
$$= \gamma^{\ell+1} - \frac{(\gamma y_1^* + \gamma^2 y_2^* + \ldots + \gamma^\ell y_\ell^*)(x_1 \gamma^\ell + x_2 \gamma^{\ell-1} + \ldots + x_\ell \gamma)}{\langle \vec{X}, \vec{Y}^* \rangle} - \langle \vec{\alpha}_n, \vec{Y}^* \rangle \cdot v_k + \delta t$$

Again, the coefficient of the unknown term $\gamma^{\ell+1}$ is

$$1 - \frac{x_1 y_1^* + x_2 y_2^* + \ldots + x_\ell y_\ell^*}{\langle \vec{X}, \vec{Y}^* \rangle} = 1 - \frac{\langle \vec{X}, \vec{Y}^* \rangle}{\langle \vec{X}, \vec{Y}^* \rangle} = 0.$$

Therefore, $D_{1,n}$ can be also computed using the knowledge of $\vec{X}, \vec{Y}^*$ and the instance $(g, g^\gamma, g^{\gamma^2}, \ldots, g^{\gamma^\ell}, g^{\gamma^{\ell+2}}, \ldots, g^{\gamma^{2\ell}})$ of the ℓ-DBDHE problem.

Challenge.

$\mathcal{A}$ submits two message M_0 and M_1 of the same length, and $\mathcal{C}$ computes the challenge ciphertext as follows:

1. Choose $\beta \xleftarrow{\$} \{0,1\}$;
2. Set $E_2 = g^s$;
3. Compute

$$\begin{aligned} E_0 &= M_\beta \cdot (\prod_{i=1}^{n-1} Z_i)^s \cdot T \\ &= M_\beta \cdot Z_1^s \cdot \ldots \cdot Z_{n-1}^s \cdot T \\ &= M_\beta \cdot e(g^s, g^{\bar{\alpha}_1}) \cdot \ldots \cdot e(g^s, g^{\bar{\alpha}_{n-1}}) \cdot T; \end{aligned}$$

4. Compute

$$\begin{aligned} E_1 &= \left((\prod_{i=1}^n g^{\alpha_{0,i}}) \cdot (\prod_{i=1}^n g^{\alpha_{1,i}})^{y_1^*} \cdot \ldots \cdot (\prod_{i=1}^n g^{\alpha_{\ell,i}})^{y_\ell^*} \right)^s \\ &= \left((g^{\alpha_{0,1}} \cdot \ldots \cdot g^{\alpha_{0,n-1}}) \cdot (g^{\alpha_{1,1}} \cdot \ldots \cdot g^{\alpha_{1,n-1}})^{y_1^*} \cdot \ldots \cdot (g^{\alpha_{\ell,1}} \cdot \ldots \cdot g^{\alpha_{\ell,n-1}})^{y_\ell^*} \right)^s \\ &\quad \cdot \left(g^{\alpha_{0,n}} \cdot (g^{\alpha_{1,n}})^{y_1^*} \cdot \ldots \cdot (g^{\alpha_{\ell,n}})^{y_\ell^*} \right)^s \\ &= (g^s)^{\sum_{i=1}^{n-1} \alpha_{0,i} + y_1^* \sum_{i=1}^{n-1} \alpha_{1,i} + \ldots + y_\ell^* \sum_{i=1}^{n-1} \alpha_{\ell,i}} \cdot \left(g^{-\langle \vec{\alpha}_n, \vec{Y}^* \rangle + \delta} \cdot g^{\langle \vec{\alpha}_n, \vec{Y}^* \rangle} \right)^s \\ &= (g^s)^{\sum_{i=1}^{n-1} \alpha_{0,i} + y_1^* \sum_{i=1}^{n-1} \alpha_{1,i} + \ldots + y_\ell^* \sum_{i=1}^{n-1} \alpha_{\ell,i}} \cdot (g^s)^\delta; \end{aligned}$$

5. Output $C^* = (E_0, E_1, E_2)$ to $\mathcal{A}$.

Phase2.

Same as Phase1.

Guess.

$\mathcal{A}$ outputs a bit $\beta' \in \{0,1\}$. $\mathcal{C}$ outputs 1 if $\beta' = \beta$; otherwise, $\mathcal{C}$ outputs 0. If $T = e(g,g)^{\gamma^{\ell+1}s}$, then:

$$\begin{aligned} E_0 &= M_\beta \prod_{i=1}^{n-1} Z_i^s \cdot T \\ &= M_\beta \prod_{i=1}^{n-1} Z_i^s \cdot e(g,g)^{\gamma^{\ell+1}s} \\ &= M_\beta \prod_{i=1}^{n-1} Z_i^s \cdot Z_n^s \\ &= M_\beta \prod_{i=1}^n Z_i^s, \end{aligned}$$

and hence $C^* = (E_0, E_1, E_2)$ is a valid ciphertext. Thus, we have:

$$\mathbf{Adv}_{\mathcal{A}}^{\text{sIND-CPA}} = \left| \Pr[\beta' = \beta] - \frac{1}{2} \right|,$$

and

$$\Pr[\mathcal{C}(g, g^\gamma, g^{\gamma^2}, \ldots, g^{\gamma^\ell}, g^{\gamma^{\ell+2}}, \ldots, g^{\gamma^{2\ell}}, g^s, T = e(g,g)^{\gamma^{\ell+1}s}) = 1] = \Pr[\beta' = \beta]$$

$$= \mathbf{Adv}_{\mathcal{A}}^{\text{sIND-CPA}} + \frac{1}{2}.$$

If T is a random element from $\mathbb{G}_T$, then the message M_β is completely hidden from the adversary's view, since E_0, E_1 and E_2 are all independently random elements. Therefore, the advantage of the adversary is:

$$\mathbf{Adv}_{\mathcal{A}}^{\text{sIND-CPA}} = \left| Pr[\beta' = \beta] - \frac{1}{2} \right| = 0,$$

and

$$\Pr[\mathcal{C}(g, g^\gamma, g^{\gamma^2}, \ldots, g^{\gamma^\ell}, g^{\gamma^{\ell+2}}, \ldots, g^{\gamma^{2\ell}}, g^s, T = e(g,g)^{\gamma^{\ell+1}s}) = 1] = \frac{1}{2}.$$

Finally, the advantage of $\mathcal{C}$ in solving the ℓ-DBDHE problem is:

$$\mathbf{Adv}_{\mathcal{C}}^{\ell\text{-DBDHE}}$$
$$= \left| Pr[\mathcal{C}(g, g^\gamma, g^{\gamma^2}, \ldots, g^{\gamma^\ell}, g^{\gamma^{\ell+2}}, \ldots, g^{\gamma^{2\ell}}, g^s, T = e(g,g)^{\gamma^{\ell+1}s}) = 1] \right.$$
$$\left. - Pr[\mathcal{C}(g, g^\gamma, g^{\gamma^2}, \ldots, g^{\gamma^\ell}, g^{\gamma^{\ell+2}}, \ldots, g^{\gamma^{2\ell}}, g^s, T \xleftarrow{\$} \mathbb{G}_T) = 1] \right|$$
$$= \left| (\mathbf{Adv}_{\mathcal{A}}^{\text{sIND-CPA}} + \frac{1}{2}) - \frac{1}{2} \right|$$
$$= \mathbf{Adv}_{\mathcal{A}}^{\text{sIND-CPA}}.$$

Therefore, if there is an adversary that wins the sIND-CPA game with a non-negligible advantage, then we can construct an algorithm $\mathcal{C}$ to solve the ℓ-DBDHE problem with a non-negligible advantage in polynomial time. □

5. Comparison

In this section, we compare our scheme with [3,5,8,11,25] in time complexity, space complexity and other security features. Among these works, [3,5,8,11] are IPE schemes and [25] is a DIPE scheme. In addition, we implement our scheme and the scheme of [25] in Python and C, and compare the execution time of our algorithms with theirs.

5.1. Asymptotic Comparisons

In Table 2, we show the encryption cost and decryption cost of each scheme. For encryption, the exponentiation computation cost is linear with the vector size, which is better than others, except [5]. In addition, we only need ℓ times exponentiation computations plus two pairing computations in decryption. Though our efficiency is not the best among [3,5,8,11], our scheme achieves decentralization while others do not. In [25], they need n times exponentiation computations plus $\mathcal{O}(k)$ pairing computations, where $k \leq 2$. Thus, both of the cost for our scheme in encryption and decryption algorithm is more efficient.

Table 2. Comparison of time complexity.

	Encryption Cost	Decryption Cost
[3]	$(4\ell+1)T_e$	$(2\ell+1)T_p$
[8]	$(2\ell+2)T_e$	$\ell T_e + 3T_p$
[5]	$(\ell+3)T_e$	$\ell T_e + 2T_p$
[11]	$(2\ell+2)T_e$	$(\ell+2)T_e + T_p$
[25]	$[(2n+1)k^2 + (2n+2)k]T_e$	$nT_e + (2k+2)T_p$
Ours	$(\ell+3)T_e$	$\ell T_e + 2T_p$

T_e: The cost of an exponentiation in multiplicative groups. T_p: The cost of pairing computation. n: The total number of authorities. ℓ: The length of predicate/attribute vector. k: The parameter of k-linear assumption. ($k \geq 2$)

The length of ciphertexts and private keys are shown in Table 3. Due to decentralization, it is normal that the private key length of DIPE is larger than that of IPE. In addition, though, we can see that [25] needs about $\mathcal{O}(nk)$ elements in $\mathbb{G}$ for a private key. Indeed, the value of k can be small in their work. However, in our work, the vector size could be large in reality. Therefore, our private key length is larger than others, which may need more storage. Nevertheless, if the value of k is greater or equal than our vector size. Then, we only need less storage than [25] in storing the private key. Note that the work of [11] achieves constant private key size. As a trade-off, their ciphertext size is $\mathcal{O}(\ell)|\mathbb{G}_T|$, which might be longer then others in the respect of the curve used in implementation.

In the comparison of ciphertext length, both our work and [5] have the least ciphertext length and only needs two elements in $\mathbb{G}$ plus an element in $\mathbb{G}_T$. It means that our ciphertext length is independent with the vector size and the number of the authorities. It can reduce the burden of connection between sender and receiver for transmitting ciphertext. However, the ciphertext length of [25] dependent on n and k. To the best of our knowledge, our work is the first DIPE scheme achieving a constant-size ciphertext.

Table 3. Comparison with the previous schemes in space complexity.

	Ciphertext Length	Private Key Length
[3]	$(2\ell+1)|\mathbb{G}|$	$(2\ell+1)|\mathbb{G}|$
[8]	$(\ell+2)|\mathbb{G}|$	$3|\mathbb{G}| + |\mathbb{Z}_p^\ell|$
[5]	$2|\mathbb{G}| + |\mathbb{G}_T|$	$(\ell+1)|\mathbb{G}|$
[11]	$1|\mathbb{G}| + (\ell+1)|\mathbb{G}_T|$	$1|\mathbb{G}| + |\mathbb{Z}_p|$
[25]	$(nk+n+k+1)|\mathbb{G}| + |\mathbb{G}_T|$	$n(2k+2)|\mathbb{G}|$
Ours	$2|\mathbb{G}| + |\mathbb{G}_T|$	$n(\ell+1)|\mathbb{G}|$

$|\mathbb{G}|$: The length of an element in $\mathbb{G}$. $|\mathbb{G}_T|$: The length of an element in $\mathbb{G}_T$. $|\mathbb{Z}_p^\ell|$: The length of an element in $\mathbb{Z}_p^\ell$. n: The total number of authorities. ℓ: The length of predicate/attribute vector. k: The parameter of k-linear assumption. ($k \geq 2$).

In Table 4, only our work, as well as [25], achieves a decentralized framework. In order to avoid collusion between users, a GID and a predicate (or an attribute) vector $\vec{X}$ are mapped to a value by a random oracle. Therefore, the security of ours and [25]'s are both proven in the random oracle model. As far as we know, there is no standard model for DIPE currently. In addition, although ours and [25]'s are both CPA secure, the latter achieves adaptive security, which is stronger than our selective model. Though all the works in Table 4 achieve CPA security, we should note that [11]'s security is proven in a relatively less used model, called a co-selective model, where an adversary outputs several vectors for querying the Key-Extract oracle in Phase 1 before seeing the system parameter. Although selective security and co-selective security are both weaker than full security, both notions are incomparable in general by definition.

Table 4. Property comparison.

	Decentralization	Confidentiality	Security Model	Group Order	Complexity Assumption
[3]	No	CPA	STD	Composite	SD
[8]	No	CPA	STD	Prime	$\mathcal{P}$-DBDH
[5]	No	CPA	STD	Prime	ℓ-DBDHE
[11]	No	CPA*	STD	Prime	M-DDH$_{\mathbb{G}_T}$
[25]	Yes	CPA	ROM	Prime	k-Lin
Ours	Yes	CPA	ROM	Prime	ℓ-DBDHE

CPA: Chosen-plaintext attack. CPA*: CPA in coselective model. STD: Standard model. ROM: Random oracle model. SD: Subgroup decision problem.

5.2. Experimental Result

In this section, we show the experimental results of our construction and the construction of [25] via Python and C languages, and analyze the execution time of the five algorithms.

Table 5 shows the system configuration and the chosen pairing group of Python. We implement our construction by Charm-Crypto library in Python. In our implementation, the pairing group is a symmetric pairing curve with a 512-bit-based field. The experiment is executed on Intel(R) Core(TM) i7-10875H CPU at 3.60GHz processor, 4 GB memory size and under the Ubuntu-16.04 operating system. In addition, we also implement our scheme and [25] in C with the pbc library, where a Type a1 pairing group is used. Table 6 shows the details for the system configuration of our C implementation.

Table 5. System configuration and elliptic curve for Python.

CPU	Intel(R) Core(TM) i7-10875H CPU @ 2.30 GHz
Memory	4 GB
OS	Ubuntu-16.04 (64-bit)
Package	Python Charm-Crypto (v0.43) library
Pairing group	SS512

Table 6. System configuration and elliptic curve for C.

CPU	Intel(R) Core(TM) i5-8257U CPU @ 1.40 GHz
Memory	2 GB
OS	Docker:Debian10
Package	pbc-0.5.14
Pairing group	Type a1

We analyze the time cost of each algorithm in our DIPE scheme below. In our experiment, the length of GID (global identity) is set to 10 bits for convenience. However, note that the length of a GID can be arbitrarily long since it is a input of the hash function. In [25], since each authority generates a partial key for an element of the predicate vector, therefore, the length of th vector size should be the same as the total number of authorities, ranging from 1 to 25 in our implementation. In addition, the value of k in [25] is set to one to minimize the cost of their work. The value of each point on the figure is obtained by executing the algorithm 1000 times and obtaining the value of the average execution time.

For the implementation using Python, Figure 1b shows that the time spent by [25] on the **AuthSetup** algorithm is more time-consuming than ours. In Figure 1d,e, we can note that the **Encrypt** and **Decrypt** algorithms are both growing linearly in two schemes when the number of authorities increases. However, ours has better performance than theirs. Then, Figure 1c exhibits that **KeyGen** is the most time-consuming algorithm due to the decentralized network. Nevertheless, we have relatively poorer performance than [25]. Since our decentralization is different from [25], in our scheme, each authority generates a partial key for a whole predicate vector instead of only an element. Therefore, the execution time of **KeyGen** is longer. Finally, in Figure 1a, the **Setup** algorithm only generates some generator of $\mathbb{G}$, some elements of $\mathbb{G}$ and the description of a hash function in both schemes. Thus, execution time is independent of the total number of authorities and vector size. In addition, our scheme has one more advantage, that is, the length of the predicate vector does not need to bind with the total number of authorities with same value.

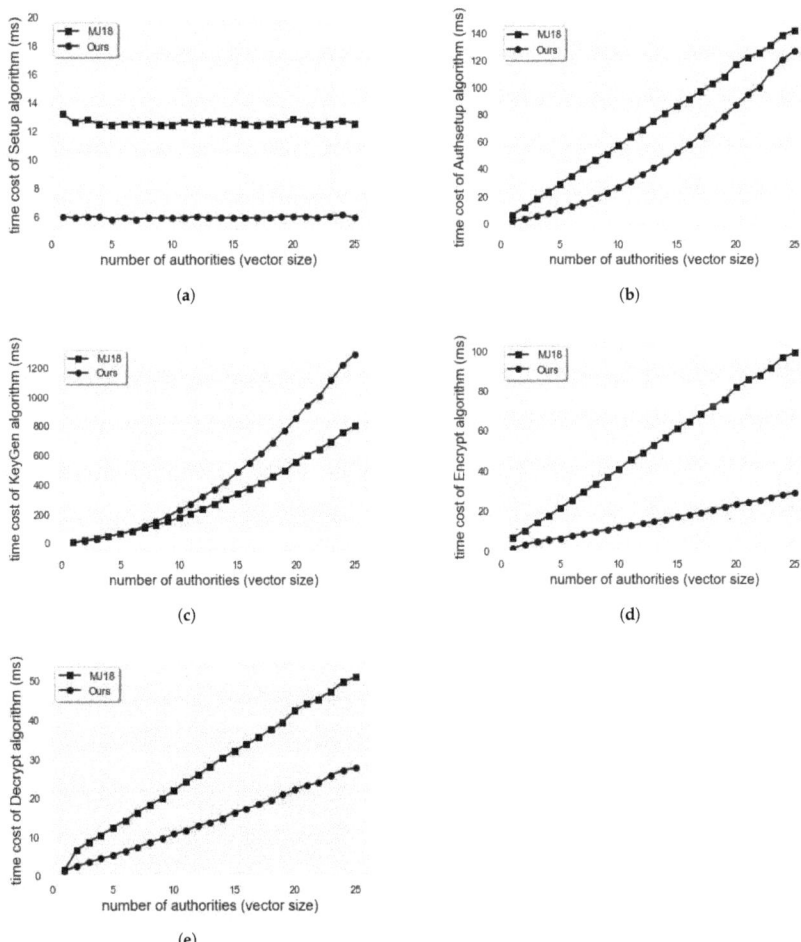

Figure 1. The time cost for Python Implementation of (**a**) Setup, (**b**) Authsetup, (**c**) KeyGen, (**d**) Encrypt, (**e**) Decrypt algorithm. (Pairing group: SS512, $|GID|=10$, # of authorities $= |\vec{X}| = |\vec{Y}| = [1,\ldots,25]$, $k = 1$).

In addition, Figure 2 shows the time cost of our scheme and [25] using C. Similar to the results using Python, Figure 2a,b show that in the comparison of the time costs of **Setup** and **AuthSetup** algorithms, our scheme is more efficient than [25]. As shown in Figure 2c,e, the costs for **KeyGen** and **Decryption** of ours are pretty close to those of [25].

Interestingly, the result of **Encryption** in C is opposite to that in Python. Figure 2d shows that the **Encrypt** algorithm of [25] is faster than ours. The reason for this might be due to the system configuration or the language. We will keep figuring out more details that may be inspired from this difference.

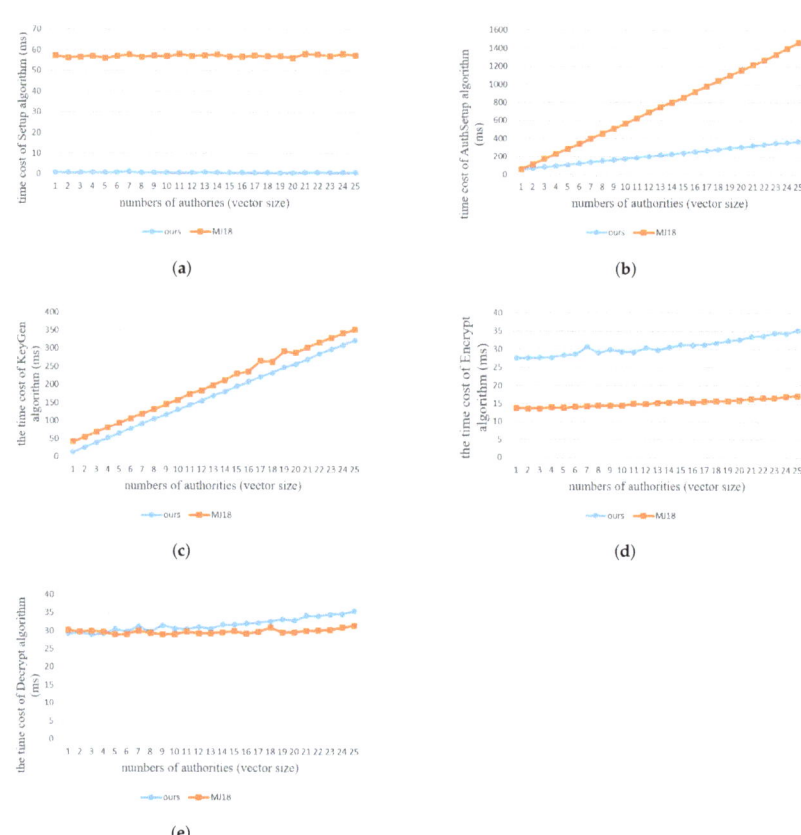

Figure 2. The time cost for C Implementation of (**a**) Setup, (**b**) Authsetup, (**c**) KeyGen, (**d**) Encrypt, (**e**) Decrypt algorithm. (Pairing group: Type a1, $|GID| = 10$, # of authorities = $|\vec{X}| = |\vec{Y}| = [1,\ldots,25]$, $k = 1$).

6. Conclusions

Thus far, there is only one decentralized inner product encryption, proposed by Michalevsky et al. in 2018. In their scheme, however, the length of ciphertexts are dependent on the number of authorities, which may become a bottleneck in the system. Therefore, we would like to solve this problem. In this manuscript, we present a novel decentralized inner product encryption which achieves constant-size ciphertexts. In addition, our scheme is proven to be selectively secure under the ℓ-DBDHE assumption. We further implement our scheme and the scheme of [25] to analyze the execution time. Except for the KeyGen algorithm, our work has better performance in the remaining four algorithms (Setup, AuthSetup, Encrypt, Decrypt). Yet, our scheme is the first DIPE scheme achieving constant-size ciphertext, and there are several potential improvements. One direction could be to upgrade the security to chosen-ciphertext security. Several generic methods [31–35] have been proposed in the literature, however, constructing a DIPE scheme with direct chosen-ciphertext security is an open problem. In addition, the security of our scheme is proven under the random oracle model. How to construct a DIPE scheme that is secure in the standard model is also a worth-fighting goal.

Author Contributions: Conceptualization, Y.-F.T. and S.-J.G.; methodology, Y.-F.T.; formal analysis, Y.-F.T.; investigation, Y.-F.T. and S.-J.G.; writing—original draft preparation, S.-J.G.; writing—review and editing, Y.-F.T.; supervision, Y.-F.T.; project administration, Y.-F.T.; funding acquisition, Y.-F.T. All authors have read and agreed to the published version of the manuscript.

Funding: This research was funded by the Ministry of Science and Technology, Taiwan (ROC), under grant numbers MOST 110-2221-E-004 -003-, MOST 110-2218-E-004-001-MBK, MOST 109-2221-E-004 -011 -MY3 and MOST 109-3111-8-004-001.

Institutional Review Board Statement: Not applicable.

Informed Consent Statement: Not applicable.

Data Availability Statement: Not applicable.

Conflicts of Interest: The authors declare no conflict of interest.

References

1. Shamir, A. Identity-Based Cryptosystems and Signature Schemes. In *Advances in Cryptology*; Blakley, G.R., Chaum, D., Eds.; Springer: Berlin/Heidelberg, Germany, 1985; pp. 47–53.
2. Boneh, D.; Franklin, M. Identity-Based Encryption from the Weil Pairing. In *Advances in Cryptology—CRYPTO 2001*; Kilian, J., Ed.; Springer: Berlin/Heidelberg, Germany, 2001; pp. 213–229.
3. Katz, J.; Sahai, A.; Waters, B. Predicate Encryption Supporting Disjunctions, Polynomial Equations, and Inner Products. In *Advances in Cryptology–EUROCRYPT 2008*; Smart, N., Ed.; Springer: Berlin/Heidelberg, Germany, 2008; pp. 146–162.
4. Lewko, A.; Okamoto, T.; Sahai, A.; Takashima, K.; Waters, B. Fully Secure Functional Encryption: Attribute-Based Encryption and (Hierarchical) Inner Product Encryption. In *Advances in Cryptology–EUROCRYPT 2010*; Gilbert, H., Ed.; Springer: Berlin/Heidelberg, Germany, 2010; pp. 62–91.
5. Attrapadung, N.; Libert, B. Functional Encryption for Inner Product: Achieving Constant-Size Ciphertexts with Adaptive Security or Support for Negation. In *Public Key Cryptography–PKC 2010*; Nguyen, P.Q., Pointcheval, D., Eds.; Springer: Berlin/Heidelberg, Germany, 2010; pp. 384–402.
6. Park, J.H. Inner-product encryption under standard assumptions. *Des. Codes Cryptogr.* **2011**, *58*, 235–257. [CrossRef]
7. Tan, Z.; Zhang, W. A Predicate Encryption Scheme Supporting Multiparty Cloud Computation. In Proceedings of the 2015 International Conference on Intelligent Networking and Collaborative Systems, Taipei, Taiwan, 2–4 September 2015; pp. 252–256.
8. Kim, I.; Hwang, S.O.; Park, J.H.; Park, C. An Efficient Predicate Encryption with Constant Pairing Computations and Minimum Costs. *IEEE Trans. Comput.* **2016**, *65*, 2947–2958. [CrossRef]
9. Zhang, Y.; Li, Y.; Wang, Y. Efficient inner product encryption for mobile clients with constrained computation capacity. *Int. J. Innov. Comput. Inf. Control* **2019**, *15*, 209–226.
10. Soroush, N.; Iovino, V.; Rial, A.; Roenne, P.B.; Ryan, P.Y.A. Verifiable Inner Product Encryption Scheme. In *Public-Key Cryptography–PKC 2020*; Kiayias, A., Kohlweiss, M., Wallden, P., Zikas, V., Eds.; Springer International Publishing: Cham, Switzerland, 2020; pp. 65–94.
11. Tseng, Y.F.; Liu, Z.Y.; Tso, R. Practical Inner Product Encryption with Constant Private Key. *Appl. Sci.* **2020**, *10*, 8669. [CrossRef]
12. Fiat, A.; Naor, M. Broadcast Encryption. In *Advances in Cryptology—CRYPTO' 93*; Stinson, D.R., Ed.; Springer: Berlin/Heidelberg, Germany, 1994; pp. 480–491.
13. Acharya, K. Secure and efficient public key multi-channel broadcast encryption schemes. *J. Inf. Secur. Appl.* **2020**, *51*, 102436. [CrossRef]
14. Chen, L.; Li, J.; Zhang, Y. Anonymous Certificate-Based Broadcast Encryption With Personalized Messages. *IEEE Trans. Broadcast.* **2020**, *66*, 867–881. [CrossRef]
15. Li, J.; Wang, S.; Li, Y.; Wang, H.; Wang, H.; Wang, H.; Chen, J.; You, Z. An Efficient Attribute-Based Encryption Scheme With Policy Update and File Update in Cloud Computing. *IEEE Trans. Ind. Inform.* **2019**, *15*, 6500–6509. [CrossRef]
16. Xue, L.; Yu, Y.; Li, Y.; Au, M.H.; Du, X.; Yang, B. Efficient attribute-based encryption with attribute revocation for assured data deletion. *Inf. Sci.* **2019**, *479*, 640–650. [CrossRef]
17. Li, J.; Zhang, Y.; Ning, J.; Huang, X.; Poh, G.S.; Wang, D. Attribute Based Encryption with Privacy Protection and Accountability for CloudIoT. *IEEE Trans. Cloud Comput.* **2020**, *1*. [CrossRef]
18. Katz, J.; Maffei, M.; Malavolta, G.; Schröder, D. Subset Predicate Encryption and Its Applications. In *Cryptology and Network Security*; Capkun, S., Chow, S.S.M., Eds.; Springer International Publishing: Cham, Switzerland, 2018; pp. 115–134.
19. Chatterjee, S.; Mukherjee, S. Large Universe Subset Predicate Encryption Based on Static Assumption (Without Random Oracle). In *Topics in Cryptology–CT-RSA 2019*; Matsui, M., Ed.; Springer International Publishing: Cham, Switzerland, 2019; pp. 62–82.
20. Tseng, Y.F.; Gao, S.J. Efficient Subset Predicate Encryption for Internet of Things. In Proceedings of the 2021 IEEE Conference on Dependable and Secure Computing (DSC), Edinburgh, UK, 22–24 June 2021; pp. 1–2. [CrossRef]

21. Rajan, M.; Varghese, A.; Narendra, N.; Singh, M.; Shivraj, V.; Chandra, G.; Balamuralidhar, P. Security and Privacy for Real Time Video Streaming Using Hierarchical Inner Product Encryption Based Publish-Subscribe Architecture. In Proceedings of the 2016 30th International Conference on Advanced Information Networking and Applications Workshops (WAINA), Crans-Montana, Switzerland, 23–25 March 2016; pp. 373–380. [CrossRef]
22. Xiong, H.; Yang, M.; Yao, T.; Chen, J.; Kumari, S. Efficient Unbounded Fully Attribute Hiding Inner Product Encryption in Cloud-Aided WBANs. *IEEE Syst. J.* **2021**, 1–9. [CrossRef]
23. Zhang, L.; Wang, Z.; Mu, Y.; Hu, Y. Fully Secure Hierarchical Inner Product Encryption for Privacy Preserving Keyword Searching in Cloud. In Proceedings of the 2015 10th International Conference on P2P, Parallel, Grid, Cloud and Internet Computing (3PGCIC), Krakow, Poland, 4–6 November 2015; pp. 449–453. [CrossRef]
24. Huang, K.C.; Chen, Y.C. Privacy Preserving Outsourced Data Integration from Inner Product Encryption. In Proceedings of the 2021 International Symposium on Intelligent Signal Processing and Communication Systems (ISPACS), Hualien City, Taiwan, 16–19 November 2021; pp. 1–2. [CrossRef]
25. Michalevsky, Y.; Joye, M. Decentralized Policy-Hiding ABE with Receiver Privacy. In Proceedings of the 23rd European Symposium on Research in Computer Security, ESORICS 2018, Barcelona, Spain, 3–7 September 2018; pp. 548–567.
26. Chase, M. Multi-authority Attribute Based Encryption. In *Theory of Cryptography*; Vadhan, S.P., Ed.; Springer: Berlin/Heidelberg, Germany, 2007; pp. 515–534.
27. Lewko, A.; Waters, B. Decentralizing Attribute-Based Encryption. In *Advances in Cryptology–EUROCRYPT 2011*; Paterson, K.G., Ed.; Springer: Berlin/Heidelberg, Germany, 2011; pp. 568–588.
28. Zhang, L.; Gao, X.; Kang, L.; Liang, P.; Mu, Y. Distributed Ciphertext-Policy Attribute-Based Encryption With Enhanced Collusion Resilience and Privacy Preservation. *IEEE Syst. J.* **2021**, 1–12. [CrossRef]
29. Boneh, D.; Gentry, C.; Waters, B. Collusion Resistant Broadcast Encryption with Short Ciphertexts and Private Keys. In *Advances in Cryptology–CRYPTO 2005*; Shoup, V., Ed.; Springer: Berlin/Heidelberg, Germany, 2005; pp. 258–275.
30. Boneh, D.; Hamburg, M. *Generalized Identity Based and Broadcast Encryption Schemes*; In Proceedings of the International Conference on the Theory and Application of Cryptology and Information Security, Melbourne, Australia, 7–11 December 2008.
31. Canetti, R.; Halevi, S.; Katz, J. Chosen-Ciphertext Security from Identity-Based Encryption. In *Advances in Cryptology–EUROCRYPT 2004*; Cachin, C., Camenisch, J.L., Eds.; Springer: Berlin/Heidelberg, Germany, 2004; pp. 207–222.
32. Fujisaki, E.; Okamoto, T. Secure Integration of Asymmetric and Symmetric Encryption Schemes. In *Advances in Cryptology—CRYPTO' 99*; Wiener, M., Ed.; Springer: Berlin/Heidelberg, Germany, 1999; pp. 537–554.
33. Fujisaki, E.; Okamoto, T. Secure Integration of Asymmetric and Symmetric Encryption Schemes. *J. Cryptol.* **2011**, *26*, 80–101. [CrossRef]
34. Koppula, V.; Waters, B. Realizing Chosen Ciphertext Security Generically in Attribute-Based Encryption and Predicate Encryption. In *Advances in Cryptology–CRYPTO 2019*; Boldyreva, A., Micciancio, D., Eds.; Springer International Publishing: Cham, Switzerland, 2019; pp. 671–700.
35. Yamada, S.; Attrapadung, N.; Hanaoka, G.; Kunihiro, N. Generic Constructions for Chosen-Ciphertext Secure Attribute Based Encryption. In *Public Key Cryptography—PKC 2011*; Catalano, D., Fazio, N., Gennaro, R., Nicolosi, A., Eds.; Springer: Berlin/Heidelberg, Germany, 2011; pp. 71–89.

Article

A Practical and Efficient Node Blind SignCryption Scheme for the IoT Device Network

Ming-Te Chen [†] and Hsuan-Chao Huang [*,†]

Department of Computer Science and Information Engineering, National Chin-Yi University of Technology, Taichung 41170, Taiwan; mtchen@ncut.edu.tw
* Correspondence: sc100@ncut.edu.tw; Tel.: +886-4-23924505 (ext. 8775)
† These authors contributed equally to this work.

Abstract: In recent years, Internet of Things (IoT for short) research has become one of the top ten most popular research topics. IoT devices also embed many sensing chips for detecting physical signals from the outside environment. In the wireless sensing network (WSN for short), a human can wear several IoT devices around her/his body such as a smart watch, smart band, smart glasses, etc. These IoT devices can collect analog environment data around the user's body and store these data into memory after data processing. Thus far, we have discovered that some IoT devices have resource limitations such as power shortages or insufficient memory for data computation and preservation. An IoT device such as a smart band attempts to upload a user's body information to the cloud server by adopting the public-key crypto-system to generate the corresponding cipher-text and related signature for concrete data security; in this situation, the computation time increases linearly and the device can run out of memory, which is inconvenient for users. For this reason, we consider that, if the smart IoT device can perform encryption and signature simultaneously, it can save significant resources for the execution of other applications. As a result, our approach is to design an efficient, practical, and lightweight, blind sign-cryption (SC for short) scheme for IoT device usage. Not only can our methodology offer the sensed data privacy protection efficiently, but it is also fit for the above application scenario with limited resource conditions such as battery shortage or less memory space in the IoT device network.

Keywords: sign-cryption; unsign-cryption; cryptography module; IoT device

Citation: Chen, M.-T.; Huang, H.-C. A Practical and Efficient Node Blind SignCryption Scheme for IoT Device Network. *Appl. Sci.* **2022**, *12*, 278. https://doi.org/10.3390/app12010278

Academic Editor: Gianluca Lax

Received: 8 November 2021
Accepted: 21 December 2021
Published: 28 December 2021

Publisher's Note: MDPI stays neutral with regard to jurisdictional claims in published maps and institutional affiliations.

Copyright: © 2021 by the authors. Licensee MDPI, Basel, Switzerland. This article is an open access article distributed under the terms and conditions of the Creative Commons Attribution (CC BY) license (https://creativecommons.org/licenses/by/4.0/).

1. Introduction

In recent years, Internet of Things(IoT for short) devices has widely applied in our daily life. From the life of human beings to industry 4.0, there are many common machines composed of several IoT devices such as the air conditioner, electronic vehicle, mobile phone, etc. These devices can collect physical signal data and transfer these data to a powerful gateway device of the IoT network through the Internet in a digital manner. When the gateway has received the sensed data from a sender node, it preserves these records in a database or cloud storage service. However, such IoT devices have limitations compared with a general gateway server, such as fewer memory space or limited computing power. This situation usually occurs in the communications between nodes of wireless sensing network(WSN for short) and IoT networks. Once an IoT device has collected physical data from a human body, it then must forward these data to the powerful gateway that can preserve the final result data into a database and perform other cryptography operations. From the above scenario, we discover that, if any IoT devices attempt to perform a heavy encryption/decryption computation such as modular exponentiation over a large prime number in a public key algorithm, then they must perform a signature operation later for concrete security protection and authentication on these sensed data. This will lead to fast power consumption and free-memory usage of these nodes.

To solve the above situation, we adopt the sign-cryption approach to let a sensing node perform the lightweight sign-cryption operation and generate the final cipher-text with its own signature simultaneously on the powerful server side. When the gateway server has received this cipher-text from a sensor node, it can decrypt this cipher-text first, then perform the validation of this plain-text with the inside signature's help for data authentication.

We consider the following situation of an IoT device called DS_i that attempts to transfer sensed data to a receiver called $\mathcal{R}$, where $i = 1 \sim l$ and l is the total number of all the sensor nodes. To keep the data confidential, DS_i must encrypt its own data first. At this time, it can adopt an efficient encryption/decryption method to generate a cipher-text. Then, DS_i can forward this cipher-text to a powerful base station (BS for short), which it equips with more computing power than all the sensor nodes in the same IoT network. However, DS_i must also consider its own memory limitation and remaining computing power to perform such encrypting/decryption computation in sequence. The node DS_i may not be able to perform the signature computation after it has generated encryption if the remaining power is not enough to perform signature generation in this time; thus, it must transfer the heavy computation to a powerful node such as the base station BS.

Due to the mentioned situations, we concluded that, if there exists an efficient method allowing IoT devices to perform encryption and signature operations on the sensed data in one operation, it could save more computing time and energy, which can then be used for other computations. In the recent literature, sign-cryption was discussed in [1–4]. The authors claimed that the sender can transfer the data only to perform one sign-cryption time, and it can output a cipher-text with a guaranteed signature within. Then, the receiver can decrypt the received cipher-text with a secret random number inside the corresponding signature. When the signature is verified by the receiver successfully, the receiver can obtain the random secret value by applying its own secret key. Finally, the receiver $\mathcal{R}$ can obtain the final data by inputting this secret random number to decrypt the cipher-text. Unfortunately, their computation efficiency are not practical to fit above situation for IoT device network. There are some research limitations in our proposed scheme. One is that the sender device $\mathcal{S}$ is already authenticated with the receiver $\mathcal{R}$; they both inherently trust each other within the same IoT network environment. The authentication mechanism is beyond the scope of this research. Another limitation is that IoT device management is also beyond our research. We can adopt other proposed authentication mechanisms [5–10] for devices to authenticate with each other in an IoT device network and also construct an IoT devices group with other devices. Our scheme focuses on the efficient signature and encryption scheme for these power limitation IoT devices such as the Zigbee chips or IoT sensor devices embedding less memory.

To provide a mechanism to generate a signature and a cipher-text for IoT devices simultaneously, we propose an efficient and practical, fair sign-cryption scheme based on quadratic residue (QR for short) for the IoT device network. Not only does it offer an efficient and practical solution to IoT devices, but it also reduces the signature and cipher-text generation cost in our methodology. We also offer the formal security proof on our proposed scheme in the Appendix A and evaluate the efficiency of our mechanism in this research.

2. Related Work and Security Definitions

Related Work

In this section, we discuss the related research proposed in [1–4]. In [1], the authors propose a $\mathcal{CPAS}$ scheme for the vehicular sensor network and assume that there exists two TAs, where one is a tracing Authority (TRA for short) and the other is a public key generation center (PKG for short) for tracing the identity and key pairs of all vehicles, respectively. The TRA can produce a pseudo-ID for all vehicles after it has verified the real identity from them. The PKG also can generate the key-pairs for these vehicles. If there is a dispute in the protocol, the TRA can determine the real identity of the pseudo-ID key-pair through the help of the PKG. At this time, each vehicle does not show its real identity through the above scheme's methodology. On the other hand, we can discover that the total efficiency computation of this scheme is $3Pa + 1SM$ for signature verification operation and $3Pa + (n + 1)SM$ for n signatures batch verification, where Pa is a pairing operation and SM is a symmetric encrypting operation. We consider that the pairing operation is demanding for comparing our scheme with others in Table 1 for Internet of Things (IoT for short) devices. From the efficiency comparison in Table 1, we can see that our approach is much more efficient than [1]. In [2], we observed that authors also claim their scheme is more efficient than those in other articles [3,4]. However, this paper [2] is still slower than our proposed approach in Table 1.

On one hand, from the data authentication aspect, the gateway is unaware of what the sensor node's data are in our approach. The sensor node will blind the forward data first before sending these data to the gateway. On the other hand, the gateway also provides its own random parameters during the signature generation of the offline-sign-cryption phase. This means that each signature is generated by the gateway's signing parameters and the sensor node's parameters after the above offline-sign-cryption and online-sign-cryption phases. Meanwhile, our approach can guarantee the situation where the signer cannot fully control the signature generation and provide the unlinkability to the signature. In [3], the authors provide an efficient sign-cryption methodology between the traditional public key crypto-system to the identity-based crypto-system and vice versa. This can be applied in the multireceiver construction for the IoT device network and provides a general prototype for this crypto-system transformation. We think that this idea is effective and suitable for the IoT device to transfer sensing data to another crypto-system construction. However, the sensing node still requires great computation effort on the paring operation and can cause a performance bottleneck on these sensor nodes. We also see in [3] that its computation cost is about $3\ Pa$, where Pa is a pairing operation on a large prime number q. Finally, in [4], the authors claim their approach is only about $4\ Mu + 2\ Pa$, where Mu is the modular multiplication and Pa is the paring operation. After converting to the final computation approximately, we discover that this scheme still costs $409\ Mu$ more than ours in Table 1. In this approach, our contribution is to construct an efficient methodology that can generate a signature and encryption based on the QR at the same time and also preserve a concrete security proof on well-known hard problems such as the RSA factoring problem [11].

Table 1. Performance comparison.

	Sign-Cryption	Unsign-Cryption	Totally	Approx.
[1]	$2Mu + 1Pa$	$3Pa + 1Ad + 1\oplus$	$4Pa + 2Mu + 1Ad + 1\oplus$	$327Mu + 1\oplus$
[2]	$4Mu + 1Ex + 2Ha + 1\oplus$	$1Ex + 2Pa + 2Mu + 2Ha$	$2Ex + 2Pa + 6Mu + 4Ha + 1\oplus$	$647Mu + 1\oplus$
[3]	$4Ha + 1Ex + 2\oplus$	$3Ha + 1Pa + 2\oplus$	$1Ex + 1Pa + 7Ha + 4\oplus$	$322.8Mu + 4\oplus$
[4]	$1Ex + 2Mu + 2Ha + 1\oplus$	$2Pa + 3Ha + 1Ad +$	$1Ex + 2Pa + 2Mu + 1Ad + 5Ha + 1\oplus$	$409Mu + 1\oplus$
Ours	$4Ha + 29Mu + 1\oplus + 1SE$	$1SD + 2Ha + 1\oplus$	$33Mu + 1SE + 1SD + 6Ha + 2\oplus$	$36.2Mu + 2\oplus$

Ex—Modular exponentiation, Ad—Addition operation, Mu—Modular multiplication, SE—Symmetric Encryption operation, Ha—Hash operation, SD—Symmetric Decryption operation, Pa—Pairing operation, $\oplus$—XOR bit operation.

3. The Proposed Scheme

The following is our proposed scheme, which contains four phases: the initial phase, blinding phase, offline-sign-cryption phase, and the unsign-cryption phase.

3.1. Preliminary

In this subsection, we provide some definitions used in our proposed scheme as follows:

- n: A large prime number, which it computes from two large primes p_1 and p_2 such that $n = p_1 \cdot p_2$, where $p_1 \equiv p_2 \equiv 3 \pmod{4}$.
- l: The total number of all Internet of Things (IoT for short) nodes.
- $\hat{n}$: A large prime number, which it computes from two large prime p_3 and p_4 such that $\hat{n} = p_3 \cdot p_4$, where $p_3 \equiv p_4 \equiv 3 \pmod{4}$.

- DS_i: An IoT data sender, which is a sensor node that forwards collected data to the receiver R, where $i = 1 \sim l$ and l is the number of all sensor nodes.
- BS: A base station, which helps to collect data sent from a sensor node DS_i, where $i = 1 \sim l$.
- R: An IoT data receiver, which receives data from the sender DS_i.
- $\oplus$: An exclusive-or operation for symmetric encryption/decryption usage.
- H_1, H_2: Two secure hash functions that each of them maps $Z_n^* \to \{0,1\}^n$ with collision-resistance and outputs the same n-bits hash strings.
- E_{pk_j}: A symmetric key encryption function for the party j with the public key pk_j, where $j \in \{DS_j, R\}$, where $j = 1 \sim l$.
- D_{sk_j}: A symmetric key decryption function for the party j with the private key sk_j, where $j \in \{DS_j, R\}$, where $j = 1 \sim l$.

3.2. Initial Phase

In this phase, an IoT node DS_l acts as a data sender; it first selects two large, distinct primes, where one is p_1 and the other is p_2 such that $n = p_1 \cdot p_2$, where $l = 1 \sim l$ and l are totally node numbers. DS_i also publishes this n and we could know that given a QR in Z_n^*; there are four different square roots (or 2 roots) of the QR in Z_n^*. From this property, we could derive the 2^ith roots of the QR in Z_n^*, where i must be larger than 1 in Z_n^*. On one hand, we assume that there exists a powerful base station as a signer BS, which also selects two large primes, where one is p_3 and the other is p_4 in the same IoT network environment. It also computes $\hat{n} = p_3 \cdot p_4$ and sets up to let $n < \hat{n}$. Then, it publishes $\hat{n}$ and its prefix string Ω. In the following, we take Fan and Lei's Scheme [12] as our reference. Nevertheless, the data receiver (R for short) sets up its own private/public key pair as (sk_R, pk_R). When the set-up is finished, it publishes its own public key to the IoT network.

- First, a node DS_i randomly chooses its own QR numbers (z_1, z_2, z_3) from Z_n^* similar with y_1, y_2 and y_3, where each of them is computed from $y_i = (z_i^2 \mod n)$ and $i = 1 \sim 3$, respectively. Then, base station BS also selects two random QR numbers α and β such that they allow ($\beta^2/\alpha^2 \mod n$) to belong to QR in Z_n^*. DS_i also publishes (n, y_1, y_2, y_3) to the signer BS. Once the signer BS has received them from DS_i, DS_i computes $\gamma = (\kappa^2 \mod \hat{n})$ with a random number κ and the identifier $\hat{z} = H_1(z)$ mod $\hat{n}$ with an identifier number z. After setting up these random numbers, BS forwards ($\gamma, \hat{n}, z, \hat{z}$) to DS_i and enters the offline-signing phase.

3.3. Offline-Signing Phase
- When DS_i has received ($\gamma, \hat{n}, z, \hat{z}$) from the BS, DS_i also computes the following messages if the checking of z is valid, where $\hat{z} = H_1(z) \mod \hat{n}$. DS_i selects a random number $r \in Z_n^*$ and computes the following:

$$\begin{aligned} C_1 &= E_{pk_R}(r) \\ C_2 &= H_1(r) \oplus m \\ C_3 &= H_1(C_1, C_2, r, \hat{z}, m) \end{aligned} \quad (1)$$

- After computing the above equations, DS_i also allows β^2/α^2 as τ and performs the following:

$$\begin{aligned} C_1' &= C_1 * \tau^2 * \gamma \\ C_2' &= C_2 * \gamma \\ C_3' &= C_3 * \gamma \\ h &= H_1(C_1', C_2', C_3') \end{aligned} \quad (2)$$

- From the above equations, we know that DS_i blinds the sensor data and computes a cipher-text (C_1', C_2', C_3'). Then, DS_i forwards ($C_1', C_2', C_3', h, z, \hat{z}$) to BS. When BS has received these messages from DS'_i, it verifies above them with z, checks the h from (C'_1, C'_2, C'_3), and enters the online-signing phase.

3.4. Online-Signing Phase

- When BS obtains $(C'_1, C'_2, C'_3, h, z, \hat{z})$ from DS_i, it could perform verification of these cipher-texts. If they are valid, then BS decrypts them with γ^{-1} as follows:

$$\begin{aligned} C_1 &= C'_1 * \tau^2 * \gamma^{-1} \\ C_2 &= C'_2 * \gamma^{-1} \\ C_3 &= C'_3 * \gamma^{-1} \end{aligned} \qquad (3)$$

- After decrypting the above cipher-texts successfully, BS computes the signature as follows with a QR number λ:

$$\begin{aligned} C'_3 &= C_3^{-2} * (\frac{\beta}{\alpha})^{-2} * (\lambda)^2 \\ C''_3 &= C'_3 * y_1 \pmod{n} \\ C''_2 &= C'_2 * y_2 \pmod{n} \\ C''_1 &= C'_1 * y_3 \pmod{n} \end{aligned} \qquad (4)$$

- The signer BS finishes the signing operation and generates the signature (C''_1, C''_2, C''_3) to the data sender DS_i. When the node DS_i has received this signature, it could unblind the signature by computing the following operations:

$$\begin{aligned} C'_1 &= C''_1 * y_3^{-1} \\ C'_2 &= C''_2 * y_2^{-1} \\ C'_3 &= C''_3 * y_1^{-1} \\ C^*_3 &= C'_3 * (\frac{1}{\alpha})^2 \\ &= C_3^{-2} * \beta^{-2} * (\lambda)^2 \end{aligned} \qquad (5)$$

- Then, the DS_i computes the final encrypted cipher-text messages (C'''_1, C'''_2, C'''_3) to the BS in the following and enters the unsign-cryption phase:

$$\begin{aligned} C'''_1 &= C''_1 * \gamma \\ C'''_2 &= C''_2 * \gamma \\ C'''_3 &= C^*_3 * \gamma \end{aligned} \qquad (6)$$

3.5. Unsign-Cryption Phase

- When BS received these cipher-text messages from DS_i, it can decrypt by the following operations:

$$\begin{aligned} C^*_3 &= C'''_3 * \gamma^{-1} \\ t &= (C^*_3)^2 * (\lambda)^{-4} \\ &= C_3^{-4} * \beta^{-4} \\ t^* &= t * y_1 \end{aligned} \qquad (7)$$

- After BS has computed this signature t from the above equation, it forwards $(t^*, z, \hat{z})$ to the node DS_i and allows the DS_i to decrypt t^* and un-blinds this signature t as follows:

$$\begin{aligned} t &= t^* * y_1^{-1} \\ S_R &= t * \beta^4 \\ &= C_3^{-4} * \beta^{-4} * \beta^4 \\ &= C_3^{-4} \quad \mod n \end{aligned} \tag{8}$$

- After DS_i summarizes the above equation, we conclude that the node DS_i has the final signature $\sigma_R = (S_R, C_1, C_2, C_3)$, where $S_R^4 = C_3 = H_1(C_1, C_2, \gamma, \tau, \hat{z}, m)$. Then, the node DS_i can forward the sign-cryption signature σ_R and cipher-text messages (C_1, C_2, C_3) to the receiver R of the Internet host.
- Once the receiver R has obtained this sign-cryption signature σ_R and cipher-text messages (C_1, C_2, C_3) from DS_i, it can perform the following steps:

$$\begin{aligned} r^* &= D_{sk_R}(C_1) \\ m &\stackrel{?}{=} C_2 \oplus H_1(r^*) \\ C_3 &\stackrel{?}{=} H_1(C_1, C_2, r, \hat{z}, m) \\ S_R^4 &\stackrel{?}{=} C_3 \end{aligned} \tag{9}$$

4. Functionality Comparisons and Security Analysis

In this section, we could provide functionality comparisons with other schemes and security analysis about our proposed scheme.

4.1. Fast Sign-Cryption Operation

The proposed scheme only needs three hash operations, one $\oplus$ operations, five multiplication operations, and one symmetric encryption in the offline-signing phase. In this situation, our proposed scheme is more efficient than [2]. In addition, the sensor node DS_i can blind the sensed data to the base station efficiently and with data confidence. The base station BS cannot be aware of the sensed data content. If the base station is compromised by a malicious attacker, DS_i can also protect this data to prevent its exposure outside the IoT network. At the same time, it also guarantees the protection of user's personal information.

4.2. Signer Fair Signature Operation

Our proposed scheme can offer the signature of sensed data after the base station BS has received the encrypted sensed data from the user. In this time, BS only can apply the square root operation on these sensed data to generate the corresponding signature under these blind and encrypted data. In the online-signing operation, the IoT device can perform lightweight operations on the user's sensed data and obtain the signing result after the offline-signing phase performed by the signer BS. From the two signing phases above, we know that the IoT device and the base station can present some random numbers in these phases to prevent the unfair situation that the signature generation is controlled by a certain party.

4.3. User Data Protection

In our proposed scheme, we use the sign-cryption method to generate the encryption data with the corresponding signature within. In this time, the signer cannot know what the plain-text is without the corresponding decryption key. Only the receiver is aware of the corresponding decryption key to decrypt this cipher-text. Thus, our sign-cryption scheme could offer privacy protection of the user's personal sensed information.

4.4. Efficiency Comparisons

In this section, we evaluate the efficiency of our approach in the following. First, there is an assumption that the prime numbers p_1, p_2, p_3 and p_4 are 1024 bits in length; Ha is computation time for one hash computation; SE is the time for a symmetric encryption operation, and SD is time for a symmetric decryption operation. Meanwhile, we also define that Ex is the computation time for one modular exponential operation in a 1024-bit module, Mu is the time for one modular multiplication in a 1024-bit module, M_{ecc} is the time for a number performing another point addition over an elliptic curve [13], and Pa is the time for the computation time of a bilinear pairing operation of two elements over an elliptic curve. Then, we assume that $Ex \approx 8.24 M_{ecc}$ for the ARM CPU to process at 200 Mhz in [14]. From the above assumption, we can discover that there exists some relation in the following, where $Ex \approx 240 Mu = 600 Ha \approx 3Pa$ and $Ad \approx 5Mu$ in [15–21]. From the above computation time evaluation, we can see that our approach total computation time is $33Mu + 6Ha + 2 \oplus + 1SE + 1SD$. Then, the result is approximate to 36 Mu modular multiplication operations. Comparing with [2], we can see that our approach is much faster under the 1024-bit prime numbers. In the following two simulation results shown in Figures 1 and 2, our approach provides the QR-signature simulation and RSA signature simulation, respectively. On the other hand, we implemented our approach on a Ubuntu 20.04 operating system with Intel Core i5-1135G7 CPU @ Base 2.4 GHz up to 4.2 GHz CPU and 8 GB memory. This simulation is carried out by using GO language and python language with "crypto/encoding/Matplotlib" library on the 10 nodes to 50 nodes, where are shown in Figures 1 and 2, respectively.

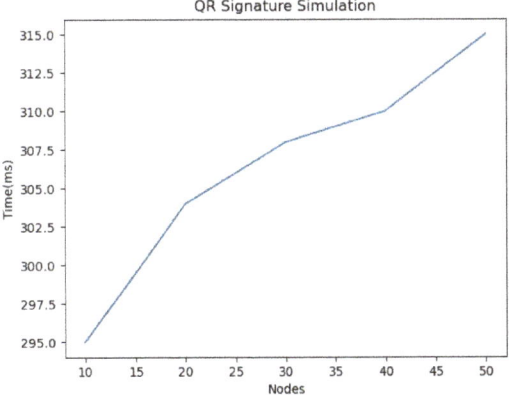

Figure 1. QR Signature Simulation on 10 nodes to 50 nodes.

4.5. Security Definitions

4.5.1. QR Signature Security

We provide the definition on the digital signature's security as follows: In the initial phase, we assume that there exists some functions used in our proposed scheme; one is the signature generating function $Sig(\cdot)$ and the other is the verification function $Ver(\cdot)$, where the signer S can input her/his signing key sk_S into this signing function with the message m. Then, we can claim that σ is the resulting output from the signing function by S and the receiver R can verify σ by the verification function $Ver(\cdot)$ with the message m and the signer's public key pk_S. The above scheme is based on well-known hard problems such as the RSA factoring problem. If there exists an attacker $\mathcal{F}$ whose goal is to forge a valid signature S' on the message m and pass the verification, i.e., $Ver(S', m, pk_S) = 1$, then $\mathcal{F}$ outputs it successfully with non-negligible probability larger than ε, we can use $\mathcal{F}$'s ability to factor the RSA factoring problem. However, in fact, the attacker $\mathcal{F}$'s advantage is less than ε.

This means that the probability of $\mathcal{F}$ to output a forged signature and for this signature to pass the verification function with non-negligible probability is less than ε.

$$Adv[S'_i \longleftarrow \mathcal{F}^{Sig(sk_S,m)} | Ver(S'_i, m, pk_S) = 1] < \varepsilon.$$

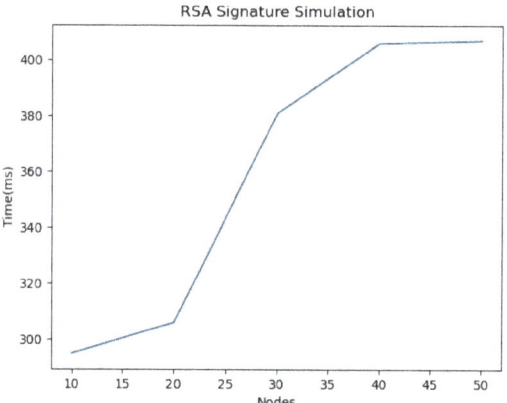

Figure 2. RSA Signature Simulation on 10 nodes to 50 nodes.

4.5.2. Unforgeability

In this proposed scheme, we provide the signature definition of our sign-cryption scheme. From the above digital signature definition, we discuss the case where there exists a forger $\mathcal{F}$ with the ability to forge a valid QR-signature on our scheme. We assume that there are some functions such that $\mathcal{F}$ can make the hash query to the hash functions $H_1(\cdot)$ and $H_2(\cdot)$, symmetric encryption $Enc_{pk_R}(\cdot)$ function and the signing function $Sig(\cdot)$. After preparing these functions, $\mathcal{F}$ can make its own query on these functions. $\mathcal{F}$ can ask i times query, where $i = 1 \sim l$ and l is the total number of IoT nodes. After the above q_s times query, if $\mathcal{F}$ can output $q_s + 1$ signatures on our proposed scheme, we can use $\mathcal{F}$ to break the RSA factoring problem.

$$Adv^{Unf}_{\mathcal{F}^{Sig(\cdot),H_1(\cdot),H_2(\cdot),RO_1,E_{pk_R}(\cdot)}}(\theta,t') \leq \frac{1}{2^l \cdot q_s \cdot q_e \cdot q_d} + \varepsilon'.$$

Lemma 1. *First, we assume that there exists a secure digital signature function $Sig(\cdot)$ and a secure hash function $H_1(\cdot)$, which could be replaced with a random oracle RO_1 and a secure hash function H_2 in our proposed scheme. We also claim that our proposed scheme with the above unforgeability (Unf for short) satisfies the following situations. In other words, if our scheme is (t', ε') unforgeable, then*

$$Adv^{Unf}_{\mathcal{F}^{Sig(\cdot),H_1(\cdot),H_2(\cdot),RO_1,E_{pk_R}(\cdot)}}(\theta,t') \leq \frac{1}{2^l \cdot q_s \cdot q_e \cdot q_d} + \varepsilon'.$$

where t' is total experiment simulation time, including simulating l as an upper bound on the number of IoT devices, at most signature oracle q_s times query, at most encryption oracle q_e times query, at most decryption oracle q_d times query, and ε' has taken over the coin toss of our scheme.

4.5.3. Indistinguishability

In this definition, we assume the Indistinguishable (Ind for short) game where there exists an attacker $\mathcal{A}$ in the following simulation, which is controlled by a simulator $\mathcal{S}$. First, we defined that there is a symmetric encryption/decryption function $E_{pk_i}(\cdot)/D_{sk_i}(\cdot)$, where $i \in \{DS_j, BS, R\}, j = 1 \sim l$, in which DS_j is one of the l IoT devices; BS is the base station, and R is the receiver of the outside network. The simulator $\mathcal{S}$ will prepare all set-up parameters including key pairs for the above parties. After set-up is complete, $\mathcal{S}$ will launch the proposed scheme simulation with $\mathcal{A}$. $\mathcal{A}$ can perform the encryption/decryption on the chosen message m. $\mathcal{S}$ also can reply the cipher-text $C = E_{pk_i}(m)$ and the original message m to $\mathcal{A}$. After the above game simulation, $\mathcal{S}$ can replace the encryption/decryption functions to an encryption/decryption oracle (τ, τ^{-1}), which performs the same action as our above symmetric encryption/decryption function. Through the above training phase, $\mathcal{A}$ sends a chosen target message (M_0, M_1) to $\mathcal{S}$; $\mathcal{S}$ will perform a coin flip b on the message (M_b, M_{1-b}). Then, $\mathcal{S}$ inputs the M_b to the encryption oracle E_{pk_i} to obtain the final result C_b. $\mathcal{S}$ forwards C_b to $\mathcal{A}$ to guess whether M_b is M_0 or M_1 on its coin flip b'—that is,

$$Pr[b' \longleftarrow \mathcal{A}^{(E_{pk_i}(\cdot), D_{sk_i}(\cdot), \tau, \tau^{-1})} | b = b'] < \frac{1}{2} + \varepsilon'.$$

4.5.4. Indistinguishable-Chosen Cipher-Text Attack (Ind-CCA for Short)

In this proposed scheme, we continue to define the chosen cipher-text attack security of our SC approach. There also exists an attacker $\mathcal{A}$, whose goal is to distinguish the cipher-text of our sign-cryption scheme. First, we assume that there is a simulator $\mathcal{A}$ to control the environment situational parameters including key pairs, security parameters, and hash length. After setting up, $\mathcal{S}$ defines the experiment in which $\mathcal{A}$ can make a query as follows.

- Phase 1: In this phase, the attacker $\mathcal{A}$ could make the encryption/decryption query on the chosen message m. If $\mathcal{A}$ makes the encryption query on the m of the IoT device i, where $i = 1 \sim l$, then $\mathcal{S}$ inputs the m into $C_{i,1} = E_{pk_i}(\gamma_i)$, $C_{i,2} = m \oplus H_1(\gamma_i)$ and $C_{i,3} = H_1(C_1, C_2, \gamma_i, m)$, where $i = 1 \sim l$. Here, $\mathcal{S}$ will preserve these parameters into the encryption oracle list $\mathcal{E}_i$ entry. On the other hand, $\mathcal{A}$ asks the decryption query on the cipher-text $(C_{i,1}, C_{i,2}, C_{i,3})$, $\mathcal{S}$ will check if there are any parameters matching this cipher-text in the $\mathcal{E}_i$ entry. If the answer is yes, $\mathcal{S}$ forwards the original message back to $\mathcal{A}$ and keeps this query in the decryption oracle $\mathcal{D}_i$ entry.
- Challenge: In this phase, if $\mathcal{A}$ chooses a target IoT device j^* and a message pair (M_0^*, M_1^*), where M_0^* and M_1^* are never asked the encryption query and decryption query before, $j^* \neq i$ and $i = 1 \sim l$. In this time, $\mathcal{S}$ will toss the coin flip b and inputs the M_b^* into the encryption oracle $E_{pk_j^*}(\cdot)$. Finally, $\mathcal{S}$ returns the target cipher-text $(C_{1,j^*}, C_{2,j^*}, C_{3,j^*})$ to $\mathcal{A}$. When $\mathcal{A}$ has received this target cipher-text, it still can make the decryption query on other cipher-texts except $(C_{1,j^*}, C_{2,j^*}, C_{3,j^*})$.

In the following, we model above the actions as game simulation steps that we played with the attacker $\mathcal{A}$.

$Exp_{\mathcal{A}, SC}^{Ind-CCA-b}(\theta)$
Phase 1
$i \in \{1, \ldots, l\}, M_i \longleftarrow \mathcal{A}^{E_{pk_i}(\cdot, \theta), D_{sk_i}(\cdot, \theta), H_1(\cdot)}$
$\gamma_i \longleftarrow \{0,1\}^*$
$C_{1,i} \longleftarrow E_{pk_i}(\gamma_i)$
$C_{2,i} \longleftarrow M_i \oplus H_1(\gamma_i)$
$C_{3,i} \longleftarrow H_1(C_{1,i}, C_{2,i}, \gamma_i, M_i)$
Challenge Phase
$b \in \{0,1\}, j^* \neq i, (M_b^*, M_{1-b}^*) \longleftarrow \mathcal{A}$
$M_{b,j^*} \xleftarrow{b} \mathcal{S}$
$C_{1,j^*} \longleftarrow E_{pk_{j^*}}(\gamma_{j^*})$
$C_{2,j^*} \longleftarrow M_i \oplus H_1(\gamma_{j^*})$
$C_{3,j^*} \longleftarrow H_1(C_{1,j^*}, C_{2,j^*}, \gamma_{j^*}, M_{b,j^*})$
$b' \longleftarrow \mathcal{A}^{(E_{pk_{j^*}}(\cdot, \theta), D_{pk_{j^*}}(\cdot, \theta), \tau, \tau^{-1})}(C_{1,j^*}, C_{2,j^*}, C_{3,j^*}, M_b^*, M_{1-b}^*)$
Return b'.

The advantage ok function of the adversary $\mathcal{A}$ where it is defined as $Adv_{\mathcal{A},SC}^{Ind-CCA}(\theta) = |Pr[Exp_{\mathcal{A},SC}^{Ind-CCA-1}(\theta) = 1] - Pr[Exp_{\mathcal{A},SC}^{Ind-CCA-0}(\theta) = 1]| < \varepsilon'$.

Lemma 2. *We defined that our sign-cryption SC scheme can withstand Ind-CCA attacks if there exists no such attacker $\mathcal{A}$ that could guess the cipher-text during above experiment Exp with non-negligible probability than ε', i.e.,*

$$Adv_{\mathcal{A},SC}^{Ind-CCA}(\theta,t) < \frac{1+\varepsilon'}{2 \cdot q_e \cdot q_d},$$

where at most t time bound, at most q_e times encryption query, at most q_d times decryption query under the θ security parameter.

Theorem 1. *First, we assume that our sign-cryption SC scheme is an Ind-CCA secure symmetric encryption/decryption scheme with a secure hash random oracle H_1 and also satisfied with the unforgeability (Unf) in the following. Then, we can say that, if SC is (t', ε') Ind-CCA secure and unforgeable, then*

$$Adv_{\mathcal{F},\mathcal{A},SC}^{Unf,Ind-CCA}(\theta,t) \leq \left(\frac{1}{2^l \cdot q_s \cdot q_e \cdot q_d} \cdot \varepsilon + \frac{1+\varepsilon'}{2 \cdot q_e \cdot q_d} \right),$$

where t is the maximum total experiment time including adversary execution time, l is an upper bound on the number of all IoT devices of at most q_s times signing query, at most encryption oracle q_e times query, and at most decryption oracle q_d times query under the security parameter θ in the experiment.

5. Conclusions

In the final result, we can see that our approach is suitable for an IoT device to compute the QR signature and encryption simultaneously. From Table 1, we also can see that our approach is more efficient than other schemes [1–4]. Our methodology not only efficiently computes the encryption and signature simultaneously, but can also support the fair protocol of two parties during communication between these IoT devices. This point also prevents allowing a single device such as the powerful gateway being compromised by attackers when IoT devices attempt to perform a signature operation or data exchange with this gateway. At the same time, this approach also provides data privacy protection for users. On one hand, our future goal is to develop a lightweight hierarchical sign-cryption scheme for IoT devices, and it can offer the authentication functionality between different levels of IoT devices with data privacy protection simultaneously. On the other hand, our approach can extend to develop a novel and real practical IoT data migration methodology for the IoT network in the future.

Author Contributions: Conceptualization, M.-T.C. and H.-C.H.; methodology, M.-T.C.; software, H.-C.H.; validation, M.-T.C. and H.-C.H.; formal analysis, M.-T.C.; investigation, H.-C.H.; resources, H.C.H.; data curation, H.-C.H.; writing—original draft preparation, M.-T.C.; writing—review and editing, H.-C.H.; visualization, H.-C.H.; supervision, H.-C.H.; project administration, H.-C.H.; funding acquisition, H.-C.H. All authors have read and agreed to the published version of the manuscript.

Funding: This research received no external funding.

Institutional Review Board Statement: Not applicable.

Informed Consent Statement: Not applicable.

Acknowledgments: This study was supported in part by grants from the Ministry of Science and Technology of the Republic of China (Grant No. MOST 109-2221-E-167-028-MY2).

Conflicts of Interest: The authors declare no conflict of interest.

Appendix A

Proof of Theorem 1. First, we define experiments of the above two security definitions and each attacker's ability, respectively. We will provide the proof of Lemma 1 and also define that there exists an attacker $\mathcal{F}$ whose goal is to forge a signature in the proposed scheme. We also define a simulator $\mathcal{S}$ that can control the experiment of the proposed scheme. On the other hand, $\mathcal{S}$ is given a signing oracle $Sig(\cdot)$, which can perform the same action as signature generation by the signer in our approach. $\mathcal{S}$ also prepares all IoT device key pairs, including the receiver's one.

Before beginning the experiment of digital signature, $\mathcal{S}$ is given a hard RSA problem in n^* and its goal is to use the $\mathcal{F}$'s ability to factor this n^*. During this time, $\mathcal{S}$ will also prepare the symmetric encryption/decryption function for the $\mathcal{F}$ encryption/decryption query. The query types are discussed below.

- Encrypting query: $\mathcal{F}$ can make an encrypting query on the chosen message m, the target receiver i and the corresponding hash value $H_1(r_i')$. During this time, $\mathcal{S}$ checks the H_1 list record and determines the random number r_i'. If there is no hash record on the list, $\mathcal{S}$ will generate the $(*, H_1(r_i'), r_i')$ entry for the random number r_i' on the list. Then, $\mathcal{S}$ generates the corresponding cipher-texts in the following:

$$\begin{aligned} C_1' &= E_{pk_i}(r_i') \\ C_2' &= m \oplus H_1(r_i') \\ C_3' &= H_1(C_1', C_2', r_i', m). \end{aligned} \quad (A1)$$

Then, $\mathcal{S}$ forwards this cipher-text (C_1', C_2', C_3') back to $\mathcal{F}$ to finish this Encryption query and records (C_1', C_2', C_3') into the H_1 list to be noted as $(C_1', C_2', C_3', H_1(r_i'), r_i')$.

- Decrypting query $Dec(\cdot)$: When $\mathcal{F}$ forwards a cipher-text (C_1', C_2', C_3') to $\mathcal{S}$, $\mathcal{S}$ will search the H_1 list to see if there is any entry in this list; if yes, $\mathcal{S}$ uses the $H_1(r_i')$ to decrypt the cipher-text (C_1', C_2', C_3'). Finally, $\mathcal{S}$ returns m back to $\mathcal{F}$.

- QR Signnature query: When $\mathcal{F}$ makes the signature query on the chosen message m, $\mathcal{S}$ will generate the following:

$$\begin{aligned} C_1' &= E_{pk_i}(r_i') \\ C_2' &= m \oplus H_1(r_i') \\ C_3' &= H_1(C_1', C_2', r_i', m) \\ S_R'^{4} &= C_3' \end{aligned} \quad (A2)$$

After generating the signature S_R' and the corresponding cipher-text (C_1', C_2', C_3'), $\mathcal{S}$ will check the signature list s_1 to see if there is any entry inside; if no, $\mathcal{S}$ preserves the signature S_R' into the signature list and stores $(C_1', C_2', C_3', S_R', H_1(r_i'), r_i', m)$ in the s_1 list. Then, $\mathcal{S}$ transfers S_R' back to $\mathcal{F}$. $\mathcal{F}$ can make the above signature query several times on the chosen message m. If $\mathcal{F}$ has made l times signature query on the message m, $\mathcal{F}$ can forge $l+1$ signatures on the message m. Then, we can have the probability of adversary $\mathcal{F}$

$$Adv_{\mathcal{F},Sig(\cdot),Enc(\cdot),Dec(\cdot)}^{Unf}(\theta, t) \leq \frac{1}{2^l \cdot q_s \cdot q_e \cdot q_d} \cdot \varepsilon, \quad (A3)$$

where there is at most q_s times signature query, at most q_e times encryption query, and at most q_d times decryption query in the polynomial t time bound under security parameter θ.

Second, we present the proof of Lemma 2 as follows. We assumed that there exists an attacker $\mathcal{A}$ whose goal is to distinguish a cipher-text (C_1, C_2, C_3) from a given message tuple (M_0, M_1) with non-negligible probability. Before simulating the experiment, we model a simulator $\mathcal{S}$, which is given a RSA hard problem n^* and its goal is to factor n^* and find the prime factor of n^*. During this time, $\mathcal{S}$ also generates all key pairs of IoT devices including the base gateway BS and the receiver R. When everything is ready, the S also allows $\mathcal{A}$ to send query types in the following.

- Cipher-text query on $Enc(\cdot)$: In this simulation, $\mathcal{A}$ can also launch a cipher-text query with an input the message m, the target receiver i, and the corresponding hash value $H_1(r_i)$ to S. When receiving this query, S checks the H_1 list records and finds out if there exists a random number r_i and other related records before. If there is no hash record on the list, S will generate a new entry $(*, H_1(r_i), r_i)$ for the random number r_i on the list. Then, S performs the following steps:

$$\begin{aligned} C_1 &= E_{pk_i}(r_i) \\ C_2 &= m \oplus H_1(r_i) \\ C_3 &= H_1(C_1, C_2, r_i, m) \end{aligned} \quad (A4)$$

Subsequently, S sends this cipher-text (C_1, C_2, C_3) back to $\mathcal{A}$ and stores (C_1, C_2, C_3) into the H_1 list to be noted as $(C_1, C_2, C_3, H_1(r_i), r_i)$.

- Plain-text query on $Dec(\cdot)$: When $\mathcal{A}$ makes a plain-text query on S with an cipher-text (C_1, C_2, C_3), S will search the H_1 list first to see if there is any entry inside or not; if yes, S uses the $H_1(r_i)$ to decrypt the cipher-text (C_1, C_2, C_3) and returns m back to $\mathcal{A}$.
- Signing query: When $\mathcal{A}$ makes an QR signature signing query on the chosen cipher-text (C_1, C_2, C_3), S will calculate the following equations:

$$\begin{aligned} C_1 &= E_{pk_i}(r_i) \\ C_2 &= m \oplus H_1(r_i) \\ C_3 &= H_1(C_1, C_2, r_i, m) \\ S_R^4 &= C_3 \end{aligned} \quad (A5)$$

After performing the above training, we defined it as the Phase 1 training phase of the experiment in the above definition. In the next phase, the $\mathcal{A}$ can send a target message tuple (M_0^*, M_1^*) and forward it to S. In this time, S will choose one of them by a coin toss on b. Then, S performs signing steps as follows:

$$\begin{aligned} C_1^* &= E_{pk_i}(r_i^*) \\ C_2^* &= M_b^* \oplus H_1(r_i^*) \\ C_3^* &= H_1(C_1^*, C_2^*, r_i^*, M_b^*) \\ S_R^{4*} &= C_3^* \end{aligned} \quad (A6)$$

After generating the above cipher-text $(C_1^*, C_2^*, C_3^*, S_R^{4*})$, S returns it back to the $\mathcal{A}$. During this time, $\mathcal{A}$ can make the decryption query except on the target cipher-text $(C_1^*, C_2^*, C_3^*, S_R^{4*})$. If $\mathcal{A}$ can distinguish the cipher-text $(C_1^*, C_2^*, C_3^*, S_R^{4*})$ computed from M_b^*, we can have

$$\begin{aligned} Adv_{\mathcal{A},SC}^{Ind-CCA}(\theta) &= |Pr[Exp_{\mathcal{A},SC}^{Ind-CCA-1}(\theta) = 1] - Pr[Exp_{\mathcal{A},SC}^{Ind-CCA-0}(\theta) = 1]| \\ &= Pr[Exp_{\mathcal{A},SC}^{Ind-CCA-1}(\theta) = 1] - (1 - Pr[Exp_{\mathcal{A},SC}^{Ind-CCA-1}(\theta) = 1]) \\ &< \varepsilon'. \end{aligned} \quad (A7)$$

Then, we can obtain that

$$Adv_{\mathcal{F},\mathcal{A},SC}^{Ind-CCA}(\theta, t) = Pr[Exp_{\mathcal{F},\mathcal{A},SC}^{Ind-CCA-1}(\theta) = 1] \leq \frac{1+\varepsilon'}{2 \cdot q_e \cdot q_d},$$

where at most q_e times encryption query and at most q_d times decryption query in the polynomial t time bound under the security parameter θ. The probability that $\mathcal{A}$ can distinguish the above target cipher-text (C_1^*, C_2^*, C_3^*) is less than ε'. We have summarized the above proofs of Lemmas 1 and 2. We can obtain

$$Adv_{\mathcal{F},\mathcal{A},SC}^{Unf,Ind-CCA}(\theta,t) \leq \left(\frac{1}{2^l \cdot q_s \cdot q_e \cdot q_d} \cdot \varepsilon + \frac{1+\varepsilon'}{2 \cdot q_e \cdot q_d}\right).$$

□

References

1. Shim, K.A. $\mathcal{CPAS}$: An Efficient Conditional Privacy-Preserving Authentication Scheme for Vehicular Sensor Networks. *IEEE Trans. Veh. Technol* **2012**, *61*, 1874–1883. [CrossRef]
2. Naresh, V.S.; Reddi, S.; Kumari, S.; Allavarpu, V.D.; Kumar, S.; Yang, M.H. Practical Identity Based Online/Off-Line Signcryption Scheme for Secure Communication in Internet of Things. *IEEE Access* **2021**, *9*, 21267–21278. [CrossRef]
3. Sun, Y.; Li, H. Efficient signcryption between TPKC and IDPKC and its multi-receiver construction. *Sci. China Inf. Sci.* **2010**, *53*, 557–566. [CrossRef]
4. Li, F.; Xiong, P. Practical secure communication for integrating wireless sensor networks into the Internet of Things. *IEEE Sens. J.* **2013**, *13*, 3677–3684. [CrossRef]
5. Hammi, B.; Fayad, A.; Khatoun, R.; Zeadally, S.; Begriche, Y. A Lightweight ECC-Based Authentication Scheme for Internet of Things (IoT). *IEEE Syst. J.* **2020**, *3*, 3440–3450. [CrossRef]
6. Choi, S.; Ko, J.; Kwak, J. A Study on IoT Device Authentication Protocol for High Speed and Lightweight. In Proceedings of the 2019 International Conference on Platform Technology and Service (PlatCon), Jeju, Korea, 28–30 January 2019; pp. 1–5.
7. Ning, H.; Liu, H.; Yang, L.T. Aggregated-Proof Based Hierarchical Authentication Scheme for the Internet of Things. *IEEE Trans. Parallel Distrib. Syst.* **2015**, *3*, 657–667. [CrossRef]
8. Kim, B.; Yoon, S.; Kang, Y.; Choi, D. PUF based IoT Device Authentication Scheme. In Proceedings of the 2019 International Conference on Information and Communication Technology Convergence (ICTC), Jeju Island, Korea, 16–18 October 2019; pp. 1460–1462.
9. Lounis, K.; Zulkernine, M. T2T-MAP: A PUF-Based Thing-to-Thing Mutual Authentication Protocol for IoT. *IEEE Access* **2021**, *9*, 137384–137405. [CrossRef]
10. Taher, B.H.; Jiang, S.; Yassin, A.A.; Lu, H. Low-Overhead Remote User Authentication Protocol for IoT Based on a Fuzzy Extractor and Feature Extraction. *IEEE Access* **2019**, *7*, 148950–148966. [CrossRef]
11. Rivest, R.; Shamir, A.; Adleman, L. A method for obtaining digital signatures and public-key cryptosystems. *Commun. ACM* **1978**, *21*, 120–126. [CrossRef]
12. Fan, C.I.; Lei, C.L. A User Efficient Fair Blind Signature Scheme for Untraceable Electronic Cash. *J. Inf. Sci. Eng.* **2002**, *18*, 47–58.
13. Koblitz, N.; Menezes, A.; Vanstone, S. The state of Elliptic curve cryptography. *Des. Codes Cryptogr.* **2000**, *19*, 173–193. [CrossRef]
14. Lauter, K. The Advantages of Elliptic curve cryptography for wireless security. *IEEE Wirel. Commun.* **2004**, *11*, 62–67. [CrossRef]
15. Bertinoi, G.; Breveglieri, L.; Chen, L.; Fragneto, P.; Harrison, K.; Pelosi, G. A pairing SW implementation for smart cards. *J. Syst. Softw.* **2008**, *81*, 1240–1247. [CrossRef]
16. Hankerson, D.; Menezes, A.; Scott, M. Software Implementation of pairings. *Identity-Based Cryptogr. Cryptol. Inf. Secur.* **2008**, *2*, 188.
17. Hohenberger, S. Advances in Signatures, Encryption, and E-Cash from Bilinear Groups. Ph.D. Dissertation, Massachusetts Institute of Technology, Cambridge, MA, USA, 2006.
18. Li, Z.; Higgins, J.; Clement, M. Performance of Finite Field Arithmetic in an Elliptic Curve Cryptosystem. In Proceedings of the 9th IEEE International Symposium on Modeling, Analysis, and Simulation of Computer and Telecommunications Systems (MASCOTS'01), Cincinnati, OH, USA, 15–18 August 2001; pp. 249–256.
19. Ramachanfdran, A.; Zhou, Z.; Huang, D. Computing cryptography algorithm in Portable and embedded devices. In Proceedings of the IEEE International Conference on Portable Information Devices, Orlando, FL, USA, 25–29 May 2007; pp. 1–7.
20. Schneier, B. *Applied Cryptography*, 2nd ed.; John Wiley & Sons: New York, NY, USA, 1996.
21. Takashima, K. Scaling Security of Elliptic Curves with Fast Pairing Using Efficient Endomorphisms. *IEICE Trans. Fundam. Electron. Commun. Comput. Sci.* **2007**, *90*, 152–159. [CrossRef]

Article

Development of Additive Fibonacci Generators with Improved Characteristics for Cybersecurity Needs

Volodymyr Maksymovych [1], Mariia Shabatura [1], Oleh Harasymchuk [2], Mikolaj Karpinski [3,*], Daniel Jancarczyk [3] and Pawel Sawicki [4]

[1] Department of Information Technology Security, Institute of Computer Technologies, Automation and Metrology, Lviv Polytechnic National University, 79013 Lviv, Ukraine; volodymyr.m.maksymovych@lpnu.ua (V.M.); mariia.m.mandrona@lpnu.ua (M.S.)
[2] Department of Information Protection, Institute of Computer Technologies, Automation and Metrology, Lviv Polytechnic National University, 79013 Lviv, Ukraine; oleh.i.harasymchuk@lpnu.ua
[3] Department of Computer Science and Automatics, Faculty of Mechanical Engineering and Computer Science, University of Bielsko-Biala, 43-309 Bielsko-Biala, Poland; djancarczyk@ath.bielsko.pl
[4] SunsetPicnic UG, 10437 Berlin, Germany; mail@psawicki.de
* Correspondence: mkarpinski@ath.bielsko.pl

Citation: Maksymovych, V.; Shabatura, M.; Harasymchuk, O.; Karpinski, M.; Jancarczyk, D.; Sawicki, P. Development of Additive Fibonacci Generators with Improved Characteristics for Cybersecurity Needs. *Appl. Sci.* **2022**, *12*, 1519. https://doi.org/10.3390/app12031519

Academic Editors: Gianluca Lax and Agostino Forestiero

Received: 28 December 2021
Accepted: 27 January 2022
Published: 30 January 2022

Publisher's Note: MDPI stays neutral with regard to jurisdictional claims in published maps and institutional affiliations.

Copyright: © 2022 by the authors. Licensee MDPI, Basel, Switzerland. This article is an open access article distributed under the terms and conditions of the Creative Commons Attribution (CC BY) license (https:// creativecommons.org/licenses/by/ 4.0/).

Abstract: Pseudorandom sequence generation is used in many industries, including cryptographic information security devices, measurement technology, and communication systems. The purpose of the present work is to research additive Fibonacci generators (AFG) and modified AFG (MAFG) with modules p prime numbers, designed primarily for their hardware implementation. The known AFG and MAFG, as with any cryptographic generators of pseudorandom sequences, are used in arguments with tremendous values. At the same time, there are specific difficulties in defining of their statistical characteristics. In this regard, the following research methodologies were used in work: for each variant of AFG and MAFG, two models were created—abstract, which is not directly related to the circuit solution, and hardware, which corresponds to the proposed structure; for relatively small values of arguments, the identity of models was proved; the research of statistical characteristics, with large values of arguments, was carried out using an abstract model and static tests NIST. Proven identity of hardware and abstract models suggest that the principles laid down in the organization of AFG and MAFG structures with modules of prime numbers ensure their effective hardware implementation in compliance with all requirements for their statistical characteristics and the possibility of application in cryptographic information security devices.

Keywords: pseudorandom sequences; additive Fibonacci generator; statistical characteristics; cybersecurity; information security

1. Introduction

Additive Fibonacci generators (AFG) are one of the types of pseudorandom sequence generators that are widely used in many technical means, particularly in cryptographic means of information protection. In their traditional design, they do not provide adequate cryptosecurity, but can be used as part of cryptographic devices [1–9]. Recently, we proposed a modified AFG (MAFG), in which the introduction to their structure and additional logic circuit, allowed us to include, in the process of arithmetic addition, the result of a logical function from the binary values of the resulting register, which significantly improved the statistical characteristics of the pseudorandom output sequence [10–15].

At present, almost all classic AFGs and new MAFGs, designed for hardware implementation, operate according to recurrent equations with modules whose values are equal to the power of two. It simplifies their hardware implementation but narrows their functionality and worsens the statistical characteristics of the output pseudorandom sequences.

In [16], we proposed AFGs that can work with an arbitrary value of a module, including a module whose value is a prime number. However, these devices do not have an additional logic circuit [10–15], which does not allow satisfactory statistical characteristics to be obtained without the involvement of additional devices.

In this article, we reveal the approach to constructing Fibonacci additive generators with modules of prime numbers. This construction method expands the capabilities of the hardware implementation of such generators and improves their output statistical characteristics, which allows them to be used effectively in cryptographic applications. A research methodology is proposed based on using abstract and hardware models of generators. Their identity is proved, which allows investigation of the statistical characteristics of such generators with the large values of arguments, which is especially important for cryptographic generators. The research results indicate that the proposed models and structures of generators can be effectively used to solve cryptographic problems of information security.

The aim of the work is to create and research the characteristics of AFGs and MAFGs with modules whose values are prime numbers. To achieve this goal, new generator structures are proposed, in which the introduction of additional structural elements allows us to ensure the operation of generators with arbitrary values of the recurrent equation modulus. This is the scientific novelty of the obtained results, which significantly improves the statistical characteristics of generators, expands their functionality, and expands the scope of their use in cryptographic means of information protection, particularly in streaming ciphers.

2. Related Works

A large number of works are devoted to the construction of AGF. In particular, analyses of the implementation of Fibonacci hardware generators on FPGA are given in [17]. There are also similar studies of Fibonacci generator implementations on FPGA in [18], and in [19], true random number generators, based on Fibonacci–Galois ring oscillators for FPGA, are considered, and the possibility of using these generators in cryptographic applications is shown. The results of research that used a combination of a hybrid of two existing generators—a linear congruential method and a delayed Fibonacci technique—are presented in [20]. The analysis of the efficiency of using a Fibonacci generator for cryptographic problems is also considered in [21,22]. Moreover, in [23], Fibonacci generators are used for the key generation algorithm with the necessary randomness and low algorithmic complexity. The work in [24] is devoted to the question of the correct choice of Fibonacci generator parameters.

AFGs operate according to the following generalized recurrent equation:

$$x_i = (x_{i-a} + x_{i-b} + \ldots + x_{i-q}) \bmod (m), \tag{1}$$

where $a > b > \ldots > q > 0$.

Usually, AFGs are used in which the module $m = 2^n$, where n is the number of generator structural elements binary bits, that simplifies their hardware implementation. Under certain conditions, the repetition period of such AFGs is not less than value $2^n - 1$ [25].

It is known [26] that, if the module $m = p$ is a prime number, then, according to the theory of finite fields, we can find such multipliers as $a_1, a_2, \ldots, a_k$, so that the sequence can be defined by the following equation:

$$x_i = (a_i x_{i-1} + \ldots + a_{k-1} x_{i-k+1} + a_k) \bmod p, \tag{2}$$

which will have the maximum possible period equal to $p^k - 1$. In this case, the following theorem holds. If the constants $a_1, a_2, \ldots, a_k$ are such that the polynomial $x^k - a_1 x^{k-1} - \ldots - a_k$ is primitive over the field $GF(p)$, and at least one of the elements $x_0, x_1, \ldots, x_k$ is not zero, then the generator period is equal to $p^k - 1$, at any initial values of the structural elements of the generator.

It is also known [26,27] that the search for primitive polynomials for prime number modules is a difficult task.

In [10–15] we proposed modified MAFGs, in which the module is determined by the equation $m = 2^n$, but they include an additional logic circuit (LC), the function of which is logical addition of the module 2 of the bits values of one of the generator registers, and then the result is added to the main operation of the arithmetic addition. This allows a significant increase in the repetition periods of the output sequences and an improvement of their statistical characteristics.

However, for today, there are no reasonable developments in which the structures of AFGs and MAFGs are proposed with an arbitrary value of the module of the recurrent equation.

3. Structure Scheme and Work Principle of AFG and MAFG with Arbitrary Value of the Module of the Recurrent Equation

Figure 1 shows the structure scheme of AFG and MAFG, which can operate with any value of the recurrent equation module. The AFG consists of registers RG1–RG6, adders AD1 and AD2, multiplexer MUX, and logical element OR. The logic circuit LC is additionally introduced to the MAFG structure.

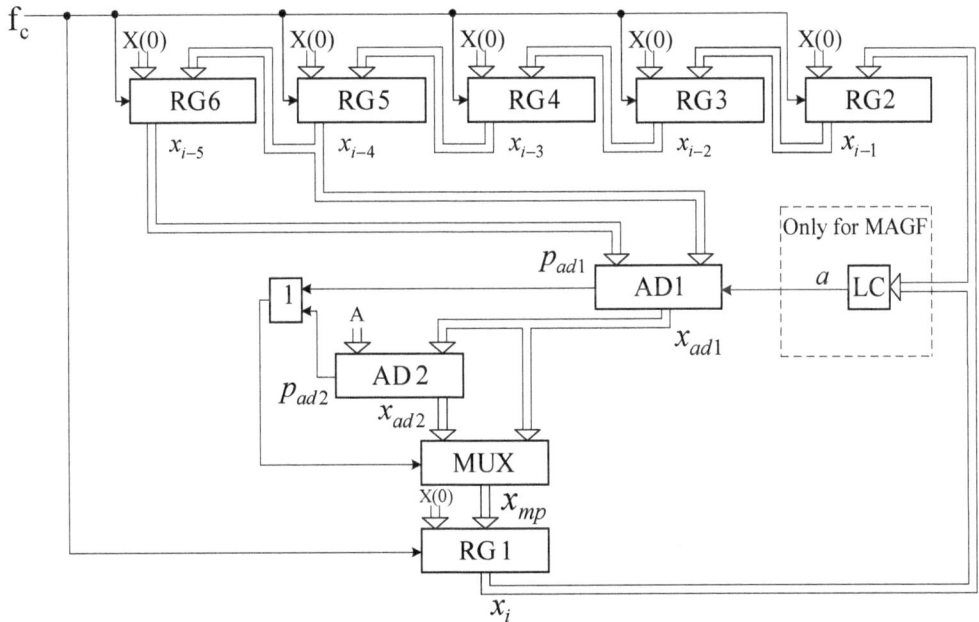

Figure 1. Structure scheme of AFG and MAFG.

The schemes are given for generators operating according to the following equations:

$$x_i = (x_{i-5} + x_{i-4}) \bmod p, \text{ (for AFG)} \tag{3}$$

$$x_i = (x_{i-5} + x_{i-4} + a) \bmod p, \text{ (for MAFG)} \tag{4}$$

where: x_i, x_{i-4}, x_{i-5}—numbers at the outputs of registers RG1, RG5, and RG6, respectively.
In Equation (4):

$$a = b_0 \oplus b_1 \oplus \ldots \oplus b_s, \tag{5}$$

where: b_i ($i = 0, 1, \ldots, s$; $s \leq n$)—values of the number x_i binary bits; n—the total number of binary bits.

With each clock pulse, new values of numbers are formed in the registers RG1–RG6, in particular in the register RG1—the number determined by the output signal of the multiplexer MUX.

At the output of the logic circuit LC, the signal a is formed in accordance with logic Equation (5). Adding the LC output signal a, in the process of arithmetic addition, implemented by the adder AD1, can significantly improve the statistical characteristics of the output pseudorandom signals of the generator.

In the absence of carry signals at the outputs of the adders AD1 and AD2, to the information inputs of the memory register RG1, through the multiplexer MUX, arrives a number from the information outputs of the adder AD1; moreover, if at least one of them is present, the number of information outputs are those of the adder AD2.

Compared with the known AFG and MAFG [10–15,28], the introduction of the second adder AD2, multiplexer MUX, and the establishment of new connections between these and other structural elements, allows changing the numbers in the registers RG1–RG6 in the range of values $0 \div (p-1)$. Thus, AFG and MAFG operate with arbitrary module values according to Expressions (3) and (4), which confirmed our research, as mentioned in the following sections.

4. Methods of AFG and MAFG Statistical Characteristics Research

AFG and MAFG, as with any cryptographic generators of pseudorandom sequences, are used in arguments whose values are enormous; therefore, there are some difficulties in determining their statistical characteristics.

In this regard, the following research methodology was used. Two models were created for each AFG and MAFG variant: firstly, the abstract, which is not directly related to the circuit design solution, and hardware, which corresponds to the proposed structure. For relatively small values of arguments, the identity of the models is proved. The study of statistical characteristics, with large values of arguments, is carried out using an abstract model.

The following algorithms represent different AFG and MAFG models. The hardware models are represented by equations that correspond to the structures' processes, shown in Figure 1. Abstract models are represented by equations that correspond to the processes that must occur in the additive Fibonacci generator when it operates with a module whose value can be arbitrary. Proving the identity of the results obtained with these models proves the correctness of the structures shown in Figure 1, in terms of achieving the desired result.

4.1. Research of AFG Models

In AFG models, the logic circuit LC is not involved in the generator structure scheme (Figure 1).

The AFG hardware model operates in accordance with the following algorithm:

$$A = 2^n - p, \quad x_{i-5} = x_{i-4}, \quad x_{i-4} = x_{i-3}, \quad x_{i-3} = x_{i-2}, \quad x_{i-2} = x_{i-1}, \quad x_{i-1} = x_i, \quad x_i = x_{mp},$$

$$x_{ad1} = (x_{i-5} + x_{i-4}) \bmod 2^n, \quad \text{if} \quad (x_{i-5} + x_{i-4}) < 2^n \quad \text{then} \quad P_{ad1} = 0 \quad \text{else} \quad P_{ad1} = 1,$$

$$x_{ad2} = (x_{ad1} + A) \bmod 2^n, \quad \text{if} \quad (x_{ad1} + A) < 2^n \quad \text{then} \quad P_{ad2} = 0 \quad \text{else} \quad P_{ad2} = 1,$$

$$\text{if } (P_{ad1} = 0), \text{ and } (P_{ad2} = 0), \text{ then } x_{mp} = x_{ad1}, \text{ or } x_{mp} = x_{ad2},$$

where: $x_i, x_{i-1}, x_{i-2}, x_{i-3}, x_{i-4}, x_{i-5}$—numbers in registers RG1–RG6, respectively; x_{ad1} and x_{ad2}—numbers at the sum outputs of adders AD1 i AD2; P_{ad1} and P_{ad2}—numbers at the carry outputs of adders AD1 and AD2; x_{mp}—the number at the output of the multiplexer MUX; n—the number of the generator's structural elements binary bits (Figure 1).

The abstract AFG model is described by the following equations:

$$x_{i-5} = x_{i-4}, x_{i-4} = x_{i-3}, x_{i-3} = x_{i-2}, x_{i-2} = x_{i-1}, x_{i-1} = x_i, x_i = x_{ad1}, x_{ad1} = (x_{i-5} + x_{i-4}) \bmod p.$$

Figure 2 shows the dependences of the current values of pseudorandom numbers X, generated by AFG on the iteration step number, i, for the hardware and abstract model with the same initial value, $X(0)$.

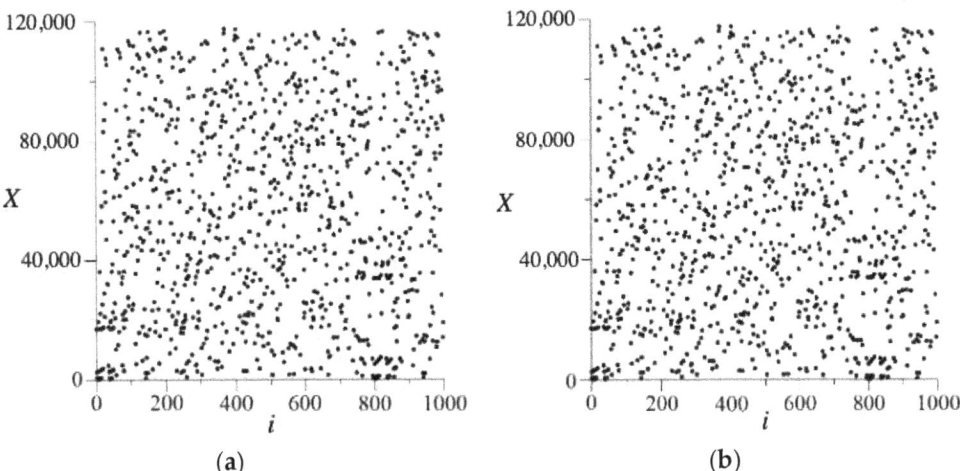

Figure 2. Current values of pseudorandom numbers X (for AFG): (**a**) hardware model: $p = 7$, $n = 3$, $A = 2^n - p = 1$, $X(0) = 1$; (**b**) abstract model: $p = 7$, $X(0) = 1$.

Numbers X and $X(0)$ are defined by the following expressions:

$$X = p^5 x_i + p^4 x_{i-1} + p^3 x_{i-2} + p^2 x_{i-3} + p x_{i-4} + x_{i-5}, \quad (6)$$

$$X(0) = p^5 x_i(0) + p^4 x_{i-1}(0) + p^3 x_{i-2}(0) + p^2 x_{i-3}(0) + p x_{i-4}(0) + x_{i-5}(0), \quad (7)$$

where: $x_i(0)$, $x_{i-1}(0)$, $x_{i-2}(0)$, $x_{i-3}(0)$, $x_{i-4}(0)$, $x_{i-5}(0)$—initial values of numbers x_i, x_{i-1}, x_{i-2}, x_{i-3}, x_{i-4}, x_{i-5}, respectively.

Figure 3 on a logarithmic scale shows the dependence of the repetition periods of the AFG pseudorandom sequence numbers from the initial values, $X(0)$.

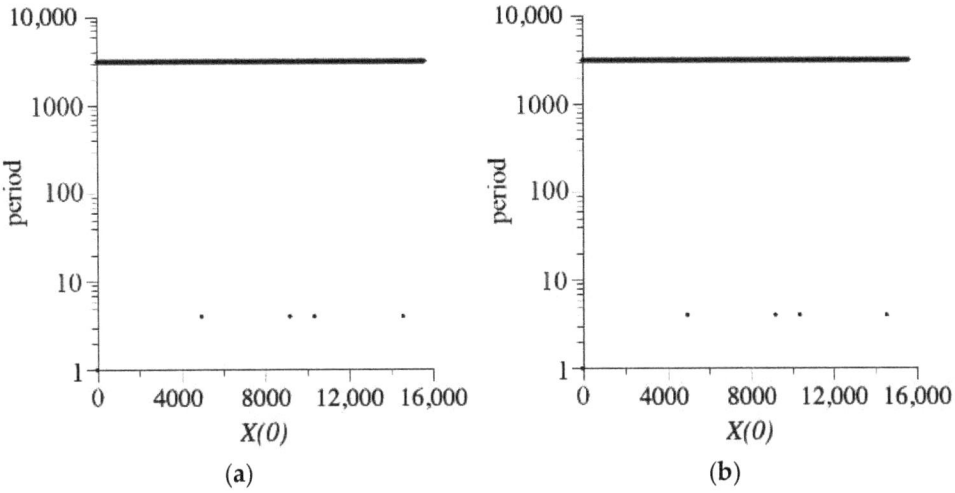

Figure 3. Dependencies of repetition periods from $X(0)$ (for AFG): (**a**) hardware model: $p = 5$, $n = 3$, $A = 2^n - p = 3$, $X(0) = 0 \div p^6 - 1$; (**b**) abstract model: $p = 5$, $X(0) = 0 \div p^6 - 1$.

The results (Figures 2 and 3) indicate complete identity of hardware and abstract models for forming a pseudorandom numbers sequence. Similar results were obtained for other p values, in particular for p values that are primes.

4.2. Research of MAFG Models

MAFG models: Figure 1 shows generator structure scheme with using logic circuit LC. The hardware model of the MAFG, operating according to the following algorithm:

$$A = 2^n - p, \quad x_{i-5} = x_{i-4}, \quad x_{i-4} = x_{i-3}, \quad x_{i-3} = x_{i-2}, \quad x_{i-2} = x_{i-1}, \quad x_{i-1} = x_i, \quad x_i = x_{mp},$$

$$a = b_0 \oplus b_1 \oplus \ldots \oplus b_s$$

$$x_{ad1} = (x_{i-5} + x_{i-4} + a) \bmod 2^n, \quad \text{if} \quad (x_{i-5} + x_{i-4} + a) < 2^n \quad \text{then} \quad P_{ad1} = 0 \quad \text{else} \quad P_{ad1} = 1,$$

$$x_{ad2} = (x_{ad1} + A) \bmod 2^n, \quad \text{if} \quad (x_{ad1} + A) < 2^n \quad \text{then} \quad P_{ad2} = 0 \quad \text{else} \quad P_{ad2} = 1,$$

$$\text{if} \quad (P_{ad1} = 0) \quad \text{and} \quad (P_{ad2} = 0) \quad \text{then} \quad x_{mp} = x_{ad1} \quad \text{else} \quad x_{mp} = x_{ad2},$$

where: b_i—values of the number xi binary bits.

Abstract model of the MAFG operating according to the following equation:

$$x_{i-5} = x_{i-4}, \quad x_{i-4} = x_{i-3}, \quad x_{i-3} = x_{i-2}, \quad x_{i-2} = x_{i-1}, \quad x_{i-1} = x_i, \quad x_i = x_{ad1},$$

$$a = b_0 \oplus b_1 \oplus \ldots \oplus b_s$$

$$x_{ad1} = (x_{i-5} + x_{i-4} + a) \bmod p.$$

Figure 4 shows the dependences of the current values of pseudorandom numbers, X, that were generated by the MAFG on the iteration step number, i, for the hardware and abstract model with the same initial value, $X(0)$.

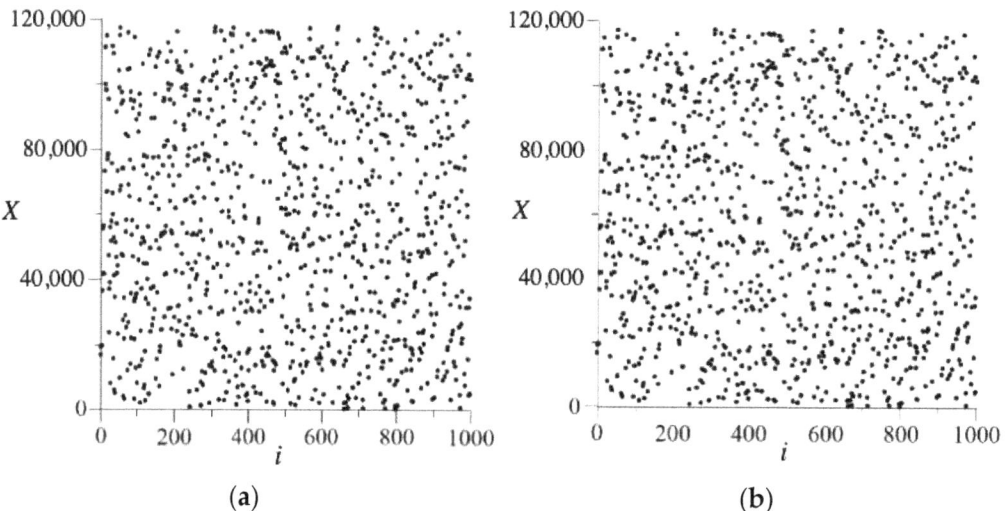

Figure 4. Current values of pseudorandom numbers X (for MAFG): (**a**) hardware model: $p = 7$, $n = 3$, $A = 2^n - p = 1$, $a = b_0 \oplus b_1 \oplus b_2$, $X(0) = 1$; (**b**) abstract model: $p = 7$, $a = b_0 \oplus b_1 \oplus b_2$, $X(0) = 1$.

Figure 5 shows, on a logarithmic scale, the dependences of repetition periods of MAFG pseudorandom sequence on the initial values, $X(0)$.

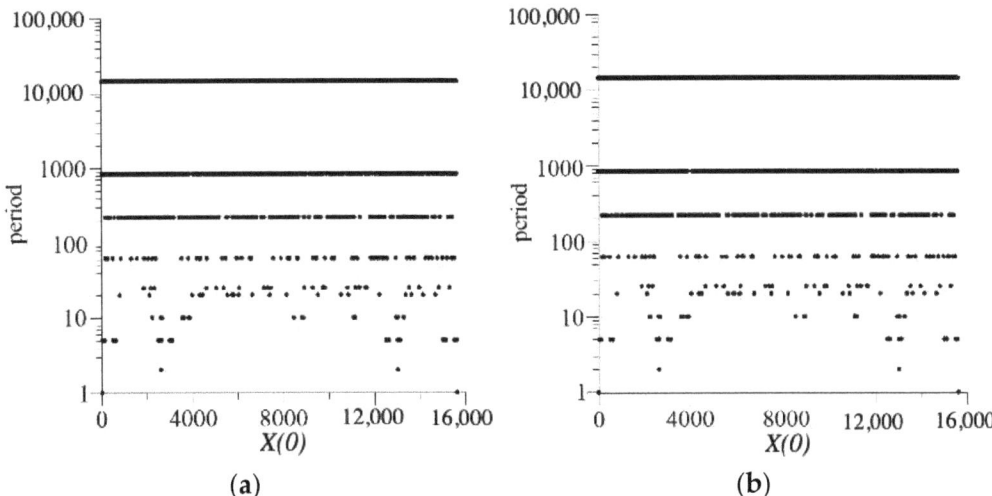

Figure 5. Dependencies of repetition periods from $X(0)$: (**a**) hardware model: $p = 5$, $n = 3$, $A = 2^n - p = 3$, $a = b_0 \oplus b_1 \oplus b_2$, $X(0) = 0 \div p^6 - 1$; (**b**) abstract model: $p = 5$, $a = b_0 \oplus b_1 \oplus b_2$, $X(0) = 0 \div p^6 - 1$.

The results (Figures 4 and 5) indicate complete identity hardware and abstract models for forming the pseudorandom numbers sequence. Similar results were obtained for other p values, in particular for p values that are primes.

5. Results

5.1. Research of Repetition Periods of AFG and MAFG Pseudorandom Sequences

The following research was conducted using an abstract model considering proven identity hardware and abstract generators models. It is necessary to speed up the simulation process.

Table 1 presents the received results of AFG and MAFG repetition periods, Tp, for a few small module p values that determined on the whole set of possible values of the initial number, $X(0) = 0 \div p^6 - 1$.

Table 1. Repetition periods of AFG and MAFG output sequences for p value on the whole set of possible values, $X(0) = 0 \div p^6 - 1$.

Some p Values	Max and Min Repetition Period Values	
	AFG (without Logic Circuit LC)	MAFG (with Logic Circuit LC)
2	63	10
		2
3	728	315
		5
5	3124	14,409
	4	5
7	2400	105,833
	24	11,360

In this case, for MAFG, the output signal value a of the logic circuit LC (Figure 1) was determined, according to Equation (5), as the sum for the module 2 for all bits of number x_i in the register Pr1.

Table 1 shows the maximum and minimum values of the period Tp. It should be noted that when $p = 2$ and $p = 3$ on the whole set, $X(0) = 0 \div p^6 - 1$ fixed only one value $Tp = p^6 - 1$. It coincides with the known theoretical results presented in Ref. [25].

Where for larger values of module p, determination of repetition period, Tp, on the whole set of values, $X(0) = 0 \div p^6 - 1$, requires a lot of machine time, all the following research was conducted for a fixed value, $X(0) = 1$. Table 2 shows the repetition period, Tp, for some p values and fixed values, $X(0) = 1$.

Table 2. Repetition periods of AFG and MAFG output sequences for some p values when $X(0) = 1$.

Some p Values	Repetition Periods Tp	
	AFG (without Logic Circuit LC)	MAFG (with Logic Circuit LC)
11	118,103	1,601,719
13	371,291	2,636,108
17	88,415	9,810,767
19	2,476,097	26,974,957
37	845,657	382,733,921
41	1679	432,850,590
43	1,116,087	5,459,242,931
73	1,401,242,835	8,949,513,501
137	4,387,429,945	$>10^{10}$

Based on the research results of the output sequences, repetition periods of the AFG and proposed MAFG, in which the modules of the recurrent equations are prime numbers, such a conclusion can be made. When $p > 3$ the repetition periods MAFG is significantly greater than the AFG. When $p = 2$ and $p = 3$, the repetition periods of AFG reach, theoretically, the maximum value, $Tp = p^6 - 1$, for all possible values, $X(0)$.

5.2. Research of Statistical Characteristics of AFG and MAFG Pseudorandom Sequences

Research the statistical characteristics of the output pseudorandom bit sequences of AFG and MAFG for some p values were carried out with the NIST test package [29–31]. Results shows in Figures 6–9. Figure 6 presents a statistical portrait of the AFG output sequence at $p = 137$.

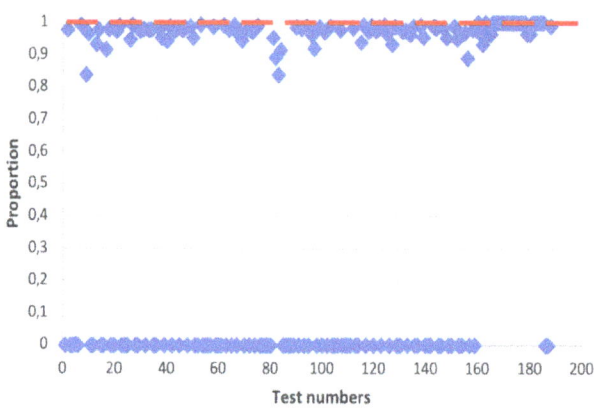

Figure 6. Statistical portrait of the AFG output sequence at $p = 137$, $X(0) = 1$.

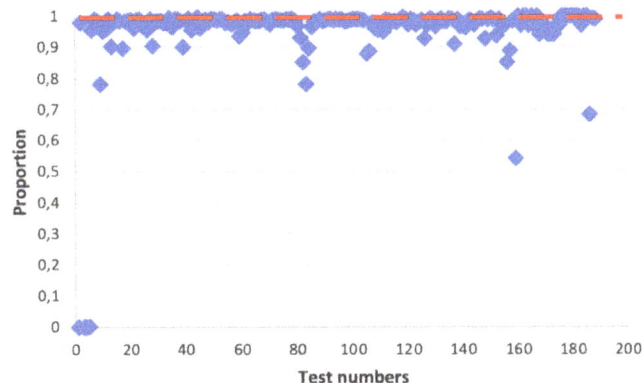

Figure 7. Statistical portrait of the MAFG output sequence at $p = 137$, $X(0) = 1$, $a = b_0 \oplus b_1 \ldots \oplus b_7$.

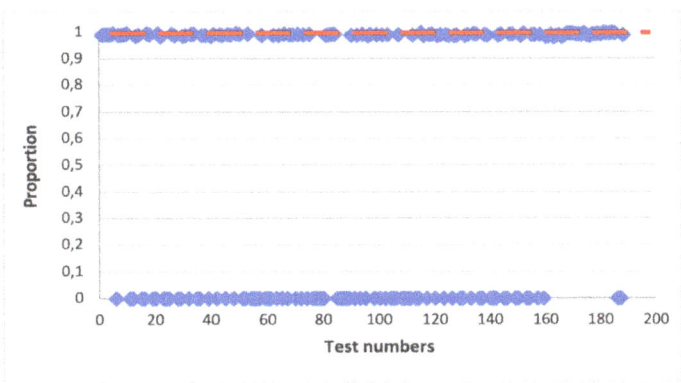

Figure 8. Statistical portrait of the AFG output sequence at $p = 65{,}537$ and $X(0)$.

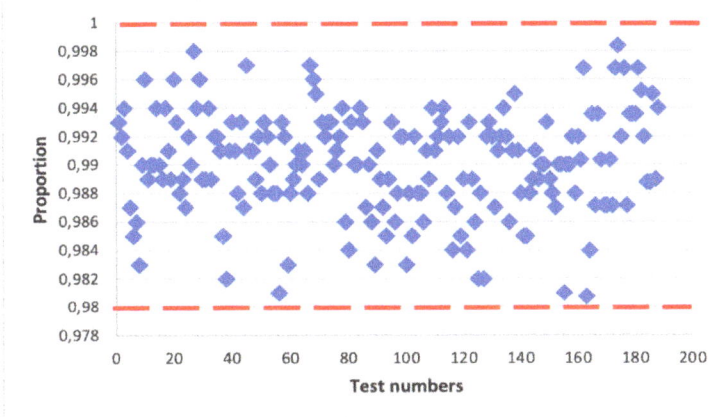

Figure 9. Statistical portrait of the MAFG output sequence at $p = 65{,}537$, $X(0) = 1$, $a = b_0 \oplus b_1 \ldots \oplus b_{16}$.

As can be seen from Figure 6, the most tests valued at 0 and did not fall within the specified interval; meaning that the sequence does not meet the randomness requirements.

Figure 7 shows MAFG using the same initial data as AFG. The sequence also does not meet the randomness requirements, but there is a significant improvement over the AFG. In particular, most test values are above 0. So, the proposed modification demonstrates positive dynamics.

Figure 8 shows the statistical portrait of the AFG output sequence at $p = 65{,}537$. The tests failed and did not meet the randomness requirements.

Figure 9 presented the statistical portrait of the MAFG output sequence using the same parameters as AFG. As can be seen, all tests are within the allowable range. It means that such sequence has high statistical characteristics and meet the randomness requirements.

Analysis of statistical portraits (Figures 6–9) shows that, with the same parameters, the statistical characteristics of the output pseudorandom sequences of MAFG significantly predominated in the AFG. Thus, at $p = 65{,}537$, $X(0) = 1$, and $a = b_0 \oplus b_1 \ldots \oplus b_{16}$ (Figure 9) MAFG statistical characteristics entirely pass all NIST tests.

The conducted research proves that the proposed Fibonacci additive generators can operate by recurrent equations, whose modules values can be arbitrary, including modules whose values are prime numbers. It distinguishes them from the known additive Fibonacci generators, whose value of the modules is equal to the power of two. That is, the class of proposed generators includes the known generators as a subclass. At the same time, the proposed generators have the best statistical characteristics and designs for hardware implementation primarily, in which will achieve their maximum speed when implementing the proposed structures in a modern element base, for example, in programmable logic integrated circuits (PLDs).

6. Conclusions

The present article proposes new structures of AFG and MAFG, in which adding additional structural elements allows the operation of the generator with arbitrary values of the modulus of the recurrent equation, in particular, with modules whose values are prime numbers.

In the present study, we proved the identity of hardware and abstract models, suggesting that the principles laid down in the organization of the AFG and MAFG structures with modules of prime numbers ensure their effective hardware implementation.

For the basic function $x_i = (x_{i-5} + x_{i-4}) \bmod p$, the MAFG selected for the research, which functions according to the equation $x_i = (x_{i-5} + x_{i-4} + a) \bmod p$, significantly predominated over AFG in the repetition period and statistical characteristics for all module values $p > 3$.

The AFG, at $p = 2$ and $p = 3$, fixed the maximum possible repetition period, $T_p = p^6 - 1$, for all possible initial values of generator registers settings.

In further research, an important task is to find primitive polynomials over the field $GF(p)$ for other values, $p > 3$, create AFG and MAFG structures for these values, and research their characteristics.

The obtained results can be used not only in the design of information security tools but also in other technology fields, such as in simulating random processes in measuring technologies.

Author Contributions: Conceptualization, V.M., M.S., and O.H.; methodology, M.S., and D.J.; validation, V.M., M.S., and P.S.; formal analysis, M.S., O.H., and P.S.; investigation, V.M., M.S., O.H., and D.J.; data curation, V.M., M.S., and O.H.; writing—original draft preparation, V.M., M.S., and O.H.; writing—review and editing, V.M., M.S, O.H., and D.J.; funding acquisition, M.K. All authors have read and agreed to the published version of the manuscript.

Funding: The research work reported in this paper was in part supported by the National Centre for Research and Development, Poland, under the project No. POIR.04.01.04-00-0048/20.

Institutional Review Board Statement: Not applicable.

Informed Consent Statement: Not applicable.

Conflicts of Interest: The authors declare no conflict of interest.

References

1. Mohamed, K.; Ali, F.H.H.M.; Ariffin, S.; Zakaria, N.H.; Pauzi, M.N.M. An Improved AES S-box Based on Fibonacci Numbers and Prime Factor. *Int. J. Netw. Secur.* **2018**, *20*, 1206–1214.
2. Belov, A.A.; Kalitkin, N.N.; Tintul, M.A. Visual Verification of Pseudo-Random Number Generators. *Keldysh Inst. Preprints* **2019**, *137*, 1–28. [CrossRef]
3. Stakhov, A.; Massingue, V.; Sluchenkova, A. *Introduction into Fibonacci Coding and Cryptography*; Publish Osnova: Kharkov, Ukraine, 1999.
4. Agarwal, P.; Agarwal, N.; Saxena, R. Data Encryption through Fibonacci Sequence and Unicode Characters. *MIT Int. J. Comput. Sci. Inf. Technol.* **2015**, *5*, 79–82.
5. Gosai, I. Fibonacci Sequence and It's Applications. *IJRAR* **2019**, *6*, 241–247.
6. Ahamad, M.V.; Siddiqui, U.M.; Masroor, M.; Fatima, U.A. Modified Playfair Encryption Using Fibonacci Numbers. *Int. J. Adv. Technol. Eng. Sci.* **2017**, *5*, 347–351.
7. Baldoni, S.; Battisti, F.; Carli, M.; Pascucci, F. On the Use of Fibonacci Sequences for Detecting Injection Attacks in Cyber Physical Systems. *IEEE Access* **2021**, *9*, 41787–41798. [CrossRef]
8. Agarwal, A.; Agarwal, S.; Singh, B.K. Algorithm for data encryption & decryption using Fibonacci primes. *J. Math. Control Sci. Appl.* **2020**, *6*, 63–71.
9. Yacoab, M.; Sha, M.; Ahmed, M.M. Secured Data Aggregation Using Fibonacci Numbers and Unicode Symbols for Wsn. *Int. J. Comput. Eng. Technol.* **2019**, *10*, 218–225. [CrossRef]
10. Mandrona, M.; Maksymovych, V. Investigation of the statistical characteristics of the modified Fibonacci generators. *J. Autom. Inf. Sci.* **2014**, *46*, 48–53. [CrossRef]
11. Maksymovych, V.; Harasymchuk, O.; Kostiv, Y.; Mandrona, M. Implementation of modified additive lagged Fibonacci generator. *Chall. Mod. Technol.* **2016**, *7*, 3–6.
12. Maksymovych, V.; Mandrona, M.; Garasimchuk, O.; Kostiv, Y. A study of the characteristics of the Fibonacci modified additive generator with a delay. *J. Autom. Inf. Sci.* **2016**, *48*, 76–82. [CrossRef]
13. Maksymovych, V.N.; Harasymchuk, O.I.; Mandrona, M.N. Designing Generators of Poisson Pulse Sequences Based on the Additive Fibonacci Generators. *J. Autom. Inf. Sci.* **2017**, *49*, 1–13. [CrossRef]
14. Mandrona, M.N.; Maksymovych, V.N. Comparative Analysis of Pseudorandom Bit Sequence Generators. *J. Autom. Inf. Sci.* **2017**, *49*, 78–86. [CrossRef]
15. Maksymovych, V.; Harasymchuk, O.; Opirskyy, I. The Designing and Research of Generators of Poisson Pulse Sequences on Base of Fibonacci Modified Additive Generator. International Conference on Theory and Applications of Fuzzy Systems and Soft Computing. *Adv. Comput. Sci. Eng. Educ.* **2018**, *754*, 43–53. [CrossRef]
16. Maksymovych, V.; Harasymchuk, O.; Karpinski, M.; Shabatura, M.; Jancarczyk, D.; Kajstura, K. A New Approach to the Development of Additive Fibonacci Generators Based on Prime Numbers. *Electronics* **2021**, *10*, 2912. [CrossRef]
17. Deshmukh, P.; Sadawarte, Y. Pseudo-Random Number Generation by Fibonacci and Galois LFSR Implemented on FPGA. In Proceedings of the IJCA Proceedings on International Conference on Advancements in Engineering and Technology (ICAET 2015) ICQUEST 2015, Wardha, India, 1–3 October 2015.
18. Zulfikar, Z.; Away, Y.; Rafiqa, S.N. FPGA–Based Design System for a Two-segment Fibonacci LFSR Random Number Generator. *Int. J. Electr. Comput. Eng.* **2017**, *7*, 1882–1891. [CrossRef]
19. Nannipieri, P.; Di Matteo, S.; Baldanzi, L.; Crocetti, L.; Belli, J.; Fanucci, L.; Saponara, S. True Random Number Generator Based on Fibonacci-Galois Ring Oscillators for FPGA. *Appl. Sci.* **2021**, *11*, 3330. [CrossRef]
20. Cybulski, R. Pseudo-random number generator based on linear congruence and delayed Fibonacci method: Pseudo-random number generator based on linear congruence and delayed Fibonacci method. *Tech. Sci.* **2021**, *24*, 331–349. [CrossRef]
21. Opoku-Mensah, E.; Abilimi, C.A.; Boateng, F.O. Comparative Analysis of Efficiency of Fibonacci Random Number Generator Algorithm and Gaussian Random Number Generator Algorithm in a Cryptographic System. *Comput. Eng. Intell. Syst.* **2013**, *4*, 50–57.
22. Mandrona, M.M.; Maksymovych, V.M.; Harasymchuk, O.I.; Kostiv, Y.M. Generator of pseudorandom bit sequence with increased cryptographic immunity. *Metall. Min. Ind.* **2014**, *6*, 24–28.
23. Amiruddin, A.; Ratna, A.A.P.; Sari, R.F. Construction and Analysis of Key Generation Algorithms Based on Modified Fibonacci and Scrambling Factors for Privacy Preservation. *Int. J. Netw. Secur.* **2019**, *21*, 250–258. [CrossRef]
24. Oduwole, H.K.; Shehu, S.; Adegoke, G.K.; Onubogu, J.L. Fibonacci Random Number Generator using Lehmer's Algorithm. *Math. Theory Modeling* **2013**, *3*, 56–62.
25. Schneier, B. *Applied Cryptography: Protocols, Algorithms, and Source Code in C*; John Wiley & Sons: Hoboken, NJ, USA, 2007; p. 675.
26. Slepovichev, I. *Pseudo-Random Number Generators*; SSU: Saratov, Russia, 2017; p. 118.
27. Beletsky, A.; Kovalchuk, A.; Novikov, K.; Poltoratsky, D. *Tables of Binary Irreducible Polynomials*; Monograph book; Agrar Media Group: Kyiv, Ukraine, 2021; p. 400.
28. Srinivas, A. Lagged Fibonacci Random Number Generators for Distributed Memory Parallel Computers. *J. Parallel Distrib. Comput.* **1997**, *45*, 1–12.

29. Faster Randomness Testing with the NIST Statistical Test Suite. Available online: https://crocs.fi.muni.cz/_media/public/crocs/sys_space_2014.pdf (accessed on 20 December 2021).
30. NIST SP 800-22 Version 1a. *A Statistical Test Suite for Random and Pseudorandom Number Generators for Cryptographic Applications*; NIST: Gaithersburg, MD, USA, 2010; p. 131. Available online: https://nvlpubs.nist.gov/nistpubs/Legacy/SP/nistspecialpublication800-22r1a.pdf (accessed on 20 December 2021).
31. Gorbenko, I.D.; Gorbenko, Y.I. *Applied Cryptology: Theory. Practice. Application*; Fort Publishing House: Kharkiv, Ukraine, 2012; p. 880.

Article

CBCIoT: A Consensus Algorithm for Blockchain-Based IoT Applications

Moin Uddin [1], Muhammad Muzammal [1], Muhammad Khurram Hameed [1], Ibrahim Tariq Javed [1,*], Bandar Alamri [2] and Noel Crespi [3]

[1] Department of Computer Science, Bahria University Islamabad Campus, Islamabad 44000, Pakistan; engrmoin.uett@gmail.com (M.U.); mmuzammal.buic@bahria.edu.pk (M.M.); muh.khurramhameed@gmail.com (M.K.H.)
[2] Lero-The Irish Software Research Centre, University of Limerick, V94 T9PX Limerick, Ireland; Bandar.Alamri@ul.ie
[3] Institut Polytechnique de Paris Telecom SudParis Evry, Courcouronnes FR, 9 Rue Charles Fourier, 91000 Evry, France; noel.crespi@mines-telecom.fr
* Correspondence: Ibrahimtariq.javed@lero.ie

Citation: Uddin, M.; Muzammal, M.; Hameed, M.K.; Javed, I.T.; Alamri, B.; Crespi, N. CBCIoT: A Consensus Algorithm for Blockchain-Based IoT Applications. *Appl. Sci.* **2021**, *11*, 11011. https://doi.org/10.3390/app112211011

Academic Editors: Gianluca Lax and Antonia Russo

Received: 15 October 2021
Accepted: 16 November 2021
Published: 20 November 2021

Publisher's Note: MDPI stays neutral with regard to jurisdictional claims in published maps and institutional affiliations.

Copyright: © 2021 by the authors. Licensee MDPI, Basel, Switzerland. This article is an open access article distributed under the terms and conditions of the Creative Commons Attribution (CC BY) license (https://creativecommons.org/licenses/by/4.0/).

Abstract: Internet of things is widely used in the current era to collect data from sensors and perform specific tasks through processing according to the requirements. The data collected can be sent to a blockchain network to create secure and tamper-resistant records of transactions. The combination of blockchain with IoT has huge potential as it can provide decentralized computation, storage, and exchange for IoT data. However, IoT applications require a low-latency consensus mechanism due to its constraints. In this paper, CBCIoT, a consensus algorithm for blockchain-based IoT applications, is proposed. The primary purpose of this algorithm is to improve scalability in terms of validation and verification rate. The algorithm is developed to be compatible with IoT devices where a slight delay is acceptable. The simulation results show the proposed algorithm's efficiency in terms of block generation time and transactions per second.

Keywords: blockchain; Internet of Things; consensus algorithm; proof of work; proof of stake; stellar consensus protocol

1. Introduction

Blockchain is a distributed database which provides decentralization and immutability of the transactions or records in a peer-to-peer network. On the other hand, IoT consists of physical devices that are connected to the internet to collect and share data. Combination of blockchain and IoT i.e. blockchain of IoT (BCIoT) will be beneficial to the world in terms of decentralization and immutability but challenges are also present with opportunities. The volume of data collected is currently tremendous and grows due to the growing number of IoT devices. Large number of IoT devices and data platforms open the door to new applications and use cases. However, IoT data security is a major concern that has slowed the technology's adoption as they are a prime target for a range of attacks. Scalability is another issue with today's IoT networks. When the number of devices linked through an IoT network rises, current centralized techniques for authenticating and linking sensor nodes in a network will become a bottleneck. If the server that handles the vast volume of data exchange goes down, the entire network can go down.

Blockchain is considered to be a game-changing technology that has the potential to address IoT security and scalability concerns [1,2]. Blockchain is a distributed ledger technology that can be used to distribute and access data in a secure and decentralized manner [3]. Every transaction may be authenticated to avoid conflicts and build trust among all network participants. However, the integration of IoT and blockchain gives rise to new challenges (Figure 1), such as scalability, big data of IoT devices, security and privacy that need to be resolved [4]. It is also necessary for blockchain and IoT to implement an encryption algorithm but both ecosystems have different computing capabilities; so, processing time and power [5] could be a great difficulty. Blockchain provides decentralization, stores transaction on every node's ledger and its size is continuously increasing with time. IoT devices have very low storage capacity [6], as this is beyond the capabilities of sensors. IoT is an open nature network and so in BCIoT, security and privacy could be a potential threat. An efficient authentication scheme by message authentication for Internet of Vehicles (EASSAIV) is proposed in [7] to resolve security and privacy concerns.

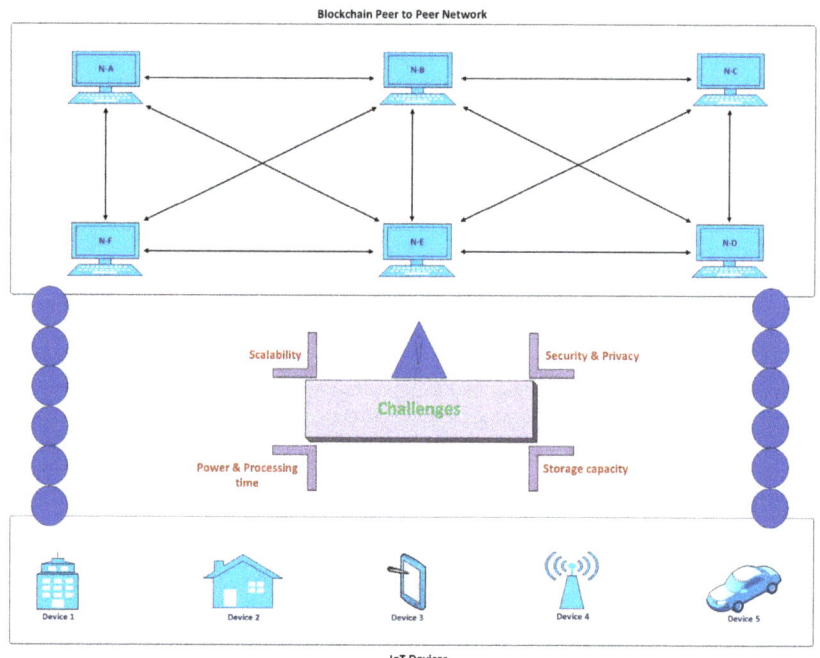

Figure 1. Blockchain IoT challenges.

In blockchain, the consensus is a process of achieving agreement on a single value in a distributed computing environment. The two most popular consensus algorithms are proof of work (PoW) and proof of stake (PoS). However, these algorithms cannot be directly used for IoT scenarios due to their scalability issues [8]. Lightweight consensus algorithms are required for IoT to adopt blockchain because current blockchain platforms such as Bitcoin and Ethereum blockchains are computationally expensive, having high bandwidth overheads and delays for IoT [9]. So, it must be ensured to solve this issue by making a suitable consensus protocol by consulting IoT problems, such as lack of security, different standards of devices, less memory of devices, and a large amount of data. Security and privacy is major concern of the IoT field but if blockchain is involved, then it has to be addressed. A novel blockchain-based approach reported in [10] is used for IoT and suggested that distributed blockchain can solve security concerns for IoT. A decentralized identity management system based on blockchain was presented by [11] which provides security and privacy of the patients for remote healthcare. An idea proposed in [12] is to preserve privacy using blockchain for medical IoT. The storage issue was addressed in [13] for industrial IoT by providing hierarchical blockchain storage structure (ChainSplitter) in which most of the blockchain is stored on the clouds. Blockchain of IoT needs lightweight algorithms to overcome the power and processing time challenges. A lightweight consensus algorithm proof of block and trade (PoBT) is proposed in [14] for BCIoT, which reduces computation time.

In this study, the scalability problem for BCIoT applications is addressed. A very comprehensive study [15] for blockchain IoT explained most of the BCIoT problems by using a mindmap in which scalability is dependent on throughput, block size and transaction speed. This mindmap also tells that throughput for BCIoT can be achieved by proper use of a consensus algorithm. In [16], a strategic approach was used to build a consensus algorithm. It needs attention before the implementation of blockchain in the IoT field. Performance, limitations, and challenges were discussed based on more than one hundred studies for IoT, and protocols which were carefully reviewed before using them for BCIoT.

In the IoT wireless sensor network (WSN), many sensors continuously collect vast amounts of data from the environment and send them to their central processing unit as shown in Figure 2. Blockchain has to validate these data more efficiently. So, several validations per second should be effective in BCIoT. The primary purpose of this study is to make a scalable consensus protocol for BCIoT.

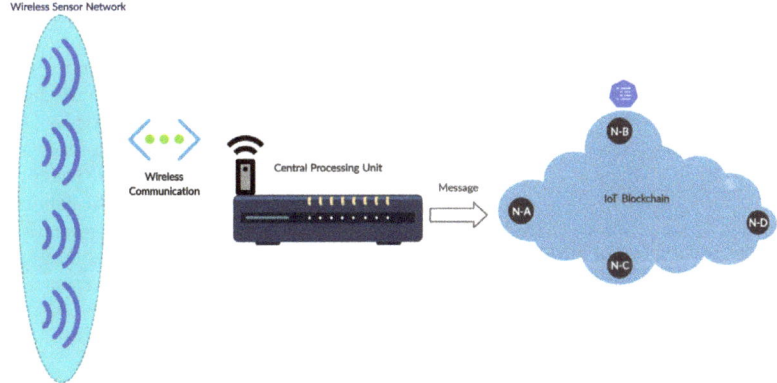

Figure 2. Blockchain for IoT wireless sensor network.

The rest of the paper is structured as follows: the related work is described in Section 2 highlighting the challenges and adopting the existing consensus algorithm for an IoT scenario. The blockchain overview is presented in Section 3 that illustrates the working, consensus, types, and some key terms of blockchain. A novel Consensus algorithm (CB-CIoT) is presented in Section 4 by making suitable changes according to the case study. An analysis is carried out in Section 5 on the proposed algorithm by using flow charts, and results are concluded with limitations. After the analysis and results, conclusions and future work are presented in Section 6.

2. Related Work

This section explains scalability and TPS (Transactions per second) problems, which are improved in cryptocurrencies by consensus algorithms. Different consensus algorithms are the core part of this section; so, a comparison between them is necessary to understand before moving further.

2.1. Scalability Problem

Applying blockchain protocols to IoT can lead us to a new set of problems due to their massive computational loads. Blockchain size grows in IoT with an increase in the number of connected devices, which generates a tremendous amount of data in real-time. This is a major difficulty for IoT blockchain to validate. Many implementations of blockchain in the current cryptocurrencies market are not so scalable according to our required scenario.

In [8], scalability problem was addressed and it was mentioned that this could be the potential barrier for BCIoT because of faster TPS.

2.2. Importance of Consensus

Consensus is very important in the blockchain. Over the period of time, many consensus algorithms have been developed to solve scalability issues. As discussed earlier, the development of blockchain in digital currencies is enormous, so many algorithms are used in this field. Proof of work (PoW) was the first consensus algorithm developed for Bitcoin by Satoshi Nakamoto in 2008 [17]. However, it is believed that this technology was conceived from Hash Cash [18] of Adam Back. He used PoW in his study before the cryptocurrency days. PoW is discussed in this section to understand the consensus in blockchain. A block created in this algorithm takes 10 min due to a large amount of computation power, and if the nodes create the block faster than other nodes, then they get the reward plus a transaction fee. It means that in PoW, the miner requires extra hashing power to get a reward; otherwise, his used resources will be wasted. Selfish mining is another problem [19] with PoW-based blockchain, but practically, it is very hard to get 51% hashing power for a mining pool. A large amount of hashing power is required for PoW to solve a complex problem, make it valuable, and cause an increase in Bitcoin price.

Proof of stake is another consensus algorithm proposed for cryptocurrency in 2011 on Bitcoin forum. It is a hybrid design [20] used to provide network security more than PoW. In this protocol, a stake is required to validate the block, which could be lost on doing a wrong validation. So, 51% attack in this protocol is nearly impossible because it is very hard to get 51% coin out of total value, and there is a threat factor also on doing a wrong validation in terms of stake loss. PoS solves the scalability issue and creates a block faster than PoW. Both PoW and PoS are basic consensus algorithms but they are complete and more decentralized, every new consensus algorithm has to be compared with these in terms of performance.

2.3. Performance Comparison

As blockchain is making progress with every day, new protocols are coming into existence. The scalability issue is also addressed in almost every concurrency. Many new consensus protocols are used in cryptocurrencies. Performance of these consensus algorithms is compared [21] in a delegated way by combining different studies discussed in Table 1. Complete comparison is available in the study, where some protocols are considered as a reference.

Table 1. Performance comparison for different consensus algorithms [21].

Consensus	Decentralization	Accessibility	Scalability	Comp. O.H.	Storage O.H.	Network O.H.	Latency	Throughput	Suitability (IoT)
PoW	High	Public, PL.	High	High	High	Low	High	Low	No
dPBFT	Medium	Private, P.	High	Low	High	High	Medium	High	Partially
Stellar	High	Public, PL.	High	Low	High	Medium	Medium	High	Partially
PoI	High	Public, PL.	High	Low	High	Low	Medium	High	Partially
Ripple	High	Public, PL.	High	Low	High	Medium	Medium	High	Partially
Raft	Medium	Private, P.	High	Low	High	N/A	Low	High	Partially
OmniLedger	High	Public, PL.	High	Medium	Low	Medium	Medium	High	Partially
RapidChain	High	Public, PL.	High	Medium	Low	Low	Medium	High	Partially
DPoS	Medium	Public, PL.	High	Medium	High	N/A	Medium	High	Partially
PoS	High	Private, P or PL	High	Medium	High	Low	Medium	Low	Partially
PoET	Medium	Private, P or PL	High	Low	High	Low	Low	High	Full
PBFT	Medium	Private, P.	Low	Low	High	High	Low	High	Full
Tangle	Medium	Public, PL.	High	Low	Low	Low	Low	High	Full

A cryptocurrency IoTA introduced a very new technology for a distributed ledger called Tangle. It is very highly scalable, with low computing and storage overhead. Moreover, it is very lightweight and specially designed for IoT devices with no transaction fee. Tangle uses DAG (Directed Acyclic Graph) in which each transaction is linked to the previous two transactions approved by it to add on the ledger through PoW. Tangle uses DAG for validation, so that is why it is not considered in the blockchain list and promises to overcome the existing barrier of decentralization for IoT resource-constrained devices. There is no mechanism in Tangle for the selection of the older two nodes to validate in IoT scenario; however, in IoTA cryptocurrency, Tangle runs an algorithm called tip selection for transactions [22]. Another problem is highlighted in [19], if a hacker acquires 33% (one third) hashing power of the total, then it can make it vulnerable and insecure.

As the most trusted platform for computing SGX, Intel proposed a new consensus mechanism proof of elapsed time (PoET) that is primarily based on Byzantine Fault Tolerance (BFT), which focuses on reducing the energy requirement. This protocol is lightweight and perfectly suitable for IoT in public and private ledger domains [23]. The suitability of this protocol can also be checked from the performance comparison table. PBFT (Practical Byzantine Fault Tolerance) is a Byzantine Fault Tolerance protocol, which is highly practical with low algorithm complexity in distributed systems [24] and contains five phases (1) request, (2) pre-prepare, (3) prepare, (4) commit and (5) reply. In PBFT, a client sends a message to the primary node which forwards it to other nodes to reach consensus. The message goes through five phases to complete the round of consensus among nodes and, finally, these nodes reply to the client. Nodes maintain common state to take consistent action in PBFT in each consensus round. PBFT creates and validates the block in DPoS to reduce the time in the consensus round [25]. The Steller consensus protocol (SCP) [26] is an improvement of PBFT which uses the federated byzantine agreement (FBA) protocol to conduct the consensus.

2.4. Continuous Growth in Crypto Market

The Crypto market is developing very fast due to establishing new studies based on new issues in the digital money market. To make digital money more reliable and fast, new lightweight consensuses algorithms emerge to mitigate new threats. A new cryptocurrency called Pi is introduced, which is in the mining phase and about to launch. It uses a very lightweight consensus protocol called Stellar consensus protocol (SCP) [26]. That is why Pi cryptocurrency can be mined easily on cell phones and does not drain the mobile battery, according to their claim. Stellar consensus protocol introduced a new consensus model called federated byzantine agreement (FBA). In a stellar algorithm, every node makes quorum slices by combining nodes on which it trusts. All these quorum slices join together to make a quorum. According to FBA, there should be 67% votes to make a transaction successful, and all the quorums must be joined together by a node to achieve consensus by federated voting. SCP works on two protocols: nomination protocol. All the nodes select transactions for the ledger by a voting process. After that, these nodes prepare and commit transactions by ballot protocol. It is a very scalable protocol for IoT in a public blockchain.

The decentralized control of proof of work and proof of stake is concluded in the previous table can also be seen in Table 2. Still, flexible trust in which users have the right to trust any appropriate combination of a party according to them, was a problem in PoW and PoS protocols. Low latency is a problem in PoW, which is solved in the Ethereum proof of stake (Casper). Digital signatures and hash families parameters are tested with large computing power which is unimaginable to protect against adversaries in Asymptotic Security. Earlier protocols such as PoW and PoS were not asymptotically secure but this problem is solved in the SCP consensus method. Another milestone achieved by SCP is decentralization which was not present in the byzantine agreement. It can be applied to IoT blockchain depending on the blockchain scenarios. If data is sent by IoT devices, after a short interval of time, then there will be a significant difference in block sizes. Another problem with SCP is that its security is highly dependent on the structure of quorum slices and [27] also proved that PBFT is better than FBA in terms of liveness and security. So, SCP could not be the better option for blockchain IoT scenarios, but in terms of decentralization, it is exceptional with the voting mechanism mentioned in its nomination protocol and ballot protocol. The libra blockchain by Facebook [28] is a decentralized and efficient cryptocurrency for billions of people to exchange. This cryptocurrency is in the development phase and will be launched soon. Libra has developed an open-source implementation prototype to validate the design and needs global efforts for advancement its new ecosystem. To discuss Libra blockchain, the challenges are the same as IoT, such as high validation rate, low CPU utilization power of computational power, and it requires a huge storage due to a large number of accounts.

Table 2. Properties of different consensus mechanisms [26].

Mechanism	Decentralized Control	Flexible Trust	Low Latency	Asymptotic Security
Proof of Work	Yes	No	No	No
Proof of Stake	Yes	No	Maybe	Maybe
Byzantine agreement	No	Yes	Yes	Yes
Tendermint	Yes	No	Yes	Yes
SCP	Yes	Yes	Yes	Yes

The raft consensus algorithm is a very suitable consensus method for IoT in a private blockchain scenario. However, it will cause difficulty in public blockchain because if attackers become successful in compromising one node and change its election time out, there will be greater chances for a malicious node to become the leader. Transactions can be manipulated after that. Security is not a prime concern in this study, but in IoT, we have to become conscious due to vulnerabilities present in IoT networks.

The blockchain technology breakthrough in the cryptocurrencies world is unimaginable. This progression starts from the first generation cryptocurrency Bitcoin and moves towards second and third generation coins (Ethereum and Cardano) by gradually resolving complications. The management of Cardano (3rd Generation) coin [29] has been succeeded in overcoming the previous digital money problems such as scalability and TPS by making the PoS protocol more perceptive. They are struggling towards new issues in digital assets. PoW and PoS can be combined together as in [30]. A novel, two-hope blockchain is proposed in it. Analysis of this study shows that blockchain is secure as long as the majority of the resources are controlled by honest players even in the case of more than 50% computing power and controlling high stakes in that system. A very comprehensive survey on consensus algorithms was presented in [31] in which consensus algorithms were classified into two groups: voting and proof-based consensus algorithms. This study proposed a performance comparison between these two categories. In voting-based consensus algorithms, a researcher considered the roles of a node as in the Raft consensus algorithm [32]. It is very famous for which node can be in leader, candidate, and follower state. A follower can discover a new candidate team and the leader. In the voting process, each node has to go to the candidate state to cast a vote. Before going into the candidate state, each node has a different election time between 150 to 300 ms. After election time out, the follower becomes a candidate. Now, the candidate node has the authority to cast a vote for itself, ask for votes from other nodes (followers), and resets their election time. Each node casts a vote on the candidate and resets its election time out. The candidate becomes a leader if it gets a majority of the votes. The leader received transactions requests from many clients and saved them into his log entry list. The leader sends his logged transactions (r) and last transaction index (pi) to followers to make secure transaction orders for all verifying nodes. After verifying that transactions are the same in the list of all the nodes, the leader will choose an index (pi) and commit all transactions before that index. If the leader does not reply to the messages between election time, the new election starts, and another candidate requests a vote to other nodes. The whole process is fine and suitable in private blockchain. Voting-based algorithms are more secure than proof-based algorithms but decentralization becomes low in voting-based algorithms except SCP, in which a voting mechanism is also introduced as discussed earlier. Executing nodes in voting-based algorithms are much less than proof-based algorithms which also causes to increase their performance and scalability in terms of transactions per second (TPS). SCP introduces a flexible trust as discussed earlier but, in Raft, trust becomes much less as compared to proof-based algorithms.

In Table 3, voting-based algorithms are compared with proof-based consensus algorithms. Voting-based consensus minimize decentralization, but security threat becomes low. Performance, scalability, and security issues are the basic problems in IoT blockchain due to maximum data handling and vulnerable IoT devices because of the small memory size and absence of standards in IoT. Blockchain protocols have become mature due to repeated use in digital currency. So, the selection of a consensus algorithm becomes easy, and we can also design our desired consensus algorithm according to our IoT scenario requirements by consulting cryptocurrencies protocols and problems related to IoT. The problem presented in this study can be solved by using a suitable consensus algorithm for BCIoT or by making appropriate changes in the existing algorithms.

Table 3. Difference between proof-based and vote-based consensus algorithms [31].

Criterion	Proof-Based Consensus	Vote-Based Consensus
Join nodes freely	Mostly	No
Decentralization	High	Low
executing nodes	Unlimited	Limited
Trust	More Trustful	Less Trustful
Award	More Serious	Less Serious
Security threat	Yes	Mostly No
Examples	PoW, PoS	Raft

In this section, consensus algorithms are discussed, which are used in a public and private blockchain. We have seen that transactions per second (TPS) were also a problem in early cryptocurrencies and improved later by different consensus algorithms. In IoT, there is a need of an efficient and scalable consensus protocol. In this study, a case study is taken in the next section, which require an efficient and scalable consensus algorithm for IoT devices by tolerating delay in communication.

3. Blockchain Overview

Blockchain is a decentralized and distributed public ledger used to record immutable transactions across a peer-to-peer network, i.e., without the need of a third party to monitor mediate transactions, and cryptographic mechanisms are used to secure transactions or blocks. This section presents an overview of the blockchain technology, including the key terms and its use-cases.

3.1. Blockchain Key Terms

To understand blockchain, it is necessary to be aware of its key terms. There are many terms used in blockchain and needed to be understand, but some important terms are discussed here. These terms are used in this study frequently, and it will not be easy to move further without understanding them.

1. Blocks: Blocks contain transaction data, which include sender address, receivers address, transaction amount, transaction fee, last block reference number (hash), and time stamp. There are multiple transactions stored in a block that a validator or miner must verify. It nearly takes ten minutes for Bitcoin to produce the new block.
2. Nodes: In a blockchain, each computer of a peer-to-peer network is called a node. These nodes float the transactions over a network for verification and store them in

their public ledger. The main objective of the nodes is to send the transaction from sender to receiver in a secure way.
3. Distributed Public Ledger: It records all the transactions so that no one can change it. If someone tries to make a change via any node, then it will not be accepted during consensus between nodes.
4. Consensus: It is a general agreement between all nodes in the blockchain. When a block is produced, all the nodes must be agreed if any of the node is changed or manipulated, the other nodes will not accept this change. The consensus mechanism creates a trust between all the nodes and a step towards blockchain immutability.
5. Flooding: Transactions reach every node by a process called flooding. When a node receives data, it sends them to all other nodes because mining will be started when a node receives all the data on the network.
6. Miner/Validator: A validator or miner is a computer that validates the transactions by calculating the hash, stores it in its ledger, and broadcasts it to the network. In bitcoin, many computers try to validate the block and the computer which solves it first gets the transaction fees and block reward.
7. Nonce: It is very easy to calculate the simple SHA-256 hash for certain data, but it becomes much more complex when the computer produces a block hash that meets certain requirements. In simple words, a nonce is a number to achieve a certain difficulty level added to the block for which the validator takes too much time and calculates several hashes until the desired result (hash) has been obtained.

3.2. Types of Blockchain

There are two main types of blockchain i.e. Public and Private, and a combination of public and private blockchain is also used which is called Consortium or Hybrid blockchain.
1. Public blockchain: A blockchain which is openly available to miners, developers and members of its community. All the transactions in public blockchain are transparent and accessible to everyone. Public blockchain is fully decentralized where no individual or entity is controlling it. Most of the cryptocurrencies blockchains are public such as Bitcoin and Etereum.
2. Private blockchain: Blockchain where only allowed persons can join the network and transactions are also available to its blockchain participants. Private blockchain is more centralized than the public one. Most of the enterprises do no want to disclose their sensitive data between groups of customers or want to hide their offers to specific customers. Ripple and Hyper-ledger are using it.

3.3. Blockchain Use Cases

Blockchain is used in almost every industry today. In this section, some interesting use cases will be discussed which are gaining more attention and causing an increase in blockchain importance. As the technology is growing every day, the adoption of blockchain is also climbing up exponentially.

Internet of Vehicles (IoV) is a fascinating topic and related to IoT in real-time response. In [33], it was mentioned that blockchain is effective for IoV due to its decentralized and distributed storage, and an outward transmission model was proposed by numerical and theoretical analysis. Security is essential in mobile-based IoV because there are large number of malicious attackers, so an authentication mechanism that is decentralized is proposed [34] based on the blockchain consensus algorithm. Car parking is another challenge for resident people and drivers in a highly densely populated area. A blockchain-based car parking system [35] which shares resources of paid parking between user and owner. Need for the third party is removed in this study, and resources are used intelligently. Supply chain management can be used in private blockchain [36] with the protocol of ultra-lightweight RFID. In this scenario, nodes of the supply chain are divided into four categories (distributor, retailer,end-use and manufacturer) which need a different level of access. In this study, the proposed protocol also provides security by reducing attacks, such as a man in the middle, reply, key disclosure, and tracking. In industry, a credit-based PoW mechanism was proposed [37] which minimizes the consumption of power for nodes and increases security for malicious nodes. A novel reporting system based on blockchain ReportCoin was proposed in [38], which is used in the smart city for the management. Security of transactions and user identity is increased due to the decentralized nature of blockchain. This study creates trust between sender and receiver without disclosing the sender's identity. PETchain [39] is based on blockchain that uses it to enhance privacy. Different hospitals lag control the electronic health records (EHRs) during the information sharing process. This problem is controlled by cloud-based EHRs in which sharing of information becomes easy, but the centralization problem of the cloud emerges. In [40], the system model of blockchain-based EHRs is highlighted to overcome centralized issues. An identity-based signature scheme is used to reduce collision attacks. An electronic health wallet (EHW) system [41] is proposed that uses decentralized technologies such as blockchain to ensure data privacy and interoperability. Due to developments in blockchain and IoT, a transaction model for accounting was proposed in [42] which is capable of collecting, uploading, and recording the data automatically. IoT (Internet of things) is globally adopted in many areas, such as medical, houses, industries, etc. The combination of IoT and blockchain is also a mature topic, and there are many studies on LightChain resource-efficient blockchain for industrial IoT [43]. Access management in IoT using blockchain [1] and authentication scheme in IoT using blockchain [44] is presented. A design for IoT blockchain [45] by using PoS protocol for Bazo cryptocurrency [46] in the presence of Lora nodes and gateways is presented, which mean blockchain can be designed for IoT using consensus protocols.

4. Methodology

A consensus algorithm is designed by considering the problem statement and dataset of IoT wireless sensor network. Changes are done in the consensus by consulting cryptocurrency algorithms and explained in this section by using suitable examples. CBCIoT is ready to test according to the scenario used at the end of Section 4. BCIoT scenario is different from cryptocurrencies' transactions. As we talked about, any consensus protocol for this kind of blockchain cannot be implemented easily. Therefore, changes in consensus protocol are required to make it intelligent for BCIoT.

- In cryptocurrencies, we deal with transactions, but a massive amount of data in IoT blockchain needs to be handled. So, the broadcast domain should be limited, and we could survive from waiting for a validation process.
- If data are distributed to all nodes in the network, they will cause the network to slow down. They should be distributed to selected nodes or groups of nodes.
- In IoT, data are used instead of coins, so a proper validator/miner selection technique should be used. A validator is selected in PoS by selection techniques in cryptocurrencies, i.e., coin age-based selection (validator is selected by multiplication age of the coins in days with several coins that are being staked) and Randomized block selection (the next validator is selected by combining the lowest hash value and the size of their stakes).
- In cryptocurrencies, the miners get the reward and punishment for doing wrong, if they are selected by the PoS protocol. So here, we cannot punish, but we can lower machine ratings. We can also apply the error detection and correction method to the validator.
- We cannot rely on a single node to validate the data in our scenario. So, there should be multiple nodes for this purpose.
- There should be randomness in the consensus protocol to make it difficult for the attacker. Although security is not the prime topic in this study, we need to keep some basics in our minds because of vulnerabilities present in IoT.

4.1. Problem Solving Strategy by Consensus

The validation rate can be increased by choosing a suitable consensus algorithm, as previously discussed. So here, we will try to develop a new consensus algorithm for BCIoT. Nodes are taken in this algorithm as follows (total number of nodes = N)

$$N = mv + 1 \tag{1}$$

v (where v = 3, 5, 7, 9....) is the number of validating nodes, m (where m = 2, 3, 4.5.......) is a multiple validating nodes. Values of m and v are to be chosen carefully. On choosing small values, randomness could be compromised, which leads to compromise the security. In the case of choosing large values, the validation rate will slow down and affect the algorithm's performance. The selection of nodes should be

$$Selection of validating nodes = (N-1)/m \tag{2}$$

An answer should be a whole number or $N-1$ should be divisible by m. In this study, we mostly use m = 3 and v = 5. For example, if N = 16, Master = 1, $N-1 = mv = 3(5) = 15$.

4.1.1. Master Node

The master node will be selected by voting, which can select five nodes for validation and verification.

4.1.2. Voting

Every node can send a token (number with time stamp) called vote to only one node randomly at a time, which helps to select the master node. Voting process is also explained in [32] but, in this study, a simple voting scheme is used to select the master for one turn. After sending the token, a node with more votes(V)*ratings(R) than others must be a master node.

$$Master node selection = V X R \tag{3}$$

4.1.3. Rating

It is a fractional number (R) between -10 to 10, which is increased by first validating the block (the same like the winner gets the reward in PoW) and decreased by doing wrong validation and verification (such as loss of stakes in PoS). In this scenario, validation reward and punishment are in terms of rating.

4.2. Procedure

Consensus in blockchain IoT (CBCIoT) is designed according to the scenario discussed in the dataset. Voting mechanisms are discussed in the previous section of related work. Some changes are needed to be made in the voting process. The procedure of working for CBCIoT algorithm is as follows.

- Every node will send data to the master node, which is selected by all the blockchain nodes in the voting process.
- Master node will receive data for 30 s (to collect maximum one time data) explained in the dataset section; after this period, a master node will send data to 5 randomly selected nodes for validation.
- Five nodes will create a block, and only one node will first send the block to the other four nodes for verification (difficulty level can be added to check the difference).
- If a block is created by more than one node at the same time, the block with greater number of verifications will win.
- After validation and verification, the block and information are broadcasted by the master to all blockchain nodes, which will be stored in their ledger.
- After a block is created, the same procedure is repeated for the next block.

- Genesis block will be created by the blockchain standard procedure.

4.3. Points of Concern

The working procedure is explained. There are some limitations that can affect the performance of CBCIoT. So, it is needed to be carefully viewed in the below points before moving further.

- All the nodes should be time-wise synchronized.
- Master node selection procedure should be fast to collect data from other nodes.
- $N - 1$ nodes have to wait a little bit to send data to master every time.
- Simulation should be flexible so that number of nodes, time, etc., can be changed to check the differences in results.

4.4. Explanation with Example

Node A is selected as a master from $N = 16$ nodes as shown in Figure 3, and it further selects five nodes for validation and sends data to 5 nodes to generate a block. All the nodes create the selection of master by a voting process. In this process, every single node can vote for one node at a time. Once a master is selected, all the blockchain nodes can send data to the master. Next, the master selects five nodes (but never selects more than one node with a rating less than 0) and sends data to them for validation. Validating nodes generate a block and, after verification, sends it back to master, which is broadcasted to all IoT blockchain nodes to store in their public ledger. Why does the master select odd (e.g., 5) nodes for validation?

- If it selects all the nodes, then validation will be slowed down as discussed in PoW.
- In case one node for validation could be a better option and blockchain performs efficiently, the attacker can insert data and validate them, if this node is compromised.
- In the case of 3 validating nodes, if one node is compromised, then the generated block will be accurate but less reliable due to one verification.
- If two nodes create two blocks simultaneously, then one block will win due to a greater number of verifications, and it is well performed in an odd number of nodes.

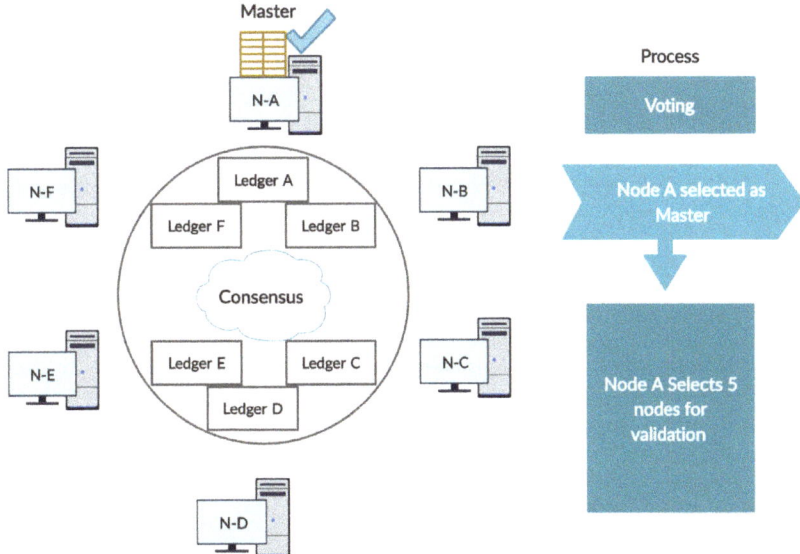

Figure 3. BCIoT working.

So, an odd number of validating nodes could be a better option, and reliability will be increased for a more significant number of verifications. In the case of validation, nodes greater than five will make the block more authentic, but the validation rate will be decreased. So, selection of validating nodes should be according to the required scenario.

4.5. Phases of Nodes in IoT Blockchain

In this proposed consensus algorithm, blockchain nodes move through different phases. The initial phase is the long phase of this consensus in which every node has no options except to collect data from IoT systems.

After the initial phase, all nodes go into a temporary phase called the election phase, in which every node has the right to cast only one vote for a random node for choosing the master node. When a master is chosen according to Equation (3), all $N - 1$ nodes go back to the initial phase.

Now, the Master node has the right to select validating nodes (v) from $N - 1$ nodes. Total validating nodes are shown in Equation (2). They are selected randomly and consult their ratings also with the master node. These validators validate and verify the block for IoT blockchain. When the block is broadcast to all blockchain nodes, all the nodes, validators, and masters return to the initial phase, and the process starts again. The whole process is shown in Figure 4.

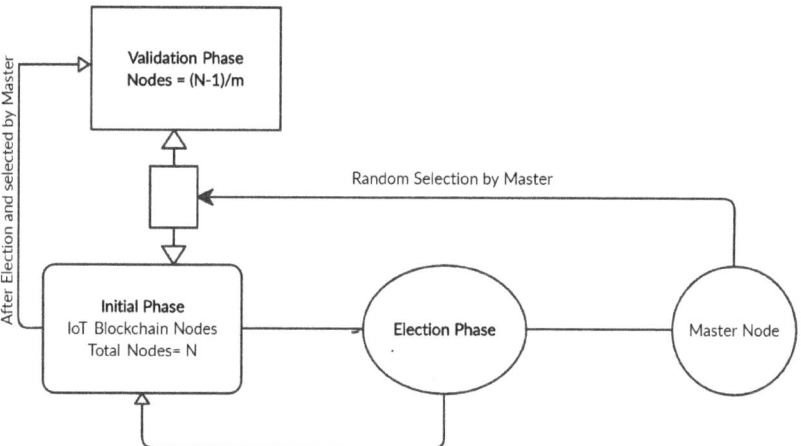

Figure 4. Different phases of BCIoT nodes.

4.6. Dataset

To verify our consensus algorithm, a dataset is chosen which is collected during deployment. This dataset is taken from the Remote Management System (RMS), also called Fuel Management System (FMS), deployed on Warid sites to control fuel theft. It is an IoT system packet with lot of information shown in Figure 5. RMS control panel makes decisions on-site (analysis and store in buffer) before sending information to the server after every 30 s. Each site sends 78 Bytes of data and the server was collecting more than 500 packets after regular intervals. An initial experiment was carried out on 1000 packets (samples) to record on the blockchain. An efficient system consists of two panels:

1. RMS Panel;
2. Fuel Sensor Box.

The RMS panel placed inside the site room to monitor phases of WAPDA (Water & Power Development Authority) and generator, room temperature, panel temperature, and voltages of the two battery banks. The code 1.1.1 means all three phases of WAPDA or generator are working. If any phase is missing, then it will show 0 instead of 1. A generator is started by using these calculations to charge batteries or to switch on the air conditioner in the room as in VTDC (voltage and Temperature-Dependent Control).

The sensor box was the second most important part of this system which is located on the fuel tank outside the site room. It has three ultrasonic sensors to calculate the fuel in the tank. Three sensors are used for correctness in the reading. It also calculates the temperature of the fuel by the temperature sensor. Sensor boxes transmit these readings to the main RMS panel to calculate theft or usage of fuel on the site.

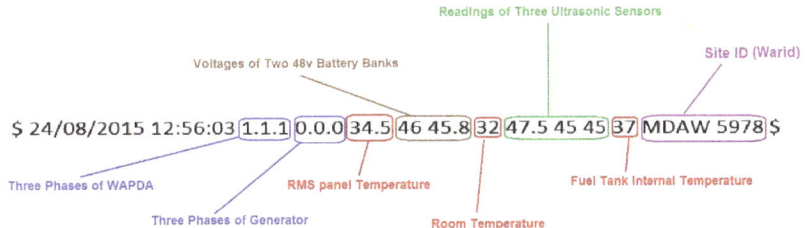

Figure 5. Remote management system.

4.7. Key Metrics of Performance

In this study, a public blockchain is used and a new consensus algorithm is proposed; so, it is needed to check its nature in terms of centralization and decentralization. Scalability of the consensus algorithm is another problem for IoT blockchain which is tested for different transactions. Throughput and verification speed of this algorithm is needed to be verified and compared with other algorithms.

5. Analysis and Results

The core section of this paper consists of a detailed analysis on the basis of its operation. Three major properties of CBCIoT algorithm are a part of this section. Worst case scenario is considered in the case study; after that, results are drawn to strengthen the blockchain IoT environment.

5.1. Sequence of Operations

In this study, the proposed algorithm's work is suitable for IoT blockchain, where a slight time delay (wait to collect data from all sites) is required. The working principle of this algorithm can be understood easily by this flow chart.

The flow chart shown in Figure 6 is used to understand the process of this consensus algorithm in the case of validating nodes (v = 5) and integral multiple (m = 3). Data receiving and voting processes are running in parallel. If the master node is selected, then data are transmitted to it, which will be further sent to validating nodes after selecting and removing duplicates from the data. Data collection by BCIoT nodes and master transmission to validating nodes is an about 30-s long process as we have seen this time delay in RMS. The master node also removes duplicate values by comparing data values. Hash for Genesis block in this consensus algorithm is created and stored in the ledger of all the blockchain nodes on the initial stages. The master node will broadcast the block to all BCIoT nodes and increase the rating of the first validator. The voting process is started to select the next master. This process runs in parallel with the previous validation process, but in this case, any prior validator or master could not be selected again. They have to wait for one turn more.

5.2. Unpredictability in the Algorithm

This consensus algorithm uses three integral multiples (m) for five validating nodes (v), which could be changed according to our scenario requirements. The selection of the master node is random by voting, and its probability is 0.0625 in case of a total of 16 nodes and goes on decreasing by increasing the total number of nodes. The master node selects additional five nodes with a probability $p(v)$ of 0.3333 for validation, making it impossible for the attacker to compromise a node. For example, in the worst-case scenario, one or two validating nodes are compromised. Still, they cannot validate the block because the other three nodes will validate and verify the block due to the majority (discussed in the case study section of this chapter).

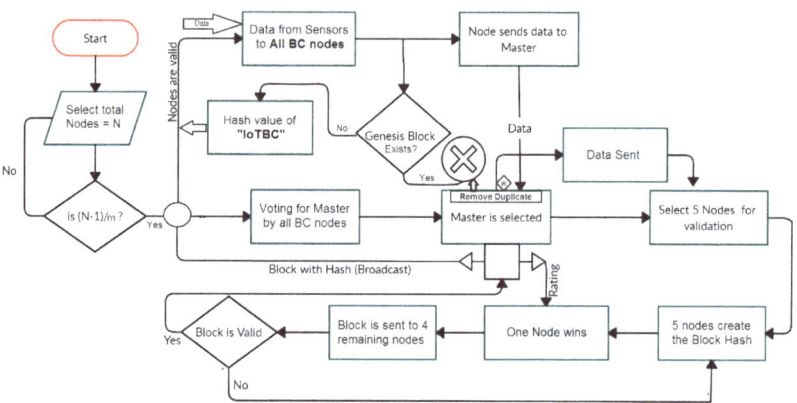

Figure 6. CBCIoT flow chart.

In this study, one node is selected as a master node, and validating nodes (v) and multiple (m) could be selected according to Equation (1) in the previous section. However, if we consider more than 5 validating nodes (v), blockchain working becomes less efficient, and computational power is increased, as we have seen in the Bitcoin scenario. Selecting v less than 5 for validating will lead the blockchain to compromise its security and fewer block verifications as security is not tested. Still, we have to assume this due to vulnerabilities present in IoT. Suppose one node produces a block and three nodes are selected for verification of this produced block. In that case, only three verifications are considered to be received in an ideal scenario. These block verifications can be decreased if one or more nodes are malicious or do not agree upon a newly generated block.

Randomness can be increased by increasing the integral multiple of validating nodes (m), increasing $N - 1$ nodes by m times for a specific number of validating nodes (v). For example, in this study, we are using $m = 3$ and $v = 5$ which means ($N - 1$) = 15, i.e., 3 times 5. By decreasing m, randomness could be decreased, and the probability of validating nodes selection by master $p(v)$ will increase and leads towards less security of the blockchain. In this case, master node selection by voting will also become more probable (e.g., 1/16 for $m = 3$, 1/11 for $m = 2$ and 1/6 for $m = 1$). That is why the value of m is greater than 2. If we select $m = 2$, then validating the node's selection probability becomes exactly half. The value of m could not be one because the probability of validating nodes selection is equal to 1. It is much easier for the attacker to manipulate the transactions by compromising 60 percent BCIoT, validating nodes and guessing the master node. Compromising a master node could be much more harmful in our CBCIoT scenario.

The probability of validating nodes selection by master $p(v)$ decreased by increasing the number of integral multiple (m) and $v = 5$ (constant). In our scenario, for $m = 3$, probability is 0.33; this is also shown in Figure 7 and goes on decreasing for greater values of m.

Figure 8 shows the total approximate time for validation and verification per block, which goes on increasing v and $m = 3$ for 7000 samples. A time delay of 30 s is included in the graph as it can be seen that every block is validated more than 30 seconds. If the master takes more nodes for validation, then one node creates a block first, and the remaining nodes verify it and send the verified block back to the master for broadcasting in IoT blockchain. Every node on the blockchain will store this new block into its ledger. So, the number of verifications is increased by increasing v, but the block producing time is also climbing up.

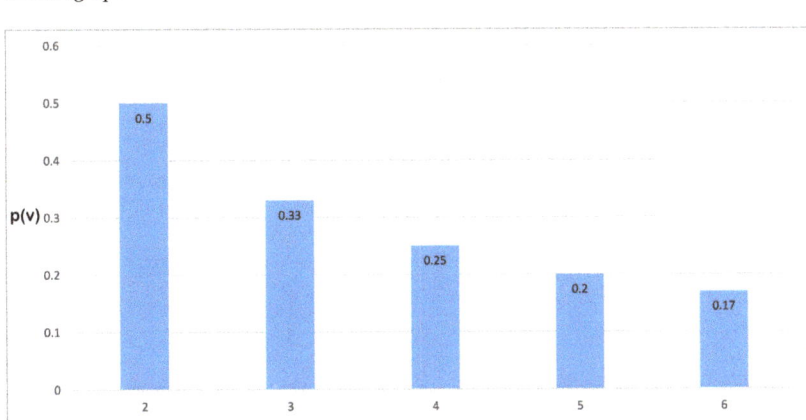

Figure 7. Probability of validating nodes.

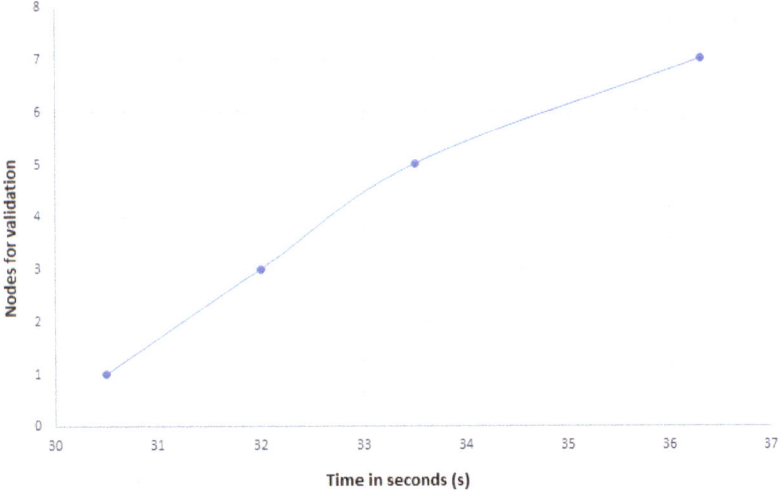

Figure 8. Total time for validation and verification per block.

5.3. Limited Broadcast Domain

It can be seen that data are transmitted to the master by all BCIoT nodes, so flooding is minimized. It could be a major threat to BCIoT, which will cause a decrease in the efficiency, validation, and verification rate. As we further see, this algorithm, validation, and verification performed by a limited number of validators will also cause an increase in the validation rate. Hypothetically, it is assumed that after validation and verification performed by all nodes, there will be greater chances of delay in the consensus.

5.4. Flexibility in the Algorithm

As it can be seen in previous sections, this algorithm is flexible and can be changed according to IoT scenario requirements. We have discussed that the integral multiplier (m) can be increased to maximize security in terms of randomness, and validating nodes (v) can also use different numbers according to the number of validations per the second requirement. The value of N, m, and v can be selected according to Equation (1) in the previous section. We choose to select integral multiplier m to increase randomness or validate nodes v according to block generation time and verification speed.

5.5. Case Study

To check the efficiency of the proposed algorithm, we assume a case study in which the attacker can compromise two validating nodes out of five and try to manipulate or insert his data. Although, it is challenging for the attacker due to its randomness, but we are taking it as a worst-case scenario. This is clearly shown in Figure 9 where the attacker takes control of two validating nodes.

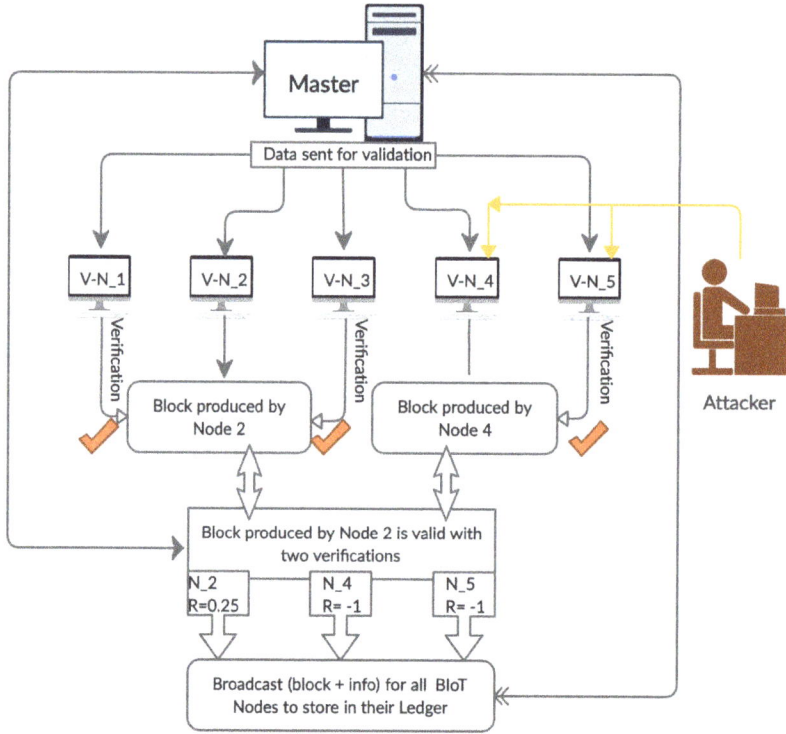

Figure 9. Case study for blockchain IoT.

Then, two blocks will be produced:
- Block produced by node 2 with two verifications;
- Block produced by malicious node 4 with one verification.

After the block is produced by node 2, it is valid due to the more significant number of verifications. So, the master increased its rating by 0.25 and decreased the ratings of malicious nodes 4 and 5 by one due to wrong validation and verification.

In the previous section, Equation (3) describes the criteria for master node selection. In our case study, the rating is decreased by -1. So, their chances of becoming masters are less than other nodes because the rating is multiplied by the number of votes, and the whole value becomes negative. These two malicious nodes can become masters only if they do four or more validations right by retaining first place in every validation. Their chances of becoming validating nodes are also affected because the master will not select more than one validating node with negative ratings. If one of them becomes a validating node again and does something wrong, its rating will be furthermore decreased in the same way.

5.6. Results

To verify our algorithm, a Java-based simulation tool is used in Ubuntu environment. This simulation tool can create a new blockchain, computer network, consensus algorithm, and changes in the existing blockchain to support PoW and PoS protocols. This simulation tool saves its output in

ROOT DIR/simulator/src/dist/output

The code 000 in hash is the difficulty level set in this blockchain 2.0. First hash

000eb84c1db7b85ffbda9315ef64ffd4c50da90cacd3a27e06c33f2ab3fc6da5

which is used in Genesis block as a previous hash, it is created by taking a hash of "IoTBC" in multiple attempts to get 000 on the leftmost position by adding a random number at the beginning of this consensus algorithm. RMS data of 1000 samples (1000 × 78 Bytes) are tested on initial level; then increased to check the performance of CBCIot. The calculated time to produce a block is different due to different amounts of data and the number of hashing performed to meet this blockchain difficulty level. The time to produce a block is about 35 s for 6–7 thousand samples, and after that, the block generation time is increased a little bit as shown in Figure 10 (slightly more than 35 s).

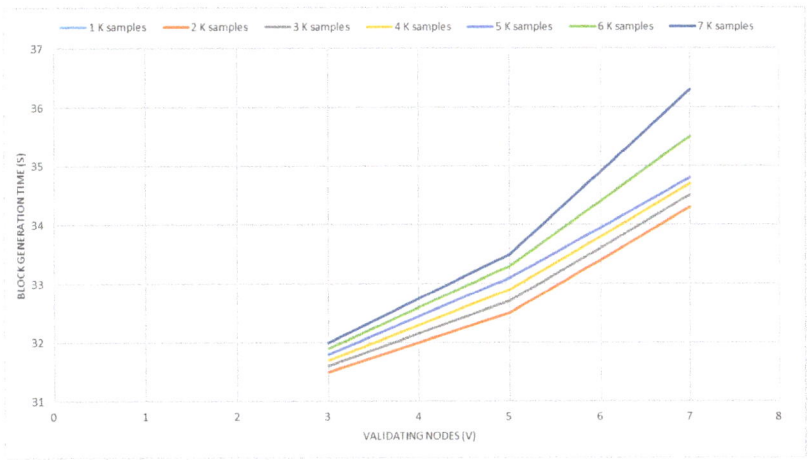

Figure 10. Block generation time for different samples.

This algorithm is tested for 5 validating nodes (v) and multiple (m) 3 on priority basis after that relation between m and v is verified according to Equation (1) by taking nodes mentioned in Equation (2). Master node selection is checked as in Equation (3) on the initial level and also verified by lower the rating (R). The performance of the proposed algorithm (CBCIoT) is fine after carefully reviewing the results, and limitations are also discussed in the next subsection.

Table 4 shows the comparisons of the proposed consensus algorithm with other consensus algorithms. Protocol data are chosen from [26,47] and compared with our proposed algorithm. CBCIoT is tested on blockchain 2.0 and it has some properties of PoW and PoS. A voting mechanism is also used for the selection of master, so it is important to compare with other voting algorithms such as SCP and RAFT. The voting process is introduced to select a master for one turn and, then, a master selects validating nodes to generate a block. In the next turn, the master and validating nodes are changed and this process is continuous for every new block. It shows that CBCIoT is decentralized in which every node has equal opportunity to become master and validator. Algorithm is tested for different samples (1000–7000) with different combinations of m and v, every time it worked perfectly fine which shows its strong scalabilty. The verification speed of the block is better as compared to other algorithms. However, block generation time is nearly 35 s in the proposed algorithm. It is not comparable because of the 30 s delay to collect data in our scenario and less data size of a single RMS system. However, if delay is ignored, then its throughput lies in the range of (250 to 1500) TPS or samples per second for 1000 to 7000 samples, which clearly indicates that CBCIoT has a high throughput. Block is verified less than 5 s for every experiment made with up to 7000 samples, and it is same like SCP and RAFT.

Table 4. Comparisons between consensus algorithms [26,47].

Characteristics	PoW	PoS	DPoS	RAFT	SCP	CBCIoT (Study)
Accessibility	Public	Public, Private	Public	Private	Public	Public
Decentralization	High	high	High	Medium	High	High
Throughput	Low	Low	High	High	High	High
Scalibility	Strong	Strong	Strong	Weak	Strong	Strong
verification Speed	>100 s	<100 s	<100 s	<5 s	<5 s	<5 s

5.7. Limitations

In this study, the proposed algorithm can be used in different scenarios; as discussed earlier, its performance is enough to fulfill the BCIoT requirement used in our described scenario (discussed in the dataset section of the previous section). However, it is simulated and has some limitations:

- Its working is fine for block size <500 KB, and performance could be degraded a little bit for larger block size as discussed in the results section.
- Difficulty level directly affects it because the number of hashes per block is increased, and it is tested on blockchain 2.0.
- Selection of master node cannot be performed twice consecutively for a single node if its block is not broadcasted.
- Validator node cannot become a Master in the next round if it is a validator in the previous block and master does not broadcast this block in the IoT blockchain.
- This algorithm is working in public blockchain and not tested for private blockchain.
- Security is kept in mind during its construction due to vulnerable IoT systems, but it has not been not tested or tried to compromise it.
- It is suitable and working fine for IoT scenarios where a little delay is present or can be tolerated.

6. Conclusions and Future Work

Blockchain has great potential in the IoT field, but issues such as scalability, security and privacy, power and processing time and storage capacity are complex and mature due to the combination of these two giant technologies. The scalability problem could be solved by designing a proper consensus algorithm. In this study, a consensus algorithm "CBCIOT" is designed for blockchain-based IoT applications, working perfectly for IoT devices that are not delay-sensitive. Limited broadcast domain causes to increase its efficiency. It can be configured according to IoT requirements due to the flexibility present in the algorithm. In this algorithm, a delay (wait to collect maximum one time data from IoT devices) is required, so it will be a great choice to use it for other IoT scenarios where delay can be tolerated. This study is only based on a consensus algorithm, so parameters that affect its scalability and throughput are addressed adequately. Results show its reliability and make it proficient in TPS and verifications (<5 s) such as present-day voting-based algorithms in cryptocurrencies. The anonymity of master node selection and validating nodes by a master make it protective against attacks. Although it has not been tried to compromise this algorithm, this could be a topic for future work.

Author Contributions: Conceptualization, M.U., M.M. and M.K.H.; methodology, M.U. and M.M.; validation, M.U.; writing—original draft preparation, I.T.J. and M.K.H.; writing—review and editing, B.A. and N.C.; visualization, I.T.J.; funding acquisition, N.C. All authors have read and agreed to the published version of the manuscript.

Funding: This work is partly supported with the financial support of the Science Foundation Ireland grant 13/RC/2094_P2 and partly funded from the European Union's Horizon 2020 research and innovation programme under the Marie Skłodowska–Curie grant agreement No 754489.

Conflicts of Interest: The authors declare no conflict of interest

References

1. Novo, O. Blockchain meets IoT: An architecture for scalable access management in IoT. *IEEE Internet Things J.* **2018**, *5*, 1184–1195. [CrossRef]
2. Panarello, A.; Tapas, N.; Merlino, G.; Longo, F.; Puliafito, A. Blockchain and iot integration: A systematic survey. *Sensors* **2018**, *18*, 2575. [CrossRef]
3. Abou Jaoude, J.; Saade, R.G. Blockchain applications–usage in different domains. *IEEE Access* **2019**, *7*, 45360–45381. [CrossRef]
4. Atlam, H.F.; Wills, G.B. Technical aspects of blockchain and IoT. In *Advances in Computers*; Elsevier: Amsterdam, The Netherlands, 2019; Volume 115, pp. 1–39.
5. Padma, M.; KasiViswanath, N.; Swathi, T. Blockchain for iot application: challenges and issues. *Int. J. Recent Technol. Eng.* **2019**, *7*, 34–37.
6. Banafa, A. 7 IoT and Blockchain: Challenges and Risks. In *Blockchain Technology and Applications*; River Publishers: Gistrup, Denmark, 2020.
7. Qureshi, K.N.; Sandila, M.A.S.; Javed, I.T.; Margaria, T.; Aslam, L. Authentication scheme for Unmanned Aerial Vehicles based Internet of Vehicles networks. *Egypt. Inform. J.* **2021**. [CrossRef]
8. Zheng, Z.; Xie, S.; Dai, H.; Chen, X.; Wang, H. An overview of blockchain technology: Architecture, consensus, and future trends. In Proceedings of the 2017 IEEE International Congress on Big Data (BigData Congress), Honolulu, HI, USA, 25–30 June 2017; pp. 557–564.
9. Dorri, A.; Kanhere, S.S.; Jurdak, R. Towards an optimized blockchain for IoT. In Proceedings of the 2017 IEEE/ACM Second International Conference on Internet-of-Things Design and Implementation (IoTDI), Pittsburgh, PA, USA, 18–21 April 2017; pp. 173–178.
10. Mohanta, B.K.; Satapathy, U.; Panda, S.S.; Jena, D. A novel approach to solve security and privacy issues for iot applications using blockchain. In Proceedings of the 2019 International Conference on Information Technology (ICIT), Bhubaneswar, India, 19–21 December 2019; pp. 394–399.
11. Javed, I.T.; Alharbi, F.; Bellaj, B.; Margaria, T.; Crespi, N.; Qureshi, K.N. Health-ID: A Blockchain-Based Decentralized Identity Management for Remote Healthcare. *Healthcare* **2021**, *9*, 712. [CrossRef] [PubMed]
12. Alamri, B.; Javed, I.T.; Margaria, T. Preserving patients' privacy in medical IoT using blockchain. In Proceedings of the International Conference on Edge Computing, Honolulu, HI, USA, 22–26 June 2020; pp. 103–110.
13. Wang, G.; Shi, Z.; Nixon, M.; Han, S. Chainsplitter: Towards blockchain-based industrial iot architecture for supporting hierarchical storage. In Proceedings of the 2019 IEEE International Conference on Blockchain (Blockchain), Atlanta, GA, USA, 14–17 July 2019; pp. 166–175.
14. Biswas, S.; Sharif, K.; Li, F.; Maharjan, S.; Mohanty, S.P.; Wang, Y. PoBT: A lightweight consensus algorithm for scalable IoT business blockchain. *IEEE Internet Things J.* **2019**, *7*, 2343–2355. [CrossRef]
15. Fernández-Caramés, T.M.; Fraga-Lamas, P. A Review on the Use of Blockchain for the Internet of Things. *IEEE Access* **2018**, *6*, 32979–33001. [CrossRef]
16. Ferrag, M.A.; Derdour, M.; Mukherjee, M.; Derhab, A.; Maglaras, L.; Janicke, H. Blockchain technologies for the internet of things: Research issues and challenges. *IEEE Internet Things J.* **2018**, *6*, 2188–2204. [CrossRef]
17. Nakamoto, S. Bitcoin: A Peer-to-Peer Electronic Cash System. Technical Report. 2008. Available online: https://bitcoin.org/bitcoin.pdf (accessed on 10 January 2021).
18. Back, A. Hashcash-a Denial of Service Counter-Measure. 2002. Available online: http://www.hashcash.org/hashcash.pdf (accessed on 16 January 2021).
19. Lo, S.K.; Liu, Y.; Chia, S.Y.; Xu, X.; Lu, Q.; Zhu, L.; Ning, H. Analysis of blockchain solutions for IoT: A systematic literature review. *IEEE Access* **2019**, *7*, 58822–58835. [CrossRef]
20. King, S.; Nadal, S. Ppcoin: Peer-to-Peer Crypto-Currency with Proof-of-Stake. Self-Published Paper. 19 August 2012. https://www.chainwhy.info/upload/default/20180619/126a057fef926dc286accb372da46955.pdf (accessed on 16 January 2021).
21. Salimitari, M.; Chatterjee, M. A survey on consensus protocols in blockchain for iot networks. *arXiv* **2018**, arXiv:1809.05613.
22. Popov, S. The Tangle. [Online] 2016. http://www.descryptions.com/Iota.pdf (accessed on 22 February 2021).
23. Corso, A. Performance Analysis of Proof-of-Elapsed-Time (PoET) Consensus in the Sawtooth Blockchain Framework. Ph.D. Thesis, University of Oregon, Eugene, OR, USA, 2019.

24. Castro, M.; Liskov, B. Practical byzantine fault tolerance. In *OSDI*; The USENIX Association: Berkeley, CA, USA, 1999; Volume 99, pp. 173–186.
25. Swathi, B.; Meghana, M.; Lokamathe, P. An Analysis on Blockchain Consensus Protocols for Fault Tolerance. In Proceedings of the 2021 2nd International Conference for Emerging Technology (INCET), Belagavi, India, 21–23 May 2021; pp. 1–4.
26. Mazieres, D. *The Stellar Consensus Protocol: A Federated Model for Internet-Level Consensus*; Stellar Development Foundation: San Francisco, CA, USA, 2015; Volume 32.
27. Kim, M.; Kwon, Y.; Kim, Y. Is Stellar as secure as you think? In Proceedings of the 2019 IEEE European Symposium on Security and Privacy Workshops (EuroS&PW), Stockholm, Sweden, 17–19 June 2019; pp. 377–385.
28. Amsden, Z.; Arora, R.; Bano, S.; Baudet, M.; Blackshear, S.; Bothra, A.; Cabrera, G.; Catalini, C.; Chalkias, K.; Cheng, E.; et al. The Libra Blockchain. Calibra Corp. 2019. https://mitsloan.mit.edu/shared/ods/documents?PublicationDocumentID=5859 (accessed on 14 April 2021).
29. Guides, T.S. Why Cardano ADA Deserves Your Attention–Cardano Cryptocurrency Strategy. 2018. https://tradingstrategyguides.com/cardano-cryptocurrency-strategy/ (accessed on 10 January 2021).
30. Duong, T.; Fan, L.; Katz, J.; Thai, P.; Zhou, H.S. 2-hop blockchain: Combining proof-of-work and proof-of-stake securely. In Proceedings of the European Symposium on Research in Computer Security, Darmstadt, Germany, 4–8 October 2020; pp. 697–712.
31. Nguyen, G.T.; Kim, K. A Survey about Consensus Algorithms Used in Blockchain. *J. Inf. Process. Syst.* **2018**, *14*, 101–128.
32. Ongaro, D.; Ousterhout, J. In search of an understandable consensus algorithm. In Proceedings of the 2014 USENIX Annual Technical Conference (USENIX ATC 14), Philadelphia, PA, USA, 19–20 June 2014; pp. 305–319.
33. Jiang, T.; Fang, H.; Wang, H. Blockchain-based internet of vehicles: Distributed network architecture and performance analysis. *IEEE Internet Things J.* **2018**, *6*, 4640–4649. [CrossRef]
34. Wang, X.; Zeng, P.; Patterson, N.; Jiang, F.; Doss, R. An improved authentication scheme for internet of vehicles based on blockchain technology. *IEEE Access* **2019**, *7*, 45061–45072. [CrossRef]
35. Hu, J.; He, D.; Zhao, Q.; Choo, K.K.R. Parking management: A blockchain-based privacy-preserving system. *IEEE Consum. Electron. Mag.* **2019**, *8*, 45–49. [CrossRef]
36. Sidorov, M.; Ong, M.T.; Sridharan, R.V.; Nakamura, J.; Ohmura, R.; Khor, J.H. Ultralightweight mutual authentication RFID protocol for blockchain enabled supply chains. *IEEE Access* **2019**, *7*, 7273–7285. [CrossRef]
37. Huang, J.; Kong, L.; Chen, G.; Wu, M.Y.; Liu, X.; Zeng, P. Towards secure industrial IoT: Blockchain system with credit-based consensus mechanism. *IEEE Trans. Ind. Inform.* **2019**, *15*, 3680–3689. [CrossRef]
38. Zou, S.; Xi, J.; Wang, S.; Lu, Y.; Xu, G. Reportcoin: A novel blockchain-based incentive anonymous reporting system. *IEEE Access* **2019**, *7*, 65544–65559. [CrossRef]
39. Javed, I.T.; Alharbi, F.; Margaria, T.; Crespi, N.; Qureshi, K.N. PETchain: A Blockchain-Based Privacy Enhancing Technology. *IEEE Access* **2021**, *9*, 41129–41143. [CrossRef]
40. Tang, F.; Ma, S.; Xiang, Y.; Lin, C. An efficient authentication scheme for blockchain-based electronic health records. *IEEE Access* **2019**, *7*, 41678–41689. [CrossRef]
41. Alamri, B.; Javed, I.T.; Margaria, T. A GDPR-Compliant Framework for IoT-Based Personal Health Records Using Blockchain. In Proceedings of the 2021 11th IFIP International Conference on New Technologies, Mobility and Security (NTMS), Paris, France, 19–21 April 2021; pp. 1–5.
42. Wu, J.; Xiong, F.; Li, C. Application of Internet of Things and Blockchain Technologies to Improve Accounting Information Quality. *IEEE Access* **2019**, *7*, 100090–100098. [CrossRef]
43. Liu, Y.; Wang, K.; Lin, Y.; Xu, W. A lightweight blockchain system for industrial internet of things. *IEEE Trans. Ind. Inform.* **2019**, *15*, 3571–3581. [CrossRef]
44. Hammi, M.T.; Hammi, B.; Bellot, P.; Serhrouchni, A. Bubbles of Trust: A decentralized blockchain-based authentication system for IoT. *Comput. Secur.* **2018**, *78*, 126–142. [CrossRef]
45. Niya, S.R.; Schiller, E.; Cepilov, I.; Maddaloni, F.; Aydinli, K.; Surbeck, T.; Bocek, T.; Stiller, B. Adaptation of Proof-of-Stake-based Blockchains for IoT Data Streams. In Proceedings of the 2019 IEEE International Conference on Blockchain and Cryptocurrency (ICBC), Seoul, Korea, 14–17 May 2019; pp. 15–16.
46. Bachmann, S. Proof of Stake for Bazo. Bachelor's Thesis, University of Zurich, Zürich, Switzerland, 2018.
47. Du, M.; Ma, X.; Zhang, Z.; Wang, X.; Chen, Q. A review on consensus algorithm of blockchain. In Proceedings of the 2017 IEEE International Conference on Systems, Man, and Cybernetics (SMC), Banff, AB, Canada, 5–8 October 2017; pp. 2567–2572.

Article

A Location Privacy Preservation Method Based on Dummy Locations in Internet of Vehicles

Xianyun Xu [1], Huifang Chen [1,2,3,*] and Lei Xie [1,4]

1. College of Information Science and Electronic Engineering, Zhejiang University, Hangzhou 310027, China; 21831091@zju.edu.cn (X.X.); xiel@zju.edu.cn (L.X.)
2. Zhoushan Ocean Research Center, Zhoushan 316021, China
3. State Key Laboratory of Fluid Power and Mechatronic Systems, Zhejiang University, Hangzhou 310027, China
4. Zhejiang Provincial Key Laboratory of Information Processing, Communication and Networking, Hangzhou 310027, China
* Correspondence: chenhf@zju.edu.cn; Tel.: +86-571-8795-1820 (ext. 217)

Featured Application: This work can used in location privacy preservation in internet of vehicles.

Abstract: During the procedure, a location-based service (LBS) query, the real location provided by the vehicle user may results in the disclosure of vehicle location privacy. Moreover, the point of interest retrieval service requires high accuracy of location information. However, some privacy preservation methods based on anonymity or obfuscation will affect the service quality. Hence, we study the location privacy-preserving method based on dummy locations in this paper. We propose a vehicle location privacy-preservation method based on dummy locations under road restriction in Internet of vehicles (IoV). In order to improve the validity of selected dummy locations under road restriction, entropy is used to represent the degree of anonymity, and the effective distance is introduced to represent the characteristics of location distribution. We present a dummy location selection algorithm to maximize the anonymous entropy and the effective distance of candidate location set consisting of vehicle user's location and dummy locations, which ensures the uncertainty and dispersion of selected dummy locations. The proposed location privacy-preservation method does not need a trustable third-party server, and it protects the location privacy of vehicles as well as guaranteeing the LBS quality. The performance analysis and simulation results show that the proposed location privacy-preservation method can improve the validity of dummy locations and enhance the preservation of location privacy compared with other methods based on dummy locations.

Keywords: privacy preservation; Internet of vehicles (IoV); location-based services (LBS); location privacy; dummy location; effective distance

Citation: Xu, X.; Chen, H.; Xie, L. A Location Privacy Preservation Method Based on Dummy Locations in Internet of Vehicles. *Appl. Sci.* **2021**, *11*, 4594. https://doi.org/10.3390/app11104594

Academic Editor: Gianluca Lax

Received: 25 April 2021
Accepted: 14 May 2021
Published: 18 May 2021

Publisher's Note: MDPI stays neutral with regard to jurisdictional claims in published maps and institutional affiliations.

Copyright: © 2021 by the authors. Licensee MDPI, Basel, Switzerland. This article is an open access article distributed under the terms and conditions of the Creative Commons Attribution (CC BY) license (https://creativecommons.org/licenses/by/4.0/).

1. Introduction

With the development and application of wireless networks, the vehicular ad hoc network (VANET) is becoming an important part of future intelligent transport system. It is expected to play an important role in the road safety [1], traffic management [2], information dissemination to drivers and passengers [3], and so on. With increasing number of vehicles being connected to the Internet of things, the conventional VANET is changing into the Internet of vehicles (IoV).

Moreover, the use of location-based services (LBS) application from mobile devices and applications (apps) is rapidly increasing [4]. When a user acquires the LBS, it needs to provide its location, which results in the disclosure of the location privacy. In addition, a vehicle may act as a provider of location services. For example, when a vehicle participates in a task based on swarm intelligence perception, it should expose the location privacy. Hence, the problem of privacy preservation in the LBS should be resolved [5].

To address the privacy-preserving issue, many approaches have been proposed over the past few years. Most of them are based on the location perturbation and obfuscation adopt well-known privacy metrics such as K-anonymity [6] and rely on a trusted third-party server [7,8]. However, K-anonymity privacy-preserving scheme is suitable for high vehicle density. When there are fewer vehicles, spatial anonymity may not be realized, or the anonymous area formed is too large [9]. On the other hand, for the point of interest (POI) retrieval service in IoV, the accuracy of retrieval results is related to the precision of provided location information. However, the location privacy-preservation schemes based on anonymity or obfuscation cannot guarantee the accuracy of location information, which affects the quality of LBS [10–13].

In the location privacy-preservation method based on dummy locations, a location set containing (or implied) the user's real location is provide to the LBS server. Hence, this method can ensure the accuracy of POI retrieval results [14]. At the same time, the generation of dummy locations does not need a trustable third-party server. In recent years, many location privacy-preservation methods based on dummy locations have been proposed [15–23]. However, due to the characteristics of vehicles, the location of vehicles is subject to the road distribution, many methods cannot be directly adopted in IoV.

In IoV, road information can be used to preprocess dummy locations by the LBS server. Since the enhanced dummy location selection (E-DLS) [18] algorithm does not take the road information into consideration, the validity of dummy locations cannot be guaranteed. In addition, due to the restriction of roads and roadside buildings, the distribution of dummy locations is constrained. Although dummy locations are generated combining with location semantic information [24], the required location distribution is difficult to be achieved under road constraints. Considering the geographical constraint, a method is proposed to generate and arrange dummy objects around users in a grid form [25]. However, the method ignores the history request information. Due to the shortcomings in the existing location privacy-preserving methods in IoV, we investigate the problem of location privacy preservation under road constraints in this paper.

In this paper, we propose a vehicle location privacy-preservation method based on dummy locations. In the proposed method, the dummy location selection algorithm is modified based on vehicle location features. The main contributions of this paper as follows:

- We investigate the problem of vehicle location privacy preservation in IoV and propose a vehicle location privacy-preservation method based on dummy locations.
- We define the concept of effective distance to represent the characteristics of vehicle location distribution. Moreover, we improve the dummy location selection algorithm by using anonymous entropy and effective distance.
- We analyze the performance of the proposed method in terms of security, computation overhead, and communication overhead, and conduct extensive simulations to evaluate the proposed method.

The rest of the paper is organized as follows. The related work about location privacy-preservation methods is overviewed in Section 2. In Section 3, we give some preliminaries and the problem aiming to be solved in this paper. In Section 4, we propose a vehicle location privacy-preservation method based on dummy locations. Performance analysis and simulation results are given to verify the proposed method in Sections 5 and 6, respectively. Finally, we conclude the paper in Section 7.

2. Related Work

The location privacy-preserving problem has been attracting wide attention from both academia and industry. This problem draws even more attention due to the booming of LBSs. Many location privacy-preservation methods have been proposed, such as K-anonymity [7–10], obfuscation [11–13], differential privacy [26,27], mixed zone [28,29], homomorphic encryption [30–32], and dummy locations [15–23]. In this work, we focus on the location privacy preservation-method based on dummy locations in IoV.

The privacy-preservation method based on dummy locations can work without a third-party server, and provides a location set containing the user's real location to guarantee the quality of LBS. Hence, this method can achieve a good tradeoff between location privacy-preservation and service quality. Sun et al. [15] proposes a privacy-preservation method based on dummy locations, where a query is submitted to an LBS provider with the actual location of a user and other dummy locations. The LBS provider searches for all the related POI locations and returns them to the user. Hence, the generation of dummy locations is the key issue in the privacy-preservation method based on dummy locations. Grid-based and circle-based algorithms for generating dummy locations are proposed to satisfy regional privacy requirements in [16]. A distributed dummy client generation method is proposed to make clients control over their privacy protection [17]. The method selects clients with movement patterns be close to user's movement pattern according to the privacy requirements. However, many dummy location generation algorithms assume that an attacker has no other background information and select locations randomly. To solve this problem, an E-DLS algorithm is proposed in [18]. In the E-DLS algorithm, dummy locations are selected to optimize the privacy-preserving effect in terms of the maximum entropy and cloaking region (CR). Based on E-DLS, Liao et al. [19] considers that when the attacker can obtain the type of service, the greedy algorithm based on entropy measurement is proposed to select the dummy locations to construct the anonymous area.

Recently, the trajectory privacy-preserving issue for continuous LBS has been becoming a hot research topic. A method named Dummy-Q is proposed for query privacy-preservation in the continuous LBS scenarios [20], where the query privacy is protected by generating dummy queries. In [21], the problem of privacy leakage under continuous LBS is studied, and a frequency-aware dummy-based method (FADBM) is proposed to ensure that dummy locations are generated around frequent areas and the time accessibility. In [22], a dummy filtering algorithm is proposed, where the spatiotemporal correlation of time-sensitive side information is used to select and generate dummy locations, and spatiotemporal correlation between locations is truncated with time accessibility and access constraints to ensure trajectory similarity. In [23], a location privacy method is proposed to prevent privacy disclosure in LBS constrained in incomplete data collection, where the anonymous candidate set is constructed with compressing sensing technology. Moreover, the differential privacy mechanism is adopted to construct the anonymous candidate set for continuous LBS.

Since the trajectory of vehicles is subject to the road distributions, the influence of road information should be considered for designing location privacy-preservation methods in IoV. Considering the geographical constraint, a method is proposed to generate and arrange dummy objects around users in a grid form [25]. However, the service request probability of locations is not considered when generating dummy locations, the effect of privacy protection is poor. Lina et al. [33] proposes a location privacy-preservation scheme based on anonymous entropy, where anonymous entropy based on location distance and request content is considered. Moreover, two algorithms are presented to select dummy users to build anonymous regions for the dense region and the sparse region, respectively. In combination with the characteristics of vehicle network, a privacy preservation algorithm converts road map into edge cluster diagram in order to hide road information and vehicle information, and constructs invisible areas based on K-anonymity and L-diversity [34]. A region-of-interest division-based algorithm is proposed to preserve the location privacy of mobile device users in location-based cyber services [24]. In this method, dummy locations are generated considering the semantic information of those locations.

We will study the location privacy-preservation based on dummy locations in IoV, in which road constraints and vehicle location characteristics are taken into consideration.

3. Preliminaries and Problem Formulation

In this section, we introduce some preliminaries including the system model, LBS query, service semantics, anonymous entropy, and adversary model. Then, the problem to be solved in this paper is formulated.

3.1. System Model

Figure 1 illustrates the system architecture of IoV that consists of a number of intelligent vehicles with onboard unit (OBU), several roadside units (RSUs), a trusted authority (TA), and an LBS server. OBU can acquire the perceived driving information of on-board sensors, calculate, process, and store the sensed data. The communication modes in IoV, namely vehicle-to-vehicle (V2V) and vehicle-to-RSU (V2R), adopt dedicated short range communication (DSRC) technology. Through V2V communication, intelligent vehicles can not only obtain driving state information through sensors and exchange messages, but also receive and forward messages broadcasted by other vehicles. Through V2R communication, vehicles can exchange information with the RSU and access the Internet.

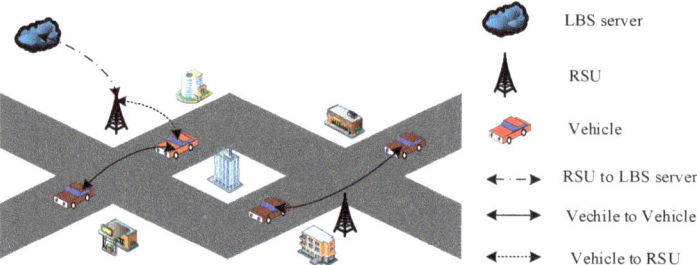

Figure 1. The system architecture of IoV.

3.2. LBS Query

An LBS query Lq is defined as $Lq = (u_{id}, \{(x, y), C, V\})$, where u_{id} denotes a user's identity; (x, y) represents the user's location information, x and y represent latitude and longitude, respectively; C denotes the user's query content; V is the user's privacy preservation level.

However, since the LBS provider may be malicious, the user's location will be disclosed if the user directly sends Lq to the LBS provider. To preserve the location privacy, dummy locations method is used to preprocess Lq. Hence, Lq is transformed to Lq' as $Lq' = (u_{id}, \{(x,y), (x_1, y_1), \ldots, (x_{k-1}, y_{k-1}), C, C_1, \ldots, C_{k-1}, V\})$, where $(x_1, y_1), \ldots, (x_{k-1}, y_{k-1})$ are $k-1$ dummy locations, C_i represents the query content sent at dummy location (x_i, y_i), $i = 1, 2, \ldots, k-1$.

From Lq', the adversary cannot determine the user's real location from $k-1$ dummy locations. By this way, the vehicle location privacy can be protected.

3.3. Service Semantics

In each location, users may request entertainment, medical treatment, transportation, or other services. The service requests sent by users are closely related to their locations, and the probabilities of various services in different locations are different. Therefore, service semantics is used to represent the relationship between location and service.

Let U be the number of services, $e_{i,u}$ represents the request probability of service u in location (x_i, y_i), $0 \leq e_{i,u} \leq 1$, $i = 0, 1, \ldots, k-1$, $u = 1, 2, \ldots, U$, and $\sum_{u=1}^{U} e_{i,u} = 1$. In this paper, the LBS server is responsible for the collection and establishment of service semantics.

3.4. Anonymous Entropy

It is pointed out in [17] that entropy can measure the uncertainty of target location in the location set. In this paper, we use entropy to evaluate the degree of anonymity.

Here, we consider set $\mathcal{G}$ including k locations, $\mathcal{G} = \{(x_0, y_0), (x_1, y_1), \ldots, (x_{k-1}, y_{k-1})\}$. The service request probability at location (x_i, y_i) is q_i, the candidate probability of location (x_i, y_i) is p_i. If the vehicle user at location (x_i, y_i) request service u, the service semantics at location (x_i, y_i) is $e_{i,u}$, and the request probability of service u at location (x_i, y_i) is q'_i, $q'_i = q_i e_{i,u}$, $i = 0, 1, \ldots, k-1$, $u = 1, 2, \ldots, U$. Hence, the anonymous entropy is defined as

$$H = -\sum_{i=0}^{k-1} p_i \log_2 p_i, \qquad (1)$$

where

$$p_i = \frac{q'_i}{\sum_{i=0}^{k-1} q'_i}. \qquad (2)$$

According to the mathematical property of entropy, it is required that the candidate probabilities of k locations be the same to achieve the maximum entropy. That is, if $p_i = 1/k$, $i = 0, 1, \ldots, k-1$, the maximum of anonymous entropy of set $\mathcal{G}$ is $\log_2 k$.

3.5. Adversary Model

The goal of the adversary is to obtain sensitive information about a particular user. There are two types of adversary model, passive adversary, and active adversary.

A passive adversary can monitor and eavesdrop on wireless channels or compromise users to obtain other users' sensitive information. A passive adversary can perform eavesdropping attack to learn extra information about a user.

An active adversary can compromise the LBS server and obtain all the information known by the server.

In this work, we assume that the LBS server and RSUs are honest-but-curious, as active adversaries. Hence, the adversary can obtain global information and monitor all the LBS queries from users. In addition, the adversary knows the location privacy-preservation scheme adopted in the system. Based on the known information, the adversary tries to infer and learn other sensitive information.

3.6. Problem Formulation

The LBS server divides the area covered by an RSU into $I \times J$ cells as shown in Figure 2. $cell_{i,j}$ denotes the cell of row i and column j, $i = 1, 2, \ldots, I$, $j = 1, 2, \ldots, J$. The location of $cell_{i,j}$ is denoted as $r_{i,j}$, and $r_{i,j} = (x_{i,j}, y_{i,j})$. The request probability of $cell_{i,j}$ is $q_{i,j}$, the service semantics of $cell_{i,j}$ is $e_{(i,j),u}$, and the information matrix $Q(r, q, e)$ for each RSU can be set up.

Figure 2 shows service request probability distribution, the area is divided into 10×10 cells. The star represents the user's real location, and the triangle represents the dummy location, and the shade in each cell represents its request probability generated based on the Borlange data set [35]. The gray block represents the road, and **R** represents the location area accessible by the road.

In Figure 2a, a vehicle user randomly generates $k - 1$ dummy locations in order to protect the location privacy. Then vehicle user uses the dummy locations and real location to send service request to the LBS server. In theory, the probability of exposing the user's real location can be $1/k$. However, using some auxiliary information, the LBS server can deduce the real location with a probability of $1/(k - k_d)$, where k_d is the number of dummy locations be filtered out through the auxiliary information.

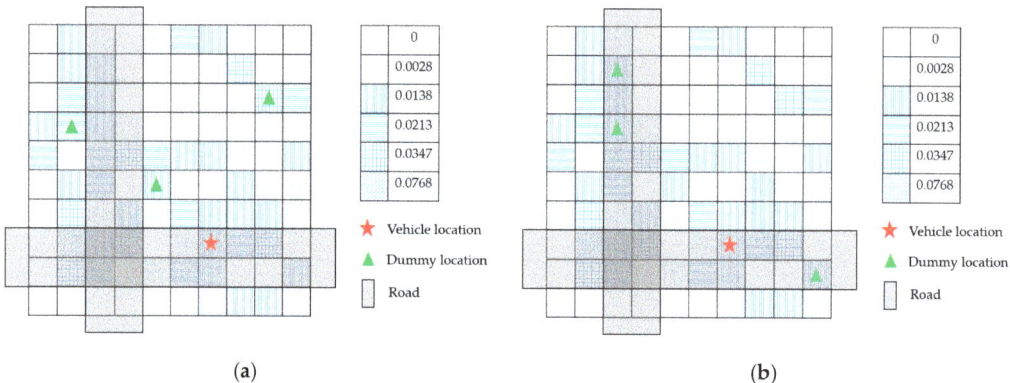

Figure 2. Service request probability distribution. (**a**) with random dummy location selection algorithm; (**b**) with dummy location selection algorithm under road restrictions.

In IoV, since the location of vehicles is restricted by the road, and the service request probability is used as auxiliary information, the validity of dummy locations generated with random dummy location selection algorithm in Figure 2a, E-DLS algorithm in [18] and Dest-ex algorithm in [25] is affected. The dummy locations filtered out by the LBS server, k_d, increases. For example, in Figure 2a, $k = 4$, and $k_d = 3$. Hence, the effect of privacy protection is degraded.

Therefore, to protect the location privacy of vehicles, it is necessary to ensure the validity of dummy locations generated. When road information, service request probability and service semantics are used as auxiliary information, set $\mathcal{G}$ is set up for minimizing k_d. The optimization problem can be defined as

$$\min_{\mathcal{G}} k_d$$
$$\text{s.t.} G(r,q,e) \subset Q(r,q,e)$$
$$\forall r_{i,j} \in \mathcal{G}, r_{i,j} \in \mathcal{C}, r_{i,j} \in R$$
$$|\mathcal{G}| = k, \tag{3}$$

where $G(r, q, e)$ is the information matrix corresponding to set $\mathcal{G}$ which consists of vehicle user's location and $k - 1$ dummy locations, and set $\mathcal{C}$ is the set of all locations of cells in the area covered by the RSU.

4. Algorithm Design

In this section, we present a location privacy-preservation method based on dummy locations in IoV, where a dummy location selection algorithm is addressed to improve the validity of dummy locations.

4.1. Effective Distance

As shown in Figure 3, due to the road restrictions and roadside buildings, the distribution of vehicles is in the form of "pipeline", and the aggregation distribution may occur. Hence, the validity of dummy locations further decreases. To ensure the validity of dummy locations, it is necessary to make the location distribution be uniform and dispersed, as shown in Figure 3b.

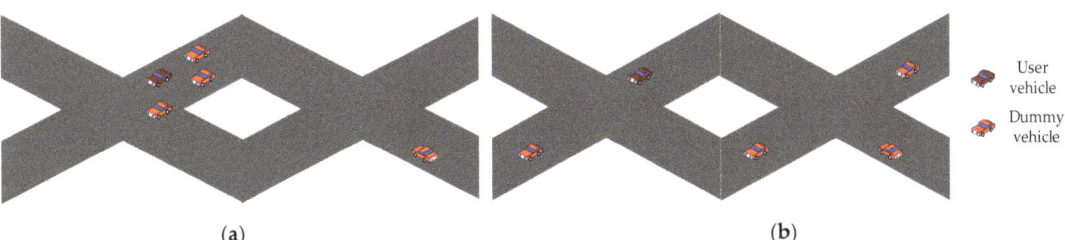

Figure 3. Schematic diagram of vehicle location distribution. (**a**) vehicle aggregation distribution; (**b**) vehicle dispersed distribution.

In order to make the distribution of generated dummy locations be uniform, we define the effective distance between locations as the minimum distance between the current location and other locations in a location set. That is,

$$d(r_i) = \min_{r_w \in \mathcal{W}, w \neq i} |r_i, r_w| = \min_{r_w \in \mathcal{W}, w \neq i} \sqrt{(x_i - x_w)^2 + (y_i - y_w)^2}, \quad (4)$$

where $\mathcal{W}$ represents a location set, r_i represents location i in set $\mathcal{W}$, the corresponding coordinates is (x_i, y_i), r_w represents location w in set $\mathcal{G}$, the corresponding coordinates is (x_w, y_w), $i = 1, 2, \ldots, |\mathcal{W}|$, $w = 1, 2, \ldots, |\mathcal{W}|$, $|\mathcal{W}|$ is the number of elements in set $\mathcal{W}$, and $d(r_i)$ is the effective distance of r_i.

From Figure 4, one finds that the larger the effective distance, the greater the spacing between vehicles, and the more dispersed the distribution.

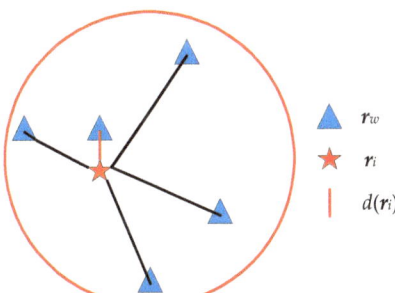

Figure 4. The diagram of effective distance.

4.2. Parameter Settings

The location privacy protection requirement is presented by privacy protection level V, which indicates the success rate of location privacy protection. That is, $V = 1 - p = 1 - \frac{1}{k}$, and $V \in [0,1)$.

Privacy parameter k is determined by privacy protection level V set by the vehicle user. That is,

$$k = \left\lceil \frac{1}{1-V} \right\rceil, \quad (5)$$

where $\lceil \cdot \rceil$ denotes the upper integer operation.

4.3. Dummy Location Selection Algorithm under Road Restriction

In order to ensure the validity of dummy locations, two conditions should be considered simultaneously for selecting the dummy locations. One is to maximize the anonymous entropy of the candidate set. The other is to maximize the effective distance of the candidate set.

Hence, the optimization problem formulated in (3) can convert to a multiple object optimization problem as

$$\max_{\mathcal{G}} \left\{ -\sum_{r_{i,j} \in \mathcal{G}} p_{i,j} \log_2 p_{i,j}, \sum_{r_{i,j} \in \mathcal{G}} d(r_{i,j}) \right\}$$
$$\text{s.t.} G(r, q, e) \subset Q(r, q, e)$$
$$\forall r_{i,j} \in \mathcal{G}, r_{i,j} \in \mathcal{C}, r_{i,j} \in \mathbf{R}$$
$$|\mathcal{G}| = k, \tag{6}$$

where candidate set $\mathcal{G}$ consists of the vehicle user's location and $k - 1$ selected dummy locations.

Obviously, the problem formulated in (6) is difficult to resolve. Hence, we decouple the problem in (6) into two sub-problems, the anonymous entropy maximization sub-problem and the effective distance maximization sub-problem.

According to the background knowledge of the LBS server and the purpose of the dummy location selection algorithm, we give priority to the sub-problem of anonymous entropy maximization. That is,

$$\max_{\mathcal{G}'} \left\{ -\sum_{r_{i,j} \in \mathcal{G}'} p_{i,j} \log_2 p_{i,j} \right\}$$
$$\text{s.t.} G'(r, q, e) \subset Q(r, q, e)$$
$$\forall r_{i,j} \in \mathcal{G}', r_{i,j} \in \mathcal{C}, r_{i,j} \in \mathbf{R}$$
$$|\mathcal{G}'| = k', \tag{7}$$

where set $\mathcal{G}'$ including the vehicle user's location and $k' - 1$ selected dummy locations is set up to resolve the sub-problem formulated in (7), k' is the number of locations in set $\mathcal{G}'$, and $k' > k$.

According to $Q(r, q, e)$, the vehicle user calculates the probability of service request at each location in $\mathbf{R}$, $q'_{(i,j),u}$, $i = 1, 2, \ldots, I, j = 1, 2, \ldots, J, u = 1, 2, \ldots, U$, $cell_{i,j} \in \mathbf{R}$. According to service request probability of content C_0, the vehicle user selects other $k' - 1$ locations whose service request probabilities are close to that of the vehicle user.

Hence, a candidate set $\mathcal{G}'$ is constructed with the vehicle user's location and $k' - 1$ selected dummy locations.

Then, the sub-problem for maximizing the effective distance of the candidate set is to resolve. That is,

$$\max_{\mathcal{G}''} \left\{ \sum_{r_{i,j} \in \mathcal{G}''} d(r_{i,j}) \right\}$$
$$\text{s.t.} G''(r, q, e) \subset G'(r, q, e)$$
$$\forall r_{i,j} \in \mathcal{G}'', r_{i,j} \in \mathcal{G}'$$
$$|\mathcal{G}''| = k, \tag{8}$$

where set $\mathcal{G}''$ including the vehicle user's location and $k - 1$ selected dummy locations is set up to resolve the sub-problem formulated in (8).

To solve the sub-problem formulated in (8), the vehicle user selects $k - 1$ dummy locations in a greedy manner.

Let $r_{0,0}$ denote the location of the vehicle user. $\mathcal{G}'' = \{r_{0,0}\}$ and $\mathcal{G}' = \mathcal{G}'' \setminus \{r_{0,0}\}$. The vehicle user chooses $k - 1$ locations with the maximum effective distance through $k - 1$ rounds.

In the ith round, $i = 1, 2, \ldots, k-1$, the vehicle user calculates the effective distance of the location(s) in $\mathcal{G}'$ to the location(s) in $\mathcal{G}''$. If $r_{i*,j*} = \arg\max_{r_{i,j} \in \mathcal{G}'} \left(\min_{r_{i',j'} \in \mathcal{G}''} |r_{i,j}, r_{i',j'}| \right)$, the vehicle user puts $r_{i*,j*}$ into set $\mathcal{G}''$ and deletes it from $\mathcal{G}'$.

Hence, set $\mathcal{G}''$ is constructed with the vehicle user's location and $k - 1$ selected dummy locations.

4.4. A Location Privacy-Preservation Method Based on Dummy Locations under Road Restriction

The specific procedure of a location privacy-preservation method based on dummy location under road restriction can be follows:

(1) Based on the historical data of service requests, the LBS server counts the number of service requests initiated by vehicle users in each cell, and the service request probability of $cell_{i,j}$, $i = 1, 2, \ldots, I$, $j = 1, 2, \ldots, J$, $q_{i,j} = f_{i,j}/F$, where $f_{i,j}$ is the number of service requests initiated by vehicle users in $cell_{i,j}$, and F is the number of service requests in the area. The service semantics of service u is $q_{i,j} = f_{(i,j),u}/f_{i,j}$, where $f_{(i,j),u}$ is the number of requests of service u initiated by vehicle users in $cell_{i,j}$, $u = 1, 2, \ldots, U$.

(2) The LBS server constructs and distributes the information matrix $Q(r, q, e)$ within the RSU's jurisdiction to each RSU.

(3) RSU broadcasts $Q(r, q, e)$ and **R** to users in its covered area.

(4) According to the privacy preservation level V, the vehicle user calculates its privacy parameter k by (5).

(5) The vehicle user generates $k - 1$ dummy locations using dummy location selection algorithm under road restriction. The details are as follows:

(5-a) Let $k' = 2k$. Within the locations in **R**, other $k' - 1$ locations apart from the vehicle user's location are selected as dummy locations by solving the problem formulated in (7). Hence, a candidate set $\mathcal{G}'$ is constructed with the vehicle user's location and $k' - 1$ selected dummy locations.

(5-b) Within set $\mathcal{G}'$, other $k - 1$ locations apart from the vehicle user's location are selected as dummy locations by solving the problem formulated in (8). Hence, set $\mathcal{G}''$ is constructed with the vehicle user's location and $k - 1$ selected dummy locations.

(6) The vehicle user generates service query Lq' including locations in $\mathcal{G}''$, their corresponding service contents, and the privacy preservation level, and then, Lq' is sent to the LBS server via RSU.

(7) Receiving service query Lq', the LBS server retrieves service results according to k locations and the corresponding service contents, and then, the LBS server returns service results to the vehicle user through RSU.

(8) The vehicle user selects the required result from service results according to its location.

5. Performance Analysis

In this section, the performance of the proposed location privacy-preservation method using dummy location selection algorithm under road restriction, abbreviated as RR-DLS, is analyzed.

5.1. Security Analysis

Since encrypt-based technologies can be easily applied to the proposed RR-DLS method, eavesdropping attack on wireless channels between users and other entities can be ignored. We focus on collusion attack and inference attack from passive and active attackers.

5.1.1. Collusion Attack

Passive attackers may collude with some users to get additional information about other users or collude with the LBS server to predict sensitive information about legitimate users. If the probability of successfully guessing the real location of a vehicle user among k locations in the service query does not increase with the number of collusion users, the proposed method can resist collusion attack.

We consider a situation that collusion occurs between a group of users aiming to acquire the user's real location from k locations. In RR-DLS method, each user can only know the service request probability and road condition collected by itself. When eavesdropping the service query sent to the LBS server, the attacker cannot filter out some invalid locations through additional information since k locations in the service query have the same or similar service request probability and are on the road.

One extreme case for the passive adversary is that it can acquire the global information by compromising the LBS server as well as RSUs. In this case, it becomes an active adversary and can perform inference attack as discussed in the following.

5.1.2. Inference Attack

The LBS server and RSUs have global information, such as information matrix $Q(r, q, e)$, road information $\mathbf{R}$ and k locations in the service query, and so on. Based on this information, the LBS server or the RSU can act as an active attacker to launch reasoning attack and acquire some sensitive information of users.

Suppose $p_G(\text{event})$ be the probability that an attacker successfully guesses that event is true. The proposed method should satisfy (9) to resist inference attack.

$$p_G(r_{i,j} \in \mathcal{B} | \mathcal{B} \cap \mathcal{G}'' \neq \varnothing) = p_G(r_{i',j'} \in \mathcal{B} | \mathcal{B} \cap \mathcal{G}'' \neq \varnothing), r_{i,j} \in \mathcal{G}'', r_{i',j'} \in \mathcal{G}'', r_{i,j} \neq r_{i',j'}, \tag{9}$$

where set $\mathcal{B}$ consists of the locations obtained by an attacker.

For any dummy location $r_{i,j}$ generated by RR-DLS algorithm, the probability of $r_{i,j}$ being guessed as the real location is

$$p_G(r_{i,j} \in \mathcal{B} | \mathcal{B} \cap \mathcal{G}'' \neq \varnothing) = \frac{p_G(r_{i,j} \in \mathcal{B}, \mathcal{B} \cap \mathcal{G}'' \neq \varnothing)}{p_G(\mathcal{B} \cap \mathcal{G}'' \neq \varnothing)} = \frac{p_{i,j}}{p_G(\mathcal{B} \cap \mathcal{G}'' \neq \varnothing)}, r_{i,j} \in \mathcal{G}''. \tag{10}$$

Substituting (10) into (9), we have

$$p_{i,j} \simeq p_{i',j'}, r_{i,j} \in \mathcal{G}'', r_{i',j'} \in \mathcal{G}'', r_{i,j} \neq r_{i',j'}. \tag{11}$$

The proposed dummy location selection algorithm under road restriction selects locations with the same or similar probability of service requests and service semantics. Hence, the proposed RR-DLS method satisfies the condition in (11), which means that the method can effectively resist inference attack.

5.2. Computation Overhead

If RSU jurisdiction is divided into $I \times J$ cells, the number of services is U and the number of results returned by the LBS server is n.

In the procedure of an LBS query, the vehicle user needs to generate k dummy locations. First, as the vehicle user selects $2k - 1$ locations based on service request probability, the computation overhead is $O(IJU)$. As the vehicle user selects dummy locations by effective distance through $k - 1$ rounds. In the ith round, $i = 1, 2, \ldots, k - 1$, the vehicle user calculates the effective distance of $2k - 1 - i$ locations in $\mathcal{G}'$ to i locations in $\mathcal{G}''$ to update the effective distance of each location, and the location with maximum effective distance of locations in $\mathcal{G}'$ is selected. Hence, the computation overhead is $O(k^2)$. Therefore, the computation overhead of dummy location selection algorithm at the vehicle user is $O(k^2 + IJU)$.

Since RSU does not need additional computation, the computation overhead at RSU is $O(1)$.

The LBS server needs to perform service retrieval for $k - 1$ dummy locations and a real location. Hence, the computation overhead at the LBS server is $O(kn)$.

5.3. Communication Overhead

In the procedure of an LBS query, the vehicle user sends service query to the LBS server through RSU. The communication overhead at the vehicle user is $O(k)$.

RSU needs to broadcast the service request probability, the service semantics and other information. The communication overhead is $O(IJU)$. At the same time, RSU needs to forward the service query to the LBS server and return kn service query results to the vehicle user. Therefore, the communication overhead at the RUS is $O(IJU + kn + k)$.

The LBS server needs to send the service request probability, service semantics and other information to RSU. The communication overhead is $O(IJU)$. Receiving the service query, the corresponding service results are returned to RSU. The communication cost is $O(kn)$. Therefore, the communication overhead at LBS server is $O(IJU + kn)$.

The performance of proposed RR-DLS method in terms of computation overhead and communication overhead is listed in Table 1.

Table 1. Performance of proposed RR-DLS method.

Entity	Computation Overhead	Communication Overhead
Vehicle user	$O(k^2 + IJU)$	$O(k)$
RSU	$O(1)$	$O(IJU + kn + k)$
LBS Server	$O(kn)$	$O(IJU + kn)$

6. Performance Evaluation and Discussion

In this section, the performance of proposed RR-DLS method is valuated. Moreover, we compare the performance of proposed RR-DLS algorithm with some existing dummy location selection algorithms, such as random dummy location selection algorithm, E-DLS algorithm in [18], Dest-ex algorithm in [25].

The simulation area and the corresponding service request probability distribution are illustrated in Figure 5, which is a region in Hangzhou with an area of 500 m × 500 m. This region is divided into 10 × 10 cells, the number of service types $U = 4$, the service request probability and service semantics are generated randomly, and orange cells represent locations that are inaccessible to the vehicle.

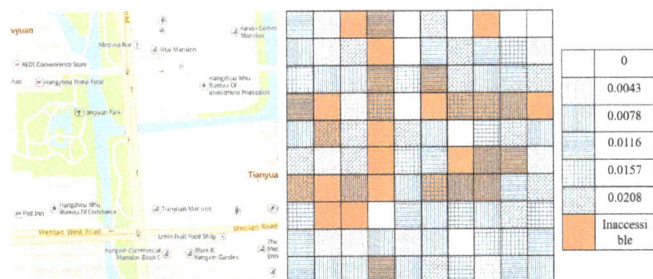

Figure 5. The simulation area and the corresponding service request probability distribution.

The simulation environment is Windows10, with 8 GB memory and AMD Ryzen 5 3550 H processor.

6.1. Computation Overhead

Figure 6 shows the impact of privacy parameter k on computation overhead in terms of execution time. From Figure 6, we observe that the computation overhead of proposed RR-DLS method is concentrated on the vehicle user side, and the execution time increases rapidly along with the increase of privacy parameter k. The computation overhead at RSU and the LBS server side is small. The execution time of RSU is independent of privacy parameter k, and the execution time of the LBS server increases linearly along with the increase of privacy parameter k.

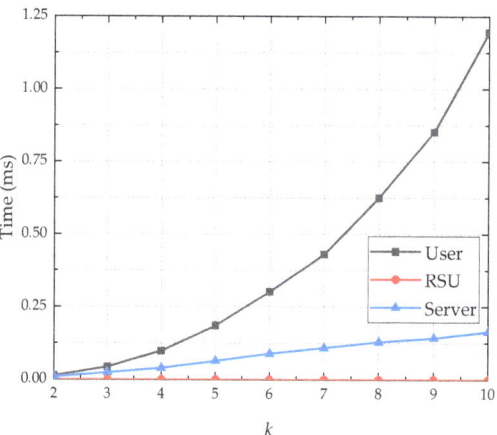

Figure 6. Impact of privacy parameter on execution time.

6.2. Communication Overhead

Figure 7 shows the impact of privacy parameter k on communication overhead in terms of data traffic. From Figure 7, we observe that the communication overhead of proposed RR-DLS method is concentrated on RSU and the LBS server, and the communication overhead at the vehicle user side is small. As privacy parameter k increases, the communication overhead in terms of data traffic increases.

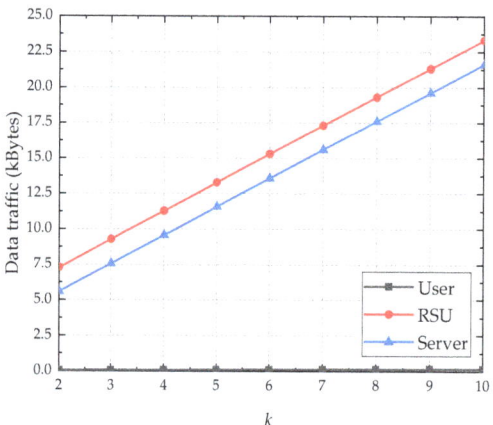

Figure 7. Impact of privacy parameter on data traffic.

6.3. Anonymous Entropy

Figure 8 shows the anonymous entropy of four different dummy location selection algorithms, the proposed RR-DLS algorithm, random dummy location selection algorithm, E-DLS algorithm in [18], and Dest-ex algorithm in [25]. From Figure 8, we observe that the anonymous entropy of proposed RR-DLS algorithm is the largest. This is because the proposed RR-DLS algorithm can ensure the validity of dummy locations. Since Dest-ex algorithm only considers the road information, the anonymous entropy of Dest-ex algorithm is smaller than that of proposed RR-DLS algorithm, and larger than that of random dummy location selection algorithm and E-DLS algorithm. Since E-DLS algorithm selects dummy locations according to service request probability and CR, some dummy locations can be filtered using auxiliary knowledge. The anonymous entropy of E-DLS algorithm is low. Since random selection algorithm selects dummy locations randomly, the anonymous entropy of random dummy location selection algorithm is the lowest.

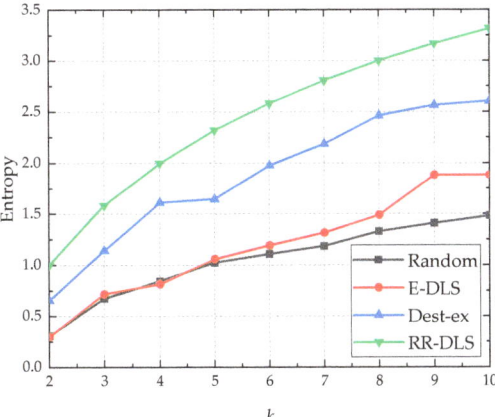

Figure 8. Anonymous entropy of different dummy location selections algorithms.

6.4. Effective Distance

Figure 9 shows the effective distance of two different dummy location selection algorithms, the proposed RR-DLS algorithm and E-DLS algorithm in [18]. For E-DLS algorithm, the anonymous area is maximized considering the query probability. From Figure 9a, the means of effective distance of two algorithms are close. Moreover, from Figure 9b, we observe that the variance of effective distance of proposed RR-DLS algorithm is much smaller than that of E-DLS algorithm. The proposed RR-DLS algorithm can guarantee the distributed and uniform distribution of dummy locations to ensure the validity of dummy locations.

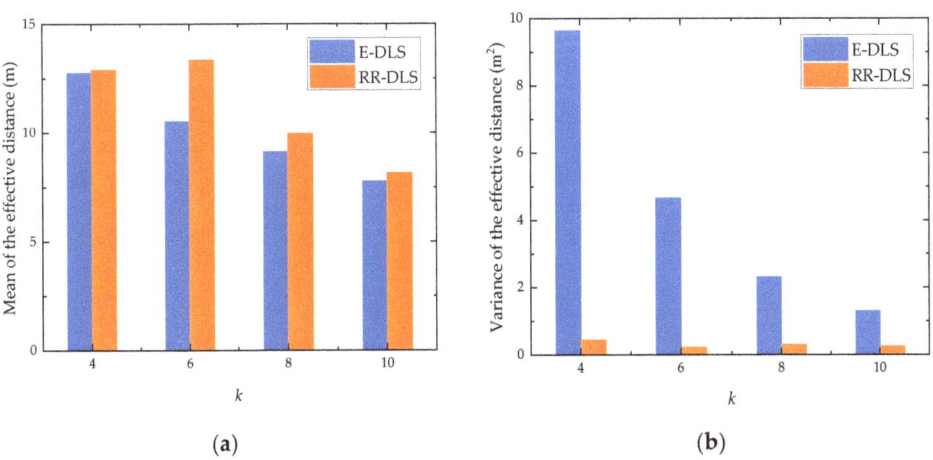

Figure 9. Effective distance of two different location selection algorithms. (**a**) mean; (**b**) variance.

7. Conclusions

In this paper, we investigated the vehicle location privacy-preserving problem in IoV and proposed a location privacy-preservation method based on dummy locations under road restriction. In the proposed RR-DLS method, the effective distance is introduced to represent the characteristics of location distribution in order to improve the validity of dummy locations. A dummy location selection algorithm under road restriction was addressed according to anonymous entropy and effective distance. Security analysis results show that the proposed RR-DLS method can resist collusion attack and inference attack effectively. Performance analysis and simulation results show that the proposed RR-DLS method can effectively protect the vehicle location privacy and ensure the accuracy of LBS service. Furthermore, the proposed RR-DLS method increases the computation overhead at the vehicle user and communication overhead at RSU and the LBS server.

In the future, we will study the problem of vehicle trajectory privacy preservation in continuous LBS scenario.

Author Contributions: Conceptualization, X.X. and H.C.; methodology, X.X. and H.C.; software, X.X.; validation, X.X. and L.X.; formal analysis, X.X. and H.C.; investigation, X.X.; resources, L.X.; data curation, X.X.; writing—original draft preparation, X.X. and H.C.; writing—review and editing, H.C.; supervision, H.C.; project administration, H.C.; funding acquisition, H.C. All authors have read and agreed to the published version of the manuscript.

Funding: This research was funded in part by the Fund of National Natural Science Foundation of China under Grant 61671410, and the Science and Technology Department of Zhejiang Province under Grant 2018R52046 and Grant LGG18F010005.

Conflicts of Interest: The authors declare no conflict of interest.

References

1. Raya, M.; Hubaux, J.-P. Securing vehicular ad hoc networks. *J. Comput. Secur.* **2007**, *15*, 39–68. [CrossRef]
2. Zhao, L.; Song, Y.; Zhang, C.; Liu, Y.; Wang, P.; Lin, T.; Deng, M.; Li, H. T-GCN: A Temporal Graph Convolutional Network for Traffic Prediction. *IEEE Trans. Intell. Transp. Syst.* **2020**, *21*, 3848–3858. [CrossRef]
3. Qiu, H.; Qiu, M.; Lu, R. Secure V2X Communication Network based on Intelligent PKI and Edge Computing. *IEEE Netw.* **2019**, *34*, 172–178. [CrossRef]
4. Sun, G.; Sun, S.; Sun, J.; Yu, H.; Du, X.; Guizani, M. Security and privacy preservation in fog-based crowd sensing on the internet of vehicles. *J. Netw. Comput. Appl.* **2019**, *134*, 89–99. [CrossRef]
5. Gupta, R.; Rao, U.P. An Exploration to Location Based Service and Its Privacy Preserving Techniques: A Survey. *Wirel. Pers. Commun.* **2017**, *96*, 1973–2007. [CrossRef]
6. Jiang, T.; Wang, H.J.; Hu, Y.-C. Preserving location privacy in wireless lans. In *MobiSys '07: Proceedings of the 5th International Conference on Mobile Software Engineering and Systems*; Association for Computing Machinery (ACM): New York, NY, USA, 2007; pp. 246–257.
7. Sweeney, L. k-Anonymity: A Model for Protecting Privacy. *Int. J. Uncertain. Fuzziness Knowl. Based Syst.* **2002**, *10*, 557–570. [CrossRef]
8. Chow, C.-Y.; Mokbel, M.F.; Aref, W.G. Casper*: Query processing for location services without compromising privacy. *ACM Trans. Database Syst.* **2009**, *34*, 1–48. [CrossRef]
9. Liu, S.; Wang, J.H.; Wang, J.; Zhang, Q. Achieving user-defined location privacy preservation using a P2P system. *IEEE Access* **2020**, *8*, 45895–45912. [CrossRef]
10. Ji, Y.; Gui, R.; Gui, X.; Liao, D.; Lin, X. Location Privacy Protection in Online Query based-on Privacy Region Replacement. In Proceedings of the 2020 10th Annual Computing and Communication Workshop and Conference (CCWC), Las Vegas, NV, USA, 6–8 January 2020; pp. 0742–0747.
11. Perazzo, P.; Skvortsov, P.; Dini, G. On Designing Resilient Location-Privacy Obfuscators. *Comput. J.* **2015**, *58*, 2649–2664. [CrossRef]
12. Kachore, V.A.; Lakshmi, J.; Nandy, S. Location Obfuscation for Location Data Privacy. In Proceedings of the 2015 IEEE World Congress on Services, New York, NY, USA, 27 June–2 July 2015; pp. 213–220.
13. Qiu, C.; Squicciarini, A.C. Location Privacy Protection in Vehicle-Based Spatial Crowdsourcing Via Geo-Indistinguishability. In Proceedings of the 2019 IEEE 39th International Conference on Distributed Computing Systems (ICDCS), Dallas, TX, USA, 7–9 July 2019; pp. 1061–1071.
14. Parmar, D.; Rao, U.P. Towards Privacy-Preserving Dummy Generation in Location-Based Services. *Procedia Comput. Sci.* **2020**, *171*, 1323–1326. [CrossRef]
15. Sun, G.; Chang, V.; Ramachandran, M.; Sun, Z.; Li, G.; Yu, H.; Liao, D. Efficient location privacy algorithm for Internet of Things (IoT) services and applications. *J. Netw. Comput. Appl.* **2017**, *89*, 3–13. [CrossRef]
16. Lu, H.; Jensen, C.S.; Yiu, M.L. Pad: Privacy-area aware, dummy based location privacy in mobile services. In *MobiDE '08: Proceedings of the Seventh ACM International Workshop on Data Engineering for Wireless and Mobile Access, Vancouver, BC, Canada, 13 June 2008*; Association for Computing Machinery (ACM): New York, NY, USA, 2008; pp. 16–23.

17. Liu, X.; Liu, K.; Guo, L.; Li, X.; Fang, Y. A game-theoretic approach for achieving k-anonymity in Location Based Services. In Proceedings of the IEEE INFOCOM, Turin, Italy, 14–19 April 2013; pp. 2985–2993.
18. Niu, B.; Li, Q.; Zhu, X.; Cao, G.; Li, H. Achieving k-anonymity in privacy-aware location-based services. In Proceedings of the IEEE INFOCOM 2014—IEEE Conference on Computer Communications, Toronto, ON, Canada, 27 April–2 May 2014; pp. 754–762.
19. Liao, D.; Huang, X.; Anand, V.; Sun, G.; Yu, H. k-DLCA: An efficient approach for location privacy preservation in location-based services. In Proceedings of the 2016 IEEE International Conference on Communications (ICC), Kuala Lumpur, Malaysia, 22–27 May 2016; pp. 1–6.
20. Pingley, A.; Zhang, N.; Fu, X.; Choi, H.-A.; Subramaniam, S.; Zhao, W. Protection of query privacy for continuous location based services. In Proceedings of the IEEE INFOCOM, Shanghai, China, 10–15 April 2011; pp. 1710–1718.
21. Liu, J.; Jiang, X.; Zhang, S.; Wang, H.; Dou, W. FADBM: Frequency-Aware Dummy-Based Method in Long-Term Location Privacy Protection. In Proceedings of the 2019 IEEE 25th International Conference on Parallel and Distributed Systems (ICPADS), Tianjin, China, 4–6 December 2019; pp. 384–391.
22. Niu, J.; Zhu, X.; Shi, L.; Ma, J. Time-Aware Dummy-Based Privacy Protection for Continuous LBSs. In Proceedings of the 2019 International Conference on Networking and Network Applications (NaNA), Daegu, Korea, 10–13 October 2019; pp. 15–20.
23. Yang, X.; Gao, L.; Zheng, J.; Wei, W. Location Privacy Preservation Mechanism for Location-Based Service with Incomplete Location Data. *IEEE Access* **2020**, *8*, 95843–95854. [CrossRef]
24. Sun, G.; Cai, S.; Yu, H.; Maharjan, S.; Chang, V.; Du, X.; Guizani, M. Location Privacy Preservation for Mobile Users in Location-Based Services. *IEEE Access* **2019**, *7*, 87425–87438. [CrossRef]
25. Hara, T.; Suzuki, A.; Iwata, M.; Arase, Y.; Xie, X. Dummy-Based User Location Anonymization under Real-World Constraints. *IEEE Access* **2016**, *4*, 673–687. [CrossRef]
26. Luo, C.; Liu, X.; Xue, W.; Shen, Y.; Li, J.; Hu, W.; Liu, A.X. Predictable Privacy-Preserving Mobile Crowd Sensing: A Tale of Two Roles. *IEEE/ACM Trans. Netw.* **2019**, *27*, 361–374. [CrossRef]
27. Zhou, L.; Yu, L.; Du, S.; Zhu, H.; Chen, C. Achieving Differentially Private Location Privacy in Edge-Assistant Connected Vehicles. *IEEE Internet Things J.* **2019**, *6*, 4472–4481. [CrossRef]
28. Lin, X.; Lu, R. Pseudonym-changing strategy for location privacy. In *Vehicular Ad Hoc Network Security and Privacy*; Institute of Electrical and Electronics Engineers (IEEE): Piscataway, NJ, USA; John Wiley & Sons: Hoboken, NJ, USA, 2015; Volume 1, pp. 71–90.
29. Guo, N.; Ma, L.; Gao, T. Independent Mix Zone for Location Privacy in Vehicular Networks. *IEEE Access* **2018**, *6*, 16842–16850. [CrossRef]
30. Al-Anwar, A.; Shoukry, Y.; Chakraborty, S.; Balaji, B.; Martin, P.; Tabuada, P.; Srivastava, M.B. PrOLoc: Resilient localization with private observers using partial homomorphic encryption. In *Proceedings of the 16th ACM/IEEE International Conference on Information Processing in Sensor Networks, Pittsburgh, PA, USA, 18–21 April 2017*; Association for Computing Machinery (ACM): New York, NY, USA, 2017; pp. 257–258.
31. Negi, D.; Ray, S.; Lu, R. Pystin: Enabling Secure LBS in Smart Cities with Privacy-Preserving Top-*k* Spatial–Textual Query. *IEEE Internet Things J.* **2019**, *6*, 7788–7799. [CrossRef]
32. Farouk, F.; Alkady, Y.; Rizk, R. Efficient Privacy-Preserving Scheme for Location Based Services in VANET System. *IEEE Access* **2020**, *8*, 60101–60116. [CrossRef]
33. Ni, L.; Tian, F.; Ni, Q.; Yan, Y.; Zhang, J. An anonymous entropy-based location privacy protection scheme in mobile social networks. *EURASIP J. Wirel. Commun. Netw.* **2019**, *2019*, 93. [CrossRef]
34. Ying, B.; Makrakis, D. Protecting Location Privacy with Clustering Anonymization in vehicular networks. In Proceedings of the 2014 IEEE Conference on Computer Communications Workshops (INFOCOM WKSHPS), Toronto, ON, Canada, 27 April–2 May 2014; pp. 305–310.
35. Frejinger, E. Route Choice Analysis: Data, Models, Algorithms and Applications. Ph.D. Dissertation, Linköping University, Lausanne, Sweden, 30 April 2008.

Article

Contact Tracing: Ensuring Privacy and Security

Daan Storm van Leeuwen [1,†], Ali Ahmed [2,*,‡], Craig Watterson [2] and Nilufar Baghaei [3,4,‡]

1. Department of Computer Science, University of Liverpool, Liverpool 11341, UK; daanstormvanleeuwen@me.com
2. School of Engineering and Computer Science, Victoria University of Wellington, P.O. Box 600, Wellington 6140, New Zealand; Craig.Watterson@vuw.ac.nz
3. School of Natural & Computational Sciences, Massey University, Auckland 0745, New Zealand; N.Baghaei@massey.ac.nz
4. School of Information Technology and Electrical Engineering, University of Queensland, St Lucia, QLD 4072, Australia
* Correspondence: ali.ahmed@vuw.ac.nz
† Current address: Mathematical Sciences Building Campus, Albany, NY 12207, USA.
‡ These authors contributed equally to this work.

Abstract: Faced with the biggest virus outbreak in a century, world governments at the start of 2020 took unprecedented measures to protect their healthcare systems from being overwhelmed in the light of the COVID-19 pandemic. International travel was halted and lockdowns were imposed. Many nations adopted measures to stop the transmission of the virus, such as imposing the wearing of face masks, social distancing, and limits on social gatherings. Technology was quickly developed for mobile phones, allowing governments to track people's movements concerning locations of the virus (both people and places). These are called contact tracing applications. Contact tracing applications raise serious privacy and security concerns. Within Europe, two systems evolved: a centralised system, which calculates risk on a central server, and a decentralised system, which calculates risk on the users' handset. This study examined both systems from a threat perspective to design a framework that enables privacy and security for contact tracing applications. Such a framework is helpful for App developers. The study found that even though both systems comply with the General Data Protection Regulation (GDPR), Europe's privacy legislation, the centralised system suffers from severe risks against the threats identified. Experiments, research, and reviews tested the decentralised system in various settings but found that it performs better but still suffers from inherent shortcomings. User tracking and re-identification are possible, especially when users report themselves as infected. Based on these data, the study identified and validated a framework that enables privacy and security. The study also found that the current implementations using the decentralised Google/Apple API do not comply with the framework.

Keywords: contact tracing; COVID-19 pandemic; security; privacy; mobile application

Citation: Storm van Leeuwen, D.; Ahmed, A.; Watterson, C.; Baghaei, N. Contact Tracing: Ensuring Privacy and Security. *Appl. Sci.* **2021**, *11*, 9977. https://doi.org/10.3390/app11219977

Academic Editors: Gianluca Lax and Antonia Russo

Received: 27 September 2021
Accepted: 19 October 2021
Published: 25 October 2021

Publisher's Note: MDPI stays neutral with regard to jurisdictional claims in published maps and institutional affiliations.

Copyright: © 2021 by the authors. Licensee MDPI, Basel, Switzerland. This article is an open access article distributed under the terms and conditions of the Creative Commons Attribution (CC BY) license (https://creativecommons.org/licenses/by/4.0/).

1. Introduction

The COVID-19 pandemic has had a dramatic impact on the world, affecting millions of people. With an increasing death toll and increased COVID variants, nations are desperately investigating ways to combat the virus [1]. However, unlike, for instance, the 1918 Spanish flu, technology is playing an essential role in the fight against the virus. It comes as no surprise that authorities have embraced new, promising, and previously unavailable technology. For instance, some cities use location and movement data to assess the population's mobility, which, in turn, is an indicator of the spread of the virus. These ventures are not without scepticism—Google's flu-tracking project famously failed and showed that some techniques are not yet mature [2,3].

With regards to COVID-19, three problems make the traditional approach difficult, such as Google's flu-tracking project, along with other manual approaches, if not impossible. Firstly, contact tracing is more complicated in urban areas. A key characteristic of urbanisation is that many people live, work, and socialise in close proximity to each other. Therefore, it is inevitable that people do not necessarily know the other people on the bus, train, gym, or marketplace. This realisation presents a challenge for a contact tracer: how do you perform contact tracing when the subject does not know most of the people they had contact with? The second problem has to do with the number of mild and asymptomatic cases that makes detection hard. The third and final problem has to do with the incubation time. The mean incubation time of 6.7 days, meaning that the time between infection and symptoms is, on average, a week [4]. This figure creates a challenge for contact tracers: when they discover a case, they might have to retrace the patients' steps for more than a week. Retracing steps becomes increasingly challenging if a patient has to rely on memory alone. The aforementioned problems combined form a deadly mix; four out of five patients exhibit no symptoms and might not even show signs for up to a week after infection—possibly longer. During that time, they are infectious to others, yet do not know they carry the disease while participating in social life in bars, public transport, and other large gatherings. If and when the condition is finally detected, manual contact tracing is extremely hard to perform. Meanwhile, for diseases such as COVID-19, with a high reproduction but low detection rate, rapid contact tracing is vital to keep cases low and the impact on society minimum [5].

Some countries were successful in their response to COVID-19. Singapore, South Korea, and China (after the initial first wave) once received high praise for their interventions. Notably, their contact tracing efforts were effective, despite the problems mentioned above (The Singapore contact tracer app also suffered from data leakage https://www.bbc.com/news/world-asia-55541001 accessed on 22 September 2021). Their approach included the use of technology, such as mobility data gathered by smartphones, giving contact tracers access to high-quality data of a person's movements before their infection. These countries were successful, as previous epidemics, such as SARS and MERS, taught them valuable lessons in handling an infectious disease [5]. South Korea even has legislation to facilitate contact tracing. With these results in mind, many states focus on digital contact tracing. Realising the power of contact tracing and the problems that come with manual contact tracing during the pandemic, governments quickly implemented digital contact tracing solutions.

The main research objectives of this paper are shown in Table 1 along with listed research methodologies to achieve them.

Table 1. The used research methodologies.

Objectives	Methodology	Method
Threats Investigation	Qualitative	Literature Analysis
Investigating Available Techniques	Qualitative	Literature Analysis
Privacy definition for contact tracing apps	Qualitative	Literature Analysis
Security definition for contact tracing apps	Qualitative	Literature Analysis
Framework Design	Prototyping	Implementation
Framework Review	Quantitative	Experimentation
Framework validation	Prototyping	Implementation

2. Digital Contact Tracing: What Is Missing?

The idea of using technology in epidemiology is not unique to the 2020 pandemic. The use of algorithms, data, and computational power to revolutionise epidemiology has been argued previously [6]. However, it was not until the publication of the work in [7] that digital contact tracing received significant attention. The authors modelled the growth of COVID-19 to assess the effectiveness of digital contact tracing. They found that the problem of pre-asymptomatic and asymptomatic cases alone is enough to sustain the exponential growth of COVID-19. If the delay between finding new cases and notification of contacts is three days or less, epidemic control is possible. Moreover, immediate notification by an application could lead to epidemic control if user adoption is 56% or higher. Lower user adoption can still contribute significantly to halting the exponential spread of the epidemic, when combined with additional interventions, such as face masks, frequent hand sanitation, and social distancing. "Digital contact tracing could play a critical role in avoiding or leaving lockdown" [7]. It is worth noting that two countries, amongst many, that successfully employed digital contact tracing solutions are China and South Korea. However, whether their methods respect privacy and security are debatable. For example, China ties its social gigantic application WeChat (https://www.wechat.com accessed on 22 September 2021) to various other governmental IT systems. Realising this threat, privacy and security advocates worldwide quickly warned of the dangers of digital contact tracing. As early as April 2020, an impressive global community of scientists released a press statement calling for digital solutions that respect privacy and security [8].

Even with the debate on privacy and security still raging, governments decided to develop contact tracing applications. Most, but not all, based their apps on the Google and Apple exposure notification (GAEN) framework. This framework is, in essence, an extra layer between the operating systems of both Google (i.e., Android) and Apple (i.e., iOS) and a third-party contact tracing application. GAEN uses Bluetooth low energy (BLE) hardware for proximity tracing. GAEN is essentially based on the decentralised DP-3T protocol and promises a privacy-preserving method to allow digital contact tracing. However, some governments remain unconvinced. The French government specifically decided to use its proprietary implementation, not wanting to rely on Apple and Google. It is argued that GAEN is inherently dangerous especially against a malicious authority [9] and is considered too restricted to perform digital contact tracing effectively. It proposes to use more, instead of less, personal information [10]. Although governments are rushing to develop contact tracing applications, often based on Google and Apple exposure notification (GAEN), the fundamental questions of privacy and security are debated and remain unanswered to this day. Although the argument continues, the question remains: what system ensures privacy and security best? This observation is troublesome considering that there are guidelines and frameworks for many other applications to ensure that those apps are safe to use, but this is lacking for digital contact tracing. In essence, what framework should app developers, governments, and healthcare providers follow when deploying a digital contact tracing system? It is worth emphasising that decentralised contact tracing apps have inherent privacy limitations [11]. It is worth noting "the Google Play Services component of these apps is problematic from a privacy viewpoint" [12] (i.e., mainly for GAEN-based contact tracing apps users on Android). This may justify why many people are reluctant to download and use contact tracing apps (i.e., The health-privacy trade-off [13]).

Known as test, trace, isolate, and quarantine (TTIQ), this strategy isolates only at-risk patients, instead of the entire population. This approach requires finding cases early, which, in the case of COVID-19, is difficult, as discussed earlier. Contact tracers in this situation require help to identify possible cases. Fuelled by the initial success that China, South Korea, and Singapore had with contact tracing [14], dozens of nations are now considering digital contact tracing solutions to identify cases quickly because "app-based tracing remains more effective than conventional contact tracing" [15].

Contact tracing consists of two components or systems: an epidemiological component, which is not the scope of this project, and a technical component [16]. Both have to work together for the systems to be effective [17]. Since smartphone penetration reaches 80% in the European Union [18], most attention concerning the technical component goes to smartphones. Contract tracing applications are mostly using four technologies or sensors on smartphones [5]:

1. Cell. Using the mobile operators cell tower information. Crude, but simple;
2. Wi-Fi. Scan for nearby devices connected to the same Wi-Fi network;

3. GPS. Using GPS and other positional data. However, these data, too, are relatively crude [19], especially in urban areas;
4. Bluetooth. Bluetooth beacons allow for short range transmission and reception and includes signal strength—specifically Bluetooth low energy (BLE).

Discussing what technology to use goes hand in hand with the question: does that technology help curb the infection, and find the effective growth rate $R_e \leq 1$? Research shows that it does if adoption exceeds 6% [7]. However, even if user adoption is significantly lower, digital contact tracing applications can have a significant contribution to stop epidemic growth—especially when combined with other measures [7,15,16]. However, speed is of the essence: the time between detection of a case and notification of contacts must be as quick as possible: "Combining traditional and digital contact tracing may leverage the advantages, and mitigate the limitations, of each approach" [17]. Given these requirements, BLE proved the best sensor to estimate the relative distance between two people—even though BLE suffers from false positives [5]. However, recording proximity between different people inherently leads to privacy and security questions [17].

3. Background Discussion

As soon as digital contact tracing surfaced, researchers began debating the privacy and security implications. Within Europe, two systems emerged from this debate: centralised and decentralised which are in the focus of this section. The first serious proposal in Europe came from the Pan European Privacy-Preserving Proximity Tracing (PEPP-PT) group (https://ercim-news.ercim.eu/en121/ib/pan-european-privacy-preserving-proximity-tracing accessed on 22 September 2021). They proposed a protocol, also named PEPP-PT, which works with BLE to record chance encounters between random individuals. The protocol functions by storing these encounters on the handset of the user. If the user receives a COVID-19 diagnosis, they can choose whether to upload the encounter data to a central server. The central server processes the encounters and notifies other, at-risk users by either a push or pull mechanism (PEPP-PT, 2020). The fact that it is the server that processes risks makes this system centralised. The French ROBERT has its origins in PEPP-PT, which drew many privacy concerns. This is why a decentralised system, where all processing takes place on the handset itself was proposed (e.g., the decentralised privacy-preserving proximity tracing (DP-3T) protocol). Unlike PEPP-PT, DP3T proposes that all infection data are publicly available and pushed to all handsets thus that every phone can assess the risk locally instead of centrally. The decentralised approach that the DP-3T-team proposed, inspired the exposure notification framework that Google and Apple jointly developed.

PEPP-PT attracted a lot of negative attention from scientists worldwide. On 19 April 2020, more than 400 scientists and researchers signed a Joint Statement on Contact Tracing, explaining a fear for mission creep in contact tracing systems stating that "It is vital that, in coming out of the current crisis, we do not create a tool that enables large scale data collection on the population" [8]. This fear is rooted in the fact that systems that process data centrally can, in theory, also produce a social graph: a detailed map that shows who has been in contact with whom. Opposed to that idea, the authors propose a decentralised system, where all processing takes place on the handset itself (e.g., the decentralised privacy-preserving proximity tracing (DP-3T) protocol). Unlike PEPP-PT, DP3T proposes that all infection data are publicly available and pushed to all handsets thus that every phone can assess the risk locally instead of centrally. The decentralised approach that the DP-3T-team proposed, inspired the exposure notification framework that Google and Apple jointly developed.

The DP-3T design forms the basis for the Google and Apple exposure notification (GAEN) API. The systems differ from PEPP-PT in that it reveals minimal information to the backend server. Where PEPP-PT calculates risk information in the backend and notifies the users at risk, DP-3T pushes at-risk information to all handsets, relying on each handset to calculate risk information and alert the user—making it decentralised. This means the user does not need to register for the service. The DP-3T protocol follows two steps. Firstly, generation and storage of ephemeral IDs. This handset generates a daily rotating key SK_t and uses a hashing algorithm to derive the EphIDs. These are broadcast to other handsets. It is impossible to recalculate the original SK_t based on the received EphIDs. Secondly, proximity tracing. Whenever a user reports positive for COVID-19, the healthcare authority publishes the SK_t for the days the user was infectious. Other phones can download and use these to re-calculate the EphIDs and compare them to the ones stored in memory.

Contact tracing applications fall within the scope of the GDPR [20]. The European Data Protection Board (EDPB) investigating both systems and confirmed they can be compliant to the GDPR, with an interesting footnote: the EDPB assesses the decentralised system better in line with the data minimisation principle. A decentralised system is preferred and it is argued that "Public health bodies are, at least in theory, more democratically accountable. On the other hand, users have, at least in theory, more robust rights to withdraw from commercial systems operating based on user consent" [21]. Even though those positions give direction to what systems to use, national privacy authorities decide if an app is admissible. For the centralised PEPP-PT/ROBERT, the French privacy authority CNIL cautiously approved the French governmental StopCovid application (https://www.cnil.fr/fr/publication-de-lavis-de-la-cnil-sur-le-projet-dapplication-mobile-stopcovid accessed on 22 September 2021). The day after this approval, however, a group of 471 French security and cryptography researchers released a statement warning of the danger of digital contact tracing, regardless of which system (https://uk.news.yahoo.com/hundreds-french-academics-sign-letter-155630916.html accessed on 22 September 2021). A few days later, on 26 April, Germany withdrew from the ROBERT framework, opting for a decentralised approach instead. However, Germany did so because of the earlier mentioned GAEN-advantage that allows for continuous background access to the Bluetooth hardware. The Netherlands, Germany, and Switzerland all received approval for their decentralised/GAEN Apps from their respective privacy authorities as well. Researchers from the University of Cambridge also looked into the decentralised (GAEN) implementation vs. the GDPR. They also conclude that GAEN is compliant with the GDPR: "the GDPR's expansive scope is not a hindrance, but rather an advantage in conditions of uncertainty such as a pandemic" [21]. However, the verdict on whether a contact tracing application complies with GDPR depends upon both GAEN and the application. That does not mean the debate about GAEN ends there. Much attention goes to the role Google and Apple play and how they expand their healthcare influence. For example, the work in [22] extensively investigates GAEN and argues that the industry practice by Google and Apple to remember which user and which handset downloaded what apps (including contact tracing apps), is against the GDPR. These debates are relevant but exceed the discussion on GDPR-compliance. The German withdrawal from PEPP-PT, the cautious approval by CNIL, and the Inria-split made the introduction of PEPP-PT controversial. The split caused reputation damage to PEPP-PT, rubbing off on the perception of privacy and security. The position of European's political and privacy bodies, supported by research, all conclude that decentralised solutions are preferable over centralised ones. It seems that decentralised technology is the best way to design contact tracing apps. However, there are other positions to consider as well, beyond centralised and decentralised, such as the DESIRE protocol [23]? The DESIRE protocol which, unfortunately, has not been comprehensively studied or used in any contract tracing application yet due to the lack of protocol software libraries.

DP-3T and PEPP-PT have data minimisation at the core, which the GDPR requires. However, outside of the European Union, proposals exist that expand, rather than limit, the amount of data collected, to increase effectiveness. It is recommended to build a voluntary system that fits the needs set forth by public health authorities. Additionally, it allows a user to enable or disable additional sensors or contextual information they want to use within the application [24]. These recommendations place a lot of trust and responsibility in the hands of the user. In other words, let the user decide how much data they want to share! The idea to add contextual information in contact tracing applications begs the question of what this would do to privacy and security. The use of contextual information in South Korea is examined and it was found that people could be the subject of "Stereotyping, stigmatisation and discrimination" [25]. It is for that, and other reasons that the GDPR calls for data minimisation and requires that actors take proportionality (is the expected gain worth it versus the level of breach?), subsidiarity (can the effect be reached by another, less intrusive method?), and necessity (is the breach necessary?) into account. From that perspective, enriching data is not a good idea since people could feel compelled or pressured to release more data than they prefer. In addition, if people want to release additional data to facilitate contact tracing, they can already do so. Typical methods could include browsing their social media history, checking their calendar, or reviewing navigation data.

With the research identified in this section, and the importance various authors placed on various aspects, it is possible to come up with a list of requirements for contact tracing applications–a framework. However, two problems remain: First, some requirements find their origin in untested research. Second, if the decentralised Google and Apple API is the best option for contact tracing, will it survive that framework? Does the Google and Apple implementation comply with the research identified so far? Additionally, the role Google and Apple play is debatable. What are they going to do with the technology they designed once the crisis is over? The same question needs answering from a governmental perspective: Somewhere, a policymaker in law enforcement already considers using this technology for law enforcement purposes.

Since contact tracing is dealing with sensitive information, this information needs to be protected against well-known attacks. Understanding the attack vector against such applications is important in securing them. Investigating the threats against both centralised and decentralised systems are demonstrated in [9,26]. It was argued that neither system protects privacy and security [9] (i.e., tracking, social graphing, identification, pressure to opt-in, replay attacks, etc.), as shown in Figure 1. Some of the threats against decentralised systems include tracking people by de-pseudonymising user's EphID, disclosing the social graph, identifying diagnosed people, pressure to opt-in, and injecting false encounters. Centralised systems suffer from similar threats.

A plus (+) indicates this schema is preferred; a minus (-) indicates this schema is not preferred.

	Centralised	Decentralised
Tracking	(-) Central server puts all users at risk; possibly theft of on device-data	(+) Infected users at risk; possibly theft of on-device data.
Social graph	(-) Central server puts the social subgraph at risk	(+) Not possible with the possible exceptation of RPI theft
Identification (de-pseudonymization)	(-) Possible by RPI reception & observations; aggravated by central server attack.	(+) Possible by RPI reception & observations.
Identification (diagnosed people)	(+) Difficult; if not impossible.	(-) Identification diagnosed people is possible. Legislation could mitigate this attack.
Pressure to opt-in	(-) Pressured user always results in privacy risk.	(+) Pressured user retains option to opt-in if the health app is designed with an OTK authorisation.
Replay attacks	(+) Replay of RPIs is possible, less opportunity for dark markets, effect measurement still possible but more labour intensive	(-) Replay of RPIs is possible, with a dark market for high likelihood infectious RPIs as a possibility. This makes it possible to measure the effect of the replay attack.

Figure 1. Overview of privacy and security attacks.

4. Framework Analysis and Design

In this section, we will introduce the framework we built and tested against several leading European implementations. Based on the comprehensive literature survey, the draft framework that preserves privacy and protects the security of users is demonstrated in Table 2. The table provides information on and an overview of requirements that have to be met to make an app that is both private and secure within the European Union. Notice that a decentralised design is required, in line with the EU and research. This (draft) framework in itself satisfies objective five, but it is unknown whether the current, leading implementations meet this framework and these requirements.

Table 2. Draft framework for privacy and security.

Identifier,	Requirement Number,	Objective
1.1	Users cannot be tracked	1 (Threat)
1.2 Exposure Keys (TEKs)	Users cannot be re-identified either after infection or otherwise. This includes when uploading infectious temporarily	1 (Threat)
1.3	Users cannot be pressured into disclosing sensitive data	1 (Threat)
1.4	Replay attacks leading to false alerts are impossible	1 (Threat)
1.5	Users cannot be identified through profiling or application use	1 (Threat)
2.1	Proximity tracing is exclusively performed with BLE	2 (Techniques)
2.2	Decentralised design conforming with DP-3T/GAEN	2 (Techniques)
2.3	The BLE beacons are pseudonymous and rotates frequently. This includes fake hardware addresses.	2 (Techniques)
3.1	Every implementation is approved by the privacy authority with a valid PIA published.	3 (Privacy)
3.2	The contract tracing system is voluntary and dismantled after the pandemic preventing mission creep.	3 (Privacy)
3.3	Google and Apple dismantle the GAEL-API after the pandemic	3 (Privacy)
3.4	The backend stores data exclusively in the EU with no data transfers outside the EU.	3 (Privacy)
4.1	The app follows a security standard to ensure continuous security evaluation	4 (Security)
4.2	The app source code is open and secured against malicious updates	4 (Security)
4.3	Google and Apple disclose the GAEN API	4 (Security)

To validate the draft framework, the project tested several leading European implementations against it. The results gathered from this paper can verify whether the GAEN-enabled implementations comply with the framework and are, as such, ensuring privacy and security. The requirements presented later, translate to the questions in Table 3 that direct further research. Note that requirement 2.2 is not tested and considered one of the future works. This requirement stipulates a decentralised design, which is an integral part of the experiments shown later. The research focuses only on decentralised designs. It is worth noting that Table 3 identifies three different research methods to investigate the answers to the questions.

Table 3. Questions to evaluate implementations.

Research Question,	Identifier,	Method
Can infected users be re-identified on uploading TEKs by sniffing their traffic?	1.2	Review Implementation
Can users be identified by IPs on uploading TEKs?	1.2	Review Implementation
Is Bluetooth the only sensor used in the application?	2.1	Review Implementation
Does the implementation have a PIA approved by the national privacy authority?	3.1	Review Implementation
Is the application voluntary?	3.2	Review Implementation
Does the backend store data exclusively in the EU?	3.4	Review Implementation
Does the implementation follow a security standard ensuring continuous security assessment?	4.1	Review Implementation
Can the source code be reviewed?	4.2	Review Implementation
Does the downloadable app match the source code published?	4.2	Review Implementation
Can GAEN API be reviewed?	4.3	Review Implementation
Are reply attacks possible?	1.4	Literature Review
Did the government have plans to dismantle the system after the pandemic?	3.2	Literature Review
Do Google and Apple have plans to dismantle GAEN after the pandemic?	3.3	Literature Review
Can users be tracked by Rolling Proximity Identifier (RPI)?	1.1	Experiments and Literature Review
Can users be re-identified by RPIs analysis?	1.2	Experiments
Can users be pressured into disclosing compromising data?	1.3	Experiments
Are the BLE beacons pseudonymous and do they rotate frequently?	2.3	Experiments
Are Bluetooth hardware addresses in the advertisement data random and rotate frequently?	2.3	Experiments
Is it possible to profile users?	1.5	Experiments

5. Framework Evaluation

It is worth noting that this research used three leading European implementations, which are not only currently in use but also were subjected to a lot of attention and debate. These implementations are CoronaMelder (i.e., the Netherlands), Corona-Warn-App (i.e., Germany), and SwissCovid (i.e., Switzerland). These Apps are mature and well-received within the privacy research community [19]. Now, let us revisit the questions in Table 3 and answer them. It is worth emphasising that, this paper focuses on those questions requiring experimentation (i.e., see Table 3), thus experiments were performed using a Raspberry Pi 4 running Raspbian Linux and an Ubertooth Bluetooth interception module. Different mobile handsets are used in such experiments.

Can infected users be re-identified on uploading TEKs by sniffing their traffic? Uploading TEKs is a sign of infection since it creates traffic to a server that is normally absent. This attack works even if traffic is encrypted. To negate this threat, the Dutch and German implementation upload fake keys at random intervals. If an attacker sniffs the traffic between the handset and the server, it is impossible to separate real uploads of keys from fake keys. This implementation prevents an attacker from identifying infected users by sniffing the TCP/IP traffic between the handset and the server. *Can users be identified by IPs on uploading TEKs?* If an attacker compromises the backend server, it is possible to re-identify infected people by IP address. This only works when it is possible to combine the IP address with infection data. The Dutch and German implementations separate the IP address from the TEKs as soon as traffic arrives at the backend server [27]. The backend stores the TEKs in a database, but it stores the IP addresses for a maximum of 15 min to allow for intrusion and attack detection. This solution shows that it is possible to separate identifiable IP information from the pseudonymous TEKs, preventing re-identification when uploading TEKs.

Is Bluetooth the only sensor used in the application? The three implementations were examined on both iPhone 11 Pro (i.e., iOS) and Nokia TA-1042 (i.e., Android). All three apps ask for no other permissions than to use the exposure notifications, mobile data for downloading TEKs and the general notifications. The investigation shows that the GAEN-enabled apps of the Netherlands, Germany, and Switzerland do not require any additional authorisations.

Does the implementation have a PIA approved by the national privacy authority? The European Data Protection Board is very clear that countries, wishing to implement a contact tracing application, need to publish a Data Protection Impact Assessment (DPIA) and have it approved by their local privacy authority. An approved DPIA exists for the German, Dutch, and Swiss apps [27,28].

Is the application voluntary? In all three nations, there is no legislation in place to make the app mandatory. GDPR also prohibits this, but in the Netherlands, additional legislation was enacted specifically forbidding private or public organisations to make the app mandatory. When installing and running SwissCovid, Corona-Warn, and CoronaMelder on both Android and iOS devices, none of these apps required registration. The privacy authorities of these countries do not allow registration since this would link personal information to the app, an IP address and possibly the TEKs [27]. The only app that did require registration is the French TousAntiCovid, in line with the PEPP-PT protocol. The European Commission (2020), parliament (2020) and EDPB confirm the importance of these criteria. The app must be voluntary and should be dismantled after use. Upon examining the DPIA of the countries investigated, it is confirmed that this is the intention [27,28]. However, the work in [29–31] make a legitimate argument that the technology cannot be un-invented and that even though national governments might dismantle the app after the pandemic, Google and Apple might not. Google and Apple claim that they will only use the technology during the pandemic, but there is no way of knowing whether this intention solidifies in reality.

Does the backend store data exclusively in the EU? When studying SwissCovid, processing data outside the European Union is undesirable, especially after the European Court of Justice invalidated Privacy Shield in 2019 [9]. Without additional safeguards and contractual clauses, the transfer of personal information to the US is illegal. SwissCovid uses Amazon servers for the back-end. Interestingly, both the Dutch and German privacy authorities agree that the backend should not be hosted on US servers. Those applications use servers within Europe, to avoid the transfer of personal data. Based on the DPIA of the

Netherlands and Germany, and the criticism on the Swiss implementation, the backend should store data within the EU which means the criterion is valid.

Does the implementation follow a security standard ensuring continuous security assessment? When designing software, a security standard helps to prevent common mistakes, forgetting critical items and review the software created. Well-known examples stem from the International Standards Organisation (ISO), the National Institute for Standards and Technology (NIST) and the European Union. The Dutch and German applications follow the NIST Cybersecurity directive, to provide cyclical security assessment and enhancements.

Can the source code be reviewed? The EDPB and various national privacy authorities stress the fact that the source code of Corona applications must be published as open source. A popular platform to do so is GitHub. Indeed, the three Apps examined all have their source code published as follows. For CoronaMelder, source code is accessible from https://github.com/minvws/nl-covid19-notification-app-ios accessed on 22 September 2021 and https://github.com/minvws/nl-covid19-notification-app-android accessed on 22 September 2021. For CoronaWarn App, it is accessible via https://github.com/corona-warn-app/cwa-app-ios accessed on 22 September 2021 and https://github.com/corona-warn-app/cwa-app-android accessed on 22 September 2021. For SwissCovid, one can view the source code from https://github.com/DP-3T/dp3t-app-ios-ch accessed on 22 September 2021 and https://github.com/DP-3T/dp3t-app-android-ch accessed on 22 September 2021.

Does the downloadable app match the source code published? Even though the software designers publish the source code online, that does not mean it matches the version of the app that is available for download in the App Store and Play Store. For instance, at the time of writing, the version of CoronaMelder at GitHub is 1.0.12, while the version on our phone is 1.0.11. Thus, how can one verify the app indeed matches the one published on GitHub? The Dutch and German App developers use an external security organisation to verify this is indeed the case [27]. Generally, this criterion is therefore valid and solvable, with a proper implementation.

Can GAEN API be reviewed? Neither Apple nor Google released the full, implemented source code of their APIs. Google did publish a "reference design" on GitHub (https://github.com/google/exposure-notifications-android accessed on 22 September 2021, https://developer.apple.com/exposure-notification/ accessed on 22 September 2021). The objective of both releases is not to allow external parties to review the code and participate in finding flaws, but to give developers an idea of how the internals of the GAEN API work. This problem is quite apparent in the literature. Many authors point out the inability to review the design choices, security and privacy of the GAEN-API [9,27,29]. The question is if there are other possibilities to review the source code. An external party could be contracted to review the code, on behalf of the health authorities.

Are replay attacks possible? Given a decentralised design, the work in [19] proved that a relay-based worm-hole attack is possible, generating false contact on a target's device. They performed their experiment in reaction to the SwissCovid app. The Swiss NCSC (2020) The attack is confirmed by the work in [9,26,28,32]. An important realisation of all these articles is that the authors replayed the RPI, not the TEK. This proves that, at least in decentralised designs, replay attacks remain possible and real danger.

The following mobile handsets were used to perform the experiment:

1. iPhone 5S incompatible with GAEN and contact tracing applications. This phone serves as a comparison between devices running GAEN, as a device that cannot run GAEN;
2. A Nokia TA-1047 running Android 10, a cheap but GAEN-compatible smartphone, in developer mode;
3. A Samsung S9 Android 9 running GAEN, a typical consumer smartphone;
4. An iPhone 11 Pro running GAEN, a typical consumer smartphone;
5. A Ruggear RG-850 Android 10 phone running GAEN, a typical smartphone used with healthcare professionals.

Are the BLE beacons pseudonymous and do they rotate frequently? The GAEN-documentation sets the time interval for RPIs at roughly 10 min. By hooking up an Android phone in developer mode with the HCI Snoop Log enabled to a computer with Android Studio running, it is possible to filter for RPI changes.

Figure 2 shows that every 10 min, the RPI changes to a new value. Deviations were observed; sometimes the RPI changes in 7 min, sometimes in 12 min. A pattern between these times could not be determined; it is reasonable to suspect that a pseudo-random generator determines a time shift. The log also shows the new *RollingProximityID* value when the RPI rotates. These values appear random; no correlation between the values was observed. The question is whether these RPIs match the ones transmitted by the phone. A single GAEN-equipped phone with the Dutch CoronaMelder GAEN application was placed next to the interception station to investigate this. The purpose of this test is to compare the transmitted RPI with the received RPI. The Ubertooth intercepted the BLE broadcasts and saved them to a *pcapng* file for later analysis. Using Wireshark for analysis, the following filter ensured that only GAEN BLE advertisements show up, which are close by ($\geq$45 dbm). Figure 3 demonstrates the output after capturing the data.

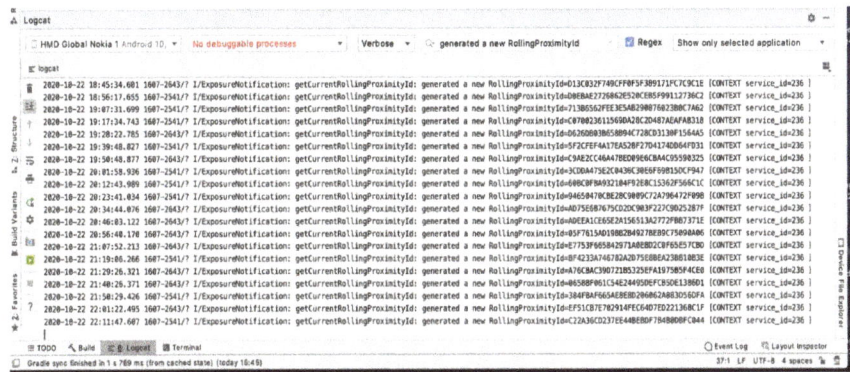

Figure 2. Time interval of RPI change.

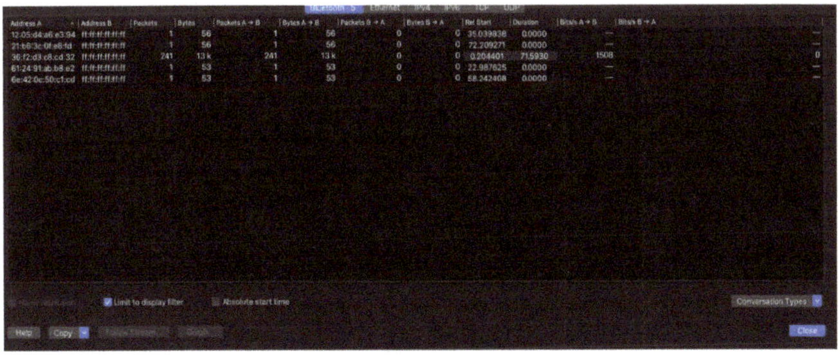

Figure 3. Wireshark Conversation.

Almost all packets were transmitted by BD_ADDR 36:f2:d3:c8:cd:32. The four packets that were transmitted from other addresses, turned out to have a faulty cyclic redundancy check (CRC), a characteristic of an incomplete interception. All other packets showed the same RPI transmitted, with exception of the AEM as shown in Figure 4. The received RPI received *f18cf5f57aff05fde6779a562cc413bd* matches the one transmitted by the telephone, as seen in the HCI Snoop Log. The experiment proved that the reported RPI in the HCI Snoop Log indeed matches with the RPI transmitted by the phone, and subsequently received by the Ubertooth. This experiment confirms the RPIs rotate frequently and are indeed pseudonymous.

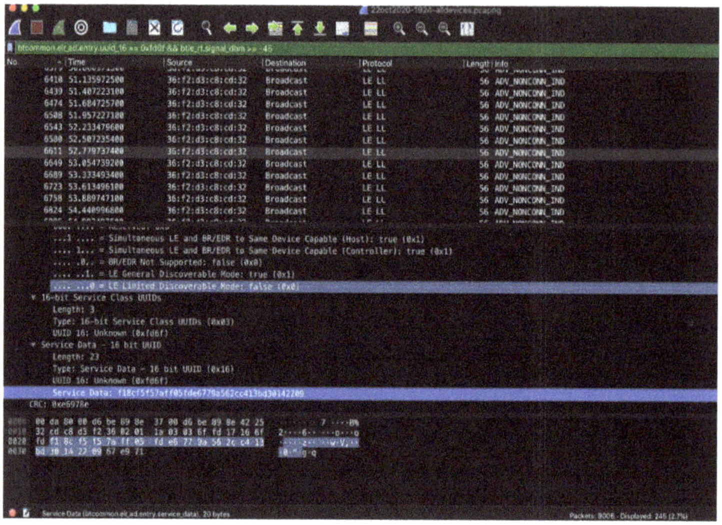

Figure 4. The Received RPI of a random package.

Are Bluetooth hardware addresses in the advertisement data random and rotate frequently? The Google and Apple specification requires the MAC address to rotate frequently (Google, 2020), to avoid device tracking. This experiment checks to see if indeed the MAC changes. The results were analysed with Wireshark below. As Figure 5 shows, address *77:8c:e9:ca:9c:55* first started transmitting 0.144961s after interception started and stopped 193.8150 s later (193,959961 s after experiment start). Interestingly, 194.498694 s after experiment start, *55:7d:89:91:fc:d2* started transmitting. Could this be a MAC address change for the same device? To answer this, one could see in Figure 6 the RPI that the first address used.

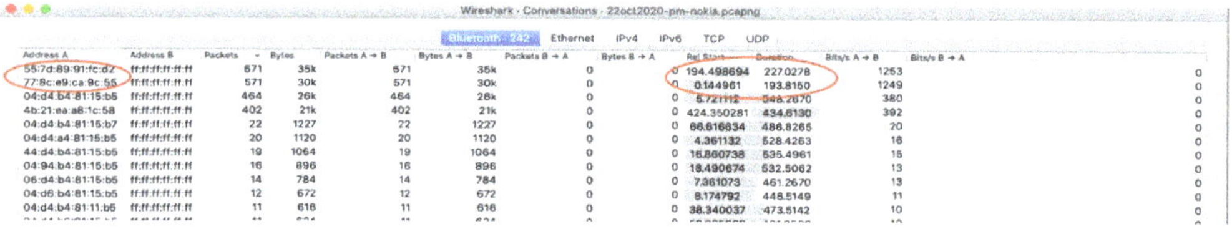

Figure 5. The Wireshark addresses captured.

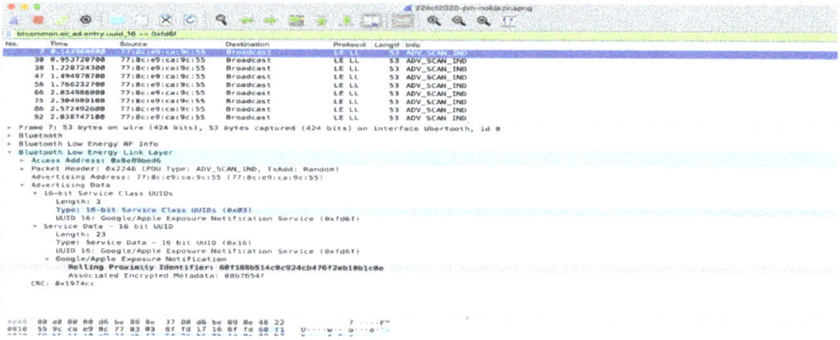

Figure 6. RPI transmitted by 77:8C:E9:CA:9C:55.

Wireshark can filter on this RPI, which shows that the new address transmitted the same RPI as seen in Figure 7.

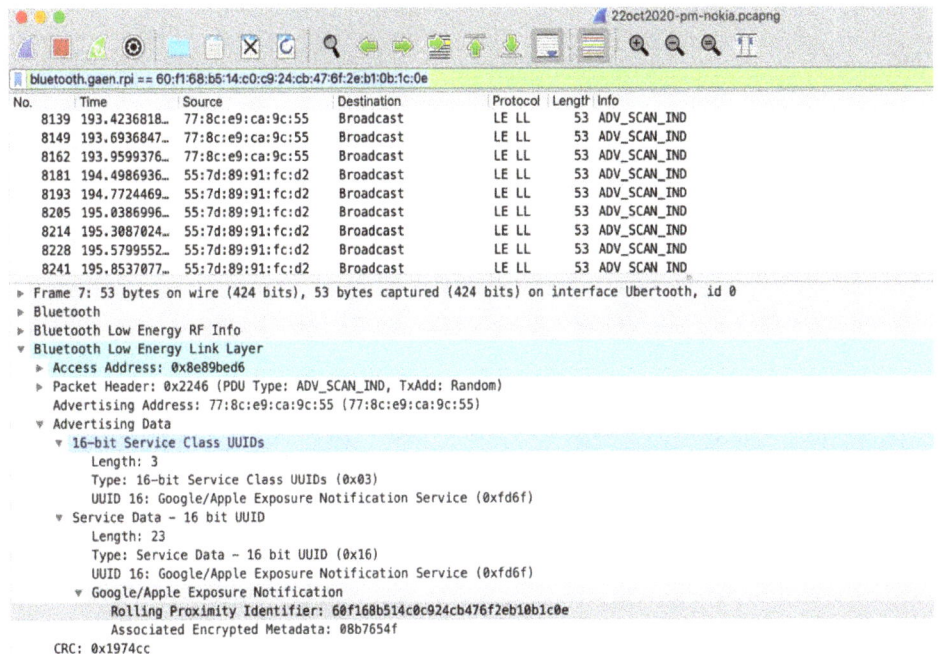

Figure 7. MAC address change with same RPI.

This experiment proves that even though GAEN randomises the MAC addresses frequently, it is possible to track the same device by using the RPI. Since RPIs rotate roughly every 10 min, and an RPI change forces a MAC address change as well, this means that an attacker has a maximum of 10 min to track a device. Even though the MAC address changes, a relatively easy analysis can tie the new MAC address to the old, by using the RPI.

Can users be tracked by RPI? Harvesting RPIs is not difficult using tools such as Raspberry Pi or Wireshark. Various projects on GitHub do exactly this: collecting RPIs. One such example is Corona-Teller (https://github.com/zeno4ever/CoronaTeller accessed on 22 September 2021). An attacker can integrate other data, such as location, date, and time, without any effort, and upload it to a central repository. This clearly shows that RPI harvesting is not difficult, and easily automated. Once harvested, it is possible to track users when they report an infection. The work in [28] proved this attack. Using the conclusions from the experiments performed above, it is possible to confirm these results: Intercepting RPIs is relatively easy and the attacker can combine them with location data, time, and date. By uploading these results to a central database, it is possible to track a user once infected.

Can users be re-identified by RPIs analysis? As discussed earlier, even though the MAC address changes frequently, it is possible to follow a specific device for a maximum of 10 min in which it transmits and receives the same RPI. This begs the question: is it possible to re-identify a user in that period? It is possible to combine phone transmissions with visual observations, as described in [9,26]. However, this experiment found a digital possibility as well. In this experiment, an attacker observes a user relatively close by and notices the user forms a Bluetooth piconet with for instance a headset, smartwatch, or another device. The attack starts intercepting Bluetooth low energy and notices the victim uses GAEN. To filter out other GAEN-users, the attacker applies a filter so only relatively close devices are shown in Figure 8.

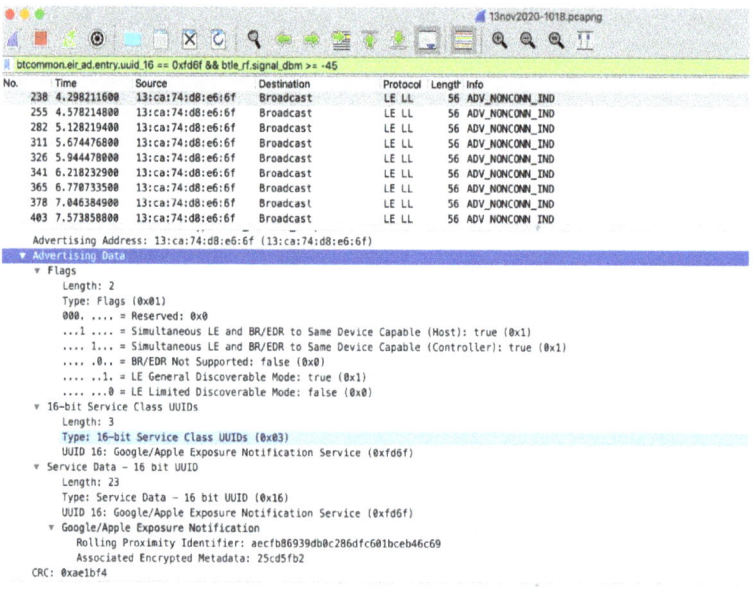

Figure 8. Victim uses GAEN; displays RPI.

The attacker can now visually link the user to the RPI, but the MAC address displayed is random. The attacker is not able to retrieve further information using this MAC. The piconet does display (part of the) MAC address, but only lower address part (LAP). To query a device, the attacker needs both the upper address part (UAP) and LAP. The attack now employs the Ubertooth to scan for networks and follow networks to try to retrieve the UAP. The attacker does that twice. The scan can retrieve the UAP and query the device, as shown in Figure 9. The figure shows, the Ubertooth successfully retrieved the UAP of the device and was able to query it. The UAP *79:93:BF:F9* matches the phone's address used in the experiment. The attack now successfully retrieved the RPI, identified the user and found the significant part of the Bluetooth address. The attacker can escalate by performing, for instance, a Bluetooth bias attack, impersonating an already paired device to retrieve more compromising information [33].

A serious consideration with this attack is that there are three limitations for it to work. First, the attack only works in a relatively closed setting, where visual observations confirm that no other devices are present. Second, the victim must use a Bluetooth piconet. Third, the attack is relatively labour-intensive.

Can users be pressured into disclosing compromising data? TEK (or SK_t) is the most compromising information. With the TEK, an attacker can reconstruct all RPIs. According to the documentation that Google and Apple provide on GAEN, it is impossible to retrieve this information since the devices store it in an enclave, or protected part of the memory. When investigating the exposure checks on both iOS and Android, the devices reveal no sensitive information. The user can check when the device downloaded TEKs, what the hash of the TEK download is, how many keys are in the file and how many match, etc. The user also has the option to delete the keys with the "Delete Exposure Log" button. However, the user cannot access sensitive information.

```
Scan results:
??:??:??:2B:28:0F
AFH map: 0xefd0023df80f01000011
??:??:79:93:BF:F9        iPhone-11-Pro-Daan
Requesting information ...
     BD Address:   00:00:79:93:BF:F9
     Device Name:  iPhone-11-Pro-Daan
     LMP Version:  (0xa) LMP Subversion: 0x4228
     Manufacturer: Broadcom Corporation (15)
     Features page 0: 0xbf 0xfe 0xcf 0xfe 0xdb 0xff 0x7b 0x87
          <3-slot packets> <5-slot packets> <encryption> <slot offset>
          <timing accuracy> <role switch> <sniff mode> <RSSI>
          <channel quality> <SCO link> <HV2 packets> <HV3 packets>
          <u-law log> <A-law log> <CVSD> <paging scheme> <power control>
          <transparent SCO> <broadcast encrypt> <EDR ACL 2 Mbps>
          <EDR ACL 3 Mbps> <enhanced iscan> <interlaced iscan>
          <interlaced pscan> <inquiry with RSSI> <extended SCO>
          <EV4 packets> <EV5 packets> <AFH cap. slave>
          <AFH class. slave> <LE support> <3-slot EDR ACL>
          <5-slot EDR ACL> <sniff subrating> <pause encryption>
          <AFH cap. master> <AFH class. master> <EDR eSCO 2 Mbps>
          <EDR eSCO 3 Mbps> <3-slot EDR eSCO> <extended inquiry>
          <LE and BR/EDR> <simple pairing> <encapsulated PDU>
          <err. data report> <non-flush flag> <LSTO> <inquiry TX power>
          <EPC> <extended features>
     Features page 1: 0x0f 0x00 0x00 0x00 0x00 0x00 0x00 0x00
     Features page 2: 0x7f 0x07 0x00 0x00 0x00 0x00 0x00 0x00
     Clock offset: 0x2b5d
     AFH Map: 0xfefffffefffffffff3f
AFH map: 0x04000000000150640101
```

Figure 9. Retrieved UAP using the Ubertooth.

6. Conclusions and Future Work

Can contact tracing applications, deployed in the fight against COVID-19, be safe and secure and, if so, what framework should designers follow to reach safety and security? This question started this research project. This paper investigated the current literature that exists on contact tracing from security and privacy perspectives. It led to the conclusion that decentralised solutions are preferable to centralised solutions. Decentralised solutions provide less attack surface because of the distributed nature of the system. The paper proposed a framework that provides a roadmap on building contact tracing applications within the EU. The framework is evaluated against the threats identified earlier using three leading European contact-tracing implementations. The results proved that the framework is valid and provides safety and security. However, the results also showed that the decentralised principle has inherent properties that lead to a breach in privacy and security.

This study intended to research and validate a framework for mobile contact tracing applications in light of the COVID-19 pandemic. The application of the research is not just limited to COVID-19, but any infectious disease. However, the research is limited in that it looked more thoroughly at decentralised than centralised solutions. Even though this study provided a comprehensive overview of contact tracing techniques and applications, follow-on work could look at centralised systems in more detail. Another suggestion for follow-on research is to develop an application that conforms to the framework: when starting from scratch, without the work that Apple and Google did, is it possible to design an application that conforms to the framework? A possible solution is to look at hybrid systems, which combine the best of centralised and decentralised systems.

Author Contributions: Conceptualization, A.A.; formal analysis, D.S.v.L.; investigation, D.S.v.L.; writing—original draft, D.S.v.L.; methodology, A.A.; software, D.S.v.L.; supervision, A.A.; validation, A.A., C.W. and N.B.; writing—review and editing, A.A., C.W. and N.B. All authors have read and agreed to the published version of the manuscript.

Funding: This research received no external funding.

Institutional Review Board Statement: Not applicable.

Informed Consent Statement: Not applicable.

Conflicts of Interest: The authors declare no conflict of interest.

References

1. Hassandoust, F.; Akhlaghpour, S.; Johnston, A.C. Individuals' privacy concerns and adoption of contact tracing mobile applications in a pandemic: A situational privacy calculus perspective. *J. Am. Med. Inform. Assoc.* **2021**, *28*, 463–471. [CrossRef] [PubMed]
2. Martinez-Martin, N.; Wieten, S.; Magnus, D.; Cho, M.K. Digital contact tracing, privacy, and public health. *Hastings Cent. Rep.* **2020**, *50*, 43–46. [CrossRef]
3. Imsanguan, W.; Bupachat, S.; Wanchaithanawong, V.; Luangjina, S.; Thawtheong, S.; Nedsuwan, S.; Pungrassami, P.; Mahasirimongkol, S.; Wiriyaprasobchok, A.; Kaewmamuang, K.; et al. Contact tracing for tuberculosis, Thailand. *Bull. World Health Organ.* **2020**, *98*, 212. [CrossRef]
4. Tian, S.; Hu, N.; Lou, J.; Chen, K.; Kang, X.; Xiang, Z.; Chen, H.; Wang, D.; Liu, N.; Liu, D.; et al. Characteristics of COVID-19 infection in Beijing. *J. Infect.* **2020**, *80*, 401–406. [CrossRef] [PubMed]
5. Hernández-Orallo, E.; Manzoni, P.; Calafate, C.T.; Cano, J.C. Evaluating how smartphone contact tracing technology can reduce the spread of infectious diseases: The case of COVID-19. *IEEE Access* **2020**, *8*, 99083–99097. [CrossRef] [PubMed]
6. Eckhoff, P.A.; Tatem, A.J. Digital methods in epidemiology can transform disease control. *Int. Health* **2015**, *7*, 77–78. [CrossRef]
7. Ferretti, L.; Wymant, C.; Kendall, M.; Zhao, L.; Nurtay, A.; Abeler-Dörner, L.; Parker, M.; Bonsall, D.; Fraser, C. Quantifying SARS-CoV-2 transmission suggests epidemic control with digital contact tracing. *Science* **2020**, *368*, 6491. [CrossRef] [PubMed]
8. Larus, J.; Paterson, K.; Veale, M.; Smart, N.; Preneel, B.; Cremers, C.; Troncoso, C.; Fiore, D. Joint Statement on Contact Tracing. Available Online: https://www.kastel.kit.edu/downloads/Joint%20Statement.pdf (accessed on 10 September 2021).
9. Vaudenay, S. *Centralized or Decentralized? The Contact Tracing Dilemma*; Technical Report; Cryptology ePrint Archive, 2020/531; EPFL: Lausanne, Switzerland, 2020.
10. Kahn, J.P. *Digital Contact Tracing for Pandemic Response: Ethics and Governance Guidance*; Johns Hopkins University Press: Baltimore, MD, USA, 2020.
11. Bengio, Y.; Ippolito, D.; Janda, R.; Jarvie, M.; Prud'homme, B.; Rousseau, J.F.; Sharma, A.; Yu, Y.W. Inherent privacy limitations of decentralized contact tracing apps. *J. Am. Med Inform. Assoc.* **2021**, *28*, 193–195. [CrossRef]
12. Leith, D.J.; Farrell, S. Contact tracing app privacy: What data is shared by europe's gaen contact tracing apps. In Proceedings of the IEEE INFOCOM 2021-IEEE Conference on Computer Communications, Vancouver, BC, Canada, 10–13 May 2021; pp. 1–10.
13. Tran, C.D.; Nguyen, T.T. Health vs. privacy? The risk-risk tradeoff in using COVID-19 contact-tracing apps. *Technol. Soc.* **2021**, *67*, 101755. [CrossRef]
14. Lee, D.; Heo, K.; Seo, Y. COVID-19 in South Korea: Lessons for developing countries. *World Dev.* **2020**, *135*, 105057. [CrossRef]
15. Kretzschmar, M.E.; Rozhnova, G.; Bootsma, M.; van Boven, M.; van de Wijgert, J.; Bonten, M. Time is of the essence: Impact of delays on effectiveness of contact tracing for COVID-19, a modelling study. *medRxiv* **2020**. [CrossRef]
16. Hinch, R.; Probert, W.; Nurtay, A.; Kendall, M.; Wymant, C.; Hall, M.; Lythgoe, K.; Cruz, A.B.; Zhao, L.; Stewart, A.; et al. Effective configurations of a digital contact tracing app: A report to NHSX. *Retrieved July* **2020**, *23*, 2020.
17. Kleinman, R.A.; Merkel, C. Digital contact tracing for COVID-19. *CMAJ* **2020**, *192*, E653–E656. [CrossRef] [PubMed]
18. Silver, L. *Smartphone Ownership Is Growing Rapidly Around the World, but Not Always Equally*; Technical Report; Pew Research Center: Washington, DC, USA, 2019. Available online: https://www.pewresearch.org/global/2019/02/05/smartphone-ownership-is-growing-rapidly-around-the-world-but-not-always-equally/ (accessed on 9 September 2021).
19. Baumgärtner, L.; Dmitrienko, A.; Freisleben, B.; Gruler, A.; Höchst, J.; Kühlberg, J.; Mezini, M.; Miettinen, M.; Muhamedagic, A.; Nguyen, T.D.; et al. Mind the gap: Security & privacy risks of contact tracing apps. *arXiv* **2020**, arXiv:2006.05914.
20. Scantamburlo, T.; Cortés, A.; Dewitte, P.; Van Der Eycken, D.; Billa, V.; Duysburgh, P.; Laenens, W. Covid-19 and contact tracing apps: A review under the European legal framework. *arXiv* **2020**, arXiv:2004.14665.
21. Bradford, L.; Aboy, M.; Liddell, K. COVID-19 contact tracing apps: A stress test for privacy, the GDPR, and data protection regimes. *J. Law Biosci.* **2020**, *7*, lsaa034. [CrossRef] [PubMed]
22. Leith, D.J.; Farrell, S. Gaen due diligence: Verifying the Google/Apple COVID exposure notification API. In Proceedings of the CoronaDef21, NDSS '21, San Diego, CA, USA, 23–26 February 2020.
23. Castelluccia, C.; Bielova, N.; Boutet, A.; Cunche, M.; Lauradoux, C.; Métayer, D.L.; Roca, V. DESIRE: A Third Way for a European Exposure Notification System Leveraging the best of centralized and decentralized systems. *arXiv* **2020**, arXiv:2008.01621.
24. Raskar, R.; Singh, A.; Zimmerman, S.; Kanaparti, S. Adding Location and Global context to the Google/Apple Exposure Notification Bluetooth API. *arXiv* **2020**, arXiv:2007.02317.
25. Ryan, M. In defence of digital contact-tracing: Human rights, South Korea and Covid-19. *Int. J. Pervasive Comput. Commun.* **2020**, ahead-of-print. [CrossRef]
26. Vaudenay, S. Analysis of DP3T: Between Scylla and Charybdis. IACR Cryptology ePrint Archive. 2020. Available online: https://infoscience.epfl.ch/record/277808 (accessed on 8 September 2021) .
27. de Winter, B.; Lute, E.; Dasselaar, A.; Frenken-Farag, M. *Duidingsrapportage CoronaMelderInformatiebeveiliging en Privacybescherming*; Technical Report 1, Stand van Zaken, Lanceringsadvies. 2020. Available online: https://www.rijksoverheid.nl/documenten/rapporten/2020/08/28/duidingsrapportage-coronamelder-informatiebeveiliging-en-privacybescherming-stand-van-zaken-lanceringsadvies (accessed on 8 September 2021).
28. Dehaye, P.O.; Reardon, J. SwissCovid: A critical analysis of risk assessment by Swiss authorities. *arXiv* **2020**, arXiv:2006.10719.

29. Sharon, T. Blind-sided by privacy? Digital contact tracing, the Apple/Google API and big tech's newfound role as global health policy makers. *Ethics Inf. Technol.* **2020**, 1–13. [CrossRef] [PubMed]
30. Wen, H.; Zhao, Q.; Lin, Z.; Xuan, D.; Shroff, N. A study of the privacy of covid-19 contact tracing apps. In Proceedings of the International Conference on Security and Privacy in Communication Systems, Washington, DC, USA, 21–23 October 2020; pp. 297–317.
31. Vitak, J.; Zimmer, M. More Than Just Privacy: Using Contextual Integrity to Evaluate the Long-Term Risks from COVID-19 Surveillance Technologies. *Soc. Media+ Soc.* **2020**, *6*, 2056305120948250. [CrossRef] [PubMed]
32. Iovino, V.; Vaudenay, S.; Vuagnoux, M. On the Effectiveness of Time Travel to Inject COVID-19 Alerts. Technical Report, Cryptology ePrint Archive, Report 2020/1393. 2020. Available online: https://eprint.iacr.org/2020/1393 (accessed on 22 September 2021).
33. Antonioli, D.; Tippenhauer, N.O.; Rasmussen, K. Bias: Bluetooth impersonation attacks. In Proceedings of the 2020 IEEE Symposium on Security and Privacy (SP), San Francisco, CA, USA, 18–21 May 2020; pp. 549–562.

Article

AI Model for Predicting Legal Judgments to Improve Accuracy and Explainability of Online Privacy Invasion Cases

Minjung Park and Sangmi Chai *

Ewha School of Business, Ewha Womans University, 52 Ewhayeodae-gil, Seodaemun-gu, Seoul 03760, Korea; mjpark6767@ewha.ac.kr
* Correspondence: smchai@ewha.ac.kr; Tel.: +82-2-3277-2780

Abstract: Since there are growing concerns regarding online privacy, firms may have the risk of being involved in various privacy infringement cases resulting in legal causations. If firms are aware of consequences from possible cases of invasion of online privacy, they can more actively prevent future online privacy infringements. Thus, this study attempts to predict the probability of judgment types caused by various invasions within US judicial cases that are related to online privacy invasions. Since legal judgment results are significantly influenced by societal factors and technological development, this study tries to identify a model that can accurately predict legal judgment with explainability. To archive the study objective, it compares the prediction performance by applying five types of classification algorithms (LDA, NNET, CART, SVM, and random forest) of machine learning. We also examined the relationship between privacy infringement factors and adjudications by applying network text analysis. The results indicate that firms could have a high possibility of both civil and criminal law responsibilities if they distributed malware or spyware, intentionally or non-intentionally, to collect unauthorized data. It addresses the needs of reflecting both quantitative and qualitative approach for establishing automatic legal systems for improving its accuracy based on the socio-technical perspective.

Keywords: online privacy invasions; personal information infringements; predicting judgments; predictive analytics; privacy act; network text analysis

Citation: Park, M.; Chai, S. AI Model for Predicting Legal Judgments to Improve Accuracy and Explainability of Online Privacy Invasion Cases. *Appl. Sci.* **2021**, *11*, 11080. https://doi.org/10.3390/app112311080

Academic Editor: Gianluca Lax

Received: 15 October 2021
Accepted: 17 November 2021
Published: 23 November 2021

Publisher's Note: MDPI stays neutral with regard to jurisdictional claims in published maps and institutional affiliations.

Copyright: © 2021 by the authors. Licensee MDPI, Basel, Switzerland. This article is an open access article distributed under the terms and conditions of the Creative Commons Attribution (CC BY) license (https://creativecommons.org/licenses/by/4.0/).

1. Introduction

Prediction of legal judgment is a long-lasting topic in the theory and practice of law to improve judicial consistency, access to justice, and administrative efficiency [1]. Therefore, various methods and techniques have emerged over time, including simple calculative models to highly advanced analytical algorithms to predict legal judgements. There have been a wide range of approaches attempted; in particular, artificial intelligence (AI)-based approaches have been increasingly utilized, with the recent advent of AI.

Legal decision systems have been established, based on AI, by predicting verdicts automatically to support lawyers.

A legal automation system called AI lawyer was invented to predict verdicts in the United States on May 2016, and since, constant efforts have been made to develop its accuracy. It reads a vast number of judgment documents and analyzes the contents based on a special algorithm to draw decisions to judge a case automatically. It becomes more difficult and time consuming for human lawyers to sentence correct verdicts in legal judgments, because there have been significantly increased numbers of lawsuits in the recent past. Thus, there is a growing need to develop systems for predicting legal judgments precisely based on a vast number of legal precedents, with the emergence of these AI lawyers and automatic legal systems based on big data. However, there is little research on big data analytics in the field of law. Therefore, our aim is to provide an AI model for establishing a system to predict legal judgments with explainability by identifying factors with high potential to cause privacy infringements and thus constitute illegal acts, as well as to compare the performance of predicting judgments.

This study focuses on the judicial cases related to privacy infringements caused by firms [2]. Since online privacy infringement cases cause severe legal consequences for firms, it is important for them to be aware of various privacy infringement with legal liability. In addition, as the number of online privacy invasion cases is predicted to increase and become more diverse, the development of an automated predictive model for legal decisions can significantly reduce the efforts of legal practitioners as well as companies. Therefore, this study is devised from the motivation to suggest the foundation for applying and interpreting a predictive model from a socio-technical perspective, along with deriving an optimal judgment model.

Legal cases related to privacy infringement are outcomes of interactions between society and technological factors, since the cases often comprise violation of law, human errors, personal information owners' perception, etc. It means that recent privacy legal cases have shown different characteristics from other legal incidents. For example, the case of stealing someone's property is always considered illegal, regardless of time and space. However, in most privacy infringement cases, it is very difficult to clearly identify a responsible party. Legal cases regarding improper usage of adware to invade an individual's privacy is a representative case that demonstrates that legal judgments may be influenced by technological and social environmental factors. Therefore, this study applied NTA (network text analysis) method, which has been used in sociology to reflect social influences [3]. In addition, we performed a comparison of AI models, including LDA (linear discriminant analysis), NNET (neural network), CART (classification and regression tree), SVM (support vector machine), and random forest, to identify a model with high prediction accuracy. The results of this study provide the foundation for developing an automated legal prediction system that could consider influences from social and technical factors that past research did not consider. This study is conducted in the following steps. The discussion of an extensive literature review of judgement prediction and algorithms for online privacy is performed in Section 2. We introduce the collected data, the characteristics of our collected data, and the five classifications methods (LDA, NNET, CART, SVM, random forests) for predicting in Section 3, the research method section. In Section 4, the comparison of the performance of each model is presented. In Section 5, constructed networks of legal judgments by NTA are discussed. We suggest concluding remarks, as well as contributions and limitations of this study, respectively, in Sections 6 and 7.

2. Related Works
2.1. Prediction of Legal Judgments

The advancement in natural language processing and machine learning is contributing to predictive models that identify various patterns in judicial decisions. Related studies in predicting legal judgments mainly take two approaches: increasing the accuracy of predictions under the present algorithms or predicting the outcome of future legal disputes by using statistics and AI in real judicial cases.

A prediction model based on contiguous word sequences (i.e., N-grams and topics) has up to a 79% rate of accuracy and is now applied to cases in the European Court of Human Rights [4]. Prior research mainly focused on textual information. However, IBP (issue-based prediction) has recently been used to predict legal outcomes. Although IBP is similar to previous computer models, in that it predicts legal judgments based on statistics and AI, it has an ability to draw an overall prediction through testing assumptions [5]. When IBP is applied to a legal case, it establishes favorable assumptions for each participant in the case. To verify the assumption, IBP infers large numbers of past legal judgments [6]. A new model, CNN-BiGRU, is suggested to have better prediction than a single CNN or RNN model [7], and we propose the generalized Gini-PLS algorithm, which is based on the simple Gini-PLS model, to develop a judicial prediction system [8].

2.2. Algorithms for Protecting Online Privacy

Research on online privacy has focused on personal information that can be leaked in an e-commerce environment and online social networks [9]. These days, a massive amount of personal information has been collected and managed online, and it has raised privacy concerns about how to manage these data appropriately [10]. Fast-developing IT technology also causes various types of privacy invasions, which could further increase related incidents. Online privacy studies in the field of engineering provide technical measures and prediction algorithms against privacy invasion. A study by Hanguang and Yu [11] developed a web-based intrusion detection system to identify external attacks and improve the overall performance of the detection system through an algorithm, Apriori. One study designed a system to detect personal information stored in a user's PC and evaluated the impact based on the possibility of data breach [12]. The research of Blei and Ng [13] explored topic modeling techniques to develop an algorithm for a privacy invasion forecast system. Further, as there are growing concerns about re-identification of personal data online, related research is also being actively conducted [14].

A lot of research has been conducted to determine a method to protect online privacy by developing protection techniques such as differential privacy (DP), which has been introduced to preserve privacy in datasets [15,16]. It is defined as a way of circumventing the problems of an adversary with auxiliary information and provides the level of privacy with superior performance [10]. DP was based on a probability model with a set of conditions that need to be met to guarantee that auxiliary information will not result in a privacy breach [17,18]. It has the ability to create useful statistics by itself, while the users' privacy is maintained in a database [19].

A new algorithm has recently emerged for lowering error by adapting to properties of the input data, so-called data-dependent algorithms [16]. Pythia proposes a meta-algorithm that does not need to understand valid algorithms or identify the subtle properties of input data [10]. Functional dependency (FD) is based on preserving probabilistic encryption scheme. It considers the frequency analysis (FA) attack and the functional dependency preserving chosen plaintext attack (FCPA) for protecting sensitive information in the outsourced data while preserving the data dependency for the data owner [20].

K-anonymity, K-privacy, and K-support techniques have been applied to data to protect the privacy of the outsourced database and the mined the association rule [17]. However, these techniques have a shortcoming, in that they are relatively expensive. To overcome this drawback, Yi and Rao [21] proposed a solution by performing association rule mining on the encrypted data in the cloud and returning encrypted association rules to the user in the same time. The data-cleaning-as-a-service (DCaS) paradigm makes users outsource their data and attain a data cleaning service by third-party service providers [20]. However, this paradigm raises the issue that it cannot be guaranteed that their private information in the outsourced data is fully protected. To solve this problem, Dong and Liu [20] designed the privacy-preserving data-deduplication-as-a-service (PraDa) system, focused on data deduplication, which is the most vulnerable in data cleaning problems. By providing privacy assurance against both the known-scheme attacks and frequency analysis, PraDa secures the server to find duplicated records from the encoded data [20].

Previous studies have predicted judicial decisions by focusing only on textual information without considering the social environment. That is, the adjudication is predicted by a fixed the pattern between words and decisions, which is constructed based on a specific word frequency. It is also made without including the characteristics of various online privacy intrusion factors. To overcome the limitations of prior studies, this study attempts to predict the judgments in a social context, focusing on each factor of online privacy invasion, and finally, to provide the explainability of our prediction models. To this end, we intend to establish a social network of the judgment and each factor of online privacy intrusion and provide a foundation for explaining how each factor affects the judgment.

3. Research Method

3.1. Data Preparation

The Privacy Act in the United States takes different approaches to the public sector and the private, unlike other regions such as Europe. This sectoral approach has the advantage that the law can promptly respond to new social issues and IT. Online privacy invasion factors vary by environment, so this study selected the legal precedents of the United States, which adopted a sectoral approach as the target of analysis. Therefore, this study analyzed United States judicial cases, which were collected from Westlaw database. Westlaw is a database that contains legal documentary data in the U.S. It classifies data based on key issues of judgments [22]. Among various classification items, this study collected 1098 cases of legal precedents (from January 2000 to December 2018) to obtain judgment documents related to privacy invasions.

We collected data from Westlaw, which include only federal law precedents among numerous online privacy invasions across the United States. A federal law is applied to the nation as a whole and to all 50 states, whereas state laws are only in effect within that particular state. Therefore, in this study, only the precedents that have been sentenced based on federal law were selected for analysis, as that can be applied equally to all states in the United States. The reason that only cases sentenced by federal law are selected for this study is that it focuses on online privacy invasions that occurred in a virtual online environment without physical territorial limitations. In other words, this study deals with cases sentenced by federal law, regulating without physical territorial restrictions to reflect the features of online spaces rather than dealing with sentences under state law, including the regional characteristics in which the case occurred. Therefore, it is expected that the results of this study can be applied to online privacy infringement cases occurring across the United States without distinction of state law.

Table 1 shows the numbers of the legal precedents each year we collected from Westlaw. The highest number of sentences related to online privacy invasions were decided under federal law in 2012 with 87, followed by 83 in 2018.

Table 1. The Numbers of Precedents of Each Year.

Year	Precedents	Year	Precedents	Year	Precedents	Year	Precedents
2000	42	2005	41	2010	51	2015	51
2001	53	2006	54	2011	53	2016	56
2002	62	2007	44	2012	87	2017	77
2003	61	2008	74	2013	56	2018	83
2004	52	2009	49	2014	62		

To examine the interconnectivity between the words extracted from text preprocessing and judgments related to privacy invasion, they were classified into two groups as follows. First, actual malicious codes generated to collect personal data from other PCs without the users' consents are classified as "type of privacy invasion". Second, words relevant to the actual adjudication of precedents are classified as "type of privacy invasion judgment". The authors classified those words into 2 categories according to the research's main objective. For example, "type of privacy invasion" mainly consists of techniques that hold possibilities of privacy threats. The case of "type of privacy invasion judgment" is composed of terminology (i.e., conviction, compensation, innocence) that is usually used in verdicts for presenting the results of litigations. Table 2 shows that words are finally extracted to construct networks and provide meaning.

Table 2. Definition and Frequency of Privacy Invasions.

Type of Privacy Invasion	Definition and Characteristics	Frequency
Adware	Refers to software that randomly shows advertisements to users but can also be used to collect personal data [23]	124
Cyberattack	An action causing damage to the other party's company by invading the user's PC through the internet. It is used as a general term for illegal access behaviors [24]	79
	A type of cyber terrorism such as leaking personal data or crashing websites for political or social purposes [25]	
Malware	A program that causes failures in system operation, acquires unauthorized access to data collection or system resources, or is used for other acts of invasion [3]	195
Spam	Refers to for-profit advertising data that are sent in unsolicited bulk, without consent, to devices such as email or cell phones of users of information and communication services [26]	212
Spyware	Software that collects personal data after being installed without the user's consent by deceiving the user [27]	137
Vandalism	Acts of destroying order in cyberspace that threaten personal data by posting another person's data with misuse of anonymity or through defamation of a specific person [28]	45
Virus	An illegal program that destroys important data or software by invading the user's system or expanding damages through self-replication, using a network [29]	184

Types of privacy invasion judgments include conviction and innocence representing adjudication in terms of criminal law, and imprisonment, penalty, and probation, which are criminal punishments. Imprisonment is a measure that restrains a person's freedom by confining the suspect or convict in a restricted space such as a detention center or prison; it indicates a prison sentence or confinement. Probation is a system that improves and rehabilitates the criminal under certain supervision and guidance with a free social life, without confining him or her in prison.

3.2. Classification Techniques in Machine Learning

Machine learning is a vast interdisciplinary field, which is based on concepts from statistics, computer science, cognitive science, engineering, optimization theory, and many other disciplines of mathematics and science. In machine learning, supervised learning algorithms—labelled training datasets—are used first to train the underlying algorithm. This trained algorithm is then provided on the unlabeled test dataset. Supervised learning algorithms that deal with classification include the following five representative algorithms: LDA (linear discriminant analysis), neural networks (NNET), classification and regression tree (CART), SVM (support vector machine), and random forests. This is used for classification analysis through a learning algorithm that makes predictions for unexperienced or future data. Classification predictive modeling in machine learning is an approach used to predict binary data. It is an approach that is used for purposes such as classifying emails into "spam" or "non-spam" to filter them automatically [30] or to predict whether it will rain or not [31]. Furthermore, classification predictive model has been widely used in various fields, for example, to predict whether to buy or not, whether or not customers belong to a group membership, or to classify images into two groups.

We select five state-of-the-art classification algorithms (i.e., LDA, NNET, CART, SVM, random forests) for which performance of binary classification has been verified on text data as well as numerical data among various models. The reason for adopting those five algorithms is, first, as the primary purpose of this study is to compare the legal judgment prediction performance of various binary classification models, it is necessary to adopt models that have been repeatedly verified in relatively various fields. Secondly, considering our data set, models that were not suitable for best performance in our data set were excluded. Traditional binary classification models such as logistic regression or stochastic gradient descent were not adopted in this study, as they rarely show high predictive performance rate compared to the other binary classification models in a small dataset, although they have been verified and improved over a long period [12]. The main purpose of this study is to discover the best prediction performance for legal predictions, since the number of our data sets in terms of cases number itself are relatively smaller than other studies using AI algorithms; algorithms such as logistic regression or stochastic gradient descent were not suitable, as they cannot used for self-training data set [12]. Naive Bayes classifier is also not applied to this study, since Naive Bayes model is not appropriate for data with binary values such as 0 and 1 due to the zero frequency problem [32]. We finally adopt five representative classification algorithms in supervised learning as LDA, CART, NNET, SVM and random forests in this paper among various models for binary classification. In the following paragraphs, each classification algorithm adopted in this study will be introduced in order of the logical flow of each definition and model construction process. It also includes the process for performing classification prediction in accordance with the purpose of this study.

3.2.1. Linear Discriminant Analysis (LDA)

Fisher's linear discriminant analysis (LDA) constructs discriminant functions that estimate discriminant values for each of subjects classified into a certain group from linearly independent predictor variables [33]. These discriminant weights are calculated by ordinary least squares, so that the ratio of the variance within the λ groups to the variance between the λ groups is minimal [34]. The decision boundary defined by LDA is linear, and that defined by QDA is quadratic. LDA is limited in flexibility compared to the other classification methods when applied to more complex datasets [35]. LDA generally shows similar performance with logistic regression [36].

3.2.2. Classification and Regression Tree (CART)

Classification and regression trees (CART) construct hierarchical decision trees by splitting data among classes of the criterion at a given node accordingly to an "if-then", applied to a set of predictors, into two child nodes repeatedly [37]. Classification trees are verified as an appropriate method for predicting the binary of target variables with high accuracy and require few assumptions about the data [38,39]. It keeps partitioning data with explanatory variables in binary split, which gives the minimal impurity until the terminal node has a predefined minimum size [40,41]. Then, it fits the response variable in each partition. The goal is to find a partition, so that the response is the most homogeneous in each partition [42]. A CART model that predicts continuous variables from a continuous or categorical predictor variable is referred to as regression model [43,44]. Decision tree-based models, including CART, have an advantage in that they are scalable to large problems and can handle smaller data sets than NN models [41]. The more complex model has the better prediction power; however, a too complex model can be hard to be interpreted, and there can be an overfitting problem [16]. Therefore, the most important aspect of constructing CART is to have balance between complexity and goodness of fit.

3.2.3. Neural Networks (NNET)

Neural networks have been applied extensively in both regression and classification problem. A neural network holds layers of interconnected nodes. Each node is a perceptron and is similar to a multiple linear regression. The perceptron feeds the signal produced by a multiple linear regression into an activation function, which is nonlinear [33]. It assumes that the response variable (output layer) has a relationship with explanatory variables (input layer) and that there is hidden layer between them in a model [16]. It postulates that input layer affects all nodes in the hidden layer, and the response is affected by all nodes in hidden layer [34]. Neural networks are differentiated from existing optimization algorithms, in that they are identified in parallel by a group of vectors, and it does not depend excessively on the initial parameter but changes stochastically [35].

3.2.4. Support Vector Machines (SVM)

Support vector machines (SVM) find a linear separating hyperplane constructed from a vector x of predictors mapped into a higher dimension feature space by a nonlinear feature function [36,37,44]. It derives classifiers, which map a vector of predictors into a higher dimensional plane through either linear or non-linear kernel functions [45,46]. SVM shows fairly good prediction accuracy based on its sound theoretical foundation in complex classification problems [36]. It is designed to perform learning in the direction of minimizing 'structural risk'; on the other hand, ANN pursues 'empirical risk management'. SVM also requires a small amount of training data called support vector, generally using only a small amount of data and being insensitive to the number of dimensions for final learning, unlike ANN [36,44]. Therefore, SVM can be relatively free from overfitting problems and offers one of the most robust and accurate methods.

3.2.5. Random Forests

Random forests are similar to a decision tree or a bagging classifier, having the same hyper-parameters [47]. Therefore, it can be explained as a way of classification by adding an additional layer of randomness to bagging [48,49]. It constructs a series of CART using random bootstrap samples of the original data sample [37,48,49]. Each tree is formed from a random subset of the total predictors who maximize the classification criteria at each node. A classification error rate can be calculated using each of the CART to predict the data not in the bootstrap sample used to grow the tree, and then mean values as out-of-the bag predictions for the grown set of trees become a "forest". Random forests methods can be easily optimized by adjusting only two parameters. It requires defining the number of random trees in the forest and the number of predictor variables in the random subset of tree at each node [35]. Random forests can be used both for two-class and multi-class problems of more than two classes, and when there are many more variables than observations [50]. It has good predictive performance, even when most predictive variables are noise [50,51]. However, random forests have a possibility to detect over-detection of real and false paradoxes in subsets of the data that do not occur in the entire dataset due to sampling error [52].

3.3. Network Text Analysis (NTA)

Network analysis is a research technique that focuses on seeking the relationship patterns between agents and their related data [53,54]. Network text analysis (NTA) is a method that creates a model of nodes and links and quantitatively analyzes their phase structure as well as the process of diffusion and evolution [55]. Therefore, the network structure established through NTA is useful for interpreting certain social phenomena beyond the dictionary meaning of the relevant text [3]. According to Bhat and Milne (2008), degree centrality analysis is the most used to understand the influence of entities and structures in a network [56]. The highest node has the strongest influence on spreading infectious diseases compared to the other nodes in the network [57]. NTA complexly connected the social network analysis technique with text analysis, and thus it simultaneously explores both knowledge and understanding of a given social phenomenon [9].

Legal verdicts inevitably reflect social phenomena (e.g., nations' characteristics, ethics, social values); thus, this study adopted NTA for analyzing precedents. More specifically, this study conducted keyword-based network analysis for in-depth analysis of legal precedents by extracting specific keywords presented in privacy legal cases, which can be considered a text aggregate of socio-structural phenomena, using NetMiner 4.0. Specifically, a concept in the network consists of one or more related words, which are nodes in a social network analysis, while links represent the relationship between two concepts. In other words, two or more concepts simultaneously appearing in a single sentence indicates that the two have a close relationship, and the association of these linkages enables implementation of a semantic map [26]. That is, co-word analysis enables calculation of co-occurrence frequency of each word, as well as classification of the subject area in the relevant field, elicitation of keywords, and determination of correlation among subject areas.

4. Performance Comparison of Machine Learning
4.1. Classification Model Construction

We adopt five classification methods by R programs for predicting the judicial decision as introduced in Section 3. All these techniques are appropriate for predicting results of binary dependent variables (coded 0: innocence, 1: conviction). To find optimized hyperparameters of each machine learning model, its value is tuned as follows. First, the hyperparameter used for the optimal SVM model is combined with the penalty parameter (C) for 0.1, kernel coefficient (γ) of 0.03, and Kernel linear function. In random forests, the best performance is identified when the maximum number of features considered for splitting a node set is 50, and the maximum levels of each decision tree are set as 3. Weight decay was tuned between 0 and 0.1 and found the optimal value as 0.09 in size 18 in a model of NNET. In CART, the best tree size is determined to be 6 in the minimum deviance, as shown in Figure 1. We complied this with a basic LDA model, as it did not require any additional tuning.

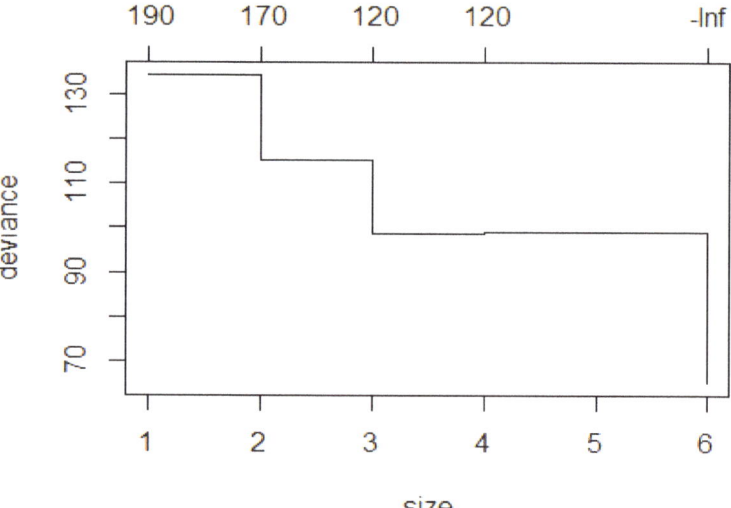

Figure 1. Deviance vs. Tree Size.

Table 3 provides the classification performance by each method as performed once. It shows the predictability, how each model can classify "real guilty case is judged as a conviction" and "real innocent case is judged as a guiltlessness". As a result, CART has the greatest prediction rate, while neural network performs worse than the others.

Table 3. Classification for Judicial Decisions.

	Classification	Innocence	Conviction	Prediction Rate (%)
LDA	Innocence	451	85	82.33
	Conviction	109	453	
CART	Innocence	460	76	83.16
	Conviction	109	453	
Neural Network	Innocence	466	70	81.79
	Conviction	130	432	
SVM	Innocence	448	102	82.69
	Conviction	88	460	
Random Forest	Innocence	463	73	83.06
	Conviction	113	449	

4.2. Model Validation and Performance Comparison

Using the above optimized hyperparameters, each model can be trained and established. To obtain independent test data and reliable results, each data set was split randomly (70:30) into a training and a test data set. In other words, we use 70% of data for training as model fitting and 30% for evaluating, among the 1098 cases we collected. The training data were evaluated and validated through K-fold cross validation. To reduce the influence of a single sampling method on model results, the seven-fold cross-validation method was adopted to select training data and test data. Seven-fold cross-validation method divided the whole dataset into seven disjoint subsets randomly and averagely. Seven subsets was identified as an optimal value in this model, among the most popular and common value (e.g., k = 3, 5, 7, 10) used in applied machine learning [33]. To compare the classification models with judicial cases, we performed 100 simulations (i.e., experiments are repeated 100 times) of each model to generalize its accuracy and compute the mean of misclassification rates, as shown in Table 4 and Figure 2. The greatest accuracy of classifications was achieved by CART, showing the lowest misclassification rate to be as same as that analyzed simultaneously. As a result, CART has the best performance rate for predicting judicial decisions.

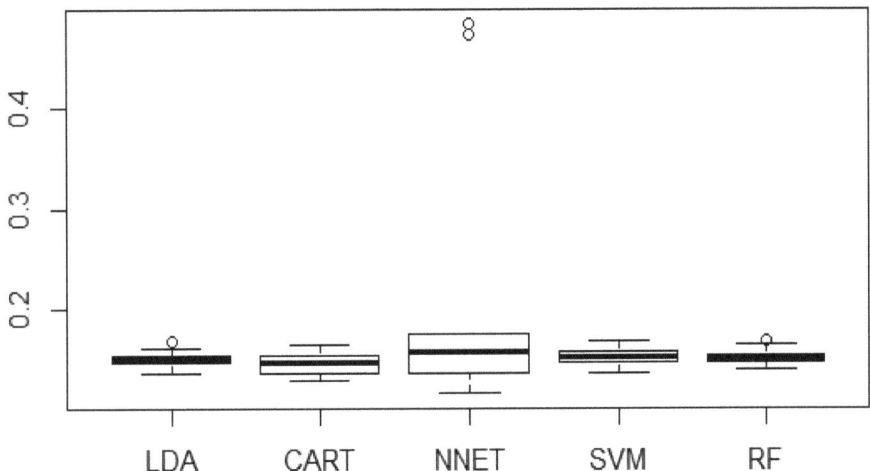

Figure 2. Misclassification Rates in 100 Simulations.

Table 4. Misclassification Rates in 100 Simulations.

Methods	Misclassification Rate (%)
LDA	11.82
CART	11.52
Neural Network	12.04
Support Vector Machine	11.90
Random Forest	11.72

5. Constructing Networks of Legal Judgments

Judicial cases refer to an aggregate of documents drawn up based on related regulations, using legal terms and focusing on specific cases or basic facts about the participants. Therefore, those forming a legal precedent are bound to have a close correlation among them. To analyze the relationship among words that form a legal precedent, this study conducted NTA. It is a descriptive modeling method for explaining the social phenomena in a macro perspective [3]. NTA is useful way to explain social issues by analyzing factors in social phenomenon [3], and it enables a researcher to identify the relationship among various confounding factors such as the factors invading privacy and the adjudication types. First, we formed a weight matrix based on co-occurrence frequency in a single paragraph as the baseline data for network analysis. Based on the elicited weight, this study also calculated the degree of centrality and concentric of the main keywords. Keywords with a greater value of degree centrality have greater influence in the overall network. This degree centrality is elicited based on an eigenvector; thus, there is a limitation, in that the frequency of the relevant keyword in the overall text is not considered. Accordingly, an analysis of concentric was conducted, additionally focused on the frequency of relevant keywords in legal precedents.

5.1. Analysis of the Possibility of Judgment According to Types of Privacy Invasion

To analyze the interrelation between types of privacy invasion and specific judgments, additional research was conducted by dividing the precedents into the possibility of conviction and innocence from the perspective of criminal law and possibility of compensation in terms of civil law.

5.1.1. Possibility of Conviction and Innocence in Terms of Criminal Law

To form a network of judgment on conviction and innocence according to the types of privacy invasion in terms of criminal law, conviction and innocence were set as the central nodes, and the relationship between the two was examined. To form a network, the degree centrality of types of privacy invasion were calculated according to conviction and innocent, which are presented in Tables 5 and 6 below.

Table 5. Degree Centrality of Conviction.

Main Keyword	Degree Centrality	Network of Privacy Invasion with Conviction
Adware	0.155	
Cyberattack	0.018	
Malware	0.278	
Spam	0.266	
Spyware	0.230	
Vandalism	0.034	
Virus	0.191	

Table 6. Degree Centrality of Innocence.

Main Keyword	Degree Centrality	Network of Privacy Invasion with Innocence
Adware	0.143	
Cyberattack	0.085	
Malware	0.221	
Spam	0.142	
Spyware	0.429	
Vandalism	0.222	
Virus	0.102	

If a certain type of invasion forms a strong connection with the node of conviction through the formed network, a conviction is more likely to occur. The types of invasion that are marked with big circles or nodes in the network and are directly linked to adjudications such as conviction or innocence are likely to receive relevant verdicts. In other words, if nodes are relatively big, such as malware, and are directly connected in primary links with conviction in the network, the invasion has a high possibility to be judged illegal. Furthermore, it can be assumed that there is a slight chance of innocence, because the types of privacy invasion with the possibility of being convicted (e.g., virus, adware, spam, cyberattack, and malware) do not form a relationship with nodes focused on innocence.

5.1.2. Possibility of Judgment of Civil Compensation by Invasion Type

Compensation generally refers to the return to conditions present before the damage was done, with the purpose of recovery and relief of violation of one's rights. It is confirmed that all of types of privacy invasion factors form a direct relationship with compensation, and especially malware, which form large nodes in the network, are likely to receive the verdict of compensation. Finally, it can be verified that even the same type of privacy invasion is likely to be subject to different judgments and types of measures depending on specific environmental factors such as current conditions. Table 7 shows the degree of centrality and network of the types of invasion that are likely to receive the verdict of compensation as a means of relief for privacy invasion.

Table 7. Degree Centrality of Compensation.

Main Keyword	Degree Centrality	Network of Privacy Invasion with Compensation
Adware	0.173	
Cyberattack	0.198	
Malware	0.231	
Vandalism	0.098	
Virus	0.102	
Spam	0.200	
Spyware	0.211	

6. Conclusions

This study performed classification methods of machine learning for predicting judicial decisions and analyzed the network. With machine learning models, it is usually very hard to explain how each factor influences the establishment of a model. Thus, this study constructed the network of judicial cases according to the privacy invasion factors by NTA. We could identify which model had the highest performance rate of prediction of legal decisions among the five classification algorithms and infer how these algorithms can predict legal or illegal activities by analyzing the network that was established by NTA.

The results of this study can be summarized as follows. First, the CART technique had the best performance of classification compared to the other methods. It can be inferred that CART algorithms should be considered a priority among various prediction algorithms for establishing the system of an AI lawyer or an automatic judicial decision machine. In other words, as CART shows the best performance within the scope of online privacy cases used in this study, it is desirable to adopt CART to predict legal disputes and judgments related to online privacy. These results have the potential to be used not only in online privacy disputes but also in resolving various legal conflicts that may occur in the online environment. However, since there is no guarantee that CART always shows the highest performance rate in predicting the guilt or innocence of numerous off-line crimes or in predicting legal decisions (e.g., probation, penalty) not covered in this study, other models should also be considered. Secondly, we can infer that malware is the most significant factor for predicting illegal decisions among various online privacy invasions. It is thereby derived that the malware node has the largest effects in the whole conviction network. If a firm invades the user's personal information based on malware for direct or indirect reasons in the process of carrying out marketing activities, there is a high chance of it resulting in conviction. Furthermore, malware can be also judged as being needed with compensation of damage in a perspective of civil law. In the case of viruses, if a firm is not able to prove that it did not create the relevant malicious code, or is not the primary distribution agent, it could result in conviction. As a result of analyzing legal precedents related to privacy invasion in the US, this study arrived at the following implications. Since it is difficult for firms to prove that they have no fault in the user's privacy invasion, it is necessary to establish drastic technical measures and management systems to prevent these issues in advance. Civil judgment of compensation is the most effective means of relief for users whose privacy is invaded by corporate activities. In particular, if invasions were made by sending spyware, virus, malware, adware, and spam, users can demand compensation for damages if they can prove the firm's negligence. Firms' obligations for accidents and users' probability for winning a lawsuit differ according to type of online privacy invasion. This study indicates possible outcomes of data privacy infringements cases in the online marketing environment. For example, this study identified that firms may have a duty of compensation for distributing adware that show ads to users and collect users' personal data. A user could also file a lawsuit for compensation for user's financial loss or psychological distress caused by an online privacy invasion originating from malware.

7. Contributions and Limitations

The overall results of this study can be applied to establish the strategy of firms as follows. Firms could have a high possibility of both civil and criminal law responsibilities if they distributed malware as a program or, spyware, which is a system to acquire unauthorized access of data collection or system resources. From now on, firms should be more cautious about sending direct messages to advertise without violating civil or criminal liability. The results of this study could be utilized as guidelines for firms to prevent incidents of online privacy infringement. This would enable firms to prevent privacy invasion accidents in the future, thereby saving costs and time required in disputes.

This study has two contributions. First, it extends the scope of research in the area of predicting verdicts by addressing the needs for accepting social perspective and statistically methodology (i.e., machine learning) at the same time. This study is differentiated from previous studies, which mainly focused on semantic-based ontology to retrieve legal information by resolving the inconsistency issue between legal terms and everyday terms. There are a few researchers developing algorithms or systems to predict verdicts accurately; however, they use statistical results that do not reflect any societal factors. Legal judgements cannot help but be influenced by social phenomena and culture, since legal provisions have been formed within social systems. Thus, we adopted NTA for reflecting social characteristics by establishing network of online privacy invasion factors and judgments and machine learning algorithms to predict verdicts. NTA is useful for interpreting social phenomena; the social influence between elements can be inferred based on the relationship formed by each element (i.e., node) in the constructed network. In this study, the online privacy infringement that changes according to social phenomena, such as the example of malware or cyber vandalism, was intended to be reflected in this study. For example, malware, which is identified with the highest probability of guilt in this study, was originally created for damage or destroy computers and computer systems. However, in recent years, as the value of data has rapidly increased, malware is mainly used for the purpose of invasion of privacy, such as access to personal information without consent or stealing personal information by misusing it beyond simple system destruction. Vandalism is also a representative factor in recent online privacy violations that have begun to be exploited to reflect the social phenomena. Although most of the factors that infringe online privacy have recently emerged due to technological advancement, vandalism has existed for a long time as a crime that harms an individual's physical property. Recent vandalism, generally, unlike in the past, involves editing online content in a malicious manner in cyberspace. Therefore, this study investigated the flow of changes in these social phenomena within the network of online privacy invasion factors and legal decisions. Moreover, this study's results indicate that there are the interrelations between types of privacy invasion factors and types of legal judgments such as criminal, civil, and compensation. Predictions with legal judgment types are very difficult for human lawyers due to massive amounts of legal documents that need to be studied to determine the conviction types.

Additionally, we provide the prediction rate of classification with the judicial decisions. Machine learning algorithms are powerful data-driven methods that are relatively less widely used in the judicial decisions and thus have not been comparatively evaluated thoroughly in the study of law. Therefore, this study addresses the need for establishing a data-driven strategy applied by machine learning and related to academic research in the field of law.

We reviewed various studies related to automated legal prediction systems that have been developed and researched to improve accuracy of prediction. In fact, a judgment has to be determined by codification (i.e., written law) and precedents; therefore, most prior studies have established data-driven prediction models by training the large data set of verdicts to predict judgments. Legal judgments, however, have a unique characteristic, in that they can be influenced by a few social factors, since they have been interpreted according to the circumstances at the time, as well as the cultural characteristics of the country. In other words, legal enforcement is decided by law but is usually influenced by social and legal environment of each country (e.g., cultures and social norms). Therefore, we adopted that both of social environments and statistically methods are needed for predicting and identifying the relationship between sentences and online privacy invasive factors. It is difficult to expect positive effects if decision-making systems are dependent on only technical computer-based systems without understanding the users or processes. This is because technology is only a means to support decision-making, and there is no consideration of the subjects making the decision and the organization and environment that the decision-making result will have. Therefore, the socio-technical system (STS) suggests that an understanding of the social structures, roles, and rights of the social sciences is required in order to induce successful adoption of information systems in organizations. From the perspective of STS, AI-based automated legal judgment prediction is also a new information system that is accepted by organizations and society, so it should reflect social structures, users, and processes. Therefore, AI-based legal judgment prediction should be introduced and developed by considering organizational policies and rules and users who interact using it based on an advanced technical system.

Secondly, we can confirm that both social environments and statistical methods are needed for predicting the verdicts related on online privacy invasions. Finally, the needs for combining both results of by NTA under the social environment as qualitative approach and prediction rate of machine learning in a quantitative approach can be provided. In other words, it can be applied to improve new AI models with higher accuracy and explainability at the same time. In most AI models, it is difficult to pursue both performance accuracy and the transparency of setting models. If they have the highest performing accuracy, they are are the least explainable, and the most explainable are less accurate.

With the improvements in machine learning methodology, the performance of AI models is reaching or even exceeding the human level on an increasing number of complex tasks. However, most AI systems cannot provide the reasons for model prediction results. Thus, explainable AI (XAI) has been revised to offer potential for users for better understanding and a trust model by producing and leveraging explainability techniques in AI models [58]. A few methods have been considered to provide explainable AI models (e.g., interpretable model, model induction, deep explanation). XAI models have been developed as modified or hybrid deep learning techniques that acquire more explainable features and generate explainable representations. This study can provide a foundation for improving XAI models by identifying the importance of feature importance of each factor, as we suggested through the results of network analysis, which have different relative values in the network.

The study only examined 1098 of the most recent legal precedents related to the Privacy Act in the US. Therefore, it is hard to generalize the results of this study to all areas of the United States. Moreover, even though privacy protection acts are enacted in most countries with similar purpose, there are bound to be differences among countries that cannot be overlooked due to the effect of the distinctive attributes of regulations. Therefore, this study selected legal precedents in the United States with a long history and that have been evaluated as favorable acts in the field of privacy protection; however, there is a need for additional comparative analysis by conducting studies on each of the countries. By accumulating the results of multiple studies considering these national characteristics, the results of the relevant studies could be utilized across diverse areas. We also have a plan to adopt more various machine learning models and identify how each model shows performance rate in legal field in future research.

This study tried to predict whether a firm's online activity is legal or illegal from the firm's perspective (i.e., defendant). Accordingly, the results of this study mainly provided implications for how firms provide online services in the range that do not infringe customer's online privacy.

Based on the conclusion of this study, finally, we can infer that, in the process of developing a system for predicting legal judgments in the future, a method that can reflect social and environmental phenomena and a scientific methodology for accurate prediction must be included at the same time. This study suggests that advanced prediction algorithms and systems may contribute to improving performance for accurate predictions but may make more appropriate judgments when times and social backgrounds are fully considered in a legal environment.

Author Contributions: Conceptualization, M.P. and S.C.; methodology, M.P. and S.C.; formal analysis, M.P.; writing—original draft preparation, M.P. and S.C.; writing—review and editing, M.P. and S.C. All authors have read and agreed to the published version of the manuscript.

Funding: This research received no external funding.

Institutional Review Board Statement: Not applicable.

Informed Consent Statement: Not applicable.

Conflicts of Interest: The authors declare no conflict of interest.

References

1. Kim, Y.-H.; Hong, J.-S.; Cha, H.-J.; Kook, K.-H. A Study of Personal Information Handler Based on Social Network Analysis. *J. Secur. Eng.* **2016**, *13*, 143–154. [CrossRef]
2. Kelbert, F.; Shirazi, F.; Simo, H.; Wüchner, T.; Buchmann, J.; Pretschner, A.; Waidner, M. State of online privacy: A technical perspective. In *Internet Privacy*; Springer: Berlin/Heidelberg, Germany, 2012; pp. 189–279.
3. Popping, R. Knowledge graphs and network text analysis. *Soc. Sci. Inf.* **2003**, *42*, 91–106. [CrossRef]
4. Ashley, K.D.; Brüninghaus, S. Computer models for legal prediction. *Jurimetrics* **2006**, *46*, 309–352.
5. Ashley, K.D.; Brüninghaus, S. Automatically classifying case texts and predicting outcomes. *Artif. Intell. Law* **2009**, *17*, 125–165. [CrossRef]
6. Bruninghaus, S.; Ashley, K.D. Predicting Outcomes of Case Based Legal Arguments. In Proceedings of the 9th International Conference on Artificial Intelligence and Law, Scotland, UK, 24–28 June 2003; pp. 233–242.
7. Branting, L.K.; Pfeifer, C.; Brown, B.; Ferro, L.; Aberdeen, J.; Weiss, B.; Pfaff, M.; Liao, B. Scalable and explainable legal prediction. *Artif. Intell. Law* **2021**, *29*, 213–238. [CrossRef]
8. Archer, K.J.; Kimes, R.V. Empirical characterization of random forest variable importance measures. *Comput. Stat. Data Anal.* **2008**, *52*, 2249–2260. [CrossRef]
9. Lame, G. Using NLP techniques to identify legal ontology components: Concepts and relations. *Artif. Intell. Law* **2004**, *12*, 379–396. [CrossRef]
10. Lax, G.; Russo, A.; Fascì, L.S. A Blockchain-based approach for matching desired and real privacy settings of social network users. *Inf. Sci.* **2021**, *557*, 220–235. [CrossRef]
11. Hanguang, L.; Yu, N. Intrusion detection technology research based on apriori algorithm. *Phys. Procedia* **2012**, *24*, 1615–1620. [CrossRef]
12. Hofmann, T.; Lucchi, A.; Lacoste-Julien, S.; McWilliams, B. Variance reduced stochastic gradient descent with neighbors. *arXiv* **2015**, arXiv:1506.03662.
13. Blei, D.M.; Ng, A.Y.; Jordan, M.I. Latent dirichlet allocation. *J. Mach. Learn. Res.* **2003**, *3*, 993–1022.
14. Amiri, F.; Yazdani, N.; Shakery, A.; Chinaei, A.H. Hierarchical anonymization algorithms against background knowledge attack in data releasing. *Knowl.-Based Syst.* **2016**, *101*, 71–89. [CrossRef]
15. Soria-Comas, J.; Domingo-Ferrer, J.; Sánchez, D.; Megías, D. Individual differential privacy: A utility-preserving formulation of differential privacy guarantees. *IEEE Trans. Inf. Forensics Secur.* **2017**, *12*, 1418–1429. [CrossRef]
16. Kotsogiannis, I.; Machanavajjhala, A.; Hay, M.; Miklau, G. Pythia: Data Dependent Differentially Private Algorithm Selection. In Proceedings of the 2017 ACM International Conference on Management of Data, Chicago, IL, USA, 14–19 May 2017; pp. 1323–1337.
17. Lundmark, M.; Dahlman, C.-J. Differential privacy and machine learning: Calculating sensitivity with generated data sets. *Comput. Sci.* **2017**. Available online: https://kth.diva-portal.org/smash/get/diva2:1112478/FULLTEXT01.pdf (accessed on 16 November 2021).
18. Dwork, C.; Roth, A. The algorithmic foundations of differential privacy. *Found. Trends Theor. Comput. Sci.* **2014**, *9*, 211–407. [CrossRef]
19. Aggarwal, C.C.; Philip, S.Y. A general survey of privacy-preserving data mining models and algorithms. In *Privacy-Preserving Data Mining*; Springer: Berlin/Heidelberg, Germany, 2008; pp. 11–52.
20. Dong, B.; Liu, R.; Wang, W.H. Prada: Privacy-Preserving Data-Deduplication-as-a-Service. In Proceedings of the 23rd ACM International Conference on Conference on Information and Knowledge Management, Shanghai, China, 3–7 November 2014; pp. 1559–1568.
21. Yi, X.; Rao, F.-Y.; Bertino, E.; Bouguettaya, A. Privacy-Preserving Association Rule Mining in Cloud Computing. In Proceedings of the 10th ACM Symposium on Information, Computer and Communications Security, Singapore, 17 March–14 April 2015; pp. 439–450.
22. Arewa, O.B. Open access in a closed universe: Lexis, Westlaw, law schools, and the legal information market. *Lewis Clark Law Rev.* **2006**, *10*, 797.
23. Takasugi, N. E-Commerce Law and the Prospects for Uniform E-Commerce Rules on the Privacy and Security of Electronic Communications. *Ariz. J. Int. Comp. Law* **2016**, *33*, 257.
24. Valdes, A.; Skinner, K. Adaptive, Model-Based Monitoring for Cyber Attack Detection. In *International Workshop on Recent Advances in Intrusion Detection*; Springer: Berlin/Heidelberg, Germany, 2000; pp. 80–93.
25. Argaw, S.T.; Bempong, N.-E.; Eshaya-Chauvin, B.; Flahault, A. The state of research on cyberattacks against hospitals and available best practice recommendations: A scoping review. *BMC Med Inform. Decis. Mak.* **2019**, *19*, 1–11. [CrossRef]
26. Lee, S.-S. A content analysis of journal articles using the language network analysis methods. *J. Korean Soc. Inf. Manag.* **2014**, *31*, 49–68.
27. Maroco, J.; Silva, D.; Rodrigues, A.; Guerreiro, M.; Santana, I.; de Mendonça, A. Data mining methods in the prediction of Dementia: A real-data comparison of the accuracy, sensitivity and specificity of linear discriminant analysis, logistic regression, neural networks, support vector machines, classification trees and random forests. *BMC Res. Notes* **2011**, *4*, 1–14. [CrossRef]
28. Mood, C. Logistic regression: Why we cannot do what we think we can do, and what we can do about it. *Eur. Sociol. Rev.* **2010**, *26*, 67–82. [CrossRef]

29. Han, X.; Tan, Q. Dynamical behavior of computer virus on Internet. *Appl. Math. Comput.* **2010**, *217*, 2520–2526. [CrossRef]
30. Alpaydin, E. *Introduction to Machine Learning*; MIT Press: Cambridge, MA, USA, 2020.
31. Haupt, S.E.; Cowie, J.; Linden, S.; McCandless, T.; Kosovic, B.; Alessandrini, S. Machine learning for applied weather prediction. In Proceedings of the 2018 IEEE 14th International Conference on e-Science (e-Science), IEEE, Amsterdam, The Netherlands, 29 October–1 November 2018; pp. 276–277.
32. Wu, J.; Cai, Z. A naive Bayes probability estimation model based on self-adaptive differential evolution. *J. Intell. Inf. Syst.* **2014**, *42*, 671–694. [CrossRef]
33. Bengio, Y.; Grandvalet, Y. No unbiased estimator of the variance of k-fold cross-validation. *J. Mach. Learn. Res.* **2004**, *5*, 1089–1105.
34. Heidari, A.A.; Faris, H.; Aljarah, I.; Mirjalili, S. An efficient hybrid multilayer perceptron neural network with grasshopper optimization. *Soft Comput.* **2019**, *23*, 7941–7958. [CrossRef]
35. Anderson, J. *An Introduction to Neural Networks*; MIT Press: Cambridge, MA, USA, 1995; ISBN 026-201-144-1.
36. Pal, M. Random forest classifier for remote sensing classification. *Int. J. Remote Sens.* **2005**, *26*, 217–222. [CrossRef]
37. Suykens, J.A.; Vandewalle, J. Least squares support vector machine classifiers. *Neural Process. Lett.* **1999**, *9*, 293–300. [CrossRef]
38. Padmanabhan, B.; Zheng, Z.; Kimbrough, S.O. An empirical analysis of the value of complete information for eCRM models. *Mis Q.* **2006**, 247–267. [CrossRef]
39. Padmanabhan, B.; Zheng, Z.; Kimbrough, S.O. Personalization from incomplete data: What you don't know can hurt. In Proceedings of the Seventh ACM SIGKDD International Conference on Knowledge Discovery and Data Mining, San Francisco, CA, USA, 26–29 August 2001; pp. 154–163.
40. Lawrence, R.L.; Wright, A. Rule-based classification systems using classification and regression tree (CART) analysis. *Photogramm. Eng. Remote Sens.* **2001**, *67*, 1137–1142.
41. Razi, M.A.; Athappilly, K. A comparative predictive analysis of neural networks (NNs), nonlinear regression and classification and regression tree (CART) models. *Expert Syst. Appl.* **2005**, *29*, 65–74. [CrossRef]
42. Tsoi, A.C.; Pearson, R. Comparison of Three Classification Techniques: CART, C4. 5 and Multi-Layer Perceptrons. In *Advances in Neural Information Processing Systems*; Kaufmann: San Mateo, CA, USA, 1991; pp. 963–969.
43. Markham, I.S.; Mathieu, R.G.; Wray, B.A. A rule induction approach for determining the number of kanbans in a just-in-time production system. *Comput. Ind. Eng.* **1998**, *34*, 717–727. [CrossRef]
44. Cortes, C.; Vapnik, V. Support-vector networks. *Mach. Learn.* **1995**, *20*, 273–297. [CrossRef]
45. Pal, S.K.; Wang, P.P. *Genetic Algorithms for Pattern Recognition*; CRC Press: Boca Raton, FL, USA, 1996.
46. Wang, C.; Jin, X. Study on Prediction of Legal Judgments Based on the CNN-BiGRU Model. In Proceedings of the 2020 6th International Conference on Computing and Artificial Intelligence, Tianjin, China, 23–26 April 2020; pp. 63–68.
47. Breiman, L. Random forests. *Mach. Learn.* **2001**, *45*, 5–32. [CrossRef]
48. Liaw, A.; Wiener, M. Classification and regression by randomForest. *R News* **2002**, *2*, 18–22.
49. Díaz-Uriarte, R.; De Andres, S.A. Gene selection and classification of microarray data using random forest. *BMC Bioinform.* **2006**, *7*, 3. [CrossRef]
50. Hua, J.; Xiong, Z.; Lowey, J.; Suh, E.; Dougherty, E.R. Optimal number of features as a function of sample size for various classification rules. *Bioinformatics* **2005**, *21*, 1509–1515. [CrossRef] [PubMed]
51. Shmueli, G.; Yahav, I. The forest or the trees? Tackling Simpson's paradox with classification trees. *Prod. Oper. Manag.* **2018**, *27*, 696–716. [CrossRef]
52. Caballé-Cervigón, N.; Castillo-Sequera, J.L.; Gómez-Pulido, J.A.; Gómez-Pulido, J.M.; Polo-Luque, M.L. Machine learning applied to diagnosis of human diseases: A systematic review. *Appl. Sci.* **2020**, *10*, 5135. [CrossRef]
53. Wasserman, S.; Faust, K. *Social Network Analysis: Methods and Applications*; Cambridge University Press: Cambridge, UK, 1994.
54. Sowa, J.F. *Conceptual Structures: Information Processing in Mind and Machine*; Addison-Wesley Longman Publishing Co. Inc.: Boston, MA, USA, 1984.
55. Wellman, B.; Berkowitz, S.D. *Social Structures: A Network Approach*; CUP Archive: Cambridge, UK, 1988; Volume 2.
56. Bhat, S.; Milne, S. Network effects on cooperation in destination website development. *Tour. Manag.* **2008**, *29*, 1131–1140. [CrossRef]
57. Christley, R.M.; Pinchbeck, G.; Bowers, R.G.; Clancy, D.; French, N.P.; Bennett, R.; Turner, J. Infection in social networks: Using network analysis to identify high-risk individuals. *Am. J. Epidemiol.* **2005**, *162*, 1024–1031. [CrossRef] [PubMed]
58. Gunning, D. *Broad Agency Announcement Explainable Artificial Intelligence (XAI)*; Technical Report; Defense Advanced Research Projects Agency: Arlington, VA, USA, 2016.

Article

Achieving Sender Anonymity in Tor against the Global Passive Adversary

Francesco Buccafurri *,†, Vincenzo De Angelis †, Maria Francesca Idone †, Cecilia Labrini † and Sara Lazzaro †

Department DIIES, University of Reggio Calabria, Via Università 25, 89122 Reggio Calabria, Italy; vincenzo.deangelis@unirc.it (V.D.A.); mariafrancesca.idone@unirc.it (M.F.I.); cecilia.labrini@unirc.it (C.L.); saralazzaro20@gmail.com (S.L.)
* Correspondence: bucca@unirc.it
† These authors contributed equally to this work.

Abstract: Tor is the de facto standard used for anonymous communication over the Internet. Despite its wide usage, Tor does not guarantee sender anonymity, even in a threat model in which the attacker passively observes the traffic at the first Tor router. In a more severe threat model, in which the adversary can perform traffic analysis on the first and last Tor routers, relationship anonymity is also broken. In this paper, we propose a new protocol extending Tor to achieve sender anonymity (and then relationship anonymity) in the most severe threat model, allowing a global passive adversary to monitor all of the traffic in the network. We compare our proposal with Tor through the lens of security in an incremental threat model. The experimental validation shows that the price we have to pay in terms of network performance is tolerable.

Keywords: anonymous communication systems; Tor; Onion; censorship resistance

---

Citation: Buccafurri, F.; De Angelis, V.; Idone, M.F.; Labrini, C.; Lazzaro, S. Achieving Sender Anonymity in Tor against the Global Passive Adversary. *Appl. Sci.* **2022**, *12*, 137. https://doi.org/10.3390/app12010137

Academic Editors: David Megías and Eui-Nam Huh

Received: 14 October 2021
Accepted: 17 December 2021
Published: 23 December 2021

Publisher's Note: MDPI stays neutral with regard to jurisdictional claims in published maps and institutional affiliations.

Copyright: © 2021 by the authors. Licensee MDPI, Basel, Switzerland. This article is an open access article distributed under the terms and conditions of the Creative Commons Attribution (CC BY) license (https://creativecommons.org/licenses/by/4.0/).

1. Introduction

The Tor overlay network [1] is the most popular anonymous communication protocol used for low-latency network applications. Tor is based on the Onion protocol [2]. This protocol is based on two concepts: rely nodes (also called *Tor routers*) and layered encryption. Relay nodes act as proxies in an Onion route. Each relay node receives its message from the preceding one and forwards it to the next, until the destination is reached. Differently from random walk [3], the route is deterministic and chosen by the sender. Moreover, the message is wrapped through layered encryption, which the sender can apply by knowing the cryptographic keys of all the relay nodes of the route. This way, each node is able to drop an encryption layer, and can see the address of the next relay node to which the still encrypted message should be forwarded. Eventually, the message with only one layer of encryption reaches the destination. According to this scheme, each node in the route only knows the address of the preceding node and the address of the next node. Therefore, by design, the first relay node knows the address of the sender. *Sender anonymity* is then not supported if we allow the adversary to control the first relay node. The practical impact of this weakness is that sole collaboration with an Internet service provider allows the adversary to detect that a user is utilizing the Tor system. Sender anonymity is obviously broken in a severe threat model with a global passive adversary, able to monitor all the traffic in the network. Anyway, breaking sender anonymity is not enough to nullify the final goal of the protocol, which is *relationship anonymity*. Indeed, the aim of Tor, as in general happens for an anonymous communication network, is to prevent the adversary from detecting that a given sender is communicating with a given recipient. Consider that, despite the fact that anonymity services are often used for criminal purposes, there are a lot of ethical applications of anonymous routing, including censorship resistance. However, relationship anonymity can be broken in Tor in a global passive adversary model.

As a matter of fact, Tor is vulnerable to many passive attacks [4,5], allowing traffic de-anonymization. It can be easily recognized that if the adversary can monitor the traffic at the bounds of the Tor circuit (i.e., the first and the last router), traffic analysis attacks break relationship anonymity [6,7], thereby fully de-anonymizing the communication.

In this paper, our aim is to overcome the above drawbacks of Tor, by achieving sender anonymity (in the sense of *communication k-anonymity* [8]) in the most severe threat model, in which a global passive adversary is allowed, which monitors all the traffic in the network. Recall that sender anonymity is enough to guarantee relationship anonymity, as stated in [7]. Therefore, we obtain effective protection of users' privacy.

The approach we use to obtain sender anonymity in Tor is to hide the sender within an anonymity set of nodes built as a *ring* of potential senders. To prevent the adversary from detecting the initiator of the communication, we equip the ring with cover traffic that the senders can opportunistically use to send their messages, by filling one or more of the circulating tokens. Thanks to probabilistic encryption, empty and filled tokens are indistinguishable for the adversary. The route Tor is then built from a proxy node of the ring to the destination. The adversary can see that a node of the ring is working as a proxy node, but it is not able to understand which node the sender is among the nodes of the ring. Traffic analysis attacks are not possible due to the cover-traffic mechanism.

Our approach can be related to *buses*[9,10], as we also consider a pre-determined route that is opportunistically used by the sender. However, there is a crucial difference. In buses, the fixed route is a Eulerian path passing through all the nodes, including thus all the possible pairs of sender–receiver. This is an impractical solution resulting in intolerable communication latency in a large network (such as the Internet).

Instead, our approach allows us to modulate the size of the anonymity set to a value that fulfills reasonable anonymity requirements, without introducing intolerable latency times, and importantly, relying on the existing Tor system. The feasibility of our approach was tested through careful experimental analysis conducted by simulations. Therefore, this research involved both theoretical and experimental analysis.

To the best of our knowledge, there is no proposal in the literature aimed at equipping the Tor protocol with sender anonymity against a global passive adversary. A proposal with some similarities to our paper (as both papers take inspiration from the original idea of buses [10], as discussed above) is given in [11]. However, their method [11], as clearly stated in the paper, does not provide protection against a global passive adversary, because the observation of the initiator of the ring construction breaks sender anonymity. On the contrary, sender anonymity against a global passive adversary in all the (even preliminary) phases of the communication is the objective achieved by our approach, which purposefully advances the state of the art. Moreover, our paper treats and solves the problem for the case of complete bi-directional communication, i.e., a request from the sender to the recipient and a response from the recipient to the sender. Observe that, in general, this is not trivial when anonymity should be maintained. Indeed, the response cannot be simply implemented as a different forward tunnel directed from the recipient to the sender; otherwise, simple intersection attacks would break anonymity. The method in [11] does not facilitate a response. This makes it applicable only for unidirectional communications, which is a very strong limitation.

The structure of the paper is the following. In Section 2, we review the related literature. We provide some basic notions needed to understand the proposed protocol in Section 3. The protocol is presented in Section 4. The introduction of a certain degree of fault tolerance is described in Section 5. The computational complexity of our solution is discussed in Section 6. The security of the protocol is analyzed in Section 7. In Section 8, we report the results of an experimental validation of our approach. Finally, in Section 9, we draw our conclusions.

2. Related Work

The issues most relevant to this paper are the vulnerabilities which Tor suffers from.

As stated by the creators themselves [1], the Tor overlay network, based on Onion routing [2], does not provide anonymous guarantees in the severe threat model of a global passive adversary [4], which is able to observe the entire traffic of the network.

Anyway, even if we relax the powers of the adversary, many attacks are still effective [5,12,13]. The most famous class of attacks is represented by the traffic analysis attacks [14–16] in which the adversary analyzes the traffic to find correlations. Among the traffic analysis attacks there are the timing attacks [17–19], in which the adversary observes the timing of the messages arriving at and leaving from the nodes to find correlations. Other interesting subclasses of traffic analysis attacks are traffic confirmation attacks [20], in which the adversary controls and observes two possible end-relays of a Tor circuit to conclude that they really belong to the same circuit, and watermarking attacks [21], in which the adversary manipulates the traffic stream by introducing an identifiable pattern. Another category of attacks target the router selection used to build the Tor circuit. Indeed, the standard selection is based on network and CPU performance reported by the nodes themselves. This enables self-promotion attacks [22]. A countermeasure can be found in [23].

The performance of Tor was investigated in [24–26]. Performance analysis in relation to de-anonymization attacks was performed in [27].

In our approach, we extend Tor achieving sender anonymity (and then relationship anonymity) [7] in the sense of *communication k-anonymity* [8], against a global passive adversary. This goal can be reached only with the introduction of cover traffic [28] (as required by our approach).

Among the approaches supporting cover traffic, the most significant are *mixnets*, originally proposed in [29], and *buses* [9,10,30].

In the literature, several proposals include cover traffic in mixnets [31–34]. The introduction of cover traffic makes traffic analysis more difficult. For example, a possible approach is to introduce cover traffic to maintain a constant transmission rate. A very recent mixnet-based approach designed for the network layer was presented in [35]. However, it does not provide sender anonymity against a global adversary. Another relevant approach in this category, even if dated (but still very solid), is Tarzan [32]. As discussed in [36], mixnets, in general, require a suitable amount of cover traffic.

More related to our work are buses, as we also consider a pre-determined route that is used by the sender. However, buses are unrealistic in a large network (such as the Internet), since the fixed route is a Eulerian path passing through all the nodes, including thus all the possible pairs of sender–receiver.

Similar considerations can be made for DC-Nets [37], based on a secure multi-party cryptographic protocol, in which it is required that all participants are involved in every run of the protocol and initially share a pairwise key.

This paper considerably extends a work-in-progress paper [38]. Reference [38] just presented the rough idea underlying the protocol. Specifically, in that paper, the approach is only sketched out, and it refers to the original Onion approach, with no fault tolerance, no real-life contextualization in the Tor system. Moreover, no detailed security and complexity analyses were performed, and no experimental evaluation was included.

3. Background and Notation

3.1. Anonymity

We recall some background notion taken from [7]. An anonymous communication network may offer:

1. *Sender anonymity*: the adversary cannot sufficiently identify the sender in a set of potential senders, called the *sender anonymity set*;
2. *Recipient anonymity*: the adversary cannot sufficiently identify the recipient in a set of potential recipients, called the *recipient anonymity set*;

3. *Relationship anonymity*: the adversary cannot sufficiently identify that a sender (in a set of potential senders) and a recipient (in a set of potential recipients) are communicating. According to [7], sender anonymity implies relationship anonymity.

Observe that the definition of anonymity given in [7], with the use of the term sufficiently, means "both that there is a possibility to quantify anonymity and that for some applications, there might be a need to define a threshold where anonymity begins".

3.2. The Tor Network

The Tor network is an overlay network, based on TCP/TLS connections, consisting of multiple relay routers called *Onion routers* (OR). Each client runs locally an *Onion proxy* (OP) which establishes a virtual circuit of ORs to communicate anonymously with the destination. To build a circuit, the OP contacts periodically a trusted server called *Directory Server* (DS) that keeps information about the state of the network and provides the OP with *router descriptors* of the ORs. These router descriptors contain the IP addresses and the public keys of the ORs, along with their network information, such as the bandwidth. Then, the OP selects, according to some strategies, a number n of OR relays that form the virtual circuit. By default, $n = 3$. The first OR is called the *entry router*, the second the *middle router* and the last the *exit router*. Once the three ORs have been selected, the OP starts a set-up phase to build the virtual circuit. This phase is performed in such a way that each OR only knows the previous and the next node of the path. Moreover, in this phase, the OP exchanges some messages with the ORs, which include some Diffie–Hellman (DH) parameters, to share a secret key. These messages are encapsulated into *control cells* of a fixed size of 512 bytes. Since the OP has to be sure about the authenticity of the ORs, the DH parameters are encrypted by using the public keys of the ORs. At the end of this set-up phase, the OP shares a secret key with each OR. These keys are used by the OP to encrypt (symmetrically) in Onion fashion the messages intended for the destination. Once the circuit is established, the OP sends the messages to the destination encapsulated into *relay cells* of size of 512 bytes. These relay cells include a header of 3 bytes in plaintext plus 11 bytes encrypted for the exit router. Therefore, the effective payload is 498 bytes.

Through this paper, for both symmetric and public-key encryption, we denote by $E_k(M)$ the encryption of a message M with key k. Similarly, we denote by $D_k(C)$ the decryption of the ciphertext C with (symmetric or public) key k. Even though we do not explicitly highlight this aspect, the encryption we consider in this paper is only probabilistic, in such a way that, for an eavesdropper, two different encryptions of the same message are unlinkable.

4. The Proposed Protocol

In this section, we describe our protocol, called Ring2Tor, which achieves sender anonymity even in the most severe threat model including a global passive adversary. We denote by *(client) nodes* the nodes that collaborate in the protocol without playing the role of Tor routers. Senders are among the client nodes. Moreover, we have in the network n_d destination hosts, which are distinct from client nodes and Tor routers.

The description of the protocol is given in three main steps. The first step is describing the ring manager and the token-based mechanism. Some management functions are illustrated, along with the basic mechanism for implementing anonymity for the sender. The second step is describing the *set-up phase*. This is the phase in which keys are exchanged, the setting of further parameters is executed and cover traffic is established. This is a preliminary step to make possible the anonymous communication, which is explained in the last step of the description, denoted as *communication phase*.

4.1. Ring Manager and Token-Based Mechanism

In this section, we describe the basic mechanism of our approach that allows us to provide the sender with anonymity against a global passive adversary.

We assume the presence of a *ring manager* (RM) that partitions the nodes of the network in several *rings*.

The ring manager selects the nodes forming a ring in such a way that the background knowledge does not allow a possible adversary to have more information than the uniform distribution of senders. In other words, given a ring, any node of the ring is potentially a sender (with no probability bias). This is achieved by selecting, for a given ring, hosts belonging to the same, even large, geographical region.

A ring is a sequence of k nodes such that each node has exactly a *preceding* (*prec*, for short) and a *next* node. In our setting, each node only knows its prec and its next node. Several messages, called *tokens*, move through the ring. There are two kinds of tokens. The first type is used in the set-up phase. The second type is used in the succeeding communication phase. The detail will be discussed next. Tokens are filled by senders to deliver their messages to a proxy node, which, once a Tor circuit is established, sends them to the destination host. To obtain that any eavesdropper is unable to distinguish an empty token from a filled token, each node encrypts the token with a symmetric key shared with its next node.

RM maintains, along with the next node, the public keys and the network addresses of each node of the network. For each ring, each belonging node receives from RM the set of the public keys of the other nodes of the ring, and among these keys, the information about which is the public key associated with the next node in the ring. In this paper, we assume that RM is a centralized entity.

4.2. Set-Up Phase

The first purpose of this phase is to exchange a set of symmetric keys between the nodes of a ring. These keys will be used to encrypt the messages without requiring the complexity of public-key encryption.

We first introduce some notation. Given a ring, we denote by $r_1, \ldots r_k$ the k nodes forming the ring, in order. Given a node r_i, we denote by $next(r_i)$ the next element in the ring, that is, $r_{(i\%k+1)}$, where % is the operator *mod*. We denote by PK_{r_i} the public key associated with the node r_i and by $addr(r_i)$ its network address.

Now, we can describe how key exchange is executed. This is done in detail next. We have two kinds of key exchange. The first is aimed at providing each node with a symmetric key shared with the next node. These keys are used to implement hop-by-hop encryption when messages turn in the ring. This key exchange is called *forward key exchange*, and it is described in detail next, in Section 4.2.1.

The second kind of key exchange is aimed at obtaining key sharing between the sender and the proxy node. However, since both roles of sender and proxy can be played by all the nodes in the ring, the key exchange mechanism involves every pair of nodes. Synthetically, each node of the ring exchanges a symmetric key with the other $k-1$ nodes. Observe that, even though a key is exchanged between two nodes A and B, a different key will be exchanged between B and A. Indeed, the two keys will be used for different purposes depending on whether the node plays the role of *sender* or *proxy*. Therefore, the two keys are called the *sender key* and *proxy key*, respectively. A requirement of this phase is that, if A exchanges a key with B, B learns nothing about the network address of A. The detail of this mechanism, called *sender and proxy key generation*, is provided next, in Section 4.2.3. Since the above keys will be included into special tokens, before describing the key generation mechanism, we describe, in Section 4.2.2, how such tokens are arranged.

4.2.1. Forward Key Exchange

Each node r_i receives from RM the set Q of the public keys of the nodes of the ring it belongs to, $addr(next(r_i))$, and among Q, the information about which public key is associated with $next(r_i)$ (the associations of the other keys with the proper network address remain unknown to r_i). The address of the next node will be used to forward tokens.

Initially, each node r_i exchanges a symmetric key called *forward key* with its next node. This key is used only to encrypt the token hop-by-hop. In detail, as the exchange of keys occurs between the OP and the first OR in Tor (see Section 3), each node r_i generates a public DH parameter y_i and encrypts it with the public key $PK_{next(r_i)}$, obtaining $C = E_{PK_{next(r_i)}}(y_i)$. C is sent to $next(r_i)$ (we recall that r_i knows $add(next(r_i))$). The latter decrypts y_i, generates the *forward key* k_{r_i} and replies to r_i with its public DH parameter $\bar{y}_{next(r_i)}$ along with the hashed value $H(k_{r_i})$ (in plaintext). In summary, each node r_i shares a forward key k_{r_i} with its next node, and the tokens can be properly encrypted hop-by-hop.

4.2.2. Token Generation

After exchanging the forward keys, at a given time t_0, each node r_i generates $k-1$ empty tokens and sends them to its next. In turn, $next(r_i)$ forwards the tokens to its next, and so on. Each token is encrypted by r_i with k_{r_i}; then it is sent to $next(r_i)$, which decrypts it with k_{r_i}, processes the token, re-encrypts it with $k_{next(r_i)}$ and forwards it to $next(next(r_i))$.

The structure of these tokens is the following: $\langle F, PDH, R, H \rangle$ where F is a flag denoting whether the token is empty ($F = 0$) or filled ($F = 1$), PDH is a field containing a public Diffie–Hellman parameter (possibly encrypted), R is a random playing the role of identifier and H is a hashed value (the exact meaning of these fields will be clear in the following). Observe that PDH, R and H are meaningful only if $F = 1$. The tokens are born with $F = 0$. Therefore, at the beginning, there are $k(k-1)$ empty tokens turning in the ring.

Starting from a time $t_1 > t_0$, each node r_i waits a random time δ_i, and then fills the first available empty token, as explained in the following.

4.2.3. Sender and Proxy Key Generation

First, F is set to 1. Then, r_i selects a random public key PK_{r_j} from $Q \setminus \{PK_{r_i}\}$. r_i selects its public DH parameter y_{ij} and encrypts it with PK_{r_j}, thus obtaining $C_{ij} = E_{PK_{r_j}}(y_{ij})$. Then, PDH is set to C_{ij}. R is set to a random value used by r_j to reply with its public DH parameter, which is needed by r_i. This DH parameter is used in the construction of the key that r_i will use to send a message by using r_j as a proxy. This key k_{ij} is called the *sender key* for r_i (with respect to r_j), and the *proxy key* for r_j (with respect to r_i). Finally, H is filled with random bits.

The token T is encrypted by r_i with k_i, by obtaining $C_T = E_{k_i}(T)$. Then, C_T is sent to $next(r_i)$.

When C_T reaches $next(r_i)$, it decrypts C_T, by obtaining T, and since $F = 1$, it tries to read the field $PDH = C_{ij}$ of T. If $next(r_i) \neq r_j$, $next(r_i)$ is not able to decrypt such a field, and then it re-encrypts the token with the forward key $k_{next(r_i)}$ shared with $next(next(r_i))$ and forwards the token. The token moves through the ring until it reaches r_j. At this point, r_j decrypts C_{ij} and obtains y_{ij}, with which it generates the key k_{ij} which is shared with r_i. The token is filled as follows. F remains set to 1. PDH is set to $\bar{y}_{ji}$. $\bar{y}_{ji}$ represents the public DH parameter of r_j that will be used by r_i to generates the key k_{ij}. R remains unaltered, and finally, H is set to the hashed value $H(k_{ij})$. This new token moves through the ring until r_i. Observe that all the nodes between r_j and r_i, after decrypting the token with their forward keys, understand that the token is used to reply to a node, but are unaware of the sender and the recipient of this token.

When r_i receives the token, it identifies the token as a reply of r_j thanks to the random R. Then, r_i can generate the key k_{ij} as r_j. This token is then disposed by r_i. Finally, r_i drops from the set Q the node r_j. Note that any external observer only knows that a key was exchanged by a given node r_i, but does not know with which node.

The entire process (which started at time t_1) is repeated $k - 2$ times, until all k_{iy} are exchanged.

When all the $k(k-1)$ tokens are disposed of, each node r_i owns (in addition to the forward key) two symmetric keys k_{ij} and k_{ji} shared with each other node r_j of the ring. The key k_{ij} represents a sender key for r_i, since it used by r_i when has to send a message by selecting r_j as a proxy node (see next section). On the other hand, k_{ij} represents a proxy key for r_j, since it is used by r_j when plays the role of proxy node.

In Figure 1, the sequence diagram of the set-up phase is depicted.

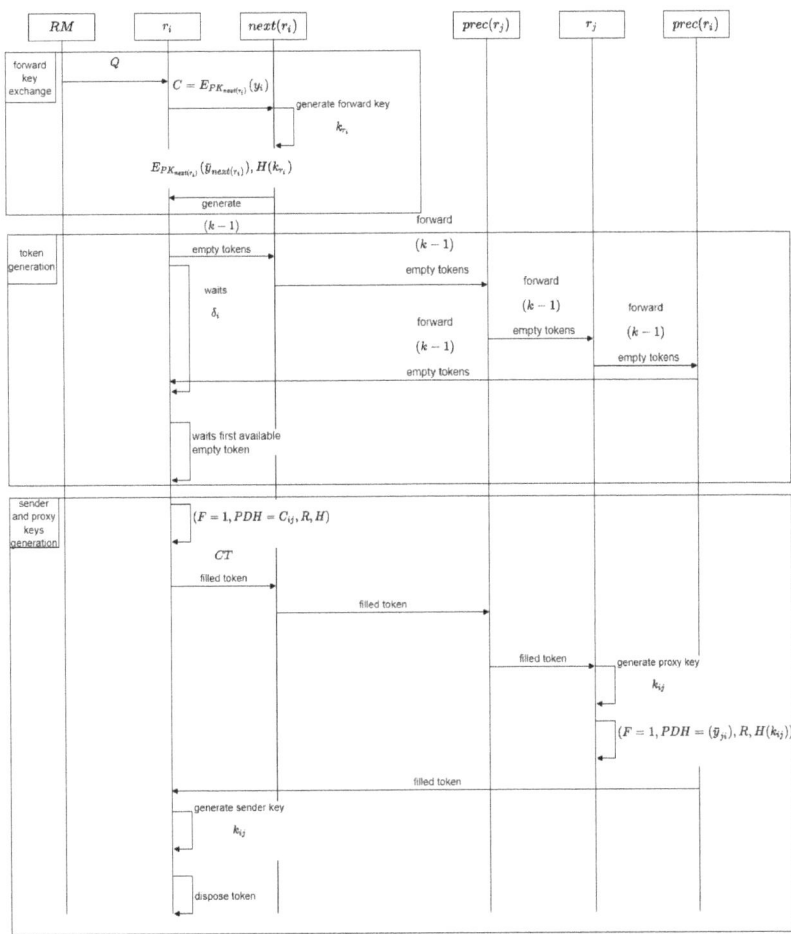

Figure 1. Set-up phase.

4.3. Communication Phase

In this section, we describe the core of our protocol, which is the communication between a sender and recipient. We remark that the communication is bi-directional, in the sense that we address both the request and the response. We split the description of the communication phase into three parts. The first part is the structure of tokens in which messages are encapsulated. Observe that these tokens are different from those used in the set-up phase, which we described in Section 4.3.1. After describing the structure of the tokens, we show how tokens are generated (see Section 4.3.2. Finally, in Sections 4.3.3 and 4.3.4, we describe how anonymous communication is established between a sender and a recipient.

4.3.1. Structure of the Token

As in the set-up phase, in the communication phase, a token-based mechanism is enabled. We assume that a given number of tokens move through the ring encrypted, hop-by-hop, from one node to the next, with the forward key exchanged in the set-up phase.

These tokens are managed (generated and disposed) by some nodes of the ring according to the network requirements (throughput, bandwidth, etc.). The specifications of these requirements are discussed in Section 8.

The structure of a communication-phase token is the following: $\langle F, HID, CI, DA, P \rangle$. In Figure 2, an expanded description of this structure is reported.

```
+----------------------------------+
|    FLAG F (1)   | ////////////// |
+----------------------------------+
|    HASHED IDENTIFIER (HID) (32)  |
+----------------------------------+
| COMMUNICATION IDENTIFIER (CI) (4)|
+----------------------------------+
|    DESTINATION ADDRESS (DA) (4)  |
+----------------------------------+
|         PAYLOAD (P) (498)        |
+----------------------------------+
```

Figure 2. Structure of the token.

As the communication phase is the core of Ring2Tor, we describe in detail how the token is organized. Its size is 539 bytes, of which 41 are reserved for the header, and 498 for the payload. The size of the payload is set to the same value as the size of the payload of the relay Tor cells.

First, we describe the meaning of the field F. It is composed of two bits (even though we reserve 1 byte for this field), with following possible meanings: 00 means *empty* token; 01 means token *reserved* for a given communication identifier; and 10 means that it is *used* for a message. A token in the state 01 (reserved) or 10 (used) is said to be *filled*.

During the description of the protocol, which we provide next, the meanings of the remaining fields are clarified.

4.3.2. Token Generation

Consider now the process of token generation. When a token is generated by a node r_g, the fields are set as follows. F is set to used (i.e., 10). r_g picks randomly from the set Q (where Q is the set of all the public keys of the ring) a public key, say PK_{r_p}, associated with the node r_p. The field HID is set to $H(PK_{r_p})$. It is used as an identifier to allow r_p to recognize that this token is intended for it. Finally, the field DA includes the encryption $\bar{S}$ with the sender key (of r_g) k_{gp} of a fixed string S different from any other network address. This string allows r_p to identify the fact that this token, if even used, does not contain any message to forward outside the ring (see below), but it has to be emptied by r_p. The reason why the token is not directly generated empty derives from security aspects. The security analysis is provided in Section 7. The other fields (CI, P) are filled with random bits.

The entire token is then encrypted with the forward key k_{r_g} and sent to $next(r_g)$. This node decrypts the token, and with the state of the token being filled, through the field HID, it checks whether this token is intended for it. In this case (i.e., $r_p = next(r_g)$), it processes the token. Otherwise, the token is encrypted, as usual, by $next(r_g)$ with the forward key $k_{next(r_g)}$ and sent to $next(next(r_g))$. The token moves through the ring until it reaches r_p.

At this point, r_p verifies that it has been selected as recipient of the token, even though it does not know that the token was generated by r_g. Therefore, r_p tries to decrypt the fields CI, DA, P with all its $k-1$ proxy keys until it finds the correct key k_{gp}. Since $D_{k_{gp}}(DA) = S$, r_p knows that it has to empty the token. Thus, r_p sets F to 00 and $HID = H(PK_{next(r_p)})$. In this case, we say that $next(r_p)$ will play the role of *proxy node* (with respect to a potential sender for a communication identifier not established yet). The other fields are set to random bits.

r_p encrypts the token with the forward key k_{r_p} (shared with its next) and forwards it to $next(r_p)$. The empty token crosses the ring encrypted hop-by-hop, as usual.

The process of generation of the tokens is represented in the sequence diagram in Figure 3.

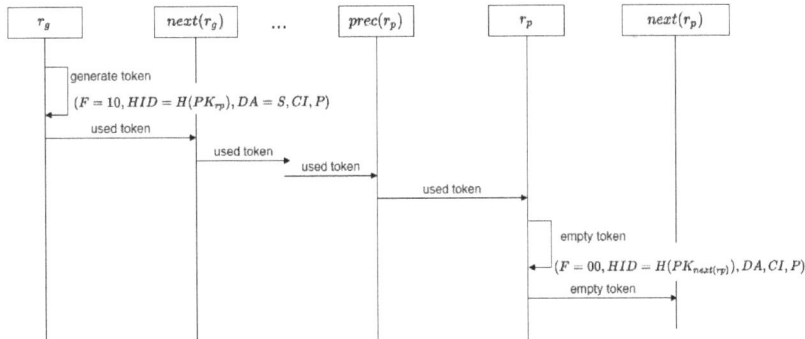

Figure 3. Process of generation of the tokens.

4.3.3. Transmission of a Message

Consider a node r_i that wants to send a message M to a destination D (outside the ring). Suppose M is already encrypted for D. First, r_i splits M into blocks $M_1, \ldots, M_q$ ($q \geq 1$) with size 498 bytes (i.e., the size of the payload P of a token). r_i waits for the first empty token (with $F = 00$). Let be $HID = H(PK_{r_j})$ (this means that r_j will play the role of proxy node for a communication session started by r_i, as we will see next). Through HID, r_i identifies the public key PK_{r_j} and the corresponding sender key k_{ij}.

The token is filled as follows. F is set to 10 (used). $HID = H(PK_{r_j})$ is unaltered. CI is set to $E_{k_{ij}}(R)$ where R is a random value identifying the current *communication session* associated with the sender key k_{ij} (note that for a given communication session, a Tor circuit will be established outside the ring). The field DA includes the encryption with key k_{ij} of the network address of the destination D. Observe that the size of this field is 4 bytes, and thus is compliant only with IPv4. Obviously, for IPv6, the size should be increased. Moreover, the TCP port is not included in this field for privacy reasons. It will be included in the payload encrypted at application layer. Finally, P is set to $E_{k_{ij}}(M_1)$ (possibly padded, if $q = 1$). The token moves through the ring (encrypted hop-by-hop) until it reaches r_j.

Regarding the other messages M_t (with $2 \leq t \leq q$), r_i waits for either (1) an empty token with $HID = H(PK_{r_j})$ or (2) a reserved token ($F = 01$) with $HID = H(R)$, meaning that the token is reserved for the communication session started by r_i identified by R.

In both cases, the token is filled as follows. F is set to 10, HID is set to $H(R)$ in case (2) (indeed, in case (1) it is already set with this value), $CI = E_{k_{ij}}(R)$, DA includes the encryption with key k_{ij} of the network address of the destination D and $P = E_{k_{ij}}(M_t)$. Additionally, these tokens move through the ring until they reach r_j. Eventually, all the blocks of the message M reach the same proxy node r_j, which will use the same Tor circuit.

We now see how such Tor circuit is established by r_j. When r_j receives the (used) token containing M_1, r_j identifies this token through $HID = H(PK_{r_j})$. Anyway, it does not know the sender r_i. Therefore, r_j tries to decrypt the fields CI, DA, P with all its $k-1$ proxy keys until it finds the correct key k_{ij}. Since $D_{k_{ij}}(DA) \neq S$ (we recall that S is a fixed string denoting that the token does not contain a message), r_j has to send the message outside the ring to the destination D through the Tor system.

Before doing this, r_j sets the flag $F = 01$ (reserved) and the field $HID = H(R)$ where $R = D_{k_{ij}}(CI)$. This means that this token is associated with the communication session identified by R. R is also stored by r_j and associated with k_{ij} in such a way that further tokens can be associated with this communication session. The random R is also used by r_j to detect further reserved tokens for this communication session. The other fields are filled with random bits and the token is then forwarded into the ring.

At this point, r_j can send the message $M_1 = D_{k_{ij}}(P)$ to the destination D. To do this, it builds a Tor circuit with destination $D_{k_{ij}}(DA)$ and sends the message M_1 to D through this circuit. The construction of the Tor circuit is performed in the standard way, by contacting the Directory Server (DS) and by selecting the entry, middle and exit nodes as illustrated in Section 3.

When r_j receives a (used) token containing a message M_t with $2 \leq t \leq q$, r_j identifies such token through HID and forwards M_t to D through the Tor circuit. The token is set to reserved ($F = 01$) and HID remains unaltered to the value $H(R)$. The other fields are set to random bits, and the token is then forwarded into the ring.

The transmission of the message M is represented in the sequence diagram in Figure 4.

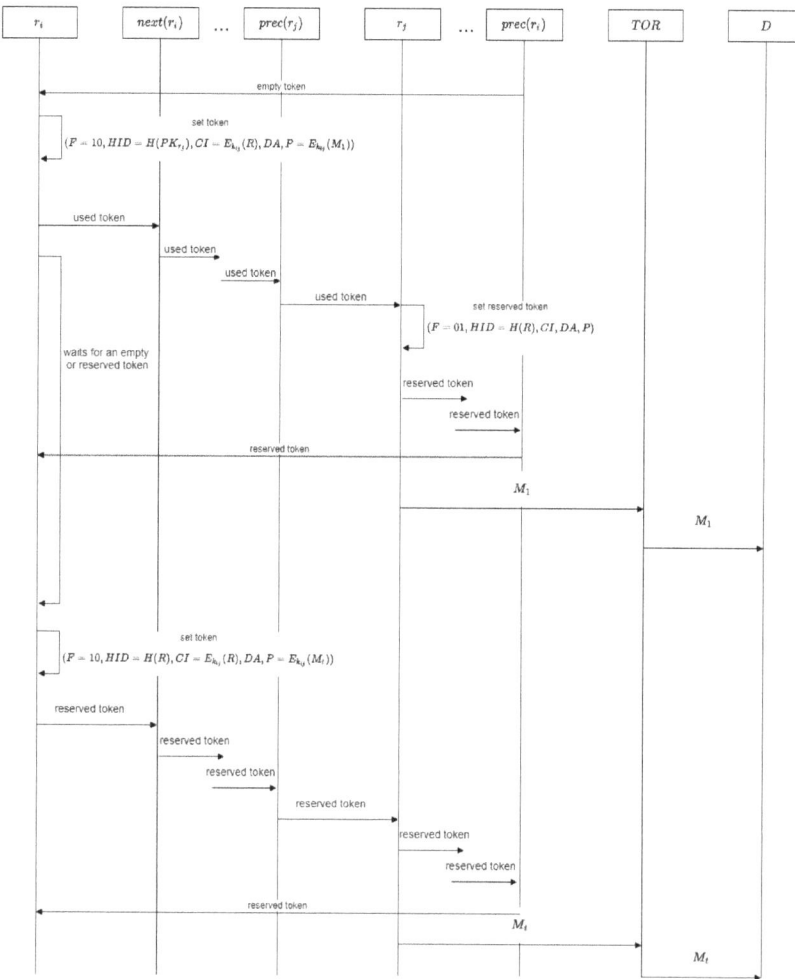

Figure 4. Transmission of the message M.

4.3.4. Transmission of the Response

When r_j receives the response M' (already encrypted by D) through the Tor circuit, r_j injects the response into the ring. Specifically, let $P'_1, \ldots P'_l$ be the Tor cells including the response M', and let denote by P_k the payload of the cell P'_k ($1 \leq k \leq l$). For each P_k, r_j waits for either (1) an empty token or (2) a reserved token with $HID = H(R)$. The token is filled as follows. F is set to 10. Only in the case of an empty token is the field HID set to $H(R)$, and the communication identifier CI, is derivable by the random R associated with the current communication session; and then, with this Tor circuit stored by r_j when the Tor circuit has been established, the field is set properly. That is, $CI = E_{k_{ij}}(R)$. The field DA is filled with random bits. Finally, P is set to $E_{k_{ij}}(P_k)$.

At this point, the token moves through the ring and is identified by r_i through HID. When r_i receives all the tokens containing the block P_k, it retrieves the entire response M'. For each of these tokens, r_i changes the state from used to reserved and forwards the token. Specifically, F is set to 01, $HID = H(R)$ is unaltered and the other fields are filled with random bits. These reserved tokens (along with other possible empty tokens) are used by r_i and r_j to exchange the other requests/responses associated with the communication session identified by R.

The transmission of the response M' is represented in the sequence diagram in Figure 5.

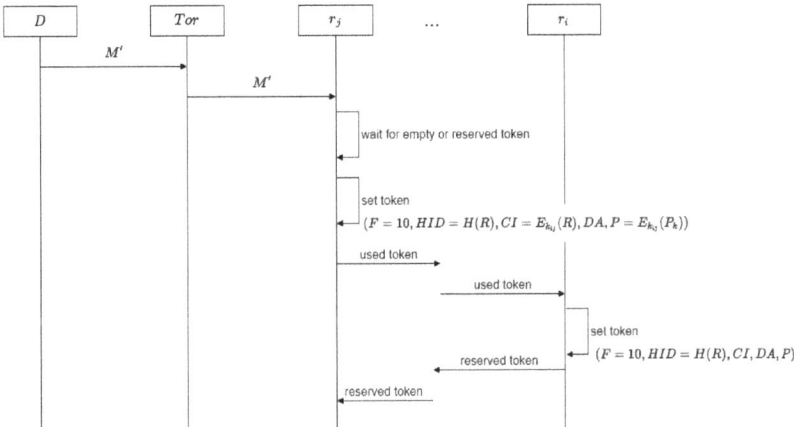

Figure 5. Transmission of the response M'.

When the communication session ends, r_i and r_j perform some actions aimed at emptying the tokens reserved for this session and destroying the Tor circuit. Specifically, for each reserved token with $HID = H(R)$, r_i fills the token in such a way that r_j recognizes that they have to be emptied. To do this, F is set to 10, $HID = H(R)$ remains unaltered, CI is set to $E_{k_{ij}}(R)$, DA is set to the encryption with key k_{ij} of S and P is filled with random bits.

When r_j receives such token, it retrieves the string S and recognizes that the session deactivation actions have to be performed. If this token is the first including S, r_j destroys the Tor circuit. For this token and the successive ones, including S, r_j empties them and forwards them into the ring. Specifically, F is set to 00 and $HID = H(PK_{next(r_j)})$. The other fields are filled with random bits.

This process of emptying the tokens and destroying the Tor circuit is represented in the sequence diagram in Figure 6.

To conclude this section, we provide a brief summary, by omitting the technical details of the communication phase. In Figure 7, we sketched a high level graphical representation of this phase.

The sender waits for an empty token, selects a proxy node and fills the token with a message. This token will be injected into the ring, in which it will move until the proxy node is reached. The path of the ring from the sender to the proxy node is represented with a red arrow. Once the proxy node receives the message (possibly, encrypted), it contacts the Directory Server (dashed arrow) to select the entry, middle and exit routers and builds a Tor circuit through them. At this point, the proxy node forwards the message through this Tor circuit until the destination. The latter will provide the response (possibly encrypted) through the same Tor circuit until the proxy node. Both the ongoing path and the return path are represented by the green arrow in the figure. Finally, when the proxy node receives the response, it waits for a number of empty or reserved tokens and fills them with the response. These tokens are injected into the ring until they reach the originator of the request. The path of the ring from the proxy node to the originator, traversed by the response, is represented with a blue arrow.

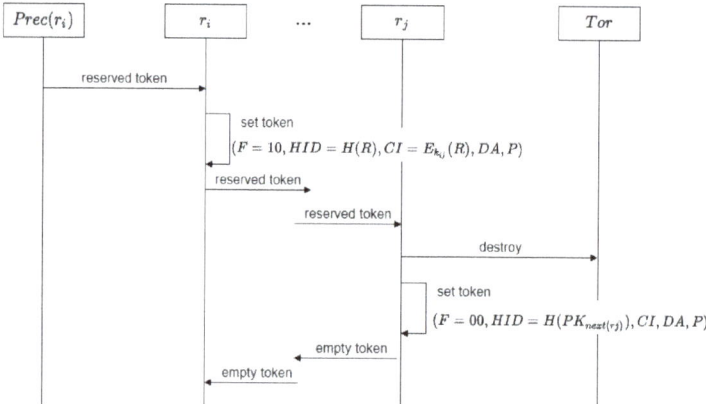

Figure 6. Process of emptying the tokens and destroying the Tor circuit.

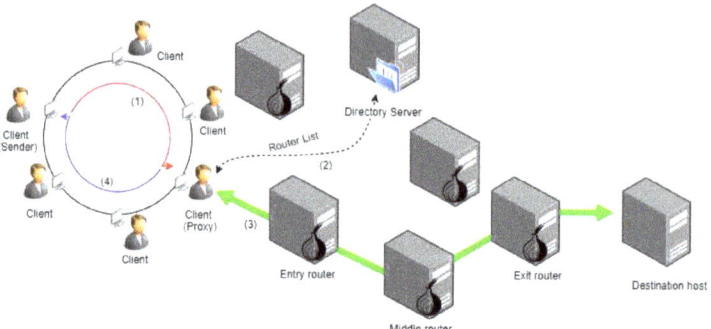

Figure 7. Communication phase.

5. Introducing Fault Tolerance into the System

Even though fault tolerance is one of the aspects that is typically missed in anonymous communication networks, we sketch in this section how a certain degree of fault tolerance can be easily introduced in a system based on our protocol. To confirm the above claim, consider the current Tor itself has no fault tolerance at all. Indeed, if a Tor router stops working during a communication, the communication is lost, and there is no a protocol to recover the communication on the fly (indeed, to set a backup Tor circuit is not enough to obtain this goal). As we focus on the part of the proposal that plays the role of *add-on*, with respect to the existing Tor system, we do not consider in this section the Tor communication occurring outside the system, between the proxy node and the destination. Apart from the fact that the fault tolerance of Tor can be considered as an orthogonal problem, it is also true that Tor routers can be considered more stable than standard client nodes involved in the rings.

The basic change we have to introduce to obtain fault tolerance is the notion of a *ring layer*. The ring manager, instead of building simply rings of k nodes, builds rings of k layers, each composed of j nodes. We can figure out that the value of j, for good fault tolerance, should be very low (for example, 2 or 3), if we are in a network with a high level of activity. Anyway, higher values of j do not result in infeasible computation, as we will see next. The nodes of each layer know each other in the sense that they are aware of the reciprocal addresses. With the notation $r_1, \ldots r_k$, used earlier for the rings, now we indicate a sequence of layers, such that $r_i = \{x_1^i, \ldots x_j^i\}$ is a set of j nodes. Besides the individual public keys of the nodes, there is also a public key per layer, called the *public layer key*. This impacts both the set-up phase and the communication phase. Concerning the set-up phase, some changes occur for the key exchange task. Forward keys are exchanged for each pair $x_p^i, x_q^{i\%k+1}$, $(1 \leq p, q \leq j)$. Thus, we have j^2 forward key exchanges per pair of consecutive layers. Instead, by leveraging public layer keys, the pair of keys used as sender key and proxy key k_{st} and k_{ts} will be established between layers instead of individual nodes. To do this, the ring manager selects one *representative* node alive per layer and informs each selected node about the other selected nodes (and then about their public keys). Then, the Diffie–Hellman process described in Section 4 happens among these representative nodes. At the end of this process, any representative node has a pair of sender key and proxy key between its layer and any other layer. These keys are exchanged with all the other nodes in the layer. Indeed, in the pre-set-up phase, the nodes of the same layer exchange a symmetric key per pair, by enacting the $j(j-1)$ Diffie–Hellman processes.

Concerning both the circulation of tokens and the communication task, the only change is that the function *next*, associating to each node of the ring the next node to forward a message, becomes non-deterministic. Specifically, a node in layer s which has to forward a message, just has to choose one alive node in the layer $next(s)$ and forwards the message to it. For the proxy node, essentially no change is required, because the encryption is done for the layer, so that any node in the layer is able to decrypt the message and then initiate the Tor circuit. Similar considerations can be made for the response.

To conclude this section, we evaluate our fault-tolerance mechanism from a probabilistic perspective, to allow the correct setting of the parameter j, once a given reliability probability is fixed. We denote by p the probability that, at a given instant, a node is alive. We assume p is the same for each node. Therefore, the probability that, given a layer of j nodes, at least one node of the layer is alive is $p' = 1 - (1-p)^j$. To guarantee reliability (i.e., the communication is not lost), at least one node per level (for the k levels) has to be alive. Therefore, the probability that the communication succeeds is $p'' = (1 - (1-p)^j)^k$. Clearly, it decreases as k increases and increases as j increases. Suppose now we set the reliability threshold to a given value τ. Then, j must set in such a way that $j > \frac{log(1-e^{\frac{log(\tau)}{k}})}{log(1-p)}$.

In Figure 8, we set $\tau = 0.999$ and show how the ratio $\frac{j}{k}$ varies for different values of p and k.

Observe that the exemplified value chosen for τ refers to a very reliable system. Indeed, according to the standard IEC 61508, this value falls into the range of probability of failure on demand (PFD), classifying the system as reliability class SIL 3, which is the second most-reliable class.

As expected, for high values of p, the number of nodes j (and then the ratio $\frac{j}{k}$) required to obtain $\tau = 0.999$ decreases. Regarding k, as k increases the absolute value of j increases but slower that k. Therefore, the ratio $\frac{j}{k}$ increases with k.

To give a practical example, with $k = 100$ and $p = 0.9$, we obtain a ratio $\frac{j}{k} = 0.05$, which means that each layer of the ring has to contain only five nodes.

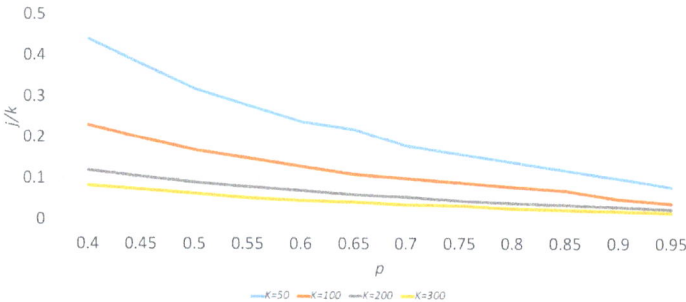

Figure 8. Ratio $\frac{j}{k}$ as k and p vary.

6. Computational Complexity

In this section, we discuss the computational complexity of our protocol. We focus on the part of the protocol regarding the ring. Indeed, for the rest of the protocol, involving just a Tor circuit, the reader may refer to the results available in the literature [1].

The communication phase requires, besides the hop-by-hop encryption of the messages (which is standard in any protocol supporting secure communication), the attempted decryptions that the intended proxy node has to perform before sending the message outside the ring. On average, there are $\frac{k-1}{2}$ decryptions applied only to the first token of a given communication (recall that the size of a token is about 500 bytes). In the worst case, there are $k-1$ decryptions. This overhead does not appear relevant, as it regards only the proxy node, and for good privacy levels (e.g., $k = 100$), the extra time required is small. Observe that the magnitude of an AES encryption/decryption is 10^2 Mbytes per second on standard personal computers.

Now, we consider the set-up phase.

First, consider the protocol without fault tolerance (see Section 4). Similarly to the Tor set-up phase, we require k key exchanges for the forward keys and $k(k-1)$ key exchanges for sender/proxy keys. For values of k guaranteeing a good anonymity level, the cost of this phase is not prohibitive. When fault tolerance is included, we pay a price in terms of complexity of the set-up phase. Indeed, we require $j(j-1)$ key exchanges per layer in the pre-set-up phase, and then j^2 forward key exchanges per pair of adjacent layers (executed in parallel) plus $k(k-1)$ exchanges for sender/proxy key exchanges. In summary, we increase the previous cost by $j(j-1) + j^2$. Due to the fact that we expect that j is very small, this computational overhead does not appear as an actual issue for the protocol. Recall that the set-up phase, differently from Tor, is not done for each communication, but it is done to set-up the network, so it can be considered an operation with a long-term lifetime.

7. Security Analysis

In this section, we analyze the security of our solution. We start by defining the threat model we consider. We introduce the following assumption:

Assumption 1 (A1). *Rings are formed in such a way that the background knowledge does not allow the adversary to have more information than sender uniform distribution.*

Observe that Assumption A1 is easily satisfied if rings are built among hosts belonging to the same, even large, geographical region.

Adversary Model (AM). We consider four types of adversaries.

- **External (E).** In this case, the adversary monitors incoming and outgoing traffic of the DS. In addition, for Ring2Tor, the adversary monitors traffic coming in and going out from the RM.
- **Weak (W).** In this case, the adversary monitors the traffic between a client node and the entry Tor router. In Tor, the client node corresponds to the OP. To be fair, for

Ring2Tor, we allow the weak adversary to monitor all the traffic between the client nodes and the traffic between the client node playing as a proxy and the entry Tor router.
- **Strong (S).** In this case, the adversary monitors the traffic between a client node and the entry Tor router and the traffic between the exit Tor router and the destination host. For Ring2Tor, in addition, the adversary can monitor all the traffic between the client nodes.
- **Global (G).** In this case, the adversary monitors all the traffic of the network.

Furthermore, for all the four adversaries, regarding Ring2Tor, we enable another capability: the adversary knows the entire composition of the rings.

Observe that the capabilities of Global, Strong and Weak adversaries are in order (i.e., Global is stronger than Strong and Strong is stronger than Weak). Furthermore, Global is stronger than External.

Both the External adversary and the Weak adversary model refer to a very feasible case in which an entity is able to control just an autonomous system. The feasibility of the External adversary can be contrasted by distributing the DS and the RM. The Strong adversary is a weak form of the Global adversary, because the autonomous systems of entry router and exit router can be very far from each other and even be in different continents [14]. The Global adversary is the standard global passive adversary.

Security properties. We analyze two security properties (see Section 3): (1) Sender anonymity (SA); (2) Relationship anonymity (RA).

In the following analysis, we discuss how Tor and Ring2Tor behave with respect to the security properties in the four adversary models. The results of the analysis are summarized in Table 1. First, we give a preliminary basic result in the following lemma.

Lemma 1. *In* Ring2Tor, *a ring of size k is a sender with an anonymity set of size k against the Global adversary.*

Proof of Lemma 1. Due to the hop-by-hop probabilistic encryption mechanism that is used to move tokens inside the ring, the only point of the ring from which the adversary can draw some information more than a random guess to identify a sender is the proxy node. Indeed, this is the only point of the ring in which the possible state transitions of a token could be in principle related to the observable incoming or outgoing traffic in/out of the proxy. Transitions occurring in other points are not identifiable with probability higher than $\frac{1}{k}$. Since reserved and used tokens cannot be filled by other client nodes different from the sender (associated with the reserved tokens), the only possibility for the adversary to identify a sender anonymity set of size less than k is to detect an empty token outgoing from a node and track it until it reaches a proxy node, which sends a message outside the ring before doing less than k steps. The only event in which the adversary can guess that a token is emptied is when a proxy node, say r_x, dismisses a Tor circuit. Indeed, according to the protocol, there is no other case in which tokens are emptied. However, r_x sets the field HID to $H(PK_{next(r_x)})$, and this means that such a token moves around the entire ring (in which it is, possibly, filled) before reaching $next(r_x)$, which possibly builds a Tor circuit outside the ring. Therefore, we can argue that the sender anonymity set is not always larger than k, even for the Global passive adversary. The proof is then concluded. □

The above lemma is the basis for the fulfillment of the security properties stated above for Ring2Tor.

This is proven through the following theorems. The first theorem states that Tor does not guarantee **SA** against any adversary. This corresponds to the first four fields of the first row of Table 1.

Theorem 1. *In Tor, any adversary breaks* **SA** *with probability 1.*

Proof of Theorem 1. Consider the External adversary. Since it observes the traffic intended to the DS, it receives the request of the sender and then the sender is identified. Since the Global adversary has the same capabilities as the External adversary, **SA** does not hold against it. Now, we consider the Weak adversary able to observe the traffic between the sender and the entry Tor router. Clearly, **W** identifies the sender. The Strong adversary has the same capabilities as the Weak adversary. The proof is then concluded. □

Now, we prove that Ring2Tor guarantees that a sender can be identified (by any adversary) with probability $\frac{1}{k}$. This corresponds to the first four fields of the second row of Table 1.

Theorem 2. *In* Ring2Tor, *any adversary breaks* **SA** *with probability* $\frac{1}{k}$.

Proof of Theorem 2. Consider the Global adversary **G**. By Lemma 1, it can identify the sender with a probability not higher than $\frac{1}{k}$. Since **G** is stronger than all the other adversaries (i.e., **S**, **W**, and **E**), we conclude that for those three adversaries also, **SA** is broken with a probability not higher than $\frac{1}{k}$. □

Table 1. Comparison between Tor (**T**) and Ring2Tor(**R2T**). Shown are the probabilities of the adversaries breaking the properties **SA** and **RA**.

	SA				RA			
AM	E	W	S	G	E	W	S	G
T	1	1	1	1	$\frac{1}{n_d}$	$\frac{1}{n_d}$	1	1
R2T	$\frac{1}{k}$	$\frac{1}{k}$	$\frac{1}{k}$	$\frac{1}{k}$	$\frac{1}{n_d \cdot k}$	$\frac{1}{n_d \cdot k}$	$\frac{1}{k}$	$\frac{1}{k}$

Now, we have to consider the remaining fields of Table 1 regarding relationship anonymity. These are covered by the following two theorems.

Theorem 3. *Let n_d be the size of the recipient anonymity set. In Tor, the External and Weak adversary break* **RA** *with probability* $\frac{1}{n_d}$. *Furthermore, the Strong and Global adversary break* **RA** *with probability* 1.

Proof of Theorem 3. Consider the External adversary. By Theorem 1, it identifies the sender SN of a communication with probability 1. Anyway, **E** has no information about the recipient R of such a communication. Therefore, **E** (without further knowledge) identifies that SN communicates with R only with the smallest probability, i.e., $\frac{1}{n_d}$.

Similarly, the Weak adversary identifies the sender with probability 1, but has no information about the recipient. Therefore, **RA** is broken with probability $\frac{1}{n_d}$.

Consider the Strong adversary **S**. Since it monitors the outgoing traffic from the exit Tor router, it can identify the recipient R of a communication with probability 1. Since S also monitors the traffic between the sender SN and the entry Tor router, it can perform traffic analysis attacks [14] and identifies that SN communicates with R with probability 1. The Global adversary has the same power as the Strong adversary. The proof is then concluded. □

Theorem 4. *Let n_d be the size of the recipient anonymity set. In* Ring2Tor, *the External and Weak adversary break* **RA** *with probability* $\frac{1}{n_d \cdot k}$. *Furthermore, the Strong and Global adversary break* **RA** *with probability* $\frac{1}{k}$.

Proof of Theorem 4. Since **SA** implies **RA** [7], by Theorem 2, it follows that **RA** can be broken with a probability not higher than $\frac{1}{k}$ by any adversary. Consider now the adversaries E and W. Even though they can identify the sender with a probability not higher than $\frac{1}{k}$, they do not have any information about the recipient. Therefore, they can only guess the recipient among all the possible recipients of the network n_d. Therefore, for E and W, RA is broken with a probability not higher than $\frac{1}{n_d \cdot k}$. For the other adversaries (i.e., S and G), the above upper bound of the success probability cannot be decreased, because both S and G are able to identify the recipient, so that the probability of breaking **RA** is the same as the probability of breaking **SA**. The proof is then concluded. □

This ends the security analysis. As is evident by Table 1, the benefit in terms of security of Ring2Tor can be measured as a multiplicative factor k, increasing the degree of anonymity provided by Tor both for **SA** and **RA**.

8. Experiments

In this section, we provide experimental validation of Ring2Tor. Specifically, our aim is to show that the network performance is not compromised by the adoption of our protocol. Our analysis was performed through the network simulator NS3 [39]. We simulated an overlay network with rings of size $k = 50$ and with no fault tolerance (clearly, fault tolerance has no impact on the communication-phase performance, only on the set-up phase). Tor routers were set as separated network nodes. Regarding the links between the Tor routers, we set a delay such that the total time to perform a download of 50KB was about 1.5 s, which represents the actual time (as of October 2021) taken to download a file of this size in the real-life Tor network [40]. The resulting delay is then 150 ms.

The above considerable delays reflect the fact that, according to the current Tor-router-selection algorithm, no two routers in the same circuit belong to the same class B network (/16 subnet) or the same family [41]. Regarding the link between client nodes, we set a delay of 10 ms, capturing that the purpose of the node-selection algorithm—to form rings is the opposite of that of Tor router selection—to obtain homogeneity among nodes in a ring (and thus an effective anonymity set). Therefore, nodes belonging to the same ring are geographically close to each other.

We used an http traffic generation model that simulates web browsing traffic according to the specification suggested by 3GPP2 [42]. We focus our analysis on three metrics: *(communication) latency*, *(traffic) overhead* and *throughput*. The communication latency is defined by the application layer, as it measures the time between the instant at which the sender sends an http request and the instant at which it receives the complete response. Observe that, to be fair, we did not consider as initial time the instant in which the sender received an available token, but the instant in which the http client generated the request. As traffic overhead, we took the average ratio between the number of empty tokens circulating in the ring and the total number of circulating tokens. Finally, the throughput was defined as per usual—that is, the average exploited data rate per node. The results are reported in Figures 9–13.

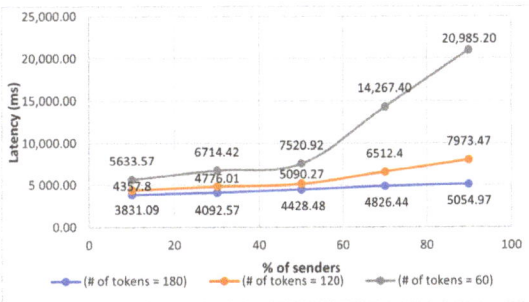

Figure 9. Latency vs. percentage of senders in Ring2Tor.

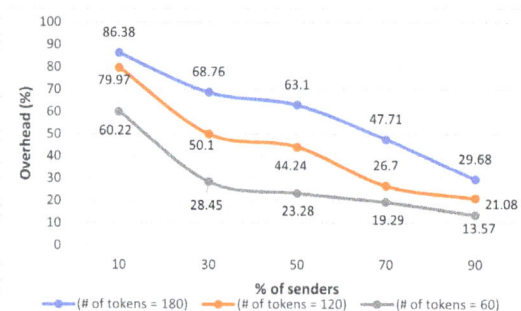

Figure 10. Overhead vs. percentage of senders in Ring2Tor.

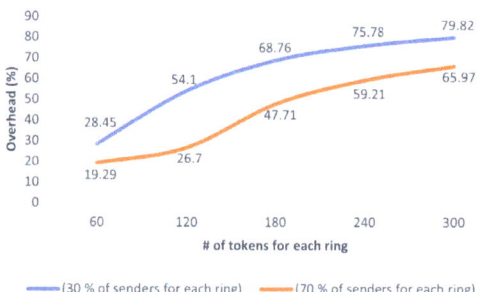

Figure 11. Overhead vs. Number of tokens in Ring2Tor.

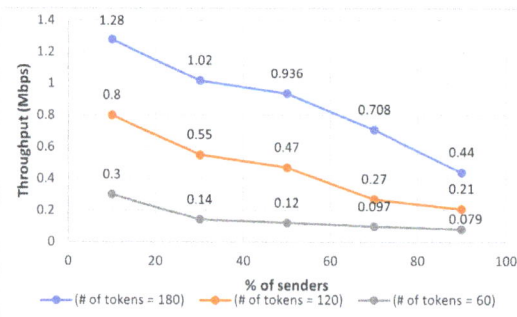

Figure 12. Throughput vs. percentage of senders in Ring2Tor.

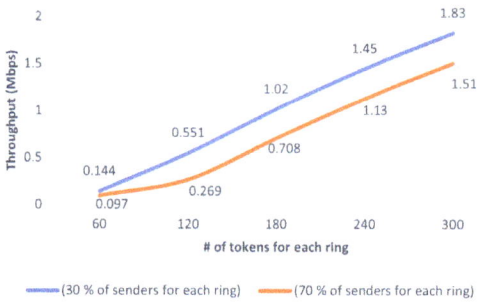

Figure 13. Throughput vs. numbers of tokens in Ring2Tor.

The plot in Figure 9 shows that our solution introduces an acceptable latency for different sender percentages. Specifically, when the percentage of senders is less than 50, the latency ranges from 3.8 s to nearly 7 s, which are values not too far from those found for Tor [43], considering the results obtained for low-volume `http` traffic.

For high volumes, the difference between `Ring2Tor` and Tor increases, because Tor's performance improves. However, the absolute values of latency experimented for `Ring2Tor` for realistic `http` traffic can be considered acceptable. As expected, the latency increases as the sender percentage does, since, in the rings, many filled (reserved and used) tokens move. On the other hand, the latency decreases as the number of tokens moving in the ring increases.

The plots in Figures 10 and 11 can be used to set the number of tokens that a generator needs to maintain in a ring. Indeed, by fixing the maximum percentage of overhead tolerable and the percentage of senders in the rings, we can find the minimum number of tokens. For example, if the maximum overhead is set to 27%, even with a high percentage of senders equal to 70%, we obtain a latency of 6.5 seconds by setting 120 tokens in the ring.

As expected, the overhead decreases as the percentage of senders increases, because there will be more filled tokens circulating into the ring. Moreover, as the total number of tokens circulating into the ring increases, with the same percentage of senders, the overhead increases since a greater number of empty tokens will circulate into the ring.

Finally, Figures 12 and 13 show that also the values of throughput are acceptable. As expected, regardless the number of tokens, the throughput decreases as the percentage of senders increases. This happens since a when the percentage of senders increases, the number of empty (available) tokens decreases and then, each sender has to wait for a longer time before sending a message. This reduces the throughput of the senders. On the other hand, as the number of tokens increases, also the number of empty (available) increases and then, with the same percentage of senders, the throughput experimented by a single sender increases.

Even though the amount of traffic overhead could appear high, we have to consider that we are dealing with an inherently difficult task, which is the resistance to a global passive adversary. It is widely recognized in the literature that a high traffic overhead is the price we have to pay in any anonymous routing protocol to achieve the above goal [28]. As a matter of fact, our protocol has a significant advantage with respect to the standard way of hiding communication against a global passive adversary. The standard way is indeed to use mixnets [29] with bi-directional cover traffic in any link of the overlay network. Instead, in our approach, cover traffic is only 1-directional and the circular overlay network, differently from mixnets, does not produce overhead amplification. To better understand this point, consider a simplified yet general model of mixnets taken from [32]. Here, as anticipated earlier, we need to enable bi-directional cover traffic over any link of the overlay network in such a way that the fan-out mechanism increases the cardinality of the anonymity set exponentially with the length of the communication path. Indeed, if we have even a simple mixnet with a degree of mixing of 2 (i.e., the traffic of two senders is mixed into one receiver at each step), for a communication path of length l, the anonymity set has cardinality 2^l. For minimum degree of nodes (which is 3, to enable the fan-out mechanism) and k nodes, the cover traffic is $2 \cdot 3 \cdot k$ (recall that the traffic must be bi-directional). Instead, in our protocol, the cover traffic involving k nodes in a ring is just k, according to the topology with no branch of the route and the fact that the traffic is 1-directional. Therefore, we reduce cover traffic by a multiplicative factor equal to 6. Observe that, in these approaches, the cover traffic is the total traffic of the network. However, when the cover traffic does not embed real traffic, it represents an overhead.

To better support the above analysis, we performed a number of experiments by implementing this simple model of P2P mixnet with 50 nodes, each with degree 3. In particular, we replicated the same simulation conditions in NS3 as those used for `Ring2Tor` (same traffic pattern, same link delay and same number of nodes). Furthermore, we measured the rate of the circulating tokens in Ring2Tor and used this value to set the rate of the total traffic for a single link of the mixnet.

In Figure 14, we show that the ratio between the cover traffic of the mixnet and the cover traffic of Ring2Tor is very close to 6 (the slight difference comes from possible imprecision of the rate setting).

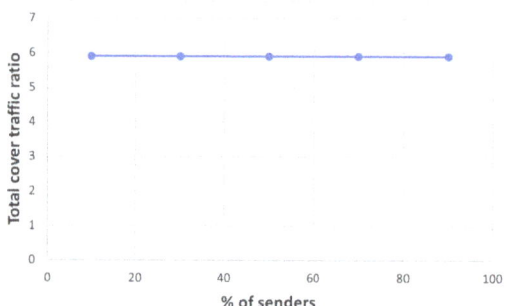

Figure 14. Ratio between the cover traffic of mixnet and Ring2Tor.

The benefits of our solution in terms of traffic overhead compared with the mixnet are highlighted in Figure 15. Therein, we consider Ring2Tor with 180 tokens circulating in each ring. For the mixnet, we obtain a very high value of traffic overhead (approximately equal to 99%). Observe that it decreases very slightly with the percentage of senders. This can be explained by considering that, for the bursting http traffic, the high volume of total cover traffic is always dominant, even when many nodes are senders.

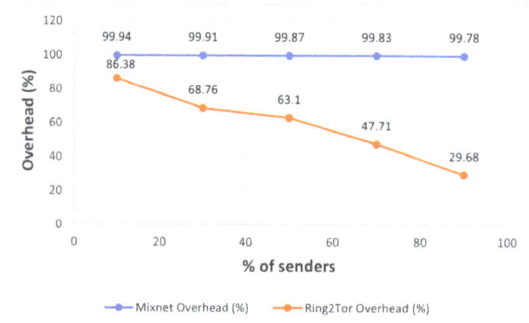

Figure 15. Overhead vs. percentage of senders in mixnet and Ring2Tor.

We expect that the benefits in terms of overhead have a price in terms of latency, as the communication path is in general much shorter in mixnets than in Ring2Tor. Indeed, in Ring2Tor, the request and the associated response go through $O(k)$ hops, but in mixnet, through $O(\log k)$ nodes. It is important to understand whether, for a significant privacy level (i.e., the cardinality of the anonymity set), the above price is tolerable or not. To do this, we performed an experiment on latency. The results are reported in Figure 16. From them, we can conclude that the latency of Ring2Tor is higher (as expected), but within a range of tolerability, for the considered application setting.

In summary, we can conclude that our protocol represents a good trade-off between latency and traffic overhead, when resistance to a global passive adversary should be achieved.

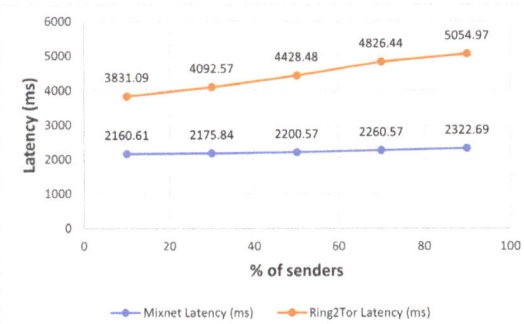

Figure 16. Latency vs. percentage of senders in mixnet and `Ring2Tor`.

9. Conclusions

In this paper, we proposed the protocol `Ring2Tor` achieving sender anonymity in Tor, and then relationship anonymity, against a global passive adversary. We conducted a security analysis, showing that the ring-based approach guarantees a sender an anonymity set the size of the ring, thereby allowing us to achieve our goal. The protocol includes also a certain degree of fault tolerance to consider the case in which not all nodes are alive and collaborative. Moreover, a computational complexity analysis of the solution was also provided. As typically happens for every k-anonymity-based approach to achieve privacy, a crucial point is to establish which is the right value of k to effectively cover the adversary monitoring. Evidently, the higher the value of k, the stronger the protection. However, an interesting question to pose is that there is a threshold to reach. The answer to this question can be acquired only from a risk-based point of view. Indeed, to guarantee k-anonymity, as our approach does, we have to provide the risk analyst with a concrete way to estimate the probability for the adversary of re-identification of a possible target. This is necessary to process risk analysis, together with the evaluation of the impact of a similar event. Therefore, the threshold may directly derive from the requirements in terms of risk we can set, depending on the application setting. In a key paper [8], some considerations about this aspect are given. Therein, the authors say that, "k-anonymity is still sufficient for a variety of applications. For example, in the United States legal system, 2-anonymity would be enough to cast *reasonable doubt*, thus invalidating a criminal charge, while 3-anonymity would be enough to invalidate a civil charge, in the absence of other evidence".

Once the specific application scenario is fixed, the risk threshold can thus established. Then, from the evaluation of the impact of a re-identification incident, the maximum allowed probability of the incident can be derived (also on the basis of the expected capabilities of the adversary). Therefore, the right privacy level k can be set.

Obviously, the chosen value of k has direct impact on the network's performance. The experimental validation highlighted that it is possible to configure the network in order to obtain acceptable values of overhead, latency or throughput, depending on the requirements. We can argue that the price in terms of network performance to obtain our strong anonymity goal is tolerable, when privacy needs are high priority. We traced the route for further investigation in the direction of more sophisticated setting of the network configuration (e.g., number of tokens, size of the rings), by enabling suitable adaptivity to better control network performance in the dynamic case.

Another direction to investigate as future work is represented by a formal validation analysis of our solution regarding dependability and security requirements. For example, reference [44] proposes an approach to validating solutions involving dynamic changes. It appears very suitable for our protocol, since it requires several message exchanges and sequential steps (generation, filling, and emptying of tokens). Another interesting framework that could be applied during the security design and development of our protocol is [45].

Furthermore, in the context of security, the analysis proposed in Section 7, combined with approach proposed in [46,47], can represent a starting point to derive specific security patterns applicable to anonymous communication networks, and thus, to our case. These patterns may involve: (1) the requirement phase, both in terms of analysis process patterns and model based patterns; (2) the design phase, by considering the design of security properties, the bridge between security design patterns and security properties and the proper domain-specific design patterns; (3) the implementation phase of the software we have to install in the nodes and in the ring manager, through secure programming guidelines, attack pattern catalog definition and secure refactoring.

Author Contributions: Conceptualization, F.B., V.D.A., M.F.I. and C.L.; methodology, F.B., V.D.A., M.F.I. and C.L.; software, S.L.; validation, F.B., V.D.A., M.F.I., C.L. and S.L.; formal analysis, F.B. and V.D.A.; investigation, F.B., V.D.A., M.F.I. and C.L.; resources, S.L.; data curation, S.L.; writing—original draft preparation, F.B., V.D.A., M.F.I. and C.L.; writing—review and editing, F.B., V.D.A., M.F.I., C.L. and S.L.; visualization, S.L.; supervision, F.B.; project administration, F.B. All authors have read and agreed to the published version of the manuscript.

Funding: This research received no external funding.

Institutional Review Board Statement: Not applicable.

Informed Consent Statement: Not applicable.

Data Availability Statement: Not applicable.

Acknowledgments: This paper is partially supported by Project POR FESR/FSE 14/20 Line A (Action 10.5.6) and Line B (Action 10.5.12).

Conflicts of Interest: The authors declare no conflict of interest.

Abbreviations

The following abbreviations are used in this manuscript:

AM	Adversary Model
CI	Communication Identifier
DA	Destination Address
DH	Diffie–Hellman
DS	Directory Server
E	External Adversary
F	Flag
G	Global Adversary
H	Hash Value
HID	Hashed Identifier
OP	Onion Proxy
OR	Onion Router
P	Payload
P2P	Peer To Peer
PDH	Public Diffie–Hellman
PFD	Probability of Failure
R	Random
RA	Relationship Anonymity
RM	Ring Manager
S	Strong Adversary
SA	Sender Anonymity
W	Weak Adversary
SIL	Safety Integrity Level
T	Tor
R2T	Ring2Tor

References

1. Syverson, P.; Dingledine, R.; Mathewson, N. Tor: The Second-Generation Onion Router. In Proceedings of the Usenix Security, San Diego, CA, USA, 9–13 August 2004; pp. 303–320.
2. Goldschlag, D.M.; Reed, M.G.; Syverson, P.F. Hiding Routing Information. In Proceedings of the International Workshop on Information Hiding, Cambridge, UK, 30 May–1 June 1996; Springer: Berlin/Heidelberg, Germany, 1996; pp. 137–150.
3. Reiter, M.K.; Rubin, A.D. Crowds: Anonymity for Web Transactions. *ACM Trans. Inf. Syst. Secur. (TISSEC)* **1998**, *1*, 66–92. [CrossRef]
4. O'Gorman, G.; Blott, S. Large Scale Simulation of Tor. In Proceedings of the Annual Asian Computing Science Conference, Doha, Qatar, 9–11 December 2007; Springer: Berlin/Heidelberg, Germany, 2007; pp. 48–54.
5. Karunanayake, I.; Ahmed, N.; Malaney, R.; Islam, R.; Jha, S. Anonymity with Tor: A Survey on Tor Attacks. *arXiv* **2020**, arXiv:2009.13018.
6. Palmieri, F. A Distributed Flow Correlation Attack to Anonymizing Overlay Networks Based on Wavelet Multi-Resolution Analysis. *IEEE Trans. Depend. Secur. Comput.* **2019**, *18*, 2271–2284. [CrossRef]
7. Pfitzmann, A.; Hansen, M. A terminology for talking about privacy by data minimization: Anonymity, Unlinkability, Undetectability, Unobservability, Pseudonymity, and Identity Management. 2010. (Version 0.33 April 2010), Technical Report, TU Dresden and ULD Kiel. Available online: http://dud.inf.tu-dresden.de/Anon_Terminology.shtml (accessed on 21 May 2021).
8. Von Ahn, L.; Bortz, A.; Hopper, N.J. k-Anonymous Message Transmission. In Proceedings of the 10th ACM Conference on Computer and Communications Security, Washington, DC, USA, 27–30 October 2003; pp. 122–130.
9. Hirt, A.; Jacobson, M.; Williamson, C. Taxis: Scalable Strong Anonymous Communication. In *Proceedings of the 2008 IEEE International Symposium on Modeling, Analysis and Simulation of Computers and Telecommunication Systems, Baltimore, MD, USA, 8–10 September2008*; IEEE Computer Society: Washington, DC, USA, 2008; pp. 1–10.
10. Beimel, A.; Dolev, S. Buses for Anonymous Message Delivery. *J. Cryptol.* **2003**, *16*, 25–39
11. Burnside, M.; Keromytis, A.D. Low Latency Anonymity with Mix Rings. In Proceedings of the International Conference on Information Security, Samos Island, Greece, 30 August–2 September 2006; Springer: Berlin/Heidelberg, Germany, 2006; pp. 32–45.
12. Salo, J. *Recent Attacks on Tor*; Aalto University: Espoo, Finland 2010.
13. Erdin, E.; Zachor, C.; Gunes, M.H. How to Find Hidden Users: A Survey of Attacks on Anonymity Networks. *IEEE Commun. Surv. Tutor.* **2015**, *17*, 2296–2316. doi:10.1109/COMST.2015.2453434. [CrossRef]
14. Basyoni, L.; Fetais, N.; Erbad, A.; Mohamed, A.; Guizani, M. Traffic Analysis Attacks on Tor: A Survey. In *Proceedings of the 2020 IEEE International Conference on Informatics, IoT, and Enabling Technologies (ICIoT), Doha, Qatar, 2–5 February 2020*; IEEE Computer Society: Washington, DC, USA, 2020; pp. 183–188.
15. Edman, M.; Yener, B. On Anonymity in an Electronic Society: A Survey of Anonymous Communication Systems. *ACM Comput. Surv. (CSUR)* **2009**, *42*, 1–35. [CrossRef]
16. Murdoch, S.J.; Danezis, G. Low-Cost Traffic Analysis of Tor. In *Proceedings of the 2005 IEEE Symposium on Security and Privacy (S&P'05), Oakland, CA, USA, 8–11 May 2005*; IEEE Computer Society: Washington, DC, USA, 2005; pp. 183–195.
17. Levine, B.N.; Reiter, M.K.; Wang, C.; Wright, M. Timing Attacks in Low-Latency Mix Systems. In *Proceedings of the International Conference on Financial Cryptography, Key West, FL, USA, 9–12 February 2004*; Springer: Berlin/Heidelberg, Germany, 2004; pp. 251–265.
18. Syverson, P.; Tsudik, G.; Reed, M.; Landwehr, C. Towards an Analysis of Onion Routing Security. In *Designing Privacy Enhancing Technologies*; Springer: Berlin/Heidelberg, Germany, 2001; pp. 96–114.
19. Gilad, Y.; Herzberg, A. Spying in the Dark: TCP and Tor Traffic Analysis. In *Proceedings of the International Symposium on Privacy Enhancing Technologies Symposium, Vigo, Spain, 11–13 July 2012*; Springer: Berlin/Heidelberg, Germany, 2012; pp. 100–119.
20. Rochet, F.; Pereira, O. Dropping on the Edge: Flexibility and Traffic Confirmation in Onion Routing Protocols. *Proc. Priv. Enhanc. Technol.* **2018**, *2018*, 27–46. [CrossRef]
21. Iacovazzi, A.; Elovici, Y. Network Flow Watermarking: A Survey. *IEEE Commun. Surv. Tutor.* **2016**, *19*, 512–530. [CrossRef]
22. Snader, R.; Borisov, N. A Tune-up for Tor: Improving Security and Performance in the Tor Network. In Proceedings of the NDSS, San Diego, CA, USA, 10–13 February 2008; Volume 8, p. 127.
23. Johnson, A.; Jansen, R.; Hopper, N.; Segal, A.; Syverson, P. PeerFlow: Secure Load Balancing in Tor. *PoPETs* **2017**, *2017*, 74–94. [CrossRef]
24. Bauer, K.S.; Sherr, M.; Grunwald, D. ExperimenTor: A Testbed for Safe and Realistic Tor Experimentation. In Proceedings of the CSET, San Francisco, CA, USA, 8 August 2011.
25. Panchenko, A.; Pimenidis, L.; Renner, J. Performance Analysis of Anonymous Communication Channels Provided by Tor. In *Proceedings of the 2008 Third International Conference on Availability, Reliability and Security, Barcelona, Spain, 4–7 March 2008*; IEEE Computer Society: Washington, DC, USA, 2008; pp. 221–228.
26. Komlo, C.H.; Mathewson, N.; Goldberg, I. Walking Onions: Scaling Anonymity Networks while Protecting Users. In Proceedings of the 29th USENIX Security Symposium (USENIX Security 20), Boston, MA, USA, 12–14 August 2020; pp. 1003–1020.
27. Cangialosi, F.; Levin, D.; Spring, N. Ting: Measuring and Exploiting Latencies Between All Tor Nodes. In Proceedings of the 2015 Internet Measurement Conference, Tokyo, Japan, 28–30 October 2015; pp. 289–302.
28. Danezis, G.; Diaz, C. *A Survey of Anonymous Communication Channels*; Technical Report, Technical Report MSR-TR-2008-35; Microsoft Research: Cambridge, UK 2008.

29. Chaum, D.L. Untraceable Electronic Mail, Return Addresses, and Digital Pseudonyms. *Commun. ACM* **1981**, *24*, 84–90. [CrossRef]
30. Young, A.L.; Yung, M. The drunk motorcyclist protocol for anonymous communication. In *Proceedings of the 2014 IEEE Conference on Communications and Network Security, San Francisco, CA, USA, 29–31 October 2014*; IEEE Computer Society: Washington, DC, USA, 2014; pp. 157–165.
31. Wang, W.; Motani, M.; Srinivasan, V. Dependent link padding algorithms for low latency anonymity systems. In Proceedings of the 15th ACM Conference on Computer and Communications Security, Tokyo, Japan, 18–20 March 2008; pp. 323–332.
32. Freedman, M.J.; Morris, R. Tarzan: A Peer-to-Peer Anonymizing Network Layer. In Proceedings of the 9th ACM Conference on Computer and Communications Security, Washington, DC, USA, 18–22 November 2002; pp. 193–206.
33. Le Blond, S.; Choffnes, D.; Zhou, W.; Druschel, P.; Ballani, H.; Francis, P. Towards Efficient Traffic-Analysis Resistant Anonymity Networks. *ACM SIGCOMM Comput. Commun. Rev.* **2013**, *43*, 303–314. [CrossRef]
34. Kotzanikolaou, P.; Chatzisofroniou, G.; Burmester, M. Broadcast anonymous routing (BAR): Scalable real-time anonymous communication. *Int. J. Inf. Secur.* **2017**, *16*, 313–326. [CrossRef]
35. Chen, C.; Asoni, D.E.; Perrig, A.; Barrera, D.; Danezis, G.; Troncoso, C. TARANET: Traffic-Analysis Resistant Anonymity at the Network Layer. In *Proceedings of the 2018 IEEE European Symposium on Security and Privacy (EuroS&P), London, UK, 24–26 April 2018*; IEEE Computer Society: Washington, DC, USA, 2018; pp. 137–152.
36. Buccafurri, F.; De Angelis, V.; Idone, M.F.; Labrini, C. Anonymous Short Communications over Social Networks. In Proceedings of the EAI SecureComm 2021—17th EAI International Conference on Security and Privacy in Communication Networks, Virtual Event, 6–9 September 2021; Springer: Berlin/Heidelberg, Germany 2021.
37. Shirazi, F.; Simeonovski, M.; Asghar, M.R.; Backes, M.; Diaz, C. A Survey on Routing in Anonymous Communication Protocols. *ACM Comput. Surv. (CSUR)* **2018**, *51*, 1–39. [CrossRef]
38. Buccafurri, F.; De Angelis, V.; Idone, M.F.; Labrini, C. Wip: An Onion-Based Routing Protocol Strengthening Anonymity. In Proceedings of the 2021 IEEE 22nd International Symposium on a World of Wireless, Mobile and Multimedia Networks (WoWMoM), Pisa, Italy, 7–11 June 2021; pp. 231–235.
39. ns-3—Network Simulator 3. 2021. Available online: https://www.nsnam.org/documentation/ (accessed on 21 May 2021).
40. TorPerformance. 2021. Available online: https://metrics.torproject.org/torperf.html (accessed on 21 May 2021).
41. AlSabah, M.; Goldberg, I. Performance and Security Improvements for Tor: A Survey. *ACM Comput. Surv. (CSUR)* **2016**, *49*, 1–36. [CrossRef]
42. 3GPP2-TSGC5. *HTTP, FTP and TCP Models for 1xEV-DV Simulations*; 3GPP2: Arlington, VA, USA, 2001.
43. Keita, B. Experimental Evaluation of the Impact of Tor Latency on Web Browsing. 2021. Available online: https://witestlab.poly.edu/blog/latency-tor/ (accessed on 21 May 2021).
44. Muñoz, A.; Maña, A.; Serrano, D. AVISPA in the Validation of Ambient Intelligence Scenarios. In *Proceedings of the 2009 International Conference on Availability, Reliability and Security, Fukuoka, Japan, 16–19 March 2009*; IEEE Computer Society: Washington, DC, USA, 2009; pp. 420–426.
45. Serrano, D.; Ruíz, J.F.; Muñoz, A.; Maña, A.; Armenteros, A.; Crespo, B.G.N. Development of Applications Based on Security Patterns. In *Proceedings of the 2009 Second International Conference on Dependability, Athens, Greece, 18–23 June 2009*; IEEE Computer Society: Washington, DC, USA, 2009; pp. 111–116.
46. Yoshioka, N.; Washizaki, H.; Maruyama, K. A survey on security patterns. *Prog. Inf.* **2008**, *5*, 35–47. [CrossRef]
47. Schumacher, M.; Fernandez-Buglioni, E.; Hybertson, D.; Buschmann, F.; Sommerlad, P. *Security Patterns: Integrating Security and Systems Engineering*; John Wiley & Sons: Hoboken, NJ, USA, 2013.

Article

A Blockchain-Based Efficient, Secure and Anonymous Conditional Privacy-Preserving and Authentication Scheme for the Internet of Vehicles

Kashif Naseer Qureshi [1], Luqman Shahzad [1], Abdelzahir Abdelmaboud [2], Taiseer Abdalla Elfadil Eisa [2], Bandar Alamri [3], Ibrahim Tariq Javed [1,*], Arafat Al-Dhaqm [4,5] and Noel Crespi [6]

[1] Department of Computer Science, Bahria University, Islamabad 44000, Pakistan; knaseer.buic@bahria.edu.pk (K.N.Q.); luqmanshahzad93@gmail.com (L.S.)
[2] Department of Information Systems, College of Science and Arts, King Khalid University, Muhayil Asir 61913, Saudi Arabia; aelnour@kku.edu.sa (A.A.); Teisa@kku.edu.sa (T.A.E.E.)
[3] Lero-The Irish Software Research Centre, University of Limerick, V94 T9PX Limerick, Ireland; Bandar.Alhamri@ul.ie
[4] School of Computing, Faculty of Engineering, Universiti Teknologi Malaysia, Skudai 81300, Malaysia; mrarafat1@utm.my
[5] Department of Computer Science, Aden Community College, Aden 8916862, Yemen
[6] Institut Polytechnique de Paris Telecom SudParis Evry, Courcouronnes FR, 9 Rue Charles Fourier, 91000 Evry, France; noel.crespi@mines-telecom.fr
* Correspondence: itariq.buic@bahria.edu.pk

Citation: Qureshi, K.N.; Shahzad, L.; Abdelmaboud, A.; Elfadil Eisa, T.A.; Alamri, B.; Javed, I.T.; Al-Dhaqm, A.; Crespi, N. A Blockchain-Based Efficient, Secure and Anonymous Conditional Privacy-Preserving and Authentication Scheme for the Internet of Vehicles. *Appl. Sci.* **2022**, *12*, 476. https://doi.org/10.3390/app12010476

Academic Editors: Paula Fraga-Lamas and Gianluca Lax

Received: 3 October 2021
Accepted: 16 December 2021
Published: 4 January 2022

Publisher's Note: MDPI stays neutral with regard to jurisdictional claims in published maps and institutional affiliations.

Copyright: © 2022 by the authors. Licensee MDPI, Basel, Switzerland. This article is an open access article distributed under the terms and conditions of the Creative Commons Attribution (CC BY) license (https://creativecommons.org/licenses/by/4.0/).

Abstract: The rapid advancement in the area of the Internet of Vehicles (IoV) has provided numerous comforts to users due to its capability to support vehicles with wireless data communication. The exchange of information among vehicle nodes is critical due to the rapid and changing topologies, high mobility of nodes, and unpredictable network conditions. Finding a single trusted entity to store and distribute messages among vehicle nodes is also a challenging task. IoV is exposed to various security and privacy threats such as hijacking and unauthorized location tracking of smart vehicles. Traceability is an increasingly important aspect of vehicular communication to detect and penalize malicious nodes. Moreover, achieving both privacy and traceability can also be a challenging task. To address these challenges, this paper presents a blockchain-based efficient, secure, and anonymous conditional privacy-preserving and authentication mechanism for IoV networks. This solution is based on blockchain to allow vehicle nodes with mechanisms to become anonymous and take control of their data during the data communication and voting process. The proposed secure scheme provides conditional privacy to the users and the vehicles. To ensure anonymity, traceability, and unlinkability of data sharing among vehicles, we utilize Hyperledger Fabric to establish the blockchain. The proposed scheme fulfills the requirement to analyze different algorithms and schemes which are adopted for blockchain technology for a decentralized, secure, efficient, private, and traceable system. The proposed scheme examines and evaluates different consensus algorithms used in the blockchain and anonymization techniques to preserve privacy. This study also proposes a reputation-based voting system for Hyperledger Fabric to ensure a secure and reliable leader selection process in its consensus algorithm. The proposed scheme is evaluated with the existing state-of-the-art schemes and achieves better results.

Keywords: IoV; authentication; security; blockchain; privacy; network; latency; scalability

1. Introduction

Internet of Vehicles (IoV) networks are able to improve driving safety, efficiency, and traffic management using On-Board Units (OBUs) for data communication, with or without prior infrastructure. As a result of the increase in the number of users and the open nature of these networks, security threats are a challenge. Security requirements such as authentication, the privacy of vehicle nodes, and audibility are necessary to avoid these networks from different types of attacks, such as impersonation attacks, and spreading of false information. Authentication of nodes in a network is the first line of defense to block any unwanted activity in a network [1,2]. If the network allows unauthenticated vehicle nodes, then malicious vehicle nodes can also join the network and undertake different types of activities, e.g., impersonate an ambulance to exceed the given speed limits. If integrity is not provided during message transmission, then vehicle nodes can misbehave and alter the content of a message. In such a case, the receiver only knows that the message was sent by a legitimate vehicle, and they would be responsible for any damage. Privacy is a core feature of IoV, but traceability is also necessary in the case of any unwanted activity in a network. In this case, the privacy of the vehicle should be revoked and punished.

Existing solutions of IoV are vulnerable to and suffer from various privacy threats. Due to this loophole, many fake messages may be delivered, resulting in numerous victims. The conventional security solutions are based on a centralized approach, which necessitates a trusted central authority and faces a single point of failure. This potential also exposes different security and privacy attacks such as hijacking and unauthorized tracking of vehicle nodes' locations. These solutions do not guarantee timely notification [3]. Another example is the broadcasting of fake information by an intruder to mislead or confuse other vehicle nodes in the network. Hence, ensuring the authentication, non-repudiation, authenticity, and traceability of messages in IoV is crucial. Vehicle privacy is also another critical challenge because a vehicle's sensitive information, such as its location and identity, should not be revealed to other nodes in the network. Conditional privacy can prevent vehicles misbehaving, via tracing and penalizing by one or many entities. Although users normally trust a third party to check the legitimacy of their transactions before bringing them into effect, a middle party may be suspected of cheating its customers. Currently, conventional security and trust methods used in smart vehicles are ineffective due to many challenges, such as inefficient communication among the vehicles, centralization, insecure communication, and untraceability of malicious nodes.

To address these issues, blockchain is one of the most promising technologies, in which an agreement called a "consensus algorithm" is shared among all entities that want to add their proposed blocks. In a blockchain, algorithms enable the different users to agree on the current state, even if they do not trust each other or there is no central authority between them. To address vehicle data-sharing issues, blockchain creates a safe, trustworthy, and decentralized intelligent transportation ecosystem [4]. Blockchain is a form of decentralization in which transactions are registered through a peer-to-peer network rather than relying on a centralized authority and centralized server. Therefore, the system is able to run without interruption in the case of any single point failure. Every entity in a network maintains the same copy of the digital ledger. If the ledger is public, it provides all the information in the ledger to all the members of the network [5]. Another exciting feature of blockchain is immutability, which ensures that anything committed on the ledger cannot be altered or changed. This is in contrast to the conventional system. Each entity in a network has a copy of the ledger. Before any information is committed to the ledger, it is first validated by the nodes. If the transactions pass the validation process undertaken by the majority of the nodes, then the transactions will be added to the ledger [6,7]. This core feature of blockchain ensures transparency. It is impossible to reverse or change the hash. If a single change is made to the input, then the hash is generated completely differently. In order for a malicious node to corrupt the data in the network it must change the data stored in the ledger on every node. This is highly complex if the network consists of millions of nodes and each node has the same digital copy of the ledger. Each transaction in a blockchain network is stored and a hash of the block is recorded in the next block to trace the transaction and ensure transparency.

The main existing privacy-preserving strategies and solutions for blockchain are identified in this paper, to provide insight into the different cryptographic primitives and privacy-preserving approaches, methods, and techniques used in blockchain. This paper proposes an efficient, secure, decentralized Conditional Privacy-Preserving and Authentication (CPPA) scheme for IoV networks. The proposed scheme is based on Hyperledger Fabric for the selection of leaders in the consensus algorithm. It also provides traceability and anonymity ensure that authorities can trace the vehicle nodes in case of disputes. Hyperledger Fabric is an open source blockchain developed by Linux foundation. Hyperledger is a permissioned blockchain technology in which all participants are identified and authenticated. Hyperledger allows the execution of smart contracts which are called chaincodes. Most importantly, it ensures privacy by facilitating confidential transactions.

The main contributions of this paper are as follows:

- The proposed scheme handles multiple transactions at once and provides scalability by using blockchain technology.
- The scheme provides multiple decentralized trusted authorities and avoids the issue of a single point of failure in traditional networks.
- The scheme provides feature traceability for malicious node detection

The remainder of this paper is organized as follows: Section 2 presents a review of the relevant literature. Section 3 presents an efficient, secure, decentralized, and conditional privacy and authentication scheme for IoV. Section 4 illustrates the results and provides a discussion. The last section concludes the paper with possible future directions.

2. Related Work

The authors in [8] proposed a Conditional Privacy-Preserving Authentication (CPPA) scheme for vehicular ad hoc networks that uses Schnorr's signature. The secret key is pre-loaded on the vehicle but a long-term secret key can be accessed by an adversary when it has physical access. In another study [9], the authors presented an Efficient, Anonymous Authentication with Conditional Privacy (EAAP) scheme based on a bilinear pairing technique, using anonymous certificates that are valid for short-term and public keys for IoV. In [10], the authors presented secure authentication solution for authentication, integrity, and confidentiality. Traceability depends on a Trusted Authority (TA). If the TA is compromised, then the entire network is disrupted. The authors in [11] presented a scheme based on blockchain to protect the security and privacy of vehicle nodes. The authors proposed a Lightweight Scalable Blockchain (LSB), without traceability of the malicious vehicle nodes. The approach uses an Overlay Block Manager (OBM), which acts as a cluster head. It also did not provide batch verification or batch authentication. The proposed model is also affected by the issues of key management, caching data, and mobility. In [12], the authors briefly described a model which has three layers: perception, service, and edge computing. It ensures the security of vehicle nodes through blockchain technology. It also offers computing capabilities and cloud services. The authors in [13] proposed blockchain-based IoV and proposes an authentication and secure data transfer algorithm. However, it does not provide traceability, batch verification, or authentication. In [14], the authors proposed a secure information sharing scheme for IoV based on blockchain. The authors achieved conditional privacy using threshold secret sharing and fair-blind signatures.

The authors in [15] presented a seven-layer architecture for transportation systems. This paper also presented delegated proof-of-stake (DPOS), which is appropriate for vehicular communication because it establishes blockchain-based vehicular networks. The authors in [16] presented a distributed trust management scheme for a clustering mechanism for IoV based on blockchain technology. In this paper, block validation is performed by proof of work and roadside units function as miners performing POW for the consensus mechanism. In [17], the authors proposed a Byzantine fault tolerance consensus algorithm for IoV. This algorithm provides a privacy-preserving incentive announcement network. By using reputation points, this announcement mechanism allows vehicle nodes to forward and collect accurate information. However, this consensus scheme faces limited scalability. The authors in [18] proposed a reputation-based data sharing scheme using a subjective logic model to improve data integrity and provide a secure data exchanging system in vehicular communication. In this paper, proof of work is utilized for exchanging information, auditing, and verification of the record. To encourage vehicle nodes, a scheme named proof-of-storage is also presented to allow and incentivize vehicles to share storage resources. An updated DPOS consensus algorithm for reliable reputation management is proposed in [19]. The authors used a multi-weight subjective logic model and contract theory to prevent internal collision among miners. The authors in [20] recognize the difference between correct and fake transactions. In addition to increasing accuracy, this recognition prevents double-spending problems in which someone may be able to create multiple correct transactions and thus combine them to create a fraudulent transaction. The third phase is the latency of the system and computing power, which is need to enable the correctness and agreement processes.

The authors in [21] adopted the properties of the POS algorithm and included additional security measures. The algorithm focuses on two properties, namely, persistence and liveness. Persistence indicates that, if a node in a network declares a specific transaction as being stable, then all the remaining nodes will report it as stable, but only if they are responding honestly. Liveness states that the transaction will be stable when an honestly generated transaction is available to the nodes in a network for a significant amount of time. To ensure the randomness of a leader in an election process, the algorithm employs the coin-flipping protocol. In [22], the authors proposed an Efficient Threshold Anonymous Authentication (ETAA) protocol for VANETs. This protocol uses a group signature and a decentralized group model, and the threshold authentication method, to obtain threshold authentication, efficient revocation, unforgeability, anonymity, and traceability for VANETs. The group signature strategy uses independent interest to provide traceability and linkability.

The authors in [23] proposed a metaheuristic algorithm for anomaly detection in IoT networks using an activity footprint-based method. This algorithm captures the semantic context and high dimensional vectors, which are assigned to the mobile agents. The isolated agents are monitored for abnormal activities and can be associated with potential intruders. The proposed algorithm was tested in a simulation environment to confirm and validate the metaheuristic algorithm. However, this algorithm was designed for IoT networks where the movement of the devices is not as fast as those in IoV networks. These types of solutions are not feasible for IoV networks. The authors in [24] presented a hybrid method for anomaly detection using metaheuristic methods for high speed networks. The hybrid method uses large scale datasets and detector generation based on multi-start metaheuristic and genetic methods. The proposed method achieved accuracy of 96.1% with machine learning algorithms. However, this method was designed for fixed networks and is not feasible for ad hoc networks such as IoV.

3. Design and Development of Blockchain-Based IoV

In this section, we present an efficient, secure, decentralized, and anonymous network model for IoV to overcome the above limitations. The proposed scheme provides traceability to identify malicious vehicle nodes. The proposed reputation scheme is based on the Hyperledger Fabric leader selection process. The scheme also satisfies the security and authentication requirements.

3.1. Network Model

The proposed scheme uses the Fabric Certificate Authority (CA) for the registration of identities. It has sufficient capabilities, such as high computation, fast communication, and enough storage. CA is also responsible for the generation of certificates for vehicles and roadside units. Additionally, once their registration is complete, the TA produces the initial security parameters for all vehicles and roadside units (RSUs), and sends them to the vehicles via TLS. Issuance of Enrollment Certificates (ECerts) is an enrollment process whereby the Fabric CA issues a certificate key-pair, comprised of a signing certificate and a private key that forms the identity [25]. The private and public keys are first generated locally by the Fabric CA client, and then the public key is sent to the CA, which returns an encoded certificate, the signing certificate for certificate renewal, and revocation. Orderers are stationary nodes deployed on the roadside. These orderers act as the RSUs. The orderer maintains the list of the organizations that can create and configure the channel, and are responsible for ordering and packaging the transactions. The orderer also obtains the certificates that represent identities, and the Membership Service Provider (MSP) contains the permission identities. The orderer utilizes a dedicated short-range communication protocol for V2V and V2R wireless communications. The MSP authenticates traffic messages from vehicles and processes them locally or forwards them to the TA. The law enforcement department may request the CA to revoke the real identity of the message sender if malicious activity is detected. Vehicle nodes are embedded with high processing, storage, and wireless communication modules. The vehicle-to-vehicle and vehicle-to-RSU communications are conducted through wireless networks. Figure 1 shows the layers of the proposed solution.

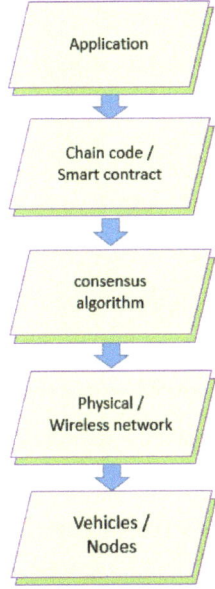

Figure 1. Layers of the proposed network.

Figure 1 shows the different layers of the proposed network, comprising the application layer, chain code/smart contract layer, consensus layer, physical/wireless network, and the ground vehicular nodes. Smart contracts are blockchain based programs that execute when certain criteria are met. The contracts are decentralized applications that respond to events by executing business logic. These are often used to automate contract execution so that all parties immediately know the outcome without the need for any intermediaries.

3.2. Enhanced Hyperledger Fabric

Vehicles with OBU and digital networking equipment are blockchain-based IoV to communicate with neighboring RSUs, to thus access vehicular networks. The OBU performs basic functions, collects local data, and sends it to the orderer via a communication channel. Vehicle nodes work as information providers and provide their information to data requesters. Vehicle nodes send their messages to the neighboring orderer. Orderers are stationed along roads to ensure that cars can connect with orderers. Orderers are roadside nodes that are stationary. According to their locations, the entire network is split into several regions. Without the help of a trustworthy third party, a group of auditors has the secret tracing key. If malicious conduct is discovered, the law enforcement department can request that group auditors revoke the true identity of the message. To retrieve the real identity of the sender, at least 't' tracers must work together. This is used to prevent misuse of power. We should mention that the CA and vehicle nodes in the scheme elect the issuers and auditors. The steps of the proposed scheme are system configuration, registration enrollment process, transaction handling, consensus process, ledger update, and traceability.

3.2.1. System Configuration

Because the certificates associated with a node must be generated before the node itself can be implemented, the first part that must be installed in the network to configure the device is a CA. After passing identity verification by the CA, any entity appears to be valid. It is not mandatory to use the Fabric CA for certificate generation. However, it is used in the current proposal because it produces MSP directories, which are required for organizations and entities to be properly defined; otherwise, we must create the MSP directories ourselves. We check that CAs are deployed in our network. All the intermediate CA's will be created by a single root CA. Intermediate CAs are an effective means of preventing the root CA from being overworked. We use a dual-headed CA consisting of a TLS CA, which necessitates setting up (1) a TLS CA and using it to create TLS certificates; and (2) an organizational CA, which is used to generate admin certificates for an entity, the MSP, and the nodes owned by that organization. For the state database, we use the Level DB because we prioritize speed. All the peer nodes on the channels are required to utilize the same state database (CouchDB or Level DB). To maintain anonymity and isolation for such transactions, channels are deployed depending on the geographical area. After the CA has been configured, it can be utilized to register and enroll vehicles. The administrator of the CA assigns a username and password for the vehicle in the first stage. The vehicles are also granted roles and associations. It now builds a directory known as an MSP, which includes the public certificate of the CA granting the certificate in addition to the CA's root of trust. The vehicle is registered and enrolled in both an 'Enrollment CA' and a 'TLS CA', much like an admin identity. The CA assigns the function of orderer or peer, rather than admin, when registering the vehicle. Peers and orderers who are owned by different organizations are now deployed; thus, these organizations are called peer organizations and orderer organizations. These organizations are connected, and smart contracts, where ledgers are stored, are installed on both peers and orderers.

3.2.2. Registration and Enrollment

In the registration and enrollment phase, when any vehicle wants to connect to the network for the first time, it requires registration from the CA. The CA generates a public/secret key-pair and sends credentials to the vehicle through TLS after verifying the information's identity. The CA stores public keys on its database. This database can be checked to determine if a car is registered in the network by looking up the public key of the vehicle in the database. The association between the public key (pk) and the vehicle's identification details is known only to the CA. Any vehicle in each area can register in the same regions in the intermediate CA. The Fabric CA automatically functions as an Idemix issuer. When the CA is started with the "init" command, two files are generated in the CA's home directory: "IssuerPublicKey" and "IssuerRevocationPublicKey". The Idemix MSP is created using these keys. When an Idemix credential is being used, the Client-Identity library is used to help the GetAttribute-Value feature. The peers only use Idemix MSP for signature authentication. Only the Client SDK is used to sign with the Idemix MSP.

3.2.3. Transaction Handling

After setting up and executing the channel, the system ensures that vehicles undergo the registration and enrollment phase with the CA and have cryptographic identities that are known for their authentication. The system also checks that the chain code is already written on all the vehicles and activated on the channel. The chain code is also given an endorsement scheme which requires that all the vehicles must endorse the message transaction. Let us suppose that vehicle (VA) wants to share the message to all the vehicles in that channel. In the first phase, VA initiates a transaction message (for example: about the road condition). A request is submitted in the channel by targeting all vehicles. Then, a transaction proposal is created. To create a transaction proposal, the vehicle uses a supported SDK. The proposal enables a chain code to be invoked with certain input parameters to read or update the ledger. The SDK envelopes the proposal of the message into a particular format and uses the user's account details to create a unique signature for it. The endorsement policy defines that all vehicles must endorse the transaction; hence, the request goes to all vehicles. Then, the endorsing vehicles verify that the transaction proposal has not been previously sent, to prevent a replay attack, and also check whether the signature is valid by using the MSP. Additionally, they confirm that the sender can execute this process on the channel. The transaction proposal inputs are transferred to the invoked chain codes by the endorsing vehicles. The chain code is run with Level DB to generate output that includes the answer-value, read-set, and write-set. At this point, ledgers are not updated. All of these values, in addition to the signatures of the endorsing vehicles, are returned as a proposal reply to VA.

In the next phase, the sender verifies the signatures of all endorsing vehicles and ensures that the proposal responses from all the vehicles are the same. It verifies that the specified endorsement rules are achieved before submission. If the sender does not inspect responses and forwards messages without endorsement, then the endorsement rules are still imposed by other vehicles in the channel and upheld at the "commit validation phase". After verifying the responses and updating the ledger, it sends a message to the RSU (ordering service). The message proposal and endorsing reply are then bundled into a message and sent to the RSU by VA. The OS does not need to search the whole content of the message; however, it simply orders all of the transactions received from the channels, and generates blocks of transactions for each channel. In the next phase, the transaction blocks are delivered by OS to all vehicles on that channel. The endorsement rules are verified by validating the message within the block. The block's transactions are classified as "valid" or "invalid". Each vehicle adds the block to the channel's chain and, if the transactions are valid, then write sets are committed to Level DB. Each vehicle notifies VA that the message has been added to the chain, and whether the message was validated. Figure 2 shows the flow diagram of the enhanced Fabric.

3.2.4. Consensus Process

The Raft consensus protocol in Hyperledger Fabric utilizes the "leader and follower" model in which a channel's ordering nodes dynamically elect a leader, and that leader forwards data to all of its followers. Because the network can tolerate the failure of nodes, including leader nodes, because several ordering nodes exist, Raft is called "Crash Fault Tolerance". For instance, if a channel has five vehicles, it can afford the loss of two vehicles. This feature of Raft provides a high-availability strategy for the ordering service. RSUs are in different locations and, if any RSU or the entire location becomes unavailable, then RSUs in other locations will continue to operate. The ordering nodes that are actively involved in the consensus process for a given channel are referred to as the "consenter set". The quorum is the minimum number of consenters who agree to a proposal to serialize the transactions.

Leader, follower, and candidate are the three possible states for the RSU. The RSU is initiated as a follower. It may approve logs from the leader or vote for the leader selection at this time. If there are no logs or heartbeats obtained for a specific amount of time, then it will be self-promoted to the candidate state. In this stage, it will request votes from other RSUs. It will be appointed a leader if it earns a quorum of votes. The leader RSU oversees generating new logs, sending these logs to follower RSUs, and determining whether logs are committed.

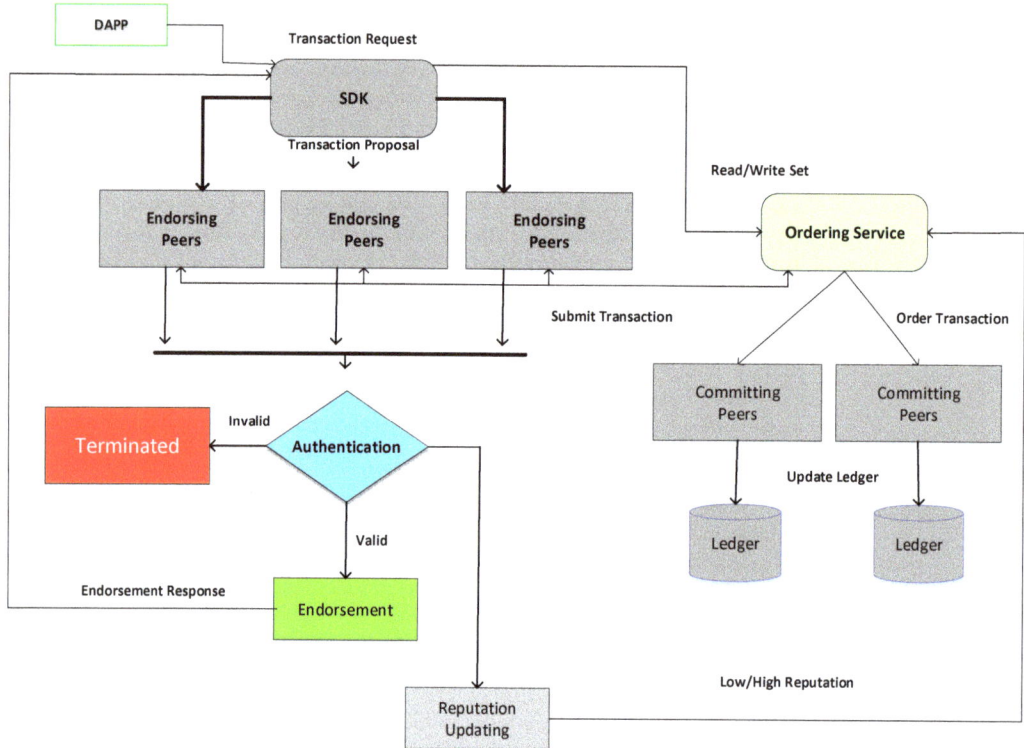

Figure 2. Flow diagram of enhanced Fabric.

3.2.5. Calculating and Updating Reputation

RSUs can calculate the reputation of all members in the ordering service. This is focused on previous experiences, in addition to new recommendations from the vehicles. To form the local opinion on each RSU, the model considers three weights based on previous experiences. The vehicular blockchain contains the most recent recommended opinions. To receive a final reputation on each RSU, each vehicle computes its local and recommended opinions. Vehicles update and review a current data block for that round of the consensus mechanism. If the information is accurate, vehicles upgrade their reputation opinions for the RSU and send their opinions to OS. The RSUs work together to apply legitimate reputation values to the vehicular blockchain through a consensus mechanism. The following security study should be used to solve the concerns of the vulnerable leader in the proposed scheme: reputation is utilized to select the RSU to indicate the trustworthiness of nodes by considering their past behaviors. A high-reputation RSU is chosen as the leader. Hence, the leader is trustable, and there is a very small chance that it will damage the system. This leader is selected for a time slot because, if a leader is compromised and tries to harm the system, then it can only harm the system in its time slot. The endorsing vehicles can also check for mistakes in the block data on the vehicular blockchain during the validation and commit phase. Then, the leader is accused and blacklisted. Figure 3 shows the blockchain-based IoV.

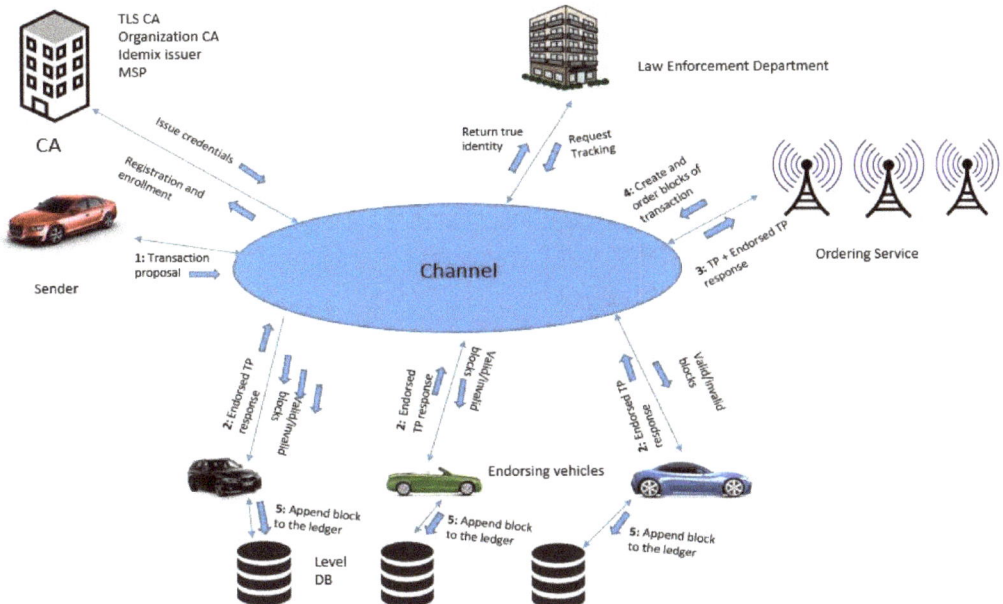

Figure 3. Blockchain-based IoV.

3.2.6. Local Opinions for Ordering Services

Suppose a peer (V_i) and an ordering service (RU_j) interact with each other. The vector defined for the local opinion of V_i to RU_j is $\omega_{i \to j} := b_{i \to j}, d_{i \to j}, u_{i \to j}, k_{i \to j}$ where $b_{i \to j}$ represents trust, $d_{i \to j}$ represents mistrust, $u_{i \to j}$ represents uncertainty, and $k_{i \to j}$ is a constant which shows a willingness to trust ordering services and is less than 1 (0.5). The values of $b_{i \to j}, d_{i \to j}, u_{i \to j}$, in addition to the relationships between them, are particularly important. Hence, $b_{i \to j}, d_{i \to j}, u_{i \to j} \in \{0,1\}$, $b_{i \to j} + d_{i \to j} + q_{i \to j} = 1$.

$$\begin{cases} u_{i \to j} = 1 - q_{i \to j} \\ b_{i \to j} = (1 - u_{i \to j}) \frac{\alpha_i}{\alpha_i + \beta_i} \\ d_{i \to j} = (1 - u_{i \to j}) \frac{\beta_i}{\alpha_i + \beta_i} \end{cases}$$

α_i and β_i are the number of good and bad experiences, respectively. $q_{i \to j}$ is the communication quality of a link between vehicle i and RSU_j. The reputation according to $\omega_{i \to j}$, $x_{i \to j}$ denotes the expected trust of vehicle V_i that RSU is trustworthy and behaves appropriately throughout a consensus period, represented as $xi \to j = bi \to j + k_{i\beta j} u_{i \to j}$.

3.3. Multi-Weight Local Opinions for Subjective Logic

Different dynamics affect local opinions by utilizing the subjective logic model [26]. Both reputation logics are handled similarly in standard subject logic. However, different reputation logics originating from different sources must be weighted correctly to be aggregated with greater precision. If the vehicle has existing experience of, and maintains more recent ratings for, the RSU, the accuracy of the reputation will be significantly improved. Regarding weighting operations, this model progresses into "multi-weight subjective logic". We use the following weights.

3.3.1. Rate of Experiences

The rate of experiences shows how much the vehicle knows about RSU. If the rate of experience is large, it indicates that the vehicle (VA) knows a significant amount about

RSU_j. The ratio of the number of times that vehicle (VA) communicates with RSU (RSU_j) to the total amount of times that the vehicle communicates with other RSUs during some time 'T' is the rate of experiences between them.

$$f_{i \to j}^i = \frac{M_{i \to j}}{\overline{M_i}} \tag{1}$$

where $M_{i \to j} = (\alpha_t + \beta_t)$, and $\overline{M_i} = \frac{1}{|Q|} \Sigma_{q \in Q} M_{i \to q}$. Q is the ordering service (group of RSUs) interacting with vehicle V_t during the time window. A high rate of experience indicates a high reputation value.

3.3.2. Recent Experiences

In IoV, the more recent experiences are given a higher weight to the RSU, which may not always be trustworthy and secure because widely spread RSUs can be vulnerable to a breach due to insufficient protection. Both the trustworthiness and reputation of V_t to Ru_j are continually changing. For local opinions, recent and past experiences have different weights. The parameters γ and δ indicate the weights of recent and past experiences, respectively. $\gamma + \delta = 1$, whereas $\gamma > \delta$.

3.3.3. Experience Effects

If the RSU has good experiences, this will increase the RSUs' reputation, and if it has/had bad experiences, it will decrease the RSU's reputation. As a result, bad experiences had a greater effect on local vehicle opinions than good experiences. Good experiences have a weight of μ, and the weight of negative interactions is ν, where $\mu + \nu = 1$, $\mu < \nu$. The weights of recent experiences and experience effects are coupled to create a new experience frequency:

$$\alpha_t = \gamma \mu \alpha_1^i + \delta \mu \alpha_2^i, \beta_i = \gamma \nu \beta_1^i + \delta \nu \beta_2^i \tag{2}$$

α_1^i and β_1^i are good and bad recent experiences with time t, which satisfies $t \leq t_r$. If $t > t_r$, α_2^i, and β_2^i are good and bad past experiences, respectively. Hence the updated rate of experience from V_i to RU_j is:

$$f_{i \to j}^i = \frac{M_{i \to j}}{\overline{M i}} = \frac{\mu(\gamma \alpha_1^i + \delta \alpha_2^i) + \nu(\gamma \beta_1^i + \delta \beta_2^i)}{\frac{1}{|q|} \Sigma_{q \in Q} M_{i \to q}} \tag{3}$$

As a result, for local opinions, the total weight of reputation is $\sigma_{i \to j} = \tau_i * f_{i \to j}^i$, whereas the parameter of the pre-defined weight is $0 \leq \tau_t \leq 1$.

3.4. Recommended Opinions for Ordering Services

Recommended opinions and common opinions are combined as:

$$\omega_{y \in j}^r := b_{y \in j}^r, d_{y \in j}^r, u_{y \in j}^r \tag{4}$$

$$\begin{cases} b_{x \to j}^r = \frac{1}{\Sigma_{y \in Y}^{\sigma_{x \to j}}} \Sigma_{y \in Y} \sigma_{y \to j} b_{y \to j} \\ d_{x \to j}^r = \frac{1}{\Sigma_{y \in Y}^{\sigma_{x \to j}}} \Sigma_{y \in Y} \sigma_{y \to j} d_{y \to j} \\ u_{x \to j}^r = \frac{1}{\Sigma_{y \in Y}^{\sigma_{x \to j}}} \Sigma_{y \in Y} \sigma_{y \to j} u_{y \to j} \end{cases} \tag{5}$$

Here, $y \in Y$ is another group of vehicles which have had experience with RU_j. Taking opinions from different vehicles and combining them is known as a recommended opinion.

3.5. Combination of Local Opinions and Recommended Opinions

When vehicles obtain the recommended opinion from other vehicles of RSU$_j$ based on their experience with them, the vehicle will use its local opinion to create the final reputation opinion, $\omega_{i \to j}^f := b_{i \to j}^f, d_{i \to j}^f, u_{i \to j}^f$ where

$$\begin{cases} b_{i \to j}^f = \frac{b_{i \to j} u_{y \to j}^r + b_{y \to j}^r u_{i \to j}}{u_{i \to j} + u_{y \to j}^r - u_{y \to j}^r u_{i \to j}} \\ d_{i \to j}^f = \frac{d_{i \to j} u_{y \to j}^r + d_{y \to j}^r u_{i \to j}}{u_{i \to j} + u_{y \to j}^r - u_{y \to j}^r u_{i \to j}} \\ u_{i \to j}^f = \frac{u_{i \to j} u_{y \to j}^r + u_{y \to j}^r u_{i \to j}}{u_{i \to j} + u_{y \to j}^r - u_{y \to j}^r u_{i \to j}} \end{cases} \tag{6}$$

Therefore, the final reputation opinion of VA to RSU$_j$ is $T_{i \to j}^f = b_{i \to j}^f + \gamma \mu_{i \to j}^f$. These reputations are utilized for leader selection in the ordering service. The RSU with the highest reputation is selected as a leader in Hyperledger Fabric.

4. Experiment Setup and Results

Hyperledger Fabric was selected for the implementation of blockchain-based IoV. The designed network consists of three categories including peer nodes, ordering services, and law enforcement departments. First, we selected the database for Fabric, and selected the Level database (DB) for the state database. After selecting the database and organizations, the dual-headed certificate was adopted as the authority that involves two CAs. One TLS CA is responsible for secure communications and generating TLS certificates. The other CA is an organizational CA, which is responsible for generating the admin certificates of an organization. After deployment of CAs, the channels are deployed and configured for the privacy of transactions, so that members on the other channels cannot access the transactions. The use of firewalls is also necessary for the deployment of IoV because nodes that belong to an organization can require access to other organizations; thus, there is a need for the configuration of advanced networking. The docker is deployed for peer nodes and other entities on the laptop. Then, the volumes are mounted for external entities where the entities are placed. Due to limited space, we used one channel. Nonetheless, the resources must be monitored to ensure that there is sufficient space for the blockchain and the database. In Hyperledger Fabric, CA is the first entity that must be deployed because the certificates of the nodes must be created before creation of the nodes themselves to identify who is the admin of this node.

The dual-headed CA is used based on different geographical locations. One CA is used for the MSP of the organization for enrollment of any node that is owned by that organization. This is also called the enrollment CA because it is responsible for enrolling nodes in the network. The other CA generates Transport Layer Security (TLS) certificates to secure communications. This CA is also known as a "TLS-CA". These certificates avoid attacks such as man in the middle attacks. Certificates of "intermediate" CAs are issued by a "root CA" or another intermediate CA that responds to a root CA. Intermediate CAs are useful because if the root CA is compromised then the entire network, including admins and peers, can be damaged. Then, Lightweight Directory Access Protocol (LDAP) is configured to manage identities. For three organizations, it is recommended to use at least three dual-headed CAs. One CA is responsible for ordering services, one CA is responsible for peers, and one CA is responsible for auditing departments.

After creating the CAs, we can create certificates for the identities using these certificates. It is important to first register the admin before enrolling it. Creating the MSP is also necessary. The CA's admin will issue a username and password for the entity. After being issued to the identity, these credentials can be used for enrollment. Two certificates are generated by the CA. One public certificate is used by other members, and the private certificate is used to sign messages and identities. The CA generates the Membership Service Provider (MSP). This is a set of folders that contains the CA's public certificate and root of trust for the CAs. MSPs assign roles to the identities, i.e., the node is either a peer node, an orderer node, or a CA. The MSP is created after the creation of the node identity. After configuring the CAs and MSPs, peers and ordering nodes must be deployed. There are different ways to deploy the nodes but the configuration file must be configured before deployment. The peer's configuration file is called "core.yaml", and that of ordering nodes is "orderer.yaml". The roles of peers and orderers must be understood before deployment. The main difference between them is that the channel's "ordering service" comprises nodes that function together to form the OS.

4.1. Performance Evaluation and Results

In the performance and evaluation phase, we tested the proposed model with existing models and evaluated the efficiency regarding different performance parameters. The performance parameters were used to evaluate the proposed architecture and were helpful in generating the results. We used MATLAB for performance and evaluation.

4.2. Security and Privacy Analysis

High-availability systems span multiple global networks. Although firewalls and physical security measures are used, it is essential that those networks are secured and do not allow an attacker to attack a vehicle's data. The compromised server cannot be used to compromise other parts of the system. Hence, some schema is needed to create trust between the vehicles in the network. The proposed system supports secure communication among vehicles using TLS. Vehicles can assign their cryptographic operations to a Hardware Security Module. This secures the secret keys and executes cryptographic functions, enabling vehicles and RSUs to sign and endorse transactions without revealing the secret keys.

4.3. Scalability

Any system must grow with the growth of the users. This requires more computational power. The system must handle short spikes and short periods of high demand. If the system is unable to respond in a sensible time, transaction flow will be affected and delayed. Hyperledger Fabric is scalable, and comprises a channel system enabling new channels to be created without disturbing the previous architecture. New nodes can be added and deleted without causing any disturbance to the existing environment. Figure 4 shows the latency in the enhanced Fabric transactions. Latency refers to block time, which is the time required to generate the next block of the transaction. Latency is the amount of time a user has to wait for its transaction to be validated and included on the blockchain.

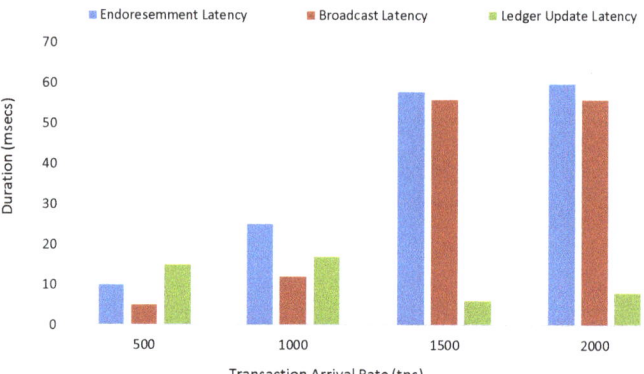

Figure 4. Latency in enhanced Fabric transactions.

4.4. Anonymity and Unlinkability

The Fabric enables advanced cryptographic algorithms and includes privacy features such as anonymity, unlinkability, and small disclosure of attributes. The Fabric uses Idemix, which is a cryptographic protocol that ensures strong features of privacy preservation and authentication. It allows users to prove their authentication without disclosing their real identities. It also enables users to send multiple transactions that are unlinkable. In addition, it is also not possible to identify multiple transactions that are sent by a single user. The actors who are involved in this protocol suite are the user, issuer, and verifier. Figure 5 shows the performance of the enhanced Fabric transactions with different block sizes.

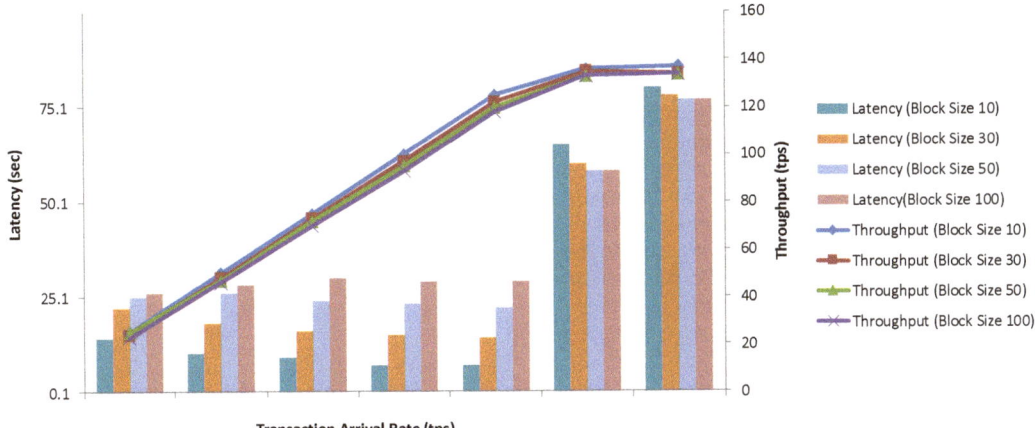

Figure 5. Performance of enhanced Fabric transactions with different block sizes.

4.5. Authentication

The Fabric utilizes access control lists (ACLs) by defining the policies to control the access to the network. These ACLs are very useful for Hyperledger Fabric because they allow only those identities that are linked with a request to be checked. Different types of policies are associated with the network for different purposes, such as endorsement policy checks to determine whether a transaction is properly endorsed. Similarly, modification policies are defined for the configuration of channels that access control and are specified in the configuration of the channel itself. In our proposed system, all the peers in a network are authentic and authorized through the MSP. Roles are defined in the MSPs to access the channels: who are you and what is your role? The system cannot be secured without certainty regarding the user's identity. The MSP gives permission to the vehicles and RSUs regarding the operations that can be executed and the data that can be accessed.

4.6. Traceability

The proposed scheme of IoV provides a conditional-privacy scheme that discloses the real identity of the vehicle if any malicious activities in the network are detected. The most significant feature of our proposed scheme is that the identity of the compromised entity must be traced by the law enforcement department (LED) to punish the intruder. Currently, including traceability and privacy preservation together in the blockchain is a challenging task. Therefore, traceability must be considered in the proposed scheme to avoid any malicious activities in the network. Hyperledger Fabric provides an audit feature. If any malicious activity is noticed, the LED can detect the vehicle's id and time stamp. The Fabric enables "ZKP" to manage privacy preservation with asset management using an auditing feature, which is also called ZKAT. This enables senders to send transactions without disclosing any information to the public. This feature differentiates Hyperledger

Fabric from other schemes available for privacy preservation. A specific auditor, who has full access to transactions of the user, is assigned to each user in a network. Subsequently, auditors are also able to check all of the history and extract the information of users who are assigned to that auditor. Auditors are not able to audit the users who are not assigned to them. In IOV, auditing is the most required feature. Unlike other privacy-preserving blockchain solutions, Fabric fulfills the requirements of the permission network by providing long-term credentials to vehicles. Hence, Fabric supports nonrepudiation, strong accountability, and a strong and secure auditing mechanism for vehicles in the blockchain network.

Figure 4 shows the different latencies of transactions, such as endorsement latency, broadcast latency, and ledger update Latency. We note that latency increases with the increase in the number of transactions per second.

Figure 5 shows the number of transactions per second, which is known as transaction throughput. The time it takes for a transaction to commit is known as transaction latency. The throughput increases linearly as the transaction arrival rate rises. The throughput becomes saturated at roughly 140 tps, and the latency rapidly increases. The latency will be the same for all block sizes. A smaller block size is faster when the transaction rate rises before the saturation point

Figure 6 shows the average delay of the BESA scheme and Ethereum with a varied number of transactions. It clearly shows that our proposed scheme has low latency compared to the Ethereum network.

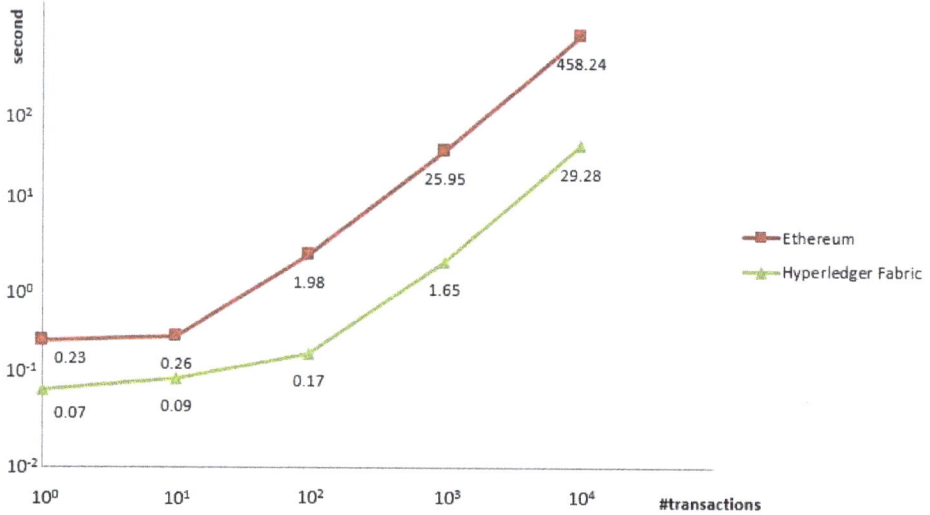

Figure 6. Comparison of enhanced Fabric with Ethereum.

Figure 7 depicts the correct probability that a data block will be verified for several successful detection reputation levels. We note that when the reputation threshold is 0.25, then the accurate probability of our BESA scheme is more than 75% higher than that of the TSL scheme. This shows that the BESA scheme based on the multi-weight subjective logic (MWSL) model can ensure secure block verification even when attackers use internal active miner cooperation. Figure 7 shows the probability of corrected data blocks whereas the Figure 8 compares the resource utilization in PBFT and SBFT.

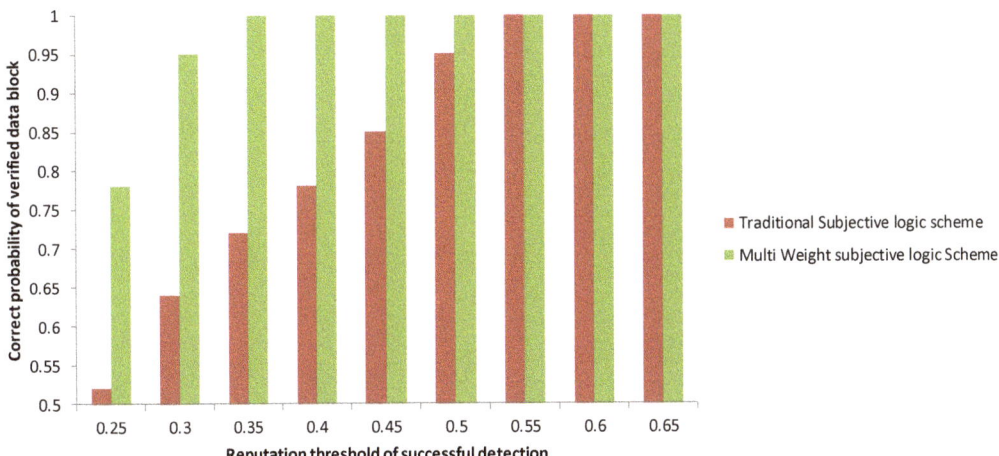

Figure 7. Probability of corrected data blocks.

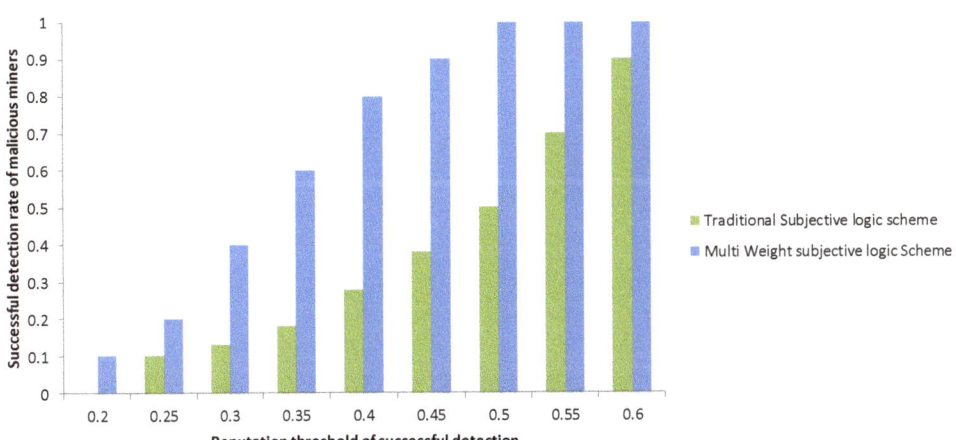

Figure 8. Detection rate of malicious miners.

We used the traditional subjective logic scheme and the proposed BESA solution based on the multi-weight subjective logic scheme to track the detection rate of 10 malicious miner candidates for 1 h. The MWSL technique had a substantially greater successful detection rate of malicious miners than the TSL scheme. We note that when we set the value of the reputation threshold to 0.5, the proposed scheme has a detection rate that is approximately 99 percent higher than that of the traditional subjective logic scheme. Because the MWSL scheme has a greater detection rate, possible security threats can be discovered and prevented more effectively, resulting in a more secure blockchain-enabled IoV.

We calculated the computation cost of the proposed BESA scheme with state-of-the-art schemes to evaluate the scheme overrun of a real-time processor. Computational cost is the execution time per time step during simulation. To estimate this time, we executed the scheme in a simulation, and measured the execution time and determined the average execution time per time step on a real-time target. It is clearly shown in Figure 9 that the computation cost of message verification of the proposed solution is lower than that of the existing schemes of CPPA [8], ATAAP [22], and EAAP [9]. Figure 10 shows the comparison of BESA communication cost with that of existing schemes.

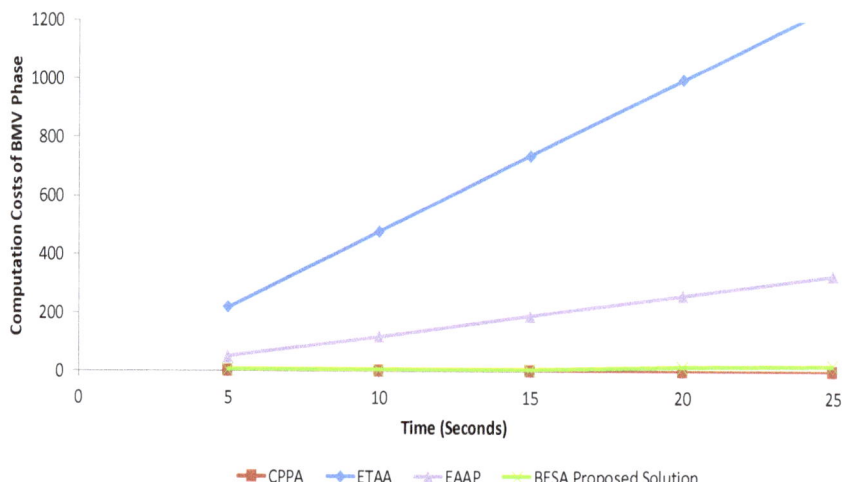

Figure 9. Comparison of BESA computation cost of message verification with that of existing schemes.

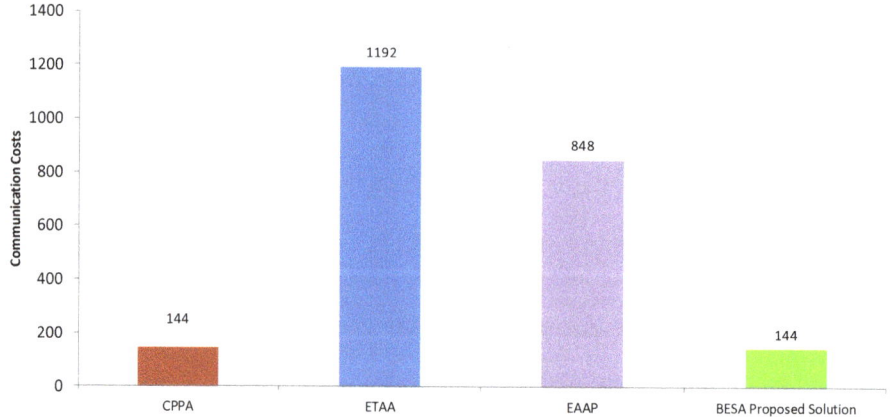

Figure 10. Comparison of BESA communication cost with that of existing schemes.

A graphic representation of the comparison results in Figure 10 is provided. In comparison to the three other approaches—CPPA [8], ATAAP [22], and EAAP [9]—the BESA solution has a lower communication cost.

Figure 11 depicts the reputation of a malicious miner candidate as seen through the eyes of a well-behaved vehicle in three scenarios: the traditional Hyperledger Fabric scheme, the traditional subjective logic scheme, and our BESA scheme. In the standard Hyperledger Fabric scheme, because there is no reputation element, vehicles are unable to identify the malicious vehicles, and thus the vehicle's evaluation of malicious candidates increases. The traditional subjective logic scheme and our BESA scheme are both based on the reputation values of vehicles; thus, we note that opinions from other well-behaved vehicles decrease the reputation of malicious vehicles in both schemes. Reputation values are below the reputation value of 0.50. It is also clear that the MWSL is more efficient because it is based on different weights. As result, our BESA scheme has a more precise reputation calculation than the TSL, which leads to a more secure leader selection process.

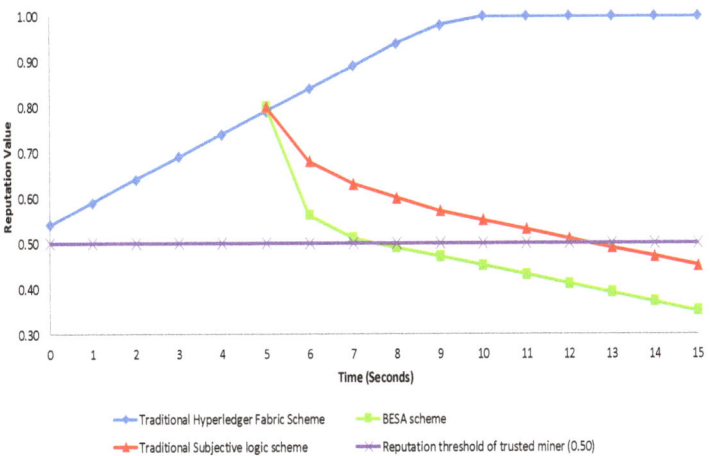

Figure 11. Reputation of a malicious miner.

5. Conclusions

In this paper, we introduced a hard security solution, i.e., the improved Hyperledger Fabric, to implement a blockchain-enabled IoV for safe vehicle information sharing. This paper comprehensively highlighted the issues related to IoV. The literature review concluded that most of the security services can be achieved by the implementation of blockchain. Hyperledger Fabric is one of the major implementations of blockchain for achieving security services. This paper provides a brief introduction to IoV, Hyperledger Fabric, consensus algorithms, privacy, and anonymization techniques, in conjunction with the additional terminology necessary to understand the problem statement and proposed scheme. Then a critical analysis is undertaken of existing consensus algorithms and conditional privacy schemes in the context of the IoV environment. The paper also discusses the non-applicability of existing schemes to the IoV environment. Thus, there is a requirement for an efficient decentralized scheme for IoV that can address security issues and fulfill the latest security requirements of vehicular communication. Hyperledger Fabric appears to be the most suitable emerging solution for a resource-constrained environment, and addresses some of the functionality issues of IoV. The security analysis indicates the proposed scheme will address some of the limitations of existing schemes and fulfill the security criteria of CPPA schemes for IoV. The two main contributions of this research relate to the manner in which it addresses the issue of the leader selection process. The first is to select leaders based on their reputation. A reputation-based scheme is utilized to calculate the accurate reputation of RSUs. Second, this paper presents an anonymous and traceable CPPA approach that can be utilized in a vehicular network. We also evaluated the performance of the proposed solution. In future work, we will choose a more effective and scalable consensus algorithm, and a more efficient scheme to increase the accuracy of the leader's reputation. We will also create a version of the suggested approach for real-world experimentation in a permissioned system, enabling us to analyze and modify the scheme to make it more realistic.

Author Contributions: Conceptualization, K.N.Q. and L.S.; methodology, A.A. and T.A.E.E.; software, T.A.E.E.; validation, A.A.-D.; writing—original draft preparation L.S.; and K.N.Q.; visualization, I.T.J.; writing—review and editing, I.T.J. and B.A.; supervision, N.C. All authors have read and agreed to the published version of the manuscript.

Funding: This research received no external funding.

Institutional Review Board Statement: Not applicable.

Informed Consent Statement: Not applicable.

Acknowledgments: The authors extend their appreciation to the Deanship of Scientific Research at King Khalid University for funding this work through Research Groups under grant number (R. G. P. 1/127/42).

Conflicts of Interest: The authors declare no conflict of interest.

References

1. Qureshi, K.N.; Bashir, F.; Abdullah, A.H. Provision of Security in Vehicular Ad hoc Networks through An Intelligent Secure Routing Scheme. In Proceedings of the 2017 International Conference on Frontiers of Information Technology (FIT), Islamabad, Pakistan, 18–20 December 2017; pp. 200–205.
2. Qureshi, K.N.; Din, S.; Jeon, G.; Piccialli, F. Internet of Vehicles: Key Technologies, Network Model, Solutions and Challenges with Future Aspects. *IEEE Trans. Intell. Transp. Syst.* **2020**, *22*, 1777–1786.
3. Zhang, C.; Lin, X.; Lu, R.; Ho, P.-H. RAISE: An efficient RSU-aided message authentication scheme in vehicular communication networks. In Proceedings of the 2008 IEEE International Conference on Communications, Beijing, China, 19–23 May 2008; pp. 1451–1457.
4. Zheng, Z.; Xie, S.; Dai, H.; Chen, X.; Wang, H. An overview of blockchain technology: Architecture, consensus, and future trends. In Proceedings of the 2017 IEEE International Congress on Big Data (BigData Congress), Honolulu, HI, USA, 11–14 December 2017; pp. 557–564.
5. Javed, I.T.; Alharbi, F.; Margaria, T.; Crespi, N.; Qureshi, K.N. PETchain: A Blockchain-Based Privacy Enhancing Technology. *IEEE Access* **2021**, *9*, 41129–41143.
6. Bonneau, J.; Miller, A.; Clark, J.; Narayanan, A.; Kroll, J.A.; Felten, E.W. Sok: Research perspectives and challenges for bitcoin and cryptocurrencies. In Proceedings of the 2015 IEEE Symposium on Security and Privacy, San Jose, CA, USA, 17–21 May 2015; pp. 104–121.
7. Javed, I.T.; Alharbi, F.; Bellaj, B.; Margaria, T.; Crespi, N.; Qureshi, K.N. Health-ID: A Blockchain-Based Decentralized Identity Management for Remote Healthcare. *Healthcare* **2021**, *9*, 712.
8. He, D.; Zeadally, S.; Xu, B.; Huang, X. An efficient identity-based conditional privacy-preserving authentication scheme for vehicular ad hoc networks. *IEEE Trans. Inf. Forensics Secur.* **2015**, *10*, 2681–2691.
9. Azees, M.; Vijayakumar, P.; Deboarh, L.J. EAAP: Efficient anonymous authentication with conditional privacy-preserving scheme for vehicular ad hoc networks. *IEEE Trans. Intell. Transp. Syst.* **2017**, *18*, 2467–2476.
10. Li, J.; Choo, K.-K.R.; Zhang, W.; Kumari, S.; Rodrigues, J.J.; Khan, M.K.; Hogrefe, D. EPA-CPPA: An efficient, provably-secure and anonymous conditional privacy-preserving authentication scheme for vehicular ad hoc networks. *Veh. Commun.* **2018**, *13*, 104–113.
11. Dorri, A.; Steger, M.; Kanhere, S.S.; Jurdak, R. Blockchain: A distributed solution to automotive security and privacy. *IEEE Commun. Mag.* **2017**, *55*, 119–125.
12. Zhang, X.; Li, R.; Cui, B. A security architecture of VANET based on blockchain and mobile edge computing. In Proceedings of the 2018 1st IEEE International Conference on Hot Information-Centric Networking (HotICN), Shenzhen, China, 17–19 August 2018; pp. 258–259.
13. Arora, A.; Yadav, S.K. Block chain based security mechanism for internet of vehicles (IoV). In Proceedings of the 3rd International Conference on Internet of Things and Connected Technologies (ICIoTCT), Jaipur, India, 9–10 May 2018; pp. 26–27.
14. Zhang, L.; Luo, M.; Li, J.; Au, M.H.; Choo, K.-K.R.; Chen, T.; Tian, S. Blockchain based secure data sharing system for Internet of vehicles: A position paper. *Veh. Commun.* **2019**, *16*, 85–93.
15. Yuan, Y.; Wang, F.-Y. Towards blockchain-based intelligent transportation systems. In Proceedings of the 2016 IEEE 19th International Conference on Intelligent Transportation Systems (ITSC), Rio de Janeiro, Brazil, 1–4 November 2016; pp. 2663–2668.
16. Kchaou, A.; Abassi, R.; Guemara, S. Toward a distributed trust management scheme for vanet. In Proceedings of the 13th International Conference on Availability, Reliability and Security, Hamburg, Germany, 27–30 August 2018; pp. 1–6.
17. Li, L.; Liu, J.; Cheng, L.; Qiu, S.; Wang, W.; Zhang, X.; Zhang, Z. Creditcoin: A privacy-preserving blockchain-based incentive announcement network for communications of smart vehicles. *IEEE Trans. Intell. Transp. Syst.* **2018**, *19*, 2204–2220.
18. Kang, J.; Yu, R.; Huang, X.; Wu, M.; Maharjan, S.; Xie, S.; Zhang, Y. Blockchain for secure and efficient data sharing in vehicular edge computing and networks. *IEEE Internet Things J.* **2018**, *6*, 4660–4670.
19. Kang, J.; Xiong, Z.; Niyato, D.; Ye, D.; Kim, D.I.; Zhao, J. Toward secure blockchain-enabled Internet of Vehicles: Optimizing consensus management using reputation and contract theory. *IEEE Trans. Veh. Technol.* **2019**, *68*, 2906–2920.
20. Schwartz, D.; Youngs, N.; Britto, A. The ripple protocol consensus algorithm. *Ripple Labs Inc White Pap.* **2014**, *5*, 151.
21. Kiayias, A.; Russell, A.; David, B.; Oliynykov, R. Ouroboros: A provably secure proof-of-stake blockchain protocol. In Proceedings of the Annual International Cryptology Conference, Santa Barbara, CA, USA, 20–24 August 2017; pp. 357–388.
22. Shao, J.; Lin, X.; Lu, R.; Zuo, C. A threshold anonymous authentication protocol for VANETs. *IEEE Trans. Veh. Technol.* **2015**, *65*, 1711–1720.

23. Forestiero, A. Metaheuristic algorithm for anomaly detection in Internet of Things leveraging on a neural-driven multiagent system. *Knowl.-Based Syst.* **2021**, *228*, 107241.
24. Ghanem, T.F.; Elkilani, W.S.; Abdul-Kader, H.M. A hybrid approach for efficient anomaly detection using metaheuristic methods. *J. Adv. Res.* **2015**, *6*, 609–619.
25. Alamri, B.; Javed, I.T.; Margaria, T. A GDPR-Compliant Framework for IoT-Based Personal Health Records Using Blockchain. In Proceedings of the 2021 11th IFIP International Conference on New Technologies, Mobility and Security (NTMS), Paris, France, 19–21 April 2021; pp. 1–5.
26. Huang, X.; Yu, R.; Kang, J.; Xia, Z.; Zhang, Y. Software defined networking for energy harvesting internet of things. *IEEE Internet Things J.* **2018**, *5*, 1389–1399.

Article

Strength Analysis of Real-Life Passwords Using Markov Models

Viktor Taneski *,†,‡, Marko Kompara ‡, Marjan Heričko ‡ and Boštjan Brumen ‡

Faculty of Electrical Engineering and Computer Science, University of Maribor, 2000 Maribor, Slovenia; marko.kompara@um.si (M.K.); marjan.hericko@um.si (M.H.); bostjan.brumen@um.si (B.B.)
* Correspondence: viktor.taneski@um.si; Tel.: +386-40-179-471
† Current address: Koroška cesta 46, 2000 Maribor, Slovenia.
‡ These authors contributed equally to this work.

Abstract: Recent literature proposes the use of a proactive password checker as method for preventing users from creating easy-to-guess passwords. Markov models can help us create a more effective password checker that would be able to check the probability of a given password to be chosen by an attacker. We investigate the ability of different Markov models to calculate a variety of passwords from different topics, in order to find out whether one Markov model is sufficient for creating a more effective password checker. The results of our study show that multiple models are required in order to be able to do strength calculations for a wide range of passwords. To the best of our knowledge, this is the first password strength study where the effect of the training password datasets on the success of the model is investigated.

Keywords: Markov models; passwords; password analysis; password strength; password score

Citation: Taneski, V.; Kompara, M.; Heričko, M.; Brumen, B. Strength Analysis of Real-Life Passwords Using Markov Models. *Appl. Sci.* **2021**, *11*, 9406. https://doi.org/10.3390/app11209406

Academic Editor: Gianluca Lax

Received: 20 August 2021
Accepted: 30 September 2021
Published: 11 October 2021

Publisher's Note: MDPI stays neutral with regard to jurisdictional claims in published maps and institutional affiliations.

Copyright: © 2021 by the authors. Licensee MDPI, Basel, Switzerland. This article is an open access article distributed under the terms and conditions of the Creative Commons Attribution (CC BY) license (https://creativecommons.org/licenses/by/4.0/).

1. Introduction

Authentication is the core of today's Web experience. The online services, social networks (e.g., Facebook, Twitter etc.) and websites require an authentication so that users can create a profile, post messages and comments, and tailor the website's content so it can match their interests. In an information security sense, authentication is the process of verifying someone's identity and typically it can be classified into three main categories: knowledge-based authentication-"what you know" (e.g., textual or graphical passwords), biometrics authentication-"what you are" (e.g., retina, iris, voice, and fingerprint scans), and token-based authentication-"what you have" (e.g., smart cards, mobile phones or other tokens). Lately, another alternative authentication method is becoming more available-the two-step verification. We focus on the first category and in particular, on the textual passwords and their security simply because the username-password combination used to be [1,2] and still is the most widely used method for authentication [3], due to their simplicity and cost effectiveness. The problems related to textual passwords and password security are not new. Morris and Thompson [4] were first to identify textual passwords as a weak point in information system's security. More than three decades ago, they conducted experiments about typical users' habits about how they choose their passwords. They reported that many UNIX-users have chosen passwords that were very weak: short, contained only lower-case letters or digits, or appeared in various dictionaries. The aforementioned problems still exist today and are still being made to solve them. However, users fail to implement the behaviours necessary to stay safe and secure, even though they are aware of the security issues. They create the easiest-to-remember passwords regardless of any recommendations or instructions and tend to trade security for memorability. Some important literature [5–9] proposes the use of a proactive password checker as a method (beyond simple dictionary lookup and composition rules) for preventing users from entering simple and easy-to-guess passwords into a computer system. The core property of a proactive password checker to be more effective and more prudent is the ability to check the probability of a given password to be chosen by the user and hence the probability to be chosen by an attacker. Some passwords are more likely to be chosen than others since certain letters and combinations of letters in any given language occur with varying frequencies.

1.1. Motivation

Some relevant literature [10–13] suggests that Markov models can be used as a tool that can aid the development of such a proactive checker since they can estimate the strength of a password by estimating the probability of the n-grams that compose the password. The estimation can be better if the model is trained on actual password datasets. However, a recent study in this area [14] suggests that state-of-the-art strength meters from academia, that are based on probabilistic context-free grammar (PCFG) and Markov models, are not enough competent at scoring weak passwords (which is basically their primary goal). They further argue (based on experimental comparison) that Markov models are no longer suitable for password scoring since they underperform compared to the PCFG technique. The authors present an explanation for this invalidation of commonly accepted belief that Markov models could be used to create better proactive password strength meters/checkers (than probabilistic context-free grammar). The provided rational states that smoothing techniques (e.g., backoff, Laplace and Good-Turing [13]) used in Markov models make them better at cracking passwords (i.e., predicting more unseen passwords), yet this, in turn, makes Markov-based strength meters subject to the sparsity problem and worse at measuring weak passwords.

Our motivation for this study is based on the weaknesses of Markov models stated and presented in [14], and the commonly known issues related to Markov models-sparsity and overfitting [9,13]. As stated in [9,14] at some point the performance of the Markov model is reduced because the model overfits the data and is not able to properly score weak passwords anymore. One possible reason (besides the ones stated in [14]) for this issue could be due to the fact that datasets used for training differ in terms of size, password types, localization etc. Furthermore, as it is clear from the literature ([9,12,15]), these models are mostly trained only on one training dataset or, at most, on a few datasets ([16]). This could limit the performance of the model in terms of properly scoring weak or very strong passwords. Since training datasets are core in developing the models, it is clear that they will have some effect in the final password scoring that the Markov model produces, which is also clearly suggested in [16]. Therefore, what we explore in our study is how significant is this effect and how other characteristics (e.g., size of the dataset, average password length, number of unique passwords etc.) affect the final password scoring.

We primarily focus on investigating the effect of different, but similar, training datasets on strength estimation. For the purpose of our study we analyse publicly available datasets of "common passwords" and process them regarding the frequency distribution of letters these passwords contain. Based on these datasets and the frequency distributions, we built different Markov models. This would help us find out if one Markov model is sufficient, or if multiple models are needed for the password checker to be effective for a wide range of passwords. To the best of our knowledge, this is the first time where the effects of the training dataset on the final password score are investigated in detail.

1.2. Goals

The goals of this paper are: (i) to find out if different Markov models (trained on different password datasets) will provide statistically different results when tested on the same password dataset, (ii) to find out if one model (that is trained on one big dataset, composed of multiple different datasets) is sufficient for creating an effective password checker, and (iii) to find out if Markov models of different orders (specifically of first and second order) will produce statistically different results. We address these goals by focusing on investigating whether there is a statistically significant difference in the scores from different models, trained on different training datasets. Furthermore, we investigate whether the order of the model has some significant effect on the success of the model.

1.3. Contributions

We make three contributions in this area. The first, and also the novelty in this research field, lies in training the models on a variety of datasets (12 in total), each with different characteristics, and testing them on the same password dataset in order to investigate the effect of the dataset on the success of the model. In particular, we show that the dataset has a significant effect on the final scoring of the passwords. The fact that different training datasets can lead to statistically different password scores, leads us to the conclusion that it is very important what kind of dataset is used to train the Markov models. We argue that one universal dataset should not be used to train one Markov model if we want to have an effective password scoring tool. The second contribution is the confirmation of our previous statement: the use of multiple different Markov models is better for efficient estimation of password strength rather than using one universal model, which is trained on one big dataset that combines multiple different datasets. Finally, the third contribution is that we showed that the difference in outputs between two Markov models with different orders (1st and 2nd) is, in most cases, not statistically significantly different. Therefore, the general conclusion here is that, without a doubt, it is important to analyse the dataset before selecting the order of the model.

Overall, we show that if we want to have an effective password scoring tool for calculating the strength of a wide range of passwords, it would be required to use multiple different Markov models, which should be constructed and trained on a particular dataset of passwords so that they can be more efficiently used on that particular password group.

1.4. Organization

The rest of the paper is organized as follows: we present and review the related work in Section 2, and we provide some background of Markov models in Section 3. In Section 4 we describe our experimental methodologies, the construction of our models, the datasets, and the processing of the datasets we used, including the choice of training/testing datasets. Next, we present the results of our study in Section 5. We discuss the results and the ethical considerations of the study in Section 6. In Section 7 we present our final conclusions.

2. Related Work

In this section, we provide a short review of relevant previous studies that deal with calculating the password strength or password cracking process and are closely related to Markov models.

The strength analysis of users' passwords has been one active research area since passwords were exposed as the weakest link in information system's security in 1979 by Morris and Thompson. There are various techniques that have been used for both calculating the strength of the password and enhancing the password cracking process.

2.1. Basic Password Strength Calculation

The basic password strength calculation is done by a simple password policy or, as it is also called-a password rule system. Such a system has the ability to estimate the strength of a given password by analysing its structure i.e., the number of upper case, lower case, or whether it contains numbers or special characters. The estimation is a binary result which tells whether the passwords meets the requirements of the policy or not. One major weakness of a password rule system is that users and their textual passwords are still considered "the weakest link". Users tend to choose weak passwords and passwords that are easy-to-guess and can be found in a dictionary [17]. Because of this, such a password rule system fails when it comes to preventing weak passwords from entering the system. For example, a password "Password1!" may be acceptable for the password rule system (it contains an upper case, a number and a special character), but it is still the most common and one of the easiest passwords to be cracked (with the use of a personal computer it can be cracked within seconds). We need more advanced password rules that can additionally check the possibility that a given password can be chosen by the attacker. This is where Markov models come to the rescue since they can be used as an aid to brute-force or dictionary password cracking.

2.2. Entropy

One of the earliest method for password scoring is entropy. In information theory, entropy is the expected value of the information contained in a message. Authors in [18] attempt to determine the effectiveness of using information entropy (more specifically, Shannon entropy) as a measurement of the security of various password policies. They accomplish this by analysing the success rate of standard password cracking techniques against multiple sets of real-life passwords. Their experiments show that password entropy does not provide a valid metric for measuring the security provided by password creation policies. Furthermore, they found that the most common password creation policies remain vulnerable to online attacks, since users are using easy-to-guess passwords that still comply with the requested policy (e.g., "Password1!").

2.3. Probabilistic Context-Free Grammars

Another tool for password cracking are probabilistic context-free grammars as an aid in the creation of word-mangling rules, proposed by Weir et al. in [19]. Probabilistic password cracking is based on the assumption that not all guesses have the same probability of cracking a password (i.e., some passwords are more probable to be guessed than others). Probabilistic context-free grammars are based on a probability distribution of user's passwords and measure the frequencies of certain patterns associated with the password strings. Authors trained this method on different sets of previously disclosed passwords. They used some of the sets for training and others for testing the solution and calculating password probabilities. As a comparison against the PCFG password cracking technique, authors use John the Ripper's default word-mangling rules. The results of the study show that this technique performed better than John the Ripper by cracking 28–129% more passwords, given the same number of guesses.

A study by Houshmand et al. [20] presents an improved PCFG for password cracking by systematically adding keyboard patterns and multi-word patterns to the context-free grammars used in probabilistic password cracking. They state that while their probabilistic password cracking approach shows consistent effectiveness, at one point it gets "stuck" in a dead end. Authors suggest that maybe at that point it is better to support Markov or brute force guessing.

2.4. Markov Models

One of the earliest use of Markov models as a password cracking tool was by Narayanan and Shmatikov in [10]. They used them as an improvement of rainbow table cracking, by training Markov models to general rules that passwords follow. They show that Markov models might have an important application for distributed password cracking. This work also is the first to hint that Markov models can be used as a tool for calculating password strength and shows that they can perform better than the Rainbow attack by recovering 96% of the passwords over the 39% recovered by the Rainbow attack.

Later, a survey of the most common techniques used in public and private tools for enhancing the password cracking process was made by Marechal [11]. The paper is mainly focused on using Markov models as a powerful tool for password cracking and as a password generator, for generating the most common passwords used as a supplement for the dictionary or the brute-force attack. The findings in this paper show that the Markov password generator, despite it being slower than John the Ripper [21] was actually performing better. According to this study, Markov tools can be included in a password-checking policy so it can be more effective than those that only check the structural content of the password.

Different password cracking techniques (attacks) were analysed by Dell' Amico et al. in [9] in order to find out what is the probability of breaking a given password. The authors compared the search space against a number of cracked passwords for guessing techniques like dictionary attacks, brute force, dictionary mangling, probabilistic context-free grammars, and Markov models. These password cracking techniques were tested on three different large datasets of passwords. Their findings show that no single cracking strategy prevails over the others: dictionary attacks are most effective in discovering weak passwords, dictionary mangling is useful when the base dictionaries are exhausted and Markov-model techniques are powerful in breaking strong passwords. The authors of the study believe that proactive password checking is a better approach in persuading the users to put more effort into choosing their password.

Markov models as a tool for calculating password strength were already mentioned in [11] where the authors showed that password crackers based on Markov models can outperform existing cracking techniques. In [12] Markov models are used as a concept for adaptive password strength meters that can estimate the password strength. Password checkers have a very important role in providing security of computer systems since they are the mechanism that should prevent bad passwords from getting into the system. This study focuses on building adaptive password strength meters based on Markov models. They measured the accuracy of their construction by comparing the scores of the meter to the scores of other meters (Google, Microsoft etc.) as well as to the ideal password strength meter. The results of the study show that their Markov-based password strength meter achieves higher accuracy and outperforms commonly used password meters.

A similar probabilistic framework for estimation of password strength is proposed in [15]. The proposed framework is based on a very large public dataset containing 75,000,000 unique passwords. As part of the framework, two different Markov models are considered and tested: simple Markov model, where the transition probability from one character to another depends only on the previous state, and layered Markov model, where the transition probability also takes into account the position of the character in the given password. Both models are analysed and tested using different independent datasets simulating a conventional password guessing attack. The authors argue, based on the results of the study, that such a probabilistic framework may be capable of providing a better estimation of the strength (i.e., the resistance to attacks) of a password. In [13] Markov models were also proven to perform slightly better than the PCFG proposed by Weir et al. in [19]. Through a systematic evaluation of many different password models using 6 real-world plaintext password datasets, with about 60 million passwords, they show that the model based on PCFG does not perform as well as the Markov model.

A related study presents results regarding the performance of Markov models that counteract with the previous ones. Authors in [14] performed an experiment where they tested existing password scoring meters from the industry (e.g., Zxcvbn, KeePSM and NIST PSM) and academia (PCFG-based ones and Markov-based ones). Their results show PCFG-based meter performs best among existing password scoring meters. Their conclusion is that the PCFG-based model is better at measuring passwords, and the Markov-based model is better at cracking passwords. Furthermore, the authors present a novel password strength meter based on a fuzzy probabilistic context-free grammar. It can react dynamically to changes in how users choose passwords.

A recent study [16] performs an extensive and empirical analysis of Chinese web passwords where the authors evaluate the security of these passwords by employing two state-of-the art cracking techniques: PCFG and Markov models. Their results show that Chinese passwords are more prone to online guessing than English passwords. Furthermore, this study explores how password scoring meters measure the password strength, which leads the authors to the claim that in order for a PSM to be accurate, its training set should be representative of the password base of the target site and that there is no single training set that can fit all PSMs. This claim is what we explore further in our study.

2.5. Neural Networks

Neural networks can be considered as a statistical technique in pattern recognition. They implement non-linear mappings from several input variables to several output variables, where the form of the mapping is governed by a number of adjustable parameters. A neural network learns how to compute a mapping by trial and error, through a certain parameter optimization algorithm. Such an algorithm, due to the biological premises of the theory of neural networks, is called a learning algorithm. During the learning process (also called training), the network receives a sequence of examples and adapts its internal parameters to match the desired input-output functionality. The knowledge to compute the mapping is therefore acquired during this learning process and it is stored in the modified values of the internal parameters. It is known that neural networks have been used for generating the probability of the next element in a string based on the preceding elements [22,23] (e.g., in generating the string *password*, a neural network might be given *passwor* and output that *d* has a high probability of occurring next).

Since password creation is conceptually similar to text generation, it was somehow inevitable for neural networks to become more commonly used as a tool for password scoring and password generation. Their main advantage over other password scoring methods is their speed and lightweight regarding memory requirements. One of the first times where neural networks have been fully and successfully applied to designing proactive password checkers is presented in [24]. This study presents a way of using neural networks in a password checker solution. The authors applied SLP (Single Layer Perceptrons) and MLP (Multilayer Perceptron) networks to the design of proactive password checking. They have evaluated the performance of several network topologies and compared the MLP networks with kernel-based and fuzzy-based neural network models. Their comparison of classification rates obtained by their solutions with previous proactive password checkers showed that proactive password checkers based on this technology have high efficiency and efficacy.

Another study [25] describes how to use neural networks to model human-chosen passwords and measure password strength. In their study authors comprehensively test the impact of varying the neural networks model size, model architecture, training data, and training technique on the network's ability to guess different types of passwords. Furthermore, this study compares the implementation of neural networks to state-of-the-art password-guessing models, like probabilistic context-free grammars and Markov models. This comparison shows that in general neural networks at high guesses outperform other models, with some exceptions which are related to the training dataset (in this case authors used a combination of datasets-one of which is the Rockyou training dataset used also in our experiment). The main contribution of this study is the client-side implementation of a proactive password checker based on neural networks. It is implemented in JavaScript and light-weighted (requires only 60MB of disk space).

2.6. Summary of the Related Work

Based on the reviewed related work regarding Markov models, we can say that Markov models can be used as an efficient tool for successful cracking of difficult passwords, even though they have some setbacks (like overfitting). We argue that they can be used as a framework for estimating password strength in a proactive password checker, as long as they are properly trained and properly developed (see Section 1.1). Our approach has a similar background as some of the related work that we described. In this work, we inspect the possibility of using one universal Markov model, or multiple different models, as a mechanism for password checking, by analysing publicly available datasets of passwords that we used to train and test our Markov models on.

3. Background

Markov model is a stochastic process where the next state of the system depends only on the present state and not on preceding states [26]. That is, only on the single present state and not the history of the states. Markov models are commonly used as a language processing tool in speech recognition systems, like in [26], but they can also be used in other fields, particularly in the context of passwords. Such Markov models have already been used before (see Section 2) as an aid to brute-force or dictionary password cracking. These models are based on the fact that particular characters or sub-strings in a particular language area have a higher frequency of occurrence than others (e.g., the string "the" is much more likely to occur than "tqe" and the letter e is very likely to follow "th"). This approach can be used to calculate the strength of the password, by defining a probability distribution over a sequence of characters, which constitutes the password. Such constructed Markov model assigns each password a probability P, which is calculated differently based on the order of the Markov model. The general equation for calculating this probability is [12]:

$$P("c_1c_2...c_l'') = P(c_i|c_1...c_n) \prod_{i=n}^{l} P(c_i|c_{i-n+1}...c_{i-1}). \quad (1)$$

and can be applied to every order of the Markov models.

The models used by Narayanan and Shmatikov are zero-order model and first-order model.

Zero-order Markov model is a Markov model, where the characters are independent of each other i.e., each character's probability is calculated according to the underlying frequency distribution and independently of the previous characters.

On the other hand, first-order Markov model is a Markov model, where each 2-gram (i.e., diagram, ordered pair, or a sub-string of length 2) of characters is assigned a probability by looking at the previous character. The probability assigned to a password "$c_1c_2...c_l$" in the case of a first-order Markov model would be ([13]):

$$P("c_1c_2...c_l'') = P(c_1)P(c_2|c_1)P(c_3|c_2)...P(c_l|c_{l-1}). \quad (2)$$

The probabilities $P(\alpha_j|\alpha_i)$ are called *conditional transitional probabilities* and denote the probability of a transition to state α_j when the automata is in state α_i. In the context of passwords that would be the probability of a character c_i following the character c_{i-1}. The conditional probabilities can be easily computed with the following formula ([13]):

$$P(c_i|c_{i-1}) = \frac{count(c_{i-1}c_i)}{count(c_{i-1}x)} \quad (3)$$

where $count(c_{i-1}c_i)$ presents the number of occurrences of the sub-string $c_{i-1}c_i$ and $count(c_{i-1}x)$ denotes the number of occurrences of c_{i-1} when followed by another character x. This character x is part of the password's alphabet A, i.e., the set of distinct characters that are identified in a particular password dataset, which is also the number of possible states of the Markov model. The number of sub-strings $c_{i-1}x$ in a particular dataset is by definition equal to: $count(c_{i-1}x) = \sum_{c_i \in A} count(c_{i-1}c_i)$. By using this substitution, the above Equation (3) takes the form:

$$P(c_i|c_{i-1}) = \frac{count(c_{i-1}c_i)}{\sum_{c_i \in A} count(c_{i-1}c_i)}. \quad (4)$$

The transitional probabilities ($P(\alpha_j|\alpha_i)$) between the states of the model (α_j being the current state and α_i being the previous state) are described by a matrix called *transition probability matrix* or simply *transition matrix*. Each value $P(\alpha_j|\alpha_i)$ denotes the probability that, given the model is currently in state α_i, it will be in state α_j in the next step.

The power of Markov models lies in the ability to use the transition matrix for determining the probability of the model being in a certain state after a certain number of steps (more than one). For e.g., if we have a transition matrix with probabilities for the various kinds of weather, we can denote the probability for the weather being rainy, sunny or snowy two, three or four days from now. This probability is denoted by $P^n_{\alpha_i \alpha_j}$, where:

- α_i denotes the current state of the model
- α_j denotes the next state of the model
- n denotes the number of steps

The probabilities $P^n_{\alpha_j \alpha_i}$ are calculated by setting the transition matrix to power n-the number of steps.

When the above statements are applied to the passwords, the transitional probabilities simply represent the probability of a character c_j appearing after a character c_i in a certain position in the password, which corresponds with the number of steps (n). Having this in mind we can transform Equation (2) into:

$$P("c_1 c_2 ... c_l'') = P(c_1) P(c_2|c_1)^1 P(c_3|c_2)^2 ... P(c_l|c_{l-1})^{l-1}. \qquad (5)$$

From the above equations, we can see that the probability P basically represents the probability of occurrence of a sequence of characters and the order of the characters in the password. This probability is obtained by analysing the frequency distribution (the number of occurrences) of these characters in a suitable training dataset.

It is important to note that the probabilities of the first characters $P_{0\alpha_i}$ are represented by an *initialization vector*. The initialization vector basically holds the probabilities of every character occurring in the first position in a password.

The final score assigned to the password is a number that is computed by using the following equation [15]:

$$S("c_1 c_2 ... c_l'') = -10 \log_{10} P("c_1 c_2 ... c_l''), \qquad (6)$$

so that the less likely it is to produce the password, the stronger it is according to the model.

Needless to say, the frequency distributions of the characters used in keyspace compression via Markovian filtering is language-specific, and the distribution used in this paper applies only to passwords chosen by English-speaking users (presumably, similar distributions can be found for other alphabet-based languages).

4. Materials and Methods

In this section we justify our decision on using first-order Markov models, we describe our method, the development of the models, give a description of the datasets we use, and present the selection of training/testing datasets.

4.1. Constructing the Model(s)

We used Equations (2) and (4) for building our models and Equation (6) for calculating the Markov scores for the passwords from the testing dataset. Our constructed models are Markov models of *first order* (the model is applied to sub-strings of length two), which means that the model keeps track only of the previous state of the system-i.e., the probability distribution of the current character depends only on the previous character in the password.

In our practical case, the number of states i.e., the number of distinct characters that we search in the datasets and used in our models is $A = 224$, coinciding with the set of ASCII characters from character code 32 to 255. This character set includes all characters from the extended ASCII table, except for the initial 32 characters which are basically unprintable control codes and are used to control peripherals such as printers. To the best of our knowledge, such a large number of possible states of a Markov model hasn't been explored and used for password scoring yet [10,12,13,15].

The output of the model is a real number indicating the password strength. Following the approach in [15], in the case of passwords that are assigned a probability of occurrence of 0 by the model, the final password strength is assigned 4000, which represents a very high strength (so we can avoid infinite values). The value 4000 was selected because the highest values that models otherwise achieved were only over three thousand (maximum value is never over 4000). Further in the paper, we refer to this situation as *the model was unable to calculate the password strength*.

For calculating the password strength we used Equation (5), which represents the probability of a character (or a character sequence) occurring after a certain number of steps of the model (i.e., a certain position in the password) and Equation (6), which represents the final score of the password.

The initialization vectors are also trained on the same database subsets as the respective models. They represent the probability that a password initiates with each of the 224 characters.

To create the model and calculate the scores for the test passwords, we first need to train the Markov model over a known distribution. This distribution can simply be a publicly available set of passwords from a previously attacked dataset. These datasets are further described in the following subsection.

4.2. Data Collections

We used 12 datasets that contain real user passwords in plaintext that were leaked and are publicly available for research purposes. These password datasets represent real user passwords, which were compromised by hackers and subsequently publicly disclosed on the Internet. We used only the password information in the datasets and we removed all additional information like user names and/or email addresses included in some datasets.

The "RockYou" dataset [27] contains over 14 million passwords leaked from the social application site RockYou in December 2009. The "10 million combos" dataset [28] contains 10 million passwords collected and cracked by Mark Burnett for research purposes. The dataset also contained user names that are connected to the passwords. In order to maintain the anonymity of these informations, we removed the related user names and focused only on the released passwords. The "PhpBB" dataset [27] contains about 180.000 passwords cracked from MD5 hashes by Brandon Enright leaked from Phpbb.com in January 2009. The "MySpace" dataset [27] includes 37.000 passwords that were obtained via phishing attack in October 2006. The "faithwriters" dataset contains 8K passwords stolen from the religious forum Faithwriters. The basic information and the sources of the rest of the datasets are presented in Table 1. For additional details, readers are referred to original works.

Table 1. Basic information of datasets.

Dataset	Size	Date Obtained	Source
rockyou	14,344,390	12-2009	[27]
10_million_passwords	10,000,000	02-2015	[28]
passwords	2,151,220	12-2011	[29]
uniqpass_preview	1,999,984	12-2011	[29]
phpbb	184,389	01-2009	[27]
scribd	106,358	Unknown	Source unknown
tuscl	38,820	Unknown	[27]
myspace	37,139	10-2006	[27]
singles_org	12,233	10-2010	[27]
10k_most_common	10,000	06-2011	[30]
hotmail	8930	Unknown	[27]
faithwriters	8347	03-2009	[27]

4.3. Data Processing

Since our goal is to create multiple Markov models and test them on the same testing dataset, we decided not to merge all datasets into one big dataset and then partitioning it into training and testing. Such an approach can also cause some frequent passwords or passwords with similar length, or some pattern distributions, to appear both in training and testing, thus introducing bias. Furthermore, since the datasets differ from each other in terms of scope, size, password security policies under which passwords were constructed etc., we were not able to decide which datasets will be used for training and which for testing, because our results could easily be biased based on the selection of the training datasets. Therefore, we decided to partition the datasets in the way that is shown in Figure 1. Before the partitioning took place, we first randomized our datasets. Then, half of the passwords in each dataset were used as a training dataset for building a Markov model and the other half was added to our common testing dataset. In the end, we have 12 different models that are trained on 12 different datasets, and a common dataset for testing the models.

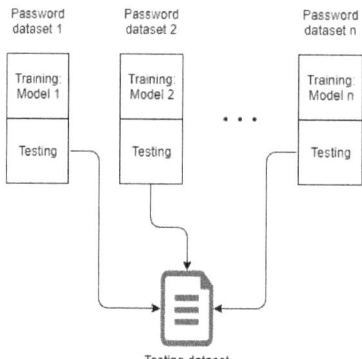

Figure 1. Graphical presentation of the process of dividing datasets and combining them into one dataset for testing.

After we partitioned our datasets into training and testing datasets and constructed our models, we run every model on the same testing dataset, which contains over 14 million passwords. The input of each Markov models is the testing dataset, while the output is a set of calculated scores appropriately for each of the passwords from the testing dataset. The process is presented in Figure 2.

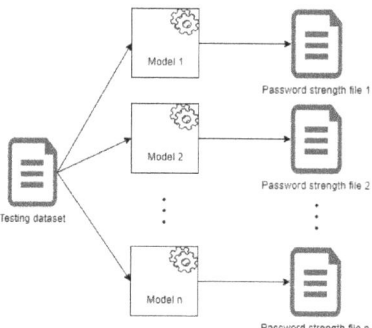

Figure 2. Graphical presentation of the process of calculating the passwords' strength with different models.

5. Results

In this section, we present the results of our study. First, we analyse the datasets and the frequency distribution of the characters inside the datasets. Then we analyse the passwords in the datasets regarding their construction like length, numerical, upper case, lower case, alphanumerical, the containment of special characters etc. Finally, we present our main results regarding our analysis of the connection between the models and the scores of the testing passwords.

5.1. Character Frequency Analysis

The character frequency distribution is the basis for constructing a Markov model for the purposes of either cracking passwords or computing its Markov score i.e., its strength. We performed character frequency analysis on our datasets of disclosed real-life passwords (see Appendix A).

Since the datasets are acquired from different sources, we expect them to differ in terms of character frequency distribution, which is important for our research, since we are trying to create different independent models. We present a couple of findings that point to this assumption. First, in almost all of the datasets, the most frequent characters are *numbers*, *lower-case letters* and *upper-case letters*, but the *10k_most_common* and *uniqpass_preview* lack *upper-case letters*. Likewise, special characters from the basic ASCII table are not present in all the datasets. Second, the RockYou dataset contains characters from the extended ASCII table, which other datasets do not, so we expect this dataset to produce significantly different password scores from the testing dataset.

In order to confirm our assumption about the statistically significant difference between the datasets in terms of character frequency distribution, we performed a statistical analysis of the character frequency for all datasets. We used the nonparametric Friedman's ANOVA statistical test for multiple repeated measures since the Shapiro-Wilk test for normality showed that all of the differences between pairs of datasets do not conform to a normal distribution ($p < 0.05$ in all cases). The Friedman's ANOVA test did find that there are statistically significant differences ($\chi^2(11) = 259, p < 0.001$). This confirms our assumption and gives us the ability to continue with our experiment and analysis since this meets the condition for diversity; this condition is met when at least one dataset is different from the others.

5.2. Data Collections Characteristics

Before we present our main results, we present some summary statistics about our datasets, regarding the characteristics of the passwords they contain. We are interested in passwords characteristics like the average length, uniqueness, the percentage of passwords that were only numerical, only lower-case letters, only upper-case letters, mixed-case letters, alphanumerical, and that contain at least one special character.

Table 2 shows a summary of the distributions of passwords and the average password length in each dataset. As we can observe, the most common passwords in every dataset are alphanumeric passwords.

Table 3 shows the percentages of passwords that appear 1–5 or more times in every dataset. As we can observe from the table, out of all 12 dataset only three (*10_million_passwords*, *passwords*, and *scribd*) do not contain a 100% unique passwords. The high percentage of uniqueness of the datasets goes in hand with our experiment, since it allows us to train our models over a wide variety of passwords.

Table 2. Passwords information.

Dataset	Digits Only	Lowercase Only	Uppercase Only	Mixedcase	Alphanumeric	A special Character *
1. rockyou	16.36%	26.06%	1.61%	1.12%	47.51%	6.82%
2. 10 million passwords	20.36%	38.25%	1.09%	2.52%	35.90%	1.10%
3. passwords	23.22%	23.85%	0.75%	1.56%	47.08%	3.02%
4. uniqpass preview	6.70%	28.96%	0.00%	0.00%	48.86%	15.48%
5. phpbb	11.24%	41.25%	0.93%	2.69%	41.19%	2.13%
6. scribd	0.27%	81.71%	0.18%	7.57%	2.94%	7.32%
7. tuscl	8.70%	42.36%	0.94%	2.38%	43.17%	1.72%
8. myspace	0.72%	6.75%	0.29%	0.18%	80.43%	10.66%
9. singles_org	8.37%	55.11%	2.26%	4.37%	29.00%	0.24%
10. 10k most common	5.54%	83.10%	0.00%	0.00%	11.20%	0.16%
11. hotmail	18.52%	41.59%	2.21%	1.05%	29.50%	6.93%
12. faithwriters	6.27%	50.15%	1.32%	3.83%	37.14%	0.53%

* the password contains at least one special character.

Table 3. Passwords frequency information.

Dataset	Size	Unique	Twice	3 times	4 times	5+ times
1. rockyou	14,344,390	100%	0%	0%	0%	0%
2. 10_million_passwords	10,000,000	44.34%	3.86%	1.21%	0.6%	1.89%
3. passwords	2,151,220	99.96%	0.02%	0%	0%	0%
4. uniqpasss_preview	1,999,984	100%	0%	0%	0%	0%
5. phpbb	184,389	100%	0%	0%	0%	0%
6. scribd	106,358	75.68%	12.12%	0.03%	0%	0%
7. tuscl	38,820	100%	0%	0%	0%	0%
8. myspace	37,139	100%	0%	0%	0%	0%
9. singles_org	12,233	100%	0%	0%	0%	0%
10. 10k_most_common	10,000	100%	0%	0%	0%	0%
11. hotmail	8930	100%	0%	0%	0%	0%
12. faithwriters	8347	100%	0%	0%	0%	0%

Table 4 shows the average password length in our datasets. The table shows that the average password length (weighted by the size of the datasets) is 8.38 characters, which is in line with findings in [17,31,32].

Table 4. Password length.

Dataset	Size	Password Length	
		Mean	Standard Deviation
rockyou	14,344,390	8.75	2.898
10_million_passwords	10,000,000	7.59	2.15
passwords	2,151,220	8.37	1.995
uniqpass_preview	1,999,984	9.92	3.51
phpbb	184,389	7.54	1.75
scribd	106,358	7.51	2.6
tuscl	38,820	7.37	1.75
myspace	37,139	8.23	2.6
singles_org	12,233	6.74	1.19
10k_most_common	10,000	6.30	1.3
hotmail	8930	8.79	2.89
faithwriters	8347	7.71	1.86
Simple average		7.9	
Weighted average		8.38	

5.3. Main Results

Each model produced 11,924,618 results. Table 5 shows the descriptive statistics for the results of all 12 models. From it we can quickly notice some distinguishable differences between the models. The mean values range from 132.99 to 3003.56, medians are between 120.22 and 4000.00, and standard deviations range from 95.21 to 1895.30. All of these differences are very big and at least one reason for this can be seen in the mode statistic. The mode of all models is 4000. This is not surprising as the models assign this value to passwords for which they are unable to calculate the strength. As the passwords that could not have their strength calculated are considered to be stronger than the rest we assigned them the highest value. In our case the value 4000 acts similarly to a ceiling value, resulting in a distribution with a ceiling effect (which, in turn, compromises the normal distribution of the models).

Table 5. Descriptive statistics for the password strengths produced by the 12 models.

Dataset	Mean	Median	Mode	Std. Deviation	Maximum
10_million_passwords	146.26	120.22	4000	257.99	4000
10k_most_common	1074.47	126.20	4000	1671.79	4000
faithwriters	1286.00	141.36	4000	1772.61	4000
hotmail	632.37	127.12	4000	1303.92	4000
myspace	487.87	132.53	4000	1111.33	4000
passwords	1656.88	161.35	4000	1895.30	4000
phpbb	174.87	128.49	4000	381.38	4000
rockyou	132.99	120.69	4000	95.21	4000
scribd	3003.56	4000.00	4000	1690.55	4000
singles_org	750.01	127.06	4000	1425.36	4000
tuscl	427.66	127.33	4000	1027.52	4000
uniqpass	657.80	126.40	4000	1332.94	4000

An example of this can be seen in Figure 3. Figure 3 shows the distribution of *myspace* model. In the right part of the graph, we can see the large increase in the frequency of the ceiling value.

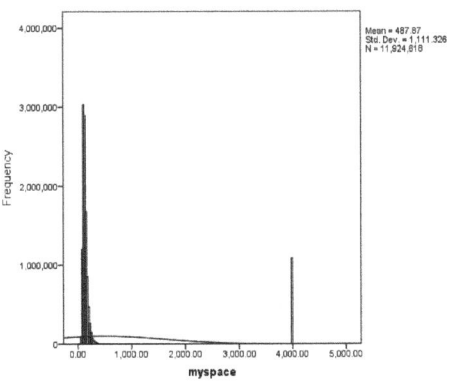

Figure 3. Distribution histogram for the myspace model.

All models produce such an effect to a greater or lesser degree. Even though the mode of all the models is 4000 it might pay to take a closer look at the frequency of this value in different models. After all the *scribd* model has a median that is the same as the ceiling value, meaning more than half the results outputted by this model were 4000. High frequencies of such values could also mean a bad training dataset that was not able to accurately measure the strength of passwords from the testing dataset.

Many ceiling values would inflate the average statistics and the standard deviation. We can see this is in Figure 4, where the number of ceiling values that each model produces is shown. Comparison between Table 5 and Figure 4 indicates that the size of the mean is connected with the number of ceiling values each model produces–the order of models, sorted by their mean size is the same as the order of models when sorted by the number of ceiling values. This will probably be the most important defining characteristic of successful models, because of the way we define a good password checking model. The best model is the one that is the most severe with the passwords it is checking (i.e., it produces the smallest values) because when dealing with the security we should always be prepared for the worst-case scenario. An excessively stringent model promotes the use of safer passwords, while an overly mild model gives good marks to less desirable passwords and creates false confidence in those passwords. Models with more ceiling values will on average and when compared, value by value, to another model be more prone to show higher password strengths and will therefore be determined to be less desirable for evaluation of password strengths.

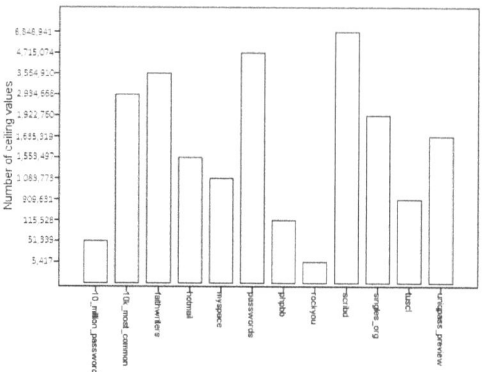

Figure 4. Frequency of ceiling values for each model.

When comparing models by their frequency of ceiling values (Figure 4), we can notice large differences between them. The most successful model at avoiding ceiling values and therefore the most successful at calculating the strength for any password turned out to be the model created from the biggest password dataset—*rockyou*. It was unable to calculate only 5417 passwords (0.045%), while on the other hand *scribd* failed to calculate the strength of almost 8.9 million passwords (74.2%).

Figure 5 shows how many models were unable to calculate individual passwords. For approximately half a million of passwords used in the testing dataset, every single model was able to successfully calculate their strength. Those are most likely the very weakest of passwords, constructed from very common characters. Of the approximate 12 million passwords used in the testing dataset, almost 2.55 million passwords failed to be calculated by one model, 4 million by two models, etc. (see Figure 5). The strength of the most complex passwords was impossible to calculate for up to nine models. This means that for every single password at the very least three models were able to compute its strength. As we have seen in the previous graph every single model had difficulties calculating the strength of some passwords. However, we have now seen that every password could be processed by at least a few models. This gives us the first indication that the use of multiple models is required in order to be able to do strength calculations for a wide range of passwords.

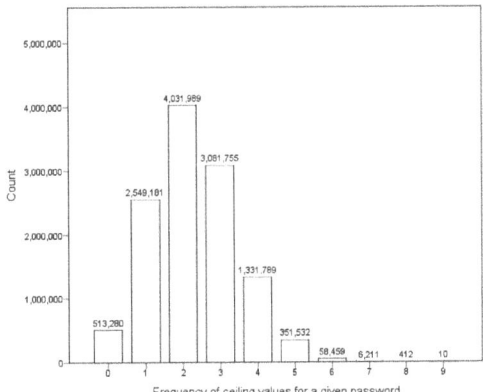

Figure 5. The number of times models were unable to calculate each passwords strength.

Friedman's ANOVA test is a non-parametric statistical test used for one-way repeated measures analysis of variance by ranks. The Friedman test was selected, because as is clear that the model outputs are not normally distributed. Considering the sample size, the significance level was set at 0.001. Test results show statistically significant differences between the distributions of Markov models trained on different datasets, with $\chi2(11)$ = 14,629,394.673 and $p < 0.0001$. Consequently, we reject the null hypothesis, stating that the distribution of scores in all models are the same and accept the alternative hypothesis confirming that at least two of the models' distributions differ.

For post hoc testing the Sign test was used, to compare every possible pair of models. When looking at the difference between all 66 model pairs none had a normal distribution and the majority of them were also nowhere close to symmetrically distributed. Because other statistical tests assume that one of the two distributions is a normal distribution, the Sign test, which makes no assumptions about the distribution, was used.

For post hoc testing the Wilcoxon Sign test was used, to compare every possible pair of models. The Sign test was selected because the data meet all the required assumptions (explained below). Figure 6 contains a selection of four differences between models with normality curves. Graph a in Figure 6, for example, shows the distribution of *10_million_passwords* model results subtracted from the results of the *rockyou model*. Here the distribution is fairly symmetrical, but as we map the differences of more diverse models the distributions become more and more skewed. When looking at the difference between all 66 model pairs none had a normal distribution and the majority of them were also nowhere close to symmetrically distributed (Figure 6a,b graphs are the closest). Because other statistical tests assume that one of the two distributions is a normal distribution, the Sign test, which makes no assumptions about the distribution, was used.

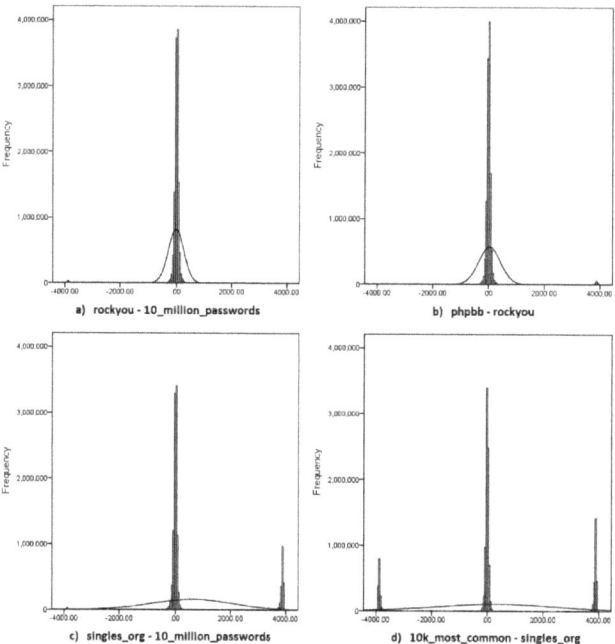

Figure 6. Four examples for the distribution of differences between two models.

Pairwise comparisons were performed with a Bonferroni correction for multiple comparisons. Statistical significance was therefore accepted at the $p < 0.000015$ level. The results for all 66 pairs can be seen in Table A1. Based on the results we reject the null hypothesis (the median of the differences between two models is 0) for all 66 pairs and accept the alternative, stating that the median of the differences between two models is not equal to 0. This was, because the sample size and nature of data, somewhat expected. For this reason, we also included effect size [33]. Effect size is a measure of magnitude or size of an effect (the observed phenomenon). Effect size is calculated with the following formula:

$$r = Z/\sqrt{N}, \qquad (7)$$

where r is the effect size, Z is the z-value produced in the sign test, and N is the number of observations. Bigger r value means a more substantial difference between the results of the two models. Using Cohen criteria, we interpret the size of the effect. Effect size between 0.1 and 0.3 is considered to be small, but definitely not trivial or something to be ignored. Bigger values that are smaller than 0.5 are said to have a medium effect, while r values over 0.5 represent a large effect. To simplify and make the effect size more understandable we also calculate the common language effect size (CL), also called probability of superiority. CL gives the probability that a random score from one model will be higher than its matching pair in the second model. CL is calculated by dividing the positive differences by the number of comparisons. The number of comparisons excludes ties (pairs where both models produce the same value). Effect size, its effect classification and CL can all be found in Table A1.

Each row in the table represents a pair of models (Model 1 and Model 2). Next two columns are the Z and the p-value results of the sign test. Following are the metrics for the effect size. Let us for example take the first pair in Table A1. For the pair *10K_most_common* and *10_million_passwords* the effect size was calculated to be 0.1092. This result is higher than 0.1 and is therefore not insignificant, however, it is not especially high, so we mark the effect as small. CL is calculated by subtracting the model 2 results from model 1. The end percentage, therefore, tells us the probability of model 1 producing a higher strength evaluation than model 2 for a random password. Looking back at the previous example, the CL is 57.73%. This means *10K_most_common* produced higher strength estimations in 57.73% of the cases, while *10_million_passwords* only had the higher value in 42.27% of the results (excluding the ties). This brings us back to the definition of a more successful model. Generally, the model consistently producing smaller password strength estimations would be better. From the example, we can see that model *10_million_passwords* more rarely generates the higher strength value of the two and for that reason, we would consider this model to be the better one. Because of the way the models are sorted into model 1 and 2 columns, the ones in the second column are always considered better. As a result, to find the best models we can simply just count the number of times a single model is written in the second column (higher the count, better the model). Following this rule, we find that *10_million_passwords* is the best model, followed by *rockyou, phpbb, tuscl, uniqpass, hotmail, singles_org, 10k_most_common, myspace, faithwriters, passwords*, and the worst of the tested models *scribd*. We summarise this and order the models in Table 6.

Table 6. Ordering the models

Order Number	Dataset	Size	Freq. of Ceiling Values	% *
1	10_million	10,000,000	51,339	0.43
2	rockyou	14,344,390	5,417	0.05
3	phpbb	184,389	115,528	0.97
4	tuscl	38,820	909,631	7.63
5	uniqpasss_preview	1,999,984	1,635,319	13.71
6	hotmail	8930	1,553,497	13.03
7	singles_org	12,233	1,922,760	16.12
8	10k_most_common	10,000	2,934,668	24.61
9	myspace	37,139	1,083,773	9.09
10	faithwriters	8347	3,564,910	29.90
11	passwords	2,151,220	4,715,074	39.54
12	scribe	106,358	8,848,941	74.21

* percents from the testing dataset.

Ordering the models from the best to the worst is not very difficult, however, it should be noted that the differences between models are not even remotely the same. For this reason, we join models with similar results into groups. As stated before *10_million_passwords* produces the best results, but *rockyou* does not lag far behind. The effect size shows that they do in fact produce very similar results. Additionally, as was shown in Figure 4 *rockyou* is the most likely to calculate the strength of any passwords. These two models we would therefore classify as very good. Not so good but still very decent are the models *phpbb, tuscl, uniqpass_preview, hotmail*, and *singles_org*. All of these are very similar to each other, as can be seen from effect sizes. While their dissimilarity to the two best models is not big enough to be of small effect, they are quite close. The same cannot be said for *10K_most_common* and *myspace*, which have a meaningful difference to the two best models. Consequently, these two models are considered not good, although they are still much better than the last group. Models *faithwriters, passwords*, and *scribd* are significantly different from any preceding model. This is especially true for the *scribd* model, which is the only one that has medium and large differences from other models (including *faithwriters* and *passwords*).

Table 7 is a summary of the big Table A1 (see Appendix B) that includes all the results mentioned and can be found in the appendix. Of the 66 comparisons between the models, in 35 cases the difference was determined to be too small to be of any importance. The remaining differences are large enough to not be ignored. Of those, 20 were classified as small, 9 as medium and 2 as large differences. The table also shows the difference in CL between classes.

Table 7. Summary of Pairwise Comparison.

Effect	#	Mean r Value	Mean CL
Trivial	35	0.044	53.14%
Small	20	0.154	61.01%
Medium	9	0.426	82.12%
Large	2	0.523	87.01%

6. Discussion

Now that we have all the data, we can look for the possible reasons, why some password datasets might be better for constructing a good Markov model.

The first dataset property that could cause differences is its size. Intuitively one might assume, bigger learning set of passwords would produce a better end result. Considering the two biggest password datasets (*rockyou* and *10_million_passwords*) managed to construct the two best models this might look very plausible. However, the *rockyou* model, even though it was constructed from more than 40% bigger dataset, is still not better than the *10_million_passwords* model. Furthermore, the third best model (*phpbb*), which was only marginally worse than the two best, was constructed from a dataset more than fifty times smaller than the *10_million_passwords* and was only fifth in the overall size, while the third largest dataset (*passwords*) created the second worst model. This leads us to believe that while the size is important, the quality of the dataset is also important. The increase in dataset size also seems to have a diminishing return on the final quality of the model. This would mean that the biggest datasets do not necessarily make a better model, while on the other hand, smaller datasets have a stronger possibility to build a weaker model. In our case, this is seen from the fact that none of the models built from the four smallest datasets is amongst the five best models. The only considerably larger datasets that performed worse have other major problems.

When looking at the password composition of models some additional reasons for the success or failure of models can be found. The easiest password property to look at is the mean length (Table 2). Password length does not appear to have any effect on the model's success. Models constructed from datasets with higher average password length can be found among the best and worst. For example, the *10_million_passwords model*, which was shown to be the best, has the fifth shortest average password length, while *rockyou* the second best model was constructed from a dataset with the second highest average password length.

The composition of the passwords themselves is somewhat more difficult to compare, but with the help of the frequency distribution of characters in datasets (see Section 5.1) and the table on password information (Table 2) some distinct differences between datasets and the resulting models become clear.

A quick overview of character frequencies shows that numerical characters are very common in the majority of datasets, while upper-case letters are fairly uncommon. This could be an added reason why datasets with proportionally smaller amount of numerical characters perform reasonably badly (*10K_most_common*, *faithwriters*, *scribd* and partially *singles_org*) and why datasets with no upper-case letters can do reasonably well (i.e., *uniqpass_preview*).

Uniqpass_preview is the third biggest dataset by the number of characters (*passwords* dataset has more passwords but they are shorter). It has decent amounts of lower-case letters, numbers and compared to other datasets it has proportionally more special characters (more than 15% of all passwords contain a special character). Even though it has zero upper-case letters the constructed model was the fifth best. This means that the model cannot calculate the strength of any password with any number of upper-case letters. As a consequence, the model cannot calculate the strength of a fair amount of passwords (7th place overall). More ceiling values would normally mean a bad result, but a healthy number of lower-case, numeric and special characters gives this model the ability to rigidly asses all other passwords. *Uniqpass_preview* is the best model built from a dataset that is completely missing a major group of characters. A helping factor for this is no doubt also the fact that the dataset was constructed for password cracking (although here we use only a part of it) and is not just a collection of random passwords.

The four datasets that were the best have one thing in common. Frequency distributions of characters show that they all have reasonable amounts (enough for the Markov model to make connections between the majority of characters) of all types of characters. The most variety in the character set definitely belongs to the *rockyou* dataset. This is the most likely reason that this dataset is the most reliable at being able to calculate the strength of any password. The *10_million_passwords* dataset is similar to *rockyou* in the distribution of characters, but it does not have such a wide range of characters. Consequently, it is better at measuring more common passwords (constructed from more commonly used characters), while it somewhat lags behind the *rockyou* in the ability to calculate the strength of any password. Third (*phpbb*) and fourth (*tuscl*) best models were constructed from a lot smaller datasets and therefore cannot compare with the first two in the number of characters, but the amount of characters here is still enough for Markov models to not have problems building connections between them and from the frequency distributions of characters it is visible that proportions between different types of character are still very similar. The built Markov models are therefore probably also very similar, resulting in password strength estimation very much alike to those of *10_million_passwords* and *rockyou* even though they were built from considerably smaller datasets.

Hotmail and *singles_org* datasets both have a good amount of lower-case letters and comparable, although a small, number of upper-case letters. *Hotmail* also has proportionally more numeric characters and it has some special characters while *singles_org* has none. As a result, *hotmail* is better at calculating the password strength for any password and is also marginally better overall. *Hotmail* model is in 6th place, while *single_org* is in 7th.

10K_most_common is the 3rd smallest dataset, but with the shortest average password length, it contains an even smaller amount of characters than the smallest dataset-*faithwriters*. It has no upper-case letters, practically no special characters and the proportion of numeric characters is small when compared to the best models. More than 83% of all passwords in *10K_most_common* consist exclusively of lower-case letters. Frequency analysis of characters would suggest *faithwriters* to be a better dataset because it contains upper-case letters and more numeric characters, however, the end results do not support this presumption. Contents of the two datasets reveal that *faithwrites* has many passwords with religious motives (the dataset was obtained from a religious forum) consequently suffering from a large number of very similar passwords. A dataset consisting of related passwords creates a Markov model that is not good at estimating the strength of any other passwords. The *10K_most_common* dataset on the other hand is a collection of common passwords. The dataset is filtered and does not contain recurrence of any passwords. Because it contains the most likely passwords it also contains at least some of the most likely combinations of letters. As a result, the *10K_most_common* model is very successful despite its size and absence of upper-case letters.

The *myspace* dataset contains a varied collection of characters, but the special characters and the upper-case letters are sparse. The constructed model is therefore fairly successful in estimating the strength of any passwords (5th best), but passwords containing any of the special characters or the upper-case letters, have their strength rated fairly high because based on the dataset they are very uncommon. These high values cause the model to be ranked fairly low (9th place). This phenomenon can also be seen in descriptive statistics (Table 5). *Myspace* results have a small mean value (because results do not contain many 4000) but a relatively high median (because on average the calculated password strength is larger).

Passwords dataset looks, on the basis of all the metrics that we have measured like it should produce a good model. The only metric where it slightly stands out is the number of numeric characters. More than 31% all characters in the dataset are numeric, but this is not far from the 25% in *rockyou* and *10_million_passwords*. Nevertheless, the results of the statistics test show that the model is the second worst model of them all. To find a reason for this we had to look at the passwords themselves. Although the dataset is fairly big, we have found that the variety of passwords in the dataset is very low. Many of the passwords are just a variation of the same password or they share a word root. As a result, the Markov model learns that those character combinations are very common (because they are often repeated in the dataset), which would be a good thing, if there was not for many other valid combinations of characters that the model never sees, and therefore cannot calculate the strength for. *Passwords* is a very good example of a dataset that on paper looks as it should perform well, but in reality, is not good at all.

In our research, the worst dataset to construct a Markov model from was *scribd*. From the frequency distribution of the characters, we can see why. Upper case, numeric, and special characters are all very rare in the dataset, especially considering that the dataset is not small. As a result, the model could not estimate the strength for almost three-quarters of the passwords in the testing dataset.

As we have seen with multiple modes the model's ability to calculate the password's strength for any password and its quality rating (how good did the model turn out to be) seem to be strongly connected. Models that were able to calculate more password strengths (Figure 4) ended up being marked as better models. It is self-evident that good models should be able to calculate the strength of any password, while the models that struggle to estimate the strength of the majority of passwords are not good. This only further substantiates our claim that multiple Markov models are needed in order to construct a proper password checker.

6.1. Solidity of the Experiment

The first-order Markov model is commonly used for password cracking [10] since it is the most easier to implement and requires less computational power. Higher order models require more computational power, depending on the level of the model (i.e., the level of history that the model keeps track of). One could argue that Markov models of higher order can be more accurate at calculating probabilities since they take into account previous states of the model, which in turn could lead to a more accurate calculation of password strength [9,16]. The counterargument to a such statement would be the fact that selecting the order of the model is a more challenging issue than it may seem. Markov models of higher order can give us a greater accuracy as long as we have enough data. Every order we add to the Markov model gives us A times more parameters, where A is the number of states (in first-order Markov model A is basically the set of distinct characters identified in the training dataset), i.e., an exponential explosion in a number of parameters. This means, roughly, that we need exponentially greater amounts of data to properly train the model. At some point, the model will overfit the data and it will run the risk of sparsity [14]. Sparsity means that transition probabilities are being computed from very small count numbers, which may be noisy [13]. So, the proper order of the model would be the one that fits the data. Furthermore, creating a higher order model can be more difficult and expensive. In the worst-case scenario, where the order k is exceeding the maximum password length, the model would explicitly list the probability of occurrence of each possible password [9]. This would require a larger training set and more storage capabilities since the required space is of the order of $|A|^k$, where $|A|$ is the size of the character set [9].

For the purposes of our study, we used first-order Markov model mainly because of the above arguments-the possibility of data sparsity or data overfit if we use the wrong order of the model. In order to back up our decision, we conducted a short experiment where we compared first-order and second-order Markov models. We were interested in the differences in the outcome of the first-order and the second-order Markov model. The models were trained on the same password datasets in order to provide consistency and statistical conditions. We used Equation (1) for calculating the probabilities of the passwords. The models were trained on datasets described in Section 4.2 and then tested on the same testing dataset (containing randomly selected passwords that do not appear in the training datasets).

Wilcoxon Signed Rank was used for testing the differences between the results from the first-order and the second-order Markov model. Wilcoxon Signed Rank test is a non-parametric statistical test that is used to compare two sets of scores that come from the same participants. This test was selected, because the outputs of both models are not normally distributed (Kolmogorov-Smirnov test indicated that the differences in the scores from both models do not follow a normal distribution, $D = 0.407, D = 0.364, D = 0.388, D = 0.434, D = 0.483, D = 0.377, D = 0.504, D = 0.501, D = 0.523, D = 0.425, D = 0.485, D = 0.446, p < 0.001$).

In only five out of twelve cases test results show statistically significant differences between the median of differences between the two models, with $Z = -14.084, Z = -227.664, Z = -386.435, Z = -348.423, Z = -736.736, p < 0.001$. In these cases we reject the null hypothesis, stating that "the median of differences between first-order and second-order equals 0" confirming that there are statistical differences between the medians of differences provided by both models. Consequently, in the other seven cases, we retain the null hypotheses (i.e., seven out of twelve cases showed no statistically significant differences).

The above tests show that the difference in outputs between the two Markov models with different orders is, in most cases, not statistically significantly different. Therefore, we argue that it is, without a doubt, important to analyse the dataset before selecting the order of the model. As long as one is not limited by the hardware and one is not facing data sparsity, one can use a higher order Markov model when necessary. Since our study is not directly related to what order of the model we use and the statistical tests showed no statistical differences in most of the cases, we decided on using first-order Markov model for our experiments.

6.2. Effectiveness of the Approach

So far we have analysed the output scores of the models and compared them with each other. Based on the statistical analysis of these scores we argued that multiple Markov models are needed in order to create an effective password checker for a wide range of passwords and that one universal dataset should not be used to train one Markov model if we want to have an effective password scoring tool. In this section, we test and prove the effectiveness of different models specified for scoring different groups of passwords. For that purpose, we performed an additional experiment as a continuation of our main experiment. The goal is to prove the effectiveness of our models for scoring passwords that are strong, medium, or weak. Furthermore, the universal Markov model was trained on one "ultimate" password dataset, which consists of multiple different password datasets put together. We then tested the cracking resistance of the passwords that our models and the universal model identified as strong, medium, or weak. We define the term *cracking resistance* as the ability of a password to resist the cracking attack-the longer the password resists the attack, the higher the password strength score.

6.2.1. Environment Setting

We tested the cracking resistance for 1500 of the best-ranked passwords from our testing dataset. We selected these passwords based on the score given by three of our models. We classified these passwords in the categories of *strong*, *medium* and *weak* in the following way: 500 of the best ranked passwords scored by our best-ranked model *10_million_passwords* were classified as *strong* passwords, 500 of the best ranked passwords scored by our middle-ranked model *hotmail* were classified as *medium* passwords, and 500 of the best ranked passwords scored by our worst-ranked model *scribd* were classified as *weak* passwords. We did a similar selection for the universal model: we selected the top 500 passwords that were scored by the universal model as *strong*, 500 that were scored as *medium*, and 500 that were scored as *weak*.

For testing the cracking resistance of the selected passwords we used Hashcat [34] and its abilities. Hashcat is an open-source tool (MIT License) and its functionalities are generally available. It can also be used in Markov mode for cracking passwords which is useful for our efficiency testing since the password guesses in Markov modes are built with the use of Markov models.

Since Hashcat works only on hashed data, we hashed the selected passwords with MD5 hashing algorithm, before we ran them through Hashcat. We performed three password cracking cycles-one for every category of passwords. In every cycle we ran the same sequence of password cracking techniques: (1) dictionary attack, (2) dictionary attack with additional mangling rules, and (3) Markov mode attack. The first password cracking technique is a basic dictionary attack, the second is a dictionary attack with additional mangling rules that are already implemented in Hashcat, while the third is a technique that is based on Markov models. It is important to note that for the dictionary-based password cracking techniques we used all our training files that we used to train our Markov models on.

We expected to crack all the weak and most of the medium passwords in a relatively short time, but for the strong passwords, we expected it would take a much longer time. For the purpose of this experiment we only need to prove that the passwords that our models identified as weak passwords can be cracked in a lot shorter period of time regarding the passwords that were identified as strong. Considering this, we decided to run all cracking techniques for the same amount of time-2 weeks for every password cracking technique-and count the number of cracked passwords from every password category. By analysing the number of cracked passwords from every category, within the same period of time, we can confirm whether those passwords are weak, medium or strong.

The last password cracking technique based on Markov models took more time to complete since the Markov model needs to be trained first. For training the model we used our best training dataset-*10_million_passwords*. Because of space and memory sparsity (the size of the final Markov file with password suggestions has grown to almost 350 GB), we let Hashcat work for 2 days and build the Markov model. We piped the generated results from the Markov model into Hashcat and performed the password cracking technique.

It is important to note that all parts (cycles) of the experiment were performed with the same technical equipment and in the same time period in order to preserve the continuity and the soundness of the experiment. We used Intel(R) Core(TM) i5-3550 processor on 3.30 GHz and 24 GB of RAM with 64-bit Windows 10 operating system.

6.2.2. Results

We started every password cracking cycle by running the passwords through Hashcat's dictionary attack process. The results of the cracking process for every cycle for the three different models are shown in Table 8.

Table 8. Password cracking results for the three different Markov models.

Password Category	Attacking Technique			Total
	Dictionary	Dictionary + Rules	Markov Mode	
Weak	462 (92.4%)	4 (0.8%)	/	466 (93.2%)
Medium	96 (19.2%)	150 (30%)	/	246 (49.2%)
Strong	2 (0.4%)	153 (30.6%)	/	155 (31%)

Table 9 shows the results of the cracking process for the universal Markov model.

Table 9. Password cracking results for the universal Markov model.

Password Category	Attacking Technique			Total
	Dictionary	Dictionary + Rules	Markov Mode	
Weak	10 (2%)	49 (4.8%)	/	59 (11.8%)
Medium	2 (0.4%)	25 (5%)	/	27 (5.4%)
Strong	1 (0.2%)	25 (5%)	/	26 (5.2%)

Multiple different models Expectedly, in the category of weak passwords we managed to crack almost all of the passwords. With the first dictionary attack, we managed to crack 462 weak passwords or 92.4%. Following, we used a dictionary attack with additional rules (these were mostly basic mangling rules) where we managed to crack additional 4 passwords (0.8%). Surprisingly, with the Markov mode, we didn't manage to crack any passwords. The first cracking cycle took one day to complete i.e., we managed to crack 466 (96.4%) weak passwords in just one day.

The second cycle of cracking passwords from the category of medium passwords gave even more promising results. With the basic dictionary attack we managed to crack only 96 medium passwords (19.2%) and with the second attack with additional mangling rules, we cracked additional 150 passwords (30%). In the second cycle we ended up with a total of 246 (49.2%) cracked medium passwords.

In the third and final cycle, we managed to crack 155 (31%) passwords that were identified as strong. We cracked the passwords with the dictionary attack followed by additional more complex mangling rules. The Markov mode attack did not manage to crack any of the strong passwords.

In the scope of this additional experiment with multiple different Markov models, we managed to crack overall 466 passwords from the weak category, 246 from the medium, and 155 from the category of strong passwords. As evident from the descriptive statistics of the results, our Markov models are able to distinguish between at least three different categories of passwords (i.e., strong, medium, or weak).

Universal model The situation with the universal Markov model was completely different. As we can see from Table 9 we managed to crack only 11.8% of the weak passwords. In the second and third cycle we cracked even fewer passwords: only 5.4% of the medium and 5.2% of the strong passwords. Most of the passwords were cracked with the dictionary attack with additional mangling rules. Surprisingly, with the Markov mode, we also didn't manage to crack any passwords. Overall, we cracked a total of 112 passwords out of 1500 selected. The number of cracked passwords with this approach is far lower than the other approach where we used three different Markov models. Even more, the number of cracked passwords between each category is almost the same, especially between the category of medium and strong passwords (27 and 26 accordingly). This gives the indication that the ultimate model has difficulties with categorizing medium and strong passwords and probably undergoes the "overfitting" process, where it can no longer distinguish between new passwords that are supposed to be strong and already known ones that are supposed to be weaker.

6.3. Ethical Considerations

Our results are from our Markov models that were trained on password datasets that are publicly and widely available. These datasets were originally collected through illegal cracking and phishing attacks. Some argue that such data should not be used by researchers because it can compromise the accounts and data of the users whose passwords were stolen. The passwords that we used were anonymised and did not contain any other data that could connect the password to its user and/or account. We use these datasets only to train our Markov models and not to use them as cracking datasets, for they do not contain any other information about the passwords (e.g., usernames or email addresses). We do strength analysis of plaintext passwords, not cracking hashed passwords which we could publish later and compromise the users and their accounts. Furthermore, since these password datasets have already been used in other research studies [9–12,15,18,19] and have been made public and easily available, using them in our research does not increase the harm to the victims. Still, there is a possibility that attackers will use these datasets as training sets for their cracking mechanisms, but since we use the datasets and our statistical analysis to improve the way password checkers work and to better assess the passwords' strength entered by the users, our use of them to assess passwords' strength and our results are more likely to be of practical use for the security and for the system administrators.

6.4. Limitations

When performing the experiments, we limit the number of states, i.e., the number of distinct characters that we search in the datasets and use in our models, to 224, coinciding with the set of ASCII characters from character code 32 to 255. This character set includes all characters from the extended ASCII table, except for the initial 32 characters which are basically unprintable control codes and are used to control peripherals such as printers.

It is necessary to note that when Markov models are used for password cracking they are usually used as an aid when dictionaries are exhausted and when the search space becomes very large. We assume that an average attacker would have access to password training sets that are as good and effective as the best of all our training sets. If Markov models are used the other way around (as a password scoring tool), one should do an analysis of the datasets similar to ours, in order to find the right way to combine the datasets and to create a more effective password scoring tool.

Furthermore, the datasets that we used in our research are publicly available datasets of passwords that were illegally collected. This increases the doubt that these datasets are partial (only a part of larger datasets that also contain stronger passwords) and biased datasets that contain only the most common and weaker passwords that are easy to predict. Since these are publicly available datasets of previously compromised accounts, we can argue that future attackers can also use only the datasets that are available online in order to build their tool and strategy for an attack. This implies that a solution for password restriction based on multiple Markov models should be able to recognize and prevent the weak passwords from entering the system. The problem in information security are not strong passwords that are not yet cracked and leaked, but weak passwords that are publicly available. A good password checker should not let weak passwords through. Hence, our models should be able to recognize and assess these passwords as weak. This implies that our models should be trained on weak, biased and similar passwords that are available for most of the attackers.

6.5. Practical Use of the Approach

Our approach can be used in a typical Web-based password-protected service. A practical example of our approach follows:

The Markov model is represented by a Markov matrix that contains the conditional transitional probabilities (see Section 3) needed for calculating the password score. This matrix is stored and available on the server-side, while the actual password checker is available on the website (i.e., the client-side). On the client-side, the user enters the password in the password field. The password entered in plain text is then sent through a secure connection (HTTPS) to the server-side. On the server-side, the Markov matrix is used to calculate the score of the password. If the password is assessed as strong or very strong, the password is hashed, salted and stored in the database. Otherwise, a warning is presented to the user, stating that the password is too weak to be accepted by the system and it requires a change. Additional instructions on how to create a secure and strong password are displayed. The levels of password strength are defined on the basis of the scores of all the passwords in all training datasets. Basically, the solution can be used as an additional step at the server-side and there is no need for additional modification of the existing user interface (i.e., the website).

7. Conclusions

In this study, we explored the possibility of using Markov models as a basis for creating a more effective password checker. The idea itself brought out the question of whether one model is sufficient if we want our password checker to be able to properly calculate the strength of a variety of passwords with different characteristics. Successively, the objective of this study was to compare different Markov models and find out whether there are significant differences between them. Our goal was to find out whether different Markov models will provide statistically different results when tested on the same password dataset, which would lead us to the answer to our main question. We used publicly available password datasets that we randomized and divided into training and testing datasets. We explored the results of every model and compared them with each other in order to investigate the statistical significance in the scores from different models. We also explored the effect of the datasets size, the average password length and other characteristics on the success of the model.

We find that of the approximate 12 million passwords used in the testing dataset, almost 2.55 million passwords failed to be calculated by at least one model. We also find that every single model had difficulties calculating the strength of some passwords and that every password could be processed by at least a few models. Hence our assumption that the use of multiple models is required in order to be able to do strength calculations for a wide range of passwords.

Overall, the results and the statistical tests demonstrate that there are significant differences in medians between all models. Size of dataset seems to be a big determining factor in the final quality of the model, up to a certain point-increasing the dataset size (number of characters) afterwards has a diminishing return. The size itself will do no good, without the right composition, the right and sufficient amount of numbers, lower and upper-case letters, and special characters.

Based on the presented results, we came to a few major conclusions:

- different Markov models (trained on different password datasets) provided statistically different results when tested on the same password dataset,
- more diverse datasets are needed to be able to calculate the strength of as many passwords as possible, since one "universal" model, trained on one "universal" dataset is less effective at classifying passwords in different categories (i.e., weak, medium, strong),
- the passwords in the dataset are also important. They should be diverse and should not repeat in any significant way,
- different Markov models of 1st and 2nd order, in most cases, give no statistically different results,
- overall, Markov models can be used as a basis for constructing a more effective password checker that uses multiple different and specific Markov models, which could be more effective if we want to cover a wider range of passwords.

The fact that different training datasets can lead to statistically different password scores, leads us to the conclusion that it is very important what kind of dataset is used to train the Markov models. We argue that one universal dataset should not be used to train one Markov model if we want to have an effective password scoring tool. Our results give the indication that the use of multiple models is required in order to be able to do strength calculations for a wide range of passwords. We further argue that if a Markov model would be used for assessing password strength, then it should be constructed and trained on a particular dataset of passwords, so it can be more efficient for that particular password group. For this manner, multiple different Markov models can be used in combination (depending on the type of the password), so the password scoring tool can effectively cover a wider range of passwords. In other words, we select the one model that is trained on a dataset of passwords that closely resembles the password creation policy.

We believe that the results of this study can be of certain aid for future password checkers, that would be based on multiple Markov models, where each is tailored for a particular password group(s). Such a password checker can easily and more effectively check the probability of a given password to be chosen by the user.

Author Contributions: Conceptualization, V.T. and B.B.; Formal analysis, M.K.; Methodology, V.T.; Resources, M.H.; Software, V.T.; Supervision, B.B.; Validation, M.H. and B.B.; Writing—original draft, V.T.; Writing—review and editing, M.K., M.H. and B.B. All authors have read and agreed to the published version of the manuscript.

Funding: The authors acknowledge the financial support from the Slovenian Research Agency (Research Core funding No. P2-0057) and the European Union's Horizon 2020 Research and Innovation Program under the CyberSec4Europe project (Grant Agreement No. 830929).

Institutional Review Board Statement: Not applicable.

Informed Consent Statement: Not applicable.

Data Availability Statement: No new data were created or analysed in this study. Data sharing is not applicable to this article.

Conflicts of Interest: The authors declare no conflict of interest.

Abbreviations

The following abbreviations are used in this manuscript:

PCFG   Probabilistic Context-Free Grammars
PSM   Password Strength Meter
SLP   Single Layer Perceptrons
MLP   Multy Layer Perceptrons

Appendix A. Character Frequency Distribution

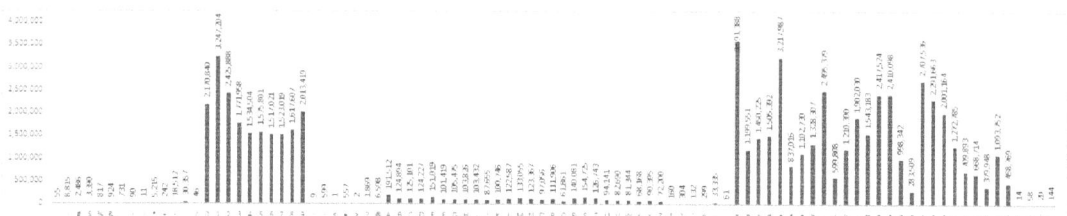

Figure A1. Frequency Distribution of Characters-Dataset: 10_million_passwords.

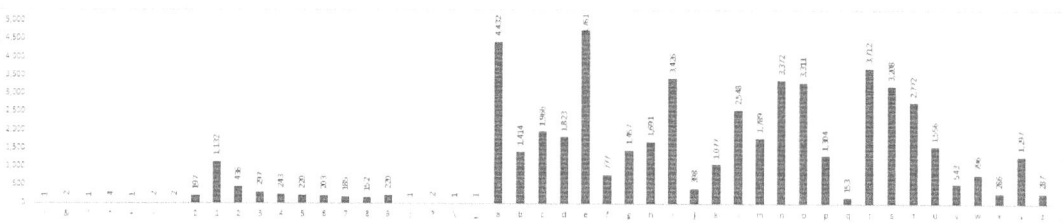

Figure A2. Frequency Distribution of Characters-Dataset: 10k_most_common.

Appl. Sci. **2021**, *11*, 9406

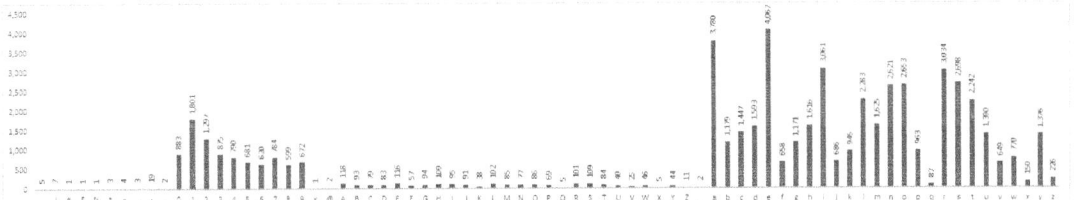

Figure A3. Frequency Distribution of Characters-Dataset: faithwriters.

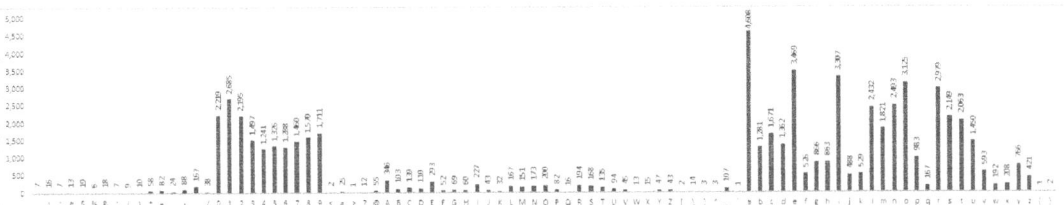

Figure A4. Frequency Distribution of Characters-Dataset: hotmail.

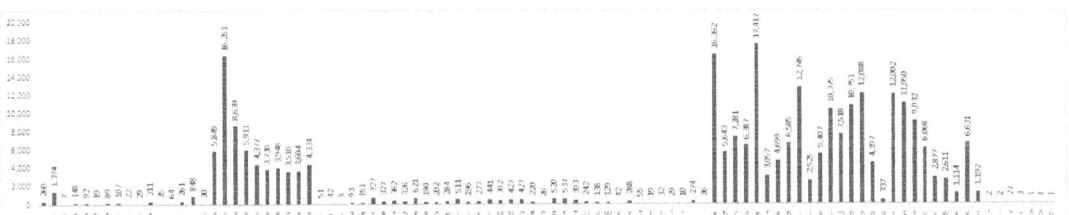

Figure A5. Frequency Distribution of Characters-Dataset: myspace.

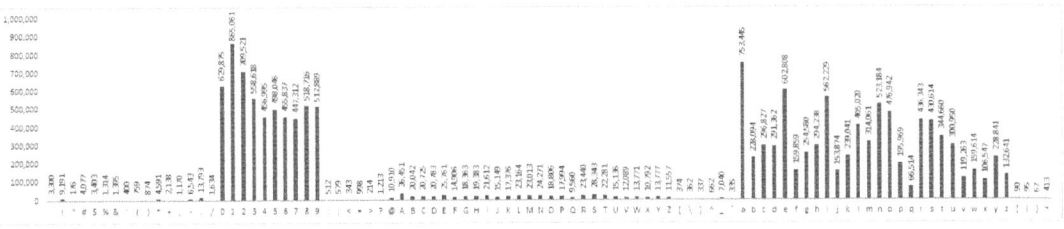

Figure A6. Frequency Distribution of Characters-Dataset: passwords.

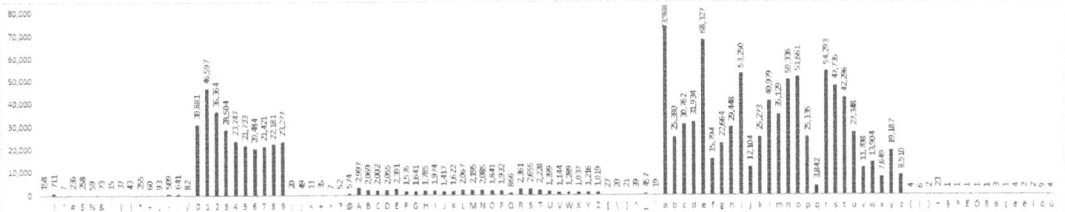

Figure A7. Frequency Distribution of Characters-Dataset: phpbb.

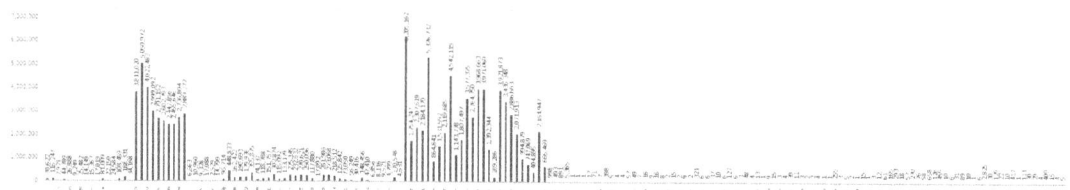

Figure A8. Frequency Distribution of Characters-Dataset: rockyou.

Figure A9. Frequency Distribution of Characters-Dataset: SCRIBD.

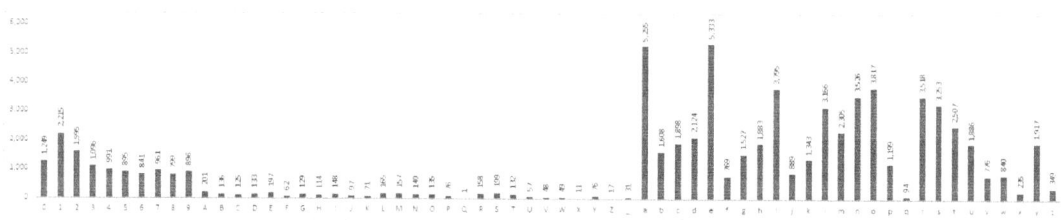

Figure A10. Frequency Distribution of Characters-Dataset: singles_org.

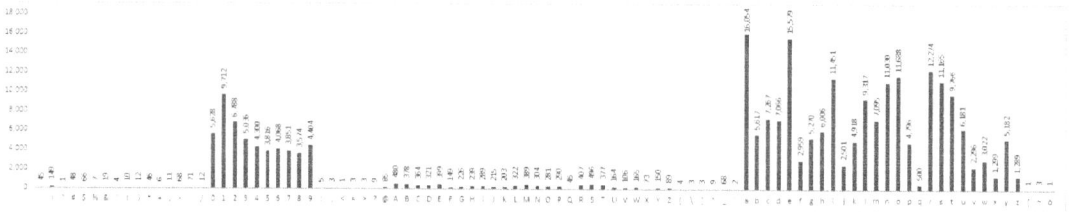

Figure A11. Frequency Distribution of Characters-Dataset: tuscl.

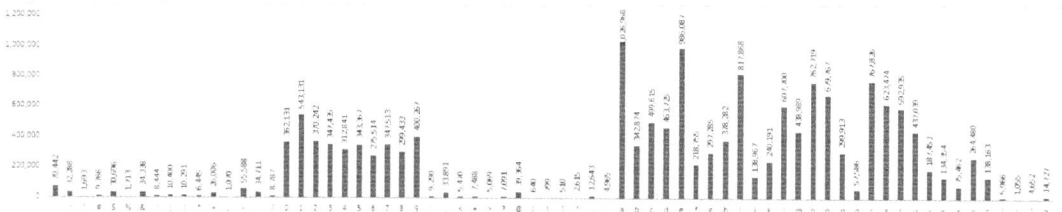

Figure A12. Frequency Distribution of Characters-Dataset: uniqpass_preview.

Appendix B. Pairwise Comparison of the Models

Table A1. Pairwise Comparison of the Models.

Model 1	Model 2	Z	p-Value	r	Effect	CL
10k_most_common	10_million_passwords	−533.29	<0.000005	0.1092	Small	57.73%
10k_most_common	hotmail	−97.42	<0.000005	0.0199	Trivial	51.43%
10k_most_common	phpbb	−170.25	<0.000005	0.0349	Trivial	52.47%
10k_most_common	rockyou	−466.12	<0.000005	0.0954	Trivial	56.75%
10k_most_common	singles_org	−54.90	<0.000005	0.0112	Trivial	50.81%
10k_most_common	tuscl	−135.87	<0.000005	0.0278	Trivial	51.99%
10k_most_common	uniqpass	−117.42	<0.000005	0.0240	Trivial	51.73%
faithwriters	10_million_passwords	−1075.77	<0.000005	0.2203	Small	65.59%
faithwriters	10k_most_common	−474.36	<0.000005	0.0971	Trivial	57.15%
faithwriters	hotmail	−641.63	<0.000005	0.1314	Small	59.47%
faithwriters	myspace	−493.29	<0.000005	0.1010	Small	57.25%
faithwriters	phpbb	−757.29	<0.000005	0.1551	Small	60.98%
faithwriters	rockyou	−1026.99	<0.000005	0.2103	Small	64.87%
faithwriters	singles_org	−579.74	<0.000005	0.1187	Small	58.61%
faithwriters	tuscl	−690.55	<0.000005	0.1414	Small	60.13%
faithwriters	uniqpass	−645.65	<0.000005	0.1322	Small	59.54%
hotmail	10_million_passwords	−473.38	<0.000005	0.0969	Trivial	56.86%
hotmail	phpbb	−44.39	<0.000005	0.0091	Trivial	50.64%
hotmail	rockyou	−397.70	<0.000005	0.0814	Trivial	55.76%
hotmail	tuscl	−32.67	<0.000005	0.0067	Trivial	50.48%
hotmail	uniqpass	−26.93	<0.000005	0.0055	Trivial	50.39%
myspace	10_million_passwords	−685.35	<0.000005	0.1403	Small	59.93%
myspace	10k_most_common	−64.28	<0.000005	0.0132	Trivial	50.94%
myspace	hotmail	−210.92	<0.000005	0.0432	Trivial	53.07%
myspace	phpbb	−284.03	<0.000005	0.0582	Trivial	54.11%
myspace	rockyou	−624.40	<0.000005	0.1279	Small	59.04%
myspace	singles_org	−173.66	<0.000005	0.0356	Trivial	52.53%
myspace	tuscl	−255.10	<0.000005	0.0522	Trivial	53.71%
myspace	uniqpass	−232.11	<0.000005	0.0475	Trivial	53.38%
passwords	10_million_passwords	−1154.46	<0.000005	0.2364	Small	66.73%
passwords	10k_most_common	−552.33	<0.000005	0.1131	Small	58.42%
passwords	faithwriters	−142.85	<0.000005	0.0293	Trivial	52.20%
passwords	hotmail	−739.00	<0.000005	0.1513	Small	60.99%

Table A1. *Cont.*

Model 1	Model 2	Z	p-Value	r	Effect	CL
passwords	myspace	−631.29	<0.000005	0.1293	Small	59.29%
passwords	phpbb	−883.09	<0.000005	0.1808	Small	62.81%
passwords	rockyou	−1106.78	<0.000005	0.2266	Small	66.03%
passwords	singles_org	−680.09	<0.000005	0.1393	Small	60.18%
passwords	tuscl	−783.45	<0.000005	0.1604	Small	61.52%
passwords	uniqpass	−749.46	<0.000005	0.1535	Small	61.15%
phpbb	10_million_passwords	−452.18	<0.000005	0.0926	Trivial	56.55%
phpbb	rockyou	−374.77	<0.000005	0.0767	Trivial	55.43%
rockyou	10_million_passwords	−85.05	<0.000005	0.0174	Trivial	51.23%
scribd	10_million_passwords	−2563.90	<0.000005	0.5250	Large	87.18%
scribd	10k_most_common	−1978.05	<0.000005	0.4050	Medium	81.69%
scribd	faithwriters	−1719.88	<0.000005	0.3522	Medium	78.20%
scribd	hotmail	−2214.09	<0.000005	0.4534	Medium	83.74%
scribd	myspace	−2228.82	<0.000005	0.4564	Medium	83.38%
scribd	passwords	−1469.32	<0.000005	0.3009	Medium	75.33%
scribd	phpbb	−2430.38	<0.000005	0.4977	Medium	85.32%
scribd	rockyou	−2542.95	<0.000005	0.5207	Large	86.83%
scribd	singles_org	−2149.37	<0.000005	0.4401	Medium	83.17%
scribd	tuscl	−2314.10	<0.000005	0.4739	Medium	84.46%
scribd	uniqpass	−2213.08	<0.000005	0.4532	Medium	83.81%
singles_org	10_million_passwords	−488.33	<0.000005	0.0999	Trivial	57.07%
singles_org	hotmail	−29.83	<0.000005	0.0061	Trivial	50.44%
singles_org	phpbb	−82.63	<0.000005	0.0169	Trivial	51.20%
singles_org	rockyou	−414.37	<0.000005	0.0849	Trivial	56.00%
singles_org	tuscl	−55.45	<0.000005	0.0114	Trivial	50.81%
singles_org	uniqpass	−52.65	<0.000005	0.0108	Trivial	50.77%
tuscl	10_million_passwords	−425.79	<0.000005	0.0872	Trivial	56.17%
tuscl	phpbb	−22.96	<0.000005	0.0047	Trivial	50.33%
tuscl	rockyou	−363.60	<0.000005	0.0745	Trivial	55.26%
uniqpass	10_million_passwords	−434.23	<0.000005	0.0889	Trivial	56.29%
uniqpass	phpbb	−26.70	<0.000005	0.0055	Trivial	50.39%
uniqpass	rockyou	−362.49	<0.000005	0.0742	Trivial	55.25%
uniqpass	tuscl	−13.70	<0.000005	0.0028	Trivial	50.20%

References

1. Loch, K.D.; Carr, H.H.; Warkentin, M.E. Threats to Information Systems: Today's Reality, Yesterday's Understanding. *MIS Q.* **1992**, *16*, 173–186. [CrossRef]
2. Tzong-Chen, W.; Hung-Sung, S. Authenticating passwords over an insecure channel. *Comput. Secur.* **1996**, *15*, 431–439. [CrossRef]

3. Creese, S.; Hodges, D.; Jamison-Powell, S.; Whitty, M. Relationships between Password Choices, Perceptions of Risk and Security Expertise. In *Human Aspects of Information Security, Privacy, and Trust*; Lecture Notes in Computer Science; Marinos, L., Askoxylakis, I., Eds.; Springer: Berlin/Heidelberg, Germany, 2013; Volume 8030, pp. 80–89.
4. Morris, R.; Thompson, K. Password Security: A Case History. *Commun. ACM* **1979**, *22*, 594–597. [CrossRef]
5. Bishop, M.; Klein, D.V. Improving system security via proactive password checking. *Comput. Secur.* **1995**, *14*, 233–249. [CrossRef]
6. Yan, J.J. A Note on Proactive Password Checking. In Proceedings of the 2001 Workshop on New Security Paradigms, Cloudcroft, NM, USA, 10 September 2001; pp. 127–135.
7. Proctor, R.W.; Lien, M.C.; Vu, K.P.L.; Schultz, E.E.; Salvendy, G. Improving computer security for authentication of users: influence of proactive password restrictions. *Behav. Res. Methods Instrum. Comput.* **2002**, *34*, 163–169. [CrossRef] [PubMed]
8. Vu, K.P.L.; Proctor, R.W.; Bhargav-Spantzel, A.; Tai, B.L.B.; Cook, J.; Eugene Schultz, E. Improving Password Security and Memorability to Protect Personal and Organizational Information. *Int. J. Hum.-Comput. Stud.* **2007**, *65*, 744–757. [CrossRef]
9. Dell' Amico, M.; Michiardi, P.; Roudier, Y. Password Strength: An Empirical Analysis. In Proceedings of the 2010 Proceedings IEEE INFOCOM, San Diego, CA, USA, 14–19 March 2010; pp. 1–9.
10. Narayanan, A.; Shmatikov, V. Fast Dictionary Attacks on Passwords Using Time-space Tradeoff. In Proceedings of the 12th ACM Conference on Computer and Communications Security CCS '05, Alexandria, VA, USA, 7–11 November 2005; pp. 364–372.
11. Marechal, S. Advances in password cracking. *J. Comput. Virol.* **2008**, *4*, 73–81. [CrossRef]
12. Castelluccia, C.; Dürmuth, M.; Perito, D. Adaptive password-strength meters from Markov models. In Proceedings of the 19th Annual Network and Distributed System Security Symposium, Hilton, San Diego, 5–8 February 2012; Volume 2012.
13. Ma, J.; Yang, W.; Luo, M.; Li, N. A Study of Probabilistic Password Models. In Proceedings of the 2014 IEEE Symposium on Security and Privacy, Berkeley, CA, USA, 18–21 May 2014; IEEE Computer Society: Washington, DC, USA, 2014; pp. 689–704.
14. Wang, D.; He, D.; Cheng, H.; Wang, P. fuzzyPSM: A New Password Strength Meter Using Fuzzy Probabilistic Context-Free Grammars. In Proceedings of the 2016 46th Annual IEEE/IFIP International Conference on Dependable Systems and Networks (DSN), Toulouse, France, 28 June–1 July 2016; pp. 595–606.
15. Galbally, J.; Coisel, I.; Sanchez, I. A probabilistic framework for improved password strength metrics. In Proceedings of the 2014 International Carnahan Conference on Security Technology (ICCST), Rome, Italy, 13–16 October 2014; pp. 1–6.
16. Wang, D.; Wang, P.; He, D.; Tian, Y. Birthday, Name and Bifacial-Security: Understanding Passwords of Chinese Web Users. In *Proceedings of the 28th USENIX Conference on Security Symposium (USENIX Security 19)*; USENIX Association: Santa Clara, CA, USA, 2019; pp. 1537–1554.
17. Egelman, S.; Sotirakopoulos, A.; Muslukhov, I.; Beznosov, K.; Herley, C. Does My Password Go Up to Eleven?: The Impact of Password Meters on Password Selection. In Proceedings of the SIGCHI Conference on Human Factors in Computing Systems, Paris, France, 27 April–2 May 2013; pp. 2379–2388.
18. Weir, M.; Aggarwal, S.; Collins, M.; Stern, H. Testing metrics for password creation policies by attacking large sets of revealed passwords. In Proceedings of the 17th ACM Conference on Computer and Communications Security-CCS '10, Chicago, IL, USA, 4–8 October, 2010 ACM: New York, NY, USA, 2010; p. 162.
19. Weir, M.; Aggarwal, S.; de Medeiros, B.; Glodek, B. Password Cracking Using Probabilistic Context-Free Grammars. In Proceedings of the 2009 30th IEEE Symposium on Security and Privacy, Oakland, CA, USA, 17–20 May 2009; pp. 391–405.
20. Houshmand, S.; Aggarwal, S.; Flood, R. Next Gen PCFG Password Cracking. *IEEE Trans. Inf. Forensics Secur.* **2015**, *10*, 1776–1791. [CrossRef]
21. John the Ripper Password Cracker. Available online: https://www.openwall.com/john/ (accessed on 16 April 2019).
22. Sutskever, I.; Martens, J.; Hinton, G. Generating Text with Recurrent Neural Networks. In Proceedings of the 28th International Conference on International Conference on Machine Learning Omnipress ICML'11, Washington, DC, USA, 28 June–2 July 2011; pp. 1017–1024.
23. Graves, A. Generating Sequences With Recurrent Neural Networks. *arXiv* **2013**, arXiv:cs.NE/1308.0850.
24. Ciaramella, A.; D'Arco, P.; Santis, A.D.; Galdi, C.; Tagliaferri, R. Neural Network Techniques for Proactive Password Checking. *IEEE Trans. Dependable Secur. Comput.* **2006**, *3*, 327–339. [CrossRef]
25. Melicher, W.; Ur, B.; Segreti, S.M.; Komanduri, S.; Bauer, L.; Christin, N.; Cranor, L.F. Fast, Lean, and Accurate: Modeling Password Guessability Using Neural Networks. In Proceedings of the 25th USENIX Security Symposium (USENIX Security 16). USENIX Association, Austin, TX, USA, 10–12 August 2016; pp. 175–191.
26. Rabiner, L.R. A tutorial on hidden Markov models and selected applications in speech recognition. *Proc. IEEE* **1989**, *77*, 257–286. [CrossRef]
27. Passwords. 2015. Available online: https://wiki.skullsecurity.org/Passwords/ (accessed on 10 March 2019).
28. Today I Am Releasing Ten Million Passwords. 2015. Available online: https://xato.net/today-i-am-releasing-ten-million-passwords-b6278bbe7495 (accessed on 15 March 2019).
29. Large Password List: Free Download Dictionary File for Password Cracking. 2011. Available online: https://breakthesecurity.cysecurity.org/2011/12/large-password-list-free-download-dictionary-file-for-password-cracking.html (accessed on 16 March 2019).
30. 10,000 Top Passwords. 2011. Available online: https://xato.net/10-000-top-passwords-6d6380716fe0 (accessed 16 March 2019).
31. Voyiatzis, A.G.; Fidas, C.A.; Serpanos, D.N.; Avouris, N.M. An Empirical Study on the Web Password Strength in Greece. In Proceedings of the 2011 15th Panhellenic Conference on Informatics, Kastoria, Greece, 30 September–2 October 2011.

32. Zezschwitz, E.; Luca, A.; Hussmann, H. Survival of the Shortest: A Retrospective Analysis of Influencing Factors on Password Composition. In *Human-Computer Interaction—INTERACT 2013 SE-28*; Lecture Notes in Computer Science; Kotzé, P., Marsden, G., Lindgaard, G., Wesson, J., Winckler, M., Eds.; Springer: Berlin/Heidelberg, Germany, 2013; Volume 8119, pp. 460–467.
33. Cohen, J. {CHAPTER} 1-The Concepts of Power Analysis. In *Statistical Power Analysis for the Behavioral Sciences (Revised Edition)*, Revised Edition ed.; Cohen, J., Ed.; Academic Press: Cambridge, MA, USA, 1977; pp. 1–17.
34. Hashcat, Advanced Password Recovery. Available online: https://hashcat.net/wiki/ (accessed on 20 April 2019).

Article

Technique for Evaluating the Security of Relational Databases Based on the Enhanced Clements–Hoffman Model

Vitalii Yesin [1], Mikolaj Karpinski [2,*], Maryna Yesina [1,*], Vladyslav Vilihura [1] and Stanislaw A. Rajba [2]

[1] Department of Security of Information Systems and Technologies, Faculty of Computer Science, V. Karazin National University of Kharkiv, 61022 Kharkiv, Ukraine; v.i.yesin@karazin.ua (V.Y.); viligura93@gmail.com (V.V.)
[2] Department of Computer Science and Automatics, Faculty of Mechanical Engineering and Computer Science, University of Bielsko-Biala, 43-309 Bielsko-Biala, Poland; rajbas@ath.bielsko.pl
* Correspondence: mkarpinski@ath.bielsko.pl (M.K.); m.v.yesina@karazin.ua (M.Y.)

Abstract: Obtaining convincing evidence of database security, as the basic corporate resource, is extremely important. However, in order to verify the conclusions about the degree of security, it must be measured. To solve this challenge, the authors of the paper enhanced the Clements–Hoffman model, determined the integral security metric and, on this basis, developed a technique for evaluating the security of relational databases. The essence of improving the Clements–Hoffmann model is to expand it by including a set of object vulnerabilities. Vulnerability is considered as a separate objectively existing category. This makes it possible to evaluate both the likelihood of an unwanted incident and the database security as a whole more adequately. The technique for evaluating the main components of the security barriers and the database security as a whole, proposed by the authors, is based on the theory of fuzzy sets and risk. As an integral metric of database security, the reciprocal of the total residual risk is used, the constituent components of which are presented in the form of certain linguistic variables. In accordance with the developed technique, the authors presented the results of a quantitative evaluation of the effectiveness of the protection of databases built on the basis of the schema with the universal basis of relations and designed in accordance with the traditional technology of relational databases.

Keywords: security; security model; security measure; security evaluation; database

Citation: Yesin, V.; Karpinski, M.; Yesina, M.; Vilihura, V.; Rajba, S.A. Technique for Evaluating the Security of Relational Databases Based on the Enhanced Clements–Hoffman Model. *Appl. Sci.* **2021**, *11*, 11175. https://doi.org/10.3390/app112311175

Academic Editors: Gianluca Lax and Antonia Russo

Received: 10 October 2021
Accepted: 23 November 2021
Published: 25 November 2021

Publisher's Note: MDPI stays neutral with regard to jurisdictional claims in published maps and institutional affiliations.

Copyright: © 2021 by the authors. Licensee MDPI, Basel, Switzerland. This article is an open access article distributed under the terms and conditions of the Creative Commons Attribution (CC BY) license (https://creativecommons.org/licenses/by/4.0/).

1. Introduction

The growth of Big Data and the vision of a data-driven world opens up many interesting opportunities, while simultaneously revealing many unresolved problems [1,2]. In particular, the new era of Big Data, which involved many researchers in the "data management game" and forced them to abandon the usual ways of designing, developing and implementing data management solutions, has exacerbated the problem of ensuring data security, since interest in the information circulating inside information systems (IS) has increased not only from legitimate users and owners, but also from attackers. For the latter, databases and data warehouses, as the most important information resources, are some of the most vulnerable and attractive elements of the IS. Security is one of the most important characteristics of the quality of the IS as a whole [3], and databases (DBs), as their main component, in particular. In this regard, the presence of an information protection system, as a complex of software, technical, cryptographic, organizational and other methods, means and measures that ensure the integrity, confidentiality, authenticity and availability of information in conditions of exposure to threats of a natural or artificial nature, has become an integral feature of any modern IS and databases. At the same time, in order to be able to verify the conclusions about the security level, it must be measured in some way.

By now there have been many major efforts to measure or evaluate security, including using the Trusted Computer System Evaluation Criteria (TCSEC) [4], Information Technology Security Evaluation Criteria (ITSEC) [5], the Systems Security Engineering Capability Maturity Model (SSE-CMM) [6], Common Criteria [7]. However, as stated by Jansen et al. [8], each attempt had only limited success. To measure the security of databases in [9], it was proposed to use such metrics as the metrics for losses that arise from security incidents, the database security control costs metric, and confidence metrics. However, specific mathematical expressions allowing to determine their quantitative value, as recommended by the performance measurement guide for information security [10], have not been given. It was also proposed to use a metric consisting of several levels to evaluate the security of databases [11,12]. A set of requirements that must be met by the system in order to achieve the corresponding level of security was listed for each level. However, this assessment was qualitative, although ranked. Neto et al. [13] proposed to evaluate the security of database configurations based on a survey of database administrators about the use of certain best practices in the system under study, followed by the definition of a security index. Developing this approach, the Oracle Corporation has developed a tool [14] to assess the security of its databases, which analyzes database configurations, users, their rights, security policies and determines where sensitive data are located in order to identify security risks and improve the state of database security. However, all of these decisions are usually based on intuition and are fragmented. In many cases, there is no integral metric to evaluate the security degree of the database as a whole.

In this connection, the objectives of our paper are:

(a) To present a technique for evaluating the security of relational databases, the security system of which is based on the provisions of the enhanced theoretical Clements–Hoffman model, and the degree of security is calculated on the basis of a determined integral quantitative metric. This metric is the reciprocal of the total residual risk associated with the possibility of implementing threat in relation to a database object when using security measures;

(b) To show the practical application of this technique for measuring the security of relational databases, including in order to identify a more secure one (in which solutions are used that provide a higher degree of database security).

The main contribution of the authors is the creation of a technique for evaluating the security of relational databases, based on the enhanced Clements–Hoffman model, which they obtained, and the integral metric of database security defined by them. The Clements–Hoffman model, traditionally considered the basis for the formal description of security systems, has been expanded to include a variety of object vulnerabilities. At the same time, vulnerability is considered as a separately objectively existing category. This makes it possible to evaluate the likelihood of an unwanted incident (threat realization) and the database security as a whole more adequately. As an integral metric of database security, the reciprocal of the total residual risk was determined, the constituent components of which characterize the strength of a certain security barrier and are presented in the form of certain linguistic variables. This made it possible to quantify the security of databases. In accordance with the evaluation technique developed by the authors and the formulated assumptions, a comparative analysis of their security was carried out on the example of relational databases created using various technologies. As analyzed databases, we researched databases designed according to the traditional technology of relational databases and built them based on the schema with the universal basis of relations (UBR) [15]. The expediency of researching a database with UBR is due to the fact that within the framework of its invariant schema, many original solutions have been implemented related to the protection of data and stored programs. This ensures that the data stored and processed in them is secure.

The rest of this paper is organized as follows: Section 2 presents related works from the literature; in Section 3, we give a formalized description of a full overlap security system (a covered security system) for databases. Section 4 presents the evaluation technique of database security. Section 5 presents the results of a comparative assessment of the effectiveness of database security measures proposed within the framework of the database schema with UBR with the existing solutions implemented within the framework of traditional relational databases (RDB). Section 6 concludes this work.

2. Related Works

Information security metrics, as noted in the NIST document [8], are an important factor in making informed decisions on various aspects of security, from the design of architectures and security controls to effectiveness and efficiency security operations. Effectiveness is understood as a property of the assessment object, representing how well it provides security in the context of its actual or proposed operational use [5,6]. Security effectiveness means the confidence that the security-enforcing mechanisms of the system meet the stated security objectives (that is, they do nothing other than what they should do while satisfying expectations for resiliency) [8,16,17]. Security efficiency denotes assurance that adequate security quality has been achieved in the system under study, meeting the resource, time and cost constraints [16,17].

A systematic survey of system security metrics is given in [18]. To measure security at the system level, the authors propose a structure of security sub-metrics based on vulnerability metrics, defenses metrics, attack metrics, and situation metrics. Each of these sub-metrics has a hierarchical structure. This paper discusses open questions in the research domain of security metrics and proposes key factors for improving security metrics from a system security perspective.

Despite the abundance of models and recommendations used for evaluating information security performance, Bernik et al. [19], referring also to other authors [20–22], point to the lack of studies that could comprehensively measure or consider information security through the use of specific positioning indicators. They criticize the existing models for their narrow focus or impossibility to apply in practice. Therefore, they propose their own multilevel model for measuring information security performance, which belongs to the scope of qualitative assessment of organizations' systems.

Based on the argumentation theory, Yasasin et al. [23] derived and showed what requirements should be fulfilled by the security metrics of information technology (IT). Katt et al. [24] proposes a quantification method that aims to evaluate the security assurance of systems by measuring the level of confidence that mechanisms that meet security requirements are present and the vulnerabilities associated with potential security threats are absent. They use this method to evaluate the security level of some REST APIs. Sanders [25], noting much work done in the development of methods for quantitative security assessment, speaks of the need for multiple approaches, including formal methods, probabilistic methods, benchmarking and experimentation, classical risk assessment, threat and vulnerability assessment, as well as informal and semi-formal methods. At the same time, for the developed metrics and approaches to be useful, their usability must be thoughtful. Various aspects of database security are discussed in [11,12,26–31].

Obtaining sufficient and credible security evidence of the system under study is one of the main challenges in information security engineering and management is noted in [16]. System developers, project managers, and executive management need information about the security status of technical systems at various stages of the system lifecycle. This study proposes a new Security Metrics Objective Segments (SMOS) model to enable the design of security metrics taxonomies. The model can be integrated with risk-based security metrics development approaches.

The studies carried out and described in [17] revealed such factors contributing to a holistic perception of security effectiveness in software systems, as evidence of (a) direct security effectiveness, (b) quality of risk assessment, (c) security correctness and system quality. However, as noted in the paper, their practical application causes certain difficulties. For example, measuring security effectiveness directly is not easy, and in practice, it is only partially possible. In this connection, further research is needed for definition of a rigorous methodology enabling systematic development of security effectiveness metrics.

Mishra et al. [32] analyze the impact of security policy, deterrence practices and system audit on the information security effectiveness. Fabian et al. [33] consider the conceptual framework for security engineering with an emphasis on elicitation and analysis of security requirements. This conceptual framework, as a guide for comparing different methods of developing security requirements, is used by the authors to compare and evaluate current approaches to developing security requirements, such as Common Criteria, Secure Tropos (Tropos is a software development methodology based on the paradigm of agent-oriented software development), Security Requirements Engineering Process (SREP), Multilateral Security Requirements Analysis (MSRA), as well as methods based on Unified Modeling Language (UML) and problem frames. Mapping the terminology of a particular method with a conceptual framework allows to assess the method scope and, therefore, its usefulness for a given purpose. This paper provides an example for comparing methods that can help practitioners and academics to choose the method that best suits their application area.

The fundamental monograph [34] and paper [35] discuss the concept of a covered security system, where at least one security measure exists for each identified penetration path. They also describe a formal model (known as the Clements–Hoffman model) that defines the protection domain, the threat domain, security measures and the relationship between them. The model systematizes the resistance, probability, and value measurement process. Resistance is taken to mean the degree to which a security technique succeeds in combating the set of threats against which it has been implemented. The measurement process is based on fuzzy set theory.

Various approaches to measuring security, which can be conditionally classified as cost, functional and based on risk analysis, with appropriate methods and metrics for evaluating the asset protection, are described in [36–41].

The basis for holding any works in the information security area, including the assessment of the protection effectiveness, are International Standards, including ISO/IEC 15408 [42], ISO/IEC 27001 [43], ISO/IEC 27004 [44]. Thus, the International Standard ISO/IEC 15408 defines a common set of requirements for the security functionality of information technology products that can be implemented in the form of hardware, firmware or software, and for the assurance measures applied to these IT products during a security evaluation. It also defines a common approach (model) to assessing security, taking into account threats, vulnerabilities, assets, and risks of harm and the choice of countermeasures. ISO/IEC 15408 is applicable to risks arising from human activities (malicious or otherwise) and to risks arising from non-human activities. It is flexible enough, enabling a range of evaluation methods to be applied to a range of security properties of a range of IT products. Therefore, users of the standard are advised to be careful that this flexibility is not misused. For example, using standards in conjunction with unsuitable evaluation methods, inappropriate security properties, or inappropriate IT products can lead to meaningless evaluation results.

The International Standard ISO/IEC 27004 provides guidelines to assist organizations to evaluate the information security (InfoSec) performance and the effectiveness of an information security management system (ISMS) in order to fulfill the requirements set out in ISO/IEC 27001. It establishes monitoring and measurement of information security performance, monitoring and measurement of the ISMS effectiveness, including its processes and controls, analysis and evaluation of monitoring and measurement results.

Thus, from the experience gained to date, it can be concluded that security measurement is a tough problem that should not be underestimated. Therefore, for its solution today various approaches are proposed, including those mentioned above. In addition, since, in the general case, the formulation of the problem of ensuring information security can vary widely, and the effectiveness of the functioning of the information protection system depends on many factors and is evaluated by a set of metrics that are in complex interrelationships, then the variety of the methods of evaluating the protection effectiveness is natural. These approaches and methods are mostly based on intuition, are empirical and fragmented, and the authors of this paper wanted to find some scientific-methodological, general approach to solving this problem. Therefore, having analyzed and summarized various, including the above-mentioned approaches and achievements in the domain of evaluating the security of information systems, the authors concluded that it is advisable to use the Clements–Hoffman model. This model is based on the theory of graphs, fuzzy sets, and probabilities. It is traditionally considered the basis for the formal description of protection systems.

Below, based on this model, after its certain enhancement, a technique for evaluating relational databases is proposed.

3. Enhanced Clements–Hoffman Model for Databases

So, let us take as a basis the Clements–Hoffman model in the form of a 5-tuple:

$$S = \{O, T, W, V, B\} \quad (1)$$

where O is the set of protected objects; T is the set of security threats; V is the set of vulnerabilities representing paths of implementing threats T in relation to objects O, determined by a subset of the Cartesian product $V = T \times O$; B is the set of barriers representing the points at which protection is required, defined by a subset of the Cartesian product $B = V \times W = T \times O \times W$.

At first, let us clarify some of these elements in relation to databases:

- $T = \{t_i\}, i = 1..I$ is the set of database security threats. According to studies [11,26,28,31,45–47], the main largest and most important threats (types of threats) to database security (to a greater extent they are associated with anthropogenic sources of threats—people or groups of persons, as a result of whose actions or inaction, the security of the considered system has been violated) are:
    - ✓ Excessive and unused privileges. For definiteness, let us designate this type of threat as t_1;
    - ✓ Privilege abuse—t_2;
    - ✓ Input injection—t_3;
    - ✓ Malware—t_4;
    - ✓ Wweak audit trail—t_5;
    - ✓ Storage media exposure—t_6;
    - ✓ Exploitation of vulnerabilities and misconfigured databases—t_7;
    - ✓ Unmanaged sensitive data—t_8;
    - ✓ Inference—t_9;
    - ✓ Denial of service—t_{10};
    - ✓ Limited security expertise and education—t_{11}.

- $O = \{o_j\}, j = 1..J$ is the set of protected database objects. Considering that database systems are information products with a dual nature (that is, consisting of two components (assets): DBMS software, independent of their scope, structure, semantic content of the accumulated and processed data, and the actual stored data), as well as the possible harmful effects on the corresponding assets, it is advisable to ensure the security of both components. For relational databases, as the most widespread (this thesis is confirmed by the results of DB-Engines and Popularity of Programming Language (PYPL) ratings [48,49], as well as reports of experts from the world-famous company Gartner, Inc. [50,51]), taking into account the possibility of various degrees of detail of these components, the following objects of protection can be distinguished [11,52]:
    - ✓ The entire database—o_1;
    - ✓ Tables—o_2;
    - ✓ Views—o_3;
    - ✓ Tuples (rows) of tables—o_4;

- ✓ Separate fields (attribute values) of rows—o_5;
- ✓ Triggers—o_6;
- ✓ Persistent stored modules—o_7 and some others.

- $W = \{w_k\}$, $k = 1..K$ is the set of security measures (also referred to in the literature [53–57] as controls), which include any process, policy, device, established practice, or other action which modifies risk [57]).

The elements of all the sets listed above are among themselves in certain relationships, at that the relationship between threats and objects is not a "one-to-one" relationship. Threat $t_i \in T$ can spread to any number of objects O, and object $o_j \in O$ can be vulnerable to more than one threat T.

Now we note one feature of the presented Clements–Hoffman model (Equation (1)). Hoffman and Clements [35], introducing the concept of vulnerability, formally represent it as a mapping of $T \times O$ onto a set of ordered pairs $v_r = (t_i, o_j)$, and not a separately objectively existing category—*vulnerability* (weakness asset or control that can be exploited by one or more threats [57]). Threats exist separately from asset weaknesses. Vulnerability in itself does not cause damage it is only a condition or set of conditions that allows a threat to harm assets. When a threat is realized, one or more vulnerabilities of an asset can be used [58]. At that, one type of vulnerability can lead to many various security threats. Therefore, it is advisable to consider threats and vulnerabilities as a whole. Therefore, it is advisable to consider threats and vulnerabilities in the complex. Only together, they can cause an unwanted incident that can harm the system (assets). Furthermore, in this case, it is necessary to correctly define threats, vulnerabilities and the relationship between them.

In this regard, we will extend the above model with full overlap to a 6-tuple by including a set of vulnerabilities (weakness) of objects (Γ):

$$S' = \{O, T, \Gamma, W, V, B\} \qquad (2)$$

where the main components of tuple (2) basically correspond to the components of tuple (1). The distinctive features are shown below.

After the corresponding clarification of the model, the set V will be the set of ordered triples $v_r = (t_i, \gamma_\psi, o_j)$, $\psi = 1..\Psi$, where $\gamma_\psi \in \Gamma$ is the vulnerability (its type) used by the threat $t_i \in T$ aimed at violating the security of the object $o_j \in O$. The set of barriers will be accordingly defined as: $B = V \times W = T \times \Gamma \times O \times W = \{b_l = (t_i, \gamma_\psi, o_j, w_k), l = 1..L\}$. Furthermore, the condition for ensuring full security will take the following form: $\forall (v_r)$, $\exists (b_l = (t_i, \gamma_\psi, o_j, w_k)) \in B$. This condition means that for each triple (t_i, γ_ψ, o_j) from the set V, a barrier $b_l \in B$ is created, which makes it impossible to implement an undesirable incident (implementation of the $t_i \in T$ threat using vulnerability $\gamma_\psi \in \Gamma$) in relation to the protected object $o_j \in O$.

In order to have a clear idea of what types of vulnerabilities are most important for databases, the authors of the paper, based on the analysis of existing taxonomies of vulnerabilities, determined a list of the main common weaknesses. It was based on the specification from the Common Weakness Enumeration (CWE) more precisely the classification of the abstract representation of the Research Concepts CWE [59] used by academic researchers, vulnerability analysts, and assessment tool vendors. Taking into account, the specifics of the aspects under consideration, due to the characteristic features of security inherent for databases and DBMS, their list included the following are the main weaknesses of a sufficiently high level of abstraction:

(1) *Improper privilege management*: incorrect assignment of privileges, elevation (escalation) of privileges, performing operations with excessive privileges;
(2) *Improper authorization*: incorrect assignment of permissions for a critical resource, missing authorization, incorrect authorization, exposure of sensitive information through metadata, exposure of sensitive information through data queries. The authorization check is not performed or incorrectly performed when an actor attempts to access a resource or perform an action;

(3) *Improper authentication*: weak password, outdated password, authentication bypass, incorrect implementation of the authentication algorithm, insufficient session expiration, use of a password hash instead of a password for authentication, etc.;
(4) *Uncontrolled resource consumption*: the allocation of a limited resource is not properly controlled, thereby enabling an actor to influence the amount of resources consumed, which ultimately leads to their depletion;
(5) *Cleartext storage of sensitive information*;
(6) *Inadequate encryption strength*;
(7) *Improper scrubbing of sensitive data from decommissioned device*: scrubbing may be missing, insufficient, or incorrect;
(8) *Use of a broken or risky cryptographic algorithm*: use of a non-standard cryptographic primitive with no proven strength;
(9) *Use of insufficiently random values*;
(10) *Insufficient verification of data authenticity*: download of code without integrity check, improper validation of integrity check value, improper verification (no verification) of the cryptographic signature;
(11) *Improper input validation*: improper validation of syntactic correctness of input data, improper validation of specified type of input data, improper validation of consistency within input, improper validation of unsafe equivalence in input. The input data are either not validated, or are incorrectly validated—without assurance that their use will not lead in the future to incorrect and unsafe data processing;
(12) *Use of prohibited code*: functions, libraries, or third party components are used that has been explicitly prohibited, whether by the developer or the customer;
(13) *Embedded malicious code*: Trojan horse, trapdoor, time bomb, logic bomb, spyware, etc.;
(14) *Violation of secure design principles*: unnecessary complexity in the protection mechanism (a more complex mechanism is used than necessary); reliance on a single factor in a security decision; insufficient compartmentalization—functionality or processes that require different privilege levels, rights or permissions are not sufficiently separated; access check is not provided on a protected resource every time the resource is accessed by an entity; insufficient psychological acceptability (the difficulty and inconvenience of using the protection mechanism often encourages non-malicious users to disable or bypass it accidentally or deliberately); reliance on security through the obscurity (a defense mechanism is used, the strength of which heavily depends on its obscurity); imperfection of the mechanism for maintaining data integrity;
(15) *Incorrect provision of specified functionality*: the code does not function according to its published specifications, potentially leading to incorrect usage;
(16) *Hidden functionality*: there is functionality that is not documented, not part of the specification, and not accessible through an interface or command sequence. Hidden functionality can take many forms, including, for example, such as intentionally malicious code;
(17) *Incomplete documentation*: there are no descriptions of all relevant elements of the product, such as its usage, structure, interfaces, design, implementation, configuration, operation, etc., which naturally complicates maintenance, indirectly affecting security due to lack of awareness, making it difficult to find and/or fixing vulnerabilities or taking a lot of time, which can also simplify the introduction of vulnerabilities;
(18) *Configuration error*: non-compliance with safety requirements during the installation and configuration of the database. Administrative, auxiliary, educational accounts are installed, which are registered in the database by default without proper analysis and changing of default passwords, no limitations on the length and complexity of passwords are set, unused accounts are not blocked, critical updates are not installed, the event audit system is improperly configured, etc.

For definiteness, we denote them, respectively, as $\gamma_1, \ldots, \gamma_{18}$.

For a better representation (understanding) of the relationship between the main elements of the security system under consideration, Figure 1 in the form of a class diagram in the Unified Modeling Language (UML) notation shows these high-level security concepts and their relationship. The relationships between the security system elements under consideration are many-to-many relationships, subdivided into so-called associations (represented by straight lines), and dependencies (represented by dashed lines).

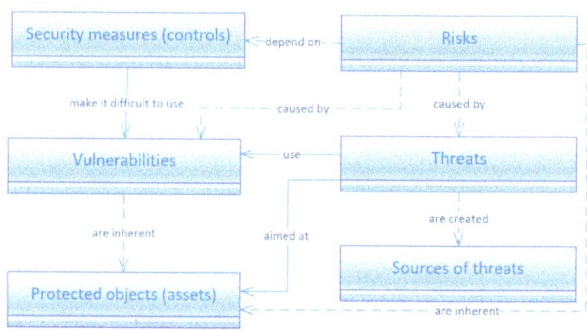

Figure 1. Security concepts and their relationship.

Ideally, each protection mechanism (security controls, security measures) should exclude an appropriate path of implementing the threat. In practice, however, these mechanisms provide only a limited amount of resistance to security threats. For example, passwords have a finite length; ciphers have different cryptographic strengths; different frequency of synchronization points between the database and the transaction log leads to all kinds of, sometimes unacceptable, recovery times in case of failures; dependence of security on the relevance and timeliness of installed updates, configuration parameters, etc.

The authors of the model [34,35] believe that for some quantitative evaluation of the security level of objects, it is necessary and possible to measure the degree of system security. As an appropriate structure for expressing such measures, they propose a linguistic variable that assumes values, which are words rather than numbers. To do this, they redefine security barriers B, each of which ($b_l \in B$) is represented as a composite linguistic variable, the components of which are linguistic variables: P_l is the probability of threat occurrence; L_l is the amount of damage (loss) in case of successful implementation of the threat in relation to the protected object; R_l is security measure resistance (the degree of security measure resistance w_k, characterized by the probability of overcoming it). At that, it is noted that these components are evaluated in the context of the specific barrier ($b_l = (t_i, o_j, w_k)$) that they form. The indices of the P_l, L_l, R_l linguistic variables are the same as the barrier index, and not the same as those of the $b_l = (t_i, o_j, w_k)$ barrier components in the basic security system—threats, objects, and security measures (controls). Clements and Hoffman [34,35] state that the resistance value determines the degree of increase or decrease in the overall system security, and an informal combination of the probability and the loss value gives the importance (weight) of the barrier in the overall rating (evaluation). In general, these values determine the contribution of the barrier to the overall system security. However, they do not say anything about specific methods of obtaining (evaluating) them.

Therefore, after analyzing the various approaches set out in relevant sources [60–62] the residual risk Rr has been selected as such an indicator (metric). The risk remaining after risk treatment (residual risk [57]) is associated with the possibility of implementing threat $t_i \in T$ in relation to the DB object $o_j \in O$ when using security measures (controls) $w_k \in W$. Naturally, that a quantitative approach to risk evaluation is preferable to a qualitative one, since it offers a more tangible value of the situation [63]. The residual risk value characterizing the strength of the barrier $b_l \in B$ can be determined as follows [60,61]:

$$Rr_l = P_l L_l (1 - R_l) \qquad (3)$$

At the same time, let us clarify that the probability P_l is understood as the probability of an undesirable incident (threat realization), as the product of the probability of the threat occurrence P_{t_i} (the so-called motivational component of the threat realization probability [64]) and the probability of successful exploitation of the vulnerability P_{γ_ψ}: $P_l = P_{t_i} \cdot P_{\gamma_\psi}$ [62]. Furthermore, the amount of damage (loss) L_l in relation to the protected object should be considered from the standpoint of the successful implementation of the threat t_i exploiting the vulnerability γ_ψ.

Residual risk is essentially a measure of insecurity asset. Then, the value of the database security can be determined by calculating the reciprocal of the total residual risk [60,61]:

$$S = \sum_{\forall b_l \in B} \frac{1}{P_l L_l (1 - R_l)} \quad (4)$$

where $P_l, L_l \in (0,1)$, $R_l \in [0,1)$.

If there are no barriers b_l in the system that block certain paths of implementing threats in relation to the objects, the degree of security measure resistance R_l is taken to be zero. From the formal point of view, this can be represented by introducing the so-called null security measure (protection means with a zero degree of providing security) w_o added to the set W. Each unprotected object is assigned such a protection means. Thus, for $\forall (t_i, \gamma_\psi, o_j) \in V$, for which $(\forall k \in K)$ $(t_i, \gamma_\psi, o_j, w_k) \notin B$, barrier $(t_i, \gamma_\psi, o_j, w_o)$ is added to the B.

- Thus, the Clements–Hoffman model was extended to a 6-tuple by including a set of vulnerabilities of objects, as a separate objectively existing category. This allows you to evaluate the probability of an unwanted incident and the security of the database as a whole more adequately. In addition, as a result of enhancing the Clements–Hoffman model, taking into account the dual nature of the relational database system and varying degrees of detail of its components, the following were determined: the main objects of protection;
- The list of the main common weaknesses (as some types of vulnerabilities);
- The main significant threats to the security of databases;
- Integral metric of database security (as the reciprocal of the total residual risk).

4. Evaluation Technique of Database Security

It is easy to see that with known values of the probability of an undesirable incident (threat realization) $P_l = P_{t_i} \cdot P_{\gamma_\psi}$, the amount of damage (loss) L_l (with the successful implementation of the threat in relation to the protected object), the degree of corresponding security measure resistance R_l, it is possible to evaluate the database security using Equation (4). However, obtaining accurate P_{t_i}, P_{γ_ψ}, L_l, and R_l values is not an easy task. This is often not possible in practice [58]. In addition, to paraphrase Zadeh [65], as system complexity increases, analytical precision decreases [35]. Therefore, as a rule, in such cases it is advisable to resort to numerical estimates in a certain range of values, especially since each quantitative range can be associated with a certain qualitative scale, with which under certain conditions it is much easier to work. A linguistic variable can serve as a suitable structure for expressing such values, as noted above. For these reasons, first of all, in accordance with the introduced changes in the model, we will redefine the security B barriers, each of which ($b_l \in B$) will be represented as a composite linguistic variable, the components of which are linguistic variables:

- The probability of threat occurrence (P_t);
- The probability of exploiting the vulnerability (P_γ);
- The amount of damage (L) in case of successful implementation of the threat in relation to the protected object;
- The degree of security measure resistance (R), characterized by the probability of overcoming it.

At that, again, we note that these components are assessed in the context of the specific barrier that they form (the $P_l = f(P_{t_i}, P_{\gamma_\psi})$, L_l, R_l indices are the same as the barrier index, and not the same as those of the $b_l = (t_i, \gamma_\psi, o_j, w_k)$ barrier components in the basic security system—threats, vulnerabilities, objects, and security measures).

We begin formalizing the corresponding components with the probability of a threat occurrence P_t. At the same time, we note that in practice, to calculate the risk, it is often not the mathematical probability that is used, but the approximate frequency of its implementation over a certain period. To avoid confusion, the standards deliberately use the concept of *likelihood* instead of the mathematical term *probability*. In what follows, we will use exactly this term.

In view of the above, the likelihood of a threat occurrence P_t can be represented as a linguistic variable:

$$\langle name, T, X, G, M \rangle \tag{5}$$

where *name* is the name of the linguistic variable (in our case, this is the likelihood of a threat occurrence P_t); T is a set of values of a linguistic variable (term-set), which are the names of fuzzy variables (α_ε, where $\varepsilon = 1, 2, \ldots$ ($\varepsilon \in \mathbb{N}^*_{\leq n}$), n is the maximum number of fuzzy variables), the definition domain of each of which is the set X—a universal set or universe (in this case, these are the numerical values of the probability of threat occurrence P_t); G is some syntactic procedure that allows you to operate with the elements of the term-set T, in particular, generate new terms (values); M is a semantic procedure that makes it possible to transform each new value of a linguistic variable, obtained using the procedure G, into a fuzzy variable, that is, to form a corresponding fuzzy set. In the considered case, we can restrict ourselves to the assumption of the trivial nature of G and M, that is, no logical connectives and modifiers will be used.

An analysis of various relevant sources on the problems of information risk management [53,58,66,67] showed that to evaluate P_t it is enough to enter three verbal gradations with the corresponding approximate quantitative estimates, without which any qualitative scale is meaningless:

- Low likelihood (L). This threat is unlikely to occur. There are no incidents, statistics, motives that would indicate that this can happen. The expected frequency of the threat does not exceed 1 time in 5 years;
- Moderate likelihood (M). There are prerequisites for the emergence of a threat (there have been incidents in the past), there are statistics or other information indicating the possibility of a given threat, the attacker has the motivation to realize appropriate actions. The expected frequency of occurrence of this threat is approximately once a year;
- High likelihood (H). There are objective prerequisites for the emergence of a threat. There are incidents, statistics, or other information indicating that the threat is most likely to realize, the attacker has motives to take appropriate action. The expected frequency of occurrence of a threat is on average once every four months or more often.

This three-level scale, as noted by some experts [53,58,66,67], is usually sufficient for an initial high-level assessment. This is explained by the fact that estimates of the expected frequency of occurrence of a threat from level to level on a qualitative scale differ significantly, so it is unlikely that competent experts would be greatly mistaken in their estimates. Nevertheless, in the future, the authors plan to expand the number of levels by adding several intermediate ones.

On the other hand, the value of the frequency estimate can be converted into the numerical equivalent of the probability of the threat occurrence, corresponding to a certain range of values. The results of the analysis of relevant sources [66,68,69] suggest that, in numerical terms, the likelihood of such a threat at the appropriate level may be in the corresponding range:

- For level L—$P_t = [0, 0.2]$;
- For level M—$P_t = [0.2, 0.6]$;

- For level H—$P_t = [0.6, 1]$.

Then, using the well-known qualitative scales used in assessing information security risks [53,58,66,67], in particular, a three-level qualitative scale, we define the names of fuzzy variables—a set of values of a term-set T: T = {"low likelihood", "moderate likelihood", "high likelihood"} = {"L", "M", "H"}, that is α_1 = "L", α_2 = "M", α_3 = "H".

As you know, when we are talking about a fuzzy variable α, we always mean some fuzzy set $A = \{\mu_A(x)/x\}$, which determines its possible values, where $\mu_A(x)$ is the membership function ($\mu_A(x) \in [0,1]$; $\mu_A(x) : X \to [0,1]$), which indicates the grade of membership of an element x in the fuzzy set A.

The most widespread in the construction of membership functions of fuzzy sets are direct and indirect methods [70,71]. In view of the fact that $x \in X$ can be measured on a quantitative scale, we will use the direct method, when an expert or a group of experts sets for each $x \in X$ the value of the membership function $\mu_A(x)$. The theory of fuzzy sets when using direct methods for constructing the membership function does not require its absolutely precise assignment [70]. Very often, it is enough to fix only the most characteristic values and the view of the function $\mu_A(x)$.

Based on the analysis of the main membership functions used to represent such properties of fuzzy sets, which are characterized by the uncertainty of types, such as: "small value", "negligible value"; "located in the range"; "approximately equal"; "large value", "significant value", for the considered fuzzy variables "L", "M", "H" trapezoidal, linear Z- and linear S-shaped functions were selected. Each of these functions can be represented as follows:

- Linear Z-shaped membership function of a fuzzy set $A_L = \{\mu_L(x)/x\}$, corresponding to a fuzzy variable "L" for a linguistic variable P_t:

$$\mu_L(x; a, b) = \begin{cases} 1, & x \leq a, \\ \frac{b-x}{b-a}, & a < x < b, \\ 0, & b \leq x, \end{cases} \quad (6)$$

where a, b are numeric parameters ($a \leq b$);
- Trapezoidal membership function of a fuzzy set $A_M = \{\mu_M(x)/x\}$ corresponding to a fuzzy variable "M" for a linguistic variable P_t:

$$\mu_M(x; a, b, c, d) = \begin{cases} 0, & x \leq a, \\ \frac{x-a}{b-a}, & a \leq x \leq b, \\ 1, & b \leq x \leq c, \\ \frac{d-x}{d-c}, & c \leq x \leq d, \\ 0, & d \leq x, \end{cases} \quad (7)$$

where a, b, c, d are numeric parameters ($a \leq b \leq c \leq d$);
- Linear S-shaped membership function of a fuzzy set $A_H = \{\mu_H(x)/x\}$ corresponding to a fuzzy variable "H" for a linguistic variable P_t:

$$\mu_H(x; c, d) = \begin{cases} 0, & x \leq c, \\ \frac{x-c}{d-c}, & c < x < d, \\ 1, & d \leq x, \end{cases} \quad (8)$$

where c, d are numeric parameters ($c \leq d$).

Figure 2 shows all three graphs of the membership functions of fuzzy variables used to determine the linguistic variable—the likelihood of a threat occurrence P_t.

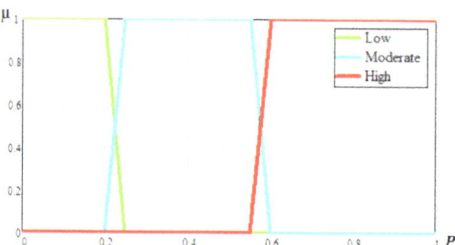

Figure 2. Graphs of the membership function of fuzzy sets A_L, A_M, A_H.

The expert based on a priori knowledge assigns linguistic values, which are the names of fuzzy variables, for each the likelihood of a threat occurrence P_{t_i}, as a component of the corresponding specific barrier b_l. In this case, these values can be represented verbally as "low likelihood", "moderate likelihood", "high likelihood" (or "L", "M", "H"). At that, since each such value is associated with the corresponding membership function with the corresponding approximate quantitative estimates, then, in principle, for each threat $t_i \in T$, it is possible to determine with a limited degree of accuracy the numerical value of this likelihood P_{t_i}, for example, as the *modal value* of a fuzzy set. If the core of a fuzzy set A (is the crisp subset of the domain X consisting of all elements of A with a membership grade equal to one [72]: $C(A) = core(A) = \{x : \mu_A(x) = 1, x \in X\}$) contains more than one element, then for such a set the modal value is calculated as the mean value of the core.

Further, using the above approach, we represent in the form of the corresponding linguistic variable—the likelihood of exploiting the vulnerability—P_γ (the likelihood that in the event of implementing threat in relation to an asset, this threat will be successfully implemented using this vulnerability). To estimate P_γ, we introduce three verbal gradations with the corresponding approximate quantitative estimates:

- High (H). The vulnerability is easy to exploit and there is weak protection or no protection at all. The likelihood of exploiting a vulnerability (the likelihood of successful implementation of a threat due to a given vulnerability) is in the range [0.7, 1];
- Moderate (M). The vulnerability can be exploited, but there is some protection. The likelihood of exploiting a vulnerability is in the range [0.3, 0.7];
- Low (L). The vulnerability is difficult to exploit and there is good protection. The likelihood of exploiting a vulnerability is in the range [0, 0.3].

As with threats, this three-tier scale may be sufficient for an initial high-level evaluation of the vulnerability. In the future, for a more detailed evaluation, the authors also plan to expand it.

Then, using the introduced designations, we define the names of fuzzy variables (β_ε, where $\varepsilon \in \mathbb{N}^*_{<n}$) is the set of values of the term-set T_γ for the linguistic variable P_γ: $T_\gamma = \{$"high vulnerability", "moderate vulnerability", "low vulnerability"$\} = \{$"H", "M", "L"$\}$, that is, $\beta_1 = $ "H", $\beta_2 = $ "M", $\beta_3 = $ "L". The definition domain of each of the fuzzy variables is a set of numerical values ($X \in [0,1]$) of the likelihood of exploiting the vulnerability. In the case under consideration, we also restrict ourselves to the assumption that G_γ and M_γ are trivial (without logical connectives and modifiers).

Based on the analysis of the main membership functions, similar to the above, for the considered fuzzy variables $\beta_1 = $ "B", $\beta_2 = $ "C", $\beta_3 = $ "H", trapezoidal, linear Z- and linear S-shaped functions were selected.

Figure 3 shows graphs of these membership functions ($\mu^v_L(x)$, $\mu^v_M(x)$, $\mu^v_H(x)$) used to determine the linguistic variable—the likelihood of exploiting the vulnerability P_γ.

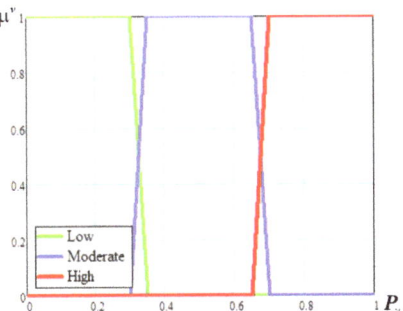

Figure 3. Graphs of the membership function of fuzzy sets $A_L^v = \{\mu_L^v(x)/x\}$, $A_M^v = \{\mu_M^v(x)/x\}$, $A_H^v = \{\mu_H^v(x)/x\}$.

The expert based on a priori knowledge assigns linguistic values, which are the names of fuzzy variables, for each likelihood of exploiting the vulnerability P_γ, as components of the corresponding barrier b_l, thanks to which it becomes possible to implement the corresponding threat t_i. These meanings are presented verbally as "L", "M", "H". Since each such value is associated with the corresponding membership function with the corresponding approximate quantitative estimates, then for each vulnerability γ_ψ, it is possible to calculate with a limited degree of accuracy the numerical value of this likelihood P_{γ_ψ}, for example, as the modal value of the corresponding fuzzy set.

By analogy, you can determine the degree of resistance of the security measures, characterized by the likelihood of overcoming them ($P_l^{ov} = 1 - R_l$). The corresponding levels of control (degrees of resistance) can be determined as follows:

– H is the high degree of security measure (mechanism) resistance (high level of control). It is unlikely that such a mechanism will be overcome. The likelihood of overcoming (bypassing) such a mechanism is in the range $P_l^{ov} \in [0, 0.4]$.

– M is the moderate degree of security measure resistance. This measure provides some protection, but it is possible to overcome it, spending some effort. The likelihood of overcoming the corresponding security measure is in the range [0.4, 0.8].

– L is the low degree of security measure resistance. This measure is quite easy to overcome. The likelihood of overcoming the corresponding security measure is in the range [0.8, 1].

Then, using this scale, we define the names of fuzzy variables (δ_ε, where $\varepsilon \in \mathbb{N}^*_{<n}$) is the set of values of the term-set T_R for the linguistic variable R: T_R = {"high degree of resistance", "moderate degree of resistance", "low degree of resistance"} = {"H", "M", "L"}, that is, δ_1 = "H", δ_2 = "M", δ_3 = "L". The definition domain of each of the fuzzy variables is a set of numerical values ($X \in [0,1]$) of the likelihood of overcoming security measures. In the case under consideration, we also restrict ourselves to the assumption that G_R and M_R are trivial.

Similar to the above approach, for the considered fuzzy variables δ_1 = "B", δ_2 = "C", δ_3 = "H" (with which the corresponding fuzzy sets are associated, defining their possible values: $A_H^{ov} = \{\mu_H^{ov}(x)/x\}$, $A_C^{ov} = \{\mu_C^{ov}(x)/x\}$, $A_B^{ov} = \{\mu_B^{ov}(x)/x\}$) were selected trapezoidal, linear Z- and linear S-figurative membership functions ($\mu_H^{ov}(x)$, $\mu_C^{ov}(x)$, $\mu_B^{ov}(x)$). Figure 4 shows three graphs of the membership functions of fuzzy variables used to determine the linguistic variable R ($R = 1 - P^{ov}$; in some sources [53] P^{ov} is called reverse of the control strength).

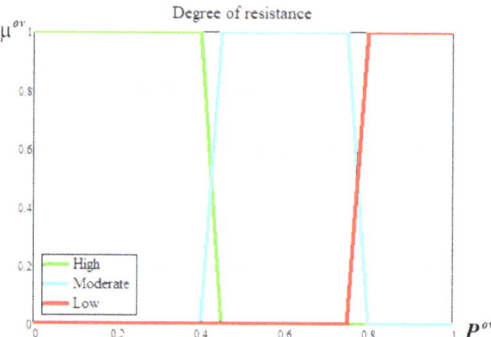

Figure 4. Graphs of the membership function of fuzzy sets A_H^{ov}, A_M^{ov}, A_L^{ov}.

An expert, on the basis of a priori knowledge of security measures used that complicate the exploitation of the corresponding vulnerability γ_ψ, due to which it becomes possible to implement the corresponding threat t_i, assigns the linguistic values ("H", "M", "L") for each R_l as components of the corresponding barrier b_l. In view of the fact that each such value is associated with the corresponding membership function with the corresponding approximate quantitative estimates, then for each security measure $w_k \in W$ of barrier b_l, it is possible to determine the numerical value of both P_l^{ov} and $R_l = 1 - P_l^{ov}$. Again, as the modal value of the corresponding fuzzy set.

The damage caused as a result of security incidents is associated with the target function of the system—one of the relevant indicators, such as lost profit, loss of competitive advantages, deterioration of the organization's reputation, damage to the interests of a third party, financial losses associated with the restoration of resources, etc. For different organizations, the importance of each of them can have significantly different meanings.

From an economic point of view, damage to assets is conveniently expressed in terms of financial losses. However, in practice, obtaining accurate quantitative values of damage is often difficult or even impossible [62]. Nevertheless, most of the losses that cannot be described quantitatively can be represented numerically by using an empirical scale of the damage level—a qualitative scale of measurement, divided into areas (ranks) corresponding to different degrees of satisfaction of the requirements under consideration, for example, on a five-point scale: from 1 to 5. Each of these levels (ranks) can be associated with the value of the term set T_L (T_L = {"Very low", "Low", "Medium", "High", "Very high"} = {"VL", "L", "M", "H", "VH"}) linguistic variable—the amount of damage L. The definition domain of each of the fuzzy variables is the set of numerical values of the damage value/damage level (in points)—$X \in (0, 6)$. In the case under consideration, we also restrict ourselves to the assumption that G_L and M_L are trivial.

For the considered fuzzy variables ρ_1 = "VH", ρ_2 = "H", ρ_3 = "M", ρ_4 = "L", ρ_5 = "VL" (with which the corresponding fuzzy sets are associated, defining their possible values: $A_{VH}^L = \{\mu_{VH}^L(x)/x\}$, $A_H^L = \{\mu_H^L(x)/x\}$, $A_M^L = \{\mu_M^L(x)/x\}$, $A_L^L = \{\mu_L^L(x)/x\}$, $A_{VL}^L = \{\mu_{VL}^L(x)/x\}$), triangular, linear Z- and linear S-shaped membership functions ($\mu_{VH}^L(x)$, $\mu_H^L(x)$, $\mu_M^L(x)$, $\mu_L^L(x)$, $\mu_{VL}^L(x)$) were selected:

$$\mu_{VL}^L(x; a, b) = \begin{cases} 1, & x \leq a, \\ \frac{b-x}{b-a}, & a < x < b, \\ 0, & b \leq x; \end{cases} \quad (9)$$

$$\mu_H^L(x; a, b, c, d), \mu_M^L(x; a, b, c, d), \mu_L^L(x; a, b, c, d) = \begin{cases} 0, & x \leq a, \\ \frac{x-a}{b-a}, & a \leq x \leq b, \\ \frac{c-x}{c-b}, & b \leq x \leq c, \\ 0, & c \leq x; \end{cases} \quad (10)$$

$$\mu_{VH}^L(x;c,d) = \begin{cases} 0, & x \leq c, \\ \frac{x-c}{d-c}, & c < x < d, \\ 1, & d \leq x. \end{cases} \quad (11)$$

Figure 5 shows the graphs of the membership functions of fuzzy variables used to determine the linguistic variable—the amount of damage L.

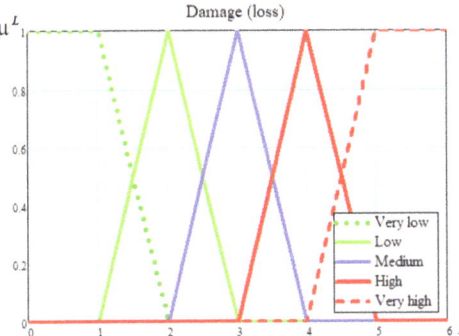

Figure 5. Graphs of the membership function of fuzzy sets $A_{VH}^L, A_H^L, A_M^L, A_L^L, A_{VL}^L$.

Table 1 presents an assessment of damage on a five-point scale and its semantic characteristic.

Table 1. The assessment of damage and its semantic characteristic.

Level	T_L	Semantic Characteristic
1	Very low	Loss can be ignored.
2	Low	The damage can be easily eliminated; the costs of eliminating the consequences of the threat implementation are low.
3	Medium	Eliminating consequences of the threat implementation is not associated with large costs.
4	High	Eliminating consequences of the threat implementation is associated with significant financial losses.
5	Very high	The organization ceases to exist.

In order for the assessment of the value of assets to make economic sense, it is advisable to correlate the qualitative scale of assessing the damage with the amount of direct financial losses. However, establishing such a correspondence requires additional research in each specific case and depends on many factors for the systems under consideration. Possible independent scales (examples) for assessing direct financial losses and their relative values ($r_{fl}^{rel} = z_{fl}/z_{fl}^{per}$, where z_{fl} is direct financial losses; z_{fl}^{per} is permissible direct financial losses) are shown in Table 2. At that, it should be understood that, depending on the tasks solved by the organization, the area, the nature and scale of its activities, the form of ownership, the value of assets, the severity of the consequences of violating their security and a number of other factors, they may be other.

Table 2. Financial damage assessment scales.

Level	T_L	Range z_{fl}	Range r_{fl}^{rel}
1	Very low	<100 $	≤0.1
2	Low	(100–1000) $	(0.1, 0.3]
3	Medium	(1000–10,000) $	(0.3, 0.6]
4	High	(10,000–100,000) $	(0.6, 0.9]
5	Very high	>100,000 $	>0.9

Thus, when developing an evaluation technique of database security, the authors, based on a generalization of experts' recommendations, determined the number of levels for the linguistic variables under consideration with their corresponding ranges, as well as the membership functions and a variant of determining the numerical value for the corresponding likelihood or damage.

Having the appropriate data using Equation (4), it is possible to determine the security value of the analyzed database.

It should be noted that the proposed technique, in contrast to some known, is characterized by a certain flexibility. This is manifested in the ability to adapt to new conditions of functioning and to take into account the emerging new actual threats, vulnerabilities, security measures that can be combined into some general groups. Including there is the possibility of choosing the number of levels of the corresponding linguistic variables. At that, the use of the introduced integral security metric makes it possible to evaluate the security value of the investigated RDB quantitatively.

5. Quantifying Database Security

In this section, the authors tried to show, using examples of relational databases developed using various technologies, the ease of use and potential of the proposed technique with explainable and non-contradictory results of evaluating their security that confirm its sufficiency.

Before proceeding to assessing the security of relational databases built using various technologies and comparing their security, we note some important aspects and assumptions.

1. As the studied databases, we consider databases designed based on the schema with the universal basis of relations and according to the traditional technology of relational databases.
2. In the DB with UBR, which can be used as an ordinary DB, a data warehouse of various subject domains (SDs) or a configuration DB of the dataspace management environment [73–75], various security measures are implemented [76–80]. These measures are based on the provisions of the theory of relational databases [8,30,81], formal access control models [82,83] and ensuring data integrity [84], the potential of the modern blockchain model [85,86], row-level security (RLS) technology [87], SQL capabilities [45]. Separate elements of these solutions can be used to protect databases and data warehouses with various models (relational, NoSQL, NewSQL [12,39,82,88–91]). However, in this case, for traditional RDBs, which are investigated below, these measures were not implemented.
3. It is believed that the likelihoods: P_t is the likelihood of occurrence of the corresponding threats $(t_1, \ldots, t_{11})$ and P_γ is the likelihood of exploitation the corresponding vulnerabilities $(\gamma_1, \ldots, \gamma_{18})$ in relation to specific protected objects $(o_j \in O, j = \overline{1,7})$ are the same for the compared databases.
4. Evaluation of the residual risk for the compared databases is carried out for the case of a "Low" amount of damage (damage level-2; Tables 1 and 2) with a relative value of possible financial losses amounting to 0.2 ($L^{\text{UBR}}_{\text{quant}} = L^{\text{RDB}}_{\text{quant}} = 0.2$, where $L^{\text{UBR}}_{\text{quant}}$, $L^{\text{RDB}}_{\text{quant}}$ are the numerical values (relative) of damage L for a database with UBR and traditional database, respectively).
5. As security measures/controls ($w_k \in W$), some generalized solutions are used associated with a certain process, policy, device, established practice and other actions aimed at modifying the risk, namely:
    - w_1—means that allow to identify and remove incorrectly assigned privileges. Such, for example, as: audit tools, utilities, scripts used by the database administrator (DBA) for aggregating user rights into a single repository, collecting information about users, their roles and behavior, as well as data privacy, identifying users who have too many privileges and users who do not use their rights, viewing and approving/rejecting the individual rights of users, tracking

all actions to access the database, real-time alerts and blocking, detecting unusual access activity, etc.;
- w_2—tools provided by the DBMS and special developed means in the DB schema with UBR (means that ensure the maintenance of a special *log-table of the modified data*, the formation of data for a *special table of users* and some others [76]), allowing to identify and eliminate incorrectly assigned privileges;
- w_3—tools provided by the DBMS and special developed means in the DB schema with UBR (means providing the formation of data from a special *table of the access privilege distribution to the data of other users* and some others [76]), allowing to identify and eliminate incorrectly assigned privileges;
- w_4—tools provided by the DBMS and special developed means in the DB schema with UBR (means providing the data formation from a special *table of restrictions on access rights to a specific data element* and some others [76]), allowing to identify and eliminate incorrectly assigned privileges;
- w_5—means that allow to identify and eliminate excessive privileges; detect vulnerabilities, missing patches from vendors; inactive accounts, modify default passwords; properly configure the event auditing system, including tracking unusual user access activity, etc. Timely installation of patches or the use of virtual patches to protect the database;
- w_6—means that allow detecting unusual user access activity and complicating the leakage of confidential data from database tables (including the use of means for masking data provided by the DBMS and proposed in [79]; the usage of means of restricting access rights to a specific data element [76] implemented in the DB with UBR);
- w_7—means to detect unusual user access activity and complicate code disclosure of confidential persistent modules (including the use of means for masking data provided by the DBMS and proposed in [77]);
- w_8—means that allow to identify and eliminate incorrectly assigned privileges, detect vulnerabilities, inappropriate session duration, improper implementation of the algorithm, authentication protocol, settings. Timely installation of critical updates or the use of virtual patches to protect the database from attempts to exploit vulnerabilities until a full-fledged and permanent patch is deployed;
- w_9—means that allow controlling resource consumption (for example, through the profile mechanism—a named set of resource restrictions that can be used by the user);
- w_{10}—means that allow controlling the integrity of the trigger code and persistent stored modules, including those based on the potential of the modern blockchain model proposed in [78] and implemented in a DB with UBR;
- w_{11}—using parameterized queries, stored procedures, least privileges; escaping user input; converting data types to the type that was assumed by the logic of the program, checking the data entered by the user for compliance with the allowed character sequences;
- w_{12}—maintenance of the list of "prohibited" functions, procedures, the usage of which should be avoided;
- w_{13}— —anti-virus software;
- w_{14}—means providing support for data integrity (both built into the DBMS and specially developed in the DB schema with UBR [76,80]), as well as implementing security models based on discretionary and role-based policies;
- w_{15}—means that implement security models based on: discretionary, mandatory, role-based, attribute policy, including those specific to a database with UBR [76];
- w_{16}—special documented diagnostic functions capable of identifying the causes of defects caused by the incorrect formation of primary keys, entering incorrect data, inadmissible entry, deletion, modification of data, unauthorized access to data, unauthorized changes to the database schema with UBR and its objects

(including using the capabilities of blockchain technology [78]); special triggers that can be used to intercept and log operations performed in the database; DBMS audit tools;
- w_{17}—audit means built into the DBMS, including specially developed means in the DB schema with UBR (means that ensure the maintenance of a special log-table of the modified data);
- w_{18}—masking data of tables based on the approach described in [79];
- w_{19}—masking of stored objects using the means provided by the DBMS, as well as based on the approach described in [77];
- w_{20}—using transparent data encryption (TDE) and cryptographically strong primitives built into the DBMS as well as national encryption standards (for example, the symmetric block cipher "Kalyna" from the national standard of Ukraine DSTU 7624: 2014);
- w_{21}—timely installation of critical updates, monitoring of the cryptographic strength of the used implementations of encryption algorithms and randomness of numbers generated by pseudo-random number generators (PRNG) that meet the specified requirements;
- w_{22}—database administrator tools built into the DBMS, as well as specially developed scripts that simplify the work of the DBA;
- w_{23}—detailed documentation on the DBMS, DB with a description of all its corresponding elements, their use, including all the main components of the DB schema with UBR;
- w_{24}—audit, blocking a response if the number of requests is incorrect.

In accordance with the above technique and the accepted assumptions, let us estimate the potential value of the database security with the universal basis of relations and compare it with the security of traditional relational databases. For this purpose, on the basis of the above-defined list of main objects, threats, vulnerabilities, available security measures, summarizing the experience of operating and building protection systems for relational databases and databases with UBR, we determine the values of the corresponding components of security barriers ($P_l = f(P_{t_i}, P_{\gamma_\psi}), L_l, R_l$). For this, we will correlate them with the quadruple corresponding most significant (from the point of view of the issues under consideration) elements of barrier $b_l = (t_i, \gamma_\psi, o_j, w_k)$ in the basic security system. Figure 6 shows a fragment of a database security system model in the form of a directed graph.

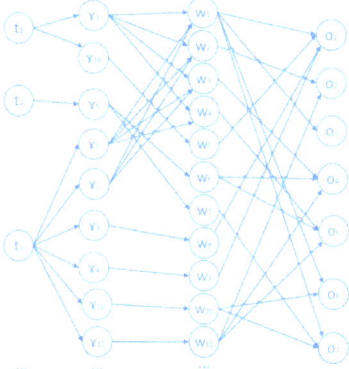

Figure 6. Fragment of the database security system model in the form of a graph.

Table 3 shows a fragment of the evaluation results of the main components of security barriers and resistance (strength) of each of them.

Table 3. Fragment of the evaluation results of the main components of security barriers.

Barrier No.	Threat (t)	P_t^{verbal}/P_t^{quant}	Vulnerability (γ)	$P_\gamma^{verbal}/P_\gamma^{quant}$	Security Measure (w)	$R^{UBR}_{verbal}/R^{UBR}_{quant}$	$R^{RDB}_{verbal}/R^{RDB}_{quant}$	Object (o)	Rr^{UBR}	Rr^{RDB}
1	t_1	"M"/0.4	γ_1	"M"/0.5	w_1	"H"/0.8	"H"/0.8	o_1	0.008	0.008
2	t_1	"M"/0.4	γ_1	"M"/0.5	w_2	"H"/0.85	"H"/0.8	o_2	0.006	0.008
3	t_1	"M"/0.4	γ_1	"M"/0.5	w_3	"H"/0.85	"H"/0.8	o_4	0.006	0.008
4	t_1	"L"/0.1	γ_1	"M"/0.5	w_4	"H"/0.8	"L"/0	o_5	0.002	0.01
5	t_1	"M"/0.4	γ_1	"M"/0.5	w_1	"H"/0.8	"H"/0.8	o_3	0.008	0.008
6	t_1	"M"/0.4	γ_1	"M"/0.5	w_1	"H"/0.8	"H"/0.8	o_6	0.008	0.008
7	t_1	"M"/0.4	γ_1	"M"/0.5	w_1	"H"/0.8	"H"/0.8	o_7	0.008	0.008
8	t_1	"M"/0.4	γ_{18}	"M"/0.5	w_5	"H"/0.8	"H"/0.8	o_1	0.008	0.008
9	t_2	"M"/0.4	γ_5	"H"/0.85	w_6	"H"/0.8	"M"/0.6	o_4	0.0136	0.0272
10	t_2	"M"/0.4	γ_5	"H"/0.85	w_6	"H"/0.8	"M"/0.6	o_5	0.0136	0.0272
11	t_2	"M"/0.4	γ_5	"H"/0.85	w_7	"H"/0.8	"M"/0.6	o_7	0.0136	0.0272
12	t_3	"M"/0.4	γ_1	"M"/0.5	w_1	"H"/0.8	"H"/0.8	o_1	0.008	0.008
13	t_3	"M"/0.4	γ_1	"M"/0.5	w_2	"H"/0.85	"H"/0.8	o_2	0.006	0.008
14	t_3	"M"/0.4	γ_1	"M"/0.5	w_3	"H"/0.85	"H"/0.8	o_4	0.006	0.008
15	t_3	"L"/0.1	γ_1	"M"/0.5	w_4	"H"/0.8	"L"/0	o_5	0.002	0.01
16	t_3	"M"/0.4	γ_2	"M"/0.5	w_1	"H"/0.8	"H"/0.8	o_1	0.008	0.008
17	t_3	"M"/0.4	γ_2	"M"/0.5	w_2	"H"/0.85	"H"/0.8	o_2	0.006	0.008
18	t_3	"M"/0.4	γ_2	"M"/0.5	w_3	"H"/0.85	"H"/0.8	o_4	0.006	0.008
19	t_3	"M"/0.4	γ_2	"M"/0.5	w_1	"H"/0.8	"H"/0.8	o_3	0.008	0.008
20	t_3	"M"/0.4	γ_2	"M"/0.5	w_1	"H"/0.8	"H"/0.8	o_6	0.008	0.008
21	t_3	"M"/0.4	γ_2	"M"/0.5	w_1	"H"/0.8	"H"/0.8	o_7	0.008	0.008
22	t_3	"M"/0.4	γ_3	"M"/0.5	w_8	"H"/0.8	"H"/0.8	o_1	0.008	0.008
23	t_3	"M"/0.4	γ_4	"M"/0.5	w_9	"M"/0.4	"M"/0.4	o_1	0.024	0.024
24	t_3	"M"/0.4	γ_{10}	"M"/0.5	w_{10}	"H"/0.9	"M"/0.4	o_6	0.004	0.024
25	t_3	"M"/0.4	γ_{10}	"M"/0.5	w_{10}	"H"/0.9	"M"/0.4	o_7	0.004	0.024
26	t_3	"M"/0.4	γ_{11}	"M"/0.5	w_{11}	"H"/0.8	"H"/0.8	o_2	0.008	0.008

Where P_t^{verbal} is the verbal value of the linguistic variable—the likelihood of a threat occurrence P_t; P_t^{quant} is the numerical value of the likelihood P_t; P_γ^{verbal} is the verbal value of the linguistic variable—the likelihood of exploiting the vulnerability P_γ; P_γ^{quant} is the numerical value of the likelihood P_γ; R^{UBR}_{verbal} is the verbal value of the linguistic variable—the degree of security measure resistance R ($R = 1 - P^{ov}$) for the database with UBR; R^{UBR}_{quant} is the numerical value of the degree of security measure resistance R for the DB with UBR; R^{RDB}_{verbal} is the verbal value of the linguistic variable—the degree of security measure resistance R for the traditional database; R^{RDB}_{quant} is the numerical value of the degree of security measure resistance R for the traditional database; Rr^{UBR} is the numerical value of the residual risk value for the DB with UBR; Rr^{RDB} is the numerical value of the residual risk value for the traditional database.

In accordance with the obtained results of assessments of the main components of security barriers and residual risk values (Figure 7), under the given assumptions, in accordance with Equation (2) the values of the security quantities of traditional databases and DB with UBR were calculated. All obtained values are presented in Figure 8 in the form of a corresponding diagram.

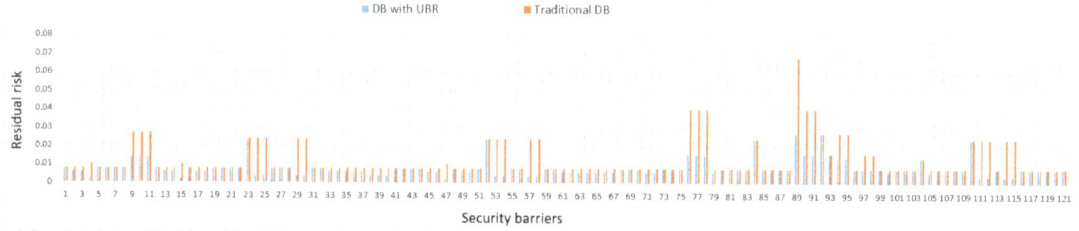

Figure 7. Diagram of residual risk values of the compared databases.

Figure 8. Diagram of security values of compared databases.

Based on the results obtained, a general conclusion was made about the greater effectiveness of the solutions proposed within the framework of the database schema with UBR in comparison with the existing solutions implemented within the framework of traditional relational databases. Taking into account the obtained quantitative assessment, the usage of the proposed solutions will increase the effectiveness of protection (as the reciprocal of the total residual risk) of databases built on the basis of the schema with the universal basis of relations by more than 1.5 times.

An analysis of various countermeasures aimed at ensuring security shows that many problems with the protection of data stored in a database often arise not due to a lack of research, the presence of theoretically developed models, methods, but due to insufficient security in the corresponding specific database implementation or applications working with it. In this sense, DBs with UBR have an advantage, since they are not designed from scratch every time and are not subject to significant modification during reengineering, including in terms of their security. The schema of such databases invariant to various SDs has already been developed, including special measures to ensure security (in the form of appropriate methods, implemented objects). This schema can be installed on the platform of some relational DBMS. When expanding the data set of the simulated SDs in a DB with UBR, unlike traditional relational databases, new basic relations, attributes, keys and other schema objects, including those ensuring its security, are not created, but a new record is simply added to one of the existing basic schema relations. This makes it possible, when reengineering databases built based on this schema, to simplify the process of their adaptation to dynamic changes in subject domains.

The results obtained indicate the objectivity of the developed technique. It is natural that if a database with UBR contains original solutions aimed at improving security, but traditional relational databases do not have them, then the resulting gain in improving the protection effectiveness is predictable.

In the future, it is planned to compare the proposed technique with other approaches.

6. Conclusions

Having analyzed and summarized various approaches and achievements in the field of assessing the security of information systems, the authors of the paper have developed a technique for evaluating the security of relational databases. The proposed technique is the result of a comprehensive combination of the enhanced Clements–Hoffman model, defined integral security metric, the provisions of the theory of fuzzy sets and risk. The Clements–Hoffman model has been extended to a 6-tuple (sextuple). The expansion was carried out by supplementing the model with a set of vulnerabilities (weaknesses) of objects, as a separate objectively existing category. This made it possible to evaluate both the likelihood of an unwanted incident and the database security as a whole more adequately. In addition, in the process of developing the enhanced model, some of its significant components were concretized. Namely:

- Identified the main significant threats to the security of databases;
- The main protected objects are determined taking into account the dual nature of the relational database system and the various degrees of detail of its components.

As an integral metric of database security, the reciprocal of the total residual risk was determined, which is essentially an insecurity measure of an asset. This made it possible to quantify the security of databases. The constituent components that determine the residual risk and characterize the strength of a certain security barrier are presented in the form of certain linguistic variables.

The proposed technique, in contrast to a number of known ones, is based on the time-tested provisions of the theories of probability, fuzzy sets, and risk, allowing at the same time to quite simply, comprehensively and quantitatively evaluate the security of RDBs. The explainable, non-contradictory results of evaluating the security of relational databases designed using various technologies with various security measures presented in the paper indicate the objectivity of the developed technique. If the database with UBR contains original solutions aimed at improving security, but traditional relational databases do not have them, then the gain in improving the protection effectiveness is natural. At that, the very value of the obtained advantage is also explainable and plausible. This is all very important. First of all, from the point of view of the possibility and expediency of practical application of the developed technique in the future for evaluating and comparing the security of various RDBs. Due to its flexibility, the proposed technique can also be used to evaluate the security of databases with various data models.

Author Contributions: Conceptualization, V.Y.; methodology, V.Y. and V.V.; software, V.Y., V.V. and S.A.R.; formal analysis, M.K.; investigation, V.Y., M.Y., V.V and S.A.R.; writing—original draft preparation, V.Y., M.Y. and S.A.R.; writing—review and editing, V.Y., M.K. and M.Y.; funding acquisition, M.K. All authors have read and agreed to the published version of the manuscript.

Funding: The research work reported in this paper was, in part, supported by the University of Bielsko-Biala, Poland, under program no. K18/1b/UPBJ/2019-2020.

Institutional Review Board Statement: Not applicable.

Informed Consent Statement: Not applicable.

Data Availability Statement: Not available.

Conflicts of Interest: The authors declare no conflict of interest.

References

1. Abadi, D.; Agrawal, R.; Ailamaki, A.; Balazinska, M.; Bernstein, P.A.; Carey, M.J.; Chaudhuri, S.; Dean, J.; Doan, A.; Franklin, M.J.; et al. The Beckman Report on Database Research. *ACM SIGMOD Rec.* **2014**, *43*, 61–70. [CrossRef]
2. Abadi, D.; Ailamaki, A.; Andersen, D.; Bailis, P.; Balazinska, M.; Bernstein, P.; Boncz, P.; Chaudhuri, S.; Cheung, A.; Doan, A.; et al. The Seattle Report on Database Research. *ACM SIGMOD Rec.* **2020**, *48*, 44–53. [CrossRef]
3. ISO/IEC 25010:2011 Systems and Software Engineering. Systems and Software Quality Requirements and Evaluation (SQuaRE). System and Software Quality Models. Available online: https://www.iso.org/standard/35733.html/ (accessed on 21 September 2021).
4. Latham, D.C. *Department of Defense Trusted Computer System Evaluation Criteria*; Department of Defense: Arlington, VA, USA, 1986. Available online: http://csrc.nist.gov/publications/history/dod85.pdf (accessed on 21 September 2021).

5. Commission of the European Communities. Information Technology Security Evaluation Criteria (ITSEC): Provisional Evaluation Criteria. Document COM(90) 314, Version 1.2. Available online: https://www.ssi.gouv.fr/uploads/2015/01/ITSEC-uk.pdf (accessed on 21 September 2021).
6. ISO/IEC 21827:2008 Information Technology. Security Techniques. Systems Security Engineering. Capability Maturity Model® (SSE-CMM®). Available online: https://www.iso.org/obp/ui/#iso:std:iso-iec:21827:ed-2:v1:en (accessed on 21 September 2021).
7. Common Criteria for Information Technology Security Evaluation Part 1: Introduction and General Model. Version 3.1 Revision 5 CCMB-2017-04-001. Available online: https://www.commoncriteriaportal.org/files/ccfiles/CCPART1V3.1R5.pdf (accessed on 21 September 2021).
8. Jansen, W.; Gallagher, P.D. NISTIR 7564. Directions in Security Metrics Research. Available online: https://nvlpubs.nist.gov/nistpubs/legacy/ir/nistir7564.pdf (accessed on 21 September 2021).
9. Juma, J.; Makupi, D. Understanding Database Security Metrics: A Review. *Mara Int. J. Sci. Res. Publ.* **2017**, *1*, 40–48.
10. NIST Special Publication 800-55 Revision 1. 2008. Available online: https://csrc.nist.gov/publications/detail/sp/800-55/rev-1/final (accessed on 21 September 2021).
11. Sandhu, R.S.; Jajodia, S. Data and Database Security and Controls. In *Handbook of Information Security Management*; Auerbach Publishers: Boca Raton, FL, USA, 1993; pp. 481–499.
12. Date, C.J. *An Introduction to Database Systems*, 8th ed.; Pearson Education Inc.: New York, NY, USA, 2004.
13. Neto, A.A.; Vieira, M.; Madeira, H. An appraisal to assess the security of database configurations. In Proceedings of the Second International Conference on Dependability, Athens, Greece, 18–23 June 2009; pp. 73–80. [CrossRef]
14. Oracle. Database Security Assessment Tool User Guide. Available online: https://docs.oracle.com/en/database/oracle/security-assessment-tool/2.2.2/satug/index.html#UGSAT-GUID-C7E917BB-EDAC-4123-900A-D4F2E561BFE9 (accessed on 21 September 2021).
15. Yesin, V.I.; Karpinski, M.P.; Yesina, M.V.; Vilihura, V.V. Formalized Representation for the Data Model with the Universal Basis of Relations. *Int. J. Comput.* **2019**, *18*, 453–460. [CrossRef]
16. Savola, R.M. A Security Metrics Taxonomization Model for Software-Intensive Systems. *J. Inf. Process. Syst.* **2009**, *5*, 197–206. [CrossRef]
17. Savola, R.M. Towards Measurement of Security Effectiveness Enabling Factors in Software Intensive Systems. *Lect. Notes Softw. Eng.* **2014**, *2*, 104–109. [CrossRef]
18. Pendleton, M.; Garcia-Lebron, R.; Cho, J.-H.; Xu, S. A Survey on Systems Security Metrics. *ACM Comput. Surv.* **2017**, *49*, 1–35. [CrossRef]
19. Bernik, I.; Prislan, K. Measuring Information Security Performance with 10 by 10 Model for Holistic State Evaluation. *PLoS ONE* **2016**, *11*, e0163050. [CrossRef]
20. Kong, H.-K.; Kim, T.-S.; Kim, J. An analysis on effects of information security investments: A BSC perspective. *J. Intell. Manuf.* **2010**, *23*, 941–953. [CrossRef]
21. Jacobs, M.A. Complexity: Toward an empirical measure. *Technovation* **2013**, *33*, 111–118. [CrossRef]
22. Savola, R.M. Quality of security metrics and measurements. *Comput. Secur.* **2013**, *37*, 78–90. [CrossRef]
23. Yasasin, E.; Schryen, G. Requirements for IT Security Metrics—An Argumentation Theory Based Approach. In *European Conference on Information Systems—ECIS*; Completed Research Paper; Paper 208; ECIS: Münster, Germany, 2015.
24. Katt, B.; Prasher, N. Quantitative security assurance metrics: REST API case studies. In Proceedings of the 12th European Conference on Software Architecture: Companion Proceedings, Madrid, Spain, 24–28 September 2018; pp. 1–7.
25. Sanders, W.H. Quantitative Security Metrics: Unattainable Holy Grail or a Vital Breakthrough within Our Reach? *IEEE Secur. Priv. Mag.* **2014**, *12*, 67–69. [CrossRef]
26. Sarmah, S. Database Security—Threats & Prevention. *Int. J. Comput. Trends Technol. (IJCTT)* **2019**, *67*, 46–50.
27. Awadallah, R.; Samsudin, A. Using Blockchain in Cloud Computing to Enhance Relational Database Security. *IEEE Access* **2021**, *9*, 137353–137366. [CrossRef]
28. Pfleeger, C.P.; Pfleeger, S.L.; Margulies, J. *Security in Computing*, 5th ed.; Prentice Hall: Upper Saddle River, NJ, USA, 2015.
29. Mousa, A.; Karabatak, M.; Mustafa, T. Database security threats and challenges. In Proceedings of the 8th International Symposium on Digital Forensics and Security (ISDFS), Beirut, Lebanon, 1–2 June 2020; pp. 1–5.
30. Connolly, T.M.; Begg, C.E. *Database Systems: A Practical Approach to Design, Implementation, and Management*; Pearson Education Limited: London, UK, 2015.
31. Kulkarni, S.; Urolagin, S. Review of attacks on databases and database security techniques. *Int. J. Emerg. Technol. Adv. Eng.* **2012**, *2*, 2250–2459.
32. Mishra, S.; Morris, R.; Chasalow, L. Information security effectiveness: A research framework. *Issues Inf. Syst.* **2011**, *12*, 246–255.
33. Fabian, B.; Gürses, S.; Heisel, M.; Santen, T.; Schmidt, H. A comparison of security requirements engineering methods. *Requir. Eng.* **2009**, *15*, 7–40. [CrossRef]
34. Hoffman, L.J. *Modern Methods for Computer Security and Privacy*; Prentice-Hall, Inc.: Englewood Cliffs, NJ, USA, 1977.
35. Hoffman, L.J.; Clements, D. *Fuzzy Computer Security Metrics: A Preliminary Report*; Electronics Research Laboratory, College of Engineering University of California: Berkeley, CA, USA, 1977. Available online: https://www2.eecs.berkeley.edu/Pubs/TechRpts/1977/ERL-m-77-6.pdf (accessed on 21 September 2021).

36. Anishchanka, U.V.; Krishtophic, A.M. Methods of evaluating the effectiveness of protecting the assets in information technology objects. *Informatika* **2004**, *3*, 95–105.
37. Maslova, N.A. Methods for assessing the effectiveness of information systems protection systems. *Artif. Intell.* **2008**, *4*, 253–264.
38. Domarev, V.V. *Information Technology Security. Systems Approach*; OOO «TID «DS»: Kyiv, Ukraine, 2004.
39. Hoffmann, R.; Kiedrowicz, M.; Stanik, J. Evaluation of information safety as an element of improving the organization's safety management. In Proceedings of the 20th International Conference on Circuits, Systems, Communications and Computers (CSCC 2016), MATEC Web of Conferences, Corfu Island, Greece, 14–17 July 2016; Volume 76, p. 04011. [CrossRef]
40. Kiedrowicz, M.; Stanik, J. Method for assessing efficiency of the information security management system. In Proceedings of the 22nd International Conference on Circuits, Systems, Communications and Computers (CSCC 2018), MATEC Web of Conferences, Majorca, Spain, 14–17 July 2018; Volume 210, p. 04011. [CrossRef]
41. Lee, M.-C. Information Security Risk Analysis Methods and Research Trends: AHP and Fuzzy Comprehensive Method. *Int. J. Comput. Sci. Inf. Technol.* **2014**, *6*, 29–45. [CrossRef]
42. ISO/IEC 15408-1:2009. Information Technology. Security Techniques. Evaluation Criteria for IT Security. Part 1: Introduction and General Model. Available online: https://www.iso.org/standard/50341.html (accessed on 21 September 2021).
43. ISO/IEC 27001:2013. Information Technology. Security Techniques. Information Security Management Systems. Requirements. Available online: https://www.iso.org/standard/54534.html (accessed on 21 September 2021).
44. ISO/IEC 27004:2016. Information Technology. Security Techniques. Information Security Management. Monitoring, Measurement, Analysis and Evaluation. Available online: https://www.iso.org/standard/64120.html (accessed on 21 September 2021).
45. Rohilla, S.; Mittal, P.K. Database Security: Threads and Challenges. *Int. J. Adv. Res. Comput. Sci. Softw. Eng.* **2013**, *3*, 810–813.
46. Imperva Whitepaper. Top Ten Database Security Threats. 2015. Available online: https://informationsecurity.report/Resources/Whitepapers/e763d022-6ee4-4215-9efd-1896b0d9c381_wp_topten_database_threats%20imperva.pdf (accessed on 21 September 2021).
47. Imperva Whitepaper. Top 5 Database Security Threats. 2016. Available online: https://www.imperva.com/docs/gated/WP_Top_5_Database_Security_Threats.pdf (accessed on 21 September 2021).
48. DB-Engines Ranking. Available online: https://db-engines.com/en/ranking (accessed on 21 September 2021).
49. TOPDB Top Database Index. Available online: https://pypl.github.io/DB.html (accessed on 21 September 2021).
50. Adrian, M.; Feinberg, D.; Heudecker, N. Gartner Magic Quadrant for Operational Database Management Systems. ID G00376881. Available online: https://www.gartner.com/en/documents/3975492/magic-quadrant-for-operational-database-management-syste (accessed on 21 September 2021).
51. Adrian, M.; Feinberg, D.; Greenwald, R.; Ronthal, A.; Cook, H. Critical Capabilities for Cloud Database Management Systems for Operational Use Cases. ID G00468197. Available online: https://www.oracle.com/explore/adw-ocom/gartner-cloud-database-management/?source=:ow:o:p:mt:::RC_WWMK200720P00100:Gartnerdatabase&intcmp=:ow:o:p:mt:::RC_WWMK200720P00100:Gartnerdatabase&lb-mode=overlay (accessed on 21 September 2021).
52. Groff, J.; Weinberg, P.; Oppel, A. *SQL: The Complete Reference*, 3rd ed.; McGraw-Hill, Inc.: New York, NY, USA, 2010.
53. Talabis, M.; Martin, J. *Information Security Risk Assessment Toolkit Practical Assessments through Data Collection and Data Analysis*; Syngress: Waltham, MA, USA, 2012.
54. Whitman, M.E.; Mattord, H.J. *Principles of Information Security*, 6th ed.; Cengage Learning: Boston, MA, USA, 2017.
55. *NIST Special Publication 800-53 Revision 5. Security and Privacy Controls for Information Systems and Organizations*; National Institute of Standards and Technology: Gaithersburg, MD, USA, 2020. [CrossRef]
56. ISO/IEC 27002:2013 Information Technology. Security Techniques. Code of Practice for Information Security Controls. Available online: https://www.iso.org/standard/54533.html (accessed on 21 September 2021).
57. ISO/IEC 27000:2018 Information Technology. Security Techniques. Information Security Management Systems. Overview and Vocabulary. Available online: https://www.iso.org/standard/73906.html (accessed on 21 September 2021).
58. Astakhov, A.M. *The Art of Information Risk Management*; DMK Press: Moscow, Russia, 2010.
59. MITRE. CWE VIEW: Research Concepts. Available online: https://cwe.mitre.org/data/definitions/1000.html (accessed on 21 September 2021).
60. Astakhov, A. *Analysis of the Security of Corporate Systems*; Open System DBMS: Moscow, Russia, 2002; pp. 7–8. Available online: https://www.osp.ru/os/2002/07-08/181720 (accessed on 21 September 2021).
61. Averchenkov, V.I.; Rytov, M.Y.; Gainulin, T.R. Optimization of the choice of the composition of the means of engineering and technical information protection based on the Clements-Hoffman model. *Bull. Bryansk State Tech. Univ.* **2008**, *1*, 61–66.
62. Karpychev, V.Y. Economic analysis of normative and technical support of information security. *Econ. Anal. Theory Pract.* **2011**, *35*, 2–18.
63. Burtescu, E. Database security—Attacks and control methods. *J. Appl. Quant. Methods* **2009**, *4*, 449–454.
64. Arkhipov, A.E. Expert-analytical assessment of information risks and the efficiency level of the information protection system. *Radio Electron. Comput. Sci. Control* **2009**, *2*, 111–115.
65. Zadeh, L.A. The concept of a linguistic variable and its application to approximate reasoning—I. *Inf. Sci.* **1975**, *8*, 199–249. [CrossRef]
66. Petrenko, S.A.; Simonov, S.V. *Information Risk Management. Economically Justified Safety*; DMK Press: Moscow, Russia, 2004.

67. NIST Special Publication 800-30 Revision 1. Guide for Conducting Risk Assessments. Available online: https://nvlpubs.nist.gov/nistpubs/Legacy/SP/nistspecialpublication800-30r1.pdf (accessed on 21 September 2021).
68. Kornienko, A.A.; Nikitin, A.B.; Diasamidze, S.V.; Kuz'menkova, E.Y. Simulation of computer attacks on distributed software. *Bull. St. Petersburg State Transp. Univ.* **2018**, *15*, 613–628.
69. FSTEC Russia. Methodology for Determining Current Threats to the Security of Personal Data during Their Processing in Personal Data Information Systems. Available online: https://fstec.ru/tekhnicheskaya-zashchita-informatsii/dokumenty/114-spetsialnye-normativnye-dokumenty/380-metodika-opredeleniya-aktualnykh-ugroz-bezopasnosti-personalnykh-dannykh-pri-ikh-obrabotke-v-informatsionnykh-sistemakh-personalnykh-dannykh-fstek-rossii-2008-god (accessed on 21 September 2021).
70. Leonenkov, A.V. *Fuzzy Modeling in MATLAB and Fuzzytech*; BHV Petersburg: Sankt-Petersburg, Russia, 2005.
71. Kruglov, V.V.; Dli, M.I.; Golunov, R.Y. *Fuzzy Logic and Artificial Neural Networks*; Fizmatlit: Moscow, Russia, 2001.
72. Piegat, A. *Fuzzy Modeling and Control*; Physica-Verlag: Heidelberg, Germany, 2001.
73. Yesin, V.I.; Vilihura, V.V. Method for Development of Databases Easily Adaptable to Variations in The Subject Domain. *Telecommun. Radio Eng.* **2019**, *78*, 595–605. [CrossRef]
74. Yesin, V.I.; Karpinski, M.; Yesina, M.V.; Vilihura, V.V.; Veselska, O.; Wieclaw, L. Approach to Managing Data From Diverse Sources. In Proceedings of the 10th IEEE International Conference on Intelligent Data Acquisition and Advanced Computing Systems: Technology and Applications (IDAACS), Metz, France, 18–21 September 2019; pp. 1–6. [CrossRef]
75. Franklin, M.; Halevy, A.; Maier, D. From databases to dataspaces: A new abstraction for information management. *ACM SIGMOD Rec.* **2005**, *34*, 27–33. [CrossRef]
76. Yesin, V.I.; Yesina, M.V.; Rassomakhin, S.G.; Karpinski, M. Ensuring Database Security with the Universal Basis of Relations. In *CISIM 2018: Computer Information Systems and Industrial Management*; Lecture Notes in Computer Science, 11127; Saeed, K., Homenda, W., Eds.; Springer: Cham, Switzerland, 2018; Chapter 42; pp. 510–522. [CrossRef]
77. Yesin, V.; Karpinski, M.; Yesina, M.; Vilihura, V.; Warwas, K. Hiding the Source Code of Stored Database Programs. *Information* **2020**, *11*, 576. [CrossRef]
78. Yesin, V.I.; Yesina, M.V.; Vilihura, V.V.; Yesin, V. Monitoring the integrity and authenticity of stored database objects. *Telecommun. Radio Eng.* **2020**, *79*, 1029–1054. [CrossRef]
79. Yesin, V.; Vilihura, V.; Yesin, V. Some approach to data masking as means to counteract the inference threat. *Radiotekhnika* **2019**, *3*, 113–130. [CrossRef]
80. Yesin, V.; Karpinski, M.; Yesina, M.; Vilihura, V.; Warwas, K. Ensuring Data Integrity in Databases with the Universal Basis of Relations. *Appl. Sci.* **2021**, *11*, 8781. [CrossRef]
81. Sadalage, P.J.; Fowler, M. *NoSQL Distilled: A Brief Guide to the Emerging World of Polyglot Persistence*; Pearson Education: London, UK, 2013.
82. Harrison, M.A.; Ruzzo, W.L.; Ullman, J.D. Protection in operating systems. *Commun. ACM* **1976**, *19*, 461–471. [CrossRef]
83. Lipton, R.J.; Snyder, L. A Linear Time Algorithm for Deciding Subject Security. *J. ACM* **1977**, *24*, 455–464. [CrossRef]
84. Clark, D.D.; Wilson, D.R. A Comparison of Commercial and Military Computer Security Policies. In Proceedings of the IEEE Symposium on Research in Security and Privacy (SP'87), Oakland, CA, USA, 27–29 April 1987; IEEE Press: Oakland, CA, USA, 1987; pp. 184–193.
85. Bashir, I. *Mastering Blockchain: Distributed Ledger Technology, Decentralization, and Smart Contracts Explained*, 2nd ed.; Packt Publishing: Birmingham, UK, 2018.
86. Antonopoulos, A.M. *Mastering Bitcoin: Programming the Open Blockchain*, 2nd ed.; O'Reilly Media: Sebastopol, CA, USA, 2017.
87. Cotner, C.; Miller, R.L. International Business Machines Corporation. Row-Level Security in a Relational Database Management System. US Patent 8,478,713 B2, 16 January 2018. N 15/343,568.
88. Meier, A.; Kaufmann, M. *SQL & NoSQL Databases. Databases Models, Languages, Consistency Options and Architectures for Big Data Management*; Springer Fachmedien: Wiesbaden, Germany, 2019. [CrossRef]
89. Harrison, G. *Next Generation Databases: NoSQL, NewSQL, and Big Data*; Apress: Berkeley, CA, USA, 2015.
90. Pavlo, A.; Aslett, M. What's Really New with NewSQL? *ACM SIGMOD Rec.* **2016**, *45*, 45–55. [CrossRef]
91. Garcia-Molina, H.; Ullman, J.D.; Widom, J. *Database Systems: The Complete Book*, 2nd ed.; Pearson Prentice Hall: Upper Saddle River, NJ, USA, 2009.

Communication

Ensuring Data Integrity in Databases with the Universal Basis of Relations

Vitalii Yesin [1], Mikolaj Karpinski [2,*], Maryna Yesina [1,*], Vladyslav Vilihura [1] and Kornel Warwas [2]

1 Department of Security of Information Systems and Technologies, Faculty of Computer Science, V. Karazin National University of Kharkiv, 61022 Kharkiv, Ukraine; v.i.yesin@karazin.ua (V.Y.); viligura93@gmail.com (V.V.)
2 Department of Computer Science and Automatics, Faculty of Mechanical Engineering and Computer Science, University of Bielsko-Biala, 43-309 Bielsko-Biala, Poland; kwarwas@ath.bielsko.pl
* Correspondence: mkarpinski@ath.bielsko.pl (M.K.); m.v.yesina@karazin.ua (M.Y.)

Abstract: The objective of the paper was to reveal the main techniques and means of ensuring the integrity of data and persistent stored database modules implemented in accordance with the recommendations of the Clark–Wilson model as a methodological basis for building a system that ensures integrity. The considered database was built according to the schema with the universal basis of relations. The mechanisms developed in the process of researching the problem of ensuring the integrity of the data and programs of such a database were based on the provisions of the relational database theory, the Row Level Security technology, the potential of the modern blockchain model, and the capabilities of the database management system on the platform of which databases with the universal basis of relations are implemented. The implementation of the proposed techniques and means, controlling the integrity of the database of stored elements, prevents their unauthorized modification by authorized subjects and hinders the introduction of changes by unauthorized subjects. As a result, the stored data and programs remain correct, unaltered, undistorted, and preserved. This means that databases built based on a schema with the universal basis of relations and supported by such mechanisms are protected in terms of integrity.

Keywords: integrity; database; database with the universal basis of relations; Clark–Wilson model

1. Introduction

Ensuring information security of databases (DBs) is impossible without considering aspects of ensuring data integrity. Many, especially commercial, organizations are more concerned with the integrity of their data than its confidentiality [1]. Integrity is more important to them. If you publish information on the Internet on a web server and your goal is to make it available to the widest possible range of people, then confidentiality is not required. On the contrary, the responsibility for providing undistorted information obtained from a database, for example, about the data stored in it from official legal, regulatory, financial, medical, and other documents of the organization, including these documents themselves, is significantly increased. The information must be authentic or genuine. Data must remain correct, truthful, and be a true reflection of reality. In general, both in a commercial and a military environment, it is difficult to imagine a system for which the properties of integrity would not be important [2].

As noted in the Certified Information Systems Security Professional Official Study Guide [1], numerous attacks are aimed at violating integrity. These are both malicious modifications performed by various malicious programs and errors in applications. Integrity violations are not limited to deliberate attacks. User error, oversight, or inept actions are the cause of many cases of unauthorized modifications of information. Events that lead to integrity violations include the modification or deletion of files, database data, entry of incorrect data, configuration alteration, errors in commands, virus introduction,

and malicious code execution. Integrity violations can occur due to the actions of any user, including administrators, either through an oversight in the security policy or due to misconfigured security controls.

The authors of the information systems security guide [1] noted that integrity can be examined from three perspectives: Preventing unauthorized subjects from making modifications, preventing authorized subjects from making unauthorized modifications (e.g., errors), and maintaining internal and external consistency of objects. Properly implemented integrity protection provides a means for authorized modifications while protecting against malicious unauthorized actions, as well as errors made by authorized users. This ensures that the data remain correct (there are no logical errors in the structure and data values), unaltered (data identity to a certain standard), undistorted (no data tampering), and preserved. When a security mechanism ensures integrity, it provides a high level of assurance that data, objects, and resources will not be altered from their original protected state. However, at the same time, it should be remembered and taken into account that integrity control requires additional resources: Time and memory. For example, the main problem in the implementation of mechanisms for controlling the integrity of file objects is their rather strong influence on the load of the computing resource of the system, which is due to the following reasons [3]: First, control of large amounts of information may be required, which is associated with a significant duration of the control procedure; second, continuous maintenance of the object in a reference state may be required. In this connection, a natural question arises: With what frequency to exercise control, since file integrity monitoring is an effective approach to detecting aggressive behavior by detecting actions to modify the corresponding critical files [4]. If it is performed frequently, it will lead to a significant decrease in system performance; if rarely, then the effectiveness of such control may be low. Therefore, one of the main tasks in the implementation of mechanisms for controlling the integrity of file objects is the choice of principles and mechanisms for starting the integrity check procedure.

Another problem of integrity monitoring is the integrity control of the controlling program itself if the integrity control is implemented in software. All of this requires a certain additional study and the adoption of appropriate decisions depending, as a rule, on the features of specific information systems (ISs). Therefore, depending on the importance of the considered aspect of integrity and the data use scope, there are various methods and means to guarantee the integrity of the data under various possible threats. Thus, the correctness, non-distortion, and non-alteration of data can be ensured by methods and means of access control technologies based on formal models of integrity. Non-distortion of data during storage and transmission in information systems can be ensured through cryptographic primitives, such as digital signature, cryptographic hash functions, and message authentication codes. Parallel transaction technologies in multi-user systems also play an important role in ensuring the integrity of a database. The concept of a well-formed transaction is that users should not manipulate data arbitrarily, but only in ways that preserve the integrity of the database [5].

The objective of our paper was to present techniques and means that ensure the integrity of the main components of the database with a universal basis of relations (UBR) [6].

The expediency of researching precisely databases built on the basis of a schema with the universal basis of relations, implemented within the framework of the relational data model, is due to the fact that, first, this will make sure that the data and programs stored in them are secure from the point of view of their integrity. Second, based on their example (in view of the fact that databases with UBR can be used as an ordinary database, as a data warehouse for various subject domains (SDs), or as a configuration database of the dataspace management environment [7]), when applying certain new approaches, it becomes possible to develop a holistic solution that ensures the security of databases and data warehouses. Separate elements of such a solution can be used to protect databases and data warehouses with various models (relational, NoSQL, and NewSQL [8–14]) as well. All of this is important for the scientific community.

The main contribution of the authors is the development of techniques and means that ensure integrity of the main components of a database with the universal basis of relations in accordance with the recommendations of the Clark–Wilson model [15] as a methodological basis for building an integrity assurance system in information systems.

2. Related Works

Figure 1 shows a diagram of the main basic relations R^{sh} of the DB schema with UBR obtained by the authors of the article as a result of many years of research on the problem of creating a standard/universal data model, which has been discussed in the database community since the late 1980s [16–21]. Universal data models can provide effective solutions to many important data management problems [18]. The basic relations R^{sh} proposed by the authors have fundamental differences in the purpose, structure, and storage location of the description of the metadata of the simulated subject domain relative to the relations created in the traditional design technology of relational databases. Their number and structure do not depend on the data set (they are invariant to SDs), in contrast to the structure and number of basic relations of schemas developed using traditional technology. This makes it quite easy to adapt the database created in this way to changes in the SD. At the same time, the structure of DB schema relations remains unchanged. The pre-unlimited variety of SD elements is distributed over a fixed set of basic relations of the DB schema, while providing the possibility of the simultaneous storage and use of data from various significantly different SDs.

In order to more strictly and scientifically state the results of applied research related to ensuring the integrity of databases built on the basis of the schema with the universal basis of relations, it is advisable to use some security model, since it is known that security is easier to achieve if there is a clear model of what is to be protected and who is allowed to do what [22].

The use of formal security models makes it possible to formulate the requirements for creating secure systems (in this case, for the database) in a clearly defined form that corresponds to the security policy adopted in the organization. In general, a security model can be obtained from scratch using a mathematical model or by expanding an existing one. Although, neither of these approaches are easy, since they require the necessary formalization and re-proof [23]. Therefore, having analyzed, taking into account the peculiarities of the aspects under consideration, the well-known integrity models Biba [24], Clark–Wilson [15], and their application [1,2,23,25–30], as well as less well-known Goguen-Meseguer [31], Sutherland security [32], the Clark–Wilson model was taken as the basis. The Clark–Wilson model takes a multifaceted approach to ensuring integrity. This model does not require the use of a lattice structure, and instead of defining a formal state machine, it defines each data element and allows modifications only with a small set of programs [1]. The Clark–Wilson model is less of a specific security policy model, but rather a framework and guideline for formalizing security policies [29]. Data integrity, in accordance with the Clark–Wilson model, is achieved through [33] authentication, audit, well-formed transactions, and separation of duties.

Briefly characterizing the Clark–Wilson integrity model, the following can be noted. This model is based on triplets: "*Subject transaction not violating integrity object.*" Subjects, in accordance with this model, do not have direct access to objects. Objects can only be accessed through the *transformation procedure* (TP). TPs are the only procedures that are allowed to modify a *constrained data item* whose integrity is controlled by an IVP verification procedure (*integrity verification procedure*). IVP is a procedure that scans data items and confirms their integrity. Data whose integrity is not controlled by the security model is denoted as *unconstrained data items* (UDIs).

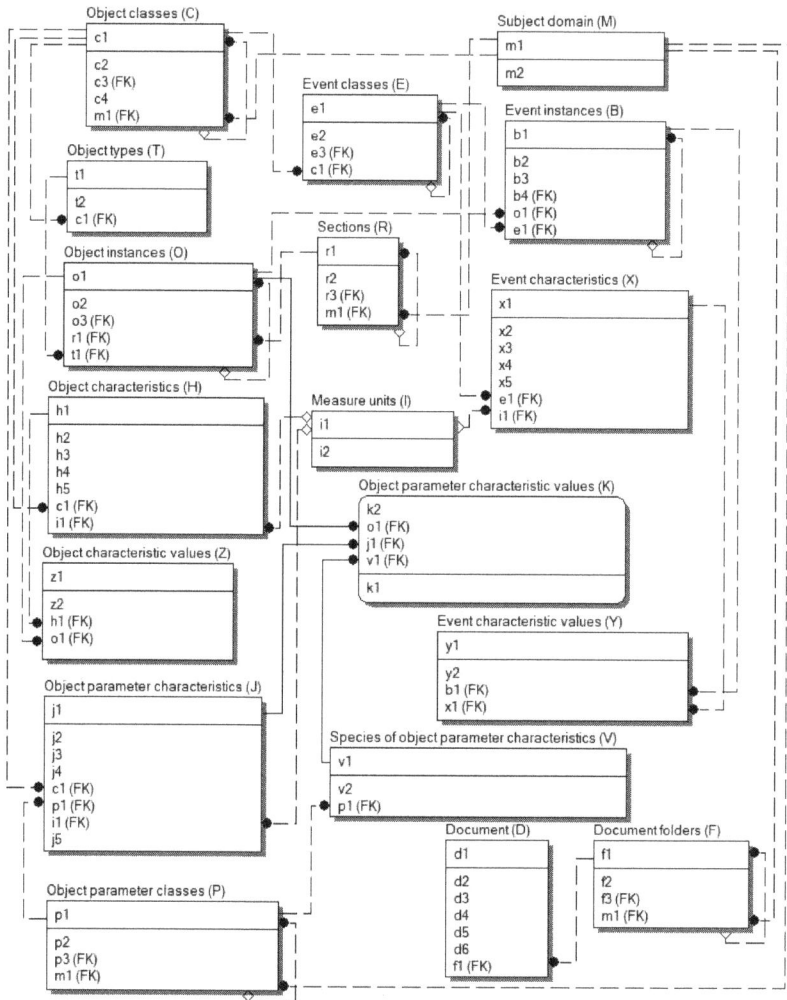

Figure 1. Diagram of the main basic relations R^{sh} of the DB schema with UBR.

The model consists of two sets of rules: Certification rules (C1–C5) and enforcement rules (E1–E4). Enforcement rules correspond to application-independent security functions, while certification rules allow application-specific integrity definitions to be included into the model. In other words, enforcement rules define the security requirements that must be supported by the protection mechanisms in the underlying system (in our case, it is a database management system (DBMS)). Certification rules define the security requirements that the application system should uphold (in this case, these are the proposed solutions within the framework of the DB with UBR schema, taking into account the features and capabilities of the DBMS on the platform on which it is implemented). Figure 2 shows a scheme of the application of these rules to data management.

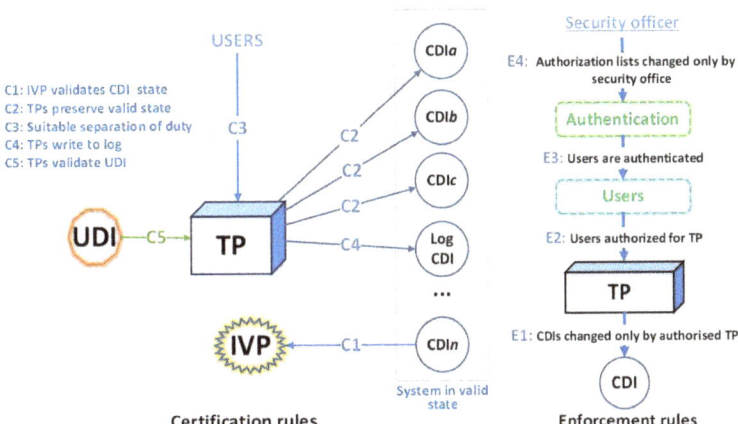

Figure 2. Scheme of applying the rules of the Clark–Wilson model.

3. Applying the Clark–Wilson Model Recommendations to Ensure the Integrity of Databases with the Universal Basis of Relations

It is known that access to the data of any modern database is possible only through the DBMS. A traditional DBMS provides authentication, authorization, transaction, data management, logging, etc. Thus, to check whether the subject (user and process) has the necessary authorization to carry out the required operation in traditional DBMS, in the so-called database manager [9], there is a special module for authorization control. Therefore, the implementation of a DB with UBR on the platform of some selected relational DBMSs automatically leads to the fulfillment of the E3 rule requirement of the Clark–Wilson model, which instructs the system to authenticate all users (each subject) trying to perform any TP procedure.

According to the E4 rule, the access rights of subjects (taking into account their functional duties) to DB objects with UBR (processed CDI elements) can be assigned and changed only by specially authorized subjects (security officers, database administrators, and DB schema owners). For this purpose, the commands (statements) GRANT / REVOKE of the SQL standard are used. In addition, taking into account the peculiarities of the schema and the possibilities of using the DB with UBR [6,7], an additional mechanism for granting privileges was developed, implemented within the framework of RLS (*Row Level Security*) technology (also known as Fine Grained Access Control (FGAC) and Virtual Private Database (VPD)) [34–39], which required the introduction of some additional relations to the existing basic schema of the database with UBR:

- User relation U:

$$U = \{(u_1, u_2, u_3) | u_1 \in U_1 \land u_2 \in U_2 \land u_3 \in U_3 \land \\ ((\forall u_1 \forall u_2 \forall u_3 (\forall u'_2 \in U_2)(U_{pr}(u_1, u_2, u_3) \land U_{pr}(u_1, u'_2, u_3) \rightarrow u_2 = u'_2)) \land \\ (\forall u_1 \forall u_2 \forall u_3 (\forall u'_1 \in U_1)(U_{pr}(u_1, u_2, u_3) \land U_{pr}(u''_1, u_2, u_3) \rightarrow u_1 = u'_1)))\}, \quad (1)$$

where U_1 is the set of user identifiers (subjects), U_2 is the set of user names, $U_{pr}(\ldots)$ refers to the predicates (predicate symbols) matching the relation U, and U_3 is the set of privileges granted to users for performing operations such as deletion, insert, update, select, as well as their combinations;

- The relation of the access privilege distribution to the data of other users G:

$$G = \{(g_1, g_2, g_3) | g_1 \in U_1 \land g_2 \in U_1 \land g_3 \in U_3\}. \quad (2)$$

The relation extension (2) is a set of tuples, each of which is associated with a specific data user/owner (g_1), which transmits its access privileges (g_3) to another authorized user (g_2).

As a rule, today, in relational DBMSs, individual records (fields and cells) are not specially protected, although there are examples known from practice when this is required. Therefore, in order to ensure such functionality, taking into account the invariance of the structure of the relations R^{sh} and based on the capabilities of the RLS technology, a special additional relation was also defined within the framework of the DB with the UBR schema. Namely, it is the relation of restrictions on access rights to a specific data element of the simulated SD:

$$A = \left\{ (a_1, a_2, a_3, a_4) \middle| a_1 \in U_1 \wedge a_2 \in U_2 \wedge a_3 \in R^{sh}_{name} \wedge a_4 \in R^{sh}_{ID} \right\}, \quad (3)$$

where R^{sh}_{name} is the set of names of database schema relations R^{sh} (Figure 1), and $R^{sh}_{ID} = \bigcup_i R^{sh}_i [K_{PK_i}]$ is the set of identifiers that are primary keys (K_{PK_i}) in the corresponding relations R^{sh}, access to which is limited for user $a_1 \in U_1$ with the name $a_2 \in U_2$.

In accordance with RLS technology, the following were defined:

- A set of declarative commands (RLS policies) that determine how and when to apply user access restrictions (in accordance with their functional duties, according to rule C3) to the tuples of the main relations R^{sh} of the DB schema with the UBR;
- A set of stored functions Ψ that are called when the conditions specified in the security policy (RLS policy) are performed;
- Predicates formed by Ψ functions that the DBMS automatically appends to the end of the WHERE clause of user-executed SQL statements.

Taken together, all of this can be represented as the implementation of the rules governing the access control to data of R^{sh} relations of the DB schema with UBR:

$$Sr = \left\{ R^{sh}_i, oper^j_i, policy^k_i, \Psi^l_i, attr^{\mu k l}_i, pat^{R^{sh}_i}_{contr} \right\}, \quad (4)$$

where $oper^j_i$ is j-th combination (from values select, update, delete, and insert) of allowed access operations (transformation procedures (TPs)) to the relation $R^{sh}_i \in R^{sh}$ (as one of the CDI elements); $policy^k_i$ is the name of the k-th RLS policy, which is applied to the base relation R^{sh}_i; $\Psi^l_i \in \Psi$ is the name of the l-th function that generates the predicate for the base relation R^{sh}_i; $attr^{\mu k l}_i$ is the value of the μ-th parameter for the k-th RLS policy and the l-th function; $pat^{R^{sh}_i}_{contr}$ is pattern of the commands for managing access to R^{sh}_i (an example of one of such patterns is given in [40] in the form of program code elements).

All of the above actions were taken so that the DBMS could control the admissibility of applying TP to the CDI elements and provide support for the list of TP transformation procedures required for specific users with an indication of the permissible set of processed elements CDI for each $TP_i \in TP$ and given subject ($s_j \in S$), in accordance with the requirements of rules E1 and E2 of the Clark–Wilson model.

For databases that support the relational data model, integrity constraints are ensured by ways of declarative and procedural support, each of which, in fact, leads to the creation and/or use of some program code that implements the constraint. The difference is only how the code is generated and where it is stored. At that, data integrity constraints must be preliminarily formally defined (declared) before the DBMS can ensure their implementation. In the case of operations that modify the contents of the database, in a traditional DBMS (in the DB manager), as a rule, there is a special data integrity checker module [9], which checks whether the requested operation satisfies all established data integrity constraints. Additionally, this module, taking UDI as input, activates TP, which either converts them to CDI or rejects (according to rule C5). The DBMS data integrity control module, controlling the admissibility of the application of transformation procedures TPs in relation to the list of elements CDIs in accordance with rule E1, monitors the correctness of the implementation of all transformation procedures TPs (according to rule C2), in the sense that these procedures should not violate data integrity. Moreover, all of this takes into account the fact that the system must have procedures $IVPs$ capable of confirming the integrity of any CDI (rule C1).

When developing the main objects of the database schema with UBR, in order to protect the database from violation of the consistency of the data stored in it, the capabilities of both methods were used. Namely, in the created schema, using the integrity support means provided by the SQL language standard, implementations of the Pr^{sh} integrity constraints obtained as a result of the mapping were defined: $\gamma : \text{Pr} \to \text{Pr}^{sh}$ (where Pr is the set of integrity constraints that are specified in the data model with UBR (M_{ubr}) [6]).

The essence of declarative support for integrity constraints is the definition of constraints using the data definition language (DDL) of SQL. The means of declarative support for integrity were used to create the basic relations of the database schema with UBR to define such types of constraints as entity integrity, referential integrity, required (not null) data, and domain constraints. Namely, as known [8,9], the entity integrity is associated primarily with the uniqueness and irreducibility of the primary key. These integrity requirements were defined for all basic schema relations as a result of mapping (applying "*primary key*" and "*unique*" constructs of the corresponding SQL statements): $\gamma_{PK} : \text{Pr}_{PK} \to \text{Pr}^{sh}_{constr_{primary\_key}}$; $\gamma_{UK} : \text{Pr}_{UK} \to \text{Pr}^{sh}_{constr_{unique}}$ Below is an example of the result for such a mapping in the form of the main lines of DDL:

```
alter table MEAS_VALUES
add primary key (MEAS_TIME, MEAS_TYPE_ID, TYPE_ID, OBJECT_ID);.
```

As a result of the mapping: $\gamma_{FK} : \text{Pr}_{FK} \to \text{Pr}^{sh}_{constr_{foreign\_key}}$ (applying "*foreign key*" construction of the "*create/alter table*" operators), to ensure referential integrity, the foreign keys of the schema relations and the action strategies when deleting data were defined. As a result of the mapping: $\gamma_{not\_null} : \text{Pr}_{not\_null} \to \text{Pr}^{sh}_{constr_{not\_null}}$ (applying the "*not null*" specifier in the "*create/alter table*" statements), the constraints prohibiting the assignment of undefined values (*null*) to the corresponding attributes were set.

By mapping a set of integrity constraints of the data model with the universal basis of relations M_{ubr}, constraints for the feature attribute domains, data types of the characteristics of the objects, events, parameters of objects, and some others were defined in the database schema invariant to subject domains (as a result of mapping $\gamma_{dom} : \text{Pr}_{dom} \to \text{Pr}^{sh}_{constr_{check}}$, applying the "check" construction of the "*create/alter table*" operator). An example of the results for such mapping is as follows:

```
alter table EVENTS add check ((event_end_time is null) or ((event_end_time
is not null) and (event_end_time >= event_time)));.
```

However, not all integrity constraints could be implemented (thereby contributing to enforcing the requirements of rules C1 and C2) using declarative support. Therefore, along with the means of this way of implementing integrity constraints, procedural support means have found widespread use, such as triggers, stored procedures, and functions (for simplicity, sometimes united by the common name SQL procedures [41]), the mechanisms of which have been significantly expanded in many commercial DBMS in recent years [14,41]. Using procedural support means, the following integrity constraints ($\text{Pr}^{sh}_{constr_{proc}}$) were implemented in the DB schema with UBR:

The constrains on possibility: Changing SD metadata entered into the corresponding relations of the schema (e.g., the maximum values of max_vals $\in at(R^{sh}_{event\_prop\_types})$) and the removal of the list values for the corresponding characteristics from the relations $R^{sh}_{pr\_vals}$, $R^{sh}_{ev\_pr\_vals}$, and $R^{sh}_{meas\_vals}$ if they are present in the relations associated with the data of the modeled SD [6];

- The constraints on the ability to enter new data that contradict the entered SD metadata (for relations R^{sh} associated with the SD data);
- Implementation of referential integrity for the schema relations R^{sh} associated with the relation R^{sh}_{docs} (a specific document from relation R^{sh}_{docs} is associated with a specific instance of the corresponding relation R^{sh} (Figure 1));

- The constraint of the maximum number of instances of objects ($R^{sh}_{objects}$ relations) for a certain class of objects ($R^{sh}_{obj\_classes}$);
- The constraint of the maximum number of values ($R^{sh}_{ev\_prop\_values}$) that can be assigned to a certain event characteristic ($R^{sh}_{event\_prop\_types}$) for the event instance (R^{sh}_{events}) of the specific class;
- The constraints on the number of events (R^{sh}_{events}) that occur with one object instance ($R^{sh}_{objects}$):

    (a) At the same moment in time with one object instance, more than one event of the same class cannot occur;

    (b) One event that occurs with one object instance can have several subordinate events with different instances of objects occurring at the same time, but the specific event instance that occurs with the object instance of the certain class can have only one "event-owner";

- Generation of unique primary key values for schema relations R^{sh} and some others.

Figure 3 shows the scheme of applying techniques of declarative and procedural support for integrity constraints, which are used in the development of objects of the database schema with UBR to ensure the integrity of its data.

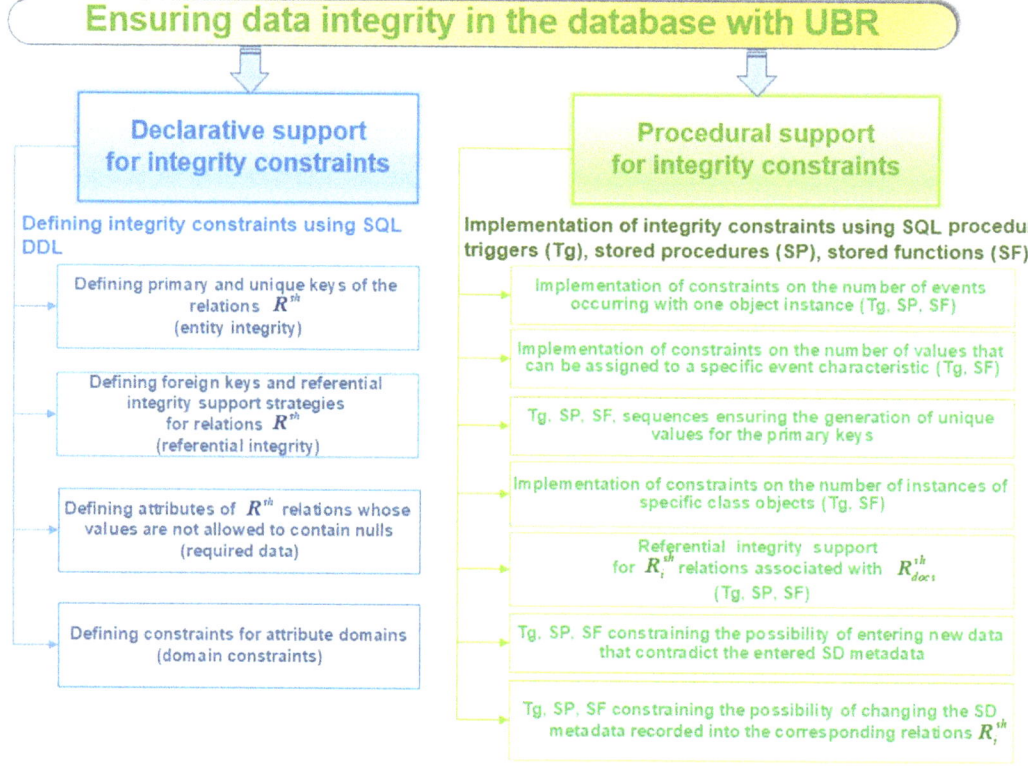

Figure 3. Scheme of using techniques of declarative and procedural support for integrity constraints to ensure data integrity in the DB with UBR.

In addition, taking into account the dual nature of database systems as an information product with two components (assets)—the actual data stored in the database, available for use, and DBMS software—as well as the possibilities of malicious impact on these assets, it is advisable to ensure the security of both of them. Therefore, below, we consider some aspects of ensuring the integrity of such important database objects performing data management as persistent stored modules (PSMs). These are specially designed programs, including SQL statements that are stored in a database, that can be invoked by applications and run within the DBMS. These include the aforementioned stored procedures, functions that can be combined into packages, triggers as a special kind of procedural code (a stored procedure that is called in response to the modification of the database contents [41]), and some others. Constant monitoring of these database objects (as CDI elements) is very important, since some of the attacks on the database (although not only on it, as, for example, you can attack the operating system through the vulnerabilities of the database server) can be detected precisely based on the modification analysis (intentional or accidental) of these objects (violation of their integrity) or their set (increase or decrease in their number) on the database server. Therefore, to ensure the possibility of monitoring the integrity of such stored modules, including those related to the DB schema with UBR, using the potential of the modern blockchain model, as shown in [42], the following have been developed:

- Structure;
- Techniques of forming the genesis and subsequent blocks;
- Verification methods (in the terminology of the Clark–Wilson model, this is IVP) of the PSM integrity, as well as two relations located in one of the privileged user database schemas, which are a mapping of the structure of blocks in the blockchain chain.

1 Relation of blockchain block headers R_{bch}:

$$R_{bch}(i_{id}, t, d_{DB}, n_{DB},\quad n_{sh}, h_{root}, h_{block}, h_{p\_block}, n_{so}, w \mid i_{id} \in \mathbb{N}^* \wedge t \in T \wedge d_{DB} \in Nm^{d_{DB}} \wedge \\ \wedge n_{DB} \in Nm^{DB} \wedge n_{sh} \in Nm^{sh_{DB}} \wedge h_{root} \in H_{Mr} \wedge h_{block} \in H_b \wedge \\ \wedge h_{p\_block} \in (H_b \cup \varnothing) \wedge n_{so} \in \mathbb{N}^* \wedge w \in W), \tag{5}$$

where i_{id} is the number of the i-th blockchain block; t is timestamp of block creation (T UTC Coordinated Universal Time); $Nm^{d_{DB}}$ is a set of database domain names; d_{DB} is the domain name of a specific database; Nm^{DB} is a set of database names; n_{DB} is the name of a specific database; $Nm^{sh_{DB}}$ is a set of names of the database schemas; n_{sh} is the name of a specific database schema (or "genesis block"); H_{Mr} is a set of hashes of Merkle roots; ($H_{Mr} = \{0,1\}^n$ is a set of all words of length n in the alphabet $\{0,1\}$); h_{root} is the hash of Merkle tree root of the i-th block ($i = 1 \ldots N_{bc}$, where N_{bc} is the total number of blockchain blocks); h_{block} is the hash of the header of the current i-th block; h_{p_block} is the hash of the header of the previous $(i-1)$-th block; H_b is a set of block hashes; ($H_b = \{0,1\}^n$); n_{so} is the number of controlled stored DB modules (as data items $CDIs$); $\mathbb{N}^*$ is a set of natural numbers without zero; W is a set of digital signatures ($w \in W$, $W = \{0,1\}^l$).

An example of a partially filled database table, which is a mapping of the relation R_{bch}, is given below (Table 1).

2 Relation of stored database modules (objects) R_{sp}:

$$R_{so}(i_{id}, p_k, \alpha_k, h_k \mid i_{id} \in \mathbb{N}^* \wedge p_k \in type_{so} \wedge \alpha_k \in Nm_{so} \wedge h_k \in H_{so}), \tag{6}$$

where Nm_{so} is a set of names of stored modules (objects), and H_{so} is a set of hashes of stored modules ($H_{so} = \{0,1\}^n$).

An example of a partially filled database table, which is a mapping of the relation R_{so}, is given below (Table 2).

Table 1. An example of a partially filled table of blockchain block headers. *

i_{id}	t	d_{DB}	n_{DB}	n_{sh}	h_{root}	h_{block}	h_{p_block}	n_{so}	w
296987922	21-APR-20 06.00.13.000000 PM +03:00	ua.xxx.com	WORKGR\ DESKTOP-QRRDTTA	genesis block	D420161F3 5294B0A64 7DD3E625 3C57AE25 8EC417D10 14EFC483A 66E7B6A9 1CE1	D420161F3 5294B0A64 7DD3E625 3C57AE25 8EC417D10 14EFC483A 66E7B6A9 1CE1		1	...
296987923	22-APR-20 02.34.01.575000 PM +03:00	ua.xxx.com	orcl	SYS	4DC69C66 60AF511F0 8D3F89FE89 9D19396269 676F657883 2EBC452EA 45F4AD56	442F64B40C 2CBA0E478 6DEC2FB9F A64C310C8 555F8E6F15 82E1651AE B7501CEB	D420161F3 5294B0A647 DD3E6253C 57AE258EC 417D1014EF C483A66E7 B6A91CE1	9799	...
296987924	22-APR-20 02.36.24.606000 PM +03:00	ua.xxx.com	orcl	user_1	3538FDE465 91936C2FF5 3D06909323 1E9F72C316 451629D44F AAE4AB221 FE2D1	F5415080C6 8CE7E671F5 262A968CE0 13B70C6B3B EC200C9E90 192D5AA22 ED6EC	442F64B40C 2CBA0E478 6DEC2FB9F A64C310C8 555F8E6F15 82E1651AEB 7501CEB	326	...
...	...	...	...	...	...	...	F5415080C6 8CE7E671F5 262A968CE0 13B70C6B3B EC200C9E90 192D5AA22 ED6EC	...	...

* The background color is used for better understanding.

Table 2. An example of a partially filled table of stored modules.

i_{id}	p_k	α_k	h_k
296987923	FUNCTION	AQ$_GET_SUBSCRIBERS	05A85236D79D0FFB86DEB 11B1F5D155C49B831A008 C6E96F4A389C3896540107
...	...	...	...

Access to these tables is limited: Only read/write and only to the owners of the corresponding schemas. In order to protect against unauthorized actions of a privileged user, as well as against illegitimate actions of attackers who illegally obtain the privileges of the owner of some schema with respect to the corresponding objects (modules), the proposed solution prescribes the creator of a specific database schema to sign "own" relevant data (see Table 1) with one of the modern digital signature algorithms. The result of the concatenation of hashed values (Merkle root hash, the timestamp, and the number of objects) is such signed data. The use of a hash tree structure, such as Merkle root, a digital signature mechanism to control the integrity and authenticity of objects stored in a specific database schema, is due to the objective need for rational use of resources, leading to savings for stored data and the computing resources of the processor.

As you know, the main disadvantage, usually mentioned for the Clark–Wilson model, is that IVP and related techniques are not easy to implement in real computer systems, in particular due to the fact that control of large amounts of information may be required, which is associated with a significant duration of the procedure IVP [30]. Thus, for example, in order to control the integrity of a specific stored module (as one of the CDI elements) in a specific database schema in the usual way, it is necessary to perform hashing and digital signature procedures, storing the corresponding data for each of them. The use of the hash tree structure allows ensuring the integrity control not only of the specific PSM being checked, but also of all other stored programs of the selected database schema, including the procedure that ensures the correctness of the formation of the values of Tables 1 and 2. Since this one data fragment is included in the general structure, changing at least one bit in it will entail a complete change in the value of the Merkle root. Therefore, Merkle trees are widely used for secure and efficient validation (control integrity) of large data structures [43–47].

On the DBMS server, the integrity control of the persistent stored modules, as described above, can be established with a certain periodicity as part of the audit with the recording of relevant information in the audit log with its subsequent analysis and taking effective measures. At that, the integrity check of a certain PSM can be initiated by any of the legitimate users of the system, who will contact the server with a corresponding request, which is described in more detail in [42].

An approach to the usage of the potential of the modern blockchain model can also be applied to control the data integrity of the relation R_{docs}^{sh}, in which various documents of the simulated subject domain can be stored. If necessary, it is also possible to provide control of the integrity of Tables 1 and 2. At that, some data of tables of Tables 1 and 2 can be converted into JSON format, after which a certain file will be formed from this data some file-ledger, which is distributed to all legitimate users. First, for the possibility of performing duplicate monitoring of unauthorized changes in stored database objects, and second, for the possibility for legitimate users of so-called lightweight nodes [43] to formulate correct queries to obtain information about the integrity of stored objects used in their applications. Using the concept of hash trees, and having certain data from the file-ledger, a legitimate user retains the ability to determine the fact of the presence of the object of interest stored in the database, as well as its integrity, by obtaining a small amount of data (as an authentication path in the Merkle tree) from the database server without the need to store or transfer a huge amount of blockchain data.

It is no secret that the audit procedure is equally important for creating a complete database security system. According to rule C4 of the Clark–Wilson model, each application of TP must be logged in a special item CDI, which is a log containing sufficient information to reconstruct a complete representation of each application of this transformation procedure, and available only for adding information to it. Therefore, to monitor the status, changes made to the database, user actions, in addition to using standard audit means of DBMS, on the platform of which the database schema with UBR is implemented, the developed special diagnostic functions implemented in the interpreter of the data model language (LDM) [48] are used. These functions can detect the introduction of incorrect data. For this purpose, triggers are also used that support the logging of operations performed in the database. In addition, for accountability of user actions, data from the log table of the modified data can be used [40]. Thanks to the information stored in the log table, which is automatically formed when the corresponding parameter of the stored procedure of the data model language interpreter is specified, the process of recovering incorrectly modified or lost data is simplified, and the procedure for determining the users, times, and nature of the modifications made by them is facilitated.

Thus, analyzing from the perspective of the Clark–Wilson model the possibilities of the above developed and implemented, including within the framework of the DB schema with UBR, techniques and means that ensure the integrity of the corresponding database elements of the CDI, we can conclude that they fully correspond to the main idea of the model. The basic theoretical principles of the integrity control policy lay out what needs to be done, and the mechanisms implemented define how these principles are achieved. Therefore, databases implemented based on a schema with UBR can be considered appropriate to the needs of databases protected from the point of view of integrity.

4. Conclusions

Using the recommendations of the Clark–Wilson model as a methodological basis for building an integrity assurance system in information systems, the authors developed techniques and means that ensure the integrity of the main components of a database with the universal basis of relations.

The proposed mechanisms are based on the provisions of the theory of relational databases, the RLS technology, the potential of the modern blockchain model, the capabilities of the SQL and LDM languages, as well as the DBMS on the platform on which DBs with UBR are implemented.

The implemented techniques and means, controlling changes of the stored *CDI* elements of the database with UBR, prevent their unauthorized change by authorized subjects and prevent changes by unauthorized subjects. As a result, the stored data and programs remain correct, unaltered, undistorted, and preserved. Consequently, databases built based on the UBR schema and supported by such mechanisms are protected in terms of integrity.

Author Contributions: Conceptualization, V.Y.; methodology, V.Y. and V.V.; software, V.Y., V.V., and K.W.; formal analysis, M.K.; investigation, V.Y., M.Y., V.V., and K.W.; writing—original draft preparation, V.Y., M.Y., and K.W.; writing—review and editing, V.Y., M.K. and M.Y.; funding acquisition, M.K. All authors read and agreed to the published version of the manuscript.

Funding: The research work reported in this paper was, in part, supported by the University of Bielsko-Biala, Poland, under program no. K18/1b/UPBJ/2019-2020.

Institutional Review Board Statement: Not applicable.

Informed Consent Statement: Not applicable.

Conflicts of Interest: The authors declare no conflict of interest.

References

1. Chapple, M.; Stewart, J.M.; Gibson, D. *CISSP Certified Information Systems Security Professional Official Study Guide*, 8th ed.; Sybex, John Wiley & Sons, Inc.: Indianapolis, IN, USA, 2018.
2. Jueneman, R.R. Integrity controls for military and commercial applications. In Proceedings of the Fourth Aerospace Computer Security Applications, IEEE, Orlando, FL, USA, 12–16 September 1988; pp. 298–322. [CrossRef]
3. Shcheglov, A.I. *Protection of Computer Data from Unauthorized Access*; Nauka i Technika: St. Petersburg, Russia, 2004.
4. Jin, H.; Xiang, G.; Zou, D.; Zhao, F.; Li, M.; Yu, C. A guest-transparent file integrity monitoring method in virtualization environment. *Comput. Math. Appl.* **2010**, *60*, 256–266. [CrossRef]
5. Sandhu, R.S.; Jajodia, S. Data and database security and controls. In *Handbook of Information Security Management*; Auerbach Publishers: Boca Raton, FL, USA, 1993; pp. 481–499.
6. Yesin, V.I.; Karpinski, M.; Yesina, M.V.; Vilihura, V.V. Formalized representation for the data model with the universal basis of relations. *Int. J. Comput.* **2019**, *18*, 453–460. [CrossRef]
7. Yesin, V.I.; Karpinski, M.; Yesina, M.V.; Vilihura, V.V.; Veselska, O.; Wieclaw, L. Approach to Managing Data From Diverse Sources. In Proceedings of the 10th IEEE International Conference on Intelligent Data Acquisition and Advanced Computing Systems: Technology and Applications (IDAACS), Metz, France, 18–21 September 2019; pp. 1–6. [CrossRef]
8. Date, C.J. *An Introduction to Database Systems*, 8th ed.; Pearson Education Inc.: New York, NY, USA, 2004.
9. Connolly, T.M.; Begg, C.E. *Database Systems: A Practical Approach to Design, Implementation, and Management*; Pearson Education Limited: London, UK, 2015.
10. Sadalage, P.J.; Fowler, M. *NoSQL Distilled: A Brief Guide to the Emerging World of Polyglot Persistence*; Pearson Education: London, UK, 2013.
11. Meier, A.; Kaufmann, M. *SQL & NoSQL Databases. Databases Models, Languages, Consistency Options and Architectures for Big Data Management*; Springer Fachmedien: Wiesbaden, Germany, 2019. [CrossRef]
12. Harrison, G. *Next Generation Databases: NoSQL, NewSQL, and Big Data*; Apress: Berkeley, CA, USA, 2015.
13. Pavlo, A.; Aslett, M. What's really new with NewSQL? *ACM SIGMOD Record* **2016**, *45*, 45–55. [CrossRef]
14. Garcia-Molina, H.; Ullman, J.D.; Widom, J. *Database Systems. The Complete Book*, 2nd ed.; Pearson Prentice Hall: Upper Saddle River, NJ, USA, 2009.
15. Clark, D.D.; Wilson, D.R. A Comparison of Commercial and Military Computer Security Policies. In Proceedings of the IEEE Symposium on Research in Security and Privacy (SP'87), Oakland, CA, USA, 27–29 April 1987; IEEE Press: Oakland, CA, USA, 1987; pp. 184–193.

16. Bernstein, P.A.; Dayal, U.; DeWitt, D.J.; Gawlick, D.; Gray, J.; Jarke, M.; Lindsay, B.G.; Lockemann, P.C.; Maier, D.; Neuhold, E.J.; et al. Future Directions in DBMS Research—The Laguna Beach Participants. *ACM SIGMOD* **1989**, *18*, 17–26. [CrossRef]
17. Bernstein, P.; Brodie, M.; Ceri, S.; DeWitt, D.; Franklin, M.; Garcia-Molina, H.; Gray, J.; Held, J.; Hellerstein, J.; Jagadish, H.V.; et al. The Asilomar report on database research. *ACM SIGMOD* **1998**, *27*, 74–80. [CrossRef]
18. Silverstone, L. *The Data Model Resource Book, Vol. 1: A Library of Universal Data Models for All Enterprises*; John Wiley & Sons, Inc.: Indianapolis, IN, USA, 2001.
19. Silverstone, L. *The Data Model Resource Book, Vol. 3: Universal Patterns for Data Modeling*; John Wiley & Sons, Inc.: Indianapolis, IN, USA, 2009.
20. Vyazilov, E.; Fedortsov, A.; Kobelev, A. Unification of data structure for field research, exploration and resources using of World Ocean. In Proceedings of the 10th All-Russian Scientific Conference "Digital Libraries: Advanced Methods and Technologies, Digital Collections", Dubna, Russia, 7–11 October 2008.
21. Vyazilov, E.D.; Fedortsov, A.A. Universal data storage model taking into account the life cycle of objects. In Proceedings of the Sixth All-Russian Open Annual Conference "Modern Problems of Remote Sensing of the Earth from Space", Moscow, Russia, 10–14 November 2008.
22. Tanenbaum, A.S.; Bos, H. *Modern Operating Systems*, 4th ed.; Pearson Education, Inc.: Upper Saddle River, NJ, USA, 2015.
23. Schott, M.; Krätzer, C.; Dittmann, J.; Vielhauer, C. Extending the Clark-Wilson security model for digital long-term preservation use-cases. In Proceedings of the SPIE 7542, Multimedia on Mobile Devices, San Jose, CA, USA, 27 January 2010. 75420M. [CrossRef]
24. Biba, K.J. *Integrity Considerations for Secure Computer Systems*; Mitre Corp: Bedford, MA, USA, 1977.
25. Whitman, M.E.; Mattord, H.J. *Principles of Information Security*, 6th ed.; Cengage Learning: Boston, MA, USA, 2017.
26. Katzke, S.; Ruthberg, Z. Report of the Invitational Workshop on Integrity Policy in Computer Information Systems (WIPCIS). NIST Special Publication 500-160. Available online: https://nvlpubs.nist.gov/nistpubs/Legacy/SP/nistspecialpublication500-160.pdf (accessed on 24 August 2021).
27. Shockley, N.R. Implementing the Clark-Wilson integrity policy using current technology. In Proceedings of the 11th National Computer Security Conference, Baltimore, MD, USA, 17–20 October 1988; pp. 29–37.
28. Toapanta, S.M.T.; Trejo, J.A.O.; Gallegos, L.E.M. Analysis of Model Clark Wilson to Adopt to the Database of the Civil Registry of Ecuador. In Proceedings of the 21st conference of the Open Innovations Association FRUCT, Helsinki, Finland, 6–10 November 2017; pp. 513–518.
29. Gollmann, D. *Computer Security*, 3rd ed.; Wiley: Hoboken, NJ, USA, 2011.
30. Ge, X.; Polack, F.; Laleau, R. Secure databases: An analysis of Clark-Wilson model in a database environment. In *Advanced Information Systems Engineering. CAiSE 2004*; Persson, A., Stirna, J., Eds.; Lecture Notes in Computer Science, 3084; Springer: Berlin/Heidelberg, Germany, 2004; pp. 234–247. [CrossRef]
31. Goguen, J.A.; Meseguer, J. Security policies and security models. In Proceedings of the IEEE Symposium on Security and Privacy, Oakland, CA, USA, 26–28 April 1982; pp. 11–20. [CrossRef]
32. Sutherland, D. A Model of Information. In Proceedings of the 9th National Computer Security Conference, Baltimore, MD, USA, 15–18 September 1986; pp. 175–183.
33. Van Tilborg, H.C.A.; Jajodia, S. *Encyclopedia of Cryptography and Security*, 2nd ed.; Springer Science & Business Media: New York, NY, USA, 2011. [CrossRef]
34. Row-Level Security in a Relational Database Management System/Curt Cotner, Gilroy, CA (US); Roger Lee Miller, San Jose, CA (US); International Business Machines Corporation, Armonk, NY (US)—N 10/233,397. US Patent 2004/0044655A1. 4 March 2004.
35. Row-Level Security in a Relational Database Management System/Curt Cotner, Gilroy, CA (US); Roger Lee Miller, San Jose, CA (US); International Business Machines Corporation, Armonk, NY (US)—N 12/242,241. US Patent 8,131,664 B2. 6 March 2012.
36. Row-Level Security in a Relational Database Management System/Curt Cotner, Gilroy, CA (US); Roger Lee Miller, San Jose, CA (US); International Business Machines Corporation, Armonk, NY (US)—N 15/343,568. US Patent 8,478,713 B2. 16 January 2018.
37. Feuerstein, S.; Pribyl, B. *Oracle PL/SQL Programming*, 6th ed.; O'Reilly Media, Inc.: Sebastopol, CA, USA, 2014.
38. Kyte, T. *Expert Oracle*; Apress: New York, NY, USA, 2005.
39. Nanda, A.; Feuerstein, S. *Oracle PL/SQL for DBAs*; O'Reilly Media, Inc.: Sebastopol, CA, USA, 2005.
40. Yesin, V.I.; Yesina, M.V.; Rassomakhin, S.G.; Karpinski, M. Ensuring Database Security with the Universal Basis of Relations. In *Proceedings of the Computer Information Systems and Industrial Management. CISIM 2018*; Lecture Notes in Computer Science, 11127; Saeed, K., Homenda, W., Eds.; Springer: Cham, Switzerland, 2018; Chapter 42; pp. 510–522.
41. Groff, J.; Weinberg, P.; Oppel, A. *SQL. The Complete Reference*, 3rd ed.; McGraw-Hill Inc.: New York, NY, USA, 2010.
42. Yesin, V.I.; Yesina, M.V.; Vilihura, V.V. Monitoring the integrity and authenticity of stored database objects. *Telecommun. Radio Eng.* **2020**, *79*, 1029–1054. [CrossRef]
43. Bashir, I. *Mastering Blockchain: Distributed Ledger Technology, Decentralization, and Smart Contracts Explained*, 2nd ed.; Packt Publishing: Birmingham, UK, 2018.
44. Antonopoulos, A.M. *Mastering Bitcoin: Programming the Open Blockchain*, 2nd ed.; O'Reilly Media: Sebastopol, CA, USA, 2017.
45. Chapweske, J. Tree Hash Exchange Format. Available online: https://web.archive.org/web/20090803220648/http://open-content.net/specs/draft-jchapweske-thex-02.html (accessed on 24 August 2021).

46. Wei, W.; Yu, T. Integrity Assurance for Outsourced Databases without DBMS Modification. In Proceedings of the IFIP Annual Conference on Data and Applications Security and Privacy, Vienna, Austria, 14–16 July 2014; Springer: Berlin/Heidelberg, Germany, 2014; pp. 1–16.
47. Niaz, M.S.; Saake, G. Merkle Hash Tree based Techniques for Data Integrity of Outsourced Data. In Proceedings of the 27th GI-Workshop Grundlagen von Datenbanken, Gommern, Germany, 26–29 May 2015; pp. 66–71.
48. Yesin, V.I.; Yesina, M.V. Language for universal data model. *Inf. Process. Syst.* **2011**, *5*, 193–197.

Article

Delegation-Based Personal Data Processing Request Notarization Framework for GDPR Based on Private Blockchain

Sung-Soo Jung [1], Sang-Joon Lee [2] and Ieck-Chae Euom [2,*]

1 Research Center, DISEC, Daegu 41069, Korea; jssdisec@gmail.com
2 System Security Research Center, Chonnam National University, Gwangju 61186, Korea; s-lee@jnu.ac.kr
* Correspondence: iceuom@jnu.ac.kr

Abstract: With the growing awareness regarding the importance of personal data protection, many countries have established laws and regulations to ensure data privacy and are supervising managements to comply with them. Although various studies have suggested compliance methods of the general data protection regulation (GDPR) for personal data, no method exists that can ensure the reliability and integrity of the personal data processing request records of a data subject to enable its utilization as a GDPR compliance audit proof for an auditor. In this paper, we propose a delegation-based personal data processing request notarization framework for GDPR using a private blockchain. The proposed notarization framework allows the data subject to delegate requests to process of personal data; the framework makes the requests to the data controller, which performs the processing. The generated data processing request and processing result data are stored in the blockchain ledger and notarized via a trusted institution of the blockchain network. The Hypderledger Fabric implementation of the framework demonstrates the fulfillment of system requirements and feasibility of implementing a GDPR compliance audit for the processing of personal data. The analysis results with comparisons among the related works indicate that the proposed framework provides better reliability and feasibility for the GDPR audit of personal data processing request than extant methods.

Keywords: GDPR; personal data; delegation; notarization; blockchain; non-repudiation

1. Introduction

Information and communication technologies can potentially create high added value in various fields owing to the use of big data. In such applications of big data, various personal data are being collected, stored, analyzed, and utilized [1–5]. These collected personal data can be used for personalized marketing and consumption trend analysis and are recognized as a new type of highly valuable asset to service providers [6,7]. However, the importance of guaranteeing privacy and protecting collected personal data is being emphasized, as accidents involving the illegal collection, illegal distribution, and leakage of personal data by the service provider have become frequent, and related damage has increased [8].

In addition, owing to the development of the Internet and distributed storage technology, personal data that are not deleted over time have been identified as a new risk factor that can lead to serious invasion of privacy. Consequently, the importance of the right to request the processing of stored personal data of each data subject, such as the right to be forgotten, is also being focused upon [9]. Moreover, with the growing awareness of privacy, many countries are refining laws and regulations on personal data protection [10–13]. The general data protection regulation (GDPR), which came into effect in May 2018, focuses on strengthening the rights of data subjects and corporate accountability, and clarifying requirements for transfer of personal data outside the EU [8,14]. Under the implementation of the GDPR, other than member states of the EU, which are required to present implementations that meet the requirements of the GDPR, countries that desire to be incorporated into the EU and many other countries are amending or replacing existing laws to reflect certain aspects of the GDPR [8,14]. To protect the fundamental rights and freedoms of natural persons and in particular their right to the protection of personal data, the GDPR sets out items on the protection and safe processing of collected data that controllers and processors must observe. In addition, it stipulates data processing policy according to the right to request processing of the private data of the data subject, and it ensures that member countries are obligated to manage and supervise compliance while stipulating that a strong administrative measure is imposed in case of violation [15,16].

However, since data subjects are guaranteed the right to request the processing of their personal data, which is stipulated in Articles 12 to 23 of Chapter 3, "Data Subjects' Rights," GDPR is a challenge. A personal data processing request is not an act entrusted to the service provider in the personal data processing consent that the data subject voluntarily proceeds before subscribing to the service to use the service provider's service. However, the records of requests such as the modification, deletion, and transfer of the data subject are managed by the service provider and used for GDPR compliance audits. Consequently, there is a risk of the service provider damaging, contaminating, or not creating the records for their own benefit. Therefore, the integrity and objective reliability of the data subject's request records managed by the service provider are not guaranteed. However, despite these problems, at present, the supervisory authority is obligated to rely on the evidence presented by the service provider for the GDPR compliance audit of service providers [17]. For example, if the data subject filed a legal lawsuit because the service provider did not faithfully comply with the regulations even though the data subject requested the service provider to delete its data under the right to be forgotten as stipulated in Article 17 of the GDPR, service providers may delete or corrupt the data subject's request record. A proposed countermeasure to this situation is a method wherein the data subject obtains a record of the requests for the processing of personal data and responses exchanged with the service provider from an external organization such as an email service provider, which are then notarized through a trusted notary organization. However, implementing this method is a challenge for any individual data subject owing to its complexity, cost, and cumbersome nature.

Thus far, several studies have researched systems and methods for safe and reliable GDPR management or audit. As analysis of that integrity and reliability of evidence data cannot be guaranteed through an existing centralized system method; certain studies focused on blockchain (BC) as a personal data storage, management, and GDPR [17–22]. However, to date, no realistic and reliable method to protect the data subject's right to request for the processing of personal data has been proposed [6,23,24]. Most of the previous systems and methods have proposed schemes to share personal data or to manage records of the processing of personal data from the perspective of service providers; this cannot guarantee the integrity and reliability of the data subject's request records necessary for the GDPR compliance audit. Data processing requests and their corresponding responses should exhibit an agreement between the data subject and service provider to ensure objectivity on credibility. The method that involves the management of data only from the perspective of the service provider cannot secure an objective view on credibility, while the method of storing all records of accessing or processing the data in a BC conflicts with GDPR regulations such as the right to be forgotten. Consequently, if further personal data are stored, the privacy problem associated with BC reproduces itself further [22–26].

This paper proposes a delegation-based personal data processing notarization framework for GDPR based on private BC technology. Figure 1 shows the conceptual configuration of the distributed storage and notarization of personal data processing request transactions using a BC-based notarization framework.

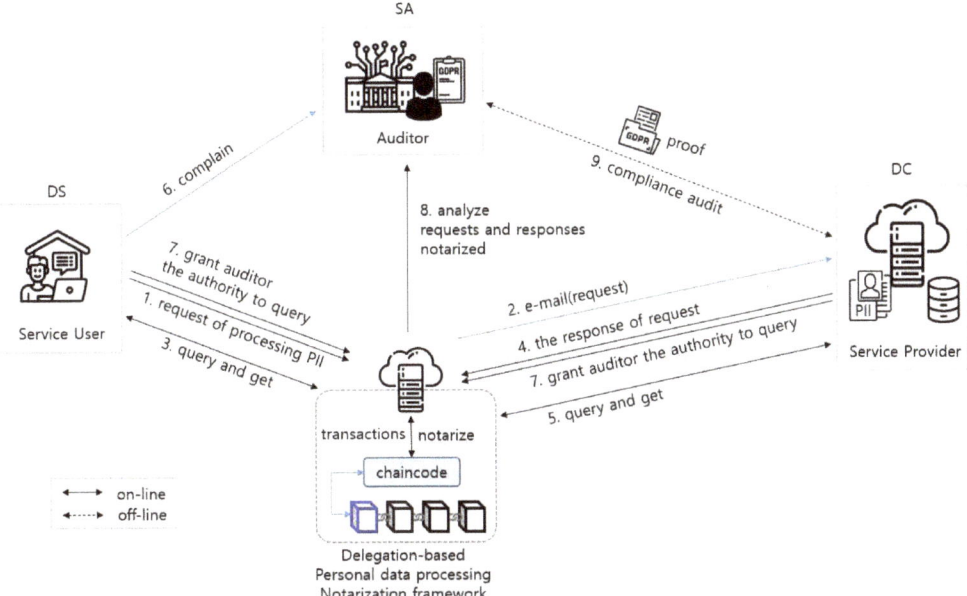

Figure 1. A procedural overview of the personal data processing request notarization framework.

When the data subject requests the data controller to process personal data, the reliability and integrity of the requests and responses can be guaranteed by notarizing the request contents via the proposed notarization framework. Furthermore, transparency and security for data management is realized by distributing and storing the ledger wherein request transactions are recorded on the BC network and allowing only the auditor authorized by the transaction creator to access the stored transactions. Moreover, the proposed framework does not store personal data but only manages requests for the processing of personal data and response records that can perform GDPR compliance audits and secures the audit data without violating the GDPR. Furthermore, it can further strengthen and guarantee data subjects' rights to the processing of personal data.

The rest of this paper is organized as follows. Section 2 presents an overview of BC and GDPR and reviews the related works. Section 3 details the devised delegation-based personal data processing notarization framework, and Section 4 presents the implementation results of the proposed notarization framework by using Hyperledger Fabric (HLF). Furthermore, Section 5 presents the analyses of the functions and attributes of the proposed notarization framework, and the conclusions drawn from the study are presented in Section 6.

2. Background and Related Work
2.1. GDPR

GDPR, which came into force as of 25 May 2018, consists of 11 Chapters and 99 Articles, and it stipulates the rules related to the protection of natural persons related to the processing of personal data and the rules related to the free movement of personal data [15]. Among the role groups defined by the GDPR, the primary role groups for GDPR compliance are as follows:

- Data subject (DS): owner of the produced personal data who possesses the right to process his/her personal data; decides on the entrustment of the processing of own personal data to the service provider; requests to view, correct, delete, suspend processing,

or transmit personal data stored by the service provider and confirm the result; and can ask the supervisory authority to audit service providers for GDPR compliance.
- Service provider (SP): organization that provides various services by collecting and managing personal information; must comply with the GDPR regulations and prepare legal evidence for all actions involving collecting and managing personal data; and present the evidence upon request from DS and supervisory authorities.
- Data controller (DC): the person who is in charge of personal data management belonging to the SP; determines the purpose and method of the processing of personal data; and is responsible for managing and proving that the data for the DS is processed in a lawful, fair, and transparent manner.
- Supervisory authority (SA): the organization that conducts GDPR compliance audits; has the legal authority to regularly oversee and investigate the compliance of SPs with GDPR regulations; is an independent public authority responsible for monitoring the application of regulations to protect the basic rights and freedoms of natural persons regarding the processing of personal data and to promote the free flow of personal data within the Union.

One of the primary requirements when collecting and processing personal data in the GDPR is the technical implementation, which is required to guarantee the rights of the DS considering the concept of personal data protection. Violations can result in strong administrative penalties, such as fines, and they may be subject to laws and regulations even when conducting business in Europe [15]. On the basis of these requirements, a summary of the main Articles and Recitals particularly related to the processing of personal data is as follows:

- Articles 12–23: The DS may request a provision of information on personal data collected in relation to oneself, correction of inaccurate personal data about oneself without delay, deletion of personal data related to oneself without delay, and transmission of personal data provided by oneself to other DCs. Moreover, the DC shall not refuse to act in response to the DS's request for the exercise of these rights.
- Recital 59: Modalities should be provided for facilitating the exercise of DS's rights under this Regulation, including mechanisms to request and, if applicable, obtain, free of charge, in particular, access to and rectification or erasure of personal data and the exercise of the right to object. In addition, the DC should provide the means for requests to be made electronically, particularly where personal data are processed via electronic means.
- Recital 66: To strengthen the right to be forgotten in the online environment, the right to erasure should also be extended in such a manner that the DC who has made the personal data public must be obliged to inform the DCs that are processing such personal data to erase any links to, or copies, or replications of those personal data. Consequently, the DC must incorporate reasonable steps, considering the available technology and the means available to DC, including technical measures, to inform the DCs that are processing the personal data of the DS's request.

2.2. Blockchain

BC is a technology that distributes and verifies data within peer-to-peer network nodes in the form of blocks having a chain-type link. It is a data forgery prevention technique wherein several blocks are connected similar to a chain such that the hash of the current block becomes a component of the subsequent block using data encryption technology [27,28]. In the traditional transaction model, a central entity with authority functions as a gate and manages and guarantees the ledger data generated between nodes. In this centralized model, when a system with a central authority is incapacitated by internal or external intentional or unintentional attacks and failures, or when data are damaged or contaminated, the damage can spread throughout the entire network. In contrast, in the BC model, a copy of the ledger is distributed and stored to all nodes in the network, thereby reducing the risk and maintaining trust by removing the central authority. Owing to this structure, the BC has four key characteristics as follows [25]:

- Decentralization: BC network transactions can be performed between two peers (P2P) without authentication from a central authority.
- Persistence: As each transaction spreading through the network must be verified and recorded in blocks distributed throughout the network, tampering is almost impossible.
- Anonymity: Owing to the absence of a central system to store the personal data of the user, each user can communicate with the BC network using the created address, thus minimizing identity exposure.
- Auditability: In the BC, each transaction can repeatedly trace the previous transaction. This improves the traceability and transparency of the stored data.

Currently, the BC system can be divided into a public, private, and consortium BCs. Among these, private BC allows only authorized nodes to process consensus, can restrict read permission, and has high efficiency, so it is often used as a framework for corporate business processing [25].

2.3. Related Works of Blockchain-Based GDPR

Features of BC such as integrity, transparency, reliability, and traceability are effective when they are applied to tasks that require compliance management. To manage personal data or GDPR compliance, many researchers have performed research based on BC [8,15–25,28–42].

For related research analysis, by the SLR (Systematic Literature Review) approach, we selected research questions and derived key search terms such as 'Personal Data', 'Blockchain', 'GDPR', and 'Notarization' from the research questions, and we used them to search and collect papers. However, many of the extracted papers provide only preliminary methodological investigations. Through the primary analysis of the collected papers, we classified the papers with solution implementation plans or implementation examples and performed secondary intensive analysis. Table 1 shows related studies that suggest blockchain-based unique technologies in relation to GDPR compliance.

Table 1. Overview of related works based on BC.

No	Research Works	Proposed Technology
R01	Liang et al. in [29]	BC-based data provenance architecture in cloud environment with privacy
R02	Yan et al. in [30]	Protecting privacy and self-sovereignty through blockchains for OpenPDS
R03	Chowdhury et al. in [31]	BC as a notarization service for data sharing with personal data store
R04	Agarwal et al. in [32]	GDPR legislative compliance assessment
R05	Truong et al. in [33]	BC-based personal data management
R06	Truong et al. in [34]	GDPR-compliant personal data management
R07	Vargas in [35]	BC-based consent manager for GDPR compliance
R08	Kassem et al. in [36]	BC identity management system to secure personal data sharing in a network
R09	Rantos et al. in [37]	Consent management platform for personal data processing using BC
R10	Faber et al. in [38]	BC-based personal data and identity management system
R11	Piras in [39]	Privacy by design platform for GDPR compliance
R12	Mahindrakar and Joshi in [40]	Automating GDPR compliance using policy integrated BC
R13	Casaleiro in [41]	Protection and control of personal identifiable information
R14	Daudén-Esmel et al. in [42]	BC-based platform for GDPR-compliant personal data management

As a result of analyzing the related studies, the main research areas of the related studies are shown in Table 2.

Table 2. Related works by research field.

Major Research Field	Related Work's Number
Data provenance	R01
Access control	R05, R06
Notarization	R02, R03, R09
Identity management	R08, R10
Compliance assessment	R04, R12
Consent management	R07, R09, R14
GDPR compliance management	R06, R07, R11, R13

As a result of analyzing works related to BC-based personal data protection and GDPR compliance management, it can be seen that various methods and solutions are being studied for the expansion of GDPR compliance by using the characteristics of the BC such as integrity, confidentiality, transparency, and audit traceability. However, most of the works that tried to solve the privacy problem using BC do not consider GDPR, so it is difficult to apply it as a method to meet the requirements according to each regulation of GDPR. On the other hand, most of the works that suggested the application of BC to meet the requirements of the GDPR only present a conceptual design and did not present a practical implementation method of BC. Even works that presented practical implementation methods did not suggest a method to address the risk that BC-based systems may themselves violate GDPR principles because of their BC nature or how the records stored in BC could be utilized by an outer auditor for compliance audits. Most of the works designed the system structure under the premise that SP stores and manages personal data. So, the proposed architecture is designed so that users go through the system of SP to access BC. Nevertheless, the issue of the objective reliability of the data stored in BC was not taken into account. Most of the systems proposed by related works are designed to link the SP's system or storage with the blockchain through API. However, considering the actual situation, there may be a problem in GDPR application scalability due to difficulties in API development and the interworking module distribution in order to link the SP's legacy personal data management system with the BC-based proposed system. However, most studies do not take these issues into account. As shown in Figure 2, BC-based GDPR compliance solutions have been proposed in various areas; however, solutions for securing the reliability of personal data processing requests and response evidence are yet to be proposed [43].

Table 3 shows the limitations of previous related works for GDPR compliance audits so far.

Table 3. The limitations of related works for GDPR compliance audits.

Limitations	Related Work's Number
Lack of proposal of measures considering detailed regulations for GDPR compliance	R01, R02, R03, R05, R07, R08, R09, R10, R11
Lack of support for outer auditors	R05, R06, R08, R09, R10
Lack of consideration of scalability issues due to legacy system linkage	R01, R02, R03, R04, R05, R06, R09, R10, R12, R13, R14
Lack of consideration of personal data protection issues in BC (risk of privacy violations due to storage of personal data and all access records)	R01, R05, R06, R07, R13
Lack of presentation of a practical BC system implementation method	R02, R03, R07, R08, R10, R11, R12, R13, R14
Lack of research on GDPR compliance with personal data processing request	All except R06, R07, and R14

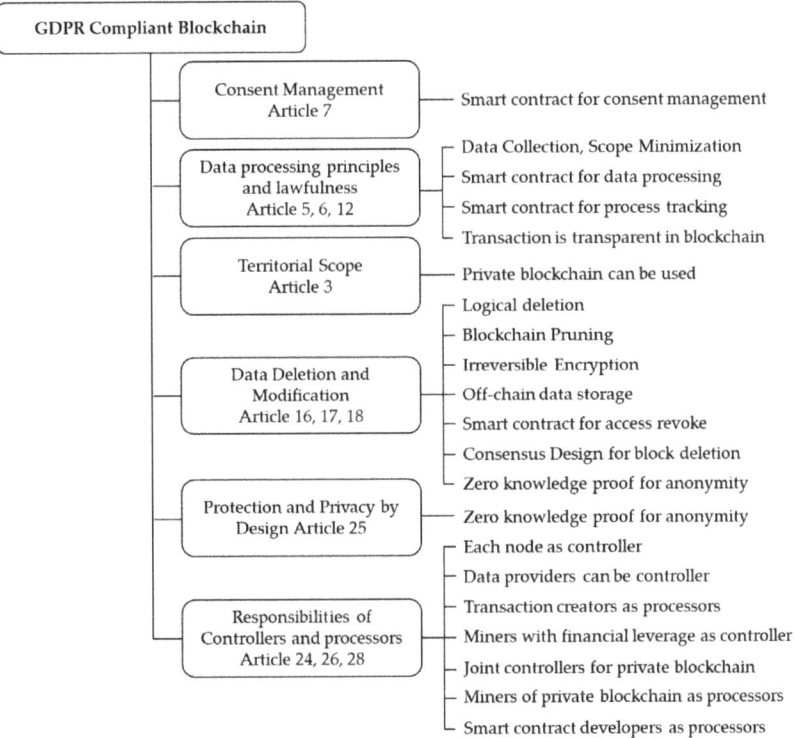

Figure 2. Proposed solutions for GDPR compliance.

3. Delegation-Based Personal Data Processing Request Notarization Framework

This section proposes a delegation-based personal data processing request notarization framework that can notarize requests by the DS for the processing of personal data and its corresponding response. This was done to guarantee reliability and integrity for the GDPR audit. The DS delegates the request for the processing of personal data to the proposed framework, which forwards the request to the SP's DC by e-mail such that the DC responds to the request. For GDPR compliance, e-mail was used for a formal request proof of the processing of personal data from DS to SP. Herein, the request and response were recorded in the BC ledger. The ledger was notarized via nodes in the BC network. Consequently, the right of the DS to process personal data as stipulated by GDPR is guaranteed. Personal information may be included in the transaction sent by DS or DC to the proposed framework, so a method to protect personal data is required. The proposed framework protects personal data by using a session key-based encryption method. In order for the user to use the proposed framework, he/she must consent to the delegation of authority for personal data processing when he/she sign up for the service. This process is the same as general consent processing, so it is omitted from the proposed framework architecture.

To design a framework for GDPR compliance, we set the following design security. Based on the framework, the auditor can perform a GDPR compliance audit of security design goals to ensure reliability and credibility of data processing among network participants.

- Confidentiality: Network participants must be able to trust the transaction data that are evidence related to the processing of personal data.

- Integrity: It must be guaranteed that the created and managed transaction data are not illegally forged or altered.
- Non-repudiation: Denying related facts based on the subject of transaction data creation and management is not possible.

To design a new notarization framework, first, this section presents a derivation of the required features for GDPR compliance data processing, and thereafter, it proposes a private BC-based notarization framework that can satisfy the derived features.

3.1. GDPR Compliance Audit Scenario of Personal Data Processing Request

This section provides a service scenario based on a centralized system as shown in Figure 3 to withdraw certain required features to ensure GDPR compliance of the personal data processing request.

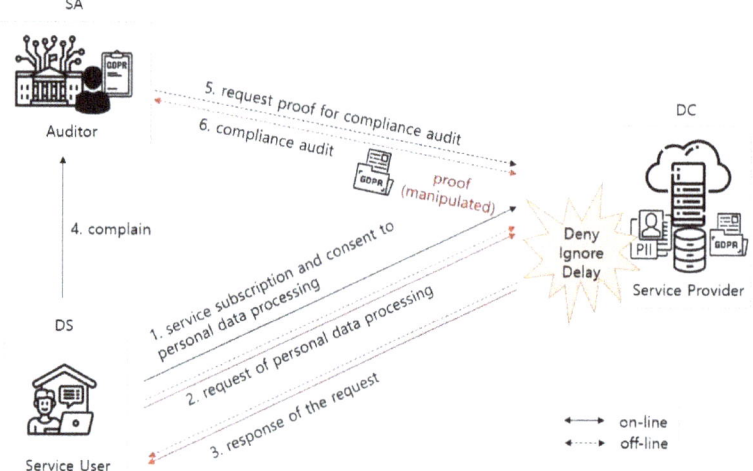

Figure 3. GDPR compliance audit scheme in a conventional centralized environment.

Consider a system wherein each service provider stores various data in its own database, which is related to the personal data processing request trusted by the DS to provide various services. In this situation, GDPR SA conducts a GDPR compliance audit based on the evidence data submitted by the service providers. The scenario where network participants perform their own actions and the SA conducts a GDPR compliance audit related to the processing of SPs is as follows:

- The DS must consent to the processing of personal data to utilize the services of an SP and subscribe to services on the system. The SP is the DC of personal data.
- SPs collect and manage the personal data of DSs adhering to GDPR regulations.
- In accordance with GDPR regulations, the DS requests the SP to view, correct, delete, stop, and transmit his/her personal data at any time if needed.
- The SP accepts the request and performs all processes without any delay. After executing the process, the results of the processing are notified to the DS. Particularly, if the DS uses their request on an electronic method, it responds to the request through an electronic method. The SP must record the processing logs and establish legal evidence data to prove GDPR compliance.
- The SA manages SP to ensure compliance with GDPR regulations and performs a GDPR compliance audit by analyzing evidence data presented by the SP to certify them.
- DSs may request a GDPR compliance audit of the SP from the SA in the processing of their personal data based on a specific situation.

- SA investigates the operation status of SPs considering the requested GDPR compliance audit and takes appropriate measures based on results obtained from the investigation.

3.2. Challenges and Requirements of the GDPR Compliance Audit for Personal Data Processing Request

In this section, through scenario analysis, we discuss the challenges and solutions for securing the reliability of personal data processing, particularly requests and responses, in GDPR compliance audits. In the scenario, the SA receives all evidence data related to the GDPR compliance audit from the SP, which is the DC of personal data. GDPR compliance verification is performed through a record of delegation-based consensus between the DS and SP; that is, it is based on the consent given by the DS to the processing of personal data, the performance of the SP with GDPR compliance in managing the DS's personal data is verified. The request made by the DS for the processing of personal data is a right attributed to the DS stipulated in Chapter 12 of GDPR, and response to the request is a duty of the SP. However, as the record can be damaged and contaminated by the SP, its reliability cannot be assured as an objective view on credibility without any consent from the DS. This is because the request is not the processing of personal data entrusted by the DS to the SP in consent. Thus, for the DS to overcome this drawback without relying on evidence provided by the SP when it responds inappropriately to requests, external notarization is the approach used to secure the reliability of the request sent by the DS. However, notarizing the requests of DS is a challenge. First, maintaining records related to requests is difficult unless electronic methods such as e-mail are used. In addition, to notarize records such as e-mail, the data on those records must be requested from an e-mail SP, and thereafter, the data have to be notarized through an organization with legal authority. Consequently, the problem of securing an objective view of the credibility on records for requests and responses can be analyzed as "the need for reliable notarization for request for the processing of personal data that can be easily used without sharing personal data and is processed in real time." GDPR regulations regarding the requests of the DS that require external notarization are Article 12 and Articles 15–21. Further, for the regulations, the functions shown in Figure 4 are required to support GDPR compliance audits related to the personal data processing request.

Considering the environment in which many countries must comply with GDPR, it is necessary to establish a notarization system that supports a distributed environment for the notarization of personal data processing requests. The following functions are required to build a notary system in a distributed environment [44]:

- Sealing of data: The sealing of data ensures data integrity and not secrecy. It must produce the same value when the data are sealed and when they are verified. A third party cannot obtain the data, modify it, and produce a new value that is acceptable when the data and value are verified.
- Accessible to all: The notary must be accessible to all who desire to seal data.
- Trusted or certifiable: The notary must either be trusted or certifiable, as must its cryptographic keys.
- Highly trusted communications: If the notary exists in a different domain, then the communication between the notary and user must be highly secure. The client must possess the means of ensuring that the data he/she has notarized are the data that were requested to be notarized.
- Authentication: It is important that the user that starts a transaction is the only user to participate in that transaction or delegate work to other users. Consequently, the user that starts a transaction can be attributed with that transaction when it is committed.

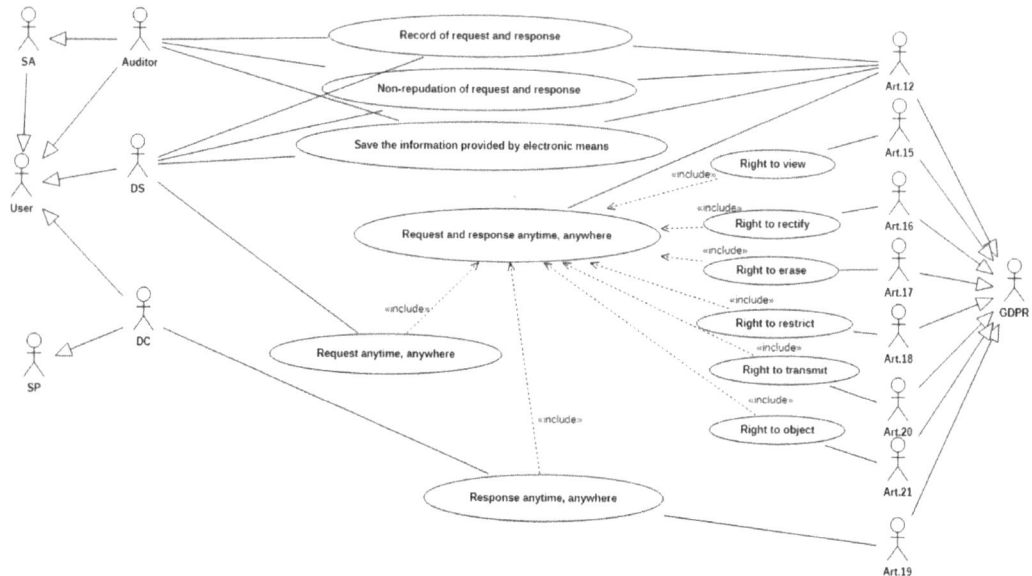

Figure 4. Requirements to support GDPR compliance audits regarding the DS's requests.

With respect to the processing of personal data, all DCs must comply with the GDPR principles relating to the processing of personal data as stipulated in Article 5 of the GDPR. This is also applicable for GDPR compliance audit management systems that deal with personal data. In particular, as deleting stored data is difficult, owing to the nature of the distributed environment in BC, the BC-based GDPR compliance audit management system is required to minimize personal data collection to not violate the GDPR principle by itself [36].

Finally, considering the reality that many SPs in various countries are operating personal data processing systems, the feasibility of minimizing modifications to the legacy system for linkage is required for the notarization framework to be applicable for GDPR compliance audit.

3.3. Design Goals

We analyzed the requirements for GDPR compliance audit management related to DS requests, requirements for a notarization system in a distributed environment, GDPR principles related to personal data processing, and the feasibility of applying to all SPs in a real environment. Based on the analysis, the design goals of the personal data processing notarization framework for GDPR compliance audit, a solution to the problem, were derived as shown in Figure 5.

The details of the functional design goals other than the security design goals mentioned previously in the derived design goals are as follows:

- Delegation for GDPR: DS must have the ability to delegate requests for the processing of personal data to the notarization system and deliver them to DC in an electronic manner. Data creators who want notarization should be easily accessible anytime, anywhere.
- Audit trail for GDPR: Requests and responses must be recorded in the form of 'who, when, to whom, and what' for GDPR compliance, and they must preserve integrity. Records must be stored in a manner such that they can be viewed by an auditor authorized by the DS and DC.

- Notarization of request for the processing of personal data: Verification of the personal data processing request and corresponding data through a number of trusted notaries should be enabled, and furthermore, the ability to notarize the integrity of the stored and retrieved data is important. The authenticity and key management of data creators and notaries should ensure that the reliability of the data cannot be denied.
- Managing permission for audit: Only the author or recipient of the data should have access to the relevant data. DSs and DCs must have the ability to authorize auditors to view data for GDPR compliance audits related to requests for the processing of personal data. However, searching for data other than the data of the approver that the auditor has authorized the inquiry authority to view should be disabled.
- Distribution of trust: The authentication of users using the notarization system and the authority that manages the ledger must be performed and mutually verified by certain trusted institutions across countries rather than one.
- Minimum collection: Personal data other than data related to requests and responses should not be collected, and GDPR compliance audits should be possible for requests from DSs without sharing them with DCs or not being provided them from DCs.

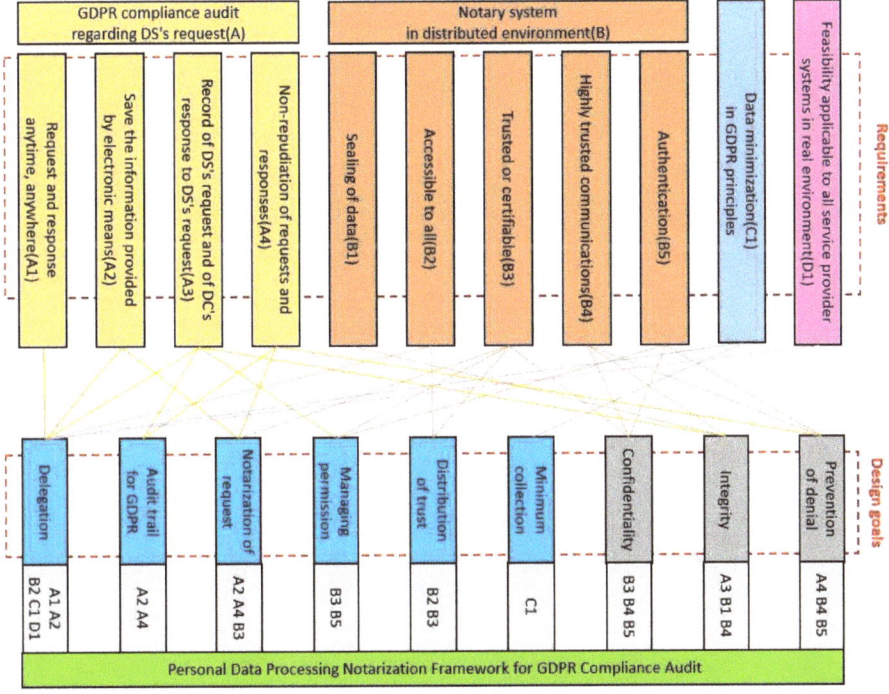

Figure 5. Notarization framework design goals.

3.4. Notarization Framework

The proposed notarization framework aims to provide an objective view of credibility assurance for evidence data of processing requests and responses for GDPR audit on the processing of personal data. Figure 6 shows the conceptual network configuration of the proposed framework, consisting of DSs (service users), DCs (SPs), SAs (auditors), and notarization systems.

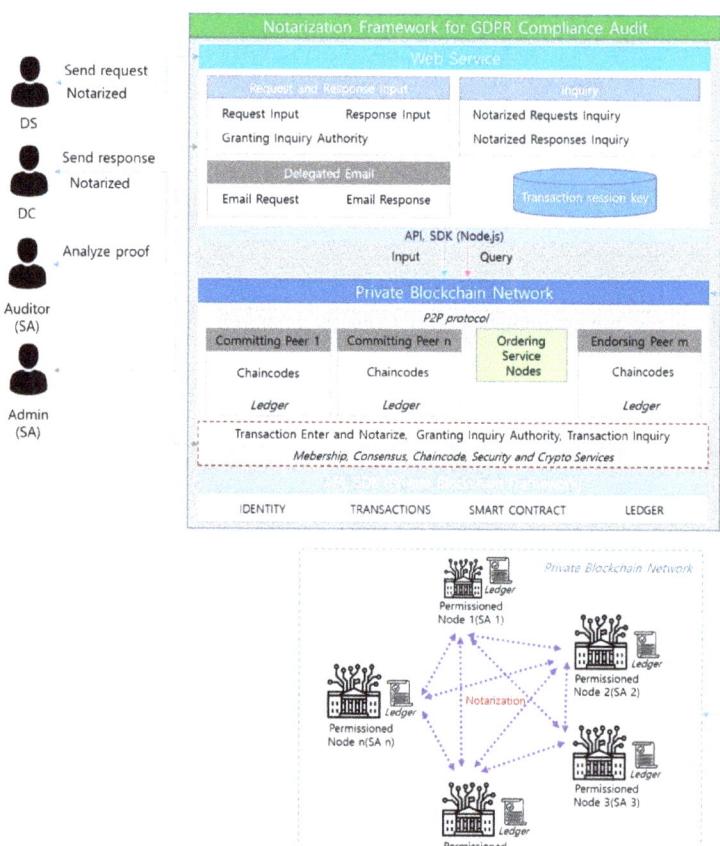

Figure 6. Notarization framework overview based on BC.

All data derived from the process of requesting and responding to the processing of personal data between the DS and DC are stored in the BC ledger through a notarization system. SAs can conduct transparent and reliable GDPR compliance audits based on the notarized ledger through the notarization system.

Moreover, for the reliability of notarization, only authoritative nodes should be allowed to participate in notarization. Therefore, the proposed notarization framework is based on a private BC framework wherein only authorized participants can participate in the BC network. The roles of the network participants are as follows:

- DS (Service user): To register request information for viewing, correction, deletion, suspension of processing, and transmission of personal information stored by SPs in the system. To query the request and the response records of the DC in the system. To complain to the SA if the DC fails to satisfactorily process the personal data of the DS against the interests and rights of the DS. To grant SAs the authority to query the records of requests for the processing of personal data through the system.
- DC (SP): To respond to requests by the DS for the processing of personal data and register responses in the system. To grant SAs the authority to query response records to requests for the processing of personal data through the system.
- Auditor (SA): With the authority authorized by the DS, to query the system regarding the records of the requests and response for the processing of personal data.

To conduct a GDPR compliance audit of the DC to determine compliance. To ensure that the DC adheres to the GDPR regulations and is authorized by the DC to inquire the data of the DC when performing an audit. To check the records of the response of the DC to the requests made by the DS stored in the system to determine the regulations are being adhered to.
- Notarization system: To provide services to the web through smart contracts, manage the BC ledger, and manage the authority of network participants. To store the data of the request in the BC when the DS registers a request for the processing of personal data in the system.

3.5. Notarized Data Structure

The main notarized data required for a GDPR compliance audit related to the processing of personal data comprises a request for data processing and a response to the request. The request, which is one of the primary data in the proposed framework, should have the request number, ID of the DS, URL of the SP, e-mail address of the SP, data processing type, and the information of the request. These are stored in blocks as a transaction and following the creation of a ledger block, the framework adds it to the BC to provide security and integrity. However, it is important to ensure controlled access and management of notarized data only by network entities who have the authority to access the framework. To realize this, a data structure should be defined for authorization control consisting of the authorization number, authorization type, authorization ID, SP URL, grantor's ID, and permitted authorization period. Details of the processing request, response on request, and authorization-related data structure for configuration of the BC ledger are as follows:

- Request: A structure requests for the processing of personal data sent by the DS to the DC.
- Response: A structure for a response to a request sent by the DC to the DS.
- Authorization: A structure of data access rights granted by the DS or DC.
- Parameters of data structures for transactions are as follows:
- Parameters of Request: The number of requests, DS's ID, SP's URL, SP e-mail, processing type, the content of the request and timestamp.
- Parameters of Response: The number of responses, the number of requests, DS's ID, data SP's URL, subject's e-mail, processing type, content of request, content of response, and timestamp.
- Parameters of Authorization: The number of grants, grantor type, auditor's ID, SP's URL, grantor's ID, and authority expiration date.

The value of the processing type, which is a parameter of the structure request and structure response, is pre-defined as reading, correction, deletion, processing suspension, and transmission, which are defined as the right of the DS to own data in the GDPR. The DS selects the type of processing, and thereafter, the request is delegated and notarized for the processing.

3.6. Identity Management

Considering that the proposed notarization framework is based on BC, a distributed environment, the entities must be uniquely identified. The proposed framework requires all entities to be authenticated via a Certificate Authority (CA) before using the proposed framework and to receive an asymmetric encryption key (public key, private key) and certificate. Furthermore, there is a need to define a unique concept of identity and the rules by which the identity is to be managed (identity verification) and authenticated (signature creation and verification) using a member service provider, which abstracts the user management functions provided by the private BC framework.

3.7. Personal Data Protection

Transactions registered with BC for notarization contain request and response contents that may contain sensitive personal data. Owing to the characteristics of the BC network, which copies and distributes the ledger, there is a risk of the sensitive personal data of transactions being exposed to unauthorized peers. Thus, to prevent this risk, the request and response contents should be encrypted and stored, and an encryption key that can decrypt data should be provided only to entities with the authority to inquire the data, such as the creator, receiver, and auditor. As shown in Figure 7, the proposed framework generates a session key for each transaction in the application before registering the request and response in BC. The transaction ID (trxId) key and {session key (sKey), DS's ID (dsId), SP's url (spUrl)} value pairs are saved to the application database. Subsequently, the request and response contents are encrypted using the session key and registered in the BC.

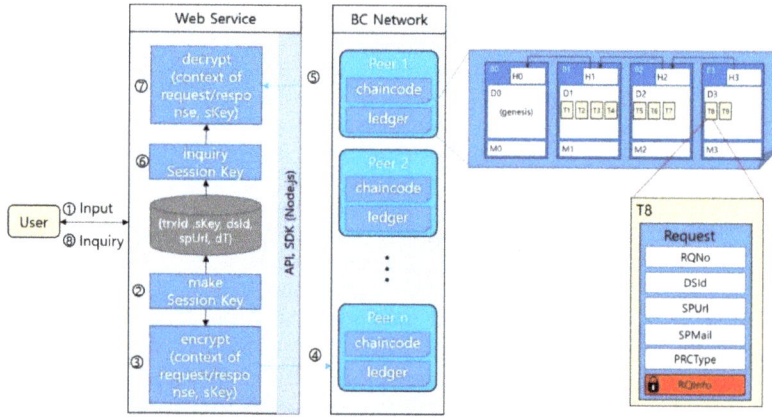

Figure 7. Personal data encryption process in transaction using session key.

The transaction ID generation algorithm is identical to the transaction key generation algorithm in the BC of the proposed framework. As in (1), the request combines {ID of DS, creation timestamp}, while the response combines {SP URL of DC, creation timestamp}. Algorithm 1 is an algorithm for generating a session key.

$$\begin{array}{l} \text{IF transaction type equal 'request' THEN} \\ \quad \text{transaction ID = DS's ID + timestamp} \\ \text{IF transaction type equal 'response' THEN} \\ \quad \text{transaction ID = SP's URL + timestamp} \end{array} \quad (1)$$

Algorithm 1. Make Session Key

INPUT: DS's ID, SP's URL, transaction ID, transaction type, private data, timestamp
OUTPUT: session key
1   **IF** transaction type equal 'request' **THEN**
2   **SET** session key to result of
         SUM result of
            COMPUTE hash encode with transaction ID
         and result of
            COMPUTE hash encode with private data
3   **SET** data array with transaction ID, session key, DS's ID, SP's URL, and timestamp
4   **ADD** data array made key with transaction ID into application database
5   **ENDIF**
6   **RETURN** session key

To retrieve and decrypt a transaction that is encrypted using the generated session key, the transaction session key is required, but only the creator or receiver of the transaction can inquire. Algorithm 2 is an algorithm for querying the session key.

Algorithm 2. Inquiry Session Key

INPUT: user ID, transaction ID
OUTPUT: session key
1 **SET** user's type to the result of **READ** user type of user ID
2 **IF** user's type is equal to 'DS' **THEN**
3   **SET** session key to the result of
              READ session key from application database
                      where user ID equal DS's ID in DB
                      and the transaction ID equals the transaction ID in DB
4 **ENDIF**
5 **IF** user's type equals 'DC' **THEN**
6   **SET** SP's URL to the result of
              READ SP's URL from the user information in the DC's session
7   **SET** session key to the result of
              READ session key from the application database
                      where the SP's URL equals the SP's url in DB
                      and the transaction ID equals the transaction ID in DB
8 **ELSE**
9   **SET** session key to null
10 **ENDIF**
11 **RETURN** session key

3.8. Notarization Process

DS transmits a request for processing personal data through the notarization system. The notarization system presents the notarization upon request and delivers it to the SP via e-mail. The SP, which is the DC, performs appropriate processing according to the request and thereafter submits the processing result to the notarization system. Consequently, the notarization system creates a block containing the processing request, processing result, and notarization content and then adds it to the ledger. Figure 8 shows the notarization process for the processing of personal data complying with the GDPR.

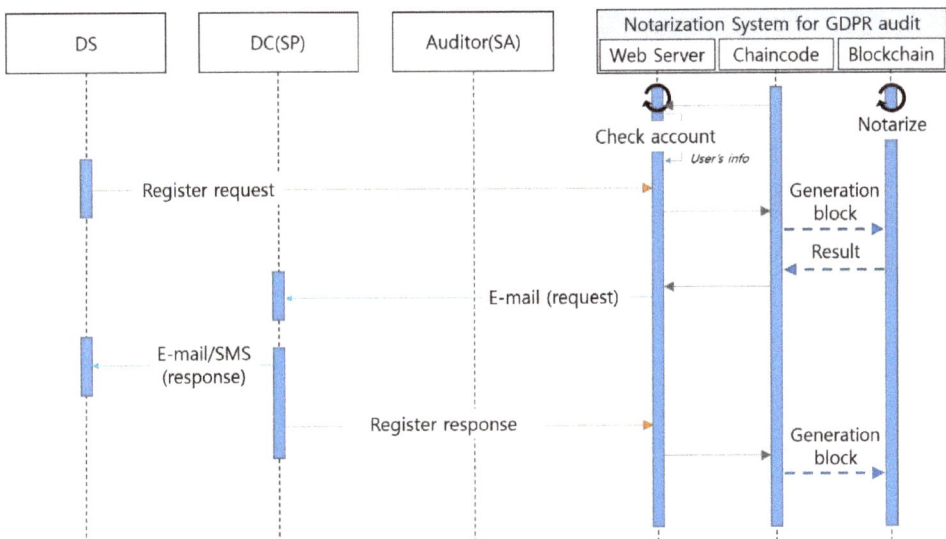

Figure 8. Notarization process of the request and response.

Algorithm 3 is the algorithm for smart contract implement of request registration in Figure 8.

Algorithm 3. Input Request

INPUT: DS's ID, SP's URL, SP's e-mail, process type, contents of request, timestamp
OUTPUT: transaction
  // make key
1 **SET** transaction key to the result of
   CALL make request number with the DS's ID and timestamp
              RETURNING request number
2 **SET** request structure with the transaction key, DS's ID, SP's URL, SP's e-mail,
                    process type, contents of request, and timestamp
3 **SET** JSON formed request to the result of
       CALL transform to JSON with request structure
              RETURNING JSON formed request
4 **RETURN** the result of
       CALL make transaction with transaction key and JSON formed request
              RETURNING transaction

Algorithm 4 is the algorithm for the smart contract implement of response registration in Figure 8.

Algorithm 4. Input Response

INPUT: request transaction key, DS's ID, SP's URL, SP's e-mail, process type,
         contents of request, contents of response, timestamp
OUTPUT: transaction
  //check request being
    1 **SET** existing to the result of
       CALL checks whether it exists with request transaction key **RETURNING** existing
2 **IF** existing is false **THEN**
3   **PRINT** "the request does not exist"
4   **RETURN** null
5 **ENDIF**
  // make key
6 **SET** transaction key to the result of
       CALL make response number with SP's URL and timestamp
              RETURNING response number
7 **SET** response structure with transaction key, DS's ID, SP's URL, SP's e-mail,
            process type, contents of request, contents of response, timestamp
8 **SET** JSON formed response to the result of
       CALL transform to JSON with response structure
              RETURNING JSON formed response
9 **RETURN** the result of
       CALL make transaction with transaction key and JSON formed response
   RETURNING transaction

Figure 9 shows the process of inquiring transactions stored in the notarization framework by an authorized participant.

3.9. GDPR Compliance Audit Process

The SA can perform a GDPR compliance audit on DC as needed. It may perform an audit by obtaining authority to inquire transactions related to the processing of personal data between DS and DC to validate the GDPR compliance of DC during the audit process. Figure 10 shows the audit procedure if the DS makes a request for a GDPR compliance audit to the SA on his/her personal data processing.

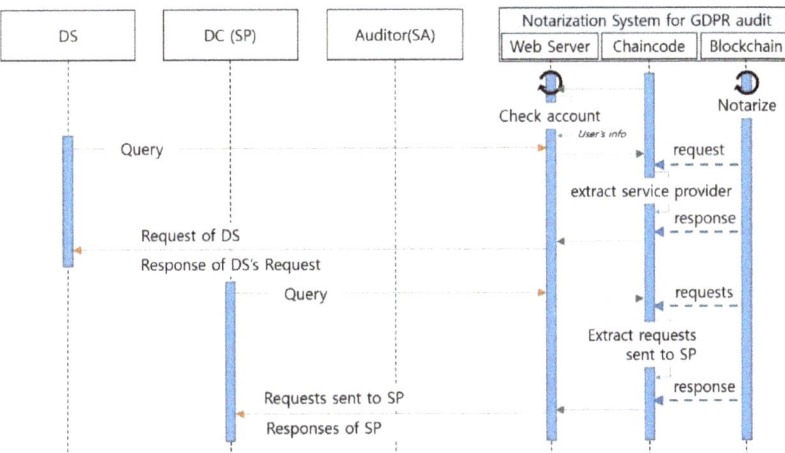

Figure 9. Transaction query process for the request and response for the processing of personal data.

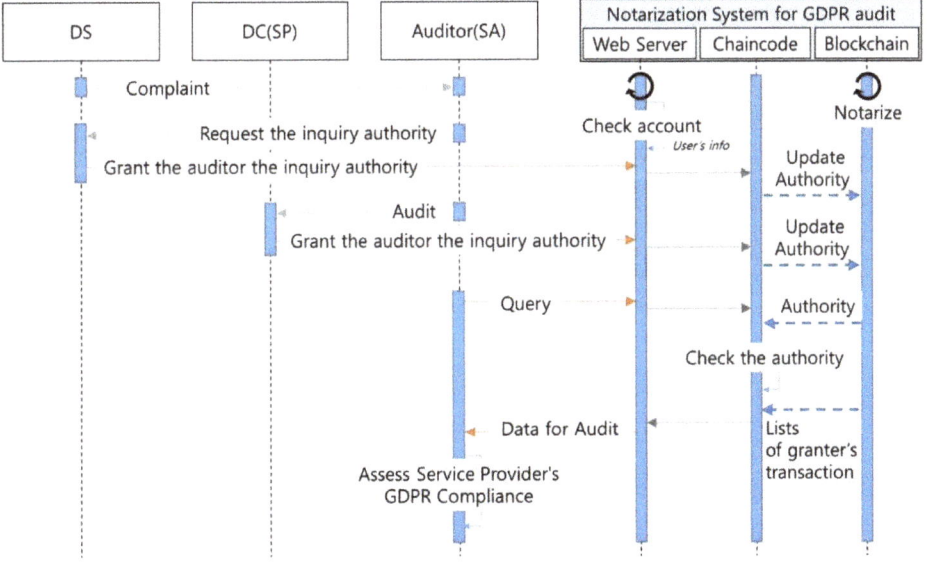

Figure 10. GDPR compliance audit process.

Algorithm 5 is an algorithm for the smart contract implement of granting inquiry authority in Figure 10.

Algorithm 5. Input Authority

INPUT: grant key, grant type, auditor's ID, SP's URL, grantor's ID, expiry date
OUTPUT: authority transaction
1   **IF** grant type equal "DS" **THEN**
2   **SET** grant key to the result of **JOIN** auditor's ID and grantor's ID
3   **ELSE**
4   **SET** grant key to the result of **JOIN** auditor's ID and SP's URL
5   **ENDIF**
    //check authority being
6   **SET** existing to the result of
          CALL checks whether it exists with grant key **RETURNING** existing
7   **IF** existing is true **THEN**
8   **SET** authority transaction to the result of
          CALL update authority with grant key and expire date
                RETURNING authority transaction
9   **ELSE**
10   **SET** authority structure with grant key, grant type, auditor's ID, SP's URL,
             grantor's ID, and expire date
11   **SET** JSON formed response to the result of
          CALL transform to JSON with response structure
                RETURNING JSON formed response
12 **ENDIF**
13 **RETURN** the result of
          CALL make transaction with transaction key and JSON formed response
    RETURNING transaction

Algorithm 6 is the algorithm for the smart contract implementation of the query of notarized requests and responses in Figure 10.

Algorithm 6. Get Notarized Lists

INPUT: grant key, grant type, start date for query, end date for query
OUTPUT: request transaction list, response transaction list
    //check authority validation
1   **SET** validation of authority to the result of
          CALL authority validation with grant key **RETURNING** validation of authority
2   **IF** validation of authority is false **THEN**
3   **PRINT** "The authority isn't valid"
4   **RETURN** null
5   **ENDIF**
    //separate and extract IDs
6   **SET** auditor's ID, DS's ID, SP's URL to the result of
          CALL extract IDs with grant key **RETURNING** auditor's ID, DS's ID, SP's URL
    // range query of DS's request
7   **SET** list of request to the result of
       CALL query by range with
          JOIN DS's ID and start date for query, JOIN DS's ID and end date for query
          RETURNING list of request
    // range query of SP's response
8   **SET** list of response to the result of
       CALL query by range with
          JOIN SP's URL and start date for query, JOIN SP's URL and end date for query
          RETURNING list of response
9   **RETURN** the result of
          CALL make transaction with list of request and list of response
    RETURNING list of JSON formed request, list of JSON formed response

4. Implementation

The proposed framework was implemented using a private BC and HLF. In this section, the implementation results are presented in the order of development environment and notarization framework implementation.

4.1. Development Environment

BC was implemented using HLF 2.2, a private framework, Go chaincode, and node.js SDK for web services. Furthermore, raft was used for the BC consensus process. The raft ordering service is simpler and faster than other consensus algorithms, as it guarantees crash fault tolerance under the assumption that all nodes are honest. For transactions, the service server forms a consortium and runs channel settings and services through configtx.yaml. In addition, for a BC-based system simulation, the security and performance of the system must be considered by configuring an effective architecture of authority management and network according to the role of network participants. We constructed the proposed notarization framework network using Docker for simulation, as shown in Figure 11.

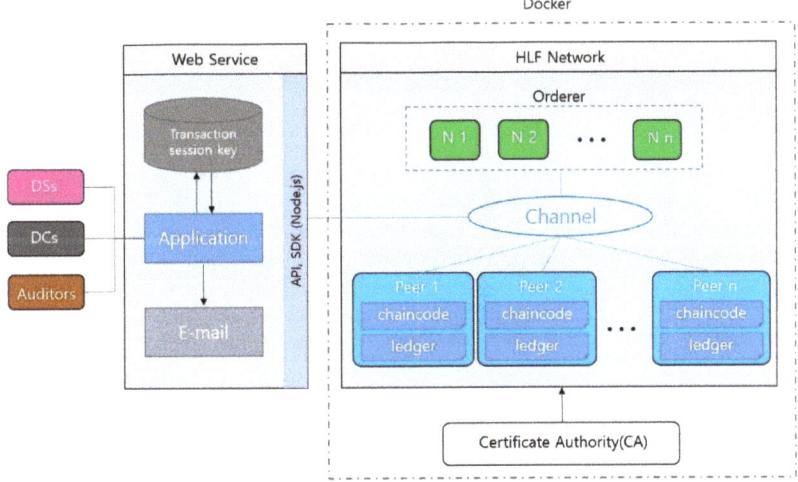

Figure 11. Simulation system architecture for the proposed framework using HLF.

4.2. Simulation

We considered the use case of conducting an audit with notarized data, using the framework proposed by the auditor of the SA when the DS requests the DC to process personal data but DC ignores the request without a good reason. Consequently, we developed and simulated a prototype of the framework.

DS, DC, and SA participated in the proposed framework for GDPR compliance audit. As shown in Figure 11, the DS and DC store the request and response transaction in the BC network through the proposed framework, and thereafter, the user DS, DC, and auditor retrieve the stored transaction through the proposed framework. Subsequently, the framework copies and forwards/verifies/distributes the transaction to each peer through the entity that ordered it. Herein, several selected peers perform the verification process and sign using their private key, which corresponds to the role of a notary public. Moreover, the peers are only operated by authorized SAs.

For authentication of all entities participating in the BC network, Fabric CA, a built-in CA provided by HLF by default was used. Fabric CA adopts a PKI hierarchical model and is used to generate X.509 digital certificates. A certificate contains an entity's key and related information. We set in docker-compose-ca.yaml, as shown in Figure 12, such that the CA service was run on port 7054 using Docker, and through this, all nodes and users were authenticated and authorized.

```
chaincode_proposal_payload": {
    "TransientMap": {},
    "input": {
        "chaincode_spec": {
            "chaincode_id": {
                "name": "gdpr2",
                "path": "",
                "version": ""
            },
            "input": {
                "args": [
                    "SW5pdExlZGdlcg==",
                    "TW9vZE1ha2Vy",
                    "d3d3LmRpc2VjLnty",
                    "bWFuYWdlcjEyM0BkaXNlYy5rcg==",
                    "RGVsZXRl",
                    "cHRnUW8xcmZoazdKMTNhbkJHSWxsWURwZWdLazU3cW9QTFpCV1VGUUJTZjRHS3dzM1hnSllMK2FrOUtBWGxNT013T3lrenNEbmhzMlJudUZDZCs2SHF6FLZ0xmOU5abSs0MXoyOFBEcVlETkJsVFllZzV2SG9qdU09qdnltbi8=",
                    "MjAyMS4wOS4wNS8xMzowNjo1MA=="
                ],
                "decorations": {},
                "is_init": false
            },
            "timeout": 0,
            "type": "GOLANG"
        }
    }
}
```

Figure 12. A transaction in a saved block viewed by peers.

The DS entered a personal data processing request including {SP's URL, DC's e-mail, processing type, content of request} through the web service of the proposed framework, and we delegated the delivery and notarization to the proposed framework. The transaction occurred in the block, as shown in Figure 12, when the json format data input by DS and delivered to the chaincode of the framework and the requested transaction are verified and agreed by the notary nodes; thereafter, the copied and stored block was inquired by the peer. Furthermore, as evident in Figure 12, the request content containing personal information is encrypted and cannot be verified by the peer.

Although the notarization framework sends the request made by the DS to the personal data manager email address entered by the DS, if there is no reasonable response from the SP, the DS requests the SA to audit the SP. Herein, the DS grants inquiry authority to the auditor such that his/her request transaction can be inquired. The auditor can perform GDPR compliance audits on SPs based on the querying request transactions.

5. Analysis and Evaluation

For the analysis of the proposed framework, the measurement of the degree of satisfaction of the requirements based on the requirements defined in Section 3 must be considered. This section details an analysis of the degree of satisfaction of the proposed framework and presents a comparison with related studies from the perspective of GDPR compliance audit.

5.1. Analysis of Meeting the Requirements of the Notarization Framework for GDPR Compliance Audits

The requirements proposed for analysis in Section 3.1 were considered as analysis elements of the system. The analysis was conducted to determine whether the functions and properties of the proposed notarization framework meet the following requirements.

5.1.1. Security Analysis

The proposed framework was designed as per the design goal of Figure 5, and all the security requirements of the notary framework for the GDPR compliance audit were achieved. Results of analysis of the satisfaction of the proposed framework with the security requirements are as follows:

- Data security: In the proposed framework, a transaction key was generated by automatically combining the DS's ID and timestamp in the chaincode when creating a request transaction, and the service provider URL of the DC and timestamp when creating a response transaction. The transaction was stored including the signature created by the private key of the creator. Furthermore, when searching for a stored transaction, the proposed framework compares the user's information (Uid, SPurl) with the stored transaction key in the chaincode. When the auditor desires to query the transaction of the DS and DC, the proposed framework checks whether the auditor has been granted the inquiry right by the DS and DC and that the authorization period is valid; then, the information (Uid, SPurl) of the approvers DS and DC is compared with the stored transaction key. The transactions are linked to each other using a hash algorithm in blocks, and their integrity is guaranteed due to it being copied and distributed to each peer in the BC network. The request and response contents that may contain sensitive personal data are encrypted and input by creating a symmetric key-type session key for each transaction in the application, and the session key is stored for each transaction in the application database. The creator, receiver, and auditor with inquiry authority can decrypt the data retrieved from the BC by inquiring the session key for each transaction. Thus, even if a transaction is exposed to an unauthorized peer in the BC network, the data cannot be decrypted unless the service is accessed through authentication in the proposed framework.
- Authentication and authorization: HLF provides Fabric CA as the default CA. Fabric CA is a public key infrastructure (PKI) based and used to generate X.509 digital certificates. All entities in the HLF must be identified by a digital ID before interacting with the BC network. An X.509 digital certificate contains key and related information of an entity and is either signed by the Fabric CA or self-signed. When implementing the proposed framework, we set the initialization value in the docker-compose-ca.yaml file and started Fabric CA using Docker. Furthermore, before interacting with the proposed framework, all entities were registered with the CA server using Fabric CA client or Fabric SDK and received the key and certificate. HLF provides an infrastructure management mechanism called "policy." Fabric policies represent the manner in which the members agree to accept or reject changes to a network, channel, or smart contract. We set policies in configtx.yaml to control all the actions each member desires to perform on the Fabric network. For example, although the DS and DC organizations allowed access to the transaction registration chaincode, the auditor group SA organization was allowed access only to the audit inquiry chaincode, while access to the notary group SA organization was not granted.
- Prevention of denial: In the proposed framework, transactions were created as blocks through the signature of the creator's private key, stored in the ledger, and shared in the BC network. In addition, by ensuring that the peers acting as the notary of the block are composed and operated only by SAs, the integrity and reliability of the stored data was increased to prevent the repudiation of notarized data.
- Accountability: In the proposed framework, request and response transactions were stored in the form of {who, when, who, what}. As the proposed framework inherits the integrity characteristics of BC, the data stored in the proposed framework can be used for GDPR compliance audits.

The proposed framework secures countermeasures against major cyberattack threats and major attack threats that may occur in BC-based systems, as shown in Table 4 by satisfying security and functional requirements.

Table 4. Countermeasure to the proposed framework for major cyberattacks on BC.

Attack	Description	Countermeasure
Race attack	Send two conflicting transactions in rapid succession.	Since it is different from cryptocurrency, multiple recipients who receive the same transaction will not be harmed if their own transaction is canceled.
Brute force attack	Attempt to decrypt any encrypted data.	Data are encrypted with an encryption algorithm recognized for stability that uses a key length of 256 bytes or more, such as AES-256. Brute force attacks on 256-byte keys are almost statistically impossible with current technology.
51% attack	After securing more than 50% of the hash computing power among all nodes, the transaction information is manipulated.	Authorizes only SAs as BC network nodes and controls malicious participants. It is possible that the proposed network is a private BC.
DoS (Denial-of-Service) attack	Sending massive amounts of traffic paralyzes BC networks and nodes.	Revokes access and authority of a party that mounts a DOS on the system since they are known identities rather than anonymous.
Unauthorized access attack	Access or modify a function or variable that should not be accessed.	Checks authentication and authority in web service and BC network. Respectively, manages authority for smart contract functions by the user group. Allows only own transaction to be accessed.
Replay attack	Copy a transaction that was added to the BC in the past and replay it in the network to distort its operation.	Users submitting a transaction with a transaction certificate should include in the transaction a random nonce, that would guarantee that two transactions do not result into the same hash.
Sniffing and capture attack	Monitoring and capturing all data packets passing through network.	TLS is used for all network sections. Encrypts the main data of the transaction based on the session key.

5.1.2. Function Analysis

The functions and properties of the proposed notarization framework were designed as per the design goal of Figure 5, and all the requirements of the notary framework for GDPR compliance audit were achieved. The proposed notarization framework receives a request for personal data processing from the DS, stores it in the ledger, notarizes it, and sends it to the DC by e-mail. In the event that the DC ignores, rejects, or delays the request without a good reason, it provides evidence to request legal sanctions, thereby guaranteeing the right of the DC to process their own data as defined in Chapters 12 to 21 of the GDPR. The proposed notarization framework assures an objective view on credibility by relaying and acting as a third party that notarizes requests and responses between the DS and DC and thus guarantees the reliability of records for GDPR compliance audits. In addition, the SPs need not modify the legacy personal data processing system or install a separate 3rd party module; thus, it is highly applicable to the actual environment. Table 5 shows the results of analysis of the satisfaction of the proposed framework with the requirements of Figure 5.

Table 5. Analysis result of meeting the requirements of the proposed framework.

A1	A2	A3	A4	B1	B2	B3	B4	B5	C1	D1
Y	Y	Y	Y	Y	Y	Y	Y	Y	Y	Y

Reasons for meeting each requirement of the proposed framework are as follows:

- Request and response anytime, anywhere (A1): The proposed framework was designed to delegate the DS's request and DC's response through the web service, notarize it in the BC network, and send it to the recipient through the e-mail service; thus, the DS and DC can make requests and responses anytime, anywhere. See Figure 6 in Section 3.4 and Figure 11 in Section 4.1.
- Save the information provided by electronic means (A2): The proposed framework stores all transactions related to personal data processing requests from DS and DC as electronic ledgers in BC. See Section 3.5 and Figure 11 in Section 4.1.
- Record of DS's request and of DC's response to DS's request (A3): The proposed framework stores all transactions related to personal data processing requests from DS and DC as electronic ledgers in BC. See Section 3.5 and Figure 11 in Section 4.1.
- Non-repudiation of requests and responses (A4): The DS and DC transmit the transaction together with the private key signature to the proposed framework, and the notary node of the proposed framework notarizes with the private key signature and stores it in BC, so the creator and notary cannot deny the stored data. See 'Prevention of denial' in Section 5.1.1.
- Sealing of data (B1): As the proposed framework is based on private BC, network participants can be managed. The proposed framework allows only the peers of the SA to participate in the network. Furthermore, the consensus procedure of HLF, which generates blocks after verification via multiple peers, has the function of notarization. Peers acting as notaries only include the signature generated by their private key in the transaction at the time of verification and do not cause any changes. Thus, the proposed framework using HLF's RAFT consensus algorithm meets the "sealing of data" requirement. See 'Data security' in Section 5.1.1.
- Accessible to all (B2): The proposed framework was designed to delegate the request of the DS and response of the DC through a web service and e-mail service. Both the DS and DC can access and use the framework after being authenticated and authorized by the CA. See Figure 11 in Section 4.1.
- Trusted or certifiable (B3): For the integrity and objective reliability of the ledger, the proposed framework restricts the nodes participating in notarization to authoritative organizations such as SAs. In the proposed framework, the algorithm that allows multiple notaries to participate and notarize inherits the RAFT algorithm of HLF, which has already been verified for stability.
- Highly trusted communications (B4): As the proposed framework uses HLF, a private BC framework, it inherits the integrity and confidentiality of the HLF's system, network, and data. HLF supports secure communication between nodes by using transport layer security (TLS) protocol, which is applied in the proposed framework.
- Authentication (B5): The proposed framework authenticates all entities using Fabric CA, which is a CA provided by HLF. See 'Authentication and Authorization' in Section 5.1.1.
- Data minimization (C1): The proposed framework only stores information for auditing the processing request transaction of the DS and DC's response to the request in the BC for the GDPR compliance audit, and it does not store any other personal data that the SPs have. See Section 3.5.
- Feasibility in real environment (D1): As the proposed framework was designed to delegate the DS's request and DC's response through a web service and an e-mail service, the SPs need not modify the legacy personal information processing system or install a separate third party module. Therefore, it can be applied as a GDPR compliance audit framework in a real environment.

5.2. Performance Evaluation

To evaluate the performance of the proposed framework, we installed Docker on Intel Core i5-8265U CPU @ 1.60 GHz, with 16 GB RAM specification system, and applied the two-peer three-order, and Raft consensus algorithm to configure and simulate the HLF network. In the performance evaluation of the proposed framework, the main issue area was found to be the BC area.

The performance of BC solutions is one of the characteristics that BC users are most concerned about. However, due to the diversity of consensus mechanisms and APIs, existing performance benchmarking frameworks cannot be directly applied to distributed ledger systems, making it very important to devise solutions to compare different platforms in a meaningful way. In order to perform and analyze the performance measurement in the BC area of the proposed framework on a consistent and systematic basis, this work used 'Hyperledger Caliper' (hereinafter referred to as 'Caliper'), which is a performance measurement framework optimized for the HLF BC environment. Caliper is a BC benchmark tool that allows users to measure the performance of a BC implementation with a predefined set of use cases. Caliper generates a report containing several performance indicators such as transaction per second (tps), transaction latency (latency), and resource utilization [45]. In this work, the performance of the proposed framework was measured by automatically generating loads by setting various use case sets of Caliper.

We increased the load from 50 to 300 tps by automatically creating a transaction and transferred it to the smart contract of the proposed framework. Furthermore, the processing result data of the proposed framework for the input data were measured, and the write and read throughput rates of the proposed framework in the BC area were analyzed. In addition, the proposed framework was designed on the basis of the assumption that SAs in various countries subject to GDPR configure peers and perform notarization; thus, performance analysis is required according to node expansion. We increased the number of peers from two to six and measured and analyzed the write and read throughput rates. This performance test was repeated five times in total, and the results were averaged. Figures 13 and 14 shows the results of analyzing the write and read throughput of the framework proposed in the BC area according to the change in the number of peers.

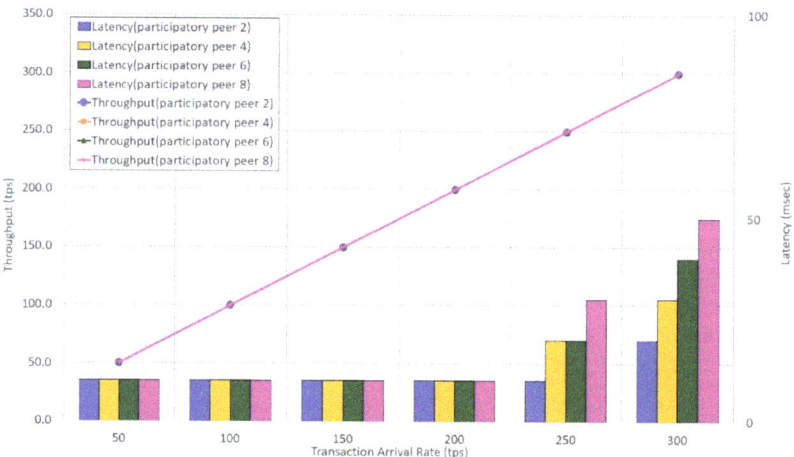

Figure 13. Performance of read in BC of proposed framework under different workloads and different number of peers.

It was confirmed that the read delay of the proposed framework increases from the peer over two peers, 250 tps area, and the write throughput is significantly reduced from the 200 tps area. Simultaneously, in the simulation, we set 50 users to continuously generate transactions. However, considering the service characteristics of the proposed framework, it is rare for users to continuously generate personal data processing requests. Moreover, considering that it is a simulation environment using Docker and there are limitations of computing resources such as CPU and memory, the performance is expected to be further improved in the actual implementation environment. In addition, considering the trade-off between security and performance according to scalability in a distributed environment, the performance decreases when nodes are increased, but security becomes stronger.

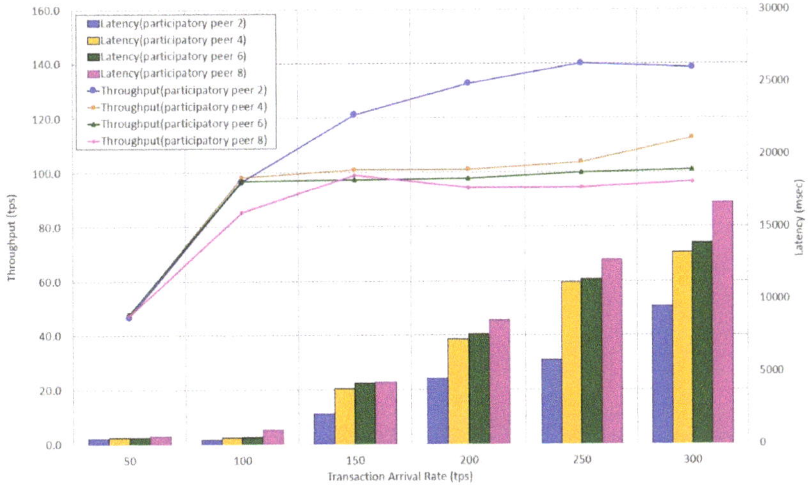

Figure 14. Performance of write in BC of proposed framework under different workloads and different number of peers.

5.3. Comparative Analysis of Related Works

The proposed delegation-based personal data processing notarization framework was designed to support the requirements of "reliable notarization of request for the processing of personal data that can be easily used without sharing personal data and processed in real time." The framework was compared with the related works, which could confirm that the reliability and excellence of the framework are satisfied.

We compared and analyzed the superiority of the proposed framework, focusing on the work of Truong et al. that includes issues on data processing requests among works related to BC-based GDPR compliance. Table 6 presents the results of analyzing whether the functions and properties of the framework proposed by Truong et al. meet the requirements in Figure 5.

Table 6. Analysis result of meeting the requirements of the platform proposed by Truong et al.

A1	A2	A3	A4	B1	B2	B3	B4	B5	C1	D1
Y	Y	N	Y	N	Y	N	Y	Y	N	N

From the analysis results shown in Table 6, it is evident that the functions and properties of the framework proposed by Truong et al. did not meet requirements, which are as follows:

- Record of DS's request and of DC's response to DS's request (A3): For an end user to request data processing to a resource server with personal data, the SP's system is the only means to achieve it. However, this has the potential to allow the SP in the middle to ignore or manipulate the end user's request. In addition, the proposed framework was designed around access control, such that although the access request for personal data processing is stored in the block chain before processing, the personal data processing is not stored until the resource server processes it. Furthermore, it is not designed to store the request contents of the DS because the scenario wherein the DS requests the SP to process it is not considered.

- Sealing of data (B1): It is possible for an end user to request data processing to a resource server with personal data only through the SP's system. However, this has the potential to allow the SP in the middle to manipulate the end user's request. Furthermore, as the proposed framework has been designed around access control, thus, the sealing and notarization process for end-user requests is not clearly presented.
- Trusted or certifiable (B3): It was assumed that a DS is "honest-but-curious", whereas SPs follow a malicious model. This indicates that the DS executes the required protocols, even though it might be curious about the results it receives after the operations. Most of the records of the processing of personal data are stored in the proposal framework by the resource server; however, if the resource server is not trusted, the data also cannot be trusted.
- Data minimization (C1): The proposed framework stores all personal data processing history of the SP. When the DS subscribes to the service of the SP, it delegates the processing of personal data to the SP. Therefore, owing to the excessive nature amount, all personal data processing of the SP delegated by DS for GDPR compliance audit and personal data related to personal data processing is also stored. Furthermore, considering the characteristics of the BC where data are replicated, distributed, and stored, and deletion is not easy, the more personal data are stored, the greater the risk of exposure and the greater the possibility of violating the principle of data minimization.
- Feasibility in real environment (D1): To apply the proposed framework, SPs must modify the legacy personal data processing system or install a separate third-party module. However, the application of the proposed framework to the real environment is difficult because enforcing it on all SPs in the real environment is a challenge.

The solution of Truong et al. is insufficient compared to the proposed framework when considering that there is no guarantee of an objective view on the credibility of the DS's request for the processing of personal data, it does not comply with the GDPR principle, and it could not directly apply to a real environment situation. The framework proposed by Truong et al. was not designed to store the personal data processing request of the DS without going through the SP. Moreover, if the SP does not add functions to the legacy personal data processing system to interface with the platform proposed by Truong et al., the problem for GDPR compliance audits remains unsolved. Thus, considering that in real situations, it is not possible to apply the platform proposed by Truong et al. to all SPs, it can be concluded that it is not an appropriate solution to the problem of GDPR compliance audit to ensure the right to request processing of personal data of DS.

Therefore, the proposed framework is superior in terms of the objective reliability of personal data processing requests, compliance with GDPR principles, and feasibility compared to solutions of previous works that allow the SP to manage the personal data processing request record of DS as in the work of Truong et al. Table 7 shows the comparative analysis results of the proposed framework and the platform proposed by Truong et al.

Table 7. Comparative analysis between this work and the work of Truong et al.

Work	A1	A2	A3	A4	B1	B2	B3	B4	B5	C1	D1
Proposed	Y	Y	Y	Y	Y	Y	N	Y	Y	Y	Y
Truong et al.	Y	Y	N	Y	N	Y	N	Y	Y	N	N

6. Conclusions

This study proposed a delegation-based personal data processing notarization framework based on a private BC to solve the problem of requiring an objective view on the credibility of records related to personal data processing requests. Furthermore, it could support the claim of the rights of DSs in a GDPR compliance audit. It can be easily used by users through the web, does not share personal data collected by DCs, adheres to the basic principles of GDPR, and is feasible. Furthermore, through the process of notarization, it is possible to secure the trust of all network participants with respect to records of the personal data processing request and response, and thus, it can be used for GDPR compliance audit. The management of the personal data processing requests in the proposed framework from the perspective of the DS and the objective view on credibility were guaranteed, thereby further strengthening the guarantee of rights of DS. Furthermore, the simulation results and subsequent analysis demonstrated that the proposed framework satisfied the functional and security requirements for a notarization system capable of GDPR compliance audit for personal data processing.

If an institution authorized by a government operates the notarization framework proposed in this paper, the reliability of the authentication and authorization of system users, including notaries, is increased, and thus, the reliability of notarization provided by the system is expected to be further increased. If the SA recommends that SPs who do not disclose the email address of the person in charge of personal data processing on the website, etc., sign up for a service using the proposed framework and disclose their email address, it is expected that the GDPR compliance for personal data processing requests will be spread just by registering as a member without forcing the SP to install an additional system. In addition, if an e-mail server of the proposed framework and the system linkage module of DC are developed and applied, DC can also delegate and notarize the notification sent to DS more easily.

For future research, studies need to be undertaken to guarantee the sovereignty of DS for personal data regarding GDPR compliance other than compliance with personal data processing, and research on notarization methods for a BC-based GDPR compliance audit is required to ensure that it does not violate GDPR regulations.

Author Contributions: Conceptualization, S.-S.J.; methodology, S.-S.J.; software, S.-S.J.; validation, S.-S.J., S.-J.L. and I.-C.E.; formal analysis, S.-S.J. and I.-C.E.; investigation, S.-S.J.; resources, S.-S.J.; data curation, S.-S.J.; writing—original draft preparation, S.-S.J.; writing—review and editing, S.-S.J., S.-J.L. and I.-C.E.; visualization, S.-S.J.; supervision, I.-C.E.; project administration, I.-C.E.; funding acquisition, I.-C.E. All authors have read and agreed to the published version of the manuscript.

Funding: This work was supported by Institute for Information & Communications Technology Planning & Evaluation (IITP) grant funded by the Korea government (MSIT) under grant no. 2019-0-01343, regional strategic industry convergence security core talent training business.

Acknowledgments: The manuscript will be used as part of the author's doctoral dissertation.

Conflicts of Interest: The funders had no role in the design of the study; in the collection, analyses, or interpretation of data; in the writing of the manuscript, or in the decision to publish the results.

References

1. Farahani, B.; Firouzi, F.; Luecking, M. The convergence of IoT and distributed ledger technologies (DLT): Opportunities, challenges, and solutions. *J. Netw. Comput. Appl.* **2021**, *177*, 102936. [CrossRef]
2. Sellami, M.; Mezni, H.; Hacid, S. On the use of big data frameworks for big service composition. *J. Netw. Comput. Appl.* **2020**, *166*, 102732. [CrossRef]
3. Campanile, L.; Iacoco, M.; Marulli, F.; Mastroianni, M. Designing a GDPR compliant blockchain-based IoV distributed information tracking system. *Inf. Process. Manag.* **2021**, *58*, 102511. [CrossRef]
4. Tamburri, D.A. Design principles for the General Data Protection Regulation (GDPR): A formal concept analysis and its evaluation. *Inf. Syst.* **2020**, *91*, 101469. [CrossRef]
5. Yang, X. Business big data analysis based on microprocessor system and mathematical modeling. *Microprocess. Microsyst.* **2021**, *82*, 103846. [CrossRef]
6. Bhattacharya, M.; Islam, R.; Abawajy, J. Evolutionary optimization: A big data perspective. *J. Netw. Comput. Appl.* **2016**, *59*, 416–426. [CrossRef]
7. Singh, A.; Click, K.; Parizi, R.M.; Zhang, Q.; Dehghantanha, A.; Choo, K.R. Sidechain technologies in blockchain networks: An examination and state-of-the-art review. *J. Netw. Comput. Appl.* **2020**, *149*, 102471. [CrossRef]
8. Parra Freund, G.; Fagundes, P.B.; Macedo, D.D.J. An analysis of blockchain and GDPR under the data lifecycle perspective. *Mob. Netw. Appl.* **2020**, *26*, 266–276. [CrossRef]

9. Eugenia, P.; Efthimios, A.; Constantinos, P. Forgetting personal data and revoking consent under the GDPR: Challenges and proposed solutions. *J. Cybersecur.* **2018**, *4*, 1–20.
10. Korea Legislation Research Institute. Personal Information Protection Act. Act No. 16930. 2020. Available online: https://elaw.klri.re.kr/eng_service/lawView.do?hseq=53044&lang=ENG (accessed on 29 May 2021).
11. European Union. Directive 95/46/EC of the European Parliament and of the Council on the Protection of Individuals with Regard to the Processing of Personal Data and on the Free Movement of Such Data. Available online: https://eur-lex.europa.eu/legal-content/en/TXT/?uri=CELEX%3A31995L0046 (accessed on 29 May 2021).
12. ICLG. USA: Data Protection Laws and Regulations. 2020. Available online: https://iclg.com/practice-areas/data-protection-laws-and-regulations/usa (accessed on 29 May 2021).
13. Gobeo, A.; Fowler, C.; Buchanan, W.J. 4 Cyber Security and the GDPR. In *GDPR and Cyber Security for Business Information Systems*; River Publishers: Gistrup, Denmark, 2018; pp. 93–116.
14. Greenleaf, G. Global data privacy laws 2019: 132 national laws & many bills. *Priv. Laws Bus. Int. Rep.* **2019**, *157*, 14–18.
15. Team, I.P. *EU General Data Protection Regulation (GDPR): An Implementation and Compliance Guide*; IT Governance Ltd.: Ely, UK, 2017.
16. Cimina, V. The data protection concepts of 'controller', 'processor' and 'joint controllership' under Regulation (EU) 2018/1725. *ERA Forum* **2021**, *21*, 639–654. [CrossRef]
17. Wirth, C.; Kolain, M. Privacy by blockchain design: A blockchain enabled GDPR-compliant approach for handling personal data. In Proceedings of the 1st ERCIM Blockchain Workshop 2018, European Society for Socially Embedded Technologies (EUSSET), Amsterdam, The Netherlands, 8 May 2018.
18. Bernabe, J.B.; Canovas, J.L.; Hernandez-Ramos, J.L.; Moreno, R.T.; Skarmeta, A. Privacy-preserving solutions for blockchain: Review and challenges. *IEEE Access* **2019**, *7*, 164922–164923. [CrossRef]
19. Sutton, A.; Samavi, R. Blockchain Enabled Privacy Audit Logs. In Proceedings of the International Semantic Web Conference, Vienna, Austria, 21–25 October 2017; pp. 645–660.
20. Feng, Q.; He, D.; Zeadally, S.; Khan, M.K.; Kumar, N. A survey on privacy protection in blockchain system. *J. Netw. Comput. Appl.* **2019**, *126*, 45–58. [CrossRef]
21. Zyskind, G.; Nathan, O.; Pentland, A. Decentralizing Privacy: Using Blockchain to Protect Personal Data. In Proceedings of the 2015 IEEE Security and Privacy Workshops, San Jose, CA, USA, 18–20 May 2015; pp. 180–184.
22. Hillmann, P.; Knupfer, M.; Heiland, E.; Karcher, A. Selective Deletion in a Blockchain. In Proceedings of the International Workshop on Blockchain and Mobile Applications (BlockApp 2020) during the International Conference on Distributed Computing Systems (ICDCS 2020), Singapore, 29 November–1 December 2020.
23. Tatar, U.; Gokce, Y.; Nussbaum, B. Law versus technology: Blockchain, GDPR, and tough tradeoffs. *Comput. Law Secur. Rev.* **2020**, *38*, 105454. [CrossRef]
24. Carvalho, R.M.; Prete, C.D.; Martin, Y.S.; Rivero, R.M.A.; Onen, M.; Schiavo, F.P.; Rumin, A.C.; Mouratidis, H.; Yelmo, J.C.; Koukovini, M.N. Protecting Citizens' Personal Data and Privacy: Joint Effort from GDPR EU Cluster Research Projects. *SN Comput. Sci.* **2020**, *1*, 217. [CrossRef]
25. Zheng, Z.; Xie, S.; Dai, H.; Wang, H. Blockchain challenges and opportunities: A survey. *Int. J. Web Grid Serv.* **2018**, *14*, 352–375. [CrossRef]
26. Rieger, A.; Guggenmos, F.; Lockl, J.; Fridgen, G.; Urbach, N. Building a Blockchain Application that Complies with the EU General Data Protection Regulation. *MIS Q. Exec.* **2019**, *18*, 263–279. [CrossRef]
27. Hewa, T.; Ylianttila, M.; Liyangage, M. Survey on blockchain based smart contracts: Applications, opportunities and challenges. *J. Netw. Comput. Appl.* **2021**, *177*, 102857. [CrossRef]
28. Asaf, K.; Rehman, R.A.; Kim, B.S. Blockchain technology in Named Data Networks: A detailed survey. *J. Netw. Comput. Appl.* **2020**, *171*, 102840. [CrossRef]
29. Liang, X.; Shetty, S.; Tosh, D.; Kamhoua, C.; Kwiat, K.; Njilla, L. ProvChain: A Blockchain-Based Data Provenance Architecture in Cloud Environment with Enhanced Privacy and Availability. In Proceedings of the 2017 17th IEEE/ACM International Symposium on Cluster, Cloud and Grid Computing, Madrid, Spain, 14–17 May 2017; pp. 468–477.
30. Yan, Z.; Gan, G.; Riad, K. BC-PDS: Protecting Privacy and Self-Sovereignty through BlockChains for OpenPDS. In Proceedings of the 2017 IEEE Symposium on Service-Oriented System Engineering, San Francisco, CA, USA, 6–9 April 2017; pp. 138–144.
31. Chowdhury, M.J.M.; Colman, A.; Kabir, M.A.; Han, J.; Sarda, P. Blockchain as a Notarization Service for Data Sharing with Personal Data Store. In Proceedings of the 2018 17th IEEE International Conference on Trust, Security and Privacy in Computing and Communications/12th IEEE International Conference on Big Data Science and Engineering (TrustCom/BigDataSE), New York, NY, USA, 1–3 August 2018; pp. 1330–1335.
32. Agarwal, S.; Steyskal, S.; Antunovic, F.; Kirrane, S. Legislative Compliance Assessment: Framework, Model and GDPR Instantiation. In *Annual Privacy Forum*; Springer: Berlin/Heidelberg, Germany, 2018; pp. 131–149.
33. Truong, N.B.; Sun, K.; Guo, Y. Blockchain-Based Personal Data Management: From Fiction to Solution. In Proceedings of the 2019 IEEE 18th International Symposium on Network Computing and Applications (NCA), Cambridge, MA, USA, 26–28 September 2019; pp. 1–8.
34. Truong, N.B.; Lee, G.M.; Lee, G.M.; Guo, Y. GDPR-Compliant Personal Data Management: A Blockchain-based Solution. *IEEE Trans. Inf. Forensics Secur.* **2019**, *15*, 1746–1761. [CrossRef]

35. Vargas, J.C. Blockchain-Based Consent Manager for GDPR Compliance. In *Open Identity Summit*; Gesellschaft für Informatik: Bonn, Germany, 2019; pp. 165–170.
36. Kassem, J.A.; Sayeed, S.; Marco-Gisbert, H.; Pervez, Z.; Dahal, K. DNS-IdM: A blockchain identity management system to secure personal data sharing in a network. *Appl. Sci.* **2019**, *9*, 2953. [CrossRef]
37. Rantos, K.; Drosatos, G.; Demertzis, K.; Ilioudis, C.; Papanikolaou, A.; Kritsas, A. ADvoCATE: A consent management platform for personal data processing in the iot using blockchain technology. In Proceedings of the International Conference on Security for Information Technology and Communications (SecITC), Bucharest, Romania, 8–9 November 2018; Springer: Berlin/Heidelberg, Germany, 2018; pp. 300–313.
38. Faber, B.; Michelet, G.; Weidmann, N.; Mukkamala, R.R.; Vatrapu, R. BPDIMS: A blockchain-based personal data and identity management system. *Int. Conf. Syst. Sci.* **2019**, *45*, 254–264.
39. Piras, L. DEFeND architecture: A Privacy by Design Platform for GDPR Compliance. In Proceedings of the 16th International Conference on Trust and Privacy in Digital Business (TrustBus), Linz, Austria, 26–29 August 2019; pp. 78–93.
40. Mahindrakar, A.; Joshi, K.P. Automating GDPR Compliance using Policy Integrated Blockchain. In Proceedings of the 2020 IEEE 6th International Conference on Big Data Security on Cloud (BigDataSecurity), IEEE International Conference on High Performance and Smart Computing, (HPSC) and IEEE International Conference on Intelligent Data and Security (IDS), Baltimore, MD, USA, 25–27 May 2020; pp. 86–93.
41. Casaleiro, R. Protection and control of personal identifiable information: The PoSeID-on approach. *J. Data Prot. Priv.* **2020**, *3*, 199–228.
42. Daudén-Esmel, C.; Castellà-Roca, J.; Viejo, A.; Domingo-Ferrer, J. Lightweight Blockchain-based Platform for GDPR-Compliant Personal Data Management. In Proceedings of the 5th International Conference on Cryptography, Security and Privacy, Zhuhai, China, 4 May 2021; pp. 68–73.
43. Haque, A.B.; Islam, A.N.; Hyrynsalmi, S.; Naqvi, B.; Smolander, K. GDPR Compliant Blockchains—A Systematic Literature Review. *IEEE Access* **2021**, *9*, 50593–50606. [CrossRef]
44. Low, M.R. *The Notary, University of Hertfordshire Computer Science Technical Report*; University of Hertfordshire: Hertfordshire, UK, 1992; Volume 153, pp. 2–5.
45. Hyperledger Caliper Project. Hyperledger Caliper. Available online: https://www.hyperledger.org/projects/caliper (accessed on 30 October 2021).

Article

Data Protection Heterogeneity in the European Union

Marko Hölbl *, Boštjan Kežmah and Marko Kompara

Faculty of Electrical Engineering and Computer Science, University of Maribor, 2000 Maribor, Slovenia; bostjan.kezmah@um.si (B.K.); marko.kompara@um.si (M.K.)
* Correspondence: marko.holbl@um.si; Tel.: +386-2-220-7361

Abstract: In light of digitalisation, we are witnessing an increased volume of collected data and data generation and exchange acceleration. Therefore, the European Union (EU) has introduced the General Data Protection Regulation (GDPR) as a new framework for data protection on the European level. However, GDPR allows the member states to change some parts of the regulation, and the member states can always build on top of the GDPR. An example is the collection of biometric data with electronic signatures. This paper aims to compare the legislation on data protection topics in the various EU member states. The findings show that the member states included in the study generally do not have many additional/specific laws (only in 29.4% of the cases). However, almost all have other/additional legislation to the GDPR on at least one topic. The most additional legislation is on the topics of video surveillance, biometry, genetic data and health data. We also introduce a dynamic map that allows for quick navigating between different information categories and comparisons of the EU member states at a glance.

Keywords: data privacy; GDPR; heterogeneity; European Union

Citation: Hölbl, M.; Kežmah, B.; Kompara, M. Data Protection Heterogeneity in the European Union. *Appl. Sci.* **2021**, *11*, 10912. https://doi.org/10.3390/app112210912

Academic Editors: Gianluca Lax and Federico Divina

Received: 14 October 2021
Accepted: 17 November 2021
Published: 18 November 2021

Publisher's Note: MDPI stays neutral with regard to jurisdictional claims in published maps and institutional affiliations.

Copyright: © 2021 by the authors. Licensee MDPI, Basel, Switzerland. This article is an open access article distributed under the terms and conditions of the Creative Commons Attribution (CC BY) license (https://creativecommons.org/licenses/by/4.0/).

1. Introduction

Digitisation has increased the volume of data collected and, at the same time, accelerated the generation and flow of personal information. Practically every facet of life and the widespread use of the Internet in both private and business settings have greatly expanded data collecting and hastened the exchange of personal information. Therefore, the European Union has enacted the General Data Protection Regulation (GDPR) [1] as a new framework to substitute Data Protection Directive 95/46/EC. The GDPR is directly enforceable and applicable because it is a regulation rather than a directive, albeit it allows the individual EU member states to change specific provisions. In contrast to directives that bind the EU member states to the outcome they must achieve whilst leaving national authorities free to choose the form and method (in practice, supplementing existing legislation or adopting new legislation), the regulation is universally applicable and directly binding for all EU member states.

Because a large amount of personal data can be easily exploited and such data is starting to gain considerable value on the market, the EU authorities have decided on single legislations to strengthen individual's rights across the EU and ensure uniform and coordinated action across the member states following years of deliberation. This has been done to prevent exploitation of the collected data and ensure a protection requirement that all personal data processors have to meet to defend against malicious actors. The final goal of the EU is to create a unified European digital market, free of regulatory restrictions imposed by the individual member states. The GDPR regulation applies to data of EU citizens regardless of the businesses' location or location of the processed data.

However, as we have eluded to before, GDPR allows some of its sections to be defined differently by the member states to better suit their needs and wishes. The prime example of this is the consent age (GDPR, Article 8, paragraph 1) set at 16 in the GDPR (persons aged 16 years and older do not require parental consent). However, the regulation allows individual countries to change this to any age between 13 and 16. Member states can also have additional legislation that builds on top of the GDPR.

In this paper, we have collected information from supervisory authorities (SA; a.k.a. Data Protection Authority—DPA) of EU member states to investigate the situation on additional legislation on data protection extending the GDPR. The aim of the research is to show the extent of heterogeneity in data protection in the EU. The member state supervisory authorities were selected as the best source of information on national legislation and policies, as they are responsible for supervising the data protection laws applicable in their country. This research enables an overview of data protection legislation on some topics in an individual member state and the possibility to compare differences between EU countries. Moreover, we created a dynamic map that visualises the aforementioned data protection legislation heterogeneity and allows an interactive and easy way of comparing legislation on specific topics between the EU member states at a glance.

In the remainder of this paper, we first address other related work that collected and studied similar information. We follow with a survey outline, where we discuss why we designed the survey in the way we did and why we chose to collect particular data. In the section on data collection, we focus on the process of collecting data and present the full list of the collected data topics. Then we move on to the presentation of the collected information, its analysis and the discussion. We conclude the paper in the final chapter.

2. Related Work

Cataloguing and/or comparing legislation between countries can be very difficult, especially when done on any larger scale. The subject itself is very complex and, at times, convoluted. When this is done internationally, the complexity of local languages (often national legislations are not translated or easily accessible) makes it almost impossible for a small group to achieve. Therefore, these types of research are usually done by large organisations which either have contacts in many countries or are reputable enough to get help in any country they need. The alternative approach we used is to survey people for each of the required locations to get them to give you the wanted information, which is not difficult to obtain for them.

For the specific field of data protection, there has not been much study of relevant legislation on a large scale (i.e., including many countries) or comparison between them. However, we have found three [2-4] such collections that include many countries. Two of the three studies are worldwide in scope and cover many countries, albeit with limited scope as they only link privacy legislation to each of the included countries. The third study remains at the same level of legislation identification but with fewer discussed countries from around the world. While in these studies, the GDPR is mentioned in the EU member states, it is not the focus of the studies and is not discussed in any detail. These studies, therefore, only contain a list of relevant legislation and not much information on what the laws themselves dictate. They are not targeting GDPR issues (and are not centred on the EU) and do not give the users anything to compare policies across multiple countries.

S. Park et al. [5] surveyed the state of data protection legislation in the selected countries in relation to the implementation of digital forensic readiness. The authors looked at, among others, the EU as a unit and at Germany as a specific representative. For the EU, the focus was the GDPR with additional legislation present in Germany and its effects. The French supervisory authority, CNIL, has prepared a solution for a very specific condition set by the GDPR (Article 45), under which the transfer of personal data to third countries is allowed if the European Commission has confirmed a suitable level of data protection provided by the receiving country's national laws. The CNIL's map [6] on data protection around the world illustrates which countries have adequate data protection laws and for which other means of sufficiently protecting the data must be guaranteed before transferring the data.

The possibility of adapting and modifying the GDPR by each of the member states with national law derogations was purposefully a part of the GDPR (e.g., Chapter III Section 5 and Chapter IX) to allow for greater flexibility. W. Long and F. Blythe [7], A. Clearwater and B. Philbrook [8], and J. Vangadesan and N. Pook [9] discuss the most probable areas for derogations in GDPR. A comparison of privacy and data protection legislation and policies in the EU (looking at eight member states, including the United Kingdom) was performed by B. Custers et al. [10]. The study also considered the importance/situation of data protection in a country by looking at the general public's awareness, media coverage, its importance in political debates, etc. However, the research was conducted shortly before the GDPR came into force. While the study did consider the upcoming regulation, it could not predict the changes in national legislation.

Finally, three studies are the closest to the work of this paper. All three are centred on identifying derogations from the GDPR and how it is supplemented in the EU. The first [11] covers 16 current member states. The second study [12] included 13 member states, while the third survey [13] collected information for 21 member states. All three were made before the UK's exit from the EU and, as a result, also include data for the UK. All three collections provide relevant information from national legislations and policies for a variety of topics. There are only two general topics present in all three that we have also included in our study—the processing of sensitive data and the designation of a data protection officer. Other topics that have some overlap with our study include information on communication with SAs, data protection for employees, consent for children, and processing of the deceased's data. All three studies present the results in a textual form. While this allows for more information, it is less than ideal for comparison (there is still a lot of work on the user to extract the necessary information and compare), especially as the level of detail is often different between countries. Our study collected more targeted information that allows for easier comparison between the member states.

3. Survey Outline

In the chapter on related work, we have mentioned some studies that have collected derogations permitted by the GDPR in the EU member states. When designing our own aspects to compare in the EU, we have decided to go a different route and focus on topics that could potentially also affect how data protection is implemented differently between the member states regardless of GDPR. One such example is the collection of biometric data on electronic signatures. Firstly, we want to distinguish electronic signatures, which we are talking about, and are typically obtained by signing your name on a type of touchscreen, from digital signatures, which are a cryptographic authentication mechanism and technically a specific subsection of electronic signatures [14]. When signing your name on an electronic device, sensors can measure the pressure of the pen, the speed, the tilt, etc., of the signing process. All of these data are considered biometric data because they are produced from the technical processing of a natural person's physical, physiological, or behavioural characteristics. Similar signature characteristics can be obtained from close examination of actual physical signatures, which is why just mimicking the look of a signature does not make a convincing forgery (at least to an expert). This is the same reason why the biometric data is collected during an electronic signature. However, some countries do not allow the processing of biometric data for this purpose, meaning electronic signatures are nothing more than images of signatures. Such differences between the member states have the potential to cause problems related to the legitimacy of signatures, where a signature could be valid in one country but invalid in another (either because it does not contain biometric data, or because it does and is consequently a case of illegal processing of biometric data).

Some important aspects of data protection that often involve personal information are not discussed much in the GDPR and could become troublesome to implement under its requirements. Here we are primarily thinking of the processing of personal data in audit trails and the problems surrounding the processing of personal data in backups. Therefore, we were interested if individual member states have made legislation to more clearly define the requirements and how they can be achieved. Note that the results are only limited to legislation and do not include any guidelines or rulings that supervisory authorities might have made on how personal data should be handled in audit trails and backups.

The inclusion of anonymisation as a form of avoiding complying with the GDPR and pseudonymisation as a method of complying with the GDPR is very interesting, especially with the open questions of when personal data become truly anonymous and how can we tell. Therefore, we were interested in whether any member states have additional legislation on the two topics where they might explain the requirements in more detail. Finally, as already discussed in the related literature, we have also included some of the topics included in the previous studies.

Collecting the data for the member states on our own was not an option. The information from foreign legislation and policies would be far too time-consuming if at all possible because they might not have an English translation. That is why we chose to use a survey. The first time, we have distributed the survey among CyberSec4Europe [15] project partners (this work was made as part of the project). With more than 40 partners, the project covers the majority of the member states. The survey was given to data protection officers (DPO) of the partner organisations. By collecting multiple responses for the same country, we were able to check for the consistency of the replies. Unfortunately, the results were very inconsistent, and we received varied feedback for the same member state. While this was a problem, it did give us an interesting insight. Even though DPOs know national data protection laws and policies fairly well, they cannot provide consistent information, indicating that this is a very complex subject. At the same time, it is understandable that DPOs, who typically deal with issues related to organisations they work in, might not have the information to the very specific questions from the survey. Ultimately we decided to scrap the collected data, and a more ambitious plan to contact all the supervisory authorities and collect the data from them was made.

4. Data Collection

To collect the best possible data quality, we chose to collect the data directly from national supervisory authorities (SA). A SA is an independent public authority that supervises the application of European data protection law, including GDPR. Each EU member state has to have a SA, which has investigative and corrective powers, provides expert advice on data protection issues, and handles any raised complaints. However, collecting responses from SAs is more difficult because there is only one per member state, and they might not be inclined to participate in unsolicited research. Even though they are the best entity to answer the prepared data protection questions, we expected to not get a response from every SA. To have the best possible feedback, we have repeatedly asked for their participation and have collected the data between April 2020 and June 2021.

The information gathering was centred around processing different forms of (special) data (e.g., biometrics) and any additional legislation or policies upgrading the GDPR requirements. The survey collected data for the following topics:

1. Any other legislation on the use of biometry (other than the GDPR).
2. Any other specific legislation on privacy, specifically with relation to:
   a. Video surveillance,
   b. hotography,
   c. Anonymisation,
   d. Pseudonymization and/or,
   e. Audit trails.
3. Any additional legislation that extends specific sections of the GDPR, specifically with relation to:
   a. Verification of parental consent,
   b. Processing data of the deceased,
   c. Processing of genetic data,
   d. Use of biometric data for the purpose of identification,

e. Processing of health data,
f. Processing of data on the sex life of individuals,
g. Processing of data on sexual orientation,
h. Erasure of personal data,
i. Data protection officer designation/appointment, and/or,
j. Supervisory authority consultations.
4. Presence of additional legislation on backing up of data.
5. Whether or not the use of biometrics is allowed for the electronic acquisition of handwritten signatures.
6. Whether or not the use of biometrics is allowed in a work environment (e.g., opening of server rooms with a fingerprint).
7. Minimum age of persons that do not require consent from a holder of parental responsibility.

5. Analysis of the Results and Discussion

In the survey, we collected feedback from 19 (Austria, Belgium, Croatia, Cyprus, Czechia, Denmark, Estonia, Finland, Germany, Greece, Hungary, Latvia, Luxembourg, Malta, Poland, Romania, Slovakia, Slovenia, and Spain) out of the 27 EU member states. The responses were collected between April 2020 and June 2021 in many repeated solicitations of supervisory authorities to participate in the survey.

We compared the collected data with the complementary data from [12,13] previously mentioned in the related work section. The most similar data collected and, therefore, the most appropriate for comparison were the data regarding the age of consent for children and the additional regulations surrounding the data of the deceased. The consent age, which we could compare with both other studies, was identical in all three studies except for the information on the Czech Republic. The result from [13] indicates the consent age is 13, while our inquiry and that of the [12] received information that it is 15. We were able to confirm from a separate source that the consent age in the Czech Republic is, in fact, 15 years of age. The information on the additional legislation surrounding the processing of deceased person data was only collected in [12], and we could therefore only compare our results to theirs. The cross-section of the collected results in the two studies did not show any mismatch. The two points of comparison give us high confidence in the trustworthiness of the data collected in our study.

Table 1 represents the collected data from the supervisory authorities. In the table columns are the 19 member states that we have collected the data for. Rows represent the topics (i.e., questions in the survey) for which we have collected data. Rows or rather topics are marked with the same numbers and letters as previously listed in the survey outline section. For example, any specific legislation on video surveillance is marked with 2a because in the previous section, "Any other specific legislation on privacy, specifically with relation to" is numbered with a 2 and "Video surveillance" is under point *a*.

The answers "yes" (the member state has additional or more specific legislation on the topic) and "no" (the member state does not have additional or more specific legislation and the original GDPR applies) that are represented by the cross-section between the member states and topics in Table 1, are colour-coded green and red, respectively.

Topics marked from 1 to 4 contain the information on whether or not a member state has additional/specific legislation on that topic. How many of the topics are covered with other or additional legislation (number of green squares for each of the member states) is summed in a row marked as "SUM". Topics marked with the numbers 5 and 6 are specific questions regarding the use of biometrics, and we do not include them in the analysis of specific or additional legislation in the member states. They are also different because the green colour of a cell in these two rows means that a member state allows the use of (not that it has additional legislation on like in previous rows) biometrics for the electronic acquisition of handwritten signatures (row marked with No. 6) or biometrics in a work environment (row marked with No. 7). The very last parameter (row marked with No. 7) is the consent age—the age after which individuals no longer need parental consent. We also produce the total number of green cells across all member states included in the survey for each topic. This information is in the far most right column (marked "SUM"). It gives information on how commonly a certain topic is covered in additional legislation (topics marked 1–4) or how frequently the use of biometrics is allowed for collecting signatures or in a work environment (topics marked with No. 5 and 6) across the member states.

Table 1. GDPR heterogeneity in the EU.

	Austria	Belgium	Croatia	Cyprus	Czechia	Denmark	Estonia	Finland	Germany	Greece	Hungary	Latvia	Luxembourg	Malta	Poland	Romania	Slovakia	Slovenia	Spain	SUM
1																				11 (58%)
2a																				15 (79%)
2b																				1 (5%)
2c																				2 (11%)
2d																				3 (16%)
2e																				4 (21%)
3a																				4 (21%)
3b																				4 (21%)
3c																				12 (63%)
3d																				9 (47%)
3e																				11 (58%)
3f																				2 (11%)
3g																				2 (11%)
3h																				5 (26%)
3i																				4 (21%)
3j																				5 (26%)
4																				1 (5%)
SUM	3	5	6	4	1	4	3	13	8	2	10	8	0	0	1	6	6	3	12	
5																				10 (53%)
6																				15 (79%)
7	14	13	16	14	15	13	13	13	16	15	16	13	16	13	16	16	16	16	14	

Red cells are "No" answers to topics defined in Section 4. Green cells are "Yes" answers to topics defined in Section 4. For full details, please refer to Section 5.

The results show that in the majority of the cases, member states do not have many additional/specific legislations. We have found that only 95 cases have additional/specific legislation (topics marked from 1 to 4) of the maximum possible of 323—which is 29.4%. This can be seen from the predominately red colour of Table 1.

The topics most often additionally covered with legislation other than the GDPR are in the area of biometry use (row marked with No. 1; in 11 of the 19 countries), video surveillance (2a; 15) processing genetic data (3c; 12), using the biometric data for the purpose of identification (3d; 9), and processing of health data (3e; 11). On the other end of the spectrum is the legislation on photography (2b) and data backups (4) which have further legislation only in one member state each. They are closely followed by additional legislation on anonymisation (2c) and extensions on GDPR rules regarding the processing of data on the sex life (3f) and sexual orientation (3g), each with legislation in only two countries.

Luxemburg and Malta are the only countries that do not have any additional legislation on the topics covered in our survey; all others included member states have at least one topic where they have other/additional legislation to the GDPR. Other countries with little additional legislation on the topics covered in this survey (topics marked from 1 to 4 in Table 1, up to a maximum of 17) include Czechia (1), Poland (1), and Greece (2).

Based on the feedback from the SAs, the most additional legislation relevant to the discussed topics are in Finland (13 green fields in topics from 1 to 4, from possible 17), Spain (12), Hungary (10), Germany (8), and Latvia (8). The use of biometrics for the electronic acquisition of handwritten signatures (row marked with No. 5) is allowed in 10 of the 19 surveyed countries—so a very even split. In contrast, only four member states do not allow biometrics in a work environment (row marked with No. 5; Greece, Malta, Slovakia, and Slovenia). This could indicate that the member states are interested in limiting the use of biometric data but do not wish to limit businesses.

The results of the survey have also been integrated into a dynamic map, enabling quick navigation through the different topics of information and comparison of the EU member states at a glance. The map has been published and can be found at [16]. The published map is depicted in Figure 1. The figure also shows what specific additional legislation is present in Spain, but naturally, users can hover over any of the countries covered in the survey to get its information.

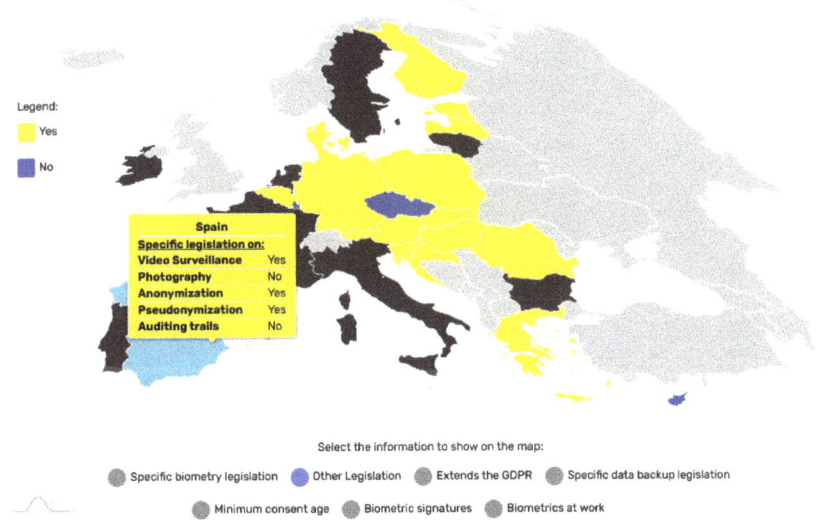

Figure 1. Map of data protection in EU, showing the additional legislation in Spain.

6. Conclusions

The GDPR privacy obligations for controllers and processors are rather extensive, and correctly implementing them takes a lot of time and work. Even if controllers and processors follow the prescribed procedures and take great care to ensure compliance, cross-border compliance challenges within the EU will persist. GDPR gives the EU member states certain leeway when it comes to data protection governance. These issues will manifest in the greater effort necessary for full GDPR compliance in all member states for cross-border service companies. This will impair service providers' overall efficiency in the Single European Market and cross-border competition in the member states.

The GDPR legislation gives the member states the flexibility to define or change specific aspects as they see fit. Member states can also always enact legislation that is stricter or has additional requirements than the GDPR. Not all member states, for example, allow biometrics to be used to obtain handwritten signatures. The use of biometrics for access control is also prohibited or restricted in some member states. As a result, services or products designed for one member state are only partially compatible with legislation in the other member states. Similarly, disparities in the minimum age for consent will necessitate service providers adapting their software and other solutions to account for differences between the member states. Though putting their software and other solutions in place may appear simple, understanding, collecting, and adhering to various regulations in all member states is not.

This paper collected and compared the legislation on data protection topics in the individual EU member states. The findings suggest that the member states do not have many additional/specific laws building on top of the GDPR. We discovered that additional or more specific laws are in place for only 29.4% of the cases discussed in this study.

Finally, we have developed a dynamic map, allowing for easy navigation among various information categories and comparisons of EU member states at a glance.

This research did have some limitations. The first limiting factor when wanting to collect data, as we have in this study, is that it is virtually impossible to collect it and check its validity by oneself. Because of the complexities involved (e.g., language barriers and learning about large amounts of legislation), the effort required would be too large without some external help. In return for relying on supervisory authorities, this workload is vastly reduced. Still, it also means we have to take whoever filled out the survey's word for it, and updating the information would require a repeated process of querying the supervisory authorities for the information. The other more obvious limitations are the missing EU member states that were not included in the study (because we were dependent on participation from supervisory authorities) and the limited number of topics we included in the survey. The last two limitations are also the basis for future work.

As such, in future work, we would like to extend the list of topics to discuss and compare between countries as well as include all of the EU member states missing in this study. Furthermore, we would like to delve into more detail for each of the topics by including lists of relevant national laws for each of the member states and potentially analysing them with the help of appropriate persons with adequate legal backgrounds from the respective countries.

Author Contributions: All authors equally contributed to the conception of the idea, the research plan's layout and participated in the literature search. M.H. led research activities, designed the conceptualisation, contributed to the investigation, defined and reviewed the methodology, performed the validation and designed as well as co-wrote the paper; B.K. performed the validation and co-wrote the original versions of the paper; M.K. contributed to the investigation, performed the validation and co-wrote the original paper. All authors equally contributed to the rest of the paper. All authors have read and agreed to the published version of the manuscript.

Funding: The authors acknowledge the financial support from the European Union's Horizon 2020 Research and Innovation Program under the CyberSec4Europe project (Grant Agreement No. 830929) and the Slovenian Research Agency (Research Core funding No. P2-0057).

Institutional Review Board Statement: Not applicable.

Informed Consent Statement: Not applicable.

Conflicts of Interest: The authors declare no conflict of interest.

References

1. European Union. Regulation (EU) 2016/679 of the European Parliament and of the Council of 27 April 2016 on the Protection of Natural Persons with Regard to the Processing of Personal Data and on the Free Movement of Such Data, and Repealing Directive 95/46/EC (General Data Protection Regulation). 2016. Available online: https://eur-lex.europa.eu/eli/reg/2016/679/oj (accessed on 11 October 2021).
2. United Nations Conference on Trade and Development. Data Protection and Privacy Legislation Worldwide. 2020. Available online: https://unctad.org/page/data-protection-and-privacy-legislation-worldwide (accessed on 30 August 2021).
3. DLA Piper. Data Protection Laws of the World. Available online: https://www.dlapiperdataprotection.com/ (accessed on 30 August 2021).
4. i-Sight Software. A Practical Guide to Data Privacy Laws by Country. 5 March 2021. Available online: https://i-sight.com/resources/a-practical-guide-to-data-privacy-laws-by-country/ (accessed on 30 August 2021).
5. Park, S.; Akatyev, N.; Jang, Y.; Hwang, J.; Kim, D.; Yu, W.; Shin, H.; Han, C. A comparative study on data protection legislations and government standards to implement Digital Forensic Readiness as mandatory requirement. *Digit. Investig.* **2018**, *24*, S93–S100. [CrossRef]
6. Commission Nationale de l'Informatique et des Libertés CNIL. Data Protection around the world. 23 November 2020. Available online: https://www.cnil.fr/en/data-protection-around-the-world (accessed on 11 October 2021).

7. Long, W.; Blythe, F.; Member States' Derogations Undermine the GDPR. Privacy Laws & Business. May 2016. Available online: https://www.sidley.com/~{}/media/publications/gdpr-derogations.pdf (accessed on 19 August 2021).
8. Clearwater, A.; Philbrook, B. GDPR Derogations and How to Prepare for Member State Variation. *CPO Magazine*, 29 September 2017. Available online: https://www.cpomagazine.com/data-protection/gdpr-derogations-prepare-member-state-variation/ (accessed on 1 September 2021).
9. Vengadesan, J.; Pook, N. United with Differences: Key GDPR Derogations Across Europe. Penningtons Manches Cooper. 26 March 2019. Available online: https://www.penningtonslaw.com/news-publications/latest-news/2019/united-with-differences-key-gdpr-derogations-across-europe (accessed on 19 August 2021).
10. Custers, B.; Dechesne, F.; Sears, A.M.; Tani, T.; van der Hof, S. A comparison of data protection legislation and policies across the EU. *Comput. Law Secur. Rev.* **2018**, *34*, 234–243. [CrossRef]
11. activeMind.legal. Data Protection Comparison. Available online: https://www.activemind.legal/law/ (accessed on 19 August 2021).
12. Bird & Bird. GDPR Tracker. Available online: https://www.twobirds.com/en/in-focus/general-data-protection-regulation/gdpr-tracker (accessed on 30 August 2021).
13. Latham & Watkins. GDPR Derogations Tracker. April 2018. Available online: https://gdpr.lw.com/Home/Derogations (accessed on 30 August 2021).
14. Mutabazi, P. What is the Difference Between Digital Signatures and Electronic Signatures? LinkedIn. 23 May 2021. Available online: https://www.linkedin.com/pulse/what-difference-between-digital-signatures-electronic-mutabazi (accessed on 11 October 2021).
15. CyberSec4Europe—European Cybersecurity Competence Network. Available online: https://cybersec4europe.eu/ (accessed on 11 October 2021).
16. Heterogeneity of Data Protection Legislation across the EU, CyberSec4Europe. 9 September 2021. Available online: https://cybersec4europe.eu/heterogeneity-of-data-protection-legislation-in-the-eu/ (accessed on 11 October 2021).

MDPI
St. Alban-Anlage 66
4052 Basel
Switzerland
Tel. +41 61 683 77 34
Fax +41 61 302 89 18
www.mdpi.com

Applied Sciences Editorial Office
E-mail: applsci@mdpi.com
www.mdpi.com/journal/applsci

www.ingramcontent.com/pod-product-compliance
Lightning Source LLC
LaVergne TN
LVHW070223100526
838202LV00015B/2080